CHIEF!

CHIEF!

ALBERT A. SEEDMAN
and PETER HELLMAN

ARTHUR FIELDS BOOKS, INC.

NEW YORK

All illustrations are from the official files of the New York City Police Department except where otherwise noted.

Diana: The Making of a Terrorist, © 1971 by Thomas Powers. Reprinted by permission of Houghton Mifflin Company.

Published simultaneously in Canada by Clarke, Irwin & Company Limited, Toronto and Vancouver
ISBN: 0-525-63004-X
Library of Congress Catalog Card Number: 72-94679
Designed by The Etheredges

*To my colleagues
in the
New York City Police Department,
the finest police officers
in the world*

CONTENTS

INTRODUCTION   1

THE BELT PARKWAY CASE   9

TO A GOLD SHIELD   22

BRASS   47

THE FALLON-FINNEGAN CASE   68

THE JOHNSON-GENOVESE CASE   109

THE MAYS CASE   147

THE GIRL IN THE BOX CASE   192

THE MELVILLE CASE   224

THE TOWNHOUSE CASE   256

THE JEWISH CONNECTION   295

THE COLOMBO CASE   345

THE GALLO CASE   396

AMBUSH   423

While all the incidents in this book are true, many of the names have been changed to protect innocent witnesses or suspects whose cases have not yet come to trial.

I want to extend thanks to Lts. Bernard Jacobs, Joe White; Sgts. John Weber, George Howard, Joe McAndrews; Capt. Angelo Galante; Insps. Eddie Jenkins, Nick NiCastro; Dets. Joe Gibney, Sam Parola, Pete Perotta, Eddie Lambert, Marty Flanagan, John Tartaglia, Tony Cordero, Sandy Tice, Clarence Crabb and Joe Gregorowicz; and especially Arthur Fields.

As for the many members of the Detective Bureau whose story this is as well as mine, no words of gratitude could possibly be adequate.

ALBERT A. SEEDMAN

INTRODUCTION

Albert Seedman kisses his sleepy wife, Henny, good-bye and walks out the front door of his modest home on Long Island. His morning-shift chauffeur, a silent man known to all as "Honey," opens the rear door of the well-polished black Plymouth. As the car heads into the early citybound traffic, Seedman lights up his first cigar of the day and scans the *New York Times*. But after five minutes, the paper is in his lap, the cigar in the corner of his mouth is out and, heedless of the crackling police receiver under the dashboard, he is dozing peacefully.

By the time the black car rolls up to the Central Park station house at 8:13, Seedman is wide awake. He pokes his head inside, and the sergeant who had been lounging behind the desk straightens up.

"Morning, Chief," he says.

"Where is it?"

"Over by Belvedere Lake. You can drive in."

"On a lovely day like this?"

Seedman walks into the park on this Indian Summer morning in September 1971. Dew still clings to the grass and the sunlight is crisp in the trees. The park seems deserted until, strolling over a knoll to the meadow beside Belvedere Lake, he suddenly comes

1

upon a swarm of patrol cars, unmarked cars, Photo unit and Medical Examiner's cars, press-media wagons, even finely groomed chestnut horses of the mounted patrol. Cops are everywhere, prowling the bushes, writing reports, taking measurements, running from tree to tree and cordoning off the area with signs that say "CRIME SCENE SEARCH AREA. STOP!"

A deputy inspector fills Seedman in on the details: A twenty-year-old Puerto Rican man and an attractive seventeen-year-old black girl just up from South Carolina—neither of whom apparently knew better than to be sitting in a remote part of the part at 2 A.M. —were accosted by two white men who grabbed the girl. When the Puerto Rican, Reuben Ortiz, tried to protect her, one of the men pulled out a gun and shot him between the eyes. Then the gunman shot his horrified accomplice in the throat (he would die in the hospital two weeks later), raped the girl, shot her too, and left her, bound hand and foot, to die by the lake. Trailing blood, it took her three hours to hop up to the road where a patrol car found her at dawn.

Seedman climbs down the steep black rocks which slope to the lake. With so many cars parked helter-skelter around the meadow and so many people rushing about, the body of Reuben Ortiz, lying down here beside the murky water, under a red-checkered vinyl cloth, seems more an afterthought, than the center of all this activity. Seedman motions for the picnic cloth to be raised; in the morning light Ortiz's body looks one-dimensional, as if it were painted on the rock.

A reporter from CBS turns away and gags. Even the Deputy Inspector keeps his eyes glued to the distant skyline of Central Park West. But Seedman stares down at the body for a long time as if contemplating a chessboard. Something is bothering him and it is not the gaping red hole in the middle of Ortiz' face. Finally he turns to the Deputy Inspector.

"Was this guy a fag?"

"As a matter of fact, the girl said he was."

Seedman shakes his head. "What in hell was a guy like this doing with a girl like that?"

It seems as though this must be an insensitive man who can gaze down at this corpse with none of the normal emotions. But Seedman has come here as Detective Chief and his job is to solve the murder of Ortiz, not to pity him. In an odd way Seedman does not even see the body. He sees a problem. Instead of the hole in the face, he sees, somehow, the traits of a homosexual. Elsewhere the observation might only be impertinent. Here it may help get the investigation on the track toward a solution, which is Seedman's sole purpose in turning up at the scene and involving himself in mechanics his subordinates can otherwise handle.

Could this murder be the work of a jealous homosexual lover? In this case it was not. But Seedman makes other observations that do get the investigation on the right track. The girl's description of the behavior of the two assailants strike Seedman as abnormal, even by criminal standards. He orders his men to check out everyone who has escaped from East Coast prisons and mental institutions during recent months. Sure enough, the murderer and his accomplice had fled from a Pennsylvania prison; they were placed at the scene of the murder by a pill vial picked out of a nearby bush by Seedman himself.

Of all the men who kiss their wives good-bye in the morning and go off to work, Albert Seedman is one of the few who says good-bye and then goes off to a murder. With the Ortiz case, it has happened for better than the thousandth time.

In the spring of 1972, after thirty years of service, Albert Seedman retired as the twenty-first Chief of Detectives of the New York City Police Department. He commanded a force of three thousand detectives—a civil investigative bureau second only in size to the FBI—and was responsible for solving some of the most celebrated and dramatic crimes in recent memory. With the city awash in front-page cases, like the shooting of Joe Colombo and the slaying of policemen by black militants, and because the investigations were directed by Seedman personally, his face appeared regularly on evening newscasts.

It was a face and a style the public liked. He didn't say much; he did not smile. Though he refused to be photographed with cigar in mouth, his was clearly a face where a cigar would be at home. He wore stylish suits—though his square shoulders gave them a padded '40s look—and white-on-white shirts with "Al" embroidered on the cuffs, usually in red script. On his right hand he wore an onyx pinky ring; on his left, a ring sprayed with tiny diamonds. In a Detective Bureau known for men of strong style, Seedman stood out.

He had a reputation for always taking over a new command just as the most memorable cases were about to break. Just after he was appointed captain in Brooklyn's 10th District in 1962, it was a double murder of two detectives, the first such case in decades. Two years later, in the 17th District in Queens, it was the murder of Kitty Genovese, perhaps the most famous victim in the city's history. Promoted to Inspector, Seedman returned to Brooklyn and had been on the job only ten days when he ran into the Mays Department Store swindle, the most masterful crime of its type in the annals of the Bureau. Moving across the East River to take command of Manhattan South detectives in 1969, Seedman almost immediately came up against the bombing campaign of a white revolutionary named Sam Melville. The big case of 1970 was the accidental destruction of a Greenwich Village townhouse by the Weatherman faction of SDS who had turned the lovely old building into a "bomb factory."

Exactly one year after the Townhouse Case, Seedman became Chief of Detectives. His record held. Only weeks after his appointment two cops were machine-gunned nearly to death in their patrol car on Riverside Drive. Two nights afterward a pair of patrolmen answering a distress call in Harlem were assassinated by black men who emptied their own guns and then jubilantly fired the cops' service revolvers into the bodies. Credit for both attacks was claimed by an ominous new group called the Black Liberation Army. On a sunny day less than three weeks later, before a crowd of thousands, Mafia leader Joe Colombo was shot in the head as he prepared to open the festivities of his Italian-American "Unity Day." In the past, entire years had gone by without producing two such sensational cases. With Seedman they were almost getting to be common occurrences.

No detective chief ever had left such an imprint on the department. Nobody had ever looked, barked, or carried himself more like a detective chief. But Seedman's legend rested, inevitably, more on performance than style. Nobody had ever conducted so many investigations with such originality, intensity, or good results.

Throughout his career Seedman often obtained his solutions by using his intelligence on the mundane, seemingly unrelated information that a record-oriented society can provide if one only knew how to use it. Several months after his retirement, for example, he arrived late for a work session on this book. He explained that he had been held up at a police conference by several small-town Connecticut detectives who wanted some help on a case.

"What sort of case?"

"In the woods just outside town they found the skeleton of a man who'd been dead for three months or so. They figured they'd find out who he was as soon as his family reported him missing, but it's been three months since he was found—which makes six months since he died—and nobody has claimed him. They don't know what to do."

"What did you tell them?"

"Once I got the answer to one question I was able to give them a method. I asked whether this skeleton showed signs of any dental work, which usually can be identified by the dentist. But according to the local cops, they said no, although the skeleton had crummy teeth. No dental work at all. Now, if he'd been wealthy, he could have afforded to have his teeth fixed. If he'd been poor, welfare would have paid. If he was a union member, their medical plan would have covered it. So this fellow was probably working at a low-paying non-unionized job, but making enough to keep off public assistance. Also, since he didn't match up to any family's missing-person report, he was probably single, living alone in an apartment or hotel. His landlord had never reported him missing, either, so most likely he was also behind on his rent and the landlord probably figured he had just skipped. But even if he had escaped his landlord, he would never have escaped the tax man.

"The rest was simple. I told these cops to wait until the year is up. Then they can go the IRS and get a printout of all single males making less than $10,000 a year but more than the welfare ceiling who paid withholding tax in the first three quarters but not in the fourth. Chances are the name of their skeleton will be on that printout."

Elementary, my dear Watson.

Once explained, the method was simple, even obvious. But nobody else had thought of it. This gift for logical deduction is one part of a great detective's makeup. Another is just the opposite—an instinct for the irrational, dark side of human behavior. Seedman flashes that instinct rarely, but when he does, it can be chilling.

It showed up unexpectedly, for example, the day eleven Israeli athletes were taken hostage by Arab guerrillas at the 1973

Olympic Games in Munich. After tense bargaining the group was given helicopter passage to a getaway plane waiting at the airport. Henny Seedman, whose family lives in Israel, followed these developments anxiously. Late in the afternoon she happily called her husband to tell him a radio bulletin had just flashed the good news that the hostages had been saved.

"Don't you believe it," said Seedman flatly.

"Al, it just came over the radio," Henny said.

"They're dead."

The words made no sense. Why deliberately upset his wife? The answer came in another hour. The first bulletin had been wrong, the hostages *were* dead.

Seedman himself cannot explain what made him anticipate tragedy. "Sometimes I just get a feeling, that's all." He shrugs.

Occasionally, what seems to be instinct is actually Seedman's Holmesian eye for fine detail. Spilled coffee on a napkin, for example, reminds him of the time he once found a body in a vacant Brooklyn lot. The man had apparently been wounded elsewhere and staggered into the lot to die, leaving a trial of blood behind. Seedman ordered a pair of detectives to follow.

"But watch out," he warned. "You might not find what you expect."

The detectives tracked the bloodstains around the corner, down one block, then two, and around another corner to a decrepit tenement. The trail led up the narrow stairs, one, two, then three flights to a landing, where, crumpled against a door, lay another man, a knife at his hand. How had Seedman known this had been a fight between *two* losers?

Seedman points to the coffee stains on the napkin. "See how the droplets point to the right? The coffee had to be moving from left to right to leave that splatter. Blood drips the same way, and in that lot I noticed that the pointed ends led *out*, so I told the detectives to follow them. Luckily, blood is more viscous and holds its shape better than coffee. . . ."

Seedman was anything but Holmesian in his approach. He did not work as a loner. Once he had taken in the crime scene with his own eyes, he preferred to move the investigation forward through his unique tool, the three thousand detectives under his command. It was the kind of tool that Holmes, as a consulting detective, obviously could not have dreamt of using, but he would have appreciated the mastery with which it was employed.

"If I do my job right," Seedman once explained, "I don't have to do anything. Everyone else is doing it. That's the way it should be. My time is too goddam valuable to spend on footwork."

All his old detectives agree that Seedman drew more work from them than any other commander ever had; more work than even they themselves thought they could produce. Gruff, glowering, he railed and cursed at them to do their best, and these proud and rugged men took from him what they would have crammed down the throat of anyone else. On the other hand, with men he did not like or trust, Seedman took pains to be polite. As Commander of Brooklyn's 10th District, for example, he maintained an unblinking calm as none other than Joe Colombo accused him of persecuting him. Even when the Mafia leader began to shout, Seedman never responded in kind. He was not about to waste any excess emotion on the likes of Joe Colombo.

None of this fully explains the special allegiance these detectives felt toward this particular Chief. That came, finally, from knowing that he cared more for their welfare than glad-hand commanders. Al Seedman might curse them, but he would never let them down.

Shortly after Seedman retired, a detective named Joe Gibney answered a call to an apartment in lower Manhattan. He raced upstairs to find a patrolman staggering in blind pain from lye that had been splattered in his face. Just then the man who had thrown it leaped out at Gibney with a carving knife. Ducking the lunge, Gibney deliberately aimed away from any vital areas and shot him.

When Gibney's superior arrived at the tenement, he looked at Gibney dubiously.

"Did you have to do that?" he asked.

"Yes, sir."

"Did you call an ambulance?"

"Yes, sir."

The questions appalled Gibney, a proud and careful man who clearly had fired in self-defense. Did he have to do that? The shot Gibney fired that day was his first in fourteen years on the force; of course he had had to do it. Had he called an ambulance? Of course he had. Wasn't he a professional?

"That captain didn't care about the poor bastard lying on the deck," says Gibney. "He was scared for himself. He didn't know what to write in the report for the boss up the line. If Seedman had still been Chief, he'd never have asked those stupid questions."

Seedman understood "walking" detectives like Joe Gibney. After all, he had been one himself. He certainly would have understood the anguish Gibney felt in firing his first shot; in all his years of service Seedman has never fired his service revolver in action. To do so would have meant that a situation had got out of control or had been improperly planned. It would have meant defeat.

Seedman often reminded his detectives that any citizen had the right to expect the theft of his missing hubcaps to be treated as one of the most important cases in the Bureau. To select twelve cases out of a file of ten thousand for this book required a somewhat different standard. Some, like the Kitty Genovese, Colombo, Gallo, and Black Liberation Army cases, would seem to be obvious choices. Yet even these, covered so voluminously in the media, would hardly bear retelling if they could not be shown now in an altogether new light. During those investigations, Seedman often prided himself on his ability to send off reporters from an interview happy with the story they got, even though he knew they had not got the full story at all. That was not mere trickery: it was the need to preserve the integrity of the investigation still in progress. Now that they are over, those same investigations can be presented here in all their dimensions.

Other cases, like the Mays and Belt Parkway, were publicized scarcely or, like the Girl-in-the-Box, not at all. But when old detectives gather, they are the ones that inevitably come up. These cases are a product of the best years of the Detective Bureau, and the very best were those when Albert Seedman was its Chief. For reasons to be explained, the Bureau is no longer the same. Such a reign as his and such cases as these are not likely to occur again.

THE BELT PARKWAY CASE

Friday morning, July 8, 1967, 8:40: a dazzler of a day in Brooklyn—not a cloud in the sky, just a hint of breeze blowing in from Sheepshead Bay, traffic moving well on the Belt Parkway west toward Manhattan. For several minutes now a detective lieutenant named Vito DeSerio, on his way to work at Staten Island's 122nd Squad, has been following behind a bright-yellow Camaro sport coupe driven by a teen-age girl. He likes watching the way the soft air off the bay swirls her blond hair. He wouldn't mind, in fact, if she'd swing out of the passing lane so he could pull alongside and steal a glance at her before having to face his fellow detectives—but she is flying.

As they pass a spot called Plum Beach the girl finally begins to drift toward the center lane. DeSerio notices she gives no signal, just keeps drifting toward the right-hand lane. He assumes she'll get off at the next exit. Except that she keeps drifting . . . drifting . . . into the service lane . . . suddenly, with a crackle and splinter, she is sideswiping the bushes at the edge of the parkway. The bumper bashes in, the hood crumples. In a tangle of foliage and hiss of steam the Camaro stops.

DeSerio mashes his brakes, pulls off the highway, and runs back to the Camaro. The girl's head is buried in her chest, her body caved over, cinched by the buckled seat belt; she is moaning. DeSerio raises her head. Though her eyes are open, the pupils are rolled back. He knows, from too much experience, it is useless to talk to her. Propping up her head, he reaches in her bag for her license. She is Nancy McEwen, seventeen years old, from Garden City. Nothing in her wallet, no bracelet on her arm to warn of epileptic seizures, diabetic collapse. Her body is unmarked. What has happened to her?

A radio car from the police Accident Investigation Unit cruises by and DeSerio flags it down. In fifteen minutes an ambulance has arrived to take the girl to Coney Island Hospital. There the doctors try everything—electrical stimulation, adrenalin injections, manual heart massage. At 11:15 they declare Nancy McEwen dead. Only then do they discover, hidden by the long hair on the left side of her head, a single small bloodless hole.

Thirty minutes later, with the sun hot now on the Belt Parkway two hundred yards west of Plum Beach, an unmarked black Ford sedan pulls alongside the Accident Investigation, Photo, and 61st Precinct patrol units already on hand. Albert Seedman, puffing his second cigar of the morning, gets out of the back seat and strolls over to the Camaro. He is a broad shouldered man of forty-eight, hair silvery-gray and lightly oiled, lips well-sculpted and slightly downturned, eyes cold green. He wears a tan summer suit. The cops respectfully make way for the unsmiling commander of all Brooklyn South detectives.

Seven years earlier, when Seedman first began to show up regularly at crime scenes as a new staff captain in Brooklyn, veteran detectives took it for granted that after a brief flurry of such appearances in cold weather and under hot sun he would soon retire to his office for all but the headline cases. He didn't, but after his promotion first to Inspector and now Deputy Chief Inspector in charge of all 300 Brooklyn South detectives, they were sure of it. The ways of detectives brass were expected to be mysterious. Former commanders had passed their whole tenures without visiting a single crime scene. But Seedman continued to hate the office, love the streets.

He did not show up everywhere, of course. Open and shut cases, even the major ones, he usually skipped. But a case with an odd twist, even if it seemed worth barely a blink in a city full of mayhem, would draw him to the scene, no matter what the hour. He did not come just to watch. Too many times for it to be a fluke now, he had shown a curious instinct for discerning a way to solve a baffling crime. Here on the Belt Parkway now, walking up to the ruined Camaro, he had come upon just such a case.

Lt. Bernie Jacobs, commander of the local 61st Detective Squad, quickly explained to Seedman the little they knew about Nancy McEwen. She had been on her way to her summer job at her father's construction firm in Brooklyn. Except for what DeSerio saw as Nancy McEwen passed Plum Beach that morning, the rest was a mystery.

"Geez," said Jacobs, shaking his head. "Who would want to shoot a sweet young kid like that?"

"Jerk," snapped Seedman. "At forty-five miles per hour nobody —not the best marksman in the world—could nail that girl with such a perfect head shot. The only way to get it off on purpose would be from a car pulling alongside at the same speed. But Vito would have seen that. Anyone coming from the opposite direction—they'd be whizzing by each other at close to a hundred. This thing had to be a crazy, one in a trillion, pure fluke."

Seedman stared at the Camaro. "Did anyone roll the windows up or down?"

"No, Chief," answered Jacobs. "That's the way it was—just the left rear window open. All the others she had up."

Since the glass in all windows was intact, the rear window remained as the only possible souce of the bullet's entry. So it must have been shot from somewhere behind the Camaro on the side of the parkway facing Sheepshead Bay. It could have come from the reeds and low dunes that sloped down to Plum Beach. It could have come from the public bath house two hundred yards back from the highway, or from the parking lot alongside the eastbound lanes, though Seedman could not imagine anyone firing a rifle from such an exposed spot in full view of the morning traffic. The shot also could have come from a boat on the bay. Or even from any of the three twenty-eight-story steel apartment tower skeletons two miles across the bay at Breezy Point in the Rockaways. From that high up, with an unobstructed line of fire, a bullet could easily reach the Belt Parkway.

But the best bet, in Seedman's mind, was those reeds and dunes of Plum Beach. Among people who commuted along this stretch regularly, even among those who use the beach, few knew that these dunes right in the middle of Brooklyn provide a hiding place for rabbits and, in season, pheasants, ducks and wild geese.

Kids hunt them with slingshots, bows and arrows, even guns. Had such a shot missed its mark at 8:40 that morning, it could have burst from the reeds to the parkway and easily caught up with Nancy McEwen.

Seedman ordered Emergency Service and Ballistic units to comb the beach and dunes for the shell casing. He knew it was an awful place to look for anything so small, but if they could find the shell, it would tell them where the shot had come from. It would also help in ballistic comparisons if they ever found the death gun.

"Tell those guys to bring their swim trunks," said Seedman. "Losing their weekend won't seem so bad if they can take a few dips."

Seedman also was interested in what had been seen by the uniform patrolmen from the 61st Precinct. The Plum Beach parking lot was a lovers' lane that they checked regularly during the midnight-to-eight shift. Maybe this time the duty patrol noticed more than just a lot of steamed-up windows.

He certainly had. Patrolman Brockstein, freshly rousted out of bed, arrived at Seedman's office at 2 o'clock that afternoon to tell an unusual story.

Brockstein had been checking the Plum Beach parking lot just after dawn when he saw something that made him gulp. Standing on a dune amid the reeds, backlighted by the low orange sun, was one of the most beautiful women he had ever seen. She was dressed in a sharply pressed khaki safari suit, and a richly colored silk scarf knotted around her auburn hair. Cradled in her arms was a double-barreled shotgun.

Brockstein walked uncertainly slowly into the sand. Mirages on a desert, yes, but at Plum Beach? He was almost to the dune when he came upon a man and woman, necks laden with cameras, crouching low to photograph her. Ignoring them, Brockstein walked straight to the woman and removed the weapon.

Courteously he explained to her that he was only doing his duty, that it was a criminal offense to discharge a firearm in city limits.

The photographers clambered up from behind the dune. "No, no, Officer," said the man. "It's only a prop. We're doing a fashion layout. This place, man, at dawn it looks exactly like the African veldt. People who see this layout in *The New Yorker* are never in a million years goings to guess it was shot in the middle of Brooklyn."

The man giggled nervously. "Sorry—I don't mean shot, Officer. The gun's not loaded. We don't need that authenticity!"

Brockstein examined the shotgun. It was a finely tooled double-barreled .410 gauge over-and-under model. Etched on the barrels was "Made in Italy" and "Abercrombie & Fitch." He checked the firing chamber to make sure the gun was empty—and handed it back to the model. A bit shamefacedly, he tipped his hat to her and trudged back to the patrol car. But before resuming his patrol, Brockstein took down the license plate number of the photographer's 1963 Buick. Two Puerto Ricans were also in the lot polishing their cars. It seemed a bit early for that, so, just to be on the safe side, he took down their plate numbers too.

"That's all there was in the lot?" asked Seedman.

"I think so," said Brockstein.

"Don't they have some kind of tow truck that sits in that lot during rush hour in case cars stall? I've seen him in there."

"He gets there about six-thirty, Chief. About half an hour after I left."

"You went and he came. That's good. We'll find out now what he saw."

"It may take us a while to dig him up," said Lieutenant Jacobs.

"Oh, yeah?" said Seedman. "You'll dig him up in the same spot at four o'clock when the rush hour starts going the other way."

His name was George Heffernan. He told the 61st Squad detectives that he too had done a double-take on seeing the beautiful girl in the dunes. He'd watched the team of photographers shoot one pose after another, until they finally left. It seemed to him they were in a big hurry. It was about 8:45, he knew, because his own shift was just about to end. Nancy McEwen had been hit at 8:50.

Late the same afternoon detectives traced the Buick's license plate to James Brooks at 896 Third Avenue on Manhattan's East Side. Brooks explained to the detectives that he and his wife, Kay, worked as a team. They had borrowed the shotgun from Abercrombie & Fitch. Yes, of course it had been empty, said Brooks, pointing out that a patrolman had checked it that very morning. The detectives asked to see the weapon anyway, so Brooks took them down to the garage. Neither of the two A & F shotguns in the trunk smelled from fresh burned powder.

Seedman knew, of course, that Nancy McEwen had not been

killed by a shotgun blast, but that made him no less suspicious of Brooks. He and his wilfe could have had—and disposed of—a third gun. It was just too coincidental that a girl had died two hundred feet from their model. Maybe they hadn't meant to kill her, but people were being shot all the time with empty guns. He had paid too many hospital calls to the kids of cops who had been shot by their fathers' supposedly empty service revolvers. If the department's top ballistics specialists handed him a gun and swore it was unloaded, Seedman would treat it exactly as if it were ready to fire.

"Let's get that broad up here right now," said Seedman.

Her name, Brooks had told the detective, was Yaffa Turner, and she was an Israeli. She was from the Eileen Ford Agency, the very best. But at 8:30 on a hot Friday night the office had long since closed. Yaffa Turner was not in the phone book and Brooks did not know where to find her. But he did remember that she was dating Richard Lefrak, son of one of the city's largest and most powerful landlords. Seedman got him on the phone at his summer home on the North Shore of Long Island. Lefrak did not know where Yaffa was either, but promised to deliver her to Seedman's office before the evening was out if it would help solve the case.

High-fashion models rarely turn up in the 61st Squad office in Sheepshead Bay, so it was no surprise when no one showed much interest in going off duty. The detectives were still there at 1 A.M. when Yaffa Turner strode in, high cheekboned and leggy, wearing the shortest pair of hot pants any of them had ever seen or imagined. To be able to look at her was worth the wait. Her information, unfortunately, was not.

"I know the gun didn't shoot," she said over and over in heavily accented English. "I never shot one since I was a private in the Israeli Army. . . ."

Seedman sat in his office alone after Yaffa left, puffing his last cigar of the day. It was still too much of a coincidence. The Brookses could have conspired with Yaffa to hide the truth. Neither of the two guns from Abercrombie & Fitch had killed Nancy, but there could easily be another gun concealed elsewhere. Yaffa had mentioned she once saw a rifle in her agent's apartment. Could that be the missing weapon?

Her agent was in Connecticut for the weekend, but Seedman didn't want to wait until Monday morning for a report. It took a little prompting, but the agent was back in the city at 5:30 that morning. He produced his gun, but it showed no signs of recent firing. Seedman had not waited around for that report. He had long since gone home to sleep.

On Saturday morning the search for the murder weapon narrowed considerably when the Kings County Medical Examiner presented the Ballistics detectives with the bullet from the left side of Nancy's head. In their laboratory in the ancient loft building at 400 Broome Street in Lower Manhattan, they identified it as a copper-coated steel-jacketed .318-caliber bullet. Like any bullet, this one had been distorted by high and low marks as it twisted, red hot and malleable, through the gun barrel. The high marks are called lands, the low ones grooves. They are nearly as individualized as fingerprints. This particular bullet had a left twist, two lands and grooves.

"This rifle," reported the excited Ballistics men, "it's very rare, Chief. We think it's either an 1884 Mauser, and 1888 Mannlicher, or maybe, just maybe, a .765 Argentine."

It was certainly possible that Brooks had borrowed a rare gun from Abercrombie & Fitch or elsewhere. "I want you to take this bullet down to your friends at the FBI lab in Washington right away," Seedman said.

"Don't you trust us, Chief?"

"Look, you dummies. This is some kind of crazy goddam gun nobody ever heard of, right?"

They nodded.

"Well, if you were a doctor who came across a rare disease, wouldn't you get a second opinion from another specialist, just to be on the safe side?"

Mollified, the Ballistics men took their bullet, and in the morning one of them left for Washington with it packed in cotton in a plastic pill vial.

Back at Plum Beach search teams had combed the sand all during the long daylight hours of the weekend without finding the shell casing.

Watching this tedious operation, Seedman suddenly recalled something he once saw in a newsclip. The GI's in Vietnam cleared mines off those jungle trails with a little machine that looked like a Hoover vacuum cleaner. Maybe the Army could lend a hand.

On Monday morning a special ordnance team from Fort Monmouth, New Jersey, began scouring Plum Beach with special metal detectors. By the time they had completed their mission, they had turned up three rusty .22s and a .38-caliber police shell—nothing that fit the Ballistic report, but at least that dirty part of the search was over. Seedman decided to explore one other possibility: if the Brookes' Buick had left quickly, as the tow operator claimed, maybe it had spun out, leaving burnt rubber behind. A tire with good tread leaves a distinct impression, and acting on Seedman's instructions, detectives did indeed find such marks. But their rib counts did not match those on the Buick tires or even on the two cars being polished by the Puerto Ricans on Friday morning. Spanish-speaking detectives had already checked them out; they owned no guns and had heard no shots fired—which just about ruled out the beautiful girl in the dunes.

As the sun went down that Monday evening, a tired, disgusted Seedman stood on the beach, scanning the marshy spur of dunes to the east, Fort Tilden and the towers of Breezy Point across the bay, the small boats heading in from sea through Rockaway Channel.

"That goddam bullet could have come from so many places besides this beach you can't even count them all," he said to Lieutenant Jacobs. "Let's get us a helicopter."

Hovering over Sheepshead Bay the next morning, Seedman for the first time noticed a shooting range at Fort Tilden—its targets facing across the water to the parkway. And those Breezy Point skeletons provided a perfect line of sight to the cars whizzing along the Belt Parkway, their windshields flashing in the morning sun. But the Army insisted that nobody had used the firing range that previous Friday. Detectives who searched the tower girders and grounds found no signs of shells.

On Tuesday morning Seedman sent detectives to Nancy Mc-Ewen's Requiem Mass in Garden City, in hopes that the man who fired the shot would turn up. An uncle promised to point out any stranger, and sure enough, one nervous young man nobody knew did take off fast after the service. But when detectives caught up with him, they found he was just a school chum of Nancy's who wanted to go to her funeral and was now in a hurry to get back to the office.

A dozen citizens called the police on Tuesday to say they also had been shot at as they drove to work in the morning on the Belt Parkway. Several demanded to know what the police were doing about this crazed, crafty sniper who was obviously on the loose. The "sniper," however, turned out to be only a large Department of Highways mowing machine that had been zinging them with stones thrown up by its whirring blades.

On Tuesday, too, the FBI returned its report on the death bullet. They confirmed that it had a left twist, two lands and grooves—just as the city's Ballistics men had said—and further identified it as a "soft-point" model made in Sweden under the brand name "Nomad" for the Norra Precision Corp. in South Lansing, New York. What startled Seedman, though, was their finding about the source of the bullet. It had been fired, not from a Mauser, Mannlicher, or .765 Argentine, but from an Enfield .303, a model that had been manufactured in England about 1940, soon after the retreat from Dunkirk. The British people were preparing to stand in the streets, if necessary, to drive back a threatened German invasion, and Enfield went on an around-the-clock production schedule. In a matter of months they turned out *millions* of Enfield Model No. 44 rifles, Mark 1 and 2, each one with a left twist, two lands and grooves! So much for the Brooklyn Ballistics men's "rare gun" theory. Seedman was furious.

Late Tuesday afternoon Seedman turned to his aide, Capt. John O'Connor, and Bernie Jacobs. "Let's go for one last look around the beach. Sometimes when you give up, you find something."

But all they found at Plum Beach was another departmental car, belonging to Ballistics. Busy plotting trajectories at the far end of the beach, the two technicians did not see Seedman and his men. Back in the parking lot half an hour later with nothing to show for the tour but sand in his shoes, Seedman glared at the Ballistics car. He was still blistering at the misinformation on the "rare gun" they had brought him. Being mislead was worse than being in the dark. Now they would be sorry.

Jacobs and O'Connor watched Seedman take out pen and notepad. Though his handwriting was normally neat and graceful, as befits a graduate accountant, he now wrote in a crude and jagged scrawl:

"STOP ME BEFORE I KILL AGAIN—THE PLUM BEACH SNIPER."

He put the note on the front seat of the Ballistics car and then drove off.

"I want a report from Ballistics this evening," Seedman ordered, back in the office. "You watch. They'll tell us all kinds of crap. But not a word about that note. They're going to try to break this case all by themselves."

At 7:30 two detectives from Ballistics knocked on Seedman's door. He was at his desk, chewing the butt of a cigar; John O'Connor and Bernie Jacobs slumped on either side of him.

"You've jerked around with this thing for five days now," Seedman barked. "What the hell did you come up with?"

The nervous Ballistics men explained how they used a sextant to inscribe the sixty-degree arc through which the shot could have come. They described their calculated rate of drop of a bullet fired from an Enfield .303 if it came from the towers at Breezy Point, the firing range at Fort Tilden, or the dunes east of Plum Beach.

"We know all that crap," Seedman said. "What else?"

The two detectives looked at each other, shifting from one foot to the other, but said nothing.

"Okay," said Seedman, "we've got work to do here. Take off."

An hour later the Ballistics men suddenly reappeared in the doorway. They were now agitated. "Sorry to bother you again, Chief," said one. "But we have something to show you."

Seedman looked up, stony-faced. "I haven't got time for you to start jerking me off now with some crazy new theory. *Get lost!*"

When Seedman wanted someone to disappear, he usually did— but one of the Ballistics men suddenly thrust forward a neatly folded piece of paper. "We were working down at Plum Beach about four o'clock," he blurted out. "When we got back to our car, we found *this.*"

Seedman grabbed the note and a look of total disgust came over his face. "You morons!" he shouted. "Did it ever occur to you two fine detectives that we could have taken fingerprints off this before you smudged it up? But no—you were going to chase this one down all by yourselves. Be the big heroes! Get out of here!"

Only after they saw the grin finally appear behind Seedman's cigar did Jacobs and O'Connor permit themselves to laugh out loud.

Seedman could use a laugh. After five days, they were nowhere. They had come up with a blank on Yaffa Turner's photo party. They had turned up no gun dealer who had recently sold an Enfield .303 or ammunition for one. They had no luck in sifting all arrest records for the last five years in which an Enfield might have figured. They had covered all the marinas, climbed the skeletons at Breezy Point, crawled around the dunes and marshes at Plum Beach, called in the Army with their mine-detecting gadgets, scouted by helicopter, checked out every wild tip that came in on the "hot line" and still had no idea who had shot Nancy McEwen, or why, or where the bullet had come from.

"What else can we possibly do, Chief?" cried Jacobs.

Seedman was well aware how much taxpayers' money had gone into the case so far with no result. He also realized that the same amount of additional expense might not bring a solution. He had elected to put many stalled investigations on ice before; as a commander, it was his duty not only to ask men to give their best, but also to judge when their best was being wasted. He had made that judgment before even in cases of clearly premeditated murder. This case did not seem to belong in that class, but someone out there had killed the girl, and Seedman was not ready to quit trying to find him. Not quite yet.

"We're going to make a canvass," Seedman said. "Starting tomorrow morning, we're going to knock on every door in Brooklyn until we find the guy who has that Enfield. He isn't talking now, but when that detective comes calling, he's going to figure we've traced that gun to him somehow and he'll come clean. He can always say he didn't know we were looking for it."

The detectives stared at each other. That was well and good. But a canvass could be a time-consuming and often boring task when they were covering just one dense block of the city. Now Seedman was talking about a borough with a population of three million! It would take longer than their lifetimes to knock on the door of every one.

"You've got to be kidding, Chief! Where would we start?"

A large map of Brooklyn was pinned to the office wall. Seedman ran his finger up and down the lower half of the borough. It landed. "Start right . . . *here.*"

Jacobs and O'Connor marked the block: Knapp Street, just north of the Belt Parkway about a mile ahead of where the Camaro had run off the road. It was not a direction from which the bullet could have come. Seedman himself could not explain then or even later why he had jabbed that particular spot.

He allotted fifty detectives for the canvass. Under O'Connor they were divided into pairs the next morning in the 61st Squad room and set out. They seemed much fresher than Seedman himself. The last several days had been awfully long. As the first teams set out, he went off for a swim.

While he was at the beach, two detectives began working the block where he had put his finger, the 2700 block of Knapp

Street. The third place they came to was a Mobil station. In the office they found the proprietor, a chunky, florid man of forty-six named Theodore DeLisi, working over his bills.

"Do you own a rifle?" the detectives asked.

"Oh, I have one down in my boat, locked away."

"What kind?"

"It's . . . an Enfield," he said, his eyes glued to his bills. "One of those British jobs."

DeLisi felt the silence. Slowly he looked up in dread.

"That girl, she was killed by a .22 rifle, right? That's what I read in the papers. Please tell me she got it from a .22. . . ."

This is the story that Theodore DeLisi told during seven hours of questioning on Wednesday at the 61st Squad office. Two weeks earlier, at the end of June, he had gone out in his boat, *Luau,* to fish for bluefish off Rockaway Beach. An experienced angler, he knew the best way to catch blues was to grind up a few dozen oily fish called menhaden and throw the pieces onto the water. Chumming, as fishermen call this kind of fishing, makes a slick that attracts fish from miles around.

Unfortunately, that day the chum also attracted sharks as well as bluefish. They scared away the blues or bit chunks out of them as they struggled against the hook. DeLisi managed to hook one of the sharks, a six-footer, but he had no way to subdue it or haul it into the boat. He had no choice but to cut it loose.

Then DeLisi remembered that when he and two other men had bought the *Luau* a few years back, a rifle had been thrown into the deal. DeLisi had not seen it for a long time. He'd never shot it. He picked up the gun from one of his partners who had been keeping it, and on Thursday evening, July 6, went with his youngest son to the Triangle Sports Shop on Flatbush Avenue. There he bought two boxes of shells for the Enfield—a fact the salesman later insisted he had forgotten when the detectives re-interviewed him.

Friday was a great day for fishing. No clouds, just a hint of wind on Rockaway Inlet. The water was blue and warm as DeLisi chugged past Buoy No. 7 in the channel and headed toward the ocean. On the south he was passing the Breezy Point towers. Far over to his other side, about a thousand yards away, the white sand of Plum Beach shone in the sun.

"I might as well see if the damn thing works," DeLisi said, picking up the rifle. Glancing around, he saw a beer can bobbing near the buoy. DeLisi took aim. He wasn't used to this. The can bobbed and sparkled, but he hit it with his first shot. DeLisi was glad to see he could do it. Any sharks messing around with his chum today would be sorry! He raised the rifle and fired one more shot before putting out to open sea.

The bullet missed the can, smacking the water beyond at a shallow angle. To a bullet traveling at that speed, the surface of the water might as well have been a sheet of steel. It ricocheted with a pop and headed north across Rockway Inlet. It whistled along almost four feet over the flat blue water, and remained at that height as it crossed the sand, dunes, and reeds of Plum Beach. Far ahead of the sound of its own report now, it sped across the parking lot and the eastbound lanes of the parkway. It just cleared the fence divider on the median strip. By now the bullet had traveled nearly a mile. It was losing momentum as it came upon the yellow Camaro. Had the left rear window been closed, the bullet probably would have glanced off. Now it had just enough force to enter behind the left ear of Nancy McEwen.

On July 18, 1967, in Brooklyn Criminal Court, Theodore DeLisi was charged with the homicide of Nancy McEwen and with discharging a rifle within city limits. The homicide charge was later dropped, but DeLisi was fined a hundred dollars on the lesser charge. Incredibly, it turned out that he and the dead girl were acquainted. Before the McEwens moved to Garden City, both families had lived in Whitestone, a small, close-knit community on the Long Island Sound in northern Queens. Often on his way to work, De Lisi waved at little Nancy McEwen.

Detectives still talk about this case because of its three amazing coincidences. The first, obviously, was that in traversing the great mile-long sweep of water and sand that separated the *Luau* and the Camaro, the bullet had found the one place where it could do fatal damage. The second was that out of the city's millions, the families of shooter and victim knew each other from a small place nowhere near South Brooklyn. But what appeared to be the greatest coincidence of all was not dismissed as such by the detectives. They had seen it happen too many times to call it anything but a particularly mysterious example of their Chief's special instinct. In the two hundred forty square miles of the borough, Seedman had put his finger precisely on the one block where the Belt Parkway case could be closed.

TO A GOLD SHIELD

Found in Albert Seedman's basement: a small, leatherbound album, cover tooled with the word "autographs," pages filled with salutations and short poems from his classmates. On a faded pink page, in a little girl's school-perfect script, is this message:

> *To Police Commissioner Albert,*
>
> *May success and happiness follow*
> *you all through life.*
>
> > *Your fellow grad-U-8*
> > *Dorothy*

The date is June 1932, the occasion Seedman's graduation from P.S. 93. He was fourteen years old.

"Whenever I was running a big case, reporters would ask me the same damn question: 'When did you decide you wanted to be a cop?' I would tell them I got sold on the career as a kid when they made me an official Stairwell Monitor at P.S. 93 in the Bronx. The reporters would always snicker. They thought I was being sarcastic. I let them think what they pleased. But I really *did* love being a Stairwell Monitor—not because it gave me a chance to boss other kids around, but because it made me feel good to see things happen right, with order and authority.

"Feeling that way I could have ended up in the military as easily as the cops. Except that in those days we rarely saw a soldier or sailor in the East Bronx. But every morning on my way to school, every afternoon on my way home, at a dangerous intersection we had to cross, I saw a cop. I never said a word to him but I knew that his job was even better than being a Stairwell Monitor. Even when I went to Townsend Harris High School, a highly competitive all-academic school where most of my classmates tended to look down on police work as a career, I still felt the way I had at P.S. 93. I would have loved to be a cop. But for what seemed to me to be solid and insurmountable reasons, I felt I'd never wear that blue and gold.

"The reasons started with my own body. I knew what a cop should look like: big, beefy, a sense of raw power perfectly under control within that uniform but ready to smash down the door of a criminal. Looking at myself, it seemed hopeless. I was a total runt. On the day I graduated from high school I weighed a hundred and twenty-two pounds. That was the least of it.

"When I was maybe three years old, I had been standing in front of the bungalow my family rented for two weeks each August up in the Catskill Mountains. A cousin of mine, twice my age, had tied a string to a coffee can filled with stones and was twirling it around his head. It was spinning in fantastic circles, and each time it came by me it cut the air with a whoosh. I'd never heard such a sound. I wanted to try it myself and came closer. As I reached out, my cousin gave this coffee can a two-handed whirl like a goddam Olympic hammer-thrower, and at the low point of its orbit it whacked me on the hip. The can knocked me up against the side of the bungalow like a cork.

"For the next two years I wore leg braces and elevated shoes. In the first months after the accident I was sent up to a hospital for crippled children in Westchester County. The place was run by an order of nuns. I guess my folks felt the location was right—just north of us in the Bronx and yet in the 'country,' with clean air and woods. They also felt that nuns would be more devoted to us kids than attendants in a regular hospital. (That was the reverse of what I found when I was a parent: Catholic cops always wanted to take their kids to Jewish doctors.) The three high points of the day at this place were mealtimes. I fed myself and then I fed another kid who who was retarded as well as crippled. I'd spoon the food in and he'd dribble it out. My parents yanked me out of this place when they discovered the nuns were making me go to Mass. For a Jewish kid it was not the way to start your day.

"I wound up at the Hospital for Joint Diseases on 42nd Street. The doctors put a chest-high cast on me for six months, which was worse than being with the nuns. But when the cast came off, I remember walking without pain into my mother's arms. Just the same, from that day on my mother was worried I'd reinjure that hip, so she never let me play any sports in school. The way I felt about my body, I figured I had about as much chance to be a centerfielder for the Yankees as to be a cop.

"The biggest barrier of all, actually, was my mother. Like most people in the South Bronx, our family was poor—not starving, but we could never afford much more than the basics. My father, David, drove a cab owned by someone else. On a bad day, he'd show up after twelve hours of work with as little as two dollars; the most he ever brought home was seven dollars. My mother was the one who brought home the big money. She was only a sewing machine operator in the garment district, but she was the best. When they needed special luxury work, she did it. Whenever she worked, the boss always tried to make her take a job as a forelady. But my mother felt her responsibility was at home, with my father, sister Frances, and me.

"My mother was determined that her only son should never know poverty. Yet the term was relative. As a child, like plenty of kids whose parents immigrated to America at the turn of the century, she had been sent out with a pail to gather coal chunks that fell from the cars in the Pennsylvania Railroad yards. Compared with her childhood, we were doing okay. But she had even higher hopes. Seeing what good money pattern cutters were making, she persuaded my father to attend night school to learn the trade. He bought a special ruler which I still use, but despite my mother's determination he never really followed through. You could say my dad was a dreamer. He loved the good life—if someone would only give it to him. Otherwise he was content just to be a sweet guy who drove a cab, played cards on his day off, and played with his children just like one of us kids. I can remember that whenever I'd go out to play pickup ball, he'd come too. And like as not he'd be chosen well before me. Everyone loved my dad.

"Even though my dad never became a cutter, my mother tried to talk me into textile designing, which paid even better than being a cutter. But her real dream was to see me go to college and enter some kind of white-collar work. She could imagine nothing more wonderful than a job where her son wore a suit and tie and sat at a desk all day without ever dirtying his hands. Then one day when I was a sophomore at Townsend Harris, I told her I was considering applying to West Point or Annapolis. She went through the roof. No son of hers was voluntarily going to put on a uniform. Part of her reaction was a mother's natural belief that to wear a uniform meant to risk getting wounded. But it was also a gut response, a Jew's traditional aversion to the uniform, any uniform. In the Old Country, Jews were not allowed to join the army, so the only uniforms they saw belonged to the Cossacks who galloped through their *shtetls*. Traditionally Jews were garment workers, butchers, small businessmen. Why should I strike out into strange territory when she had so many contacts, like my aunt Mae, who was an officer of the silk screen printer's union?

"My reaction to all my mother's fears was to keep my mouth shut. The idea of going to West Point or Annapolis, I dropped. It would cause too much grief at home. Besides, I also suspected my parents were right that a Jewish kid in the service might miss out on the promotions he deserved. Even so, in college I joined ROTC. But the first time I came home in uniform, my mother made me take it off. Good-bye ROTC.

"Luckily, an alternative turned up. One Saturday afternoon I saw a movie starring James Cagney as an FBI agent. All of a sudden I thought, why couldn't *that* be for me? I wouldn't have to wear a uniform, which would satisfy my mother. And in the FBI promotions were not nearly as important for your career. In the Army it mattered plenty whether you were a major or a lieutenant colonel, but in the FBI being an agent was all that mattered. Most important to me, here was a job where you didn't have to be brawny, tough, and rugged like an Irish cop. What with all the undercover sneaking around and espionage work FBI agents did, you'd be a lot better off *not* looking like a cop.

"In my senior year at Townsend Harris, I wrote away to Washington for information about joining the FBI. The brochure they sent back cleared up something that had been worrying me for a long time. FBI agents, I knew, usually had legal training. But my father was having heart problems, and even though I had just been admitted to the tuition-free City College of New York, I would have to take a part-time job in college to help support the family and get a full-time job the moment I graduated. So a law degree was out. Now, reading through the FBI material, I discovered that an accounting degree, which I could easily take as an undergraduate, was just as good. Years later when I got to be Chief of Detectives, people would say to me, 'Al, you love the streets so goddam much, you hate the paperwork. What in hell made you want to be an accountant?' I tell 'em it's all on account of a Jimmy Cagney movie.

"I admit I may have been a bit of a romantic about this FBI business, but I was also enough of a realist to understand that I could not hope to graduate from City College and get invited to come up and see J. Edgar Hoover—just like that. I'd have to find a job—preferably one in civil service. The attraction was not so much the pay as the security. I'd grown up seeing how even the best workers in the garment center had to expect sudden layoffs during bad times. I'd seen my father come home exhausted on bad days with only a few bucks to show for hours of cruising. If he got sick, nothing came in, not even two dollars. If my mother got sick, nothing came in for either of them. Civil servants coasted along from paycheck to paycheck. In case of sickness, there was always insurance and pension relief. Even in the worst of times, you knew you would eat.

"So at the same time as I was attending classes in college, I worked up to thirty-five hours a week in the garment center on a job Aunt Mae got for me. I also bought study manuals for a buck and took civil service exams right and left. I passed every one. By the time I was a senior in college I was on the list for firemen, meterologist, messenger, clerk, even forest ranger, fifteen exams in all. The only one I never bothered to take was the test for the NYPD. Even in college I still felt that between my family's objections and my own physical inadequacies I would never be a cop. If just one person in the family had been on the force, or even if I'd just known someone's dad who was, that might have given me the impetus to go ahead. As it was, I was twenty years old, a graduate of P.S. 93, Townsend Harris High, and now City College, and I had never said one single word to a cop—or, God help me, been spoken to by one. To think that I could walk down a city street myself in a blue jacket with gold buttons, twirling a nightstick, was incomprehensible.

"Then a silly thing happened. A college friend of mine asked me to take the police exam with him. This kid was even skinnier than me. More to the point, he was just another Jewish boy whose father owned a little stationery shop. If he could do it, I damn well could, too, though frankly, I didn't expect either of us to pass. This patrolman's exam, given on April 29, 1939, was taken by 33,000 applicants including lawyers, engineers, dentists, doctors, psychologists, even psychiatrists including one who worked for me as a patrolman in the Bronx. Years later he went on to write a bestseller with his wife called *How To Be Your Own Best Friend.*

"Naturally my mother was miffed that I took this exam. She and Dad had worked themselves silly to help me get this accounting degree so I could do nothing more arduous than sit at a clean desk and keep columns of numbers straight. No night work, no machines clattering in my ears. So now what did I want to do? A job even more dangerous than any factory work. She couldn't believe it.

"I said to her, 'Ma, I took this exam with 33,000 people, plenty of whom made me look like an illiterate, and not one out of thirty of us are going to make it. Even if I do pass the written part, I'll never pass the physical exam.' She looked dubious; her instinct turned out to be better than mine.

"I forgot the police exam almost as quickly as I took it and concentrated on choosing another job from the list of exams I had passed. Incidentally, I was incensed to discover that people who had scored below me on the messenger's exam were already being hired and I dashed off an indignant letter of protest to the Civil Service Commission. Before I could get a reply I received word that I had been selected to take the physical examination for the NYPD. Standing with that letter in my hand, all the feelings that had built up over the years were suddenly awakened. I forgot all about being a messenger, meteorologist, clerk, forest ranger, and even, for the time being, in the FBI. If there was any way in the world I could make my body pass that physical, I was determined to find it.

"The first step was arranging a six week postponement of the physical. Then I signed up at the Delehanty Institute, a private school on Fifteenth Street where cops still prepare for advancement exams. Every minute I could spare I worked out in the gym with barbells, pulleys, parallel bars, whatever would build me up. As I was exercising, I thought about the possibilities of a career on the police force. Most of the command structure was Irish, but I knew that all promotions, from patrolman to captain, were based primarily on written tests. If you scored high enough, you got the promotion. Even if I never went further than captain, the highest rank you could go on competitive exams, that was fine with me. If it didn't work out, I could always switch over to the FBI. The one thing I never bothered to imagine was that I might some day be a detective.

"One morning, after nine hours sleep and a three-egg breakfast, I took the subway up to New York University's Bronx campus, where the police physical was given. I hit the scale exactly at the minimum weight of a hundred and forty pounds. Most of the other fellows, I noticed, were twenty pounds over that, but I was astounded to see some of them huff and puff to lift weights I had no trouble with. Then we jumped hurdles, zipped through sprints, scrambled over walls and under pipes on the obstacle course. I kept waiting for them to pass by me, but all they did was fall back. At the end of the exam, I'd scored one hundred percent on everything but the mile run, where I was off the mark by three seconds. Going home on the subway I was dumfounded. Gone was my lifelong image as a physical weakling. In its place was a cop."

On March 16, 1942, Seedman assembled in formation with his class of three hundred recruits in the hall of the Police Academy, then on the third floor of the 84th Precinct on Poplar Street in Brooklyn. Lined up according to size, Seedman was near the end. The class was then divided into three groups under a fiery old captain named John Murray. Much later in his career, square-shouldered Al Seedman, with the inevitable fat cigar stub jutting from his firm jaw, would be known among his men, though never to his face, as "Big Al." But that day in March 1942 he was fiercely proud to be known as one of "Murray's Mighty Midgets."

Police training in those days was relaxed—a smattering of criminal law and long recitations of past mayhem and bravery by cheerful Irish lieutenants in their Old Country brogues. Once classwork was over, the recruits were sent out for a few hours of patrol duty with a veteran flatfoot. Real learning was reserved for the streets.

"One day toward the middle of May," remembers Seedman, "I was told to pick up my uniform at the tailor shop and get ready for my first four hours of patrol in the Forty-sixth Precinct. At home I slipped on the blue wool trousers and jacket, pinned the silver shield to the left side of the breast—I still remember my number, 19485—and settled the blue uniform cap with its silver emblem on my head. Outside the kids were playing stickball, but when I walked out for that first tour, they put down the stick and ball and just stared. It was one of the best moments in my career."

The desk sergeant at the 46th assigned Seedman to a beat with Patrolman Scanlon. As soon as they were on the street, Scanlon asked the recruit whether he had seen the feature film at the Paradise Theater, flagship of the Bronx movie houses.

"Not yet," piped up Seedman, thinking this was get-acquainted talk. "Maybe if my work's caught up, I can go on Sunday afternoon."

"You can see it on me and save some money, my boy," said Scanlon. "Now."

He wheeled Seedman into the Paradise, ignoring the ticket window and brushing past the deferential ushers. "I'll pick you up at nine-thirty," Scanlon said, and tossed him a dime. "Here's for pop-corn. You be good."

Seedman spent his first tour in blue slumped in his seat, glad at least that the theater was practically empty so no one could notice him.

"After that disgrace," says Seedman, "I made sure every recruit who ever went out on patrol got his ass run into the ground. I didn't want any silly kid ever to feel the way I did that night."

They were nearing the end of the three-month course—the time recruits begin to speculate on their assignments—when a strange captain walked into class.

"That one," Seedman heard the captain whisper to Murray, pointing to him. "He looks like an underage Guinea squirt. He'll fit in just right."

Altogether the captain picked two dozen men for a new plain-clothes detail in the office of the Commissioner and Chief Inspector. Seedman was one of four chosen from Murray's Mighty Midgets, and the only one dropped.

"Once this captain realized I wasn't Guinea but Jewish," says Seedman, "I think he backed off. Plainclothes, I'd learn later, was not exactly a stronghold of the few Jews there were in the department then. But not getting that job turned out to be a lucky break. Some years later a kingpin gambler named Harry Gross was caught distributing payoffs right up the line to the Mayor's office. The bag-men for the top brass of the police department turned out to be some of those very same guys from our class.

"Coming in as rookies, it must have knocked their eyeballs out to see the kind of cash they were being offered simply to allow men like Harry Gross to run their gambling empire. We were all taking home forty-three dollars twice a month, uniform or plainclothes, but their pay was augmented by as much as $5000 a month. Mind you, this wasn't for letting kids shoot up their arms with dope. It was just for permitting gentlemen to place a wager on a sporting event.

"As a young kid new to it all I'm glad I wasn't put in that situation; it would have been hard to find the way out. Once you get a little seasoning, of course, there's no excuse. Later on, when I was a desk sergeant myself in the Bronx, an inspector in command of a division—that's four precincts—dropped over to my station house one night and asked if I wanted to become his sergeant supervisor of plainclothes. I asked for a day to think it over. But I didn't have to think. By then I knew the score. Plainclothesmen were not detectives but patrolmen out of uniform assigned mainly to police gambling and other types of vice. Often they ended up aboard the gravy train. They'd fly out to Chicago or Cleveland for a World Series game, and if the Series went more than four they'd be out and back twice in the same week. Who could afford that? In those days not one cop out of twenty had ever been on a plane! To us guys who wore a uniform and allotted ourselves twenty-five cents for lunch, it was fantastic. Way too fantastic. I called this inspector back the next day and told him no thanks. I wasn't that crazy about baseball anyhow."

On the morning in June, when graduation assignments were issued for his class, Seedman ran down to the corner candy store for the early edition of the *Times*, which then published all Special Orders of the Police Department. He'd drawn the 48th Precinct in the Bathgate section of the Bronx, which was predominantly black even then, though it made up for its lack of downtown glamour with plenty of action. But Seedman was hardly to get a taste of the 48th. He had barely begun to familiarize himself with the neighborhood when he was inducted in the Army late in 1942.

He was assigned, predictably, to the MPs and after a brief tour at Camp Phillips, Kansas, he was sent to the University of Chicago for a year's intensive study in French language, European geography, and culture to prepare him for military government duty once he got overseas. Though he had left the 48th the greenest cop on the beat, his classmates at Chicago apparently already sensed the style and substance of later years. His capsule description in the mimeographed yearbook:

> Le flic . . . his eye has not lost its cunning . . . sees everything . . . says nothing. . . .

A few days after D-Day, Seedman was packed into a landing craft off Utah Beach with his Civil Affairs unit, awaiting the order to go ashore. Characteristically, his concern during those hours was not the resistance they might encounter ashore but that his jeep should not stall in several feet of swirling water. As methodically as he would later deal with murder suspects and clues, Seedman spent the night checking seals and casings around ignition parts, the battery, and the six-foot-high exhaust-pipe extension. At dawn, as other jeeps around him stalled out or gurgled fitfully in the hood-high water, Seedman's jeep chugged easily through the waves to the beach.

During the advance inland over the following weeks, Seedman would search at the end of each day for a suitable trench or foxhole to sleep in, since stretching out under the jeep provided too inviting a target for strafing *Fokkers*. He would cozily line the sides of his hole with stones, the floor with straw, and cover the top with sticks or more straw before going to sleep.

After two months of slow progress across France, Seedman's unit headed toward Paris as the city was being liberated. Seedman found himself in the middle of a vast truck convoy, and fastened his eyes on the red "cat's eyes" taillights of the vehicle fifty feet ahead. Around midnight the lights suddenly vanished and the next thing Seedman knew he was leading the thirty trucks and jeeps behind him toward the Tuileries gardens in the heart of Paris. Somehow he managed to find their objective, and at two o'clock he bedded down under his jeep, a few yards from a French tank. When he awoke in the morning, he saw a pretty young girl, shoes in hand, climb out of the tank hatch, as hairy arms braced her from below. Now he *knew* he was in Paris.

After ten days in Paris, Civil Affairs pushed north to Nivelles, a town in Belgium close to Waterloo. Seedman was quartered ("appropriately, on Rue des Juifs") in the comfortable home of a man named Laloux, a pigeon-breeder. It was in Nivelles that Seedman's uncanny instinct for smelling out inconsistencies overlooked by others may have first surfaced.

One evening he was invited by members of the Armée Blanche, the Underground, to celebrate the liberation of Brussels at a town bistro. Another guest of honor was an English operative who had parachuted into Nivelles a year before to make contact with the Underground and to provide intelligence for the Allied advance in Belgium. As the Germans retreated the Englishman came out of hiding and rode with Armée Blanche squads seeking out pockets of German stragglers.

The Englishman was thin and pale, with calm blue eyes and impeccable manners. He regaled them with tales from his Highlands boarding school, where the boys were forced to take bracing ice-water showers each morning, and he reminisced nostalgically about summers in Glyndebourne at the opera festival and winter Saturdays spent browsing along Charing Cross Road's musty bookstalls.

Seedman got along well with the Englishman, and the next morning invited him for a ride in his jeep. As they stopped to look over a schoolhouse abandoned by the Germans, Seedman wondered aloud how that great German army, so well trained and led, could continue to lose. Perhaps soon it would regroup for a triumphant counter-offensive.

The Englishman eyed Seedman with interest.

After all, Seedman went on, the Aryan race was clearly *superior*. Seedman had been leaning against a tree—but suddenly he snapped to rigid attention. "Heil Hitler!" he cried.

The response was instinctive. The "Englishman" clicked his heels in a Nazi brace.

Seedman said nothing, just stared at the man with the same flat, steady, unnerving gaze and concentrated calm that would later become his trademark. The man looked wildly for a direction, any direction, in which to run. Seedman put his hand to his pistol and the man's face crumpled.

"I had a feeling this guy wasn't right when we met," Seedman recalled later. "At first it was only his English—it wasn't quite right, something the Belgians couldn't be expected to catch. But then they started telling how he'd gone out with them to flush out enemy stragglers. On one of these sorties a squad had been ambushed and this Englishman was the only one to get back alive. It just smelled all wrong.

"He turned out to be a German who had spent a few years in London as a voice student and was now waiting only for the right moment to slip out of Nivelles. I handed him over to my friends of the Armée Blanche who promised he would receive quiet but absolute justice."

Seedman began to make it a nightly habit to nurse a drink in the same bistro until close to midnight; his French was fluent now, and it was a good place to find out what was going on. One night he noticed an old man at the bar who was shaking his head and muttering to himself.

Seedman softly asked him what was the problem.

"*Alors*," the man sighed. "I am seventy-one years old and suddenly I am going crazy. It is an embarrassment to my family. We have never had a crazy person for generations, and now there is me. . . ."

"What gives you such an idea?"

He gestured to his temples. "Every night I am awakened at two o'clock exactly by wireless signals in my head. Dots and dashes, dashes and dots filling my head for an hour, sometimes two hours."

"Did you ever ask anyone else to listen?"

"Of course. My wife, my son, my two daughters, they all listened. But if they could hear it, *mon ami*, would I be sitting here telling you how I'm going crazy?"

"You have a point," Seedman said, nodding. "Listen, I don't have anything pressing at two o'clock. Could I come up to listen?"

"It won't do any good," the old man insisted.

Seedman accompanied him anyhow to his flat, which was on the third floor of an old building above a *boulangerie*. At two o'clock they were sipping cognac when the old man suddenly sat bolt upright. He looked at the visitor expectantly, but Seedman had to shake his head reluctantly.

The next morning Seedman rounded up two Signal Corps technicians who returned with him that night with a direction-finding receiver. Once again the cognac was poured and at two o'clock on the button the old man tuned in precisely on schedule. The technicians twirled their dials. Within a few seconds dots and dashes crackled harshly from the receiver. The strongest signal seemed to come from the direction of a theater a few blocks away which had been closed since the invasion.

Leaving the old man and his wife beaming, Seedman and the two men from the Signal Corps cased the theater until they found an unlocked door. Inside the place was musty and black, but Seedman was sure he had seen a dim light, like a shrouded flashlight, snap off in the balcony as they came in.

Seedman and one signalman made their way upstairs while the other covered them from below. In the projection room they found a fellow hunched over a transmitter, as he had been at two o'clock each morning since the Germans had left him behind several weeks earlier.

"Like the other spy," says Seedman, "he was set up with English official papers, which allowed him to move around by day gathering information for his two-o'clock report. The old man just happened to have his inner ear tuned to the same frequency. The next night at the bistro we toasted him to a full night's sleep."

The Civil Affairs unit followed the front line forces down the eastern border of Belgium and France, crossing into Germany from Wiltz on February 17, 1945. Now that they were in enemy territory, their title changed to Military Government, and Seedman found himself investigating the alleged rapes of civilian women by American soldiers and the occasional murder of a GI, usually by a prostitute or her pimp. Arriving in Munich on June 2 with the city in full bloom, Seedman was assigned the job of clamping down on the black market that was running rampant in basic necessities, to say nothing of luxury items.

"Since we were strangers ourselves," he says, 'it seemed to me the best tool we could use was someone who could fit right in with the black market—a guy we could put on a long leash and let sniff out the operators. Of course, we had to give him an incentive to work for us."

With another investigator also named Al, Al Graff, Seedman drove to the Bavaria Penitentiary in search of a prisoner with a likely crime profile. The warden opened the cell door on a stocky, bald, sharp-eyed little man who looked like an imitation Peter Lorre. Seedman was surprised to discover he was a Polish Jew, fluent in German, who had been released from two years at Buchenwald only to go on a spree of burglarizing Munich apartments and robbing citizens in hallways. That is what had landed him back in civilian jail. His name was Nathan Wald.

"Wald," said Seedman, "either you can rot in this place or you can go to work for us. If you do it well and fast, maybe we can persuade the authorities here to be lenient with you."

Wald's eyes glittered as Seedman explained that they wanted him to infiltrate the black market. To someone like Wald, the assignment sounded too good to be true.

"We started him off with a stake of ten cartons of Lucky Strikes," says Seedman. "By the next evening he had turned over the names and operating posts of three black marketeers. They were the first of many. By the end of the week he invited Al and me up to his new apartment for an *apéritif* and offered us a choice of Scotch or Canadian whisky, vodka, or Dom Perignon, and on our way out he handed back the ten cartons of Lucky Strikes. I noticed several dozen more, of assorted brands, where that came from."

"Another fellow we used in the same way was a French Jew named Willi Korn. He had also made it through Buchenwald. Like Wald, he had a natural penchant for underhand dealing, but he also had a streak of violence, Mafioso-style, which Wald lacked. When the husband of his mistress began to complain that she was spending too much time away from home, the guy simply disappeared.

"Korn had been dealing in black-market butter, a business he found so lucrative that he demanded a full partnership from the owner of the creamery. Like any talented shakedown artist, he tried to convince the fellow that his management techniques would mean his new half-share of profits would exceed his full share before. Korn wasn't kidding. By distributing production directly into the black market and eliminating the legal middleman, profits would soar. Of course, if the owner didn't see it his way, Korn could always deliver more convincing arguments.

"Not surprisingly, the owner took Korn's deal. But when he came to us secretly to complain, we made our own offer to Korn. Either he could sniff out black marketeers for us or we would turn him over to the civil authorities. Willi did well for us. He was especially good at locating dealers in fake ration cards and travel papers, since he had dealt in this merchandise himself. Like many violent men, Willi was quite charming, but after a while he began to carry out his work with excessive zeal, so one night I drove him to Stuttgart and delivered him to the French command. I understood that he was soon doing well in Paris as a silent partner in several of the best nightclubs. Years later, in New York, I thought of him again when I came up against our own shakedown artist with special flair, Joe Gallo. If ever two men were soulmates, it was Willi and Joe."

Seedman quickly learned that Korn had no monopoly on the tactics of muscling in. While passing through a checkpoint in southern Bavaria one day, Seedman realized that the woman in the car ahead was Hilda Laussen, secretary to General Charles Keegan, a Bronx Councilman who was Seedman's overall boss in Military Government in Bavaria. Wondering how a secretary had wangled the raft of papers necessary to travel so far from Munich, Seedman walked over to her car just as the MPs were about to wave her through.

Hilda handed her papers over to Seedman with a pleasant smile. She had all the proper passes, all right, but something about them bothered Seedman—the handwriting of the authorizing signatures did not look American. Noticing that the man sitting beside Hilda seemed to be enjoying her sudden discomfiture, Seedman decided to question him instead, and the story quickly tumbled out.

Hilda had approached him and offered to double the profits of his baking business by the simple expedient of denying rations, travel privileges, even supply contracts to his competitors—something that as secretary to General Keegan she could arrange easily. In return, she asked only for a modest piece of the business. On Monday morning Charlie Keegan had a new secretary.

On the sunny, brisk morning of December 15, 1945, amid the sweet clatter of horns and garbage cans, Seedman was back walking the beat on Boston Road he had barely begun three years before. Along with him on the midnight-to-eight shift he carried ten pages torn out of the study manual for the sergeant's exam. He was still green at the job, but he couldn't help feel he was better qualified for higher rank than many of the more experienced patrolmen in the 48th. After all, he was a college graduate, an accountant, and now he had an extra year of intensive language training from the University of Chicago. On a practical level, he had spent the last two years investigating a full range of crimes in Military Government.

Under the Bronx street lamps in the quiet morning hours, Seedman would check store front doors with his right hand, while holding in his left the study pages, which he read aloud, discussing with
himself problems that might arise in the life of a sergeant supervisor.

But the road to promotion was not to be as simple as tearing
pages from a study manual. Up to now he had encountered no problems as a Jew in a predominantly Irish police force. Italians, Jews,
and even the few blacks and Puerto Ricans mixed easily with the
Irish in the intimacy of the locker room, even exchanging racial
jokes with unforced good humor. So he was especially disturbed
when a sergeant named Charlie Hess began bearing down on him
harder than on other young patrolmen.

After being "turned out" at the start of a shift, for example, it
was customary for patrolmen to be checked out by the supervising
sergeant twice—usually two hours after the tour had begun and two
hours before it ended. This was called "giving a see." But Charlie
Hess checked Seedman incessantly, sometimes doubling back after
only ten minutes in hopes of catching him drinking coffee or warming himself in a doorway. Hess might give Seedman a "see" as often
as eight times on a tour. Seedman did not worry that he would be
caught off post, since he was determined not to commit even a minor
infraction while Hess had the duty, but the knowledge that he was
being singled out nagged him.

One night in February 1946 Hess pulled alongside Seedman in
his patrol car. It was a miserable, blowy night and Seedman was
walking his beat along Tremont Avenue. Hess rolled down the
frosted window just enough to stare at the patrolman whose coat
and cap visor were coated with wet snow.

"Tell me the truth, Al," Hess said. "You really don't like this
job, do you?"

"I love this job," Seedman replied. "I never had a shift that I
couldn't wait to get to work."

"Even on a night like this? You can level with me, Al. Even *I*
don't like coming to work on a night like this."

Seedman motioned to the pelting snow. "It's real clean stuff,
sir." Hess rolled up his window and drove away.

Just before dawn one morning in spring Seedman was checking
storefronts along Boston Road when he discovered the door of a dry
cleaner unlocked. Nothing seemed amiss inside, though the cash
register was empty. But when he called the old man who owned

the place, Seedman was surprised to learn that the twenty dollars left under the cash register tray was missing.

Soon after the old man met Seedman at the store, Hess turned up. Putting an arm around the proprietor's shoulder, he said, "Your store never would have got burglarized if this patrolman had done his job. Why, you discovered the bust-in yourself, didn't you?"

The old man shook his head. "The station house called me up at five-thirty to tell me what happened. This officer was watching over the store when I got here. I don't want to dispute you, Sergeant, but I think he did his job."

Hess glared at Seedman. "Somebody out there knew you were a lazy bastard on your post. That's why they knew it would be easy. If Mr. Levitas here understood that, he could file a complaint and I'd bring you up on departmental charges."

Hess looked at his watch. "Now I'm late getting out of here because of you," he said. He stalked out.

But even without Hess's badgering, Seedman was beginning to have serious second thoughts about becoming a sergeant. That had been his ambition ever since returning from the Army; he had practically ruined his eyes straining to read his manual pages under the street lamps, and though the exam was still a year off, he could not help but feel confident.

But now he thought about what life would be like once he was promoted. As a sergeant he would "turn out" the patrolmen at the start of each tour. He would give them their "sees," log in all their tours, make changes and substitutions, figure out vacation schedules. He would sit behind the precinct desk, write notations in the blotter, take telephone complaints, act as a funnel for cases that had to go up to the second-floor Detective Squad room. Whatever recordkeeping had to be done, and there was plenty, would be his responsibility. If he had learned one thing in accounting classes, it was how to keep neat records; he knew he would make a good sergeant, a good supervisor. It certainly would be an advance over patrolling Boston Road at dawn.

But Seedman's thoughts were elsewhere now. He was remembering his experiences with the phony Englishman in Nivelles; the old man with dots and dashes in his head; the crooked Hilda Laussen; the charming and lynxlike Willi Korn; the battle against the black-marketeers. At the time it had been fascinating, but Seedman had assumed that was because he was doing exotic things in faraway places where he had never dreamed of going. Anything there would be fascinating to a boy born in the Bronx. As he walked along Boston Road morning after morning, Seedman began to realize that it wasn't just the foreign locales, it was the work itself. He had been an investigator, he had done the work not of a patrolman, but of a detective. All at once his feelings were clear. He realized that despite his hours of cramming for the sergeant's exam, despite the fact that he would surely do well on it, despite even the promotion it represented, he did not want to be a sergeant like Charlie Hess or even like sergeants he admired. He wanted to be a detective.

On his next day off, Seedman visited his old commander in Military Government at Munich, Bronx Councilman Charlie Keegan. All through his career Seedman would hit it off well with Irishmen, and Keegan was no exception. He promised Seedman his highest recommendation. A week later Seedman was called to the office of the Chief of Detectives. It was the first time he had been to the Rennaissance-style headquarters building that stretched a full block on Centre Street. Mike Ledden, a detective captain, saw him.

"You got a good record, a good 'rabbi,'" Ledden said. "We'll try you out."

"Twenty-five years later," explains Seedman, "detectives would be selected by a committee which weighed their oral expression and street performance. But in those days there were only two ways to get into the Bureau, neither of which had anything to do with committees. You could be a hero in a shootout, foiling a bank robbery and killing or capturing the desperados. If the newspapers played it up with photos, you could be a third grade detective the next morning. I used to dream about doing that, we all did. But that was like waiting for a thunderbolt, and just about as predictable.

"The other way was to have a sponsor, a 'rabbi,' as even Irishmen called it. You had to know someone who could get the ear of the Chief of Detectives or one of his deputies. Where police work ran in the family, which was true of so many Irish cops, your 'rabbi' could be a departmental veteran, even though he may never have gotten high up himself. If he was known, trusted, and liked, that's all that mattered.

"Today we have a more objective selection system for detectives with people outside the Bureau, such as First Deputy Commissioner and the Chief of Personnel involved. But the 'rabbi' system had its value. The 'rabbi' was giving his personal stamp of approval to the man. If he turned out to be a bad detective, the Chief of Detectives would make note of his 'rabbi,' and it reflected as poorly on the 'rabbi' as on the man. So everyone was very careful with recommendations. You might say it's the difference between personal and corporate responsibility."

Seedman received his first assignment as a detective while technically still a patrolman; he had three months to go before he could exchange his "white" shield for gold. Seedman was told to guard the brother of Joseph Scottoriggio, an East Harlem Republican district captain who was set upon by thugs while walking to his polling place on Election Day 1946. They gave him such a beating that he died five days later.

The Scottoriggio case caused a national scandal. Governor Thomas E. Dewey visited the obscure politician at the hospital before he died. On the floor of Congress, John Rankin of Mississippi threatened to lead a House movement to unseat Representative Vito Marcantonio, the Democrat Scottoriggio had campaigned against. Frank Hogan personally directed the DA's investigation. Mayor William O'Dwyer promised to detail one thousand police to the departmental investigation. When the case was not quickly solved, Police Commissioner Wallender fired an assistant chief inspector in charge of East Manhattan and transferred the commander of East Harlem detectives and most of his men.

The reason for the nationwide uproar was that the killing of Scottoriggio had struck at the very heart of democracy. A man should be able to walk freely and safely to his polling place to cast his vote, and anything that threatened his precious right of franchise was not to be tolerated.

"I was assigned to guard Joe's brother, Natale Scottoriggio," says Seedman. "For two months I sat outside the door of his office, at night I took him home. I waited until he and his wife were tucked in bed and I heard him snoring, and then took my pajamas from my briefcase and went to sleep on the couch.

"That assignment taught me early how fantastically expensive protective custody can be. Natale, at least, had a job and a home. In later years we often had to put up material witnesses in good hotels, support their families, pay their medical bills, even pick up the tab for a diaper service. Most of these expenses could be slashed, obviously, by putting the material witness in civil jail, but it is hard to blame someone who has not committed a crime for not wanting to go to jail—even if it is a civil jail, where he doesn't have to mix with felons.

"Once we put in protective custody a two-hundred-pound waitress who was the lone witness to the murder of a Queens nightclub owner by some shakedown artists. They promised to do the same to her if they could, and without her the state had no case. She wanted to stay in her mother's apartment, so at least we were spared the expense of hotels. But her safety required us to guard her with two detectives teamed in eight-hour shifts—that's six men per day every day for months before the trial, and months, often years after. Several of these detectives were first grade, earning more than $20,000 a year, exclusive of medical and retirement benefits— and that waitress, incidentally, was not a light eater.

"At any moment today in New York City as many as two dozen citizens may be scattered in hotels and apartments under protective custody. In the Scottoriggio case fifteen material witnesses and others were under full-time guard. The Federal authorities have even more elaborate methods of protective custody, especially in narcotics conspiracy cases. The bill for protecting a single witness can pile up to more than a million dollars.

"The saddest part of this whole business is not the cash that rolls out. This is merely painful. It is watching good detectives who thrive at their jobs having to sit and sit in front of a hotel-room door as if they were on the porch of a home for the aged. Yet this kind of responsibility can't be entrusted to a guard hired from Brink's. If the moment ever does come when an attempt is made on a material witness, these men who are skilled in handling violent confrontations are the only ones who can be counted on to fend it off.

"The solution to the whole miserable situation, I'm convinced, is a place we could call Material Witness City: a resort with plenty of recreational facilities to put people in a cooperative mood, but with a fenced and patrolled perimeter, a single access road and entrance. Several dozen guests could be protected at least as well as they presently are individually with only a fraction of the manpower. And if ever the guest roster got low, police officers could bring up their wives and kids for an inexpensive vacation."

After three months of hanging around Natale Scottoriggio, Seedman was ordered to report to the Safe and Loft Squad. Though he did not appreciate it at the time, this was the best duty a fledgling detective could hope for. The squad had been formed in the 1920s, when the criminal elite were safecrackers like Johnny Valentine who were virtuosos at listening to tumblers and probing locks with needles, disdaining such crude roughhouse tactics as lighting off a charge of TNT.

These safecrackers were considered the gentlemen of their profession. Most had a horror of violence. They did their work in the morning hours, often on the long narrow floors of loft buildings which could not afford night watchmen and were often connected, enabling a safecracker to slip in one building and walk across rooftops to the next. Good safecrackers always planned their route well in advance.

"The detectives who tracked down these criminals," says Seedman, "were members of Safe and Loft. Unlike regular squad or even Homicide detectives, they could roam all five boroughs of the city. They also handled hijackings and a wide range of other thefts. In fact, before the Department had an Internal Affairs unit to investigate wrongdoings by members of the force, these sensitive cases were investigated by Safe and Loft. The reason was that Ray McGuire, the captain who had run the squad for years, was famous for his integrity. He ran the cleanest show in town, but if he had to, he could find the dirtiest."

One Friday just before Christmas in 1947, Seedman helped lug into the Safe and Loft office dozens of cartons of toys that had been recovered from a hijacking case. There were dolls, teddy bears, stuffed animals of all kinds.

Ray McGuire, busy overseeing the operation, suddenly looked up and saw that it was close to three o'clock.

"I'm never going to get to lunch," he said. "I was going to stop at Macy's to pick up some toys for my girls."

One of the detectives mentioned he had to do the same at Macy's. McGuire handed him a twenty-dollar bill.

"Pick up a pair of dolls for me, will ya?" he said.

"If there were two dolls in that office, there were two thousand," remembers Seedman. "Yet I doubt it ever occurred to McGuire that a pair would never be missed. Or that the owner would be delighted to make them a gift. One example like that is better than a year's supply of lectures, memos, and threats from the Commissioner's office on the need for honesty in the ranks."

Since he was fluent in French, one of Seedman's first assignments from McGuire was to monitor the tap on the phone of Du Midi, a restaurant on West 48th Street where several regular patrons were suspected of smuggling. The "wire," as detectives call it, was set up in a linen closet behind the ballroom of the Belvedere Hotel, around the corner from the restaurant, and Seedman spent day after day cooped up in that cramped space under a twenty-five-watt lightbulb, scribbling down every word of what never amounted to anything more than idle chatter.

McGuire next assigned Seedman to investigate the hijacking of a shipment of fine Irish lace from the West Side docks. After a day of checking garment center workshops for any sign of the stolen goods, Seedman returned to the squad room to find two veteran Irish detectives questioning a Hassidic Jew they had nabbed for a similar theft.

"Hey," said one of the detectives to Seedman. It was the first time either had addressed him. "This fellow here, your *Landsmann*, he speaks only Yiddish. See what you can get out of him."

Seedman took the man to a corner, where they couldn't be overheard and it wouldn't be apparent that he knew little Yiddish.

The Hassid leaned close. "Don't worry," he whispered, "I speak English as good as you, but I didn't want them to know."

Seedman whipped out a sample of the stolen lace he had been carrying around ever since being assigned to the hijacking. "You know anything about a hot load of lace that looks like this?"

The Hassid rubbed the swatch between his fingers, plainly hesitating.

"You'll only be helping yourself." Seedman motioned to the other detectives. "Remember the *pogroms* in Russia where the Cossacks came trampling through the *shtetl* on horseback?"

The man nodded.

"Well, they don't have *pogroms* only in Russia!"

The Hassid nervously looked over at the hulking detectives. "Go to a fellow named Stone," he whispered rapidly. "Owns three yard-goods stores. Two here, one in Queens. Lives in Jamaica Estates. A very rich man. But where he gets his merchandise, it's not all kosher."

That evening, after finding the lace, Seedman and two other detectives, Phelan and Phyffe, drove out to Stone's house in Jamaica Estates. It was as elegant as any section of the city and Seedman, who had grown up in a Fox Street tenement in the Bronx, had never imagined that such stately homes, with broad lawns, huge shade trees, and lush flowerbeds, even existed within the borders of his city.

A slender dark man wearing a blue silk smoking jacket answered the door himself. Even before they had flashed their gold shields, he understood who they were.

"I don't know what evidence you have against me," said Stone. "I'm confident that in a court of law I would be found innocent, but you always lose when you go to court, even when you win. And I just don't like to lose."

Stone stared coolly at the detectives, then went over to the liquor cabinet to offer them a drink, Seedman assumed. But instead the liquor cabinet doors opened to a safe. Stone calmly twirled the dials and removed a thick packet of bills which he handed to Bill Phyffe. Something about them looked odd to Seedman. Then he realized they were hundred-dollar bills—he had never seen one before.

"That's $10,000 for each of you," said Stone as if he were giving his children their allowance.

The two older detectives looked over the bills and then whispered between themselves for a moment.

"Okay," said Phyffe, "that's for us." He gestured with his thumb to Seedman. "But what about the kid here? I mean, after all, he's the little bugger who broke this case."

Stone sighed wearily. "You saw the blue Cadillac in the garage?"

"Yeah?"

"That's for him."

"Tell you what, Mr. Stone," said Howard Phelan. "We know how it is when you have kids and the wife, so we won't do anything tonight. You just be in our office at 400 Broome Street tomorrow morning at nine o'clock and we'll lock you up then."

It was almost eleven o'clock when they drove back to the city. Sitting in the back seat, Seedman remembered how he had heard of cops being bribed back in the Bronx. There were stories of the fruit man tossing a patrolman an apple with a 50-cent piece cut into it.

But there had been more disturbing incidents that Seedman had seen with his own eyes. He remembered being ordered to stand guard at a meat market that had been broken into in the early-morning hours. Around 4:45 the duty sergeant—for once, it wasn't Charlie Hess—walked in.

"They get the safe open?" he asked.

"No."

The sergeant scratched his chin. "Sometimes they'll get in and then lock it back up nice and neat so it takes the owner longer to find out how much is missing."

He knelt down. "Let me just give it a few jiggles." The sergeant was on his knees working with the tumbler dial for forty-five minutes, but he couldn't get the safe open. He walked out unable to straighten up.

"Even employees have their own methods of profiting from inflated loss claims," says Seedman. "Not far from that bar was a grocery store that had just been robbed. As I entered I was sure I'd heard the cash register ringing."

"The bastard cleaned out my register, every cent," the manager told Seedman.

"What were you just ringing up?"

"A few items for a customer. She's an old lady. She calls in her order."

The manager saw that Seedman was skeptical. He took a twenty-dollar bill from his apron pocket and handed it to him. "That should do it, huh?"

"Nah, it doesn't do anything," answered Seedman.

Just then the boss rushed in. Seedman took him aside and explained that the manager may have rung up extra sales since the robbery.

"I knew it!" the man yelled. "I knew that bum was cheating on me all these years! Well, he's gonna get fired. . . ."

But even as the boss carried on, Seedman realized that the manager would not be fired, that he had done just what he was supposed to do, that the boss was not angry at all.

"This manager simply had been ringing up small sales on the register. Later, once business was back to normal he could ring up 'No Sale' on actual purchases, pocket the money, and claim the sales had been made before the robbery. And the insurance company would have to pay out the full amount listed on the cash register tape the moment the police arrived. So this employee had not done his boss a bad turn. Instead of getting fired, he probably stood to make an even split on the extra cash.

"Riding back into the city late at night with Phelan and Phyffe, the two old-time detectives from Safe and Loft, I felt fantastically elated," Seedman recalls. "I'd watched my two partners look at more cash than the three of us made together in a whole year—and not even blink. My own salary then was $3808. It was true, of course, that these were Ray McGuire's men, they were the best. Not all detectives from all squads would have handed back that packet of C-notes.

"Even though we'd skipped dinner and I was starved, I never felt better about being a cop. Or—as I had to keep reminding myself, I was a detective."

BRASS

Seedman got his first introduction to the Mafia from a coalbin behind Mulberry Street in lower Manhattan. It was late summer 1947, and he was transcribing the phone calls of a felon named Carmine Galente. In those days all conversations off the "wire" had to be written down in longhand, not taped. Many detectives just couldn't write fast enough to keep up. Those who could were not always able later to read what they had scribbled down. But ever since the Du Midi restaurant taps, when Seedman had managed to capture everything in his neat flowing hand—in French, no less—Ray McGuire decided he had the knack.

Seedman was not altogether overjoyed at the honor. In the linen closet behind the Belvedere Hotel ballroom he had only had to contend with moths and a few roaches. Here in this coalbin underneath a tenement a block from Galente's place, rats scooted along the timbers. Sitting on a cold "wire" early in the morning, black as a chimneysweep, Seedman got as close as ever to firing his .38 in the course of duty. He would draw a bead on the bright-eyed rodents, perched on their rear legs, listening, sniffing, as they gnawed a chunk of coal. He would have liked nothing better than to blow them away one after another.

Carmine (Lillo) Galente was an associate of Joe Bonanno, then the longest-reigning don in any New York crime family. Since he was a sixteen-year-old growing up in Brooklyn's Bay Ridge section, Galente had been arrested periodically for such crimes as robbery, assault, and murder. Twice in 1930 he had been arrested for shooting at policemen during robbery attempts. The first time a patrolman named Walter de Castillia died of wounds, and though Galente was widely reported in underworld circles to be the killer, he was let go for lack of hard evidence. Four months later, on Christmas Eve, a patrolman named John J. Meenahan wounded Galente as he attempted to take the payroll of the Leibman Breweries in Brooklyn. This time Galente was convicted; he had served nine years in prison when he was released on parole.

At 9 P.M. on January 13, 1943, one hour and fifteen minutes after Galente had made his weekly report to his parole officer at 80 Centre Street, Carlo Tresca, editor of the leftist Italian-language newspaper *Il Martello* (*The Hammer*) was shot dead as he walked out of the paper's office at Fifth Avenue and 15th Street. Several minutes later a new Cadillac was found abandoned with doors open in front of the subway station at Seventh Avenue and 18th Street. Galente's parole officers noticed that he had not been his usual cocky self during the interview—he had fidgeted and stared out the window—so while normally they would not have followed him, this time they did. He took the elevator to the lobby, but instead of going to the subway he was spirited away at the curb by a waiting car—the Cadillac abandoned at the subway entrance seventy-five minutes later.

Yet when Galente was picked up the following day, he swore he had taken the subway to a movie theater, then gone uptown to visit a "broad who had a good name with her husband" so he did not want to divulge her name. Lacking any positive identification by witnesses at the murder scene or any fingerprints in the car, Galente was allowed to go free.

"This Galente had no politics of his own," says Seedman. "He had spent most of his adult life in jail. But Carlo Tresca, through *Il Martello,* was an outspoken critic of Mussolini, and after the murder word filtered back from Italy that Vito Genovese, deported by the U.S. for his narcotics dealings, had promised *Il Duce* to have Tresca silenced.

"It is hard enough to prove who ordered a Mafia 'hit' in New

York, but in Italy it's virtually impossible," says Seedman. "We could not connect the murder to Genovese, nor even to Galente. But higher-ups in the Police Department felt if we continued to watch Galente, he might slip up somehow and provide us with the link. Which is why I was assigned to tap his phone in the late summer of 1947, almost five years after the crime."

Seedman was sitting on a folding beach chair in his coalbin in the early morning of September 4 when he overheard Galente agree to pick up an illegal still at a tinsmith's shop in Brooklyn. Bootleg alcohol was then a profitable racket and Seedman was delighted to hear that Galente and a trucker would meet in an hour. Even though it had nothing to do with the Tresca matter, here was a chance to put the screws on Galente. Normally Seedman would have called Safe & Loft for help, but at 1:30 in the morning, with only a single duty man in the office, there wasn't time. Instead, Seedman called the local 84th Precinct and asked the desk sergeant to post patrolmen at the streets leading to the tinsmith's shop, where shortly before 3 A.M. Seedman was able to arrest Galente and several henchmen who had come for the still.

It seemed as if he had done the right thing. But in the morning McGuire was furious. "Goddam it!" he shouted. "Why did you have to call in the uniform boys?"

"But, sir," Seedman said, "if any of them got away, Patrol would be there to nab them."

"You're a young fellow," said McGuire more softly. "You didn't know any better. But you do *now*. Detectives never, *never* ask a goddam patrolman for help in making an arrest or anything else."

In later years Seedman would often remember that upbraiding. He understood that McGuire believed heart and soul in the absolute superiority of the Detective Bureau—a man could aspire to nothing higher—and it was from Ray McGuire that Seedman himself later learned how much to demand of his own detectives. But on that September morning Seedman felt he hadn't deserved the dressing-down he got from McGuire.

From listening to Galente wheel and deal over the phone, Seedman had anticipated meeting someone with style, but under the street lamps at the tinsmith's he had confronted a dumpy hood with no class at all. Yet Galente appeared to carry considerable clout. Seedman had expected to be called up soon to testify at Galente's trial—after all, the man had been caught redhanded, and the wiretaps were corroborating evidence. But he waited and waited and began to wonder. Another phase of the wiretaps soon made him very doubtful he would ever see Galente go to jail.

Seedman and his partner, Vince Baliunas, picked up word over the "wire" that several of Galente's henchmen were about to deliver an order of bootleg liquor to a Harlem after-hours club on 124th Street. Using the subway, Seedman and Baliunas got there first. They watched from the shadow of a doorway on Lenox Avenue as a prewar Buick, riding low in the back, pulled up to the club, where two whites got out and knocked on the door in a rhythmic pattern. Two blacks came out. The Galente men were about to open the trunk of the car when they realized they were being watched.

The detectives had no alternative but to move in. Baliunas took one of Galente's men, Seedman the other. In the trunk they found eight five-gallon cans of home-brewed alcohol. It was the real stuff, all right. Seedman almost fell over from a single whiff.

Since the blacks had not yet accepted the goods, only Galente's henchmen could be charged with illegal possession of alcohol. As with the arrest of Galente at the tinsmith's shop, the case appeared to be nailed shut—and this time it was called promptly to trial.

The defense lawyer made an imposing figure in his suit and vest as he called Seedman to the stand.

"You arrested my client, Officer?"

"Yes."

"And you saw fit to charge him with illegal transport of alcohol?"

"Yes."

"Did he have this alcohol on his person?"

"No. It was in the trunk of the car."

"How did you learn my client got out of this car, Officer Seedman?"

"I watched him."

"Watched him from where?"

"From a doorway on 124th Street, just off Lenox Avenue."

"How far was that from where the auto stopped?"

"About sixty feet."

"Tell me, Officer," continued the lawyer, "how were you able to identify my client at that distance on what the almanac will show was a moonless night?"

"There was a street lamp."

"How far from where the car stopped was this lamp?"

Seedman thought a moment. "About twenty feet."

The lawyer fixed Seedman with an interested stare for a long moment. Then he walked over to the defense table, where an assistant handed him a scroll tied with a blue ribbon.

"Your Honor," he said, pulling off the ribbon with a flourish, "I have here a diagram of the intersection in question prepared by a licensed civil engineer. It shows that the nearest lamppost to the point where this Officer Seedman claims to have seen my client step from a car is exactly. . . . forty-six feet, eleven inches. I must respectfully submit to the officer that no lamppost exists where he has stated. It is not, I might add, a quibbling difference. His error on this point is more than *double!*"

The lawyer approached the bench. "Now, if Officer Seedman had been standing as close to the man he *thinks* was my client as I am right now to you, Your Honor, I might be more willing to concede that he could possibly, just possibly, have identified my client without benefit of direct light. But by his own estimate, this officer was at least sixty feet away, peeking from a dark entranceway. It would take the eyes of an Indian scout to accurately identify a man at that distance at night. As it turns out, Officer Seedman couldn't even identify the position of a lamppost. Under these circumstances, can we point the finger of guilt at this or any man?"

"You've made your point, Counselor," said the judge. "I find the accused Not Guilty."

"As the judge banged down the gavel," Seedman says, "I knew I'd learned three lessons. The first was never hesitate to say 'I don't know' to a tricky question like the lamppost measurement. The second was to stay the hell out of court. The third was that a man I had seen commit a crime with my own eyes could, with the help of a fancy lawyer and maybe an assist from a judge, go free. That was not only true of Galente's henchman; it turned out to be true of Galente himself. I had nabbed him with both hands on the still, but he never even came to trial."

In 1957 Galente got a speeding ticket near Binghamton, New York, not far from Apalachin, where the crime "summit meeting" was held—a meeting to which Galente had been invited. He did not want to pay the speeding ticket. First he hired two detectives from across the Hudson to try to bribe the state troopers to tear up the ticket. When that failed, the Summons Bureau and even the court itself were hounded by a horde of politicos, including several State Assemblymen and the Speaker of the Assembly, all imploring that the ticket be quashed. When he heard of all that pressure brought to bear for a simple speeding ticket, Seedman marveled that he had not been drummed out of uniform for daring to arrest Galente eleven years earlier.

As a detective working out of Safe & Loft, Seedman could not imagine ever wanting any other job. Still, partly out of reflex, partly to keep his hand in, he went ahead and took the sergeant's exam when it was given in 1947 and, to his dismay, found he had scored near the top. Soon he was officially promoted and ordered to sergeant's duty in the 44th Precinct in the West Bronx.

"But I don't want to be a sergeant," he told McGuire.

"It'll be good experience for a young fellow," said McGuire. "Besides, you'll take home more money."

"I don't want more money. If there's any way you can swing it, I want to stay here."

"I can't help you," said McGuire. "You were the guy who took the exam." Seedman knew that highly revered as he was, McGuire had never done too well on exams. That was why he was still an acting captain.

McGuire put an arm around Seedman's shoulder, a gesture he had never made before. "Cheer up, Al," he said. "You'll enjoy a restful tour up there in the Forty-fourth for a bit, then we'll get you back in the Bureau."

Seedman could only hope that McGuire was right and that his tour as a patrol sergeant would be mercifully short. As it turned out, he would not return to the Detective Bureau for another ten years—but when he did, he would never leave it for the rest of his career.

Nobody in the 44th Precinct bothered Seedman the way Hess had in the 48th. The hours were far shorter and more regular than at Safe & Loft; he could actually tell his wife when to expect him home. The pay was also better. Yet he took no pleasure in this work.

"First, you spent four hours at the switchboard, taking all calls that came in to the Precinct," he says. "You sent patrolmen where they were needed. You routed calls upstairs to the detectives. You wasted time talking to nuts, drunks, and lonely people who wanted to tell you either how great or how lousy you were doing your job. After four hours as a switchboard operator, you got to actually go out to check your men at their posts while the other sergeant took over the calls. My best days were when he called in sick. Then I was allowed to spend the whole tour in the streets myself.

"The only good part of the job was that it made me anxious to study for the lieutenant's exam. I was dying to be a lieutenant just so I didn't have to be a sergeant. The only ranks for which a competitive exam is required are sergeant, lieutenant, and captain; the rest are appointive. Since the jobs go to the highest scorers, the guys who are hungry for them spend every available moment studying. If you were working the four-to-midnight shift, you'd leave early to get in a few hours' drilling at Delehanty's. If you worked the eight-to-four day shift, you'd get home late because you had stopped off at Delehanty's. With half the effort, you could be a brain surgeon."

Seedman again scored high on the lieutenant's exam in 1951. After only four years as a sergeant he reported to the 112th Precinct in Maspeth, Queens, as a lieutenant. Again he sat at a desk. Again he had no trouble with bosses. The hours continued to be regular and not nearly as long as when he was a third grade detective, but he disliked this job even more.

"As a sergeant, at least I got out on patrol," he says darkly. "As lieutenant, they keep you chained to the desk right through. Instead of working the switchboard, you sit in front of a blotter and enter each man's tour, when he calls in sick or goes on vacation, when he goes to the bathroom. After eight hours of this, they let you out for sixteen. The month to look forward to is November, when they let you out for an entire tour *twice*—to keep the peace on Election Day and at Macy's Thanksgiving Parade. I knew I'd have to get out of there. This wasn't work for a so-called superior officer, it was for a chimpanzee."

One night at 11:30 Seedman was desultorily working on his blotter when a man he recognized but had never met walked into the 112th. It was Steven P. Kennedy, then the Chief Inspector, later to become Police Commissioner.

"What's doing, Lieutenant?" he asked.

"Two patrolmen collared a burglary suspect an hour ago," Seedman answered, putting down his cigar. "Otherwise, it's quiet."

They walked up to the detective squad room, where the suspects were being fingerprinted and questioned. The two patrolmen who had made the arrest were standing amid the detectives as nervously as Seedman had done as a young patrolman in the 48th.

"Those are two pretty good flatfeet," said Seedman. "They make a lot of collars and they stick. They're looking to become detectives one day."

"They got names?" asked Kennedy.

"Ringswald and Shengel," answered Seedman.

"Would you recommend them now?"

"Without reservation."

Kennedy nodded. As Seedman walked him back to the street, Kennedy asked, "How are you enjoying your own work, Lieutenant?"

Looking straight at Kennedy, Seedman considered the question. "I have no complaints," he said after a moment, "except that I'd rather be doing something else."

Kennedy again nodded and drove off, leaving Seedman to consider whether he should have said more or less to the Chief Inspector. He decided he was glad it wasn't more. A few days later Ringswald and Shengel got word of their impending promotion to the Detective Bureau. Seedman himself got called down to Headquarters to see Kennedy.

"I can put you in a lieutenant's slot in the Police Academy, Al," he said.

Seedman thanked him, even though the job would not get him back onto the street. He'd be farther than ever from crime scenes, in fact, but at least he would be free of that godforsaken blotter.

To his own surprise, Seedman began to thrive the moment he reported to the Police Academy in July 1954. After three months he was assigned to write a new recruit curriculum. Though Ray McGuire's prophecy had yet to be fulfilled, Seedman found himself after six more months in charge of Departmental detective training.

"I tried to balance the training between the mundane chores of a detective's day, like identifying and preserving evidence at a crime scene," he explains, "and the handling of rarer but potentially fatal situations, like disarming a holed-up gunman. To make the problem more realistic, I designed a model hotel room and then set up this mobster with guns all over his body—even complete with a crotch holster. Under the arm of his jacket he had rigged a gun and attached it to his lower arm so that when a detective ordered him to put his hands up, it would automatically fire in the direction he was facing. We did not think up any of these devices: they all came from inventive characters we had come up against in the street.

"In the crucial matter of evidence collection and preservation, which often can mean the difference between conviction or acquittal, we explained the correct way to handle blood samples, hair, stray matchbook covers, newspapers—and, of course, fingerprints. We had no trouble with the detectives; but the assistant DAs who were assigned to the cases, often fresh out of law school, were another story. They didn't know how to use the evidence the detectives gave them, so we held weekend seminars for the local DAs and the sessions were packed."

Since his own front-line experience in many areas of detective work was nil at the time, Seedman did not hesitate to call in experts to lecture to the detectives. Among them was Ray McGuire. This man who'd had to quit school at age fourteen took special pleasure in being invited to appear as guest scholar. The same went for many other gruff veterans—who were all, incidentally, useful contacts for Seedman.

The best of those contacts was Steve Kennedy, who had sprung him from the 112th and brought him to the Police Academy, and who was now, three years later, the Commissioner. An often abrasive man with a short temper and a whiplash wit, Kenendy was widely feared—but not by Seedman, who continued to get along with the Department's Irish with Kennedy no exception.

In 1959, for example, the Commissioner put Seedman on the Host Committee for the convention of the International Association of Police Chiefs that was being held in New York. When he heard that, an old friend of Seedman's, Mack Bernsley, a plumbing contractor from Brooklyn, asked if Seedman could arrange to have Kennedy accept a police shield from General Ramirez, the Police Chief of Mexico City. Bernsley had met Ramirez in Mexico and had led him to believe he was a man with big contacts in New York. Now he wanted to prove it. He promised to supply the shield himself: solid gold, encrusted with three and a half carats of diamonds.

"One other thing I'd be grateful for, Al," said Bernsley, "is if you could arrange for me to be in the picture when the presentation is being made."

Seedman explained the situation to the Commissioner's press officer, who arranged the ceremony. At the appointed hour, Kennedy received General Ramirez, Seedman, and Mack Bernsley in his circular office on the second floor of Police Headquarters. Ramirez looked imposing in his decorated uniform, Bernsley was beaming. But just as the Commissioner was about to accept the shield from Ramirez, Kennedy nudged Seedman.

"Who's that? he whispered, motioning to Bernsley.

Seedman could imagine what Bernsley had told Ramirez; he couldn't see it coming apart for him now. "That's an Honorary Police Chief from Mexico," Seedman whispered back.

"Just as long as he's not a bookie," Kennedy said. Everyone smiled as the photographer snapped away.

At a cocktail party that evening Ramirez pulled Seedman off to a corner.

"You know, Lieutenant, in my country it is not exactly like here," the Mexican said. "If the men choose to go out late, the wives do not always come along."

Seedman could guess what was coming.

"So what I and my friend were hoping," the General went on, "is that you could arrange a little outing for us this evening after the ladies retire."

"Sure," answered Seedman. "I'll pick you up in front of the hotel at ten-thirty." But inside he was boiling. Why hadn't Bernsley arranged their after-hours entertainment? He knew where to find hookers, of course, but that was a job for a bellboy, not for him. Seedman decided to compromise, and arranged for a front-row table at one of the night clubs on 52nd Street which feature a modest strip show.

Even though he was fifteen minutes early, Seedman found Ramirez and his underlings already waiting in the lobby of the hotel.

"This is wonderful what you did," he said, when Seedman told him what he had planned. "I am grateful. But I would be even more grateful if we could do the thing I've been thinking about every night since I was in your city four and a half years ago."

"What's that?" asked Seedman warily.

"We were downtown on the East Lower Side—"

"Lower East Side."

"—and we went to this place called . . . *Rifner's.*" The General leaned forward, grinning expectantly.

"You mean Ratner's?"

"That's it. Ratner's, Lieutenant. It was there I was introduced to cheese blintzes. I never ate anything so delicious. Crisp golden outsides . . . white soft crumbly insides. . . ."

Seedman thought the cigar would drop out of his mouth. "That's *all* you want to do—go to Ratner's?"

"Sí."

That night on Delancey Street, under the hard white lights of Ratner's, as feisty, muttering old Jewish waiters heaped the linoleum tabletop with an endless assortment of blintzes with sour cream, blintzes with cinnamoned apple sauce, a blissful General Ramirez, polished off order upon order until he could eat no more.

In late 1958 the Narcotics Squad, then still part of the Detective Bureau, was undergoing one of its cyclical shakeups when Ray McGuire got the chance to fulfill his prophecy. James (Lefty) Leggett, the Chief of Detectives, was combing the Department for an absolutely clean lieutenant to take command of the sensitive East Manhattan area from the Battery to Spanish Harlem. Leggett asked McGuire for his recommendation.

"Get Seedman from the Academy," said McGuire.

"Put a Jewish lieutenant in narcotics?"

"You asked for the best lieutenant," said McGuire.

That afternoon Lefty Leggett called Seedman to his office. "You had a good 'rabbi' when you came here as a silly kid eleven years ago," he said. "You got a better one now. I don't know if you want to leave the Academy for a job in Narcotics. It's messy. You'll have to go down some real shitholes. The class of people is the worst. I don't know that you want this, Al."

"I want it," said Seedman.

In 1958 narcotics were spreading through New York like a plague, and the number of addicts was multiplying alarmingly. Estimates of the addicted ran to twenty thousand, but as he made his rounds with his squad of eighteen detectives, Seedman figured there were at least that many in his own assigned area, particularly East Harlem. Add in the junkies of West Harlem, the Bronx, and

Brooklyn, and Seedman estimated that the city's total addict population could not be less than sixty thousand.

"Those were still the days when we could conduct searches with relative freedom," says Seedman. "If we wanted to check out an apartment for drugs, we just went in. If the people were home, they could watch. If not, we knocked the door down. When drugs were found, we arrested the residents, otherwise we left. Nobody ever complained.

"Though we trained detectives at the Academy in how to make a thorough search, I learned a few refinements in the field that made all the difference in coming up with the goods. Before we'd raid an apartment for narcotics, I'd send a detective down to the basement fifteen minutes beforehand to turn off the plumbing water. Then if anyone tried to throw the goods down the toilet, the toilet wouldn't flush. More than once, we'd head straight for the bathroom to find the bowl afloat with glassine bags."

Leggett had certainly called it: the level of misery Seedman saw during narcotics raids was worse than all the blood and mayhem he would encounter in years to come.

Seedman continued to study regularly for the captain's exam—the highest rank open to competitive appointment and the position to which he had aspired when he entered the Department after the War. Once again he scored high and was promoted to captain in December 1959. Three months later he was ordered to the Brooklyn North Detective Command as staff supervisor. Though his predecessors had regarded it primarily as a desk job, Seedman saw his new post as a ticket to roam the borough, providing high-level expertise wherever needed. Except that, for the first months, his subordinates would have to be the experts.

On his first day at work, he reported to a basement in the Bedford-Stuyvesant section of Brooklyn where a black "policy" operator lay dead on his back, sliced open from top to bottom by a bread knife. The murder weapon lay in the sink. The squad detective and Homicide specialist who had caught the "squeal" (received the complaint) were already examining the scene. Though Seedman had given lessons in how to handle this situation for years, this was his first murder.

"What do you think, Captain?" asked the Homicide man.

Seedman looked up from the gaping corpse. He was acutely aware that his own book knowledge was being tested against this veteran's street experience. To anyone but a dolt, it was obviously no contest.

"I don't think anything," Seedman answered. "You proceed and I'll watch."

It was the right answer.

From then on hardly a week passed by without Seedman's being called out of his office or home by two or three homicides. He had never dreamed of homicide when he thought of becoming a cop—mostly he saw himself walking down the street dressed in blue, or at worst chasing bank robbers—but he found that the odor of death and the wailing of the bereaved did not upset him. Instead, they made him all the more determined to find out exactly what had caused an ordinary situation to erupt into violence.

To a man who was scrupulous in the personal details of his own life, who had once embraced the precision and neatness of accounting ledgers, a corpse was a challenge to his sense of order, an error in the books. Fortunately, Albert Seedman also turned out to have a great instinct for who done it.

One spring afternoon when Seedman was called to a small apartment house on Flatbush Avenue where a middle-aged woman lay dead on the stairs below the second landing. Her blood-coated groceries were scattered all over the stairway, her left leg was blown off at the thigh.

"The nut who did this must have followed her in," said the local detective who had caught the squeal. "She tried to make a dash for her apartment and he let her have it."

Seedman shook his head. The leg had been blasted off by a shotgun. He could see the pellets in her flesh. The blast must have come from close range—not more than a few feet—since the full charge had hit in a dense mass before it could disperse. And if he was that near, the killer could have just as easily grabbed her as shot her. But the shotgun didn't make sense at any range. Who would dare stalk a woman down bustling Flatbush Avenue in the middle of the afternoon with such a conspicuous weapon? Why risk a shotgun when a pistol or knife would do the job? And what was the job?

Her pocketbook had not been touched, so robbery was out. The only other motive that immediately occurred to Seedman was jealousy. But the residents insisted that their dead neighbor would have been the last to get involved in an affair. Since the death of her husband, she had never been seen in the company of another man.

Seedman was perplexed. If it wasn't robbery, if she hadn't jilted a lover, then why was she lying dead on the stairway?

Down on the stoop a woman was sitting on a small caned chair.

"That your chair?" Seedman asked.

"It belongs to the gentleman who lives in an apartment on the street floor," she said. "He's retired. He likes to sit here on nice days and watch the people go by."

"Where is he now?"

"He usually goes to a bar around the corner for a few beers about this time each day. He'll be back by about four to greet the people coming home from work. He's friendly like that."

"You mean this guy sits here when nothing happens, but when there's a murder he misses it?" Seedman sent two detectives to the bar where the man took his beers, but the bartender had not yet seen the man that afternoon.

Seedman asked the super if he had a key to the man's apartment.

He shook his head.

"How about a ladder?"

"In the basement."

Seedman told one of the detectives to climb the ladder and look in the living-room window. But to keep his gun drawn.

"The place is empty," he called down.

He knocked a pane out of the window and he and his partner went inside and opened the door for Seedman. The place was plain but neat. Seedman motioned to the bedroom door.

"Push it open," he said. "Just don't get in front of it."

The detectives looked at him. Wasn't he making too much of this? Feeling slightly silly, they positioned themselves on either side of the door, guns drawn, just as they had been taught at the Academy. One detective turned the knob and pushed.

The man was hanging from the light fixture in the center of the ceiling. A chair was kicked to one side, the shotgun lay on the bed.

"We learned from further questioning," says Seedman, "that the victim had complained that this fellow kept asking her to his apartment for a cup of coffee whenever she passed him on the stoop. She didn't want to give him ideas or to seem rude, so she always offered an excuse. The last few times her excuses had been more pointed. He was a lonely widower, why wasn't she a lonely widow? He brooded about it. One day he just spilled over. He knew her schedule to the minute, and when she came up the stoop he was waiting at his door. He just walked up to her and pulled the trigger.

"If not for the shotgun, I wouldn't have suspected him so quickly. But he couldn't have carried it down the street at that hour. It had to be an inside job. If so, was this man still waiting in his apartment with the reloaded shotgun pointed at his front door? He had to be totally flipped out to do what he'd already done, and quite capable of blowing away anyone else who came after him. I'd rather those detectives thought I was taking too many precautions than to find themselves splattered all over the bedroom walls."

One morning in the spring of 1961 Seedman ran into Mike Ledden, the man who had first interviewed him fifteen years earlier, when Seedman had first sought to enter the Detective Bureau. Now Ledden was Chief of Detectives.

"I hear good things about you, Al," he said. "What district you got now?"

"No district. I'm working Brooklyn North as a detective supervisor."

"You ought to have a district, Al. The Tenth is coming available. You up to handling that?"

"Yes."

"Only one thing bothers me, Al," said Ledden frowning. "You play golf, right?"

"Right."

"Well, there's a nice course in the Tenth. . . ."

"I know," said Seedman.

"See to it that you use it."

Less than a month later, in May 1961, Seedman took over the 10th District in Brooklyn South. It covered six squads in Coney Island, Sheepshead Bay, Bath Beach, Borough Park, and Park Slope. Remarkably—and something unique in those days—Seedman had never commanded a squad himself or even been a squad detective. Now taking his first field command, he found himself in charge of more than a hundred detectives.

One of the few cases that required him to mobilize most of them began most unpromisingly at 9 P.M. on July 26, 1962. The weeping parents of nine-year-old Blanca Nievies came into the 7th Squad office to report her missing. They had taken her to the beach at Coney Island with her brother and sister, and in the crush of a half-million bathers she had disappeared.

After an hour's futile search, they turned to a patrolman on the boardwalk who directed them to a special area where a regiment of lost children was brought each day. Blanca was not among them. The family was told that a missing child is often taken home by bathers who live in her neighborhood—especially when the other family is also Spanish-speaking, as the Nievieses were—but when Blanca did not show up by nine o'clock, her parents finally went to the local station house.

"If a lost child was seven years old or under," says Seedman, "the rule book mandated calling out all available manpower for the search. In practice, we often did the same for kids even older. What happens in most cases is that the child wanders off, covering far more distance than anyone thinks possible. Even an infant who can barely crawl has tremendous range. When they get tired, they tend to find a cozy hideaway to curl up in and fall asleep. They may be no worse off even if they have been abducted. The city is full of lonely people who see an obviously lost child and take it home to their empty apartment. They feed it, bathe it, treat it like royalty. When the police come, they claim only to have done the child a good turn."

By dawn, when all the hundreds of children lost at Coney Island were safe in their own beds except for Blanca Nievies, Seedman began to treat her case as if the worst had happened—accidental drowning or homicide. Of the two, drowning was less likely; the beach had been too dense with bathers that day for a child who got into trouble not to have been scooped out. Besides, Blanca had been last seen not on the beach but at 13th Street and Stillwell Avenue in the center of Coney Island.

That morning Seedman borrowed every available detective and uniformed patrolman from other precincts in Brooklyn South for search teams to comb Coney Island for Blanca. Each apartment house, amusement stand, boarded-up shed, every crevice beneath the boardwalk was to be covered. A police helicopter went up to inspect the rooftops. When this produced no sign of Blanca, Seedman told the teams to switch areas and start over again. All day a patrol car fitted out with a public-address system wove through the streets, describing Blanca in English and Spanish: Four feet tall, weighing fifty pounds, short brown hair, and brown eyes. Dressed in a one-piece red bathing suit with a yellow diagonal stripe from shoulder to hip.

At three o'clock that Friday afternoon, another pair of weeping parents, the Glovers, turned up at the Coney Island station house. Their son, Lennie, had disappeared that morning from the front yard where he was playing. He was five years old. With every Coney Island block already covered, it took less than an hour to locate him, wandering on the boardwalk. He was cheerful and apparently unharmed, but a medical check showed signs of sexual abuse.

"It isn't easy to get specifics out of a five-year-old," says Seedman, "especially when his young mind may already have blocked out something unpleasant. But Lennie did well. He told us he was in a truck with a man who had a blanket in the back seat. The man was nice to him, but he didn't like him. Did he see a little girl—or what to him was a big girl? Lennie said he did not."

Near dusk that evening a pair of detectives cruising 21st Street noticed a young balding white man fast asleep in the cab of a panel truck. They had a hard time shaking him awake. He identified himself as David Kahn.

"You always sleep in a truck?" asked a detective.

"I was up most of the night," answered Kahn. "I was on my way out to Nathan's for a hotdog. All of a sudden, the curtain just came down." He waved a hand down over his pale, calm eyes. "It's better to take a nap than cause a wreck, right? Especially with so many kids playing in the street." Kahn smiled.

The detectives did not care for that smile. Neither did Seedman as Kahn flashed it in the 60th Squad office. Usually suspects brought here were indignant, fearful, or resigned. Kahn did not seem to mind being in the squad room at all. That was a bad sign. Beyond that, Seedman had a curious sensation—as if an unhealthy heat prickled beneath Kahn's damp forehead.

Acting on his hunch, Seedman wasted no time in cursory questions. He leaned close to Kahn, who did not draw back.

"My friend, what did you do with that little girl?"

Kahn looked up brightly. "Oooh. . . . I played with her."

The detectives in the room winced.

"And after you got tired of playing with her?"

"Then we drove back there to Coney Island Creek. I threw her in."

"Was she alive?"

"I think so. But frankly, she wasn't in the best shape."

"What time was that?"

"Just before it got light out this morning."

"Why did you let the little boy go?"

"I like little boys."

It was nearly dark when David Kahn took the detectives to the spot where 23rd Street dead-ends at Coney Island Creek, a dirty brown backwater of Gravesend Bay, which separates Coney Island from the Brooklyn mainland. Seedman arranged to hire two hard-hat divers who worked in tunnel construction and at dawn they began searching the mud for Blanca. They went down in shifts all day Saturday but found no sign of her.

"You lied to us," Seedman said to Kahn that afternoon.

Kahn thought for a moment. "So I lied," he said. "I didn't throw her in the creek. I buried her in the backyard of a bungalow on 37th Street."

Half the backyard where Kahn took the detectives had been dug up for tomato plants and lettuce. The rest was covered with well-tended grass. The couple who lived in the bungalow had never heard of David Kahn.

"Oops," he said. "Guess I got the wrong house. Along here they all look alike, you know."

"Where did you put her?" Seedman asked evenly.

"Okay, this is the *real* truth," said Kahn. "I drove around in my truck until I saw the sanitation truck working a block. Then I drove ahead to the next block and rolled her up in an old rug I had. When the truck came by, I told the guys, 'I'll throw this in.'"

"You'd like to see us scrounge in the dump for a couple of days, wouldn't you?" said Seedman. "That would give you a big kick. Well, forget it."

He could feel the desire mounting in his detectives to throttle this Kahn. But that was just what the man wanted, knowing all too well that he held the top card. If Kahn did not want to reveal where he had taken Blanca Nievies, they might never know. Seedman felt that all he could do for now, maddening as it would be, was to play along with Kahn until he got tired.

"Maybe I didn't throw her in an sanitation truck," Kahn was saying now. "But I did put her in a rug. Only, then I took her to a private dump on Ralph Avenue. I can show you right where I threw her."

But after forty-five minutes of poking through charred mattresses, splintered dressers, and plain garbage under the Emergency Service portable lights, Kahn shook his head.

"This isn't it, this isn't where she is at all."

His eyes were fixed on the ground. Seedman waited. After several moments, Kahn looked up brightly. Seedman noticed that even though he was looking directly into the Emergency Service spotlight, Kahn was not squinting.

"Jesus Almighty!" he said. "I am *dying* for a couple of those Nathan's hot dogs. That's where I was going when I fell asleep in the truck, you know."

"Show me the girl. Then you get the hot dogs."

"Captain, you're an intelligent man. Let me ask you, where is the *logical* place to put a person who is no longer among the living?"

"You tell me."

"In a graveyard, Captain."

"Yeah? What graveyard?"

"The one I'd just come from when you guys woke me up. Washington Cemetery."

"Where's the shovel? It wasn't in the truck."

"I left it out there."

At 3 A.M. a manacled David Kahn led Seedman and six detectives into the vast old Washington Cemetery in central Brooklyn. He directed them to a tract of crumbling and tilted tombstones. Every dozen yards Kahn would stop to get his bearings. Finally he asked Seedman to take off the handcuffs so he could pull apart the tall weeds obscuring the inscriptions. Deciding to let him play his game to the end, Seedman agreed.

Kahn chose a knoll crowded with elaborate mausoleums to make his dash. He took off with startling speed. But he was no match for Bill Bett, a leggy detective from the 60th Squad who, years later, would be shot in the back during a holdup attempt.

Bett slammed Kahn against a tombstone, and ground his nose into the earth for good measure. When Bett let him up, Kahn smiled through the dirt on his lips.

"No hot dogs, no more games," said Seedman now, as the party of detectives stood around Kahn in the moonlight. "I don't even want you to tell me where that little girl is any more."

At dawn, with Kahn locked up behind him in the "cage" of the 60th Squad office, Seedman called the New York Harbor Coast Guard Station. He wanted a mariner's opinion of how wind, tide, current, temperature, and type of sea bottom might act on a small body thrown into Coney Island Creek. Over coffee in the Coast

Guard office in lower Manhattan, Lieutenant Olsen, head of the Navigational Aids section, plotted for Seedman the movement of water between the Creek and Gravesend Bay. If the child had been thrown in just before dawn on Thursday, the outgoing tide at 6:33 would have rolled her along the slime bottom of the Creek into the bay within two or three hours. If she had no air in her lungs, Olsen felt, her body might stay down a few days until gases would bloat it and send it to the surface.

The officer pointed to a spot on the chart several hundred yards off the mouth of Coney Island Creek in Gravesend Bay. "My guess is that if she was thrown in the creek at 23rd Street when you think she was, she'll surface at about this spot on Tuesday. If it's sunny, maybe a bit sooner."

Olsen thought a moment. "I can tell you about the tides," he said to Seedman. "Can you tell me why a man would do that?"

"Not this time," said Seedman.

All day Tuesday under a slight gray haze police motor launches crisscrossed the Coney Island end of Gravesend Bay. But it was a fisherman named Salvatore Corravo, heading in to beat the dark, who saw the figure in a red bathing suit with a yellow diagonal stripe floating low in the water at 8:45 P.M. He knew who it was from radio reports. Circling around the body, he leaned to lift it out. But he could not make himself do it. He sped to his marina in Coney Island Creek and called the police.

A pair of detectives from the Bath Beach Squad, Ed Quilty and Tom Grandinetti, roared out in a launch as the last shimmer of daylight lay on Gravesend Bay. They scooped out Blanca three hundred yards west of the mouth of Coney Island Creek. Seedman was standing on the pier when they came in. Though the water had been cruel to the body, Seedman felt as if he had seen Blanca a hundred times before.

"David Kahn made no secret of how much he enjoyed playing with us," Seedman says. "He got a real kick out of sending us off on one fruitless search after another. But as we dragged him out of Washington Cemetery early on Sunday morning, I thought back to when he first took us down to the 23rd Street creek. He didn't get any kicks out of that trip. Compared to how he acted later, he seemed to be most truthful then. I asked him in the car whether he hadn't told us the real story the first time. He smiled but didn't answer. Just the same, I decided to operate on the assumption that he had indeed thrown Blanca in the creek.

"Later, I asked him why he had sent us off on so many wild chases after telling us the truth the first time. He said he felt we didn't believe him; otherwise, why hadn't we found her? So he decided to punish us. He didn't realize that tide and current would carry her into the bay.

"Kahn obviously had loose wires in his head. His mother claimed he'd never been normal since a childhood fall; his ex-wife said he was full of quirks. Kahn wound up going to a mental hospital instead of to trial."

Seedman had mobilized helicopters, divers, boats, Coast Guard expertise, and a hundred detectives and patrolmen from six precincts in the search for Blanca. It was unusual for such resources to be called up and orchestrated by a mere captain. But Seedman had already gotten a taste for directing a major operation just two months earlier, in May 1961. Then he had mobilized the detective resources of not just one district, but of all Brooklyn. It was Seedman's first great case. It marked him in the vast reaches of the Department as a man to watch.

THE FALLON-FINNEGAN CASE

I: THE KILLINGS

"The first radio report at 3:48 on Friday afternoon, May 18, 1962, was routine enough," Seedman recalls. "My driver, Eddie Mathews, had just pulled away from the Sheepshead Bay station house on our way to Bath Beach when it came: '10-30 . . . 10-30 at 1167-48th Street.' That means a felony in progress.

"All I could tell from the address was that it was in a mixed Italian and Jewish neighborhood called Borough Park. The robbery had to be in a store or factory since the banks closed at three o'clock. Friday afternoons are a good time to do stickups. Receipts are normally heavy before the weekend, and many businesses also have their payroll on hand. On a Friday like this we might expect as many as a dozen stickups.

"I knew that a sector car would be on the way to the scene and if detectives were needed, patrol would call for them. As District Commander, I could not run to every holdup in our six precincts, but I had a strong feeling, almost like a premonition, that I'd better go to this one.

"It was unnaturally hot for so early in the year, and the air rushing in the window felt good. Eddie cut on the siren as we sped up Ocean Parkway. I hoped we wouldn't be stuck too long at this thing. It was my anniversary, and I'd promised to take my wife to a show and late dinner to celebrate.

"At three-fifty, two minutes after the first report, came the second: 'Two men shot at 1167-48th Street.' That was serious but not unusual. People often shoot each other in Brooklyn, especially in the heat. Just before we got to 48th Street, the last report crackled over: 'Two MOFs [members of the force] shot at 1167-48th Street.' That was *more* than usual. In fact, I'd never heard such a report before.

"Eddie whipped around the corner from New Utrecht Avenue to 48th Street at three-fifty-five. The trip from Sheepshead Bay normally took fifteen minutes; he had cut it to five. Number 1167 was a shabby storefront called Borough Park Tobacco Company. A radio car had just pulled up. No crowd outside, no action of any kind. *Too* quiet. I slipped into the dark building from out of the bright sun and blinked. One step inside the front door I pulled up short. . . .

"Holy Jesus! On the floor inside the front door was one of my best veteran detectives, Luke Fallon, lying dead on his face. My gaze froze on him for an instant. Then I caught sight of a pair of police shoes sticking out of an office doorway. I hopped over Fallon and dashed over to find a great young detective, big John Finnegan, lying face up, eyes open, just as dead as Fallon.

"Stunned as I was, standing over the bodies of my two detectives, let me tell you this: I had a pretty good idea of who had done this to them. In fact, I had photos of the suspects right in my shirt pocket."

Two brothers named Robert and David Goldberg ran Borough Park Tobacco, a business started by their father. Located in a long, narrow, sagging loft building, it had crowded aisles and shelves stacked high with cartons of cigarettes, cigars, and candy it sold at wholesale to local shops. In the center of the place was a machine that affixed New York State cigarette tax stamps with a special red ink.

Though the Goldbergs did not sell to the public, they were glad to sell to policemen. The gesture was more than good will. Doing business mostly in cash in a neighborhood which had never been the best, they were designated a "robbery-prone location." So the Goldbergs were happy to have patrolmen and detectives constantly stopping by, even for a pack of crackers. It was cheap insurance.

"With so many hoods in the Tenth District who'd learned to sniff out cops almost since birth," says Seedman, "I had to resort to certain new tactics to keep them guessing. One of the best was the taxi decoy patrol. Using a borrowed old Checker cab, a team of detectives took turns playing passenger and driver. It was one way to keep them cruising without being too obvious." The detectives assigned to the patrol that Friday were Fallon and Finnegan.

From the preliminary facts he was able to gather from witnesses, Seedman reconstructed what must have happened as follows: at 3:30, half an hour before the end of their tour, Fallon and Finnegan pulled up at Borough Park Tobacco. Fallon wanted a few packs of Luden's cough drops for a summer cold. Finnegan picked out a Whitman's Sampler for his wife; they had been married a year to the week. The detectives paid David Goldberg in cash and walked out. They were about to get back in the cab when two men, one fat and one thin came around the corner from New Utrecht Avenue.

"After thirty years' work in this neighborhood," says Seedman, "Fallon would not have to look sideways to see this pair of young quiffs were up to no good. They were both wearing wraparound sunglasses and wide-brimmed hats and their chins were tucked into their chests—no way for honest people to go about their business when it's ninety degrees outside.

"The detectives hopped into the cab as if they didn't notice a thing. The two fellows strolled past the tobacco store, watching the cab bounce down to the end of the block and turn left on Twelfth Avenue. What they didn't see was Finnegan make a few more turns and pull up four minutes later in front of the tobacco store.

"No sign of the two quiffs. Fallon wanted to look into the store without being too obvious, but the two front windows were covered by blinds. Fallon practically had to press his nose against the pane to get a decent look. He saw nothing—no Goldbergs, no clerks running around. Where the hell was everyone? Fallon knew something was wrong. Finnegan moved up beside him and they drew their service .38s.

"The reason nobody was up front, we later learned, was that

the moment these two saw the cab turn the corner, they slipped handkerchiefs over their mouths and with drawn guns entered the store.

"It's a stickup!" shouted the thin gunman. "Hands up! Everybody march to the back!"

They herded the Goldbergs and their six clerks to a rear storage room whose heavy steel door could be latched from either side. The gunmen shoved everybody inside except for David Goldberg, who was marched up to the front office to hand over the day's receipts. Goldberg saw that both men were nervous. He was glad to give them the $1200 in the cashbox if only that would keep their gun hands from shaking.

But they wanted more. While the fat bandit covered the front, the thin one went back to the storeroom to empty the pockets of the prisoners inside. But they had bolted the door.

"Open up, you fucks!" he screamed.

"Fuck *you!*" came back the muffled chorus.

The bandit shook the door so hard his handkerchief-mask started to come undone. Trying to keep it in place, wrench open the door, and hold on to his gun at the same time became just too difficult. With a tremendous roar that resounded throughout the high-ceilinged store, the gun fired straight up.

"Just an accident," shouted the gunman. "Just open the fucking door and nobody will get hurt. . . ."

By now the detectives had returned and taken up positions at either side of the entrance to the store. Rather than barge in, they planned to grab the gunmen as they ran out: that was the procedure Seedman taught at the Police Academy. "It's worse if they stormed in," he says. "A gunman could be crouched out of sight and gun my men down. Even if he was out in the open, they'd be bound to start shooting at each other and usually it's the innocent bystanders who get hurt. It ends up much cleaner to get the drop on the gunmen as they rush out the door.

"Then the shot rang out. With that sound, the complexion of the job changed. It was no longer a routine robbery. Somebody inside might be dead or dying. His .38 aimed straight ahead, Fallon kicked open the front door and dashed in."

The fat gunman, dressed in a white open-collar sport shirt and baggy slacks, stood to the right of the office, guarding the front. Fallon was wearing a brown suit from Bond Clothes, but the gunman almost certainly knew who he was. David Goldberg remembers that he turned pale.

"Don't shoot!" he pleaded. "I give up!" Letting his gun fall, he thrust his hands straight up.

"In this hypercharged confrontation," says Seedman, "Certain officers might well go ahead and blow this gunman's head off, hands up or not. It's the safest way to deal with an armed bandit who is asking for whatever he gets. It's also not a bad notation to have on your record when it comes promotion time. Your superiors see that you faced this ultimate confrontation and did not panic. You shot an armed desperado instead of him shooting you.

"But to shoot can also mean trouble. Once two patrolmen came upon a liquor store as it was being held up. The fleeing bandits saw the cops and threw up their hands, but the cops shot them anyway. It caused a great deal of commotion, as it should have. Once the culprits put up their hands the game of cops and robbers is over. That's the way Luke Fallon knew it was supposed to be."

Seeing the fat gunman's hands go up empty, hearing his gun clunk to the floor, Fallon raced past him toward the back, where the shot had sounded. He knew his partner would be right behind to cover him, but Finnegan delayed a second before charging in. In that second the gunman ducked down and swooped up the gun, a .38-caliber revolver similar to police issue.

Fallon must have sensed it. Even as he wheeled around a single shot hit him square in the chest. He fired off a wild shot of his own. But the gunman's bullet had cut his aorta. His chest filled with blood. As David Goldberg looked on in terror, Fallon fell dead astride the office doorway. A second too late John Finnegan rushed in to protect his partner. As Fallon must have done, he too probably had to blink to adjust from the hard white afternoon sunlight to the darkness inside. It was one blink too many. A step inside the doorway Finnegan was met by two fast slugs. One hit him in the upper chest, the other entered at his right elbow and traveled up his arm to his heart. Finnegan fired off all six shots in his revolver. They hit the ceiling, shelves, floor—everything but the gunman. Finnegan started to reload. He did not know he was dead. He fell on his face just inside the front door.

David Goldberg immobilized, stared at the two bodies of the policemen whose last sale he had rung up only minutes before. In back the thin bandit whose nervous shot had triggered the massacre forgot about his prisoners and looked for an exit. Behind the store-room door Robert Goldberg, sick with fear for his brother's safety, decided to break out. "I don't care what happens to me," he said to himself. Prepared to be shot, he heaved open the heavy door and raced toward the front.

In the aisle he collided with the fat gunman. Thinking fast, the man screamed at Robert Goldberg: "I'm a cop!" Goldberg did not know who was who any more. All he wanted was to help his brother if he was still alive.

In the office David had at first remained rooted to the spot in shock. Suddenly he remembered the hidden Holmes silent alarm at the front counter. He set it off and then rushed to a Laundromat across the street to call the police.

A moment later, Robert Goldberg saw the bodies of Fallon and Finnegan and dashed into the office—fearing he would find his brother's corpse. Where was it? Just then the fat bandit rushed by him, waving his .38. Robert thought this time he would get it. But the bandit rushed right past, still bellowing "I'm a cop!" on his way out the door. The thin bandit followed right behind.

A salesman from Phillip Morris had been sitting in his car, fig-uring up his day's orders when the two bandits first entered the store. Busy with his computations, he noticed neither them nor the two men in the taxi who pulled up again a few minutes later. But at the first shot his pencil went skittering to the floor and he leaped out of the car just as an old woman came out of the Laundromat across the street. She started to cry. He took her hand and together they ran around the corner of New Utrecht Avenue to phone into the police what had happened.

The only other witnesses were two boys named Gorsina and Cohen who were playing stickball at the far end of the block. They came running after the first shot and saw the big man charge into the store after the second shot. They stared as he spun around in the doorway. When they saw blood pour from his mouth, they ran away.

"Only the radio car from the Sixty-sixth Precinct had beaten us to the scene," says Seedman. But after the third radio message, it would only be moments before uniform men and detectives, even traffic cops, began pouring to the block. "I didn't want them all barging into the store like a bunch of women heading for the sale tables. This scene had to be preserved exactly as it was—dead detectives, all the crap lying around—so that Fingerprint, Photo, Emergency Service, Ballistics, and Medical Examiner teams could do their work.

" 'Stand at the door,' I told the dazed patrolman from the radio car. 'Don't let anyone in but detectives.' We had plenty of work for everyone on the outside. The surrounding blocks had to be shut off to outgoing traffic as quickly as possible. Any driver wanting to leave would first have to satisfy us he knew nothing about the crime. The same went for pedestrians among whom we might find the killers. I was prepared, if necessary, to stop every person from leaving that neighborhood by wheel or foot for the next week.

"Late that afternoon there was an amazing sight on the sidewalk across from the tobacco store. Detectives from five boroughs, dozen upon dozen, had gathered to volunteer their help in their off-duty hours. I guess after thirty years Luke Fallon in particular had about as many friends as any man on the force. For most of them this was the first time they'd found *themselves* behind police barricades.

"They understood, of course, they would only be in the way in the store. Dozens of guys tramping around, dropping cigarette butts, were not going to help solve the case. I remember once at a homicide scene finding a matchbook imprinted with the name of a motel. It looked as though the dead woman must have had a trysting partner, but after hours spent checking the motel records, the only name we could turn up was that of a patrolman from the local precinct. He had reported to the scene, taken one look at this dead broad, lit up a cigarette, and dropped the empty motel matchbook."

The only officer to brush past the door of Borough Park Tobacco was a deputy inspector from Patrol. He paced between the bodies, muttering curses.

"Can you give a hand outside, Inspector?" asked Seedman.

"Don't tell me what to do, Captain!"

"You're the boss on the street. I'm boss in here."

Glowering, the deputy inspector walked out.

Seedman was delighted when Bill Averill, a canny and methodical captain from the Borough Commander's staff, walked in a moment later. While Seedman remained in the store, Averill took over detective operations outside. He soon had men taking down license numbers of all cars within four blocks, searching gutters, bushes, garbage cans, and rooftops for any item the bandits might have dropped or thrown away in their dash to escape. Averill also coordinated the canvass of the neighborhood. Each resident would be interviewed, several times if necessary, until every detail they had heard or seen was recorded.

Inside the store Seedman had assigned a detective to interview each of the six clerks, who were allowed out of the store only long enough for their loved ones to see that they were unharmed. Even with the store under such tight control, Seedman found it hard to keep things as they were. Robert Goldberg, for example, was about to pick up a check that had fallen to the office floor from the cash register when Seedman saw him.

"Don't touch it!" Seedman ordered. Though neither of them could know it then, the check contained a fingerprint of one of the bandits.

"In that first hour," says Seedman, "we gathered a good deal of useful evidence. A .32 caliber revolver and a black short-brimmed felt hat had been dropped as the bandits ran out. The .38 caliber murder gun turned up in a rosebush around the corner. Two blocks away a teacher who had just come home from school uncovered her trash can to dump the garbage—and stopped when she saw on the bottom a pair of sunglasses, a black fedora, and a towel stained red. She assumed it was blood. It turned out to be the tax-stamp ink."

Seedman did not immediately show the clerks the photographs in his pocket of the men he felt sure were part of the job. Not that he wasn't anxious to do so, but he knew he must proceed with unusual caution in this, the biggest case he had ever walked into. The last time two officers had been slain together in the line of duty had been in 1927, when Sgt. Ben Cantor and Patrolman Morris Borkin were shot down during the robbery of a restaurant on the Lower East Side. Seedman was wary of introducing evidence that might provide the solution to the case until his own boss was there to share the credit.

The Brooklyn Detective Commander was Ray Martin, a good investigator as well as a talented orchestrator of the police press. Martin had been the Squad Commander in 1948 when Seedman, as a young Safe & Loft detective, had solved a major case that Martin's men had been unable to crack. Ray Martin had not been pleased with that *coup*. He would be even less pleased now if Seedman were to plunge ahead before he arrived. So Seedman let the pictures burn a hole in his pocket and sent to his office for a hundred mug shots. When Martin arrived, Seedman filled him in before taking out the photos.

All the photographs—Seedman's two and the hundred mug shots—were laid out on the long worktable used for wrapping shipments of cigarettes and candy. One by one the Goldbergs and each clerk were brought over to examine them. It was a stroke of luck that neither bandit had been able to keep his handkerchief over his face, because each witness pointed to the same photo in the middle of the pile. It was of a thin sad-faced twenty-four-year-old named Jerome Rosenberg.

The other photo Seedman was hoping they could identify belonged to Anthony Dellurnia, one of a family of eight Brooklyn brothers also known as the "Mariann" boys. Most had spent time in jail. Anthony was on parole and was supposed to be in Connecticut, where he lived with his wife and children. "I had information he and Rosenberg did stickups together," says Seedman. "But one thing I couldn't hang on Dellurnia was being fat. None of the witnesses even lingered at his photo. That didn't necessarily put him out of the picture. I felt he might have driven the getaway car, though we hadn't yet got a report of one speeding from the scene."

"To explain why photos of Rosenberg and Dellurnia had been in my pocket," said Seedman, "I have to go back to a weekend two weeks ago, when I was covering the district next to mine while its commander took a holiday. That Friday a tobacco store in his district had been robbed. After a little checking I found it wasn't the first such job in recent months. A string of wholesale suppliers who dealt mainly in cash and were located off primary retail thoroughfares were being held up regularly all over Brooklyn.

"I returned to my own district on Monday, but while the case was no longer mine, I stayed interested in it just the same. I told my detectives to keep an ear out for anyone who might be involved —and, sure enough, they picked up the names of Dellurnia and Rosenberg, who'd been bragging to friends how well they'd been scoring. Tony Dellurnia's brother Red operated a candy store supplied by a wholesaler like Borough Park Tobacco, which may have given them the idea of hitting such places. As with all active cases, I kept a spare set of photos of the suspects with me to query detectives, other suspects, or just people in the neighborhood. You never know when something could turn up."

As Friday evening came detectives who had known Fallon and Finnegan, many of whom had just finished their normal workday, still arrived to stand by patiently, waiting to be assigned work. Seedman spotted one of the best, Marty Flanagan, a big Irishman who had raced over from the Brooklyn DA's office when he heard the news. Flanagan was forever rattling off jokes that began, "Did you hear about the guy who. . . ?" One was worse than the next, but this was a day when Flanagan would tell no jokes.

Seedman handed him the black fedora found in the neighbor's trash can. "Here, Marty," he said. "Put this hat on somebody's head."

"This particular hat was by no means a cheap piece of work. I figured it to sell for not less than ten dollars. On the inside of the crown it said 'Knox University Style,' and along the leather sweatband was printed 'Stadium Club . . . Size Seven . . . Joe Silver, Clothier and Haberdasher, Brooklyn, N.Y.' From the lack of sweat stains, you could see it had not got much wear."

Flanagan hurried to Silver's store on 86th Street, hoping to catch him before he left for the day. The place was closed. So Flanagan went to Silver's home in Flatbush, where he looked the hat over.

"If I'm not mistaken, I did sell a hat like this to a customer last Friday. He came in with two other fellows. He also bought other merchandise. I think he has a charge account with us."

"You wouldn't remember whether his name happened to be Rosenberg?"

"No, that wasn't it," Silver said firmly.

"Let's go to the store and look up that charge record," said Flanagan. "It can mean a lot to us."

It was after nine o'clock when Silver snapped on the lights in his darkened store. Thumbing through the previous week's charge records, he began to refresh his memory.

"The customer with the charge was a well-dressed fellow," said Silver. "The other two weren't so sharp." He stopped at a bill dated Friday, May 10. It listed a pair of dress slacks, two sport shirts, a belt, and a black fedora priced at $11.95. The bill was signed by Joseph De Mercurio. All but the slacks were marked "Taken."

"Does that mean the slacks are still here, or what?" asked Flanagan.

From the alteration rack Silver pulled out a pair of gray checked slacks. The scrawl on the tag said "To be picked up. J. Rosenberg."

"Frankly, I thought he'd have come in already," said Silver. "They've been ready since Tuesday."

"Don't expect him too soon," said Flanagan.

Even before the witnesses had picked out his photo, Seedman had sent detectives to Rosenberg's home on 18th Street. His parents said they had not seen him for days. They were distraught; of their three children, Jerry was the only one who gave them trouble. They were not even surprised that he was suspected in a murder case. As a teen-ager he had already been a prime suspect in the murder of a local florist. According to street sources, Rosenberg had headed for his estranged wife's home in Texas City a few days before. That sounded a bit too convenient to Seedman. Just the same, he dispatched a pair of detectives to Texas at once.

Looking across 48th Street that Friday evening, Seedman spotted another crack detective named Eddie Lambert. He was a well-spoken, thorough investigator who had been a first-grade detective for almost his entire career thanks to a dazzling number of arrests he had made as a patrolman and rookie detective. He was currently assigned to what had become known as the "Pizza Squad" —seven hairy fairy godmother detectives who rented an apartment across from the buildings at 49 and 51 President Street in Brooklyn where the Gallo gang was under siege by the family of Joseph Profaci.

Eddie Lambert had been on President Street when the news about Fallon and Finnegan "came down." Twenty minutes later he was waiting for orders in front of the Laundromat on 48th Street. Seedman had a delicate job in mind. "No witness had yet identified Anthony Dellurnia," he explains. "But I knew he hung out at his brother's candy store on 76th Street in New Utrecht. I hoped we might pick up information about Dellurnia and maybe Rosenberg at this place. In New Utrecht an Italian candy store is like an Irish bar—an information center. But not for outsiders. It would take a guy with tact and more than a little cunning to ferret it out. That was a job which suited Eddie Lambert."

Lambert pulled up to Dellurnia's candy store at 5:30 Friday

evening. He found it indistinguishable from five thousand others in Brooklyn: milk crates stacked up outside for newspapers; windows dirty, with a sagging rack of dusty sunglasses on display; inside, a soda counter with eight stools on one side, six initial-carved booths on the other. It was a place to buy bubble gum or a soda or a nail file or a yo-yo. But Lambert knew from his own childhood in Brooklyn that it was also a place to hang around in. Kids came in at lunch hour, after school, even during school if they dared skip a class. They dragged on cigarettes, which their parents would slap out of their faces if they caught them at home.

The kids sensed who Lambert was as soon as he walked in. The man behind the counter was John ("Red") Dellurnia. Like most of his brothers, he had spent time in jail.

"Hello, Red," said Lambert. "Where's your brother Tony?"

Red looked up from drying a Coke glass. "Geez, Detective, I haven't seen him for quite a while. He's been living up in Connecticut with his family, you know. Got a good job and all."

Lambert nodded. He knew Dellurnia was back in Connecticut only because parole regulations required he stay. Lambert did not feel like wasting time. "Red, some detectives are waiting in a car down the street. I think maybe we can clear up a few things a little easier if you go with them down to the station house." In the mirror behind the fountain Lambert saw the kids stiffen. He *wanted* them to know what might happen to them if they did not cooperate.

But the kids were not much more helpful than Red. They too could not remember when Tony Dellurnia had last been around. In fact, they didn't even know him by that name: to them he was "Johnny Mariann." Jerry Rosenberg? They looked at each other blankly. Lambert was patient. With the kids he had to be. He knew their parents could cause him more trouble than it was worth if he bore down on them. But if he kept at it gently, he felt, he might coax something out of them. At 6:30 the pay phone on the wall rang. One of the kids jumped to answer it.

"Leave it, I'll pick it up," Lambert said.

"Hello, Red's place."

"Ummm . . . is Red there, please?"

"Sorry, he's not. Who's calling, please?"

"It's just a friend of his. . . ."

"Tony, baby—is that you?"

"Yeah. Who's this?"

"It's Detective Lambert, Tony. I want you to come down here so I can talk to you."

"How come you want to talk to me?"

"We had some trouble over on 48th Street, you know. We're looking for a guy. We thought maybe you could help us out."

"Listen, I'm on parole from Connecticut. I'm not supposed to be hanging around Brooklyn. I got to get back to Norwich if there's been trouble."

"Come to your brother's place now, Tony. It'll be better for you."

Lambert could hear Dellurnia thinking hard. "Okay," he finally said, "I'll be over in ten minutes."

Lambert waited. He chatted with the kids. He looked around the place—behind the counter, at the unkempt back room, in front.

"You looking for something special?" asked the kid Red had left in charge.

"Should I be?" asked Lambert. A pall had settled over the candy store. Ten minutes passed, then twenty, then an hour. The kids began to drift home for dinner. At 8:30 the phone rang.

"Red's place," answered Lambert heartily.

Silence on the other end.

"Hey, Tony, it's Detective Lambert again. How come you didn't show?"

"Believe me, Detective, I'm just tied up and I can't. Listen, is my brother there now?"

"He's with my colleagues at the station house. Since you didn't come around, we had to run him in. Why don't you come over and have a talk with me? Then we can let Red go home."

"I will now," Dellurnia said, a little penitent. "I'll be there in half an hour. It's not that I got something to hide, you know. It's just my parole officer I got to worry about."

"It's not gonna be me who tells him you were here, Tony."

"Okay. I'll be over in half an hour."

At eleven o'clock, the boy Red left to mind the candy store told Lambert he had to close up. Dellurnia had not showed. Lambert drove back to Borough Park Tobacco to find the place finally quieting down. The Photo unit had finished snapping away at the bodies from all angles, the Medical Examiner had briefly examined them, and they were at last sent to the morgue. The only technicians left were the Fingerprint men, who continued to dust all surfaces, and the Ballistics men, still on ladders and stools, digging bullets out of the walls and high ceilings.

The Chief of Detectives had come and gone. So had the Police Commissioner. Now Seedman could proceed without further interruption. When Lambert walked in, he showed him a pair of sunglasses.

"We picked these up at the scene, Eddie," said Seedman. "It's a standard pair with no brand name, like you could buy anywhere. But it has the letters G-E-E scratched into the frame with a pin. Does that ring any bells with you?"

Lambert looked at the frame. "This is going to sound crazy," he said, "but I could swear those letters were carved in with all the other crap by the pay phone at the candy store. I'll get right back and check it now."

"If it's there, it won't go away overnight," Seedman said. "Go get some sleep. I'd rather have you there fresh when the place opens at seven o'clock."

"As that Friday ended," says Seedman, "the only suspect we'd locked tight into the crime was Jerry Rosenberg. All the witnesses had identified his photo. We had his hat and I was hoping the lab would come up with his fingerprints from the tobacco store. It was just a matter of turning him up. Dellurnia was another matter. No witnesses had placed him at the scene, yet our informants had indicated that he was a prime candidate to be getaway driver. If he'd been standing behind the counter of the candy store that evening, polishing Coke glasses like his brother, I wouldn't have been so sure. But so far as I was concerned, he gave himself away with those phone calls to Eddie Lambert. Any of the kids in the candy store would have known to play it cooler than that.

"The one we'd drawn a blank on so far was the bushy-haired, slope-shouldered gunman who had killed Fallon and Finnegan. I guess we were hungrier to get him than any man I can remember.

"I was sure we'd soon flush out the killers. Too much manpower had been thrown into the search for them to stay hidden away. I don't mean just police, either. Ordinary citizens were pulling up to stop lights in Brooklyn and staring into the car in the next lane.

" 'What're ya looking at buddy?'

" 'No business of yours. What're *you* looking at?'

"More than a couple of fights started that night between good people of Brooklyn who were keeping an eye out for the scum that killed two family men from the force."

When the boy came to open Dellurnia's candy store at 7:30 on Saturday morning, Lambert was waiting. In the *Daily News* he'd just read that a pair of sunglasses marked "GEE" had been found at the scene. Seedman had told him those letters would not go away overnight, but they had. Lambert was not entirely surprised: it just meant they were in the right place. He was sure now the kids knew even more than he'd hoped.

"Tell me who 'Gee' is," said Lambert.

"Is that a person or what?" asked the boy.

Lambert walked behind the counter and took him gently by the arm. In a friendly voice he said, "Listen to me, now. You know a terrible thing happened yesterday?"

The boy nodded.

"Those two detectives were my friends," Lambert went on. "Now I want you to tell me who this 'Gee' is. This minute. Otherwise, I'm going to take you down to the station house for questioning. It might be a while before you go home."

The boy was aware that Red Dellurnia had not been seen since he went to the station house the night before. "If I show you where Louie 'Gee' lives, will you let me go?" he asked. "And swear not to tell anyone I told you?"

Lambert nodded. They walked around the corner to 76th Street. The boy pointed to a well kept brick row house. The mailbox said "Farrara."

At the door Louis "Gee" Farrara's father was not surprised to see Lambert.

"I thought you might be around to talk to my boy, Detective. I've already instructed Louis to tell the truth, whatever you ask him. He's a good boy. He obeys me. You can talk to him here or at your office. The only thing I insist is that I'm not gonna let my boy out of my sight. Not for a minute."

Lambert knew that Mr. Farrara had a point.

Louis was standing on the stairs behind his father. He was a dark Italian boy of sixteen with pimples. "Are you going to answer this officer with the truth, Louis?" his father asked sternly.

"So help me God, Pop."

But when Louie "Gee" and his father were led into the 66th squad room at noon on Saturday it did not take the detectives long to find out otherwise.

"Louie," asked Seedman, "when did you lend Jerry Rosenberg your sunglasses?"

"I didn't lend them to nobody. I lost them a couple of weeks ago. They dropped off my belt."

"Do you know Jerry Rosenberg?"

"I seen him around."

"Did you see him yesterday, by chance?"

"Not that I remember. I was in school anyhow."

"Did you see Tony Dellurnia?"

"Who?"

"Tony Mariann."

"No, sir."

"That's how it went for quite a while with Louie 'Gee,'" says Seedman. "We went around and around with him several hours a day that day and the next. His old man ran a pizza parlor in the neighborhood. It wasn't a big place—I imagine he could hardly afford to leave the business so much—but he stayed with his son every minute we had him.

"I understand Louie's point of view, too. He comes from generations of a family which taught: Keep it in the family. Don't talk to outsiders. Back in Italy 'outsiders' meant other Italians. In New Utrecht it meant other Italians—and Jews, Irish, Swedes, and above all the police. A boy also learned that he must not 'rat' on his friends. If you did, even on a casual friend, then he had a perfect right to make a reprisal. If he was not as big as you, his brother would do it. Or he and all his brothers. Besides getting beat up, something even worse happened. You became an outcast.

"So Louie and each of those kids who hung out at the candy store had been bred to silence. They knew we wouldn't beat them into talking. You don't change them overnight. It took us about three days, but bit by bit, with a little help from Louie 'Gee' and a few of his friends, we began to wear him down until finally we could shape out a picture of what happened in the candy store that Friday:

"Jerry Rosenberg and Tony Dellurnia had indeed been in and

out of the place all day. At noon a few of the kids noticed Rosenberg walk in, carrying the morning newspaper. When he put it down it went 'clunk.' When he set it on a shelf behind the counter a moment later, a gun fell out and he had to grab for it in midair. I'd say that was rather odd, but these kids didn't even think it was worth mentioning to us until the following Tuesday.

"At about three o'clock Rosenberg and Dellurnia were joined by a third fellow. We'll get to him. A few minutes later, Tony borrowed the keys to his brother's Chevy Impala convertible parked outside and they left. A seventeen-year-old girl named Lucille Giusti went along too. We'll get to her also. At about three-thirty-five, just Dellurnia and Lucille came back. They stayed at the candy store only long enough to take a phone call in the booth five minutes later. Dellurnia borrowed the keys to Red's convertible again, even though as a parolee he wasn't supposed to be driving. When they came back again at three-fifty-five, both he and the girl looked upset. Tony left the keys for his brother and hurried out of the store.

The next morning Seedman was shaving in the 66th squad shower room with a razor borrowed from patrolman Lennie Schniper when Vic Kaufman, boss of the homicide squad came in.

Kaufman explained that a slender, shy young patrolman named Carl Loicano had come to see him at dawn. "I don't know if I'm out of line, Lieutenant," Loicano had said, "but I'd rather tell this to you than to my own precinct lieutenant. I know an old woman who lives three blocks from where the detectives were shot. She sits at her window and watches the street all day. She asked me to swear in Italian I wouldn't tell her name and I swore on all the saints. Then she tells me she saw a fellow running down the street at four o'clock. A fat guy, sweating and puffing. She knows him by the name 'Baldy.' "

Seedman rinsed off the shaving cream, dressed, and went to look up "Baldy" in the Nickname File at the district office. "It is an essential index," he says, "because half the hoodlums in Brooklyn know the other half only by a nickname. The kids at the candy store, for example, weren't fooling when they drew a blank on the name Dellurnia. They had heard only 'Mariann'—a name for which we had several entries.

"We also had half a dozen 'Baldies' on file, but only one was pudgy, 5′ 7″, 180 pounds with light-brown bushy hair. He had a string of arrests for assault and robbery going back to when he was sixteen. His name was Anthony Portelli and I was sure he was our man. But I wanted to see if we couldn't quietly tie him tight into the case before we released his name to the world.

"All the witnesses were in another room at that moment, helping a police artist make up a composite sketch of this unnamed gunman. I sat off to one side with this Portelli's photo in my palm and watched them put the picture together.

" 'No, no, his jaws are fatter,' they'd say. '. . . eyes closer together . . . more pouchy . . . hair more bristly. . . .'

"They worked like that for an hour. By the time they were done, the portrait was practically a dead ringer for the photograph in my hand. I ordered copies to be released to the newspapers for their Sunday editions so that his face would be so well known that anyone watching the ball game at Yankee Stadium on television would be able to pick him out from the middle of the crowd. Meanwhile, we'd use our own resources to find him before he knew we were looking for him by name."

Once the detective interrogation teams had Portelli's name to work with, they began to find Rosenberg's and Dellurnia's friends more cooperative. They located one who now admitted he had lent Baldy and Rosenberg his car to rob a Key Food supermarket the week before, though he insisted he did not get a piece of the take for his risk. Rosenberg and Dellurnia had visited this same fellow on Friday morning about 9:30 at a spot called Mister Donut. They wanted to borrow his car again to hit a tobacco store.

"It's broke down," he told them. "It needs a fuel pump."

"Can't you fix it by this afternoon?"

"I don't want no part of it."

"You fucking punk!" Dellurnia shouted as they left. He had good reason to be mad: now he had to ask his brother Red for his car.

Anthony Portelli, arrested nearly forty times in five years, had worked occasionally as a gas station attendant. He lived on Lake Street in the Bensonhurst section of Brooklyn with his mother and stepfather. They claimed not to have seen him for several days. His mother was a buxom woman with tired eyes. She wore her gray hair pulled tightly back and she dressed in black in the Italian tradition. She showed the detectives pictures of Anthony with his arm around her, Anthony with his cheek to hers, Anthony standing proudly behind as she sat in a garden.

"My son is a goodhearted boy," she insisted.

"We can't agree with you, ma'am," answered the detectives.

By Sunday afternoon the detectives who knew the Brooklyn underworld best were squeezing their connections for information on Portelli harder than anyone could remember. Something had to give. It did, finally, at nine o'clock, when the phone rang in the 66th squad room.

"Check out Pellegrino's Bar on Bay 8th Street," a voice said. "You'll find four guys at a table in back. One of them is Ritchie Melville. He knows where Baldy is."

Fifteen minutes later four detectives entered the shabby bar. The four men at the back table fell silent and remained silent as the detectives swiftly escorted Melville to their car. They knew him to be a small-time bookie hoping to get bigger. A good-looking man himself, he had a tiny, strikingly lovely wife and four children. It took some time at the station house—all Sunday night and Monday morning—before Melville admitted that he had been playing with his kids on Saturday evening when a friend named Frank Lino called him.

"Ritchie," said Lino. "You can do a guy the favor of a lifetime. It's for Baldy. He needs a place to hide out for a few days until the heat cools off."

"It ain't *never* gonna cool off for what he did," said Melville. "I don't want him."

"He's a buddy, Ritchie. He needs us."

"So, bring him over," sighed Melville. "But by tomorrow morning, he's gotta vanish."

Frank Lino picked up Portelli, his pale and heavily stubbled face buried deep in a newspaper at a subway entrance at 10th Street. Lino noticed that he was shaking as if the shots had just been fired. But while Mrs. Melville cooked him his first meal in two days, Portelli suddenly became expansive and told Lino and Melville what he had done.

"I'm covering the front when I see that cabbie all of a sudden peeking through the blinds," Portelli said. "I said to myself, 'Oh, shit, I *knew* they was cops!' Then that idiot Jerry has to shoot his gun."

"So you had to shoot *yours*, jerk?"

"I panicked. I mean, wouldn't you? When I was standing there with my hands up, I was thinking how they were gonna put me in the can, this time for maybe five fuckin' years. The cop had gone past me. Then I just did this thing like I saw a guy do on television one night: I swept my hand down and around and pulled up the gun. As he turns back around I pulled the trigger. The other cop runs in and I kept on pulling the trigger. It was so easy."

Portelli held his stubby hands to his ears. "So help me," he said, "they're still ringing."

Then Portelli told Melville and Lino something that Seedman had suspected: both gunman had dashed out of the store, expecting to jump into a waiting getaway car driven by Anthony Dellurnia, but it was gone. They had sprinted instead to the end of the block, Portelli not quite able to keep up with Rosenberg, and then split in different directions. Portelli had hidden in the basement of an apartment house on the far end of Borough Park until after dark, when he had crept off to a double feature—Audie Murphy in *Renegade Priest* and *To Hell and Back*. He had hidden in hallways and ridden the subways the rest of the night and into Saturday. The newspaper he perpetually kept in front of his face began to feel like lead. It also did not help to keep rereading about cop killers on the loose. When he could no longer take it, he had called his friend Franko Lino, who had called Melville.

"Did you at least get the money?" asked Melville.

"Two hundred dollars from the register. I guess Jerry got the rest. That dumb bastard. If he didn't shoot first, none of this would have happened."

Belly filled with Mrs. Melville's spaghetti, Portelli finally fell into a deep sleep on Melville's couch at three o'clock that Sunday morning. Meville himself had slipped off to stay with his friend Tom Verici: in case the police swooped down on his place in the early hours he wanted to be elsewhere. At ten in the morning he came home to find Portelli staring at his own portrait on the front page of the *Daily News*.

"That don't look like me one bit," he said.

"Oh, no?" said Melville. "I'd say you must have left your fuckin' photo in that tobacco store."

Though Portelli did not seem upset, Melville was. He had done his part. Now he wanted Portelli to go somewhere else quickly. He sent his wife out to buy a Color-Comb, which would turn Portelli's hair from the light brown described in the newspaper to black. While she was gone Melville snipped off Portelli's hair until it was much shorter than in the portrait. Frank Lino was on the phone, meanwhile, arranging for another friend named Babe Accarino—he had served time for a robbery committed with Anthony Dellurnia in 1946—to drive Portelli to Union City, New Jersey, that afternoon. He would stay overnight in a motel, take a morning flight from Newark to Chicago, check in at the Lido Motel in Franklyn Park under the name Jim Davis. From then on, with slightly less than $200 in his pocket, he was on his own.

Only Babe Accarino and Frank Lino were visible in the front seat of Accarino's car as they started out from Melville's at 3:30 on Sunday afternoon. Portelli was humped over on the floor in back, afraid even to peek out the window. As they approached the Battery Tunnel toll booths, Lino said, "Jesus, they're for sure going to recognize Baldy when we go through. Let's go back and take the Brooklyn Bridge. They got no tolls."

"We got to go through the Holland Tunnel to get to Jersey anyway," said Accarino. "They got toll booths there too."

"Better to chance it with one toll booth than two," Portelli piped up from the back. "Take the Brooklyn Bridge."

When Accarino and Lino left Portelli in front of the motel in Union City, he was wearing a white shirt, brown slacks, gold tie, and salt-and-pepper sports jacket several sizes too large. "He can't say we're fair-weather friends," Lino said on the way back to Brooklyn.

"No," answered Accarino darkly, "but I'd say we sure are a pair of dumb bastards to get mixed up in this."

It was nearly dawn on Monday when the detectives finally put together the story of Portelli's escape with the help of Melville, Lino, and Accarino. But the detectives who raced to the motel in Union City arrived forty-five minutes after Portelli had checked out. They dashed on to Newark Airport, where an American Airlines ticket agent recognized a photo of the man to whom he had sold a ticket to Chicago on the nine-o'clock flight under the name Jim Davis. He had been airborne for sixteen minutes.

Luckily, Portelli had taken a slow flight. It was delayed two extra hours by engine trouble, which forced it to make an unscheduled stop at a small airport in Ohio. Seedman called ahead to ask the Chicago police to watch Portelli from the time he finally stepped off the plane, then sent two of his own detectives to Chicago on a direct flight. They were Lt. Eddie Shea, an officer known for his caution, and Herman Frigand, known, in Seedman's words, for his ability to "wrap a guy up into a pretzel real fast."

At three o'clock Shea and Frigand, with five Chicago detectives as backup, picked up a spare key to room number 7 from the desk clerk at the Lido Motel. Frigand slipped the key into the lock. It was tight. He jiggled the key and cursed, knowing Portelli could heard him. But it didn't matter, since he also knew Portelli had left his gun in the rosebushes in Borough Park.

"You got visitors, Baldy," said Frigand. "Don't even breathe."

They found Portelli cowering in the bathroom, tearing up a paper on which Melville had written his phone number. Shea was right behind Frigand as Portelli threw up his hands, fingers spread. Though Portelli was not armed, the gesture made them nervous— it had been the last one Fallon ever saw. But Portelli only looked from Frigand to Shea imploringly.

"Why's everyone so mad at me?" he asked.

Several hours earlier that Monday morning, Seedman had felt the case was solid enough to issue a public bulletin for Rosenberg, Dellurnia, and Portelli who, he knew, would be bagged shortly anyway. Feeling also that maximum fear might hasten the surrender of the other two, he added to the bottom of the bulletin: "The suspects have stated *they will not be taken alive.*"

On Tuesday morning, as Portelli was signing a statement of voluntary extradition in Chicago, the police got a call from a lawyer named Sabine Tammbora. His brother-in-law, Anthony Dellurnia, would surrender at his home in Norwich, Connecticut, at noon. He had been hiding in the woods since Friday, but had got scared when he read in a newspaper about not being taken alive.

"I been living like a rat," he told the police as he walked out of the woods. "I don't want to die like one."

The next morning Seedman was standing in ranks with five thousand other policemen at John Finnegan's Inspector's Funeral when Rosenberg called a *Daily News* photographer named Gary Kagan, a friend of his from high school. Since shortly after the shooting, he had been holed up with an elderly aunt in the Bronx and now agreed to surrender himself that evening at the Daily News Building on 42nd Street.

"But that is not quite the whole story," says Seedman. "Solving the murders of Fallon and Finnegan was certainly a classic operation by a detective force working at peak form, making its own breaks and picking up others as gifts. Yet we were publicly damned as well as praised for what we did."

II. THE BEATINGS

Q: *Joe, you been treated good here?*
A: Yes.
Q: *Coffee, cigarettes—you got no complaints against us? This is for the record, you know. This is all of your own volition?*
A: That's right.
Q: *Nobody forced you to do this? Why did you . . . why did you want to level with us?*
A: Because—
Q: *No. Honestly, from your heart, Joe. Tell us why you are telling us these things.*
A: Because two detectives were killed in cold-blooded murder.
Q: *And you don't go for that, huh?*
A: No.
Q: *Thank God, we got people like you around, Joe.*
A: (inaudible)

> *—from a taped interrogation in the 66th Squad office, Brooklyn, May 21, 1962, approximately 4 A.M.*

This beating would do credit—if I can call it credit—to a Gestapo wretch in Hitler's concentration camp.

> *—JUDGE SAMUEL LEIBOWITZ, Supreme Court, State of New York, commenting on Richard Melville's testimony about his interrogation. The trial of Portelli, Rosenberg, and Dellurnia, January 25, 1963*

"Eight months after we wrapped up our end of the case," says Seedman, "Judge Leibowitz opened the trial of the three defendants. He was no shrinking lily. He had long been celebrated as one of the fairest but toughest criminal judges in the country who did not hesitate to send convicted men to prison for life or to the electric chair. Yet he was shocked at our methods of interrogating the key accomplice, Richard Melville. I can't say I blame him.

"What exactly happened to send Judge Leibowitz through the roof? Well, Melville testified that on the evening of May 20, 1962, he was brought from Pellegrino's Bar to the 66th Precinct station house, where, during the night, he told my detectives how he had harbored the fugitive Portelli in his house for sixteen hours. Only the story didn't just roll out effortlessly. To jog his memory, Melville testified, he had been beaten by hand and stick and burned on the back with cigarette butts. He said that as he stood naked in the basement of the station house a string with a weight had been tied around his testicles. He said he had seen Red Dellurnia lying on a bed in the squad dormitory and Red didn't look too good to him either.

"Melville wasn't the only one. Others who were close to the wanted men had been beaten too—some less severely, a few maybe a little worse. Yet these beatings were not typical of New York City detectives. Neither was the murder of two of their colleagues. In fact, the Detective Bureau and the underworld of Brooklyn long had unwritten rules on the way to play the game of cops and robbers. A pair of hoods might steal a load of tires off a truck. Our detectives, who often grew up on the same block with these quiffs, would find and arrest them. Or these same two quiffs might fight over dividing the loot and one kills the other. That's all in the family, naturally, but still we'll do our damnedest to see that the murderer spends the rest of his life in prison. Now detectives still walk around Brooklyn after putting away a thousand such criminals and nobody was after their scalps—not the prisoner's relatives or lifelong friends. And the detectives would hold no ill will against the hoods, either. Each side did what he was supposed to do—the hood committed a crime, the detectives caught him. No hard feelings. That's the way the game was meant to work.

"But the murder of Fallon and Finnegan had broken all the rules. Nothing like that was supposed to happen, *ever*. It was unthinkable for even the most bloodthirsty mobster to put out a contract on a cop. If he had dared to suggest any such thing, his friends would have put out a contract on *him*. That weekend of May 18 the Mafia was as shocked and unhappy about the killings as the detectives—but for their own reasons. The rules had been broken on their side with grievous results. They knew our detectives would want to solve this case, heart and soul—not just professionally but personally. And if that meant breaking the rules to extract crucial information, we might just do it. Breaking rules meant breaking heads. Of course, anyone who had volunteered information willingly never would have been touched. That brings up another strategy of the game.

"Each person who took a drubbing in the station house knew it could have been avoided by telling us right off what he knew. But even if they had wanted to, these hoods couldn't afford to do that. Any person labeled a 'rat' or 'fink' is not going to have a very successful life in Bath Beach or Borough Park. He may not have a life at all. If another hood goes to jail because he squealed, the family will avenge him. If the guy is part of the mob, he has the kind of family that will be *sure* to square away his debt.

"On the other hand, if this hood walks out of the station house all covered with bruises, he can wear them like badges of honor, especially if he is just starting out to make a name for himself.

" 'Jesus, Nicky,' the hangarounds will ask at the local bar, 'What happened to you?'

"And Nicky will smile through swollen lips and tell how they wanted him to fink on some guys but he wouldn't. From then on Nicky has a reputation worth trading in his part of Brooklyn. He's a guy the cops couldn't make into a squealer no matter how hard they pounded him, a guy with guts, a young man who can be trusted with bigger things.

"But suppose we haul in a hood who doesn't even *like* the guy we want to know about. He still may not want to talk—or at least let it be known that he talked. Sometimes we can get him out of that bind neatly enough. When one of Rosenberg's buddies left the station house after a couple of hours of rough questioning, his lawyer took him straight to a photographic studio.

" 'Take his portrait,' the lawyer says.

" 'You like a head-and-shoulders view in black and white?'

" 'Full body in the nude, true-to-life color,' the lawyer answers.

The photographer looks at this hairy ugly animal and shrugs. He takes the picture.

"The lawyer comes to us next day with his client. The portrait he shows us is real All-American—red welts, white skin, blue bruises.

" 'Here's the deal,' says the lawyer. 'My client will tell you what you need to know on condition you do not make him testify at any trial. Or let it be known he ever opened his mouth. If you do, we are going to bring charges of police brutality against you.'

"Since we needed his information more than we needed his testimony, we took his deal. In the society this guy chooses to live in, I guess he waltzed out with his reputation intact. Anyhow, looking at those photos, I'd say any case he brought against us he might have won.

"That was the exception. Most of these guys never threaten suit. If they were upstanding citizens, it would be different. They have chosen instead to be a special kind of citizen, so they take it all as part of the game. One fellow questioned for almost two days about the Fallon–Finnegan case left the station house and checked into a hospital, where he stayed ten more days. But he never complained. You can get a feeling for the cordiality of the Fallon–Finnegan interrogations from this taped exchange that took place at the *end* of the interview with Red Dellurnia:

Q: *How's the sandwiches in the station house, Red? Do you find any better ones around? Where you are? In your store you got better sandwiches than this?*

A: Well, I make a hamburger, you know.

Q: *That's all?*

A: Hamburgers, meatballs, minute steaks, got an electric grill. . . .

Q: *If we go to your store, would we be welcome or would you put arsenic in—*

A: Why not? Why wouldn't you be welcome? You're a customer, you're a customer. You're a welcome man. That's why I built the business, to make money.

Q: *We understand. We can talk about these things lightheartedly. Naturally, we want to see you do good. As you know, you haven't been under any duress here, is that correct?*

A: Yes.

Q: *And you haven't been around too long, so that you know we're doing the right thing, as far as you're concerned and as far as we're concerned, in arriving at a certain set of stipulated facts. Is that correct?*

A: Yeh.

Detectives working on the Fallon and Finnegan murders took care not to conduct their rougher interrogations while superior officers were on hand. They usually waited until the hours before dawn, when everyone had gone home. Later, if someone lodged an official complaint, those same superiors could "impartially" investigate the "alleged" brutality since they had not been party to it. Most often, such complaints against the police came to nothing.

Special questioning procedures hardly began with the Fallon–Finnegan case, of course. A veteran detective on the case, for example, remembers being introduced to them by two old-time colleagues in the basement of a Manhattan station house in 1945. They were trying to induce a suspect to explain how a closely guarded witness could have been poisoned just before Mafia boss Vito Genovese was to stand trial for the murder of another Mafioso named Ferdinand Boccia. The government had gone to great trouble to bring Genovese back from Italy just to try him—though the murder was alleged to have taken place years earlier, in 1934.

The three detectives were "questioning" the man intensively about how the poison got into the witness's apple pie, when suddenly the man fell to the floor. His eyeballs rolled out of sight and he stopped breathing.

"Holy Jesus!" whispered the then young detective.

"He must have had a weak heart," muttered one of the veterans. "Why didn't the bastard warn us?"

The three men agreed that they could not tell anyone, not even their sergeant, since that would make him an involuntary party to the mess. They considered what to do. Were any of the suspect's friends aware that he was being questioned? No. He had been walking down a dark street when he was snapped up.

That gave them their answer. First, they would seal off the basement so nobody could get in. Then one man would get four cement blocks and a hank of rope from a nearby construction site, and before dawn they would pitch the suspect into the East River. Whoever found him would assume that Genovese's men had got to him before the police did. Even most of Genovese's men would assume it.

While they were planning, one of the detectives suddenly noticed the victim's chest move.

All three detectives knelt over him. One puffed air into his mouth, the other two pushed on the man's sides with the palms of their hands. Soon he was breathing on his own.

The suspect smoked a cigarette shakily, took a nap for an hour, then after a few more questions went home in the dawn of a pleasant day.

"No hard feelings," he told the detectives. "You guys done what you had to do."

"My own first taste of violence came as a rookie working with the Transit Police," says Seedman. "I took the job while waiting to be appointed to the Police Department. One hot Saturday night during the summer of 1941 I was assigned to the elevated station at Coney Island. Up comes a drunk with a broad on each arm, obviously whores. He caught sight of me and for some reason I set him off.

" 'See that skinny little twerp?' he snarled to the girls. 'I'm going to hit him over the head with his own nightstick.'

"The girls laughed as he came staggering over to me. He had a point—I *was* a skinny little twerp. He took a swing, but I ducked and managed to get the handcuffs on him. The girls thought it was a scream. Just as I was about to lead him down the steps to the street, my partner came running up, demanding to know what was going on.

" 'This guy called me a few names,' I explained. 'He was going to take away my nightstick.' I was embarrassed. This was the first time I'd put handcuffs on anyone other than another recruit in Police Academy drills.

"My partner's blue eyes went narrow, and all of a sudden, socko!—he hit this poor bastard so hard on the jaw that he cartwheeled all the way down the stairs to the street. The girls were now screaming, they thought it was so funny.

" 'Did he get run over?' the desk sergeant asked when we dragged him into the station house.

" 'Nah. He fell down the stairs when we were bringing him in. Cut up his face a little.' My partner winked. In the morning this guy woke up without remembering anything about the beating, but when he found that his wallet was gone, he started yelling: 'Those godamn whores! I was watchin' my pants every minute! But I knew they'd get that wallet!'"

Seedman went into the Army after that incident. But a year after he got out he had another brief taste of how someone could get hurt in the station house. In November 1946, a week after Election Day, he was just starting up the stairs of the East 103rd Street station house to report to work on the Scottoriggio case, his first assignment as a detective. Suddenly, he was almost smashed flat by a suspect flying down. "Stay out of the squad room, kid," the detective at the top of the stairs called down. "We still have one more interrogation to finish up *privately.*"

"It used to be that hoods *expected* to be hit if they were in the wrong," Seedman says. "Certainly it was true of most of the guys hauled in during the Fallon–Finnegan case. My own introduction to that mentality came one afternoon in 1947, when I was working the garment district as a new detective in the Safe and Loft Squad."

Seedman had nabbed a wizened Irishman who had been stealing packages from Railway Express wagons at a freight terminal. As soon as he was brought into the squad room, the old man turned to the wall and put up his hands.

"I ain't about to tell ya where the packages are," he said. "I ain't, no matter what. So go on and gimme m'licks."

"Who's hitting you?" asked a surprised Seedman.

The Irishman's eyes were squeezed shut. "No, no," he said, "gimme m'licks and get it over with."

Seedman was embarrassed. "Will you sit down in this chair, goddam it! You get booked like anyone else. If you don't want to tell me where the packages are, that's okay by me, you stupid ass. You'll just get a tougher sentence from the judge."

"Even in those years, abuse of prisoners was rare," says Seedman. "Most of the time it was the work of a guy with a mean streak who liked to see blood flow or hear a helpless prisoner cry out. In a force of thirty thousand beefy men a few closet sadists will inevitably slip through. About the time of the Fallon–Finnegan case I got wind of a detective in the Tenth District who was regularly kicking prisoners around; he was dismissed from the department as soon as I was able to get the goods on him.

"Despite undeniable cases of police brutality in this city, the average prisoner, whether he tells the truth or not, never will be beaten or even threatened. The so-called 'third degree' is a myth, but one the police like to see perpetuated. Too often, a typical interrogation goes like this:

" 'Did you do it?'

" 'No sir.'

" 'Do you know who did it?'

" 'No sir.'

" 'Were you at the scene?'

" 'No sir. I was at my mother-in-law's.'

"Now the DA may get this prisoner to cooperate by offering to drop certain charges or recommend immunity in exchange for the truth. But detectives have no such inducements, only the fear of the dreaded 'third degree.' So if the prisoner is convinced that he is about to be hauled to a windowless room, tied to a chair beneath a naked light bulb and whacked with a rubber hose, the detectives do not go out of their way to comfort him. Even though beatings are no longer in order, the fear of beatings can still be useful in getting the truth."

The detectives of the 10th District were censured by the Supreme Court in 1966 for their methods of interrogation in the Fallon–Finnegan case—though many found that mild after Judge Leibowitz's tongue lashing. But the Court did not overturn the convictions obtained. If detectives had manhandled the accused murderers as they had Melville and others, the Court might have viewed their appeal differently, but Seedman took care to be sure not a finger was laid on them. In fact, the detectives who brought Dellurnia and Portelli into the 62nd Precinct squad room that Tuesday night felt their boss was acting like a mother hen.

"They don't look comfortable," Seedman said, staring into the cell. "Go get them some pillows."

"The only pillows we have are in our own dormitory," said one of the detectives.

"So, get them," ordered Seedman.

"But, Captain, we have only *three*. And three of us have got to be here all night."

"Then I guess you take your own naps without pillows," snapped Seedman. For the first time since they had been booked, Portelli and Dellurnia smiled out at him from behind the bars.

While there was no public outcry over the rough treatment of Melville or others, Seedman himself was publicly slapped down for an incident with Dellurnia. It was one of only two times in his thirty years on the force that he was reprimanded for his conduct.

It happened when Dellurnia was brought back to Brooklyn under detective escort after signing his extradition papers in Connecticut. He was spirited so quickly through the ugly crowd massed at the 62nd Precinct station house that the horde of waiting press photographers missed their shots. When they complained loudly, Seedman agreed to give them a second chance. Gripping Dellurnia firmly by the arm, he led him from the captain's office into a grid of flashing bulbs. But Dellurnia's head was bowed and sunk so low that nobody could photograph it.

"Hold his head up so we can get at least one good shot!" someone shouted.

Seedman did what he knew instantly he would regret: he gripped Dellurnia under the chin and raised his head—as the flashbulbs went off, dozens of them.

"Don't print that!" hollered Vic Kaufman, Commander of the Homicide Squad. The photographers did not even bother to answer.

The next morning Seedman was shaving again with Lennie Schniper's razor, when Schniper rushed into the dormitory shower room with the *Daily Mirror*. Staring off the front page, apparently in great pain, was Dellurnia. Standing behind the prisoner, cigar stub wedged in his impassive face, Seedman saw himself. Where he was holding Dellurnia's face, the flesh appeared to stretch like pizza dough. Seedman knew the photo would cause him trouble.

The New York Civil Liberties Union demanded that Seedman be severely disciplined. Michael Murphy, the Police Commissioner, called in Seedman on Friday morning. Seedman was ushered into the office through the handsome rotunda-style waiting room on the second floor at 240 Centre Street. It connected directly to the office of the Chief of Detectives, which to Seedman that morning seemed the last spot on earth he would ever occupy.

The Commissioner was working on papers and did not look up. After a few moments, he began to shake his head.

"How could you do something like this, Al?" he asked finally, lifting a pile of papers to reveal the *Daily Mirror* photo.

"I don't know, Commissioner. I guess I just lost my head."

The Commissioner put his head in his hands. He seemed weary. "That's all, Al," he said after a few minutes.

Seedman opened the door to leave. The Commissioner said, "Tell me one other thing."

"Yes, sir?"

"Did you have to hold on to such a crummy-looking end of a cigar? Couldn't you light up a new one instead of smoking it to the dregs?"

That afternoon the Commissioner announced to the press that Seedman had been admonished for what he had done. At the end of the day a vacant slot for a deputy inspector was filled. Until he had yanked up Dellurnia's head, Seedman knew that slot had been waiting for him.

"One last point should be made about the Fallon–Finnegan investigation," says Seedman. "Our detectives were not operating in a vacuum. The revulsion they felt over the murder of their colleagues was shared by the whole city. Everyone was hopping mad. Here is the gist of a letter I got from a *Daily News* staff reporter.

'I want you to know the working press applaud
your handling of this rotten son of a bitch.
The entire nation is with you. . . .'

"The event at Borough Park Tobacco seemed to bring out everyone's worst feelings. It even pervaded the judicial process. Neither Babe Accarino nor Frank Lino appeared to be in the best health as they hobbled into the hearing room the afternoon we arraigned them as accessories after the fact for helping Portelli to escape. The presiding magistrate, Benjamin Schor, did not seem to notice anything unusual about them, but Anthony Lino, Frank's brother, did.

" 'Frankie! Frankie!' he shouted out. 'Is that what they did to you? They broke your head! Is that justice?'

"Magistrate Schor looked down at the prisoners with great cool. He saw their arms in slings, their black eyes and bruises.

" 'Maybe they called this upon themselves by resisting arrest,' he said.

"The magistrate probably knew better, but he was caught up

in the same wave of revulsion that touched every decent citizen. Like our detectives, his emotions led him to take liberties he would not consider under ordinary circumstances. It was the feeling that the public was secretly behind them that gave the detectives license to take the measures necessary to find the killers of their colleagues.

"In this case, they knew the evidence was available to convict them. But in many other cases, not enough hard evidence could be presented to a jury to get a conviction. In those cases, the only punishment the culprit might *ever* get would come late at night, deep in the station house basement, doors locked and windows shut tight. . . ."

III. LUCILLE

"Lucille Giusti was a dark-eyed seventeen-year-old business-school student with nice manners and a good head. As we'd learn, her head worked faster than some of our detectives' did.

"It didn't take us long to find out from the kids at Dellurnia's candy store that Lucille could provide the key to what Rosenberg, Portelli, and Dellurnia had been up to that Friday. Though we had plenty of physical evidence—guns, sunglasses, fingerprints, hats—the DA would depend on the testimony of witnesses like Lucille to persuade the jury. Assuming, that is, that Lucille wanted to testify.

"More than any of the others, she had hung around with Jerry and Tony when they popped into the candy store or drove around. For two weeks in April she had even fancied herself Jerry's girl-friend. But she was seventeen and he was twenty-four, and it was probably more in her head than his—he never so much as took her to the movies or out to eat. It didn't matter, compared to the excitement of just being around a couple of sharp guys.

"The blood had barely dried at the tobacco store before Lucille's mother sent her to stay with her aunt in Cocoa Beach, Florida. I told Mrs. Giusti we had worked closely with the Florida police. Either she could bring back her daughter or we'd send down a team of detectives to talk to her there.

" 'It isn't that I'm trying to keep Lucille from you,' she said. 'It's just that people in the streets—friends of those men—might want to hurt her.'

" 'The detectives who'll be assigned to keep her from harm,'

I explained, 'are men to whom I'd entrust my own ten-year-old daughter, Marilyn.'

"That seemed to make her feel better. 'I'll call Lucille's aunt in Cocoa Beach, then,' she said. 'They can start driving back in the morning.' "

Two detectives picked up Lucille in a motel on Long Island's Sunrise Highway six days after the shooting. Though she had been on the road for two straight days, she insisted she was not tired, so the detectives took her directly to the 66th squad room for the first of what would be many days of questioning. Seedman was especially interested in what Lucille would have to say about Dellurnia, since the case against him was not as solid as that against the other two suspects.

"Like her friend Louie 'Gee' Farrara," he says, "Lucille was only too happy to tell us what happened on May eighteenth. The catch was that, like him, she was feeding us a line. Not completely, of course. But at key points in the story we felt sure she wasn't giving us the real dope.

"We did learn that after coming from business school to the candy store at twelve-thirty, she had seen Tony Dellurnia and Jerry Rosenberg go in and out. One of those times Jerry was carrying a small paper bag with something heavy in it.

"During the next few hours Lucille and her girlfriend Angela Carlo jumped in Red Dellurnia's Impala convertible more times than you can count. They went to Mister Donut, they went home to change clothes, they went over to Tony and Jerry's while *they* changed clothes. But when it came down to those crucial forty-five minutes between three-fifteen and four o'clock. Lucille seemed to have become marvelously uninvolved. She claimed to be sitting in a booth at about five past four, when Tony and Jerry rushed into the candy store, looking nervous and upset. Tony tossed his brother's car keys on the counter and they both walked out. Though Lucille had no such recollection, I felt she must have gone along on that last ride, too."

For days Lucille sat in the 66th squad room, encircled by detectives and a policewoman, while they did their best to trip her up. Looking up with wide brown eyes, she fielded all the questions with ease. Yes, she had seen Red's Impala leaving the candy store for the last time at 3:15 with Dellurnia, Rosenberg, and Portelli. No, she had not gone with them herself.

After twenty-three hours of questions spread over several days it was plain to Seedman that Lucille would not be worn down. If anyone was beginning to show signs of being frazzled it was the detectives. Seedman felt the time had come to go for broke by springing a ruse. It began with the ringing of a phone at the start of the fourth day of Lucille's interrogation.

"Hello," said Lambert curtly. "Unless it's important, tell me about it later. We're busy here." Drumming his fingers, he listened for a moment, then his face began to light up. "Yeah. . . . No kidding? Why didn't you say so in the first place? . . . I was hoping for something like this. . . . Don't worry, she's going to be right here when he comes over."

Though he had cupped the receiver and turned away as he talked, Lambert knew that Lucille was straining to listen. But she resisted asking him any questions. Ten minutes later two detectives escorted in a seedy little man with dandruff on his shoulders. He walked straight to Lucille and squinted.

"No doubt in my mind, Officers," he said. "That's her."

They escorted him out.

The questioning droned on. Lambert could see that Lucille was striving to contain her curiosity, but after an hour, the effort was too great.

"Would you mind telling me who that was?" she asked suddenly. "And what did he mean, 'That's her'?"

"I don't think we can tell you right now," said Lambert.

"Why should I tell you things if you won't tell me?"

The detectives looked at each other. "You got a point," said Lambert. "But I'll have to get an okay from the Captain."

When Lambert returned from Seedman's office, he played out the rest of the ruse. "I'll come straight to the point, Lucille," he said. "That guy is a salesman for Phillip Morris. He was parked at the curb across from where you and Tony were waiting in the car. He heard the shots, just like you did. He saw you pull away. You sped right past him."

Lucille bowed her head. For the first time in all the hours of questioning her composure evaporated. She seemed to be just a scared seventeen-year-old.

"If you want," she said at last, "we could go for a ride. I'll show you where we went after we left the candy store. I'd have told you the truth before, but I'm so afraid someone will get me."

With Lambert driving, Lucille pointed out the subway stop at 86th Street and New Utrecht Avenue where she and Dellurnia had dropped off Portelli and Rosenberg at 3:15 that Friday. They would take the train to 51st Street and call into the candy store before walking the three blocks to the Borough Park Tobacco Company.

"They look like a pair of regular guys going to work, don't they?" snickered Dellurnia as the two men walked up the steps to the subway. With their sunglasses and hats pulled down over their eyes, they looked anything but that to Lucille.

Five minutes after they returned to the candy store Tony Dellurnia took a call in the booth. Lucille was fidgety. She and Tony drove off again alone to a spot which she now pointed out to the detectives on Twelfth Avenue, half a block from the tobacco store. They waited. Lucille saw that Dellurnia was getting more nervous by the second. Suddenly the unmistakable sound of shots rang out.

"That fucking Jerry, he'll never learn, never learn!" Dellurnia snarled. He zoomed off for a few blocks, then slowed down. He drove aimlessly while Lucille said nothing.

"I'm going to cruise by the place real slow," he said finally. "You keep an eye out for Jerry and Baldy. Maybe we can still pick them up."

But when Dellurnia cruised down 48th Street, he saw that a patrol car had just pulled up. "Trouble," he said, and kept on moving. Back at the candy store, he left Lucille and the keys for Red and took off.

"On the day she'd come back from Florida," says Seedman, "we moved Lucille Giusti to a suite on a high floor of the St. George Hotel in Brooklyn Heights. As a material witness she was guarded twenty-four hours a day by teams of three detectives assigned to the Kings County District Attorney's office. Even that level of security does not necessarily keep a witness safe. One night in 1941, for example, a member of Murder, Inc., a material witness named Abe Reles, managed to fall out a window at the Half Moon Hotel in Coney Island, in this same Tenth District.

"Lucille's aunt had decided to stay with her rather than return to Florida, even though the trial would not be starting until January. Her mother often stayed at the St. George too; but any time they didn't happen to be around, a female detective had to be on duty. That protected the male detectives from any allegations of hankypanky, and vice versa.

"Women detectives have been a fantastic asset to the Bureau. Often they are the key to carrying out critical parts of investigation which a man simply can't do. But one night when I stopped off at the St. George to see how things were going, who should I see but the last female detective in all New York I wanted on this job!

"Three years ago, when this broad was still a patrolwoman, we found an old lady who'd been beaten to death in her railroad flat near the Brooklyn Navy Yard. After the Medical Examiner had released the body, we took it to the Kings County Morgue, where it still had to be stripped and searched. Since only a policewoman is allowed to do that, we keep a woman on duty at headquarters all night to search any female prisoner or, in this case, a corpse.

"This patrolwoman happened to be on duty that night. At one-thirty in the morning I sent her and a male detective to the morgue to search the body. They spent a hell of a long time at it. Too long. The detective didn't walk back into the office until almost six o'clock.

" 'What took you so long?' I asked.

"He answered me with a stupid grin. I could imagine the whole story right then.

"Here it was, three years later, and this same policewoman is now a detective. Christ! But I didn't want to pull her off the St. George job strictly on the basis of past events, especially if she had a knack for keeping the fellows awake.

"Instead, I replaced one of the male detectives on duty with the most upright detective in all Brooklyn, a Christian gentleman named Anthony Dolby. Every time that woman had the duty, I made sure Dolby had it too.

"This Dolby was such a straight arrow that it became a real problem a few years later, when I wanted to promote him to first grade detective. At the time, one of the requirements I myself had established for a well-rounded detective of that rank was that he collar at least one bookmaker. For most men this was a breeze. Any rookie patrolman could walk into a Brooklyn bar and pick out the bartender or barmaid who was making book—but not Dolby. He didn't even understand how to make a bet. He trudged from bar to bar, but for the life of him he couldn't make that arrest.

"I even thought about looking up Ritchie Melville and sending Dolby over to him. He was an up-and-coming bookie who wanted to continue doing businees even while being held as a material witness in the case. I thought he'd be ideal to tutor Dolby, but unfortunately it was not feasible. On the other hand, I couldn't wait forever for Dolby to make his pinch. Finally, I picked a broken-down, nearly retired third grade detective to shepherd Dolby to a bar.

" 'See that guy with the pad and pencil on the phone?' he whispered to Dolby in a dive on Atlantic Avenue. 'That's not his milk order. He's taking bets on the action tonight at Roosevelt Raceway. That's illegal. Now, go get'm!'

"Dolby loped off like a dog after a stick. He nabbed this guy and in court the gambling charge actually stuck. Two weeks later Dolby made first grade detective. But he was most useful to me in those eight long months from May to January when Lucille Giusti was waiting to testify as star witness at the trial of Rosenberg, Portelli, and Dellurnia.

"By the end of the summer season, we'd moved Lucille, her aunt, and attending detectives to a bungalow at Manhattan Beach, a block from the ocean. It was cheaper and more isolated than the St. George. At odd hours I'd make surprise stopovers at the bungalow to keep everyone on his toes. But there was no need to worry. I could sleep easily at night, knowing that Dolby was there.

"It took time, but I finally got rid of our lady detective. One morning several years later I was shuffling through the reports of overnight action when I came across what appeared to be an accidental shooting. An off-duty female police officer had been cleaning her gun when a bullet somehow found its way into her boyfriend's shoulder at five A.M. These things do happen, though not so often at that hour. But the woman involved was this same detective, and after further investigation she was dismissed from the force.

"A more difficult problem than Lucille's security was keeping up her will to testify during those eight months of waiting for trial. Several powerful currents pushed against us. One was her natural instinct to silence. But another was her very real fear of testifying against her former friends who were now accused murderers. They would not forget. It required many long walks out in the cold ocean air that winter with men she respected, like Lambert, to keep her spirits from flagging.

"Lucille was not the only key witness who did not rush to

testify. The Goldberg brothers themselves were not anxious to point a finger from the witness stand.

" 'What's to stop one of their people from walking in our store one day like that Friday and plugging my brother or me?' asked David Goldberg.

" 'I'll put a detective in your store for as long as you feel you need him' I answered. 'He'll work alongside you. Only he'll be carrying a loaded .38.'

" 'It could be years,' said Robert Goldberg.

" 'Then you've got him for years.'

" 'But what about when you leave the district, Captain?'

" 'You'll still have him.'

That detective, Phil Kissel, stayed with the Goldbergs until he retired, four years after they had testified at the trial. Though the brothers could have asked for a replacement, they did not.

Kissel, spelled by another detective named Sam Sklar, passed his days on the public payroll hauling cigarette cartons and stamping them with the tax machine. Seedman felt that if citizens were encouraged by this to come forward and tell what they knew about a crime, it was time and money well spent. He hated to see the Goldbergs cowed, yet he understood their point. It had been driven home to everyone in Borough Park a few years earlier by the experience of a solid citizen named Alvin Schuster, who had fingered the notorious bank robber Willie Sutton. For performing his civic duty, Schuster had been gunned down outside his home. In case anyone missed the point, as Schuster lay on the ground, the mobsters shot out his eyes. They were never caught.

Year later, when the tobacco store case came up, people shook their heads and said, "Why should I stick my neck out? Maybe what happened to that guy Schuster will happen to me."

But at the joint trial of the three men which opened before Judge Leibowitz in Supreme Court in Brooklyn on January 15, 1963, the key witnesses for the people did not hold back. Especially Lucille Giusti. Each defendant had three lawyers who did their best to shake her testimony. Dellurnia's lawyers were particularly hard on her, since she was the only witness who could place him at the scene, but during the days she sat for cross-examination she remained cool and respectful. Even under the most withering attacks by the defense she did not falter. The detectives were not surprised. Having gone around and around with her for so many days back in May, they knew she could stand up to anything but a good ruse.

Judge Leibowitz kept a firm hand on the proceedings, though Dellurnia and Rosenberg shouted out several times that they were being railroaded. But on the sixth day a wrench was tossed into the trial by Sabine Tammbora, the attorney married to Dellurnia's sister. He was on the stand to dispute the testimony of a gun dealer from a little town in Maryland who had identified Dellurnia as the purchaser of the murder weapon from his shop in April.

Tammbora claimed his brother-in-law could not have been in Maryland that day because he was at family birthday party in Connecticut. "I also had talked to Tony's parole officer that day—" Tammbora began.

At that the defense counsel jumped up to demand a mistrial. Now that the jury knew his client had some kind of previous conviction, he argued, Dellurnia could not get a fair trial. Especially since the prime evidence against him was only in the head of Lucille Giusti.

To the dismay of the District Attorney and the detectives, Judge Leibowitz strode into the courtroom after a weekend of mulling it over and ordered Dellurnia's trial to be separated from that of Rosenberg and Portelli.

"I don't want a mistrial," Dellurnia shouted. "I've been locked up for eight months. I want to get this over with."

"Take Dellurnia away," ordered Judge Leibowitz. As the cuffs were snapped onto his wrists, Dellurnia scarcely realized that he was being given the best break of his life.

"Everyone on both sides of the case had been impressed with Lucille's poise and brains at the first trial," says Seedman. "But during the month's wait for Dellurnia's own trial to begin, we found out that a ruse could work both ways."

Lucille was finishing up her business-school training that spring, and one morning she went out for a job interview in an office building on Court Street. Naturally, two of her guardian detectives accompanied her, but as they entered the elevator to see her upstairs, she hesitated.

"It's going to look funny if I walk in with two big men . . . even if they are handsome," she said. "They're sure to ask who you are and when I tell them, they'll be scared. I'll never get the job." She looked up at them with huge pleading eyes. The detectives understood her point. So they waited in the lobby until she came down twenty minutes later.

"It went great," she said, all smiles. "Thanks, fellas."

"A few weeks later, at the second trial," says Seedman, "Lucille Giusti finally let us down. It was at the end of the proceedings, when everything seemed wrapped up. Suddenly the defense offered into evidence a statement in which they claimed Lucille retracted her original version of what happened in Red Dellurnia's convertible that Friday afternoon.

"The statement was signed but not sworn to. The DA did not ask her to swear to it in court. He must have thought it wasn't necessary. I guess he thought that no jury would ever believe she could give the beautifully detailed testimony she had in the first trial unless it was true.

"But the proper element of confusion had apparently entered the minds of the jury. They found reasonable doubt that Dellurnia was guilty. While his friends Rosenberg and Portelli began serving prison terms which could last the remainder of their lives, Dellurnia walked away free."

The defense lawyer who had introduced Lucille's statement denying her previous testimony maintained that it had been dictated at his desk. His law office was located in the building on Court Street to which Lucille had gone for her job interview.

"I was disappointed in Lucille, of course," says Seedman. "If she'd finally been eaten away by worry that one day she might end up on the sidewalk like Alvin Schuster, that would have been understandable. We couldn't guard her every second of her life, forever. Even if we could, she would not want it. But I don't think that's why we lost her.

"Once I read a story about a kid who found a baby owl that fell out of a nest, and he domesticated it. At least, he thought it was domesticated: it sat around the house, eating hamburgers with ketchup with the family. But one evening that owl rustled its wings and flew off to the woods and never came back.

"The bird just answered a call from within. A voice it had to answer. I can't help feeling that Lucille finally could not shut out a voice within her, bred over generations in Italy and then in Borough Park. It was a call to *omerta,* to silence."

THE JOHNSON-GENOVESE CASE

"Many crimes have grabbed more headlines at the time they occurred than the murder of Kitty Genovese on the morning of March 13, 1964—certainly, the shooting of Fallon and Finnegan did. In fact, her murder did not grab any headlines at all. It appeared at first not to be much different from a thousand other knifings in a city full of blades. But as weeks passed, and the public learned that thirty-eight of Kitty's neighbors awoke to her screams as she was being stalked, but never heeded them, the case took on special meaning. Instead of fading from their minds like most cases, including Fallon–Finnegan, this one grew stronger and more unsettling. A book, a play, TV shows, and a ballad were written about it.

"Yet despite all the publicity, the story of how Kitty came to die was never really revealed, in detail or even in broad outline. It existed only in the heads of the Queen detectives who worked to find her murderer in the days well before the case gained notoriety. They worked on it just as hard before the case became well known as after.

"After a dull first tour as a desk lieutenant in the Maspeth section nine years earlier, I returned to Queens in May 1963 as a newly appointed deputy inspector in command of the Seventeenth

Detective District, where the case was resolved. That promotion had been delayed a year by the hoopla over the news photo of Anthony Dellurnia and me snapped the previous May. The way the scheduling worked out, if there hadn't been a delay, I never would have been in Queens for this case, which it now seems may well be remembered longer than any other I ever worked on."

The case begins not in the stylish Kew Gardens section of Queens where Kitty Genovese had lived, but to the south in the drab Jamaica section. It is February 29, 1964, a miserable Thursday in Queens. At eight P.M. Sgt. Joe McAndrews finishes up a day of "catching squeals" in the 103rd Detective squad room in Jamaica, which is part of the 16th District and adjacent to Seedman's 17th. McAndrews looks out the window, sees that the wet snow has begun to freeze and rut the road; so instead of risking trouble on the way home, he calls his wife and tells her he will sleep over in the squad's dormitory down the hall. Then he slogs across the street to the Terrace Restaurant, eats a quick steak sandwich, and lingers over a Rob Roy. At 9 he goes back to the office to finish the paperwork which is one of the headaches of being squad sergeant, and by 11:15 he has climbed into the top bunk nearest the phone and tucked in.

It is disconcerting to see this big Irish cop, his piece slung over the bedpost, his feet hanging over the end of the bunk, sleeping soundly under a brightly stenciled cow jumping over a smiling quarter-moon. The other bunks are similarly stenciled—with ugly ducklings, three little piggies, and a big bad wolf. Children's furniture is what Gertz, a local department store, had on sale when the detectives of the 103rd Squad chipped in to buy bunks.

At this same hour a hard-working brick-solid black man from South Carolina named Calvin Johnson crawls into bed beside his wife, Annie May. Their white shingled home in South Jamaica is only a five-minute drive from the 103rd Precinct station house. Calvin has to get to bed early because at 2:45 his alarm will go off. By 3:30 he will be at work in the kitchen of Interplant Food Service near LaGuardia Airport, preparing big urns of coffee for the morning flights. Since Annie May needs their car to run errands on Friday, she will have to drive him to work and then bring the car back. If she is lucky, she can grab a few hours' sleep before doing her morning shopping. The Johnsons have no children of their own, but Annie May's younger twin sisters, Arline and Earline, live upstairs with Earline's infant daughter, Gloria. Like most of the family men on the block, Calvin works hard to keep up with expenses. He has a house, a car, and five people to support on a hundred dollars a week. The Johnsons make love and are quickly asleep.

Just a few minutes away from the Johnsons, in this same section of Queens, another black man—a man who will remain nameless for the moment—kisses his wife good-bye this Thursday evening as she goes off for night duty at East Elmhurst Hospital, where she is a registered nurse. Like Calvin Johnson, this man also works hard to pay the bills for a house, two cars, and a family of four on the hundred dollars a week he makes as a Remington Rand accounting-machine operator for the Raygram Corporation. Of course, with his wife bringing in almost an equal amount, things are a little easier, and unlike Johnson, he works a normal nine-to-five day. So now he puts the two children to bed, kisses them good night, feeds his dogs, especially his big dog, Wolfie. Then, like a million other family men in Queens, he takes a sixpack of beer out of the refrigerator and settles down in his favorite chair for an evening of television.

Six hours later the first one to smell the smoke in the Johnson house is baby Gloria. She cries out. Arline and Earline awaken, smell smoke too, and in that cold hour before dawn pick up the child and hurry down the stairs. Concerned only about her baby, Earline dashes next door with Gloria, but as Arline is about to follow, she pulls up short. In the middle of the living room floor she sees Annie May, naked except for a long green scarf coiled atop her stomach. The scarf is smoking. "Wake up!" screams Arline. "Please wake up, Annie." Grabbing her sister under the arms, Arline drags her out on the porch. Next door at the Myerses', Earline is pounding the storm door so hard that she puts her fist through it. Claude Myers yanks open the door and hands the baby, wrapped only in a sweater, to his wife. "Sister, come help me!" cries Arline, kneeling over Annie May. Myers and Earline run back through the snow to the porch, where they help Arline carry Annie May to her 1959 Chevrolet parked in front and lay her down gently on the back seat.

When Sgt. Joe McAndrews gets to the house at 7:30, the fire trucks have already left. The two duty detectives from the 103rd Squad, Baker and Ramsey, are already here. Sloshing through the caved-in living room, the fire marshal shows them charred remains of newspaper piles where the fires had been set. The scarf that lay on Annie May is still there, smelling of wet burned wool. Out at the car McAndrews looks Annie May over, then shakes his head. Annie May's legs stick up over the front seat, bent at the knees, which are spread wide apart. Her burns are not severe, and a slight mark on her stomach doesn't look fatal either. McAndrews assumes the Medical Examiner's report will show that Annie May died of asphyxiation. Maybe, the detective figures, this poor woman had taken a few drinks to warm the cold away and couldn't wake up fast enough.

But the Queens Medical Examiner, another big Irishman named John Furey, figured otherwise. Working with a cigar in his mouth to cut the smells wafting from the autopsy table, he found that Annie May had died of internal hemorrhaging caused by eight stab wounds in the chest and belly, probably inflicted by an ice pick. That report came to McAndrews and the other detectives late Friday morning. Despite McAndrews' original estimate of death by asphyxiation, the detectives were already at work, canvassing the neighborhood. "If there's any chance of foul play, we don't wait for that ME's report," explains Seedman. "Every minute that ticks by after the crime occurs makes it that much harder to recreate exactly what the scene looked like at that instant—who was there and what they were doing. But if you have to make a canvass, a residential neighborhood like Ozone Park is better than 42nd Street in the middle of Manhattan, where everybody is running like hell to get someplace else. You could have a hundred and fifty witnesses to a shooting on the sidewalk in front of the Automat and they'd all disappear into Grand Central before the first cop turns up thirty seconds later. That's why we solve more murders in the Bronx, where lots of people are hanging out windows all day, than on business blocks, where people are in transit.

"A good canvass takes patience. The men have to go back to knock on the doors where nobody answered the first time. They have to go back to the ones who *did* answer because sometimes people will not tell them what they know the first time—maybe they want to talk to a friend before they decide to say anything, maybe they're just dumb and need prodding. Even after you've talked to every person on the block where a murder occurred, you aren't done with the canvass. Maybe a guy from five blocks away happened to be walking his dog on this block when it happened. I remember that the mob once decided to hit a poor bastard and took him up to a deserted park in the north Bronx at three A.M. to be shot and dumped. They figured, at that hour who's going to see? But some nut and his wife were out walking an Irish setter and they saw everything. So because that couple picked a dog that's got to be run all the time, we knew the killers drove a dark-green Cadillac and got enough of the plate number to identify it.

"Besides the neighbors, you always have service people who are on some kind of route. Maybe the milkman or breadman was delivering. Maybe a bus was going by. Then you've got all the local merchants to ask what they know about the victim's habits. You've got sewers and vacant lots to look into and gutters to sweep. The area right around a murder scene often can turn up something interesting. A guy who's fanatically neat and never forgot a thing in his life will drop a pair of sunglasses from his shirt pocket or forget his hat out of sheer excitement from putting some broad away. We've closed murder cases with nothing more than that to go on: a pair of prescription sunglasses or a hat—especially one that's been blocked and cleaned."

But whoever killed Annie May and set her house on fire in that dark morning hour had left no helpful signs. He had neatly stuffed her clothes into the kitchen trash can, but since fabric does not take fingerprints, that was no help. If the killer had left any good fingerprints on a hard surface, the firemen had washed them away. McAndrews and the other detectives had no better luck with their canvass. One man across the street had heard shouting or screaming at four o'clock, but had been too groggy from drinking to see anything more than two figures standing on the sidewalk in front of the Johnsons'. The rest of the neighbors heard nothing until the wail of the fire engine sirens. No buses had gone by. No cabs from the local cabstands had been dispatched to the block. The regulars at the local bars knew nothing of the Johnsons. Neither did the proprietors of the grocery store, beauty parlor, or liquor shops. The druggist at the corner where Annie May sometimes used the pay telephone shrugged at her photo and said, "They all look the same to me."

The only logical suspect the detectives could come up with was Calvin Johnson. He had been the last person to see his wife alive. Few other people would have been up at that hour. It hardly made sense that anybody had been wandering around South Jamaica in the snow and cold in the middle of the night looking for a woman to kill, and had just happened to end up in the Johnsons' living room.

Besides, husbands and wives kill each other all the time. Maybe Calvin Johnson had ben jealous. The detectives knew that Annie May had not always been faithful. Before marrying Calvin two years ago, she had been dating a city sanitation man nicknamed Kelly, and up to two weeks before her death Kelly often would stop by to see Annie May on his day off. Slow to anger as he was, maybe Calvin had grown increasingly riled by those visits. Tired and unhappy to be going to work that snowy morning, he may have suddenly hit his violence point. Once Annie May lay dead, why not set his own house on fire to make it look as if an intruder had done it? What did he care about Arline and Earline and the child—he had supported them long enough. By leaving the Chevy at the curb and finding another way to race to work before the firemen came, he would have an alibi. In fact, when the police called Interplant Food Service at 5:15, a delivery man named Nat Gordon was bringing twenty cartons of bread into the kitchen as Johnson was wheeling out coffee urns to a station wagon headed for LaGuardia. "My house is on fire," Johnson said, racing from the phone. He jumped into the food service's station wagon and sped off.

Checking routinely to see if Johnson was insured, detectives found he had taken out a policy with Metropolitan Life in October. He had paid $7.62 for that first month, then nothing until January, when he paid up for three months. On the day of Annie May's death the policy was in arrears but still in a grace period. Johnson would be due a thousand dollars for his wife's death. It wasn't much— just enough to add to the detectives' suspicions. They also noted that Mrs. Myers, the next-door neighbor, was not letting her children talk to Calvin Johnson. Apparently she thought he had killed his wife. Maybe she had seen fights or heard something she was not telling about.

But Calvin Johnson took the murder of his wife calmly, and just as calmly insisted he did not do it. After an especially long grilling, he turned to McAndrews and said in a faint but firm voice, "Listen, if I'd killed her, I'd tell you I did. So help me." Joe McAndrews, looking straight at Johnson, measured that plain statement and right then determined that Johnson was telling the truth.

The next best suspect was Kelly, the sanitation man. McAndrews didn't care for him because he had so obviously relished the photos of Annie May even though they showed her only from the waist down, straddlelegged over the seat of the car. He had plenty to look at. The Queens detective commander, Frederick Lussen, had upbraided the Photo unit for not taking pictures from enough angles at the last murder in Queens. This time they hadn't taken any chances. But now Lussen was even madder. "Why the hell did we get all these crotch shots?" Lussen demanded. Respectfully, he was reminded about last time.

"But I didn't ask for pictures taken by a goddamn pervert!" he shouted.

Even though they didn't like the way Kelly had ogled the pictures, the detectives couldn't tie him to the crime any better than they could Johnson. Next, they walked the Van Wyck Expressway, all the way from the Johnson's to Interplant Food Service, and looked into every hundred-gallon oil drum that blocked off a construction lane, hoping to find either the murder weapon or a few missing pieces of Annie May's clothing. But after a week of no results from that or any other phase of the investigation, McAndrews began to get the discouraging feeling that they would never solve the murder of Annie May. Not unless the killer somehow revealed himself.

At 2:55 on Friday morning, March 13, two weeks almost to the hour after Annie May died, a compact, dark-eyed and well-shaped barmaid named Katherine Genovese said good-bye to the regulars at Ev's 11th Hour Bar on Jamaica Avenue in the Hollis section of Queens and walked out to her red Fiat parked at the curb. She had left it there at six o'clock while she went out on her night off for a first date with a young man named Louis Respo. After dinner at his brother's home in Brooklyn, they stopped for a late drink at a bar called the Nitecap. Respo invited Kitty for one last drink at his place, but she declined. At two o'clock he dropped her back at Ev's, where, after chatting a bit with the regulars, she was ready to go home and sleep late.

She drove across Jamaica Avenue to the Grand Central Parkway, apparently not noticing a small white car making the same turns she did. She sped west on the parkway to the Queens Boulevard exit, turned into 82nd Road, a quiet shaded street of two-family homes in the area called Kew Gardens. At Austin Street she turned left and drove for a block to the Kew Gardens station of the Long Island Railroad, where she usually parked in the lot in front of the station, deserted at this hour. The railroad didn't like residents to do that, but Kitty's apartment was over an upholstery shop in a row of small stores right next to the parking lot, and it was close. Above each store were two apartments, called "taxpayers," with entrances in the rear. Kitty simply had to walk behind the stores to 82–70 Austin Street, then up a narrow stairway to the small flat she shared with Marie Lozowsky—a mere forty steps.

But as she paused by her car in the absolute silence of the windless morning hour Kitty sensed that something was wrong. Instead of walking those steps to the rear entrance, she hurried from the lot along the sidewalk in front of the stores and, her heels clicking in the stillness, started up toward Lefferts Boulevard. She may have been heading for the police callbox on the corner. She may have felt that the broader well-lighted boulevard was safer. Maybe she hoped that Anthony's Bar, in the middle of the row of stores, was still open. Whatever she had in mind, she got only as far as the card shop, the fourth store up.

On the seventh floor of the apartment building directly across from the card shop, Milton Hatch awoke when he heard the first scream. Bolting to the window, rubbing sleep from his eyes, he saw a girl kneeling on the sidewalk and a smallish man in an overcoat standing over her. "Help me! Help me! . . . Oh God, he's stabbed me!" she wailed.

Hatch leaned out the window, his wife beside him now. "Let that girl alone," he shouted down.

The man looked up For a few seconds nobody moved. Then the man suddenly turned and ran, pumping his knees high. He ran back on Austin Street to a car parked under the trees on the other side of the railroad station, jumped in, and backed into the next block, 82nd Road, one way the wrong way. That put him out of sight of Hatch. But in a private house on 82nd Road, Isaac Hartz had also been wakened by the screams. Though a hedge blocked part of his view, he thought the car that had backed into a bus zone in front of his house was a gray or white compact car with a flat grill—maybe a 1960 Rambler.

In front of the card shop now, Kitty was being watched by others beside the Hatches. Some were in the same seven-story building, some in the sixteen apartments over the stores, some in the apartment house on the far side of the railroad parking lot. So many eyes were on Kitty as she lay under the yellow street lamp that she might have been spotlighted on a stage. For some of her neighbors she really was. One woman went to the window to see what the screams were about, but could not quite make out the scene below. "Turn off the lights, dumbbell," her husband said, "*then* you can see." The woman did see better with the lights out. She and her husband pulled chairs up to the window to watch.

Alone on the street now, though followed by eyes all around, Kitty got up. On the second floor of the Hatches' building Molly Leffler glanced at her alarm clock. It was exactly 3:20. Kitty walked slowly back past the card shop, the liquor store, the dry cleaner, and turned the corner toward the back of the stores. As Kitty left her line of sight, Frances Hatch noticed that the girl was not staggering. If anything, her step was almost dreamlike.

In his apartment building with a side view of the parking lot Emil Power picked up Kitty where the others had lost her. He *did* see Kitty stagger as she rounded the corner. She made it past the first doorway, the entrance to the closed Interlude Coffee House. At the second entrance, a few doors from her own, she slipped inside. The door shut behind her. She may have thought that her friend Harold Kline, the strapping young man who lived upstairs, would come to help her. A woman leaning out her window a few doors down is sure she heard Kitty call Harold's name. She could not get up the stairs. She fell on her back in the narrow stairwell.

Ten minutes later the neighbors saw the man in the overcoat return. Frances Hatch noticed that he was walking normally, as if he didn't have a care in the world. Three floors below, Georgette Share was surprised to see that, while before he had had on a stocking cap, now he was wearing a Tyrolean hat with a feather in the band. Walking slowly, looking from side to side, he peeked into the doorway of the card shop. Nothing. He walked past the liquor store and the dry cleaner, and turned the corner. Molly Leffler ran from one to another of her three windows facing Austin Street to keep him in view. He crossed the parking lot without even glancing into the locked Fiat. He gave a push at the door of the waiting room of the Kew Gardens railroad station and found it open. He spent only a minute inside. Emil Power picked up the phone to call the police but his wife, Elaine, said, "Don't. Thirty people must have called by now." Power saw the man wearing the Tyrolean hat come out the side door of the Long Island Railroad waiting room and head for the rear walkway. He tried the first doorway, 82–60. Nothing. He went to the second, 82–62. Power held his breath. It had been twelve minutes since the last scream. As the man pushed open the door, only a few neighbors could hear a low cry, too weak for a scream, as the door closed behind him.

The neighbor closest to what was happening to Kitty now was Harold Kline, the young man who lived at the top of the stairs. A poodle-trimmer by profession, he often chatted over a drink with Kitty at her place or his. He had even sold her a poodle. The first attack had come almost right under his window. Now he didn't know what to do. He paced . . . went to the door . . . put his ear to it . . . unbelievable! He mustered his courage, opened the door, shut it quickly, went back to pacing. Should he call the police? Should he do nothing? He called a friend who lived in Nassau County who advised him to call the police. But from his own phone? He called old Mrs. Lucchese, who lived three doors down. She called Mrs. Morris, two more doors down. She called Evelyn Lozzi, who lived across the hall from Kitty. Often Evelyn would come in to answer the phone when Kitty was out. But now what *should* they all do? Rather than take the stairs and confront the horror in the vestibule, Harold Kline hoisted himself out his window and scooted across the steep Tudor roof to Mrs. Lucchese's. From there, at 3:55, he called the 102nd Precinct to report that a girl had been attacked in the hallway in back of 82-62 Austin Street. From the time of Kitty's first scream in front of the card shop, thirty-five minutes had elapsed.

The first patrol car from the 102nd swung into the parking lot beside Kitty's Fiat two minutes after Kline called. He and the three old women also now came down. A few minutes later, at 4:05, Mitch Sang and Mike Pokstis, the duty detectives from the 102nd Squad, pulled up in their black Ford. Kitty was lying where she had fallen —on her back at the bottom of the stairs in 82-62. Her suede jacket and blouse had been ripped open. So had her skirt and undercloth-ing. Her legs were spread. Kitty was moaning very softly. It looked like maybe a case of rape. Then Evelyn Lozzi, who had reached her first, picked up Kitty's head and felt the blood underneath. Kitty was still alive when the ambulance came, but by the time it reached Queens General Hospital a few minutes before five, she was dead.

In the morgue at dawn the police put Kitty Genovese on a steel table. They undressed her and listed her clothing: tan suede jacket, turquoise blouse, grey flannel skirt, black half-slip with lace trim, girdle, white cotton panties, tennis shorts, nylons, black leather shoes. The bra, girdle, and panties had been torn apart. The two cuts in her back were deep but not fatal. On her front were the fatal wounds—slits in the stomach and chest which had caused her chest to fill with blood, collapsing her lungs. Slashes, common to victims trying to shield themselves from a knife, also had been made on the palms of her hands; they are called "defense cuts." Other slashes also ran across Kitty's right breast and her throat. Back at Kew Gardens neighbors were now pouring out of the buildings on Austin Street, despite the early hour and the late-winter chill to watch the police begin their investigation.

The number of police grew rapidly in the early morning. The radio car had been first, notified by the desk patrolman who had taken the call from Kline. The patrolman also called up to the second-floor squad room to Sang and Pokstis, the duty detectives. They had notified their squad boss, Lt. Bernard Jacobs, who rolled out of bed and was at Austin Street by 4:30. Sang and Pokstis had also called the two duty detectives from the Queens Homicide Squad, John Carroll and his partner, Jerry Burns. Lieutenant Jacobs put in a call for duty detectives from the thirteen other Queens squads to lend a hand. Since the killing of a girl in a nice section like Kew Gardens was unusual, Jacobs also called his boss, Frederick Lussen. Stern-faced and known to smile only rarely, he was known simply as "The Dutchman." Calls also went out for the Emergency Service Unit, the Photo and Fingerprint Units, who roped off the parking lot. By seven o'clock on that chilly Saturday morning forty detectives and technicians milled about the scene of Kitty Genovese's death.

Right away the investigation got off on the wrong foot. Though the detectives didn't yet know how many of her neighbors had watched the stalking of the girl, they did sense that *someone* could have called the precinct sooner than Kline did. No one felt this more strongly than Mitch Sang, who was trying to interview Marie Lozowsky in her apartment at seven o'clock. In her best moments, Marie seemed as if she must be shy and withdrawn. Now she was practically stone. Kline had already come up to be with Marie. Though he claimed to be consoling her, in Sang's words he was only "swilling vodka and acting obnoxious." It occurred to Sang that if Kline had done more for Kitty than listen to the awful sounds at the bottom of the stairs, he would not need to console Marie. Now Sang suggested that Kline leave. "If Marie wants me to stay, I can stay," Kline said huffily. When Marie stayed silent, Sang, a tall barrel-chested man with a shaven head, politely propelled Kline out the door and down the steep stairs. As Sang walked back up, he heard curses, then a loud thump, and wood splintering behind him. Kline had kicked in the bottom panel of the door. That did it for Sang. He raced down the stairs again and hauled the cursing Kline off to the precinct house, where he was booked for disorderly conduct. Sang was mad at himself for letting Kline get to him that way. Yet he had never felt such disgust as for these people who had done nothing to help pull a girl back from death.

On the other side of the parking lot at 82-60 Austin Street, where Emil Power had watched Kitty and her killer go around to the back, Lieutenant Jacobs and his men were doing no better than Sang. Only 82-60, of all the buildings on the the block, had an all-night elevator man. If at 3:15 he had been in the lobby, where he was supposed to be, he would have seen the killer pull up almost directly in front of his door. But it was now seven o'clock and the elevator man was not giving any information. Not even his name.

"This is a homicide investigation," said Lieutenant Jacobs. "I think we have a right to know who you are." The man looked away sullenly.

"Okay, my friend," said Jacobs. "We'll take you down to the station house until you decide to tell us a little about yourself and what you saw." At the 102nd Precinct the man sat for twenty-one hours before giving his name as Robert Bodec. As for the murder on his shift, he insisted he saw nothing because he had gone down to the basement for a coffee break. For almost an hour? asked Jacobs. Bodec nodded. The detectives could get no more than that, and let him go. But Jacobs was sure that Bodec's "massive stubbornness" was a sign of having seen plenty.

Other neighbors were more cooperative than Bodec. As they knocked on doors that Saturday morning, detectives found very few who had not seen or heard something. By nine o'clock they had been able to reconstruct almost every detail but the final moments, when the killer joined Kitty in the stairwell of 82-62 Austin. Even that finale, the detectives felt, might have been observed from the upstairs apartment of Harold Kline, though he claimed to have opened his door only enough to listen. When they totaled it up, they found that the number of people who had been aware of what was happening to Kitty came to a shocking thirty-eight. How many others who claimed to have slept through it all had also been jolted awake?

The only person who had picked up the phone early in the attack was Georgette Share, a shy French girl. She had dialed the 102nd Precinct, but as the duty patrolman came on she felt her voice stick in her throat and she hung up.

On March 14 the *New York Times* ran a four-paragraph item on page 23 under the headline "Queens Woman Stabbed to Death in front of Home." It was not until March 27, five days after Police Commissioner Mike Murphy mentioned the case over lunch to *Times* Metropolitan Editor Abe Rosenthal, that a front page story ran on how not one of Kitty's neighbors had gone to her aid or even picked up the phone to call the police until the attack was over. It was a story that caused that leafy section of Queens to become notorious around the world. In Moscow *Izvestia* called it a case of our "stone jungle morals." *Witness,* a play based on the event opened in San Francisco. In New York, Mike Wallace did a nationwide CBS special, "The Apathetic American." Nightly at the Interlude Coffee Shop, a few doors down from where Kitty had lived, a folk singer named Al Casey strummed "The Ballad of Kitty Genovese." Abe Rosenthal wrote a little book, *38 Witnesses,* asking whether he would have done more himself.

"What those thirty-eight people saw, or think they saw, would make a good classroom exercise at the Police Academy in how to cut the crap from what's valuable in a witness's story," says Seedman. "You take those people with windows looking down on Austin Street, across from the first attack. They all had the same view except for the angles. Yet some thought they saw a light-skinned black and others swore they saw a swarthy white man. A few of them thought it might even have been a woman. The detectives came across one old lady, who said the guy was black. They asked her if she was sure, since her neighbor down the hall thought he was white. The old dame got offended. 'Listen, I worked for fifteen years at Monticello Raceway,' she said. 'I'd see the exercise boys running alongside the horses. Let me tell you—black boys and white boys run different. Black boys pump their legs up higher and closer together than white boys. I *know* that. You want to make a bet I'm right? Put your money right here. . . .

"This old broad may no longer have the eyes of her youth," Seedman continues. "If she took a few nips before bed, that didn't sharpen them either. But because she still uses her eyes with great discrimination, like an Indian scout, it pays to listen to her carefully. We had a similar situation when the witnesses described the killer's car. One guy tells us he saw a sports car of some type. What type? He doesn't know for sure—maybe a Jaguar or a Corvette. So you listen to this guy a little less hard. Any idiot who thinks he saw a car that is either a Jaguar or a Corvette is not discriminating. But then we get this guy who says it was a compact car and it had a flat grill and it might be a 1960 Rambler. Maybe he's wrong—he *was* wrong—but you have to listen to him. He's tuned in to the fine differences."

The thirty-eight descriptions of the killer sifted down to a slender man of 120 to 140 pounds who could have been black or white. He wore a dark overcoat and a stocking cap during the first attack but came back the second time wearing a Tyrolean-style fedora. He drove a light-gray or white compact car. He could have been any of a million New Yorkers. It was lucky the detectives got this much of a description as quickly as they did. In the days and weeks after Kitty died, most of her neighbors grew resentful that the world had singled them out, and most stopped talking to reporters. Some vilified them. "You've ruined our community. You've given us a bad name all over the world which we don't deserve," whispered a woman through a crack in her door at a *Long Island Dispatch* reporter. "You should be ashamed."

Whoever killed Kitty had done a clean job of it, despite thirty-five high-pressure minutes in which to trip up. The Emergency Service team searched the nearby bushes, sewers, trash cans, and miles of railroad track, but they found no murder weapon. The canvassing detectives checked with the local bartenders to see if any of that night's patrons answered the description of the killer. They could point to nobody. The conductor of the last train into Kew Gardens, at 2:45, saw nobody get on or off. The bus driver of the Q-10, which passed on Lefferts Boulevard at 3:55, could offer no help—at that moment the killer would have been with his victim in the stairwell of 82-62 Austin anyway. John Ferrante, who delivers Bellacicco's Italian bread on the block between three and four A.M., had seen nothing. John Valez, night man at the pizza parlor on Lefferts, around the corner from Austin, had closed at 2:30 instead of 3 o'clock because the night was so quiet.

But a key witness did come out of all this. A milkman named

Tom Daley was making his normal stop at a delicatessen on Lefferts Boulevard at 4 A.M., when a young man appeared from the walkway that ran behind the stores on Austin Street. Under the street lamp Daley saw him clearly but hardly noticed him because he seemed relaxed and in no hurry. He turned the corner at Austin Street and disappeared. The police were in no hurry to disclose Daley's testimony. If the killer were to pick up the paper and read that he had been seen so clearly, Daley might end up on the sidewalk at dawn some morning soon, with his milk bottles splattered over him.

A sensitive fact about Kitty Genovese emerged as soon as the investigation turned to the people in her own life: she was a lesbian. "You might think that doesn't have a thing to do with a case like this," says Seedman, "but it does. Or at least it can. Our experience is that one of the most common motives for murder is jealousy. Everyone knows that. But it's also our experience that homosexual romances produce more jealousy by far than 'straight' romances. More jealousy means more chance for violence. Women, in fact, can be more possessive toward their lovers than men.

"Several years ago, for example, I was in a downtown restaurant with a fellow who knew the proprietor. She came over to our table to say hello. At her side was a breathtaking blond girl. Even our wives couldn't take their eyes off her. Introductions were made all around—except for this girl who just stood there, looking blank and beautiful. The proprietor was very warm, very friendly, but she acted as if the girl were invisible. The whole scene seemed odd, and later my friend mentioned it to the bartender.

" 'Listen,' he whispered, 'that's the boss's new girl. That's not to talk to. That's her *property*, man. Nobody talks to her without the boss's permission.' "

Several of those who had looked out their windows on the morning of March 13 had thought that Kitty's attacker might have been female. One was even sure of it. All agreed that he or she weighed no more than 140 pounds. One hat or the other always hid the attacker's face. To cover every possibility, the detectives rounded up all the women Kitty had known, just as they would have picked up all the men if she had been "straight." The women were not happy to be in the station house, especially the tougher types the detectives call "butches." Bernie Jacobs knew it would require great tact to keep up their good will as they were questioned. Jacobs had it, but he knew the Borough Commander, Fred Lussen, was less than *simpatico* with these types.

Just the same, Lussen decided to question one of Kitty's especially rugged friends himself. Asking her name and address went smoothly. Then Lussen stared at her sternly.

"And which *way* do you go?" he asked.

The woman returned the look. "The same way *you* go, baby," she answered.

They glowered at each other in silence. Then Lussen turned and walked out of the squad room, his face cold white. He left the rest of that phase of the questioning to Jacobs.

Kitty Genovese's family had moved from Brooklyn to New Canaan, Connecticut, when she was a child. After high school she married an Army man, but the union was annulled after two months. She had come to New York in 1960. At first she worked in office jobs around town, then as a barmaid. Her small size and pert, boyish features were a good foil for her shrewdness and toughness. All the regulars at Ev's said that nobody could tell a man he'd had his last drink as firmly as Kitty—and without having him turn sour on her. She also had a good business head and did all the bookkeeping for the place. Her father, Vincent Genovese, later told the detectives he had never had to support his daughter after high school: from the start she had always made as much money as a man.

Each patron of Ev's who had ever talked to Kitty was checked out by the detectives. They also searched for every man she might ever have known named George, since one neighbor thought she'd called out that name as she staggered to the back hallway. They pored over the files of known criminals to see if any had a *modus operandi* like the killer's. But even the oldest detectives in Queens could not remember a killer with an MO like this one.

It reminded Seedman of a story he had read a few years earlier about a shark that attacked a girl in the California surf. At her first scream the swimmers near her formed a protective circle around her and dragged her toward shore. The shark circled round and round the circle of men. They felt its rough hide as it pushed between their bodies to slash at the girl again and again, even as she was hauled to the foot of the beach. It wanted her and would not be diverted.

"It's the same with our guy," says Seedman. "He wanted only Kitty and was willing to risk coming back to finish her off. The only difference was that those people in the surf did what they could to save that girl. They didn't let her down. In my experience, they were the exception to the way people usually act."

On the weekend of March 13 and well into the next week forty detectives worked over each shred of information the witnesses had given them. If just one person had jotted down even a part of the killer's license plate, if only Anthony's Bar or the pizza parlor on Lefferts Blvd. had not closed earlier than usual . . . but after all the intensive sifting and questioning the detectives were no further along than before. They began to feel the same way the detectives over in the 103rd Squad had with the case of Annie May Johnson: the killer of Kitty Genovese would not be found unless he struck again.

At eleven o'clock on Thursday morning, March 18, one of the first mornings of the year that seemed like spring, a man named Dan Fulton, who lived at 23-46 102nd Street in the East Elmhurst section of Queens, heard noises across the hall in the apartment of his neighbors, the Hoffmans. Nobody was supposed to be home there, so Fulton went to investigate. As he opened his door he saw a slender young man lugging out the Hoffmans' television set.

"It's okay, I'm just giving them a hand moving," the man said. He smiled. Fulton had heard of no such plans. He closed his door and went to the front window. He saw the man put the television set in the back seat of his car, a 1960 Corvair, and lock the door. Whistling a tune, he came back into the building. It didn't make sense. If this fellow was a burglar, why hadn't he seemed nervous when Fulton confronted him? Why the hell would he be coming back up again?

Fulton called a friend on the block named Jack Green. It sounded just as crazy to him that a burglar would stick around after being questioned. Maybe the Hoffmans really *were* moving. But the two men decided to take no chances. While Fulton called the 114th Precinct, Green went down to the white Corvair at the curb, opened the hood, ripped off the distributor cap. He slammed the hood and returned to his own apartment to wait. A minute later the young man appeared. He carried nothing. The two men watched him try to start the car. When the ignition would not catch, he got out and locked up. Casually he walked off down 102nd Street. A few moments after he was out of sight, Patrolmen Daniel Dunn and Pete Williamson pulled up in their radio car beside the Corvair.

It was 11:25 when Fulton and Green, acting as spotters from the back seat of the radio car, pointed out the man who had come out of the Hoffmans'. He was strolling along Twenty-third Avenue, six blocks away, with the same nonchalance as before. He didn't try to run as they pulled up beside him. Though Dunn and Williamson searched him warily, he carried only a screwdriver in his right pocket. They all rode back to the Corvair, where the police found, besides the Hoffmans' television set, a second television set in the trunk, several small appliances, and a batch of pornographic pictures.

At noon Dunn and Williamson brought their suspect into the 114th Precinct station house. Standing at the desk sergeant's high counter, he gave his name willingly: Winston Mosely of 133-19 Sutter Avenue, Richmond Hill, Queens. It was nice for the two patrolmen to get this easy "collar." The more collars they were credited with, the better it made them look at evaluation time. But plucking a routine burglar off the street without a fight hardly reflected any special valor or resourcefulness. Capturing a ferocious bankrobber after a shootout and chase, on the other hand, as young Albert Seedman had dreamed of doing while walking a quiet beat in the Bronx, would be worth a hundred burglary collars as a way to push up the ranks—maybe even to the Detective Bureau.

Dunn and Williamson now walked their suspect upstairs to the 114th Detective squad room where the duty detective, John Tartaglia, was doing his paperwork. Tartaglia was a bearlike man with dark features and a resonant voice. During his thirteen years on the force, he had built up a splendid arrest record. He had the reputation of a man who would take on the most vicious criminal with pleasure. Four years earlier, at age thirty, he had been promoted to second grade detective, one of the youngest in the Bureau.

Now Tartaglia was looking across his desk at the prisoner, a slight Negro nearly as light-colored as himself. Mosely's features were fine and catlike. Sitting still and small, his eyes cast down, he conveyed an odd air of gentleness to Tartaglia. Calm and gentleness. They did not seem the traits required to pull off the brazen burglary he had been accused of. It would be very hard for Tartaglia to work up his well-known Italian fire with this kind of suspect.

Besides, Mosely readily admitted to burglarizing the Hoffmans'. Not only their apartment, but another family's apartment earlier in the morning, which is where the television set in the car's trunk had come from. Mosely explained he took the sets to his father's television repair shop on Northern Boulevard for resale. Why had he returned to the apartment once Fulton had discovered him? Mosely looked up. "Oh, when I got to the car, I remembered I'd left my screwdriver up there. I thought I'd better go up and get it. I hate to leave things around." What about all those pornographic photos which Williamson was now busily—in Tartaglia's view, *too* busy—vouchering? They had come from the earlier burglary. "I'd never buy any of that stuff myself," said Mosely.

For an hour Tartaglia questioned Mosely about his burglaries. The answers came readily, well formulated. He had done twenty, thirty, possibly even forty jobs over the past year in Queens, almost always settling for just the television set. The two forays this morning were the exception to his customary MO of working only between midnight and dawn. He'd done his very first burglary on impulse the previous summer while riding down a residential street at 2 A.M. "I saw a side window open in a house. The place was all dark and I knew they'd be sleeping. I just had an urge to climb in and find out how hard it would be. It was easy. I tiptoed upstairs and listened to the people breathing in the bedrooms. Then I came down and took the television out through the window."

Something about this burglar did not sit well with Tartaglia. It was one thing to take a television set from an empty apartment, as Mosely had a few hours ago. But to go into a home at night where people were sleeping took a kind of icy cool most burglars lacked. But that wasn't all that bothered Tartaglia. Mosely was too smart to have been caught so easily. It didn't even make sense for him to be a burglar at all. He had a good job as a Remington Rand accounting machine operator for the Raygram Corporation in Yonkers, and not just pushing buttons, either. Mosely lost Tartaglia as he explained how he programmed elaborate inventory schedules, a task for which he earned a hundred dollars a week. Tartaglia was feeding his own family of six on not much more than that, while Mosley had only two children and a wife who worked as well. He owned his own home. He paid taxes. He had kept the same job for ten years. In short, he was everything a common burglar should *not* be.

All these signs should have pointed to a law-abiding citizen rather than an habitual burglar, but what troubled Tartaglia even more was the calm and lack of any roughness in the man. That and his well-ordered intelligence. Those qualities seemed to set him apart, not only from a stupid burglary but from any crime. Almost too far apart. Maybe, just maybe. . . .

Tartaglia did not say what he was thinking. First he had to attend to the burglary matter. Mosely claimed that he took the stolen television sets to his father's repair shop on Northern Boulevard, where he helped out making housecalls for a few hours every evening after his day at Raygram. Alfonzo Mosely was working at his repair table when his son led the detectives to him a few minutes after two o'clock. Gray-haired and dignified, he seemed ruled by the same sense of calm as his son. Tartaglia hated to do it, but he would have to arrest Alfonzo Mosely for receipt of stolen goods. A half-dozen television sets in the place had come from his son's forays. But what Tartaglia really wanted was to question Mosely about the suspicion that had been in the back of his mind ever since Dunn and Williamson had told him Mosely was driving a white 1960 Corvair.

At 3:30 Tartaglia sat Mosely down in the battered captain's chair back in the squad room. Like every good detective, he kept a mental file on all the crimes recently committed in the borough, especially those still unsolved. Right now he had in mind a woman named Suzanne Vernon. At midnight three Sundays ago, she had been waiting in her idling car for her husband in front of their Jamaica apartment building, when the door opened on the driver's side. She assumed it was her husband until she felt a rifle barrel jammed in her stomach.

"Don't say a word or I'll blow you apart," a slender young man said. He tried to shift into gear but the floor console confused him just long enough for Suzanne Vernon to jump out her side. She ran screaming down the street to where a neighbor was parking his car. Though he knew Suzanne Vernon, he did not open his window as she beat on it and pleaded for help. But once he had finished parking, he had no alternative to getting out except to sit in the car while she drummed the window. "He's going to kill my husband!" screamed Mrs. Vernon as he finally did get out. But the attacker had left her car idling and empty.

One hour later, at 1:15 in East Elmhurst, Laura Foxx was walking up to her front door when a man appeared from nowhere and put a rifle in her stomach. She grabbed the barrel and screamed. Even as the man used one arm to punch her in the eyes and jaw, she held fast. Finally he used both hands to wrench away the gun and bounded into the dark.

Both Suzanne Vernon and Laura Foxx told police they had been attacked by a light-skinned Negro of slender build, about 5' 8" and 135 pounds, wearing a dark overcoat. The description fit Mosely exactly. Yet it did not seem possible that he had the ferocity or the guts to assault those women. On the other hand, who could have guessed he would be brazen enough to go back upstairs for his screwdriver?

"Let's forget burglaries for a minute," said Tartaglia, "and start remembering assaults." He let Mosely contemplate that for a moment before going on.

"On March first you stuck a rifle in that woman's stomach over in Jackson Heights, didn't you? You'd have done *more* than that if she hadn't jumped out of the car when you fucked up the gear shift." Looking hard at Mosely now, all that Tartaglia could read in his face was calm.

"I guess I did do that."

"Then you decided you'd try to do a little cleaner job over in East Elmhurst, right? But you did it even messier. You beat up that woman in the face when she wouldn't let you stick a goddamn rifle in her gut."

"I guess I did that too."

For the first time, Tartaglia began to sense something creepy in this expressionless calm.

Tartaglia had kept Mosely to himself now since noon—four hours. It was going better than he dared hope. But while Mosely had been quite willing to admit to burglary and even to assault, the going was bound to get harder. He would need help. Using a phone out of Mosely's earshot, Tartaglia called John Carroll of the Homicide Squad and Mitch Sang at the 102nd Squad. Then he called his own detective district boss, Albert Seedman. But while they were on their way, he had other cases to ask Mosely about. They were uglier than what had happened to Suzanne Vernon and Laura Foxx.

At 5:45 on the cold morning of January 31 an American Airlines clerk named Roberta Dufek was walking briskly from her home in South Ozone Park to a candy store on Rockaway Boulevard, where she always caught her ride into town every morning at 6 o'clock. A small man appeared out of nowhere. As she described it, "He put a long screwdriver to my neck and said, 'Back down . . . back down. . . .' When he got me to a vacant lot on Inwood Street, he told me to lie down. I said, 'Please, people will be coming . . . my family. . . .'" The man unzipped his fly, forced her to "suck it," then ran off.

Two weeks later, on the only night in the week her husband worked a night shift, a Jamaica housewife named Celia Friml awoke at 1:30 to find a man standing over her. The man ordered her to stand up in the bed and lift her nightgown. "Please don't—not in front of the children," she pleaded. She pointed across the room to where her two children were sleeping. The man debated a moment.

"Okay. Then get downstairs," he said. At the bottom of the stairs he ordered her to lift her nightgown and pressed his mouth against her.

"Please, leave us alone," she pleaded when he was done. "I cashed my husband's payroll check today. You can have it."

She went into the kitchen to look for it while the man rummaged in the hall. As he did, Mrs. Friml dashed out the back door. She banged frantically at her next-door neighbor's front door. Nobody stirred. Two doors down she banged again, sobbing loudly. This time the lights went on. As they did, she saw the intruder walking briskly down the street. Rushing back to her own house, she raced upstairs to check the children. They had never even awakened.

"Now let's forget the burglaries *and* those two assaults for a little while," Tartaglia said to Mosely. "Let's get to the bad stuff. The real scummy jobs. You remember that woman you had in the parking lot off Rockaway Boulevard on the first day of January?"

Mosely shook his head.

"You should. You made her suck you off. And what about that woman in Jackson Heights? That one you went down on."

Mosely shook his head. "I didn't do any of that stuff. I already told you all the things I did. I leveled with you."

"You better not say that," said Tartaglia as he hovered over Mosely, his huge arms tensed. "Because we're going to bring those women down here and they're going to identify you faster than you can blink. Make it easy on yourself."

"Okay," Mosely said. "I did those two jobs. But that's everything now. It really is."

"The hell it is!" Tartaglia wheeled around suddenly and pointed to a "wanted" poster on the far wall. "That's you, isn't it?" he shouted. He knew that Mosely could not see the small print which said the man was wanted for a string of taxi robberies. Now he just wanted to watch how Mosely would react.

"That *is* you, Mosely."

"I told you, I did those burglaries and I assaulted those women. That's all I did. I don't know what you're talking about now."

"Okay. Then let's go back to the burglaries again and see what we missed the first time around."

By 5:30 the squad room of the 114th, normally a quiet place late on a Friday afternoon, was beginning to fill up. Johnny Carroll and his partner, Jerry Burns, had arrived from Queens Homicide. Mitch Sang, the lumbering bare-skulled duty detective from the 102nd, was there with his partner, Mike Pokstis. The boss of Tartaglia's own squad, Joe McCormick—so dynamic that his men called him "Jumping Joe"—was darting around. The highest-ranking officer to arrive was Seedman, commander of four squads in Northern Queens. Other detectives had brought in victims of the assaults, all of whom had identified Mosely as their attacker. Now that everything was established, it was time for the last item of business.

Seedman and Carroll and Tartaglia gathered around Mosely. For the first time he looked apprehensive. He drew his small frame into the chair, as if he thought that now they might hit him. But instead Carroll suddenly grabbed his slim wrists and held up his hands to the yellow light overhead. They were mocha-brown, hairless, well groomed, and remarkably slender, the fingers tapering almost to points. They curved in smoothly like long talons.

"What are those cuts on your ring finger and your index finger?" asked Seedman.

"Those? I scratched them working around the house," answered Mosely.

"No, that's not how it happened," said Seedman. He, Carroll and Tartaglia leaned even closer to Mosely, the cigars clenched between their teeth almost touching his face. "You got those cuts from Kitty Genovese when you were putting the knife in," said Carroll.

The room filled with silence. Mosely looked around almost shyly, a bare curl of a smile shaping on his lips. It was 5:57. "Okay. I killed her," he whispered.

It seemed too good to be true. Just a few hours ago the investigation into Kitty's murder had been stalled cold. It could still turn out too good to be true. Certain weird individuals got their kicks from confessing to crimes they did not commit. This mild-seeming man sitting in the battered captain's chair could easily be one of them. It would soon come out whether Mosely was telling the truth. That was why Tartaglia had called in the detectives who worked the case. They would know if the details of Mosely's story jibed with the facts of the crime—details the newspapers had left out.

"Let's start on March twelfth, right at the beginning of the day," Seedman said.

"Well, I went to work at eight o'clock like I usually do," Mosely began. "Then in the evening I went straight out to my father's shop. I always go there for a few hours after work. I do all the housecalls for him."

"Did you come back later to steal TVs from those places?"

Mosely looked up reproachfully. "I'm not that kind of creep," he said. "I *never* would do that."

"What did you do?"

"I went home about nine o'clock. My wife was just going to work. Usually we just have time to kiss because she's going and I'm coming. Then I fixed up the food for the dogs and made myself a sandwich. I watched some TV in the living room after the kids were in bed, drank some beer. I guess it was a little earlier in the evening that I started thinking about going out later to . . . kill a girl and rape her. A white girl."

"Did you want to rob her too?"

"Well, that was not primary, but it was in my mind. I decided mainly that I wanted to kill and rape a girl, if I could find the right one."

"What do you mean, 'the right one'?"

"I wanted to find a girl who was alone. Two girls would be out of the question. If she was with a man, that was out too. I thought I'd just ride around after midnight to see if it worked out."

"Weren't you concerned to leave your kids home alone?"

Mosely looked startled. "With dogs in the house? Mine are trained to bite anyone who gets near the house. Especially Wolfie. That's my best dog. Anyway, who would come in the house and hurt children?"

"You've got a point, Mosely," said Seedman.

"So a little before one o'clock I went out riding around. I was going down Jamaica Avenue when I saw this girl getting into her car alone. I drove on two more blocks, keeping her in my rearview mirror. When she started out, I made a U-turn and followed her from fairly far back. I didn't want her to notice. She pulled on to the Grand Central Parkway, moving at a real good clip. I followed her down to the Queens Boulevard exit. Then she took a little turn into a quiet dark street. It was what I was hoping for. She took a left turn after a few more blocks and went into the parking lot at the railroad station. I parked under the trees, half a block back. But I was out of my car much faster than she was. I had my hunting knife in my coat pocket. When she saw me, she was locking her car. I thought maybe she'd try to get back in, but she didn't. She started to run up the street. She ran fast but I can run much faster. I caught up with her in front of one of the stores. The knife was in my hand now. I jumped on her back and stabbed her a few times."

"Did you say anything to her?"

"No. Maybe I might have if she wasn't running so fast. I just jumped on her back and stabbed her. She fell down on her knees. She was screaming. I was looking for a place to drag her and shut her up when I noticed lights going on in some of the apartments. Then I heard somebody shout down from a window. I looked up but I couldn't quite understand what he was saying. It seemed like I better get the car out of there right away. So I ran back and put it in reverse and backed around the corner of the next block. It was quiet. I didn't hear anybody coming out or doors slamming. I waited about ten minutes. It was still quiet. So I changed into another hat I had and I went back around the corner to see if anybody was there. The girl wasn't anywhere I could see. So I walked back toward where I first caught her. But she wasn't in any of the doorways. So I started back to the parking lot."

"Wait a minute, Mosely," Seedman broke in. "Weren't you scared those people up there had called the cops? Didn't you think they were on the way?"

The detectives saw that faint smile curling on Mosely's lips again. He looked up at Seedman. "Oh, I knew they wouldn't do anything. People never do. That late at night, they just go back to sleep."

"Then what?"

"Well, I decided to look in the waiting room. She wasn't in there. I tried the restrooms but they were locked. I did happen to see out of the side window a kind of walkway going up behind the buildings, so I went over to look around. I tried the first doorway but she wasn't there. I thought maybe she'd made it home safe. But I went to the next doorway anyhow."

Mosely looked up and saw all the detectives were still. They seemed to be holding off from breathing, just as Emil Power had done that night as he watched the man in the overcoat go to the doorway of 82-62 Austin.

"So I opened the door and she let out a scream. I jumped down on her quick. I had the knife out. I cut her across the throat to stop her from screaming any more. It did, except for some little moans she was making."

"Was she trying to escape?"

"She was twisting and turning underneath me. But she couldn't get away. I cut open her jacket and her blouse. But when I cut through the center of her bra I saw she wasn't as big as I thought. She was wearing falsies. I guess it made me mad. I cut her across the right breast. She was still trying to fight me. I stabbed her four, maybe five times in the stomach. That got her still. Then I cut open all her clothes down below. She had on a lot of layers—skirt, pants, slip, shorts. I cut through it all. She was wearing a sanitary pad. I threw it off to the side and put my head between her legs and licked her. Then I opened my own pants and lay on top of her."

"Did you get into her?"

"No."

"Did you come?"

"I didn't have an . . . erection. But I did have an orgasm."

"Then what?"

"I stabbed her in the stomach a few more times. I slipped the knife up in between her legs, then got up off her. Her pocketbook was lying on the floor. I took her wallet out, also some keys and a few pill packages. The cosmetics I left in. She had seventeen dollars in the wallet, I think. Then I noticed one of her falsies had finger-marks in blood on it from where I pulled it off. I thought maybe you could get my fingerprints from it, so I took that with me too. I decided it would be better if I didn't go back the way I came. So I kept on up the stairway to the boulevard and came around to the car on a different block. On the way home I threw the falsie off into some bushes where Van Wyck crosses Hillside Avenue."

"What about the wallet?"

"I tossed it in some bushes next to the lot where I park at Raygram."

"The knife?"

"It's in my toolbox at home. I washed it first."

The detectives knew for sure now this man had killed Kitty Genovese. Nobody knew that one of Kitty's falsies was missing—except the detectives, the Medical Examiner, and the man who had taken it.

"Did you know that girl's neighbors saw everything you did except for when you killed her in the hallway?" asked Carroll.

Mosely shook his head. "It's not true. The guy who lives upstairs saw me."

"*What* guy, Mosely?"

"Well, I was, you know, lying between her legs and I heard the door open at the top of the stairs. Out of the corner of my eye I saw a man peeking out at us. But he shut the door real quick." Mosely smiled. "I wasn't worried. He wasn't going to help her any more than the others."

Mitch Sang, the veins on his shaven head standing out, pounded his fists together. "That bastard. I *knew* he saw exactly what happened." Mosely could only be talking about Harold Kline, who had been drinking vodka with Marie Lozowsky the morning Sang booted him out.

"Did that guy just open the door and listen or did he stick his head out?" asked Sang.

"I told you. I saw him."

"Could you pick him out?"

"Sure."

The detectives looked at each other. The whole thing was upside down. Here was the murderer pointing a finger at a key witness. Everything was now in place. They were elated. Yet they could not help but be guarded too. Each of them had listened to men confess to crimes calmly, to crimes like burglary, car theft, swindles, even armed robbery. Murderers, on the other hand, almost always grew flushed and excited as they relived what they had done. But Mosely had ticked off these details as matter-of-factly as if they came out of a television repair manual. The detectives had never seen a man so disconnected from what he claimed to have done.

"Tell me, Mosely," said Seedman, "besides Kitty, who else did you kill?"

Mosely contemplated a minute. The smile came. "You remember that woman in Jamaica, Annie May Johnson? I shot her."

The detectives threw up their hands. They stomped the floor. "Oh, Jesus! Oh, shit! Goddamn! You lie, Mosely!" they shouted. "She wasn't shot. She was stabbed with a fucking ice pick. You lied to us about Genovese too, didn't you? You're nothing but a two-bit small-time burglar." Several detectives walked out of the room in disgust. It *had* been too good to be true.

"Do you understand, Mosely?" asked Tartaglia. "You didn't shoot Annie May Johnson. Nobody did. She was stabbed."

Mosely did not look flustered. His face did not fall. He had the knowing look of a teacher waiting patiently for his perplexed class to catch on to a problem he has given them. "I read the papers too," he said. "They were wrong about her being stabbed. I shot her."

Unlike the others, neither Seedman nor Tartaglia had thrown up their hands at Mosely's flub. They were just mystified. Something was wrong, but the fault did not have to lie with this man who had all the rest of his facts in such good order.

"Let's hear how *you* say it happened, then," said Seedman.

Mosely explained that late in the afternoon on Friday, March 1, the urge to find a woman to kill and rape started taking hold. Even the falling snow did not dissipate the urge. He watched television, drank beer, and thought about catching a woman. Long after midnight, when the snow had let up, he went out. The bad roads would keep him close to home. After over an hour of roaming, he saw a woman alone in a Chevrolet come off the Van Wyck Expressway only a few minutes from his own home in South Ozone Park. He followed her to 133rd Avenue in a neighborhood much like his own— small homes owned by hardworking blacks. As she parked in front of 146-12 133rd Avenue, Mosely pulled in behind her. He walked toward her with a rifle pressed vertically against his side. Thinking she would make things simple for both of them, apparently she held out her pocketbook. He took it, pointed the rifle at her stomach and shot her. She fell down on her knees.

"It's one of those single-action .22's," Mosely explained. "You have to reload it after every shot. She held out her keys to me while I reloaded. She said, 'Please, help me get into my house.' I helped her get up and with her arm around me, I got her up to the porch. I shot her again there, maybe four times more. She was lying on her back now. I took the keys and went in. Upstairs I could hear people asleep. I found one hundred dollars in a dresser drawer in the empty bedroom. Then I came back downstairs and shot her a few more times. Then I tried to drag her in, but she was hard to handle. I had to roll her into the house. In the living room I undressed her. It was all those clothes that made her so hard to drag in. Then I had relations with her. . . ."

The men in the squad room had again become riveted by Mosely's flat monologue. Blood and gore they could take. But the woman had been dead. Mosely looked around and sensed their disgust.

"Did you muffdive her or what?" asked Frank Baker, the detective who had been first to turn up at the Johnson fire.

Mosely looked blank.

"Did you go down on her too?"

"Oh. I did both things," he answered. "I licked her and then I lay on top of her.

"After I lay on her I took the clothes and put them in a trash can, except for her scarf. I stuffed that between her legs. The place had newspapers lying all around. I made some piles and I lit them all off and got out of there."

It had the chill of real life. Mosely had again ticked off details that had been held back from the newspapers, like the theft of one hundred dollars from the Johnsons' bedroom. The trouble was, he still had the biggest fact of all wrong: Annie May had died by the blade, not by gunshot. The Medical Examiner did not make that kind of mistake.

"If you want, I could draw you a diagram of where I left the body in the house," Mosely volunteered. On a sheet of Tartaglia's yellow notepaper he drew a downstairs floorplan. At exactly the spot where Arline first caught sight of her sister through the smoke, Mosely drew in a straddlelegged stick figure. Seedman had the feeling Mosely knew what he was talking about. So should the Queens Medical Examiner, John Furey. The only way to settle it would be to exhume Annie May.

Ever since John Tartaglia had called them four hours ago, the detectives from the 102nd Squad had wanted to get Mosely over to their station house, where he could be booked for Kitty's murder.

Tartaglia himself could have made the arrest at the 114th Precinct, but it was traditional and only right for him to hand over the prisoner to the boys who had done the work. Bernie Jacobs was waiting patiently now over at the 102nd. Mitch Sang was waiting not so patiently at the 114th. But Winston Mosely had come in as a dull little burglar and would go out as one of the worst fiends in the annals of the Bureau. Each patrolman and detective who had participated in the investigation or capture wanted due credit and recognition for the part he had played, however small. So now at seven o'clock in this crowded squad room a delicate issue had arisen: the intricate and touchy politics of a major arrest.

Who deserved credit for Mosely's capture? It was Jack Green who had started it all by ripping Mosely's distributor cap. But Daniel Dunn and Pete Williamson had actually brought Mosely in. Dunn was a favored young patrolman in the 114th; his patrol boss was "looking to push him." This arrest, easy as it was, would be valuable to him. So Dunn was here now in the squad room, while Williamson, who seemed more interested in vouchering the pornographic pictures, had been sent home promptly at four o'clock, the end of his shift. Later, Williamson would show up at the 102nd station house to claim credit, only to be sent home again.

Should John Carroll and Jerry Burns from Queens Homicide get the collar? They had caught the case and worked hard on it. John Carroll did not need the collar. He was already a first grade detective, making as much money as a lieutenant; he was among the elite of the Bureau and could go no higher before retirement. But his partner, Jerry Burns, was only second grade. A major arrest could mean his own promotion to first grade. So Carroll tried to step back and let his partner take the credit.

As for Mitch Sang, he was a third grade detective. He had doggedly pursued every detail of the case almost without rest since he had first looked down, shivering, at Kitty Genovese fading fast in the doorway of 82-62 Austin Street. Now he felt he deserved credit as much as anyone. That meant, at the very least, taking Mosely back to the 102nd in *his* car. To make sure that the homicide detectives or anybody else didn't whisk off the prisoner, Sang now handcuffed himself to Mosely.

"What the hell are you doing?" Seedman asked.

Sang looked at the detective chief resolutely. "It's our case. I just wanted to take him back."

If there was going to be this kind of jockeying for the privilege of bringing Mosely over to the 102nd, Seedman knew how to end it. He and John Tartaglia delivered the prisoner to Bernie Jacobs at eight o'clock in Seedman's own car. Tartaglia had been just about the only man that afternoon who did not look for favors. He would also end up the only man to get a promotion. Later in the year he became first grade detective.

As quietly and patiently as before, Winston Mosely went through the details of his burglaries, rapes, and murders in the squad room of the 102nd. It was now after 9 o'clock and he had been answering questions, often thundered at him, continuously since noon. Bernie Jacobs wanted to keep Mosely fresh, especially since he would soon be taking him over to Kew Gardens to walk through the steps of the murder. "How about something to eat, Mosely?" asked Jacobs. "A little snack?"

Mosely thought for a moment. "I'd like a double hamburger, very rare, coffee light with no sugar, and a piece of French apple pie . . . *warm.*"

Jacobs liked his own food exactly a certain way too. He saw to it that Mosely got what he asked for. He even offered to let Mosely take a break from answering questions. "Oh, no, I don't mind talking while I eat," he said. That is what Mosely did: ate his hamburger and washed down his French apple pie with coffee and chatted about murder. It seemed to Jacobs, in fact, that Mosely must be glad to get this whole netherlife off his chest. He asked Mosely if he hadn't secretly wanted to be caught.

For the first time Mosely's thin face tightened. The sloping eyes fastened on Jacobs. "What the fuck do you think I'd want to do that for? I could get the electric chair for this." It was the first time during the long day that Mosely had cursed.

Mosely's story checked out with the precision of the inventory schedules he produced at work each day. Kitty's wallet was found where he said it was, in the rear of the Raygram parking lot in Yonkers. Her falsie, smeared with bloody fingermarks, turned up under the Van Wyck Expressway at Hillside Avenue, along with a few pill containers from the pocketbook. At Mosely's home on Sutter Avenue his bone-handled hunting knife lay clean and polished in his neatly arranged toolbox in the kitchen pantry, exactly as he had described it. The riddle that remained was Annie May Johnson.

In direct opposition to Furey's official findings, Mosely stuck by his story. He had shot her eight times with a single-action .22-caliber rifle and never touched her with blade or pick.

Annie May was buried in a cemetery at Monk's Corner, South Carolina, a few miles from where she had been born. On the morning of March 20 three men from New York—an assistant medical examiner, an assistant district attorney, and a lawyer for the accused —watched on a windy knoll as three black gravediggers heaved Annie May's pine coffin out of the red clay. They took her in a hearse to the University of South Carolina Hospital in Columbia, where on a stainless-steel table she was X-rayed front and back, head to toe. The medical examiner and the lawyer watched, but the district attorney stayed outside. He knew he would be sick.

The X-rays showed eight pieces of metal inside Annie May. The medical examiner probed and found six bullets and two fragments of bullets. A .22 can leave a small hole, small enough to pass for a stab wound, especially when the flesh closes over it. From that day on the Chief Medical Examiner of New York City, Milton Helpern, ordered all homicide victims from Queens to be shipped to his office in Manhattan for examination under his supervision. In any case of suspicious death in any borough, X-rays were to be made as a matter of course. For John Furey, the bluff and likable Irishman, March 20 was a most ignominious day.

After a few hours' sleep in the cage of the 102nd squad room, Winston Mosely was arraigned before Judge Bernard Dubin in Queens Criminal Court early on March 19. The accused stood meekly with his eyes down, his slender fingers curved in and relaxed.

"I can only say it's lucky that our system provides for a trial for a monster like you," Dubin said. "What you've done makes me want to vomit."

Except to ask the court to appoint a lawyer for him, Mosely said nothing. Dubin assigned Sidney Sparrow, a veteran of the local criminal courts, to be chief defense counsel. Though born in New York, Sparrow had an inexplicably heavy English accent. Combined with a pencil-thin mustache and a penchant for formalized language, it gave him a supercilious manner that belied his ability as a shrewd no-nonsense nuts-and-bolts defender. Among Queens detectives he was known as a lawyer who defended a number of bookmakers. Just by chance he'd been representing Kitty Genovese on a numbers charge at the time of her murder—a common annoyance for barmaids and bartenders who provide this service for their regulars. Driving to work on the morning of March 19, Sparrow heard the radio report of the capture of Kitty's killer. He had a feeling that he would be appointed Winston Mosely's defender.

The defense's first move was to have Mosely sent to Kings County Hospital for a psychiatric examination. Was he a madman? To do what he had done was hardly a mark of sanity. On the other hand, as Sparrow and two assistant defense counsels listened to Mosely calmly and precisely make the horror explicit, he did not seem mad at all. Walking out the hospital door after that first session, one of the young assistants went to the curb and vomited. Sparrow's strategy was clear. He would not minimize what Mosely had done, but maximize it. The crazier he looked, the better. If he was judged sane, the electric chair awaited him. But if he was judged insane, he would be committed to a mental hospital for life. The key lay in the psychiatrists' reports.

On May 28, 1964, Mosely went on trial at the Queens County Courthouse on Queens Boulevard, just a block from where he had followed Kitty's red Fiat off the Van Wyck Expressway. Many of the people who filled the courtroom had walked over from Austin Street, a few blocks away. Many heard Kitty scream at 3:15 that Friday morning and with their own eyes had seen Winston Mosely stalk her. Representing the People of Queens County was Frank Cacciatore, a folksy, voluble, immensely skilled Assistant District Attorney of the old school. His case was simple. Mosely was an admitted killer, possibly the most fiendish in memory. He knew what he had done, and now he deserved the electric chair.

Sidney Sparrow knew better than to deny the enormity of his client's crimes. He set out instead to show the jury that Mosely was one of those rare humans who contained not one but three distinct personalities. He compared him to the subject of the popular movie *The Three Faces of Eve*—a woman who switched unconsciously from demure housewife to harlot to child. Sparrow saw three faces of Winston Mosely. The first was that of loving father to his wife and children. Second was the hard worker at Raygram whose ten years of loyal work had been reflected in his steadily raised pay; a man so trusted he often drove the boss's daughter home from school. The third face had been hidden except to the doomed. One woman saw it emerge from the blowing snow before dawn; another looked up from a stairwell floor to see it materialize as a door swung open in the night.

Sparrow explored Winston's childhood to show the events that he suggested had fed his hate for women. When he was eight, Winston's mother, Fannie, had gone to the hospital for an operation, telling him that a tumor would be cut from her stomach. Fannie Mosely did not come back to her husband after that operation. Her desertion marked the end of a stable home for Winston. From then on he was shuttled between relatives in Detroit, Pittsburgh, and New York. He learned that his mother, a handsome, youthful and spirited woman, had taken up with other men. From time to time she came back to her husband, Alfonzo. Mosely watched his parents fight, drew tighter into himself. One day when Winston was seventeen, Alfonzo told him that he was not even his own true son.

At nineteen Winston married Ethel, who bore him a child but soon began to flirt openly with a bartender at the bar below their apartment in Detroit. Sometimes Mosely could sit alone in his living room and hear the laughter below. One afternoon when Ethel came up from the bar, Winston was pointing a gun at her as she opened the door. For a moment they were silent. Mosely put the gun down. Ethel picked it up and pointed it at him. "Go ahead," he said. "I don't care." Ethel shivered, knowing he really didn't care. A few months later, Mosely sued for divorce on the grounds of adultery.

Mosely lived a harmonious life with his second wife, Elizabeth, in their neat home on Sutter Avenue. She was a good mother to their two sons, a good housekeeper and, like himself, a diligent worker. They had a normal sex life, though both testified that in recent months he needed to be stimulated by cunnilingus before he could enter her and complete the sex act. But he was happy with Betty. He loved her. On the witness stand he thought for a moment, smiled to himself, and said, "I think she is perfect."

Alfonzo, Fannie, Ethel, and Elizabeth all testified to Winston's lifelong and abiding love for animals. He did not like cats because they scratched, but he had always had dogs. At the time of his arrest he had five, two of whom slept under the bed each night. Elizabeth was always amazed that her husband would work at the stove to fix up special meals for the dogs, but often forgot to feed himself. His parents remembered that he had kept white mice, hamsters, chickens, and snakes as well as dogs as a young boy.

When Mosely got on the stand he added to the list: "Japanese beetles and a couple of white rabbits."

Other than dogs, the only constant pets Mosely kept were ants. Ethel recalled that after their honeymoon to Pittsburgh her groom had brought home bottles of ants he'd collected in a park. They lived in a glass terrarium in the living room.

"Once the ants tipped over," Ethel testified. "Winston chased us all out of the house so we wouldn't step on them. He picked them up, one by one."

"And what did he feed these ants?" asked Cacciatore.

"He fed them sugar, bread crumbs, and roaches."

"Dead roaches or live roaches?"

"No dead roaches ever. He had to see how—" Leaping up to object, Sparrow cut her off.

Sparrow tried to show that Mosely, coming from this background, had never had much of a normal life and had steadily withdrawn from the little he did have. He grew to be a man with an ill mind. The unfaithfulness of his mother to his father and of his first wife to himself, argued Sparrow, turned Mosely against all women. But he targeted his greatest hatred on women who were black, like those who had done him wrong. That is why he picked out only blacks to assault, rape, and finally murder his first times out. Kitty had been the first white woman. It was also no accident, argued Sparrow, that Mosely had aimed both knife and gun at his victims' stomachs. The connection traced straight back to the day of his mother's operation, when cutting out that tumor in her stomach severed the family life he had known.

Two psychiatrists outlined this theory for the defense. One labeled Mosely an outright schizophrenic, the other concluded only that he suffered a "serious mental disorder." But to judge Mosely insane the jury would have to be convinced that his state of mind during the murder fell under one of three categories of the venerable M'Naghten Rule, which has been used by New York and California courts since 1843 as the test of legal insanity: the accused must have been unaware of what he was doing; or conscious of his act but unaware it was wrong; or aware of both his act and its immorality—but unable to withstand a so-called irresistible impulse. According to M'Naghten, it would be possible for a man to commit a crime, know it was against the law, not want to get caught, *yet still have no comprehension that the act itself was morally wrong.*

So it was quite possible for Mosely to have backed his car out of Austin Street to keep Kitty's neighbors from jotting down his license plate number, to wear a different hat when he returned, to look at the bloodstained falsie in the heat of murder and speculate on whether it had been "imprinted"—and yet, even though these were the precautions of a man who knew what he was doing, he might be totally out of touch with the immorality of what he had done. Would a sane man go out into a snowy night looking at random for a woman to kill? Hadn't Annie May Johnson offered him her housekey, thinking that even the most ruthless mugger would take pity and help her into the house? Would a sane man then shoot her again and commit an act of oral necrophilia? Did it make sense for him to reappear in full view of dozens of people to finish killing a woman? Was it the act of a sane man to go back after a stupid screwdriver when he had been caught in an act of burglary?

Sparrow's problem was that Mosely in no way appeared insane as he sat on the witness stand. He did not claim, as he might have, that irresistible impulses swept over him or that secret voices talked to him, saying, "Kill! Kill!" He answered all questions put to him thoughtfully, framing his answers in lucid English. He discriminated on a fine line, saying that he "loved" dogs but only "liked" people. He was "not sorry" for any of his victims but "was sorry that he had been caught." Asked if his motive had been divided evenly between robbing and raping and killing, Mosely answered, "I took their money but I would not have felt bad if I didn't." It seemed difficult to believe Mosely had not understood in depth what he had done; in fact, it was hard to imagine that Mosely had *ever* failed to understand in depth *anything* he had done.

Often during the trial Frank Cacciatore had made the defense witnesses squirm with his shouting, leaping-about, and folksy derision. He had so emotionally pummeled one of the defense psychiatrists that the doctor defecated in his pants on the witness chair. But no matter how he tried, Cacciatore could not shake Mosely's icy restraint. When Cacciatore once reached out to make some connection between Mosely and the queen ant in his colony, the defendant set him straight:

Q: *And there would be a queen ant, directing the operation?*
A: There would always be a queen ant, but they don't direct the operation.

Q: *Oh, they don't?*
A: No.

Q: *What does a queen ant do?*
A: The queen ant is only to produce more ants. The workers and the soldiers take care of the business of the ant colony.

Fannie Mosely had been living in her son's home at the time of his arrest, and while she was there, Alfonzo Mosely had got a gun and threatened to come and shoot his wife. Winston talked him out of it. "Come on, Daddy. You know that's not going to do any good," he said. In those last few months, Fannie and Elizabeth testified, Winston had not been himself. He had sat for hours, staring at nothing, saying not a word. Always scrupulously clean, Betty testified, the last weeks she had to tell him to take a bath. He even began to let her cut his hair, a job he'd always entrusted to a barber. As Fannie Mosely described it, "We said, 'Winston, what's wrong? How can we help?' But he only sat there and stared."

It certainly sounded like a man drifting far from sanity. If it had been almost any other man, the jury might have been persuaded. But the light of reason shone unflickering in Winston Mosely. Even his own definition of his mental state, drawn out of the sparring with Cacciatore, came out with an aloof and Cartesian logic:

Q: *Well, do you really feel you are insane?*
A: I never really thought that I was insane—but after listening, for instance, to your summation of what I have done, it doesn't seem like something an ordinary person would do.

Q: *You mean you rationalize it so that you feel whatever you did must have been done by some kind of nut?*
A: No. I didn't say that. I just don't feel that it was something normal, as you call normal.

On June 8 the jury filed into the courtroom after eight hours of deliberation. They had found Winston Mosely guilty as charged. A handful of women in the courtroom, many of them Kitty's neighbors, broke out in applause before the guards could hush them. As Mosely was led out of the courtroom, eyes down, his mother and wife wept. Judge Shapiro rejected a defense motion to change Mosely's plea from "Guilty" to "Guilty by Reason of Insanity."

Three weeks later, he sentenced Mosely to death in the electric chair.

Intoning the sentence, the judge omitted the traditional words, "May God have Mercy upon your soul." Instead he told Mosely, "I'd like to pull the switch myself."

Three months later the state Court of Appeals commuted Mosely's death sentence to life imprisonment, saying that Judge Shapiro should have allowed the defendant to change his plea to "Guilty by Reason of Insanity." In 1968 Mosely escaped from Dannemora Prison near the Canadian border by overpowering two guards in the parking lot of the hospital, where he had just been treated for self-inflicted knife wounds. Before surrendering to three hundred armed law officers who had surrounded the suburban home where he was holed up, Mosely raped one of his hostages. He is now a maximum security prisoner at Attica State Prison.

Seedman notes that of the six women Mosely attacked, at least three were menstruating at the time. "You know how certain animals can sniff blood in the wind from a mile away?" he says. "That's Mosely. An animal who could smell blood."

One final paradoxical note about Winston Mosely that he told to Tartaglia. On the morning of March 13, ten minutes after leaving the dying Kitty Genovese, he was on his way home after having just tossed the bloodied falsie in the shrubs at Hillside Avenue on the Van Wyck Expressway. Waiting for a traffic light at that hour before dawn, he noticed a man asleep in his idling car. Mosely pulled over to the curb and walked back to where the man dozed. He tapped on the window gently, in order not to startle the man.

"Listen, mister," said Mosely, when the sleeper had rolled down the glass. "You shouldn't be sleeping here like that. The carbon monoxide builds up. Or somebody could come along and do something bad to you."

The man shook his head free of sleep. The face he saw peering in was calm, gentle, concerned. "Yeah, you're right, buddy," the man said. "Just drifted off. You're a good fella. Thanks."

Mosely drove home, checked his dogs and his children, washed his knife, and went to sleep.

THE MAYS CASE

The regular Thursday-night card game is still going strong at 4 A.M. in the shuttered basement of a Long Island home when the player beside Larry Desso deals himself out.

"Got to get out the store payroll tomorrow," he says. "I need a few hours' sleep or I'll make mistakes."

"What store is that?" asks Desso.

The big man looks at Desso oddly. It is not considered good etiquette to ask specific questions of other players. But Desso seems to want to know badly.

"Mays Department Store," the man replies.

Desso soon leaves for his own suburban home and waits impatiently until an hour after daylight before calling his friend in Manhattan. "Got your man, baby. He works in the accounting office of Mays. Not as big as Macy's, but enough."

"Don't tell me about Mays, tell me about the guy," the voice asks groggily. "Is he hungry?"

"He's hungry, all right. I heard him mention he's getting killed paying alimony to his first wife. But believe me, the lousy way he plays, he's not taking extra dough out of our game."

"Perfect. He's what I need to get this thing rolling."

In the Aqueduct Raceway clubhouse a week later, between the fourth and fifth races, a strapping ex-basketball player and fixer named Jack Molinas nudges the nondescript man at his side.

"See that guy?" He points to a balding, jowly man on the far side of the clubhouse. "If he isn't at the track, he's at his stock broker's. Never makes a dime either place. Now he's trying to sell his house. He sounds just right for the job you have in mind."

"Is he smart enough to do exactly what he's told, but dumb enough not to know what he's doing?"

"That's Ray Leone on the button."

The nondescript man looks relaxed now as he sprawls on the expensive living-room sofa in his posh Manhattan apartment. He waves his hand imperially at his visitor in the wing chair. Like Ray Leone, the visitor seems like a middling, highly immemorable business type. Clearly, the two men in the apartment are friends from way back.

"Steve," says the man on the sofa, his eyes closed, but still waving his arms, "what I want is to create a brand-new person out of you. You'll start at the top, like a regular corporate maven. Except that instead of being head of just one company, you'll have a *dozen* companies. You'll open an account for each, and you'll be moving one hell of a lot of funds. But you've got to act fast—two months tops—then you close up shop. All the shops. I'll extinguish you. Just like that."

And he snapped his fingers.

Standing amid the gleaming chrome on a used-car lot in Manhattan, the nondescript man looks over a salesman.

"You got a nicer suit than that, I hope," he says.

"Sure, Woody."

"Well, put it on this Sunday. Take this Florida driver's license I filled in for you under a new name and rent a nice car. Something with class. Maybe a white convertible. I want you to go house-hunting."

"Any particular place?"

"Obviously. A little place on the Island called East Meadow. . . ."

The last man he talks to, one evening later in a bar off Seventh

Avenue, is of a much different caliber. A slender man, he wears a perfect gray suit, quiet but expensive jewelry, as befits the emissary of men of wealth, power—and danger.

"The thing is set up now like a fine watch," says the rumpled man named Woody, looking by comparison more nondescript than ever. "Set up, tuned, and wound so tight I don't need to touch it any more. I can just walk away, and every dollar the family so generously spent in seed money is going to sprout like a beanstalk. And every bean is going to be green and crinkly."

The man in the gray suit smiles coldly. "Wait till Junior finds out about this. He'll shit a brick. But it won't help. Because Woody, you're with *people*."

The empty champagne bottle is turned upside down in the silver bucket. Moonlight floods in from over Central Park. The songstress is on the edge of sleep, but the man called Woody is wide awake.

"Honey, I'll tell you how perfect this crime is," he is saying. "I could slip on my coat now, go over to the desk sergeant at the nearest station house and confess. I could write out a confession, and there's nothing they could do to me. They couldn't even book me. Fran, it's perfection . . ."

Two months later—August 3, 1964—Max Shulman looked up in confusion from the canceled green-and-yellow checks spread over his desk. Then he reached over and dialed the 84th Precinct in Brooklyn.

"This is the President of Mays Department Stores," he said tensely. "I want to report what appears to be a swindle."

"What kind of swindle?" asked Curtis Bell, the detective catching squeals on the evening shift.

"Somebody has apparently been counterfeiting company checks. I'm looking at a dozen right now, and they're beauties. A signature I can't tell from my own is on every one, but they are made out to companies we don't do business with."

"How much did you lose?" asked Bell.

"Too early to tell. God knows how many more are yet to come in."

"The ones on your desk now, sir—how much do they add up to?"

"Over half a million dollars," answered Shulman.

Bell gave a low whistle. "I'm going to send a man over right now. But this sounds like it's going to be one for the Inspector.

Following a year's delay over the Dellurnia photo incident, Seedman's promotion to Inspector of the 11th Detective District in Brooklyn had finally come through just three weeks earlier. On the morning after Bell took the complaint, the new Inspector appeared at the executive offices of the Mays Fulton Street Store, flagship of the nine-unit chain, to find Shulman staring at the checks as incredulously as he had when he first discovered them.

"Like most big stores," he explained, "we spread our business among several banks. Keeps them sharper when they have to compete against each other. These fake checks are written against two of those accounts. One is with Underwriters Bank and Trust Company, the other with First National City Bank."

Laying the bogus checks alongside genuine ones, Seedman could not detect the smallest difference. He held them up to the light and they matched exactly. The safety paper on which they were printed appeared identical, right down to the subtle underprinting of a crow's-feet pattern, pink-toned for Underwriters Trust, green for Citibank. The weight and texture of the papers was the same. So was the lettering. Even the serrations at the edges of the checks matched exactly, as if they had been torn from Mays' own checkbooks. At the bottom of each check the numerals identifying the bank branch and the account must have been printed in the correct magnetic ink or they would have been rejected by the computerized check-processing equipment. All in all, Seedman could see no reason—except Max Shulman's word—to believe the checks were phony.

"Each check had been written to the order of a company rather than an individual," explains Seedman. "Twelve companies in all. They had names like Park Lane Furniture Company, Excelsior Knitwear, Happy Time Toy Company. To a teller handling the Mays account, these names would sound exactly like any of the hundreds of suppliers dealing with a big department store. The amounts also sounded legitimate—$14,621.77 to Superior Sales Company, $18,552.90 to Excelsior Knitwear, $20,772.85 to R & L Trading Company. Even in the Mays offices these checks went unsuspected for several days.

"This was hardly the first time I'd come across a case of forged company checks. In most cases, the method was fairly standard: a new shipment of checks would be intercepted in the company mailroom or stolen from a desk at lunch hour; the culprit would fill in amounts small enough to be easily cashed and then forge an authorized signature. The checks themselves were real—only the signature was faked. The average forger wouldn't have the vaguest inkling of how to manufacture a set of bank checks from scratch.

"Yet here was just such a case—one I certainly had *not* ever come across before. Whoever had perfected these checks, right down to the serrations, hardly would have skimped on the operational details. Any scheme that had taken so much time and care to design was bound to take time and care to unravel."

All day following the discovery detective teams fanned out to comb the bank accounts of the twelve companies to whose order the bogus checks had been written. At the seven which were in Brooklyn they got the same story. Each account had been opened early in June by a fortyish, slightly overweight man who seemed friendly and joked easily. He was, to all appearances, a typical businessman. He gave his name as Bertram Williams, his residential address as 248 East 90th Street in Manhattan, and his business address in care of Mark Lanham, an attorney on Joralemon Street in Brooklyn.

At Central State Bank, Williams had opened an account for Park Lane Furniture Company, at Franklin National Bank for Superior Sales Company, at Lafayette National Bank for Excelsior Knitwear and National Carpet Distributor Companies, at Manufacturers Hanover Trust for Happy Time Toy Company, at Kings County Trust for Meyerhoff Furniture Company, and at Chase Manhattan for New York Novelty Company.

For each account opened Williams presented a bona-fide New York State Certificate of Incorporation and a cash deposit of $700. He asked for a power-of-attorney card to take back for his partner to sign. The next day he returned the card. The seven signatures on the cards were Harold Parker, Jerome Blumenthal, Abe Feldman, Ernest Glick, Karl Mitler, Milton Sobel, and Peter Fine. No teller remembered ever having seen any of these partners.

One month after Bertram Williams opened his seven accounts, another fortyish man—slightly slimmer and darker than Williams, but no more distinctive—walked into five banks in suburban Nassau County and opened five other accounts. They were R & L Trading Company at Franklin National Bank in Hempstead, Neiman Company at Chemical Bank in West Hempstead, A & N Company at Long Island Trust in Merrick, Raymond Products Company at Citibank in Old Westbury, and Teglon Holding Company at Hempstead Bank in Hempstead.

This man gave his name as Raymond Leone of 252 West Street in East Meadow, no more than a twenty-minute drive from any of the banks. He listed no business address and authorized nobody but himself to make transactions. In each case the opening deposit was a check for a hundred dollars, drawn on one of the seven Brooklyn accounts set up the previous month by Bertram Williams.

On July 6 Williams and Leone began to deposit Mays checks in the accounts. Soon a blizzard of checks were flying among the twelve accounts, drawn on Mays and on each other. All were deposited by the two smiling businessmen. On July 15 Underwriters Bank and Trust notified Mays that its checking account was overdrawn. Neither the bank nor the store was much concerned. In that account Mays tried to keep only enough to cover payments to its suppliers, while holding surplus cash in interest-bearing accounts. Occasionally payments would exceed the deposits in the checking account. As soon as Mays got word, it would send over a messenger with a check to put the account in the black. In this case the overdraft was $300,000. That was larger than usual. By the end of the month, though, the account was sure to balance out. It always had.

But seventeen days later, on August 2, as Underwriters Bank and Trust was about to send out the Mays monthly statement, the account again bounced checks. That was crazy. The additional $300,000 deposit should have more than covered all payments. This time Max Shulman went through the checks himself, prepared to fire every soul in his accounting department for such incredible laxness. Then he noticed the first check made payable by his own signature to a company he had never heard of. With each additional one he felt sicker. By the time he had gone through the Underwriters' statement, he had discovered thirteen bogus checks. When the statement from Citibank came in the next day, he picked out fourteen more. All had been deposited between July 6 and 31. None had been questioned. They came to a staggering total: $924,868.

"The first checks had been deposited the day after both banks had closed out the Mays accounts for the previous month," says

Seedman. "That gave the swindlers a full month to write checks before new statements would go out. Either at Mays or the banks somebody had told them exactly when to start the blitz.

"I was almost positive that Bertram Williams and Raymond Leone would turn out to be shadow figures. But at the end of the first day of investigation, one fact struck me as especially curious: for all seven accounts Williams had given his business address in care of Mark Lanham. This man was certainly no shadow figure. Hardly a lawyer in all Brooklyn was as well known in criminal court circles. I had met Mark Lanham myself. Undoubtedly he represented some people who were capable of this swindle. But he would be crazy to let his own good name get mixed up in a time-bomb like this, ticking away until it blew up in public. Had he gone nuts?"

When Lanham walked into his office the next morning at 9:30, he found a pair of detectives waiting.

"If it's about any of my clients, I can't help you, gentlemen," he said, pegging the men for detectives even before they had shown their gold shields.

"Is Bertram Williams a client?"

Lanham scratched his head. "Williams . . . Bertram Williams. Yes, yes, it comes back to me now. Please come inside. Normally I *don't* talk about clients, but I'll tell you what I know about this one."

Lanham explained that one morning back in May Bertram Williams had phoned for an appointment. Until that day Lanham had never seen or heard of him. Williams explained that he was actually coming on behalf of his brother-in-law, an assistant to the chief buyer for Mays Department Stores. After nine years of buying from others, he felt it was about time to do himself some good, and his plan was to set up a series of companies to compete with other suppliers for certain of Mays' business.

"Are you asking me if that is legal?" Lanham had asked warily.

"I don't have to," Williams had answered. "It's common custom in the trade. Fur buyers put their wives in charge of wholesale fur companies. Lingerie buyers set up their 'nieces' in one-room offices to buy lingerie on Seventh Avenue. If they can't sell cheaper than the next guy, they just don't get the business, that's all. If they can, they do. What I'd like you to do is set up seven little companies for my brother-in-law. They need to be incorporated and they need local business certificates. That's all I need to have done."

Lanham could see that the operation of such companies, if not downright illegal, certainly would strain the brother-in-law's ethics. He wanted no part of that. But as for the initial mechanics of establishing the companies, that was possible. That and no more. Lanham stated a fee and Bertram Williams had paid it at once in cash.

"One last thing," Williams had said as they shook hands. "It'll be another few weeks before we get an office set up. Could I possibly use your office as a temporary mailing address?"

"If it's only temporary," Lanham had replied.

Several days later a local office supply company delivered an IBM electric typewriter and an R.C. Allen adding machine to Lanham's office, rented to Bertram Williams, who promptly picked them up.

"It crossed my mind after he left that I didn't know where this Williams came from," Lanham now told the detectives. "But frankly, after you've been knocking around in this business for as long as I have, you get a reputation. People just walk in on you cold. Besides, I had no reason to be suspicious. The services he needed were standard."

Lanham smiled to himself. "I will say, though, gentlemen, that if this Bertram Williams hadn't been so quick to pay his fee in full, I wouldn't have been so quick to let him use my office for deliveries."

While the detectives were listening to Mark Lanham, another team had driven to Yorkville, the old German section of Manhattan, where they knocked on the door of Mrs. Kurt Schmitt. She managed the dreary tenement at 248 East 90th Street which Bertram Williams had listed as his home address for all seven accounts.

"I rented to him, all right, but I never had a tenant like that one," said the old lady, shaking her head. "He took the apartment on the first of May without so much as looking at it. He paid cash in advance for two months' rent—$180—then I never saw him any more. At the end of June, I got worried, so I did something I rarely do. I used my passkey and looked around his apartment. How was I to know he didn't have a stroke and die in there? But it was empty. No furniture, no nothing."

"Nothing?"

"Well, in May he got some cartons delivered by United Parcel Service. *I* wasn't going to lift them, so I told the men to put them in the basement. You can have them."

Downstairs, under a single dim bulb, the detectives cut open the two cartons. Sent from Moore Business Forms, Inc., of New

York, both were filled with reams of a long form in triplicate headed "Appraiser's Report, National Auto Appraisers, 245 East 80th Street." The detectives might have thought the delivery was a mistake, except that 245 East 80th was also the address of the Blue Circle Answering Service, whose number Williams had listed on the bank applications.

At Blue Circle, ten blocks away, the woman manning the single switchboard told detectives that Bertram Williams had rented the service for May, June, and July. She did not remember any of the messages he got, nor did she keep any record of them. As soon as they were passed on to the customer, she explained, she threw them in the trash can under the switchboard.

Thanking her, the disappointed detectives were preparing to leave, when the operator remembered something else—a final message that Williams had never picked up. On July 31 a Mr. Grossman had called and left a number where Williams could reach him. Hoping this might be the break they were looking for, the detectives left excitedly.

The number belonged to Mrs. Hilda Grossman, 210 East 163rd Street, in the Bronx. She opened the door just enough to say firmly that she had never heard of any Bertram Williams. Possibly her son Harry might have—they could ask him when he came home.

Harry Grossman was a young man working as an accountant at the Sheraton-Atlantic Hotel. When the detectives flashed their shields and asked why he had called Bertram Williams, he turned pale.

"I didn't do anything wrong," he pleaded. "You see, I'm trying to get on my feet as an accountant, and I heard that this man had started a group of new companies. So I called him blind to see if he needed an accountant—that's all."

"How did you know he was starting new companies?"

Grossman looked down uncomfortably. "I have a friend in the County Clerk's office, where they register business certificates. I know that information shouldn't be given out, but it's so hard to get started in this field. I don't want my friend to get in trouble. I take full responsibility."

"Just be glad Bertram Williams never called back," said the detectives as they left. "Then you'd know what trouble really is."

"At this point," says Seedman, "all that remained of Bertram

Williams was seven bank accounts stripped of over a half-million dollars, the bogus checks, and the memories of the bank employees who had dealt with him. The checks produced no helpful fingerprints. The tellers certainly remembered Williams. All during July they had seen him at least twice a week when he made deposits. They had accepted his checks, dishing out as much as $21,000 cash in a single withdrawal. But all they could offer was a general description of a highly average businessman. Bland as he was, Williams evidently was highly skilled at charming people. He had conned Mark Lanham, who was no pushover. With one exception he had also conned all the bank personnel who never asked a single question about the size of his transactions and frequency of his money shuffling."

The exception was an officer of the Lafayette Bank, who stopped Williams on his way out after making a $14,000 withdrawal.

"Excuse me, sir, but we do like to know just a little about our more active customers," he said apologetically.

"I'm surprised you didn't ask sooner," answered Williams. "I'm in the business of buying large consignments at distress auctions. For example, last week I bought a manufacturer's entire overstock of ladies' bathing suits for Mays Department Stores. I do that quite often for them. That's why you see all their checks coming in on the deposit side. The reason I take out so much cash is also easy to explain. In the auction business, you never know whether you're going to spend $30,000 or zero; but whatever you need, it's in cash on the spot. That's what auctions are all about, right?"

"Right, Mr. Williams," said the officer. "I didn't mean to pry."

Several other banks did provide one other special favor to Williams. After large withdrawals they sent a bank guard to escort him to his taxi or car. They did not want anyone preying on such a good customer.

Seedman took it for granted that Williams' counterpart in Nassau County, Raymond Leone, had totally vanished. So he wasn't surprised when the Nassau County Police reported that 252 West Street, the only address listed on the five accounts, did not exist. Raymond Leone probably did not exist, either. But a surprise was in store for the pair of detectives staked out at the quiet Hempstead Bank on the morning of August 5, the second business day after the swindle broke. At 11:50 a teller nodded to them in a prearranged signal to indicate that the jowly man walking into the bank was Raymond Leone.

Griping casually about the hot weather, Leone withdrew $14,000 from the account of Teglon Holding Company. He was back at his car when the detectives moved alongside him. He seemed genuinely startled to see their shields.

"We'd like to you to come over to Brooklyn to answer a few questions," said Detective Curtis Bell.

"About what?"

"About the Mays checks you've been dumping into your five accounts."

"What the hell business is it of yours?"

"It's right up our line," said Bell. "You ought to know that. The checks were fake."

Leone clapped his hands to his head. "Oh, Jesus," he moaned, swaying as though he were on a rolling ship. "I should've guessed this thing was all fishy. I smelled it right off. Listen, officers, I don't blame you for wanting to pick me up. Whatever you want to know, I'll be glad to tell you. . . ."

All the way to 76th Precinct station house, Leone moaned, "Oh, Jesus, was I ever stupid." Normally the questioning would have taken place in the 84th, where Mays was located. But Seedman preferred the 76th on such a hot day because it was the only squad room in Brooklyn with air-conditioning. He suspected that Leone's story was going to be a long one.

It had all begun less than two months ago, said Leone, on the afternoon of Flag Day, June 14. He had been sitting in his tilt-back living-room lounger, watching television, when he saw a brand-new Dodge Polara convertible stop in front of the "For Sale" sign on the lawn of his modest bungalow at 252 West Street in East Meadow. Contrary to the initial reports of the Nassau County Police, the address was real. With home prices booming in East Meadow, Leone had decided to sell the bungalow at a profit and buy a bigger place farther out on the Island.

The man who now stood in front looking the place over was nattily dressed in checkered sportcoat, well-pressed white slacks, pale-blue open-collared shirt. Leone was glad to see him finally walk toward the door. He seemed like the perfect prospect.

"I saw your sign," the stranger said. "My name is Paul Neiman. Would it be a bother if I looked around?"

"That's why the sign is out there," answered Leone.

Paul Neiman looked upstairs, downstairs, in the furnace room, and out in the backyard. He inquired about heating bills, taxes, garbage collection. Mrs. Leone thought Paul Neiman was not only a natty dresser but a nice fellow.

"Can I get you men a drink?" she asked.

"I hate to impose," answered Neiman.

"Aw, come on, don't be shy," said Raymond Leone. "What kind of day is this to turn down a nice cold beer?"

Sitting at the patio table out back, they had several beers. The Leones were especially interested to learn that Neiman was moving back to Long Island after ten years in Los Angeles. They had considered moving to California themselves, but without contacts or a promised job, it was too risky.

"Must be great to have the kind of job where you can switch so easy," said Raymond Leone.

"Frankly, that's no problem," said Neiman. "On the Coast I had some good investment advice. I made some moves which allow me to live pretty well right now."

"Yeah?" said Leone, lighting up. "I play with the market myself. What kind of winners did you have, if I can ask? I'll be happy to tell you some of my losers." He laughed self-consciously.

"Well," said Neiman, "I sank a wad in Chrysler early in 1962. Rode it right up. Since then it's split three shares for one—*twice*—and I hung on all the way. Then I picked up this little color television stock last year, National Video, that's doing so good now. Started buying it at seven, bought some more at twelve and twenty-three. Now it's floating around ninety. When it cracks a hundred, I'll unload. . . ."

Neiman rapped gently on the patio bench. "Here's hoping my luck lasts. Meanwhile, I don't worry about working." Neiman paused. "In fact, my worries are just the opposite. Maybe I shouldn't be telling you this, but I made a bad second marriage. This woman was a secretary in the brokerage house on Wilshire Boulevard where I watched the tape every day. She saw how well I was doing. Anyway, we got married and it was lousy from day one. Now we're getting divorced and I'm determined to keep as much of my money as possible out of that little bitch's greedy hands and sock it away, out of her reach. Getting back to the East Coast is a start. I'm also planning to set up some companies where I can spread the cash around. In fact, I'm looking around for someone whom I can trust to set up the financial structure, and keep my name out of it."

"Listen," cut in Leone, "I happen to be between jobs myself. Maybe we could work something out."

"Well, the job is going to involve setting up accounts for the companies, transferring funds on a precise schedule, handling stock transactions. The main thing I don't want is for my name to show up anywhere. I'm willing to pay well, of course. I was going to put a want ad in the Sunday *Times*.

"Save your money," said Leone. "Try me."

Neiman appraised Leone for a long moment. Then he broke into a smile and extended his hand. "This house isn't quite what I'm looking for," he said. "But maybe I found something better—a good man. I'm sure it'll work out between us. In the morning I have to run back to the West Coast, but I'll be back in two weeks. You can figure the job starts as of July first."

Good to his word, Neiman called Leone two weeks later to give him his first tasks. Though Leone invited him to his home, Neiman insisted on meeting in a local diner. In a rear booth he handed Leone five business certificates for the "dummy" companies to register with the Nassau County Clerk. Leone was to use his own name and address. Neiman also gave him five checks, each for one hundred dollars, to open five accounts in five different banks. Each check was drawn on the account of one of five other companies: Park Lane Furniture, Excelsior Knitwear, Superior Sales Company, New York Novelty Company, and Happy Time Toy Company. The names rang no bells with Raymond Leone.

"Now for the next thing," said Neiman. "Do you have a brokerage account where you trade on the stock market?"

"Sure," said Leone. "I use the Richard J. Buck office over in Hempstead. I got a customer's man there."

"Good. In a few days, you're going to make some big deposits in your account. Then, when I tell you, you're going to buy stocks in the morning and sell them just before the close."

"What stocks?"

"You pick 'em."

"You mean *any* goddam stock I want?"

"I trust your judgment, Ray."

"Yeah, but every stock I pick isn't going to go up automatically. You don't want to sell at the close if it's lower, do you?"

"That's exactly what I do want you to do. In and out the same day. Win or lose. Just be sure you get a check from the brokerage house as fast as you can and deliver the cash to me. For every completed transaction you get paid a hundred and fifty dollars. That may happen three times a week."

"You're the boss," shrugged Leone. Even as they got up he was thinking of the stocks he'd been having a good feeling about. Three days later, at the diner, he received the first checks to deposit in his five new accounts. All drawn on the accounts Williams had opened in Brooklyn only a month earlier, the checks totaled $168,000.

As the afternoon wore on, Leone explained his daily routine to Seedman and the detectives in the 76th squad room. As soon as the ticker started running at 10 o'clock in the morning, he would begin buying as much as $30,000 worth of stock, then sell it just before the market closed at 3:30. More often than not, he cleared a few hundred dollars, even after commissions. He paid for the stock purchases with cashier's checks drawn on the five Nassau bank accounts. The brokerage house paid him for stock sales with their own cashier's checks.

Leone did not understand what Neiman was doing, but he was sure his employer was some sort of financial genius. As Neiman had predicted, by the middle of July he was making as much as $450 a week. As he strolled into the office of Richard J. Buck & Company each morning the staff and tape-watchers looked at him with new respect. No one had ever looked at him that way before. Coming out of the Hempstead Bank on August 5 with a $14,650 cashier's check to pay for the morning's stock purchases, he had all but forgotten any initial qualms he may have had about what his boss was doing. Then he saw the shadows of the two detectives fall in beside him.

As the crestfallen Leone finished his story now, Seedman patted him on the back. "Don't take it so hard, pal," he said. "If all this is true, it's easy enough to clear yourself. Just tell us where to find this Mr. Neiman."

"This is going to sound like I'm bullshitting you," answered Raymond Leone. "But I swear, he never told me where he stayed. He always called me and told me to meet him. Mostly it was in diners. Once I asked him for a phone number in case I needed to reach him. He told me he moved around too much to make it worthwhile."

Leone slumped further down in the squad commander's battered oak armchair. "Everything was going so good. Would you believe two days ago my wife and me put down a deposit on a gorgeous home we were going to build right over the water in Merrick Cove. Eight thousand dollars for the lot, $26,440 for the split-level we'd picked, the nicest model. For the first time in my life, I was gonna be able to swing a big deal like this. Two weeks ago I even bought my wife a Corvette convertible—another $2700. Now I'm going to lose the deposit on the house. I'll try to cancel the deal on the car, but I'm gonna have nothing."

Leone looked up at Seedman imploringly. "Just tell me, why did that bastard do this to me?"

Seedman, listening raptly to this recital, understood very well what Neiman had done. It was a brilliant job of "laundering." The large amounts of cash coming into the twelve accounts by way of the fake Mays checks had been "dirty." They had to be "cleaned." The first rinse cycle, so to speak, consisted of juggling the money from one account to the next. But the real scrubbing was accomplished through Leone's daily stock trades. He paid for his purchases in the morning with a cashier's check drawn against the "dirty" deposit. When he sold at the end of the day, Richard J. Buck & Company paid him with its own spanking-clean check, which could be cashed anywhere and could never be traced further than Leone. Whether Leone made or lost a few hundred dollars hardly mattered. It was a cheap price for doing the laundry.

Trained as an accountant, Seedman could hardly fail to appreciate the beauty of this phase of the scheme. Yet it only confirmed what he had felt when he had first looked at the checks on Max Shulman's desk. This was the work of a master, and it was just beginning to unfold. In fact, despite the entry of this new player, the so-called "Paul Neiman," Seedman suspected that the master himself had yet to come out of the wings.

In State Supreme Court that night, Judge Cullen ordered Raymond Leone held as a material witness in the Mays swindle. He was put under detective guard at the St. George Hotel (where Lucille Giusti, a material witness in the Fallon–Finnegan case, had been kept two years earlier). Unlike Lucille, Leone was probably not in much danger of being silenced. Whoever had plotted the Mays swindle relied on brains, not muscle. But now, while Leone read paperbacks and ordered meals from room service, Seedman would check out whether or not he was the total dupe he claimed to be.

If Leone's story was true from the beginning, then other people as well as Leone and his wife must have noticed the white Dodge Polara convertible that rolled down the quiet block on Flag Day. Sure enough, detectives did find several neighbors who had admired the car, and one pair of teen-age girls who had been asked by the natty driver whether they knew of any houses for sale in the neighborhood.

Since that was the only time Leone had seen the convertible, Seedman's detectives checked the city's rental agencies to see if such a car had been rented on Flag Day. At Discount Rent-A-Car on Queens Boulevard, the records indeed showed that a white Dodge Polara convertible had been rented at 1:50 P.M. by a party giving his name as Paul Neiman. He presented a Florida driver's license, left a twenty-dollar cash deposit. Returning three hours later, he was billed $9.27. The agent gave him a check for the difference of $10.73, but it was never cashed. The Florida police reported that no license had ever been issued to Paul Neiman.

"The most striking item on the rental application was Neiman's home address—245 East 80th Street," notes Seedman. "It was also the address of Blue Circle Telephone Answering Service, as well as the letterhead address on the forms for National Auto Appraisers, Inc. Our next step was to track down those two cartons of forms from Mrs. Schmitt's basement."

At the office of Moore Business Forms, detectives located James Coleman, the salesman who had written up the order. On May 5, he explained, an unsolicited call from Bertram Williams had been referred to his desk.

"I run a little business in Los Angeles," Williams told him. "My agents do independent auto damage appraisals for the insurance companies. Now I'm ready to open an East Coast office and I need to have a form made up. Can you meet me tomorrow with your samples?"

"Sure. Where's your office?"

"I don't move in until next month. Why don't we meet at ten-thirty at the corner of 69th and Second Avenue. We can talk about it over coffee."

The man who Coleman found waiting for him on the corner was slightly rumpled and slightly overweight. But his face was friendly, and as they sat over coffee in a luncheonette he seemed to be a good prospect. Williams explained that he wanted to "simplify" the appraisal report form his investigators used in California, leaving more space for them to fill in the actual details of the collision and damage. At the top he wanted the company letterhead, then blanks for the names of the drivers, place and time of accident, and autos involved. Then a large space was to be left blank for the "Investigator's Report," with a signature line at the bottom.

Bertram Williams was not happy with any of the standard paper samples Coleman showed him. "My *real* problem," he explained, lowering his voice, "is that I'm afraid a few of my people may be doing a little cheating on our clients. The way they work it is to fill in one estimate for the insurance company and a different one for the auto repair shops after the report has been approved. What I really want, I guess, is some kind of safety paper which will prevent that."

"No problem at all," said Coleman, beaming. "You should have said that in the first place." From his briefcase he took a folio of special paper samples. Williams riffled through them and pulled one out.

"This is nice," he said. "Dignified but not too fancy. Could I get it in green for my East Coast office and pink for the West Coast?"

"No problem. How many of each?"

"Five thousand of each for a start. How soon can I get them?"

"I'll have to check with the factory in Niagara Falls. I can let you know in the morning."

"Let me know then what the bill comes to. I like to pay my debts fast."

Coleman nodded with satisfaction. He could use more customers like this.

The next morning, at the same luncheonette, Coleman promised delivery by the first week of June. "Send them to 248 East 90th Street," Williams said. "That's where I'll be living through June. If I'm not home, the landlady will take delivery." He paid Coleman with a cashier's check drawn on Kings County Trust Company for $540.

"I hope it'll be cheaper when I reorder," he said.

"Repeat business is cheaper business," said Coleman.

But at the end of the first week in June, Williams sounded worried indeed. He called Coleman to complain that the forms had not yet been delivered. "You promised," he said. "I counted on it. I got business here already and I need those goddam things. Now I'm sorry I paid you so fast."

"I'll check it out," said Coleman. In an hour he called back to say that the order was being printed that very day. It would be delivered in New York by the end of the week.

"Where did you say the factory was?" asked Williams testily.

"Niagara Falls. Why?"

"Because my people already got business and I need those goddam things. I'll fly up this afternoon and get them myself."

Late that day a clerk at the shipping bay of the Moore plant was surprised to see Williams climb up on the loading dock to demand the order for National Auto Appraisers.

"How big is the order?" the clerk asked.

"Ten thousand forms."

"Look, buddy, that could be buried under some really *big* order, like a *million forms*. I can't be digging it out from all that."

Williams pressed a fifty-dollar bill into the man's hand. "I don't even need 'em all," he said. "Just a handful from the top of the box to keep my people working."

"You shoulda said so in the first place," said the clerk.

"The sheaf of appraiser's forms which Williams brought back to New York," says Seedman, "were underprinted with the crow's-feet pattern he had chosen. It was the same safety paper which Mays used for its checks, the same colors, the same brand. Mays used green for First National City Bank and pink for Underwriter's Bank and Trust Company. If you divided the blank space for Williams' 'Investigator's Report' into three equal parts, they were exactly the same size as three Mays checks.

"Our next stop was Printing Industries of Metropolitan New York, Inc., where we learned that if a genuine Mays check could be borrowed for an hour, the rest was easy. Once a photo of the check was snapped, the check could be returned and the rest could be done at leisure. First, a lithographic plate was made from the photo. Except for magnetic symbols at the bottom of the plate, all the details could then be run off on a standard office multilith machine, with the symbols added separately by letterpress in magnetic ink. A portable serrating machine had apparently cut the edges of the checks to correspond with the way they appeared in a Mays checkbook. The typewriter that the store's accounting department used to make up the checks was the same IBM electric model that had been delivered for Williams at Mark Lanham's office.

"Less than three weeks after Williams flew back from Niagara Falls with the handful of National Auto Appraisers forms, he deposited the first Mays check in the amount of $19,847.67. It went through the banking process as flawlessly as would all the rest.

"Were Bertram Williams and Paul Neiman the same person? It seemed reasonable enough. Both had given the same address. Both were superb con men. Both roles could have been played by the same actor. Yet Raymond Leone's final description of Neiman did not quite match the description of Williams given by Mark Lanham, the salesman Coleman, and the tellers of seven Brooklyn banks.

"Leone insisted that the man who drove up to his house on Flag Day was slightly thinner, fairer, and younger than they had described Williams. I wished we could have found someone besides Leone who had seen Neiman regularly. No sooner had we released to the media a composite sketch of both men than Leone decided that Neiman's likeness was not quite right."

"Now that I'm looking at the sketch in the newspaper," Leone told detectives at the St. George Hotel, "I'd have to change just a few things. . . . Neiman had a lighter complexion . . . his nose was thinner and the top surface was a little flatter . . . his neck was also a little thinner . . . his chin was shorter or maybe it just needs to be squared off . . . his cheekbones started a little higher . . . I guess his mouth wasn't quite that full, either. . . ."

"How about his ears?" interrupted one of the detectives. "Nothing wrong with them?"

Leone scratched his head and held the sketch away from him. "Now that you mention it," he said, "his ears were definitely shaped more delicately and they lay closer to his head . . . also his hair had a soft wave and the forehead wasn't quite so—"

"Oh shut up!" the detective said.

"We still had found nothing to suggest that Leone's story as it pertained to Neiman's role was false in any detail," says Seedman.

"As for himself as total dupe, I had my doubts. For one thing, his change in life style was striking—certainly nothing that could be attributed to his salary and stock commissions. Before taking on the job as Paul Neiman's financial man, he had last worked as a chicken salesman for Zorn's Poultry Farm in Bethpage, Long Island. He had not lied to Neiman on Flag Day about being between jobs. Just a week earlier his supervisor at the chicken farm had taken him aside to say that his work was not satisfactory. Leone quit on the spot. Few of the people in his circle had even known where he worked. But he was less discreet about his new job."

On August 1 the manager at the poultry farm had been surprised to see his old employee strut in, dressed sharply and smiling. Leone bought six packages of chicken drumsticks and breasts, paying for them with a fifty-dollar bill.

"See that little honey out there?" he said, pointing to the white Corvette in the lot. "I bought it last week for my wife. $2700 cash."

Leone's former boss rang up the sale in silence. "I'm in financial management now," Leone continued, his voice greased with superiority. "Those fucking chickens weren't my line." Revving up the Corvette, he blasted out of the parking lot with tires squealing.

But Leone had failed to mention his activities on the evening before he was arrested. At the Hill & Tree Golf Course in Huntington, detectives discovered, Leone had tossed a loosely tied package to the clubhouse attendant. "Hold this for me while I play a round, will ya?" he said.

The attendant put the package on a shelf and went back to reading his newspaper.

"What do you think's in that package you're letting sit in plain sight?" Leone asked.

"If I asked, you'd probably tell me to mind my own business, Ray."

"Well, it's $35,000 cash," Leone said loudly and walked off.

Several minutes later the night manager arrived. Not wanting to be responsible for the package, he sent the day attendant off to look for Leone. He found him telling the snack-bar girl that his new Corvette would do 140 MPH in second gear.

"We can't keep the package for you any longer, Ray," he said. "It makes the night man nervous."

"Frankly, even if it did get lifted," shrugged Leone, "it would hardly make a dent. But I don't want to make a guy nervous." He left the course, dangling the package carelessly by the string. Asked about that incident in the station house, Leone insisted he had turned over the $35,000 to Neiman that same evening at a Sunrise Highway hot-dog stand.

But the most glaring discrepancy in Raymond Leone's portrait of himself as such an innocent dupe was provided not by Leone, but by a gas-station owner from Hempstead named Ben O'Connor, a worried man who walked into the Brooklyn DA's office flanked by two attorneys soon after the Mays story broke in the newspapers.

"I've been keeping these for Raymond Leone," he said, dropping two packages on the desk, "I don't know where he got them, but he told me they contain $10,000 cash each."

O'Connor explained that one evening in the third week of July, his casual friend Leone had stopped by the station to ask him to keep a package overnight in the safe. The next night Leone brought over a second package.

"Hey, Ben," he said, "would you believe there's $10,000 in each package?"

That got O'Connor nervous. He promised to keep it there for the night. In the morning, though, he insisted on taking it to his safe-deposit box at the Hempstead Bank.

"As soon as I read what Ray got himself into, I hustled it right over here," O'Connor now told the DA.

When confronted at the St. George with O'Connor's story of the $20,000, the detectives expected Leone to react sheepishly.

Instead, he jumped up in a rage. "The bastard! The filthy bastard," he shouted. "I gave him $30,000, not $20,000—$15,000 in each package. The fuckin' thief—"

Seeing how the detectives were gaping, Leone calmed himself as suddenly as he had blown up. He smiled sagely. "Hey, guys, I know what you're thinking. You think I was squirreling away this wad of Mr. Neiman's cash on the sly. Well, that's not how it is at all."

When Leone brought his cash to the gas station for safekeeping, he explained, O'Connor had suggested that Leone's boss might want to invest some surplus cash in a small credit company that O'Connor ran on the side with two other men. O'Connor assured Leone that his boss, whoever he might be, could expect a high return on investment, and that his name would never have to be revealed. O'Connor also recommended investing in a closed-circuit-television company that was being established by a "hot" young engineer he knew.

"I talked to Mr. Neiman about it, and he said I should check around a little. If the people looked reliable, I could invest $17,000 in the credit business and $12,000 in the closed-circuit-TV company.

"So tell that bastard to give back the other $10,000!" he said, his voice once again moving up to a shout.

"A few days later the inevitable happened," says Seedman. "Raymond Leone lost his room at the St. George when a grand jury indicted him on six counts of forgery, two counts of grand larceny, and one of attempted grand larceny. Unable to make the $100,000 bail, he was transferred to plainer quarters in the Tombs. Since the Corvette had been purchased with $2700 in stolen funds, we confiscated it. Leone was crushed, but it was all his own fault. If he had been satisfied with his salary, plus the rather generous $150 Neiman was paying him for each stock transaction, we would not have been as inclined to press all the charges. But he could not resist trying a swindle within a swindle. Actually, with the money dumped into his hands it should have been easy, but Leone did not begin to have his master's touch."

"Meanwhile, neither Leone nor O'Connor had brought us any closer to the mastermind behind the scenes. Hoping for a break, we ran the sketches of Paul Neiman and Bertram Williams in the newspapers. They brought in only the usual dross except for a report from an Avis Rent-A-Car clerk named Margaret Gershaw that twice in July she had rented a car to Bertram Williams. He had presented a New York driver's license and a Board of Elections registration card. The license gave his home address as 248 East 90th Street.

"At the Board of Elections on Varick Street we learned that Williams had walked in one morning in May to register. He swore that he was thirty-six years old, that he had been born in Springfield, Massachusetts, that he had been graduated from Springfield Day School in 1941 and Springfield High School in 1945, and that he now lived at 248 East 90th Street. With that Board of Elections card in his wallet, he had done more than get himself a legitimate driver's license: he had brought himself into existence. Now that his work was done, he had extinguished himself.

"Even with so many such details of the scheme uncovered, its solution seemed far away as ever. Except for the disposable player, Raymond Leone, we still did not know the names of any of the cast. By receiving payments from a legitimate stock broker, Neiman had insulated himself from having his funds traced to the Mays checks. We could not even be sure if the so-called Bertram Williams or

Paul Neiman or both were the brains of the scheme. If the top man was smart enough to use Leone as he had, I suspected he was also smart enough to use players for the other roles. Why do any of it himself if he could assign good people to do it for him? His task was only to lay out with precision the plan others would follow. As a detective chief, I understood that principle very well. It was one I tried to abide by myself."

"Into the vacuum of the Mays case, one day in August, walked a low-level convicted thief and punk named Leon Frainer. Currently under indictment for yet another theft, he was prepared to offer information on the Mays case in return for a bit of consideration from the DA. As he well knew, any consideration would depend on the value of what he told us, and I'd have thought he was the last guy who could deliver us a key to the swindle. I was wrong."

In the same air-conditioned squad office where Raymond Leone had told his story, Frainer now recalled how six months ago he had decided to sell a portfolio of savings bonds which he had stolen a year earlier from an Army officer in New Jersey. Since he was a thief rather than a fence, he had needed an outlet. At his regular Thursday-night poker game he had found one.

A player named Larry Desso expressed an interest, but wanted to look the bonds over first. Frainer agreed to bring them to a bar on Queens Boulevard two nights later.

Judging by the sharp way Desso played cards, Frainer felt it might be wise not to go to the meeting alone. He asked along two other felons, who also brought with them a packet of stolen securities they were hoping to sell. At the dark end of the bar Frainer saw that Desso too had brought along two brawny co-negotiators. They inspected the bonds and additional securities. Though all were negotiable, anyone attempting to cash stolen instruments of this kind would be running a major risk. Still, Desso's group agreed to buy the batch for 50 percent of face value.

"We got only one minor problem, Leon," said Desso. "Right at this minute, we don't got the money. It happens to be invested in another terrific play. We're gonna knock off Mays Department Stores in a big swindle. That's what we're tied up in now. So instead of cash, we'll give you ten points [i.e., 10 percent] of the job. Understand, we *could* get the cash in a couple of days, easy. That's no problem. If that's what you want, you can have it."

Desso put an arm around Frainer's shoulders. "I won't give you no bullshit, Leo," he continued. "Ten points of the Mays job will be worth a hell of a lot more than any cash up front now."

Frainer suddenly remembered that when one of the other poker regulars mentioned he was an accountant for Mays, Desso had been most interested in that fact.

"Okay," Frainer said. "I'll wait."

"Now, six months later," says Seedman, "Frainer and his friends had read about the Mays swindle in the newspapers. They still hadn't gotten their ten points. If they had, I doubt Frainer would have come to us. He would have pocketed at least $50,000 and taken his chances with the DA.

"Men who sit in on the same poker game for years do not customarily know much about the other regulars. Frainer, for example, knew little more than the name of the man who took his $30,000 in bonds. But he had once dropped him off at home in Huntington when his car wouldn't start after a game. He also knew that Desso was a bookmaker, which caused some complications for me. Normally, I'd have called the local police routinely to find out what they knew about a suspect, but bookmaking was the one line of work where I didn't dare. In those days more than now, a bookmaker could not operate without at least tacit approval of local police. He paid for the right. It was the same everywhere. Like the folks who bet, most cops just do not regard gambling as a genuine crime. That's why so many of them can justify not enforcing the law in this one area. In any event, I was afraid that asking the Suffolk County Police about Larry might be like shouting in his ear, so early one morning in September I drove out to the house in Huntington where Frainer had once dropped the bookie off.

"It was a beautiful place, done up in brick and redwood and set into the woods. I couldn't think of anyone I knew who owned such a palace. The only thing out of place was a couple of trucks parked around the side. One was a tank truck, the other a dump truck labeled 'Royal Sewage Co., Huntington.' The house was closed up tight. A weathered note someone had left for Larry Desso was pinned to the door. Now that Labor Day had gone by most people had finished their vacations. It would be interesting to learn whether Larry had a special reason for taking his now.

"Later in the morning, back at the office, I asked the telephone company for a list of Larry Desso's toll calls. Even when we don't need to bypass the local police, this is one of our best investigative tools. Some highly cautious people check their phones each time they come home to be sure they weren't tapped while they were gone. But many then think nothing of dialing a toll number, which is automatically clicked into telephone company billing records. Since that information does not fall into the same realm of privacy as the actual content of the conversations, we can usually get toll call records without much red tape. Naturally, finding out who dialed who doesn't prove anyone's guilt. But it sure helps narrow down the field for further investigation.

"The number Larry Desso called most often in July and early August was that of the elegant Hotel Navarro, a first class place on Central Park South. Once the calls passed through the switchboard, they were no longer traceable to individual extensions in the hotel's 250 rooms and suites. But the register did show that on August 12, the last day Desso called the Navarro, a guest named Mal Reif checked out after a month's stay. Leon Frainer had told the detectives that one of the three men who bought the stolen securities in the Queens bar had been called 'Mal.' Also known to the police as 'Abe Levine,' Mal Reif had been arrested under one name or the other eight times since 1937, for grand larceny, assault and robbery, and violation of the Federal narcotics laws. But the arrests stopped in 1949. For the last sixteen years he had been clean."

The staff at the Navarro remembered Mal Reif as a muscular man, wearing well-cut dark suits. He had craggy features and strikingly deep-set hard eyes. He usually went out evenings with a blonde on his arm, and rarely the same one twice. His bill for the month was $570. When he checked out, he paid with traveler's checks and drove off alone in a white Cadillac with Florida license plates, leaving no forwarding address.

The Navarro's billing records showed Mal Reif's favorite phone number during his stay, and Larry Desso had called that same number several times from Huntington. Unlisted, it belonged to a party named Melvin Kahn of East 74th Street, an expensive neighborhood on Manhattan's East Side. But the doorman of the apartment house at that address told detectives that after living in apartment 8C for five months, Melvin Kahn had moved out suddenly only two days ago, owing two months' back rent.

Except for a few pieces of motel-style furniture, the place had been stripped. But a young detective named Donald Harding picked out of the bathroom trash can a crumpled "Executive Lease" agreement from Avis. It was in the name of Mal Reif.

An hour later the Avis leasing manager explained that in January Reif had leased a Volvo sedan for twenty-four months. Two days ago he had tried to cancel, but the lease did not permit that. Instead, the manager agreed to sell the Volvo outright, providing Reif was willing to pay a penalty for breaking the lease.

"Whatever it comes to," said Reif, "meet me at four o'clock tomorrow afternoon at 400 East 74th Street, apartment 8C. Bring all the papers. I'll pay you then."

When he arrived the next afternoon, the manager found the place almost bare, without even a table to lay the papers down.

"As you can see," Reif said, gesturing around, "I'm getting transferred out of the city in a rush." He glanced at the bottom line of the sales contract, took a roll of bills from his pocket and peeled off $3250.

"Shift the registration to my firm, the Lansing Company at 162 Broadway," he said "By the time you do that, I'll be out of here. We can meet tomorrow in the lobby of the Mayflower Hotel at five o'clock. If you hit any snags, you can call my associate, Harriman Whitt, who will be registered there."

Now, as he finished telling detectives this story, the Avis man looked at his watch.

"It's three-thirty," he said. "I'm supposed to meet him this afternoon in ninety minutes."

"Do it," said the detectives.

From the far end of the Mayflower lobby they watched the manager give the new registration for the Volvo to Mal Reif. Except that this could not be the Mal Reif who had cut such a fine figure at the Navarro. Where were the muscular build, craggy features and well-cut suit described by the hotel staff? This man was slightly built with bland, drooping features. His brown suit was shapeless, and he wore no tie. Was this Harriman Whitt?

After the small man had gone back up to his room with the papers, the detectives checked the register. He was indeed Harriman Whitt. But where was Mal Reif? And just who was this Whitt? Thoroughly confused, the detectives called Seedman from the lobby.

"Does this Whitt resemble Melvin Kahn?" he asked.

"Come to think of it, Chief, he does look like the guy the doorman at 400 East 74th described."

"Check the handwriting in the hotel register against the signature on the apartment lease to be sure. But wait until I send over somebody to relieve you. We don't want this guy to slip away."

Later that evening, detectives compared the two signatures. They were a perfect match.

"So now we had two new players," says Seedman. "It was possible that Mal Reif had assigned this little fellow to play himself while he fled the city, just as he had assigned all the other roles in the Mays cast of characters. But Reif's previous record with us indicated that he was the type with more flash than brains—I just didn't think he was up to hatching such a grand plot.

"The more interesting character was this Harriman Whitt or, apparently, Melvin Kahn. It was a case of simple geometry. By tracing Larry Desso's toll calls from Huntington to the real Mal Reif, we had our first connection. Then we traced Reif's calls from the Navarro to Melvin Kahn, which gave us a second connection. When Larry Desso also called Kahn, we had our triangulation. As in navigation, two bearings give you a general fix on your position, but three bearings make it exact. In this case, the lines from Huntington and the Navarro intersected at 400 East 74th Street, apartment 8C.

"That geometry tipped me off to Kahn before we had even seen him. Now it turned out he looked exactly the way I'd imagined—just a little fellow utterly lacking in charm, energy or strong physical presence, a type who often learns to make up for all those deficiencies with plain old brains. What he enjoyed was sitting back and pulling the strings.

"I had one more check to make before I could feel sure about this fellow whose real name we still did not know. I sent for the handwriting samples from the hotel register and the apartment lease. Sure enough, they also matched the handwriting on the power-of-attorney cards Bertram Williams' 'partner' had filled out for each of the seven Brooklyn banks. Melvin Kahn was Harriman Whitt was Harold Parker, Jerome Blumenthal, Ernest Glick, Karl Mitler, Milton Sobel, Abe Feldman, and Peter Fine. We had found our mastermind."

In the first days after the swindle was discovered, Seedman had ordered a portfolio of known forgers to be assembled for the witnesses to view. But they had failed to pick out anyone who looked like Paul Neiman or Bertram Williams. Now Seedman went back to the portfolio, looking for the man known as Melvin Kahn, Harriman Whitt, *et al.*

"Thumbing through the mugshots, we came across a forger

arrested in 1950 for passing a bad check at Macy's. His name was Herman Witt, now thirty-nine years old. Though he had more hair and less jowls, the detectives were sure he was the same man they had seen talking to the Avis Manager in the lobby of the Mayflower Hotel.

"Our next step was to give him all the string he needed to float free. Eventually, I was sure, Herman Witt would open all the dead ends he had built into his puzzle."

The detectives on Herman Witt's track soon discovered that this drab little man led a colorful life. Though he never worked, he managed to frequent high-priced restaurants, nightclubs, and Broadway shows. His constant date was Fran Warren, a tiny dark-eyed pop singer who had sung fifteen years earlier with the Art Mooney, Charlie Barnet, and Claude Thornhill bands. Though she had even recorded a hit version of the torch song "Cry Me a River," she never quite made it to the top. With the demise of big bands Fran Warren looked mainly to summer-stock musicals and the resort hotels for work.

Hitting the night spots in high style with Witt and Fran, Seedman's detectives were quickly running through the Bureau's special expense account. The stakeout teams changed from evening to evening, so that Witt could never look across a nightclub floor and see familiar faces at another table. At all times, they stayed well back. If a situation arose where continued surveillance might make Witt suspicious, Seedman's order were to let him go off on his own. But despite all their care and vigilance, so far the stakeout was not paying off. It was as if Herman Witt had designed the characters of Paul Neiman and Bertram Williams right down to built-in vanishing buttons. Having successfully heisted over half a million dollars from the Mays accounts, they had disappeared without a trace. After a week of twenty-four-hour surveillance, the detectives had not seen Witt with anyone who looked like either man. They had not even glimpsed his friends Larry Desso and Mal Reif.

A phone tap and listening device placed by court authority in Herman Witt's room at the Mayflower produced better results. One night late in September, Witt took a call through the switchboard from Hallendale, Florida, a little town north of Miami Beach.

"It's Mal," said the caller.

"Hey, what's doin' down there?" said Witt.

"Something terrible."

"What's the matter?"

"They found me. I slipped out of town to get away and they followed me down here. You just can't give them the slip."

"*Who* found you, Mal?"

"Christ, do I have to tell you? Junior and Mac barged in here. They slapped me around. They think they're entitled to $20,000. I gave them $5000. They slapped me around some more. They'll be back for the rest. I think they got Larry too."

"Getting slapped around is the least of it. They'll blow your fuckin' head off if they don't like the way your hair cream smells. There's no point even trying to reason with them. The only ones who can call them off are the real biggies. I have somebody working on that for us right now, Mal."

"If you ask me, they don't answer to no rickety old man out in Brooklyn, either. They do whatever the fuck they want."

"They'll answer," said Witt. "Everybody is scared of somebody."

Hearing the names Junior and Mac, Seedman could almost feel a twinge of sympathy for Witt, Reif, and Larry Desso. With the law closing in on one side, they were also being hunted, it now turned out, by none other than Carmine "Junior" Persico and Hughie MacIntosh, the most feared collection team in Brooklyn now that Joe Gallo was doing time in prison for extortion. In fact, when Gallo's elder brother Larry had been garroted at the darkened Sahara Lounge in 1959, Persico had been the one who tightened the silk cord just one notch short of fatal. Then, as now, MacIntosh was his constant companion. A quiet, enormous man, Mac wore a size-52 suit. But nobody ever called him fat.

If Persico and MacIntosh were now swooping down on these two members of the Mays swindle, it told Seedman something about Witt: even the mastermind was not perfect. Witt might have dreamed up every intricacy of this fantastic plot, but he had apparently neglected the even greater intricacies of underworld politics. Somehow, he had gotten in trouble with the most ferocious wing of the Brooklyn Mafia.

Shortly after two o'clock on the morning after Mal Reif's plaintive call, Witt heard from Larry Desso at the Thunderbird Hotel in Miami Beach.

"Hey, Woody," he said, his voice high and strained on the tape. "Speaking of animals, guess who's down here?"

"I know, I know," answered Witt. "Junior and Mac. What do they want?"

"Twenty-five thousand dollars. I laughed in their faces. Or I tried to, anyhow. 'My piece of this whole score don't come to that,' I told them. So right away the guns come out in the right hands and they slap me around with the left. Finally I said, 'Junior . . . Mac, I'm gonna walk over to this bed and take out $7,000. That's what's left of what came down to me from that Mays score. I'm gonna give it to you. Then kill me. Because there *is* no more.' They took it. Then Junior says to me, "There's more. If it didn't come down to you yet, you go up and get it from your Jewish friend up in the city. Don't let him hold back. That scumbag is rollin' in dough. After you send $10,000 more over to us, the rest is yours. Is that the way you see it, Larry?' 'I see what you see, Junior,' is all I could tell them. Then they put their guns away. Jesus, Woody. Is there anybody who can pull these guys off?"

"Like I already told Mal tonight," answered Witt, "I got somebody big working on it. For all of us."

At ten o'clock the next evening Witt received a caller at his hotel room—a slender man with clean-cut features, wearing a lightly checked olive suit, buffed shoes, and horn-rimmed glasses. To the detectives posted in the lobby, he looked too young to be the "somebody big" whose help Witt had promised the two scared men in Florida. But he could well be an emissary.

"I'm glad to see you, Sam," said Witt, unaware that his room was bugged. "You don't know how glad."

"That means you got a problem."

"I still got the same problem from before, Sam. It just doesn't go away. But let me explain the whole situation from the start. That way, you'll see my position. If you think I'm in the wrong, you can tell me how. If you think I've played it square, then maybe you can lend a hand."

"I'm listening," said Sam. "But if you turn down the fuckin' TV set, I'll be able to listen even better."

Several rooms away the detective listening to the bug felt the same way.

A few days after the Mays swindle broke in the newspapers, Witt explained, he got a call at the East 74th Street apartment from Junior. They had dealt together only once before, when Witt ar-

ranged to warehouse temporarily a truckload of hijacked air-con-
ditioners. That deal had left Witt with no taste for any more deals
with Junior. It was not a good sign that Persico had managed to
get this unlisted phone number, which Witt had given to only a few
of his associates.

"Congratulations on that Mays score!" said Junior.

"Thanks," answered Witt cautiously, thinking how it was also
not a good sign that Junior knew he deserved congratulations. He
had taken pains to set up a scheme in which his own role would be
strictly hidden.

"It was such a nice score," Persico continued, "that I want you
to come over and tell us about it."

"How about coming over here?" said Witt. "We can have
drinks, maybe dinner at a nice place. I'll lay it out for you. Be my
guest."

"No. You be *my* guest. Meet me at the corner of Atlantic and
Fourth Avenues in an hour."

"I've got no car."

"Take a cab. We'll pay the fare." Persico hung up.

Knowing it would be unwise to miss the date, Witt showed up
on the corner of Atlantic and Fourth Avenues, where he was escorted into a waiting car. He was pushed to the floor of the rear seat
and blindfolded. It did not come off until, in what appeared to be
the basement of an apartment building, Junior Persico shook his
hand. So did Hughie MacIntosh. A half-dozen other men stood behind them, looking at Witt curiously.

"You eat dinner yet?" asked Persico.

"No."

"Go get us two pizzas from that guy around the corner," Persico said to one of the henchmen.

"What do you like on yours, Junior?" he asked, running to the
door.

"Extra cheese, that's all. That okay by you, Woody?"

"Sure."

"While them pies are cookin', let's get started. I wanna hear
how you did this caper. Detail by detail. But first I wanna hear the
final score."

"The papers blew it way out of proportion," said Woody. "It
wasn't anything like a million dollars. In fact, the inside man at

Mays messed us up so we lost a few days we thought we had to play with at the end. Three hundred thousand dollars was still sitting in those accounts when the whistle blew."

Persico slapped Witt hard on the face. "I said tell me the final score."

"The final score," said Witt, unwilling to put a hand to his stinging cheek, "is going to be less than half a million. This took a lot of people to do, and it's got to be split up so they each take down their share."

"They all knew their share in advance?" asked Persico.

"To the point."

"So how come I didn't know my share?"

Witt looked blank. "I don't understand, Junior. I mean, I want to, but I don't. This isn't like that hijack we worked together. If you were part of this score, you know you'd get your points. But you weren't in the picture on this one."

Persico shook his head for a long time. Mac and the others stared at Witt as if he were the class dunce. Finally, Persico put a hand gently on Witt's shoulder. "I got to explain you something basic," he said. "I'm *always* in the picture. You sit down here and be comfortable and I'm going to tell you why that is."

Witt sat down. At that moment, the pizza man was led into the basement, carrying two jumbo cardboard boxes already stained through with oil. He was a dark, stocky little man still in his apron, his tee shirt soaked with sweat.

"What's on them pies?" asked Persico.

"I made up my special for you, Junior," said the pizza man, smiling proudly. "Peperoni, a little fresh green pepper, anchovies, even a little prosciutto—"

"What did I ask for?" said Persico, cutting him off in a level voice.

The pizza man's face fell. "You ask for extra cheese . . . but I figured you'd like—"

"Didn't you ever hear the old motto that the customer is always right?" said Persico, taking out his gun.

"I just thought—"

"Hold those fucking Chinese pizzas up high," ordered Persico. The pizza man raised them on his stubby shaking left arm.

"Please, Mr. Persico, I—"

Three shots rang out. The pizza boxes danced in the air and Witt saw three holes in the cardboard bottoms gurgle with tomato paste as they fell.

"Now, go mak'm right," said Persico, turning back to Witt.

"You comfortable?" he said to Witt.

"You bet."

"You remember where I left off?"

"It was about how you're always in the picture, Junior. "

"You got a nice memory, Woody. Now this is what I want you to understand. When you get a job with the telephone company or maybe even Mays Department Store, they take something out of every paycheck for taxes, right?

"Right."

"And every year, it gets to be a little more. Now, people gripe, but they pay those taxes, Woody. They pay it, because if they don't, the government is going to tromp down on them. It's a fact of life. Now why, you may ask, does the government have a right to make you pay taxes? Well, it's a fair question."

Persico shook his finger at Witt like a schoolteacher. "The answer to that question, Woody, is that you pay taxes for the right to live and work and make money at a legit business. Does that make sense?"

"Yes."

"Well, it's the exact same situation," said Persico, spreading his hands and smiling. "You did a crooked job in Brooklyn. You worked hard and you earned a lot of money. Now you got to pay your taxes on it just like in the straight world. Because we let you do it. *We're* the government. That's why I say we're always in the picture. Am I making sense, Woody?"

Witt slumped and looked at Persico glumly. "Yeah, sure it makes sense. It's just that. . . ."

"Just what? I mean, I want this to be fully understood."

"Oh, nothing. Tell me what you want, Junior."

"You mean, what do your taxes come to? Well, let me point out something. If you'd come to us up front and told us about this job, then we'd have quoted you the normal rate. But you didn't do that, Woody. We had to find you and bring you to this here tax court. So now you got to pay a penalty on the arrears."

Persico looked sternly at Witt as he pondered. The basement lapsed into respectful silence. "Your taxes," he finally said, moving in close to Witt, "come to one half the Mays take."

"My God, Junior," wailed Witt. "Be reasonable. All the risk here was on the part of—"

Persico suddenly reached behind the chair and pulled it over, tumbling Witt on his back. Closing his eyes, Witt bunched up as best he could while he was kicked and beaten. A flurry of punches in his stomach made him want to double over, but the others held him upright.

When the blows stopped he heard Persico say, "Stop crying and look at me like a man." Witt opened his eyes but jags of pain continued to rip his insides.

"You think about the situation for the rest of the night," Persico said quietly. "My boys here will keep you company. You let me know how you feel about it in the morning."

Persico patted him on the cheek and walked out with Hugh MacIntosh. Witt pulled his knees up to his chest and rocked back and forth for a while. Later one of Persico's men knelt over him.

"I remember you from the hijack," he whispered. "You're an okay guy. I take my orders from Junior but I wanna say I'm ready to do you one favor when the time comes."

"What's that?" asked Witt, looking up hopefully.

"Well," he said, taking out his own revolver, "if I see that Junior decides to give it to you . . . I'll make sure that it comes first from right here." He pointed to the barrel solicitously before going on. "Sometimes guys really suffer, you know? I once saw a guy get shot right up the ass. Man, did *he* suffer. But I promise I'm gonna aim so it won't hurt you none at all."

"Thanks, pal," Witt said. "Let me impose on you for one more favor if the time comes?"

"Sure, Woody. Anything I can."

"Normally, you'd put cement blocks on me and throw me in the Gowanus Canal, right?"

"That's what we usually do."

"Well, this one time maybe you can arrange to have my body thrown in the street. That way, my family won't have such a hassle collecting my life insurance."

"Relax," said the henchman. "It's no problem either."

In the morning, Witt promised a smiling Persico half the proceeds from the Mays swindle as soon as he finished laundering the money. At Persico's insistence he also supplied a list of the other participants and the number of "points" going to each. At ten o'clock that morning a Cadillac dropped Witt off at his 74th Street apartment.

As Witt finished his story, Sam shook his head in wonder. "I know I could have said right up front to Junior that I'd already taken care of taxes," Witt continued. "Except that I took care of them with you and your people—not with him. But I didn't even want to mention your name. That would have really teed him off. You see what I mean, Sam?"

Sam shook his head again sadly. "This Junior has got big balls," he said. "But now he's stepping on his own. Apparently, he don't understand you're with the biggest people around. They ain't gonna be happy to hear about this inconvenience that was caused you."

"So will you tell him that personally, Sam?"

"When I say big people, Woody, I'm talking about people even bigger than *you* know. Just this past Monday I was in the chambers of one of the judges on the state Court of Appeals. He sits me down on his big leather sofa and says, 'Anything I can do for your people, you pass me the word.' That's why I say this stupid Junior is stepping on his own balls."

"So, Sam, will you say something to get him off my back?"

"I'm going to say to him, 'Junior, there isn't anyone in these United States or Europe that can put a claim on Woody. Because he's with *people*."

"Our Intelligence unit identified this visitor," explains Seedman, "as Sam Agro, an emissary from the powerful upstate Mafia family of Stephen Maggadino. From other conversations we learned that he had supplied Witt with $30,000 in venture capital to get the Mays scheme off the ground in unhurried and thorough style. Most of that sum was used to set up balances in the various accounts for Williams and Leone so that they could cash the first Mays checks at once without having to wait for them to clear.

"This was where Witt had slipped up. He had misfigured simple political necessities. The scheme was flawless, the seed money from an impeccable upstate source, the players expert. But Mays was on somebody else's turf. That was why Witt had run head-on into Persico. No matter how big Agro talked, the only people who were going to save Witt and his accomplices from the Brooklyn mob was us, the New York detectives.

"The place to start was in Florida. If the detectives I had in mind did the con job they were capable of, Mal Reif and Larry Desso would hand us all the remaining parts of the puzzle. The part I wanted most, now that we'd pinpointed the mastermind, was the real identity of Bertram Williams.

"Aaron Koota, the DA, agreed on the need for the Florida trip. But he had less confidence than I in the ability of my detectives to carry out a mission of such delicacy. It could turn into a joke."

"You go down with the detectives, Al," he said. "You give the orders. That'll make me feel better."

"Okay," said Seedman. "But I'm going to give the orders from the clubhouse phone at the golf course."

"As long as you're giving them," said Koota.

Seedman planned to take Detectives Tom Rice and Marty Flanagan with him. Both had worked on the Fallon–Finnegan case. Both were Brooklyn-born, canny, mean-looking, and large. Above all, they were superb at what detectives refer to as "jerking off" a subject.

Calling for a weather check on the evening before their departure, Seedman was disturbed to learn that a hurricane was moving slowly up the Carribean. If it kept to its present course, in thirty-six hours it would hit Miami Beach.

Seedman turned to Flanagan and Rice. "You know what to do," he said. "So go do it. Every time something happens, call me here."

"You're not coming, Chief?"

"What's the use if I can't play golf. I'll just get in your way. But please remember one thing."

"What's that, boss?"

"Raincoats."

Seedman and Koota agreed that Flanagan and Rice would have a far easier time if the New York police finally yanked in the long string on Herman Witt. Early the next afternoon, while the two detectives were airborne for Miami, other detectives watched Sam Agro pull up to the residential hotel on West 86th Street where Witt had moved two days earlier. Witt and Fran Warren joined Agro in the front seat of the white Cadillac. They drove to a Manufacturers Hanover Trust Company branch on the other side of town. Leaving Fran Warren and Agro in the idling car, Witt entered the bank alone.

From a safe deposit box listed under the name of Harold Woods, Witt removed $1090 in bills and slipped them between the buttons of his white open-necked shirt. Whistling softly, he was about to slam the box shut when Donald Harding, the young detective who had done so much footwork on the case, put out his hand.

"Leave it open, Mr. Witt. You're under arrest."

"What is this, a joke?"

"No, sir," said Harding, snapping on the cuffs. At the same moment other detectives then moved on the Cadillac to take Sam Agro and Fran Warren into custody.

Late that afternoon, at a hearing in Brooklyn Criminal Court, Witt and Agro were held in $50,000 bail each for grand larceny. forgery, and conspiracy. Fran Warren was released pending a later hearing, though District Attorney Koota told the judge she had "full knowledge" of the conspiracy. Although pleased at the clean arrests, Seedman was frustrated to learn that "Harold Woods'" safe deposit box contained only another $11,000. Where was the bulk of the Mays haul? Neither Witt nor Agro would tell. They were still claiming never to have heard of the Mays swindle. Any new details of the case would have to come out of Flanagan and Rice's work in Miami.

At Miami International Airport, Flanagan and Rice were greeted by a Dade County detective sergeant and old golfing pal of Seedman's named Paul Rosenthal.

"Where to first?" said Rosenthal.

"Let's go to the Dunes Hotel," said Flanagan. "We can check in and see if any of our friends are there."

"What kind of friends you got at that place?"

"Junior and Mac from Brooklyn. They have business with the same two guys we do."

At the Dunes, the detectives found no record of Persico or MacIntosh in the register, but they did find a bellhop who remembered bringing breakfast to a pair of men who had checked out three days earlier. One was big, the bellhop remembered. Very big. The other was smaller but muscular. When he reached for his wallet, he seemed to have trouble with his left arm.

"That's Junior," said Rice. He knew that Persico had been wounded in the left arm by Larry Gallo in retaliation for Persico's attempt on his life at the Sahara Lounge. Flanagan slipped the bellhop ten dollars. It was the most he had ever tipped anyone, but the bellhop barely nodded thanks.

"That morning I brought them breakfast," he said, "it came to

$4.70 for the two of them. The one you call Junior paid with a fifty-dollar bill. When I told him I'd have to go to the cashier for change, he says, 'Did I ask for change?' "

"Are you saying that a paltry sawbuck isn't good enough for you?" said Flanagan. "Because if it isn't, I'll stick it in your mouth to use for chewing gum."

"I'm grateful, I'm grateful," said the bellboy and backed away.

Under a lowering sky, Rosenthal drove them next to Hallendale, where they hoped to find Mal Reif hiding out at his mother's apartment. She lived on Golden Isle Drive, in Hallendale's nicest apartment tower. They rode the elevator in silence to the top floor.

Rosenthal knocked while Flanagan and Rice stood to one side.

"Who's there?" came Reif's voice after the third knock. Even through the door, they could hear a note of fear.

"It's the Dade County Sheriff's Office," thundered Rosenthal. He held his badge to the peephole.

Reif hesitated, then unlatched the door. When he saw Flanagan and Rice, his deep-set eyes widened. He tried to slam the door shut, but Rosenthal was already in. "These gentlemen are with me," he said. "They're here to help you out with the problem we know you have."

"I got no problem," said Reif. He was wearing a blue silk dressing gown.

"Yes, you do," said Flanagan. "And Junior and Mac are only *one* of your problems."

"If you're with them or someone else, it doesn't matter," said Reif. "They took all the money already. So how about leaving me alone?"

Suddenly, Rosenthal was embarrassed to realize that Reif assumed he was a crooked cop escorting somebody else's heavies.

"I said we're here to do you good," said Flanagan. "We'll help you make the best of a situation you made bad yourself. If you help us."

"Help you *how?*"

"We want you to come clean on how Woody put together this Mays caper."

"Who?" snapped Reif.

"Come on, Mal, no more games," said Flanagan as he and Rice flashed their own gold shields. "Woody was already grabbed in the city today. All your moaning to him about Junior and Mac is on tape."

Reif gaped at them. Rice felt this was the moment to drill in.

"Pick up the phone, Mal," he said. "Call Larry. Tell him you got a call from Woody and you got to meet right now to talk. Say you'll meet him at the delicatessen off Collins Avenue at 54th Street, south side. It's called Mannie's. Not Wolfie's, Mannie's. It's a little place. Tell him to meet you at seven o'clock."

Flanagan put the phone in Reif's hand.

"Look!" shouted Flanagan. "You're going to get pissed on anyway! But this way, you get pissed on the least. Now dial."

On the way back down to 54th Street, the two New York detectives looked at the palms bordering Collins Ave. They were bending gracefully but deeply in the mounting wind. "Do they always blow that way?" Flanagan asked.

"Only when a hurricane is heading in," said Rosenthal. "They say we'll get the brunt in about eight hours. In fact, we may have to clear out of the Beach right after this meet at the deli."

"The best thing could happen to a guy," Reif said glumly, "is to get blown away by the fuckin' hurricane."

"Unless you do like we tell you," said Flanagan, "I'll hit you with a fuckin' coconut. Now listen. When you get in the deli, tell Larry you heard from Woody that the big guys are headed down here again. They think you held out on them. This time it's going to be bad for you both. Suggest that maybe both of you should go to some other town, like Pierre."

"Where's that?" asked Reif.

"North Dakota, South Dakota, who the hell knows? Tell him to go to Casper, for all I care."

"Where's that?"

"Wyo— Listen, if you act like a wiseass, we'll turn you over to the big guys ourselves," said Rice.

At 7:45, as the first drops of rain mixed with the steadily rising wind, Reif left the delicatessen with Larry Desso. When Rosenthal grabbed Reif from behind, he kicked and clawed like a crazy man. The detectives couldn't have asked for a better performance. He even screamed, but the wind swallowed it. As Rice moved to help Rosenthal, Flanagan took Desso on himself.

"We're gonna take a drive in your car," he said, gripping Desso by the arm with a grip that had to hurt. "If you want to fight like your friend, it'll be over for you right now." Desso stood for a moment, watching as the two detectives wrestled Mal Reif into the back seat.

"Holy Mary, Mother of God," squeaked Desso. He climbed into the car, shaking as if he were in a deep freeze. Watching him tremble, Flanagan was afraid the steering wheel might come off in his hand.

"Drive to 182nd and Collins," the detective ordered. "The Suez Motel."

"I got a wife, a house," said Desso as they drove up the deserted avenue. Great palm fronds were now being torn from the wildly swinging trees. "If I'm going to be hit, I'd just like to tell them that—"

"Shut your mouth," said Flanagan. Once, as they drove the rest of the way to the Suez, he caught himself humming the refrain from "Cry Me a River."

At the hotel, Flanagan and Rice whisked their men into separate rooms. "Sit in that corner," said Flanagan. Desso sidled toward a motel chair against one wall of the room.

"I didn't say sit in the chair," said Flanagan, "I said sit in the corner." Desso huddled down on the floor, crossing himself.

"Where is the Mays money?" said Flanagan.

"Junior and Mac got it all, I swear."

"Listen, it was supposed to be better than a half-million-dollar score. Right?"

"I hear that it was. But it ain't in my pocket."

"Your friend Mal says it isn't in his pocket. Woody says it isn't in his pocket. That's what *all* you fucks say. Somebody is slinging the shit."

"It ain't me."

"Then who?"

Larry Desso held out his hands in despair. "What about the inside man at Mays?" asked Flanagan.

"Yeah," said Desso, hopefully. "It could be him."

"What's that fuck's name, anyway?"

"Grubert," answered Desso. "Freddie Grubert. He's a real big fellah."

"He could be King Kong, it won't matter if we decide to take him down to size," said Flanagan. "Where do you know him from?"

"I found him for Woody, for Christ's sake. He played cards with me on Thursday nights out on the Island. The guy is into the shylocks for all kinds of dough. He's paying alimony. He was the perfect setup for this deal. None of this would have happened if I hadn't introduced him to Woody. He had to have an inside man."

"How many points did he get from the score?"

"Him and somebody else was supposed to split fifteen."

"Who's the somebody else?"

"A guy who bagged the money for Woody. He works for a Buick dealer selling used cars, I think. I never met the guy. If I knew his name, I'd tell you."

"It doesn't matter," said Flanagan. "Between the two of them, their fifteen points isn't the big shitload. Who else had a piece, Larry?"

"Woody took down the biggest share, being as he thought it up," said Desso.

"I know that, you idiot," said Flanagan. He noticed he was shouting. But he had to. The wind had picked up to a high, steady moan. At that moment, he heard pounding on the door. He opened the door, assuming it was Tom Rice, who was drilling Mal Reif with the same questions in a room down the hall. But it was the assistant manager.

"Excuse me, sir," he shouted. "But the storm-watch center has warned everyone to get off the Beach. We've made arrangements for you to go to a motel inland if you have no other place."

"When you go, we'll go," shouted Flanagan and closed the door. He turned back to Desso, who now seemed more frightened of the weather than of him.

"Maybe we should go, like he said," Desso shouted.

"You'll never go till all the points add up to a hundred. You told me about Grubert and the used-car guy. I know all about Woody. I know about Sam. But that adds up to sixty at the most. Who else, Larry?"

"He don't tell me everything. He says it's better for security when the right don't know what the left is doing."

"What about the other bagman? Who's this Bertram Williams that had his picture in the newspapers?"

"Woody never told me. I swear."

"Okay," said Flanagan, crouching down in front of Desso. "Let's go over it from the beginning. How did you get into this thing in the first place?"

Desso looked up at him sharply. "Hey, you a cop?"

Grinning, Flanagan wiggled his gold shield in Desso's face. Larry had spilled so much already that there would be no point in his holding back the rest.

"What'd you come on like a mob guy for?" he demanded indignantly.

"Did I? That's a problem in your psycho head. But now it's the least of your problems, Larry. We took Woody today."

"I bet he ain't saying nothing. I said too much already."

"You don't understand, you stupid fuck," shouted Flanagan. "I know and you know that he's the brains. But he's sitting in the cage in the 84th station house, claiming it's you and Mal. He's pissing all over you, Larry. How do you think we knew where to find you two? Woody spit it right out! Now do like I asked and start—"

Suddenly the other side of the room, the floor-to-ceiling waterfront window blew out in a hail of angry glass. The curtains stood straight out, vibrating. Sheets of water slammed in. Desso got up to run, but Flanagan pushed him back in the corner.

"Start at the beginning I said," he bellowed.

"Are you crazy?" Desso shouted back. "You want us both to die?"

"That only happens if you don't tell me every detail of the story from the beginning."

Desperate, Larry finally shouted out the rest of the story. Mal Reif had introduced him to Herman Witt at the Thunderbird Hotel the previous November. Witt had talked about a foolproof department-store swindle he had figured out. But before he could put it into operation, he needed a man to work on the inside of the accounting department. He also needed two front men with spotless records and nice appearances.

In March, Desso had called Witt to say he had found just the right inside man. Freddie Grubert was badly in need of cash to pay his gambling debts and alimony. He kept hoping to make a buck during Desso's Thursday-night card games, but that was just getting him in deeper. Front man Raymond Leone was pointed out to Witt at the racetrack by a friend, Jack Molinas, who shortly went to jail himself for fixing a basketball game. Witt never met Leone; he dealt with him only through the used-car salesman whom he had sent out to West Street on Flag Day.

The other front man, Bertram Williams, was an old friend of Woody's, brought in from the West Coast for this job. Woody had started him off with a Board of Elections card and Williams had built his character's life around that. As soon as his part was over, Williams had left town. That was all he had to tell, Desso claimed, since Woody had been careful to keep members of the scheme away from one another.

By now an inch of water had seeped in beneath Flanagan and Desso. The wind had stepped up from a moan to a howl and the curtains were lying in tatters in the midst of the shattered glass.

"I spilt *everything*, I swear on everything holy," Desso bellowed. Flanagan had to admit that the story had come fast. He had even been forced to slow Desso down several times so he could get the details straight. But there was the missing part to the puzzle.

"You left out one thing!" he shouted. "Who is Bertram Williams?"

"I told you, a guy from California."

"His *name*, dummy. What's his name?"

"Steve—Stephen Hirschorn. He worked out of a residential hotel on 72nd Street, except I think he headed back to LA as soon as you guys put his picture in the papers."

Desso wrung his hands at Flanagan. "Please, please. . . . I mean, we could get cut off here. The water will come up right over us."

Flanagan could not tell whether Desso's cheeks were wet with water or tears. He extended a beefy hand and pulled the bookmaker to his feet. As they left the room, it took both of them to shut the door. In the lobby on the leeward side of the Suez they met Rice and Reif, whose interrogation had finished a few minutes before. They sat in easy chairs and listened to the wind scream until dawn, when it dropped back to a moan. They knew the hurricane was moving on.

"We picked up Frederick Grubert at his home at Greenlawn, Long Island, on October 15, while the hurricane still blew in Miami," says Seedman. "Nine thousand dollars of his share was in the house. He hadn't done much to earn it. Besides furnishing Witt with a genuine check to photograph, he was supposed to monitor the company accounts to be sure they were not overdrawn in the month of the check-writing blitz. But on July 15 the Underwriters Bank and Trust account went into the red. Luckily for the forgers, Max Shulman threw in an extra $300,000, with no questions asked. But the account also went into the red two days before the end of the billing cycle. During those two days Witt had planned to extract the last few hundred thousand from his twelve accounts.

"The elusive Paul Neiman was played, as Desso said, by a used-car salesman named Mike Punty. He had bagged all Raymond Leone's laundered funds for delivery to Witt. Desso was right about something else: Witt had never met Raymond Leone. He never wanted to. Leone could hardly implicate a man he had never seen or heard of.

"As for Hirschorn, it took us an extra few weeks to find him in California. Donald Harding and an assistant DA named Ed Panzarella flew out to arrest him. Witt had brought him in to handle several of the most delicate jobs—fooling Mark Lanham, a man not easily conned, getting the safety paper by pulling off the National Auto Appraisers ploy, opening and then cannibalizing the seven big Brooklyn accounts. He did it all flawlessly, but was somehow careless enough to leave a forwarding address at his residential hotel on West 72nd Street. He wanted his furniture sent out to the Bel Air section of Los Angeles. I sent out detectives instead.

"From Hirschorn's point of view, though, a forwarding address may not have seemed all that careless. His friend Witt had devised a seamless, perfect plot. As long as the players acted out their parts as directed, no one would be found out. Why not leave a forwarding address? Witt could even permit Raymond Leone to be caught and after investigation be found innocent of anything but being a dupe. If Leone had been satisfied with what Neiman was paying him, he would have come out okay. Instead he started socking away brown paper packages of money. In one of his conversations with Agro, Witt took the measure of this man he'd never met. 'This guy was a legitimate sucker,' he told Agro. 'He got larceny, but he was a legitimate sucker.'"

"Of the $948,000 written on bogus Mays checks, a four-year investigation by the DA's office turned up only about $300,000," says Seedman. "Twenty thousand was found behind the bathroom tiles in the house Witt built for his parents in New Jersey. Much of the rest, apparently, was invested in second mortgages that paid a high rate of return. Witt himself wasn't in jail for long. Sentenced to two and a half to three and a half years by Judge Dominic Rinaldi, he served less than half that. Hirschorn got two to three years, Raymond Leone one and a half to two. Mal Reif, Larry Desso, and Frederick Grubert got one year apiece. The same judge handed Agro a suspended sentence. Mike Punty, who had played Neiman, cooperated with the prosecution and was never tried. Before going to Sing-Sing, Witt married Fran Warren on Mother's Day, 1965. Eight years later, Judge Rinaldi was removed from the bench for questionable behavior. The official report specifically noted his light sentences in the Mays case."

Late one night before he was arrested, Witt talked about the plot with Fran Warren in his room at the Mayflower. They had been dining and drinking happily, but now she was worried that with all the publicity about the Mays case he might be caught.

"Honey, I'll tell you how perfect this crime is," he said. "I could slip on my coat now, go over to the desk sergeant at the nearest station house and say, 'I confess to the Mays swindle.' I could *write out* a confession. But there's nothing they could do to me. They couldn't even book me. They can't just take my word for it, Fran, they need corroboration and they haven't got it."

"I still can't help being a little worried," whispered Fran Warren.

"Relax," said Witt. "One of these days, baby, we're going to be using nothing but hundred-dollar bills. The rest we'll throw away. That day is coming, Fran. I've got a scheme building in my head that could take $20,000,000 out of the Federal Reserve Bank in Philadelphia for us. Twenty *million*, and that's low. It could go as high as a *billion*. But say it's only $20,000,000. If I run around the country and divvy that up between a couple of hundred savings banks, do you know what that comes to in interest alone? Just a mere $800,000 a year . . . a lowly $15,000 a week . . . a sniveling $2200 a day. . . .

"Ah, Fran, all I know how to do is make a load of money, sit tight and relax, lean back and enjoy life. That's all I'm good for. In every other way, I'm a complete flop. . . ."

"No, honey. You're wonderful in *every* way."

"Well, I'm going to do right by you. It won't be long before we're using nothing but those hundred-dollar bills. . . . Hey, honey —how about we buy an island down there in the Bahamas? They have thousands. We'd pick just a little one with palms and a white beach . . . we could build a beautiful nightclub just for you and me and our friends. For the grand opening we could fly everyone in on charter planes . . . only nice people. We could bring in the finest jazz bands, Ellington, Kenton, the Count . . . and you would stand out in front and sing . . . and it would all be free. No money allowed on our island, no money at all!"

THE GIRL IN A BOX CASE

The coldest wind of the season was blowing across the Red Hook section of Brooklyn when Joe Areneda came home from working the late shift. It was 2:40 on Saturday morning, November 20, 1966. He had shivered all the way from the subway. Now he found that somebody had left an oversized cardboard carton squarely in front of the stairway to the basement apartment he shared with his mother at 174 Bergen Street. He was so irked that he kicked the carton hard enough to sail it twenty feet. It did not budge.

Areneda grabbed the carton at the edges and dragged it out to the curb. It did not rattle, did not thump. It was just heavy. Curious, he pulled away the twine, opened one top flap, and peered inside. For a moment he was transfixed. Then he bolted for his own door. His hands were shaking so badly he could hardly insert the key. Once he made it inside, he woke his mother and called the police.

Six minutes later a patrolman named Christopher, his sector car idling at the curb, pulled open the rest of the flaps. The hard white beam of his searchlight fell on a pretty girl, slender, perhaps twenty-one or twenty-two, hair black and straight, skin pale olive, eyes shut. She was doubled up in the box, her knees against her chest, her modest skirt hiked up over the tops of her stockings. She wore a garter belt and panties. Dropped in beside her was a vinyl hand-bag, a pair of black shoes, and an umbrella with a gold handle. The patrolman snapped off his light and called for the duty detectives from the 76th Squad and the Homicide Squad.

At that moment the duty detectives, Tony Ricci and Tony Cordero, were busy with a problem of their own. During the night two cops on patrol had been waiting at a red light alongside an expensive new car driven by a teen-ager who was visibly nervous and probably underage. When one of the patrolmen got out and reached through the window for his registration, the boy had stomped the gas pedal, dragging the cop. His partner fired his .38 twice, smashing the windshield and the boy's leg before the car finally stopped after half a block. It was not the patrolmen's most brilliant performance. Plenty of answers would be demanded by their superiors in the morning. Ever since midnight Ricci and Cordero had been interviewing the principals and a half-dozen witnesses.

Leaving Cordero at the hospital to talk to the boy when he came out of surgery, Tony Ricci went alone to Bergen Street. George Kane, the Homicide duty man, was already there. A cold wind like tonight's always flattened the homicide rate, even on a normally busy weekend, and Kane had no other assignments in Brooklyn South. Lifting the handbag by a tip of the strap in order not to smudge the buckle, the detectives found that it belonged to Carmen Roldan, 268 New Lots Avenue—all the way on the other side of Brooklyn in East New York.

Under emergency service lights, the Photo unit snapped pictures of the carton, inside and out. No police officer could declare Carmen Roldan legally dead, of course; only the Medical Examiner could do that. But the Deputy ME on duty sent word he would not come over, so shortly after five o'clock a morgue wagon took Carmen Roldan to him. The detectives hung on to her handbag, shoes, and umbrella.

Tony Ricci picked up his partner, Tony Cordero, at the hospital and drove to 268 New Lots Avenue. It was a tenement far shoddier than the one at 174 Bergen Street. At apartment number 42 Carmen Roldan's mother answered at the first knock. She was draped in a shawl. They didn't have to say a word. She understood them right away: her daughter Carmen was dead.

At 8:45 on this cloudy and cold Saturday morning, Albert

Seedman, now a Deputy Chief and Commander of all Brooklyn South detectives, took a call from Tim Dowd, Captain of the 10th District, the job Seedman had held when the Fallon–Finnegan case broke four and a half years earlier. This weekend Dowd, just as Seedman had done, was covering the 11th District for its vacationing boss.

"We got a girl in a box on Bergen Street, Chief," Dowd said.

"Addressed to who?"

"No address, just a body. Looks like she was strangled. A few marks on her face, but nothing too bad. A real pretty face."

"Ask the ME to hold off moving her until I get there."

"They already drove her away, but we didn't let them take her personal effects. We've got them here at the Seventy-sixth."

Seedman hated getting to a scene after the body was removed. Even after gazing down at corpses regularly for years, he had yet to forget one: he could still see the angle of each limb, the expression on each face. That was where you started from. Otherwise you were just picking up the case like someone coming into a movie after it had begun. You could be told in detail exactly what had happened before you came in, but it was never the same as seeing it yourself from the very beginning.

"I still want to see where the box was," said Seedman. "Meet me there in fifteen minutes."

At Bergen Street detectives who had been canvassing the block since before dawn had found an old woman who said that at about eight o'clock Friday evening she had seen a light-colored car pull up to the curb, and two men jump out, heave a carton from the trunk to the sidewalk, and zoom away. From her squint, the detectives guessed her vision was not the best. But her timing seemed reliable. Other neighbors had noticed the box, but none before eight o'clock. Several children had played with it briefly. They seemed to know better than to open it.

A procession of squad cars had carried Mrs. Roldan and nine of her thirteen surviving children who still lived at home to the 76th squad room that morning. Interrogating them separately, Spanish-speaking detectives attempted to account for Carmen's friends, habits, and every second possible of her last day. None had seen her after 8:30 on Friday morning, when she left to make her weekly appearance at the local unemployment office. Then she had planned to stop off at the vinyl factory, where she had been dismissed after four years, to see whether she could get her job back. Even allowing for window-shopping, Carmen surely would have been home by suppertime.

"Did your daughter have a gentleman friend?" asked a detective named Joe Solis. This could be a touchy matter in a Spanish-speaking home.

Mrs. Roldan lowered her head. Carmen was the best girl a mother could want, she explained. She always obeyed, she believed in God. But for several months she had been keeping company with a man named Carlos. It was nothing serious. He had never brought her home later than nine o'clock, even on Saturday night. She would never get in trouble with him, if that was what Solis was thinking. Her daughter was upright. She did not wear any makeup. In her whole life, Carmen had never even been to a movie theater.

"From our own point of view," says Seedman, "we figured this boyfriend was bound to be involved. When it turned out he was married with three children, I felt it was as good as sealed. We learned that one of Carmen's sisters had taken a call from Carlos about one o'clock on Friday afternoon. He had been anxious for her to call him back before he left work at five."

But Carlos was an instant disappointment to Seedman. A neatly dressed little man who worked at the counter of a hot-dog stand, he was agitated but respectful as he was questioned in the 76th squad room. Yes, he did look forward to seeing Carmen two or three times a week for a few hours after work. But only to talk on a bench in Prospect Park. Yes, he had also called the Roldan home the day before at one o'clock. But only to ask Carmen if they would be having an early dinner, as they usually did on Friday evenings. He always dropped her off early enough so that he could have a second dinner with his own family at home. He also had always been a gentleman to Carmen. She had told him she was a virgin. He believed it, and unlike many men, respected her for it.

Since Carmen had never returned his call, Carlos said he had gone home straight from work. Even before his movements had been checked out, Seedman decided that Carlos, such a promising suspect, did not have the qualities of a killer.

The only other available suspect that Saturday was a girl named Marie, who had worked beside Carmen at the vinyl factory. Carmen had told her younger sister Demaris that they had fought several times, and the last time Marie had threatened to kill her. It was those fights that had led to Carmen's dismissal. Eyes flashing as she was brought in, Marie was in no way cowed by the squad room. She freely admitted fighting with Carmen, but only because she slacked off on the assembly line. While she may have threatened to kill Carmen, in truth she wouldn't even spit on her. Besides, she had not even seen Carmen since she was fired. This girl was as much a firebrand as Carlos was a waffle. But she was also not a killer.

Late on Saturday afternoon the Medical Examiner reported that Carmen Roldan had been strangled, probably by a length of heavy twine. She had been dead since about noon on Friday. Carmen was not pregnant—a possibility that might have implicated Carlos: as a married man carrying on secretly, it would have posed a serious dilemma. Robbery could not have been the motive. The few dollars with which Carmen had left home were still in her pocketbook. She had not been molested. Why then had she been killed?

Seedman would have settled at this point for knowing *where* Carmen had been killed. He had not been entirely kidding when he asked Tim Dowd to whom the box had been addressed. At least that detail would provide a starting point. Tracing it did not turn out to be difficult. The label showed the four-by-four heavy cardboard box had been used to ship a dining-room chair from a factory in Pennsylvania to a furniture store on Rockaway Avenue. Mr. Goldberg, the proprietor, had uncrated a set of four early Friday morning and had put all the empty cartons at the curb. Scavengers often took the best ones before the trashman did. Mr. Goldberg had no idea who had taken the one in which Carmen was packed.

The first break came at 1:06 on Monday afternoon, when a detective named "Red" Russo, catching squeals that day, took a call at the 76th Squad duty desk.

"I'm a cabbie," said a nervous Brooklyn-accented voice over the din of traffic. "Don't try to trace the phone because it's in a booth. I just wanna say that I been hearing about this dead girl on the radio. Well, on Friday night I took a fare with a box from Blake and Union in Brownsville to 174 Union Street. The box was so heavy I busted a gut getting it in the trunk. I let him take it out all by himself. It was a $2.50 fare. He gave me three dollars with the tip."

"What did he look like?" asked Russo. But on the other end the phone had already clicked.

Seedman sent detectives to the corner of Blake and Union at once, but while they missed the caller they returned to report that the location looked promising. It was just a few blocks from Mr. Goldberg's furniture store. It was also within walking distance of the unemployment office where Carmen had checked in early Friday morning. The cabbie's call was a good break, but Seedman wanted to ask him much more. The chance came later in the day when Russo again picked up the phone and held up his hand in warning.

"I . . . I'm the guy who called before . . ." the voice began haltingly.

"Yes, sir, yes, sir," said Russo. "It's nice of you to call back. We were hoping you might." Russo waited. He was not about to scare the cabbie away. The man could take his own time.

"I feel bad for that girl," the cabbie went on. "I'd like to help you fellows out, but I got my own family to think about. This guy could put *me* in a box. You understand my position."

"If I was in your shoes, I'd be looking at it the same way," Russo said. "But let me say this: the Chief is sitting right across from me. He's been directing this case personally. He already said that if you call back, to tell you he'll pick out the ten detectives in Brooklyn South who look most like King Kong to protect you any time you feel you need it. That means you'll even get the Chief himself."

Seedman glared at Russo.

". . . There's not a hell of a lot more that I can tell you, actually," said the cabbie.

"You don't have to tell us anything," said Russo. "I'm not even going to ask your name. But listen—if you can see your way clear to drop by here and have a cup of coffee with us, it sure might help us get to the murderer of that poor girl."

Thirty minutes later a middle-aged worried-looking man walked into the squad room.

"I'm probably a jerk to do this, but here I am," he said. "My name is Simon Lipton."

Chain-smoking, ignoring the black coffee Russo set in front of him, Lipton explained that he was making change for the lady he had just dropped off at the corner of Union and Blake about 8:30 on Friday night, when a heavy-set, apparently Puerto Rican man about forty years old jumped into the back seat. He was breathing heavily.

"Go down there," he ordered in accented English, pointing to the next block of Union Street. "I have a package to pick up."

"Hold up, buddy," Lipton said, irritated, and finished giving the lady change.

The box was sloppily tied with several turns of twine. It bulged slightly at the sides. Lipton and his passenger heaved it into the trunk.

"It's too high," said Lipton. "It won't close."

"It'll mash down," answered the passenger.

The passenger directed Lipton west on Union Street. Noticing that he continued to breathe in harsh gasps, Lipton offered him a cigarette. A moment later the cab was filled with an odd smell.

"You ever smoke before, mister?" asked Lipton.

"Yes, sure."

"Well, you just lit the filter end of the cigarette."

Lipton passed back another cigarette. In the rear-view mirror he saw that the man's hands were shaking as he lit it. They drove on in silence until the passenger told him to stop on a dark and totally deserted block of Bergen Street.

"My back's a little popped out," Lipton said. "You're gonna have to heave out that carton yourself."

Whatever was in it, Lipton could see it wasn't fragile. The man let it hit the curb in front of number 174 with a thud. He paid the $2.50 fare with a five-dollar bill and asked for two back. Lipton was glad to pull away from him and the empty block. It was the kind of spot where cabbies got robbed.

"By the time Lipton left us," says Seedman, "I'd divided the work into several parts. The focus of our canvass now shifted from Bergen Street in Red Hook to the area where Lipton had picked up his fare in Brownsville. Several days of door-knocking produced the woman Lipton had dropped off. Since the fellow had nearly knocked her flat jumping into the cab, she had got a good look at him. Together she and Lipton helped the police artist sketch a composite portrait of the suspect. He was dark, with short curly hair and a mustache, slightly heavier than average, but otherwise no different from ten thousand other Puerto Rican men in the departmental files. Just the same, the portrait was distributed to all station houses in

Brooklyn. The Spanish-language newspapers, which were following the case much more closely than even the *Daily News,* all put the portrait on their front page."

Since Carmen had last been seen alive at about 9:45 at the unemployment office, Seedman dispatched another group of detectives to interview every other person who had reported in that morning. Carmen could have been drawn into conversation with someone else who was waiting on line and they might have left together or she might have been followed. She certainly was attractive enough. Anyone who didn't report on the following Friday was in for a double-check.

Seedman also sent detectives to interview everyone who had worked in the vinyl plant with Carmen, including those who had since left. Since the assembly line was manned mostly by Puerto Ricans, this virtually monopolized the services of his small group of Spanish-speaking detectives.

"Everyone agreed Carmen was the nicest girl they knew," says Seedman. "She would never knowingly mix with the wrong people, and alone among her girlfriends, refused to wear makeup. But she had one quirk—she was nuts over spiritualists. Every time she felt a tic, she was off to see her favorite spiritualist of the moment. Carmen Roldan must have patronized more Spanish-speaking spiritualists than anyone else in Brooklyn. It was something to look into.

"We found these spiritualists did an unbelievable business. In Brownsville and East New York they must have outnumbered liquor dealers and they were at least one to a block. They operated out of private apartments and shops called *botánicas,* where they sold herbs and religious artifacts, blending occultism with straight religion. I doubt if they ever paid a city tax.

"These women didn't miss a trick, so when our detectives came to visit them, they all admitted they had counseled Carmen. They had seen danger for her that Friday. If only the poor girl had listened to them and stayed home . . . prophesies whose accuracy would not be lost on other clients."

Since few spiritualists advertised, or were listed in the phonebook, Seedman told the detectives to ask each spiritualist about others Carmen might have visited. Most dismissed their colleagues as charlatans, but one specialist in card-reading did say that when it came to removing or casting spells, Edith Berrios of Brownsville was the best in Brooklyn. Even at fifteen dollars per visit, a stiff fee at the time for her mainly low-income clientele, her days were always booked up.

None of Carmen's friends remembered her mentioning Edith Berrios, but the detectives were highly interested to learn she lived at 40 Tapscott Street. That was just around the corner from Blake and Union, where Lipton had picked up his fare with the box. Seedman sent over Joe Solis and Eddie Colon, his most trusted Spanish-speaking team to the tenement at 40 Tapscott.

"Berrios? They no live here no more," said the superintendent.

"When did they move?"

The super scratched his head. "It was Sunday, two weeks ago," he said.

The detectives did their own figuring back. That would have been November 21, two days after Carmen died. "Did they give notice?"

"People here, they never give notice. They wait until the rent is due, then they sneak away," he snorted.

"Did the Berrios do that?"

"No."

"Where did they go?"

The super shrugged.

"How many in the family?"

"Let's see," he said. "Mrs. Berrios always paid the rent. Then there was her husband, two little girls, and another fellow. I think he was Mrs. Berrios' brother."

"I wonder if we could take a look around the apartment?" asked Solis.

"People already moved in," said the super. That could be a problem. Without a warrant, detectives could not search the premises unless they were given permission. But the new tenants were so pleased to meet a pair of Spanish-speaking New York detectives that they gladly let them in. The small apartment, facing an inner courtyard, seemed much too cramped for the Berrios family of four plus the brother. As Solis came out of the rear bedroom, he found Colon standing in the middle of the living room.

"Wha'cha staring at, Eddie?" asked Solis.

"Look at the blinds."

It took Solis a minute to see it. Then he whistled. The tilt cord was cut halfway up. Just such a cord could account for the marks burned into Carmen Roldan's throat.

Despite intensive interviews of everyone living at 40 Tapscott, nobody could remember having seen the dead girl in the building. But a few did think the police sketch of Lipton's passenger resembled one of the two men living in apartment number 8. Most important, one woman told the detectives she had heard an odd noise on the stairs one evening several weeks ago. Opening the door a crack, she had seen the man from number 8 thumping a big carton down the stairs, one by one.

"Catching up with a whole family on the move is not usually a major problem for us," explains Seedman. "If the super doesn't know where they went, we can check with the Post Office. We can ask Con Ed, Brooklyn Union Gas, and the telephone company where they've switched the account. If the family had children in school, as the Berrios did, we can find out from the Board of Education where their records were transferred. Often the easiest way is to find the fellow who moved them. But even with all these leads, we still found no sign of the Berrios family. For all we knew, they had gone back to Puerto Rico.

"While this search was under way, we got a tip that Carmen's killer was Hector Lopez, who could be found managing a Laundromat in East New York. That was maybe the two hundredth tip we had received since announcing a special number for the public to call. Like all the rest this one had to be checked out, so a pair of detectives brought in Hector Lopez two hours later. He had already confessed on the way over. I was ready to write him off until we got his record: he had killed his first wife in San Juan eight years before. That looked promising enough to ask Lipton to come in for a look. We put Lopez in with five detectives of similar build and coloring in an interrogation room at the 76th. Lipton took one look through the one-way mirror and shook his head: his passenger had been a far bigger man than any of them.

"Lopez was indignant. 'Who'r'ya gonna believe—him or me?' he demanded.

" 'Take this guy to the nuthouse for observation,' I said in disgust.

"We got another tip," he continues, "that the killer was a man named Jesús, now working as a dishwasher in a restaurant in Connecticut. We brought him down, but when he walked in the squad room door he was smiling. He had good reason. Right behind him was his brother, Perfecto, an identical twin. Unless we could match

Jesús's prints, we'd never convince a jury that he was the culprit and not Perfecto—or vice versa."

Seedman had sent detectives to check all the real-estate agents in Brooklyn who dealt with Spanish people. None had rented to the Berrios family. The detectives moved on to Manhattan, working the Puerto Rican enclaves off Central Park West and in Spanish Harlem until, on December 10, they found an agent who remembered renting Edith Berrios apartment number 7 at 578 East 163rd Street in the teeming South Bronx.

Climbing the sagging stairs of the tenement, Colon and Cordero, who had first caught the case, could hardly see how this was any improvement over Tapscott Street. Opening the door of number 7, Edith Berrios was not in the least flustered to see them. A homely, comfortable woman with an open smile and not a hint of mystery, she invited the detectives in. The mantelpiece, windowsills, and television top were lined with statues of the saints.

"Did you know we've been looking everywhere for you?" Colon could not resist asking.

She looked at them reproachfully. "Gentlemen—if I knew that, I would have been at your doorstep. But we don't know any more what goes on in the old neighborhood. It seems further to Tapscott Street than to Santurce. Now that I know, I am at your service."

Cordero, as a matter of routine, handed her the police sketch of Lipton's passenger, though he had little hope that she would recognize him. Mrs. Berrios' two small daughters clustered by her side to peer at it.

"Mama, it looks like Uncle Miguel," piped up Diane, the seven-year-old.

"It does look like my brother," said Edith Berrios without hesitation.

The detectives were startled. After three weeks of trying to track down this elusive woman, they had expected her to be cagier than this. Maybe she really had not tried to elude them. The city could have simply swallowed her up.

"Your brother's name is Miguel—"

"Ocassio. My maiden name."

"Do you know where we can find him?"

"Well, he used to live with us on Tapscott Street. He was with us a few days here too, but it was too crowded so he moved out one day. I haven't heard from him since."

"Who else might have heard from him?"

"His wife, Ima, and he are not living together. But they talk. Maybe she knows."

"How about your husband?"

"Eduardo is at work in a restaurant in Manhattan. I will be glad to ask him when he comes home."

The detectives were puzzled by Mrs. Berrios' reactions. They had appeared without notice. They had told her it had been a long search. Without saying why, they had brought a sketch which she had readily admitted looked like her brother. Yet she had not asked how they found her or why they had the sketch. She had not asked anything at all about why they had come. She seemed in no way surprised, hostile or afraid. Cordero and Colon wondered whether that might change when they asked her certain questions—questions they also wanted to put to Eduardo Berrios—*before* the two of them could put their heads together to decide on their answers. For now, Cordero asked if she could take a ride with them to the office.

"But the children. . . ."

"Bring them along. They'll have a great time." Cordero hoped they might even be helpful.

Though Edith Berrios spoke English, Seedman suggested the interrogation be carried out in Spanish. Knowing that Colon and Cordero alone among all the detectives milling around the squad room could understand her, she might turn to them in confidence when it came to the ticklish questions.

"We'd like you to tell us what your family and Miguel did on Friday, November 19," said Colon. "The last Friday you were at 40 Tapscott."

Mrs. Berrios rolled her eyes. "Such a long time ago? I don't think I remember anything. But if anything special happened, that I would remember."

"It doesn't have to be anything special," said Colon. "Just your normal day."

Slowly, with obvious effort, Edith Berrios reconstructed that Friday. Miguel had left first, about eight o'clock, to start out early looking for a job. A few moments later Eduardo had kissed her good-bye. Then she had walked the children to P.S. 189 on East

New York Avenue, and then had spent the rest of the morning shopping for the weekend. Around noon she toted the grocery bags upstairs and fixed herself lunch. It was a pleasure to have an hour alone in the house.

At about two o'clock Miguel had come back—as usual without having found a job. If he weren't her favorite brother, she'd have asked him to leave long ago. The apartment was too cramped and she had already spoken to Eduardo about moving to a bigger place, maybe in Manhattan, so that he could leave for work a half-hour later and get home that much earlier. She was determined to move before the weekend was over. Once her mind was set, she moved decisively.

"Go down to the market and get me a half-dozen cartons," she ordered Miguel. "We're going to find a new apartment this weekend. I want to be packed and ready to get out, *pronto*."

He came back shortly with four standard Campbell's Soup cartons and a fifth box three times as big as the others.

"If I fill that monster, who's going to lift it?" Edith demanded. "It's for sure *you* won't be around. Get it out of here." She walked out to pick up her children at school. At about 5:30 they came home to find both Miguel and the unwieldly box gone. In its place he had provided three more standard-sized cartons. The family was eating dinner around seven o'clock, when Miguel came back. He was upset and wanted to borrow twenty dollars, but refused to say why. Eduardo gave him eight dollars. Shortly before midnight he returned to ask for another ten dollars. Eduardo and Edith were in bed, and she did not appreciate this.

"We can't keep giving you money, brother," she said firmly. But Miguel began to weep and beg, claiming he was in big trouble. Unwilling to listen any longer, Edith Berrios took five dollars from under one of the religious statues beside the bed and gave it to him. When she awoke in the morning, Miguel was asleep in his clothes on the couch. He smelled of stale booze, as he often did when he was not working. She and Eduardo assumed he had drunk the money away.

As Seedman now watched in the 76th squad room, Eddie Colon asked Edith Berrios the most critical question of all. He did it by simply handing her a maroon leatherette photo album and opening it to a portrait of Carmen Roldan in her high-school graduation gown.

Mrs. Berrios looked at the portrait for several moments. "Such a sweet-looking girl," she finally said. "But I never saw her. And I remember all my clients."

As she looked up, the detectives saw that her eyes were wet. They seemed to be giving a different answer. The detectives also noted that Edith Berrios had answered the precise question which had never been asked in words.

In another interrogation room Eduardo Berrios, brought over from the restaurant kitchen where he worked in Manhattan, sketched in the first and last hours of Friday, November 19, much as his wife had. He remembered Miguel's leaving in the morning and his two demands for money in the evening. As for what happened during the rest of the day, he had no way of knowing. He had never seen Carmen Roldan or any sign of an oversized box, but he did agree that Miguel had been highly upset that Friday night.

That afternoon, a pair of detectives found Ima Ocassio in a rear tenement apartment not far from her in-laws' place in the South Bronx. Hands on hips, she told them that if they found her husband, Miguel, she wished they'd let her at him. First he had two-timed her, then he had run out altogether. He had fallen behind in the meager support payments the court had ordered, and when she swore out a warrant for nonsupport, he had disappeared totally. Now she was forced to go on welfare. She claimed that it had been nearly a year since she last saw Miguel, but the old woman who lived in the apartment directly below Ima Ocassio told the detectives she had seen him within the week.

"When that fellow needs services from his wife," the old woman snorted, "he bangs the door like a hammer. Bangs it and bellows. A big heavy animal. I have seen him. I have also heard him." The old woman pointed to the ceiling. "All night long this last Tuesday . . . jiggle . . . jiggle . . . jiggle. . . ."

The detectives could hardly blame Ima Ocassio for insisting that she had not seen her husband for nearly a year. If the Welfare Department knew he was coming around, her checks would cut off. If the court knew he was coming around, it might put him in jail. That would mean no more occasional visits which, after all, she did not reject.

Three days after they talked to Ima, the detectives found Miguel in the apartment of a woman in the South Bronx. She too had been abandoned by her husband and was on welfare. Though it was mid-afternoon, they were in bed. Miguel was in no condition to offer any resistance.

"Before questioning him," says Seedman, "I decided to call Simon Lipton down to the 76th once more to look over a lineup. This time, through the one-way mirror, he did not hesitate to identify Miguel Occasio as his passenger with the box. We explained to Miguel in Spanish and English that he did not have to make any statement without a lawyer's advice. Few suspects say a word after that warning—after all, we are practically telling them that they would be dopes to do so—but Miguel insisted on making a statement anyhow.

"On the Friday in question, he claimed to have remained home all day except for a quick trip to get boxes for his sister. In anticipation of moving day, he had loaded the biggest box with junk he no longer needed and thrown it out. He showed us how he had bumpety-bumped it down the stairs. Friday night he claimed to have gone to bed quietly at nine o'clock.

"We had now established that Miguel Ocassio had packed up a large box at his sister's apartment. Edith Berrios had seen it and Miguel himself confirmed it. We had found a neighbor who could testify that she had seen Miguel thumping the box down the stairs that evening. Miguel also confirmed that. We also had a cab driver who had identified Miguel as the man with a box he had taken from Union to Bergen Street. Any jury would be convinced of that much. The only hitch was that we could not connect Miguel to Carmen Roldan that Friday. We could not even show that they had ever seen each other or that Carmen had been anywhere near 40 Tapscott Street. Unless that connection was made we had no case, so on the advice of District Attorney Aaron Koota we told Miguel to go about his business. He walked out of the 76th smiling like a tomcat.

"I didn't mind forgetting about Miguel Ocassio for the time being. We could now focus on his sister, Edith. If Miguel had ever seen Carmen Roldan, I felt the information would come from Edith. But she was a strong woman who would have to come around in her own good time. I assigned Eddie Colon and Tony Cordero to stick by her in case that time came."

Several times each week the two detectives visited Edith Berrios. Sometimes they just talked about their own families, at others they went back over the details of November 19. One afternoon just before Christmas, Edith suddenly remembered an odd detail she had put out of her mind. When she had come home for lunch that Friday, an unpleasant smell hit her nostrils as soon as she opened the door. When Miguel came home shortly after, he claimed to smell nothing, but Eduardo had wrinkled up his nose when he got home that evening. Late Saturday night, as they were finishing packing, Edith checked the breadbox. She found an Italian bread bag filled with what looked like human excrement. The detectives agreed that they too would push the incident out of their minds.

Early in January the Berrios family again moved, this time to a nicer apartment further north in the Bronx. Colon and Cordero pitched in to help pack up boxes, but though they tried not to show it, they were discouraged.

Edith Berrios picked it right up. "What's the matter, fellows?" she asked.

"I'll be frank," said Cordero, a man with the strong features and slick black hair of a bullfighter. "For nearly a month now we've been hoping you'd remember something more to help us. But nothing seems to be happening. Maybe we should forget about Carmen and get on to other cases."

"You are doing right," Edith said firmly. "I am sure you will bring justice to the poor girl and her family if you do not give up."

Several days later, on the morning of January 19, Edith Berrios met the detectives with a smile. She had remembered something else. When she came home for lunch that Friday, she had found a black ski jacket draped on a kitchen chair. She had mentioned it to Miguel, who claimed not to know to whom it belonged. But when he went out to fetch the cartons, she noticed that the jacket was gone too.

Back in Brooklyn, Colon and Cordero asked Mrs. Roldan whether Carmen had owned such a jacket. As a matter of fact, she did. Nobody had noticed what Carmen wore when she left home that morning, but the black ski jacket was nowhere to be found. Though it had not turned up in the box with the rest of her clothes, it was too cold outside for Carmen to be wearing just a blouse and skirt.

The next morning, when the detectives turned up at the Berrios apartment, Edith Berrios said her daughter Diana had something to tell them.

Diana Berrios was a shy, bright seven-year-old who adored Tony Cordero. Now in the living room she perched on his knee.

"I remember on the day before we moved, me and my sister were playing in Uncle Miguel's closet. We were making knots in a cord we had found in there. Then he came in and grabbed it away. He grabbed us both and said that if we ever told about the cord, we'd be sorry. Then when Mama saw the cord was cut on the blind, she got mad at *me*. I told her I didn't do it. But I was afraid of Uncle Miguel so I didn't say anything about when we were playing with it in the closet."

"Are you still afraid of Uncle Miguel?" asked Cordero. Diana, not looking up, nodded her head.

Cordero put his arm around the girl. "Well, from now on, you can call me Uncle Tony. And you don't have to be afraid of anyone. Uncle Tony will take care of you."

"I had forgot about blaming the girls for the cord," said Edith Berrios. "It was such a small thing. Besides, we were moving anyway." When detectives had asked her about the cut tilt cord weeks ago, she had remembered nothing about it.

The next morning Edith Berrios asked Colon and Cordero if they would be interested in attending a seance that night.

"We respect your abilities in this area," Colon said gently, "but it's really not our thing."

Mrs. Berrios nodded and smiled. "I know that. I know you don't believe in the power of the saints. That's why I thought you might want to come. If you come with an open mind and not to make fun of us, it may even be profitable."

"How do you mean, profitable?"

"I mean that if the saints smile on our efforts tonight, maybe it will help to bring justice to Carmen."

"If there's any chance of that, we'll come."

"Which of Carmen's sisters was she closest to?"

"Demaris, the seventeen-year-old."

"Perhaps you could bring her along. The saints will look for the heart that loved Carmen most dearly."

They arrived with Demaris that night at ten o'clock. The children were asleep and Edith had asked Eduardo to leave for the evening. She wore a freshly ironed white cotton dress. The detectives noticed that she seemed full of anticipation.

A table in the center of the living room had been covered with fresh linen and lined with white candles and statues of the saints. Suddenly Demaris let out a low cry and grasped Cordero's arm. On the arm of one of the chairs at the table was a black ski jacket.

"Don't be afraid," said Mrs. Berrios. "It's not the jacket your sister wore." She asked Demaris whether she would be willing to wear it tonight if that would help bring Carmen justice.

Her head bowed, Demaris nodded.

"And if it would also help your sister, would you be brave enough to get in a box while I try to reach the saints?"

Demaris began shaking. It was too much. Mrs. Berrios put her hand on the girl's shoulder. "If it scares you so much, never mind," she said. "It will be enough to wear the black jacket."

Demaris slipped on the jacket. Mrs. Berrios directed her to sit at the end of the table while the detectives took seats on each side. She turned out the lights, lit the three candles at the head of the table. Moonlight iced the window. Mrs. Berrios crossed herself and began.

"Tonight, we are gathered to ask the saints to help us bring justice to the body of Carmen Roldan. We ask this, not of all the saints, but only of those who were also martyred in the days of their youth. They are the ones this sweet girl's soul has already joined in heaven, and now her soul is at perfect peace. We know that and are thankful. But now we ask for justice for her poor body here on earth. I pray to the saints on their martyred bodies that they send us a sign, a vision which will help bring justice to the body of Carmen on earth while her own soul is blessed in heaven. . . ."

Mrs. Berrios crossed her palms over her breasts, twining a gold crucifix chain in her fingers. Her eyes closed, her breathing became deep and even. The others sat in silence. Minutes went by. Suddenly, Mrs. Berrios took the crucifix in her hands and held it tightly.

"I see . . . I see . . . the bedroom of my brother," she said in a calm voice. "It is empty but filled with sadness. . . . My brother comes in now . . . he gets down on his knees beside the bed. He reaches under. He pulls out by the feet the body of . . . Carmen. . . ."

Demaris began to weep, but Edith Berrios did not seem to hear.

". . . My brother picks up the broken body. . . . He lifts her up high and lowers her by the feet into the carton. . . . He takes a purse, umbrella, shoes from under the bed . . . puts them in the box . . . wraps the box up with twine. . . . He drags the box out of the bedroom and closes the door. . . . The room is still heavy with sorrow. . . ."

Mrs. Berrios opened her eyes. Her breath, which had been coming in deep gasps, suddenly was normal. Her face glistened with sweat, though the living room was anything but hot.

"I feel so weak," she said. "I feel almost as if I had delivered a child. Did I say anything?"

The detectives gaped at her.

"Did you *say* anything?" asked Cordero. "You don't know what you said?"

Mrs. Berrios smiled serenely. One by one, she blew out the candles. "When I am blessed with a trance, I am lifted out of this place into another," she said. "But when I awake, I never know where it was or what I saw." She turned on the lights.

The detectives did not visit Mrs. Berrios the next day. They felt the need for some perspective. Did she really expect to reveal such crucial information and now get away with claiming she didn't remember it?

"What do we do, Chief?" they asked.

"Stay with her," answered Seedman. "Let her follow her saints on her own timetable. But whatever you do, just don't accuse her of faking it. After all, it was the only way she could figure out to finger her brother and live with it later."

"Still no memory of the trance?" asked Colon the next morning.

"No. It was a vision granted for those moments by the saints and then taken back."

The detectives nodded glumly. Mrs. Berrios smiled. "But I do have a surprise for you today, gentlemen."

"I can't take any more surprises, Edith," said Cordero.

"You'll like this one. For these last two months, I have wanted to tell you certain things. But I did not because I feared for my daughters, my husband, and even for myself. I feared for all of us because of what my brother might do if I told you these things.

"But now I'll tell you a secret. I do remember one thing from my trance. The voices of the saints told me I no longer need be afraid for my family. The saints have placed their protecting hands over us all, so I will tell you the story, as much as I know, of when Carmen was killed."

While Colon and Cordero sat motionless, not even daring to take a note, Edith Berrios told how on Thursday morning she had been about to go out to the bank when she heard a gentle knock on the door.

"Mrs. Berrios?" asked a slender, pretty, and well-scrubbed young girl. She apologized for turning up without telephoning, but she was just in the neighborhood and so many people had told her how Mrs. Berrios had helped them with their problems. "I've been hurting from stomach cramps these last few weeks. The doctor can't find any problem but I am sure you could help me."

"I will be glad to try," said Edith Berrios. "But now is not a good time. Why don't you come back tomorrow?"

"That would be perfect. I have to be in the neighborhood anyway to sign in for unemployment. I can stop by right after."

As Mrs. Berrios shut the door, she was aware of her brother, Miguel, standing behind her. He said nothing but his breathing was heavy. As she went back inside, she heard Miguel go out.

Friday morning was nasty and cold, but Edith Berrios was resolved to go into Manhattan to find a better apartment for her family. Feeling that it was better to have a man along, she insisted that Miguel escort her and the girls. They all bundled up and left 40 Tapscott Street at nine o'clock. Miguel was dragging as if he did not want to make this trip.

Edith spotted two of her girlfriends in front of the Associated supermarket on Sutter Avenue and introduced them to the brooding Miguel. They all got on the elevated subway together, but when the friends got off at Nevins Street, Miguel, claiming it was too raw a day to go apartment-hunting in Manhattan, also got off too. Just as the train doors closed, Edith and the girls hurried out to join him. Maybe he was right. The girls were already shivering. They took the train back to Sutter Avenue.

"The girls and I will go look at shoes," said Edith on the platform. Miguel nodded and, without a word, he walked quickly to the stairs to the street and left them. As she was shopping later, Edith remembered she had promised to see the pretty girl who had turned up yesterday morning. But she would be back. As the girl herself had said, Edith Berrios had helped people with problems no one else could solve. They always came back.

At noon, when Edith came home with her daughters, she could barely open the door because of a large box just inside the living room. It was tied with twine, firmly but sloppily.

Edith was irritated. "What is this thing?" she shouted toward Miguel's closed bedroom door.

He came out looking drawn and shaky. "Since you're so anxious to move, I though I'd pack up all the junk I'll never need." He dragged the box back to his bedroom.

"And what's that stink in here?" Edith called after him.

"I don't smell a thing," he said. Edith thought she saw an odd grin twist her brother's face as he closed the door. As she fixed lunch in the kitchen, she saw a strange black ski jacket hanging on a chair.

She gave the girls a bite of lunch, and took them to a neighbor's apartment down the block to play. When she returned at about 12:45, the box was gone. The smell remained. Miguel came back a half-hour later.

"It doesn't look to me like you packed *anything*," she said as she dried the lunch dishes with a towel. "What did you put in that huge thing to make it so heavy?"

"What thing?" asked Miguel pleasantly.

"Oh, come on. You had a huge box. I could hardly open the door because of it."

"You're a crazy women. You fool too much with those saints. I didn't have any box."

"The girls saw it too," Edith said.

Miguel grabbed the towel, twisted it tight, and looped it around his sister's neck. "Don't say another word to anyone about a box," he snarled. "I will kill you with this towel or my bare hands if you do." Miguel stalked out of the apartment, taking the ski jacket with him.

Later in the afternoon Edith heard a thumping on the stairs. She opened the door enough to see Miguel struggling with the box on the landing just above. Apparently he had hidden it up there for the last several hours. She closed the door quietly.

The rest of Friday evening took place exactly as she had told the detectives earlier. The next day she rented the apartment at 535 East 163rd Street, and on Sunday they moved.

"One funny thing," Mrs. Berrios now told the detectives. "Miguel slept on the sofa again Saturday night. But when the mover came in the morning and started to drag the mattress off his bed, Miguel jumped at the poor man. He wouldn't let anyone touch the mattress. He insisted that we should leave it behind because it was no good. I said to my brother, 'Miguel, we only just bought that mattress.' But he wouldn't let anyone near it. I said, 'Miguel, you'll have to sleep on the floor in the new apartment.' He said, 'I don't care.' We didn't have all day to argue with him, so it was left.

"Miguel stayed with us for three days at the new place. Before he left, he grabbed me by the throat again. 'If you tell anyone that I've been here, or if you say anything about the box, I'll kill you,' he said. On the way out, he knocked all my saints to the floor.

"That's why I have feared my brother these last two months," Edith Berrios said to Colon and Cordero. "But now I know that even though he might knock over their statues, he can't stop the saints from protecting me and the family. That is what they told me in the trance the other night."

"Now that Edith had supplied the details of Thursday's visit by Carmen and the events of Friday," says Seedman, "it was not too difficult to reconstruct what must have happened.

"Miguel had dashed home from the Sutter Avenue train platform before ten o'clock that morning. Carmen Roldan, meanwhile, had checked in with the unemployment office at nine-forty-five. It was only a ten-minute walk to 40 Tapscott Street. Miguel opened the door when Carmen knocked. He told her to come in to wait for his sister, she would be right back. He knew that he had time— Edith was taking the children to shop for shoes—and he began to paw at Carmen. She fought. In a fury, he beat her on the face as he dragged her to his bed. Unexpectedly, she fainted. Miguel would be in big trouble when she revived. If she revived.

"Miguel cut a length of the venetian-blind tilt cord and strangled Carmen with it. As she died, her muscles relaxed and the bedroom was filled with the smell of excrement.

"He ran to the kitchen to find something to put it in. The Italian bread bag had only a stub left, so he took back the bag and scooped up the mess. But what should he do with the bag? Put it back in the breadbox. He picked Carmen up and rolled her under his bed. The mattress was stained, so he flipped it over and rushed out to find a box. He remembered seeing a large one in front of a furniture store on Rockaway Avenue. Luckily, it was still there.

"Back at the apartment, he pulled Carmen out from under the

bed and stuffed her in. As soon as it was dark he would drop off the box in another neighborhood. Even if his sister saw it, he could say that it was full of his personal junk. He cursed the girl for resisting him, but he had the feeling that if she had lived, she would not have kept her mouth shut. It served her right for being such a goody-goody."

Although Edith Berrios' statement went far toward firming up the case against Miguel Ocassio, District Attorney Koota was still not quite ready to present the evidence to a grand jury. He hoped to be able to find Carmen Roldan's black ski jacket and the mattress. Seedman had already sent detectives to ask the new tenants at 40 Tapscott if the Berrios' had left behind a mattress, but there was no sign of it. In the rear courtyard the detectives found several shredded mattresses. None matched the description of the one the Berrios had bought for Miguel.

"Since Demaris Roldan had taken home the ski jacket Mrs. Berrios gave her at the seance," says Seedman, "I had the Photo unit snap a picture of her wearing it, then superimpose a photo of Carmen's head. All the Spanish-language newspapers ran the picture on the front page, but no one came forward who had found the jacket wherever Miguel threw it. It had disappeared.

"Aaron Koota finally decided we would go ahead with what we had. On February 9 we booked Miguel Ocassio at the 76th. At his trial he claimed he could not have killed Carmen on Friday morning, November 19, because he had gone with his sister to cash an insurance-settlement check at the Chemical Bank branch on Court Street, clear across the borough."

Koota produced a photostat of the check, in the amount of $528, stamped for deposit the day before, on Thursday, November 18.

"That seemed to settle the matter. But Miguel's lawyer argued that the bank clerks must have made a mistake. The DA let him argue. It seemed farfetched to worry that the jury would be swayed. But with so much of the evidence linking the defendant to the victim circumstantial, the jury came back hopelessly split."

At the retrial the District Attorney presented detailed testimony from Chemical Bank officers to show that the $528 check could not have been cashed any day other than Thursday, but this time Miguel wasn't even interested in that alibi. He tried to pin the blame for the murder on a nephew he now claimed had been in the apartment that Friday. The jury was not persuaded. They found him guilty and he was sentenced to seven and a half to fifteen years in prison.

"Back when we were groping for a handle to this case, in the first weeks after Carmen was found in the box," says Seedman, "I had assigned teams of detectives to check out every one of Carmen's friends, every co-worker at her old job in the vinyl factory, every spiritualist we could find. In all, I threw over a hundred crack detectives into the case. Yet Carmen's murder was only briefly noted by the newspapers and quickly forgotten. The exception was *El Diario* and the smaller Spanish-language papers published for the Puerto Rican community.

"Just as the team of detectives involved in the Gallo–Profaci wars in 1960 was known as the Pizza Squad, the Spanish-speaking team in the Roldan case was known in the Bureau as the Rice-and-Beans Squad. Tony Cordero from that squad still stays in touch with the Roldan family, giving the kids the kind of advice and encouragement only a father can provide. The one who counted on him most was Demaris. When her marriage day comes, I suspect it will be Cordero who gives the bride away."

Albert Seedman at his desk in the cavernous Centre Street office of the Chief of Detectives. (Ken Regan/Camera 5)

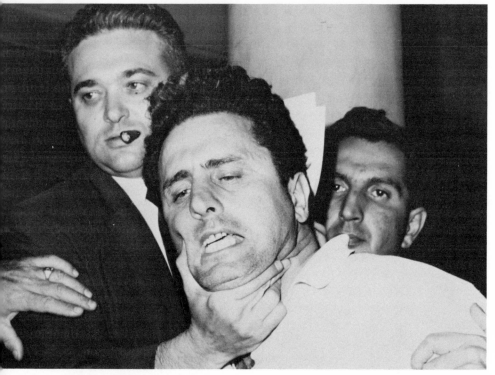

TOP: *As a young sergeant in the Bronx, Seedman collared this burglary suspect as he was clambering down a fire escape.*

BOTTOM: *The photo that cost Captain Seedman a promotion: he complies with photographers' requests for a clear head shot of Tony ("Red") Dellurnia, a suspect in the 1962 Brooklyn killings of Patrolmen Luke Fallon and John Finnegan.* (New York Journal American)

OPPOSITE: *Setting for murder. As she lay in the dingy vestibule at the foot of these narrow stairs, an already wounded Kitty Genovese was finished off by Winston Mosely as thirty-eight neighbors listened unheeding to her screams.* (Dave Sagarin)

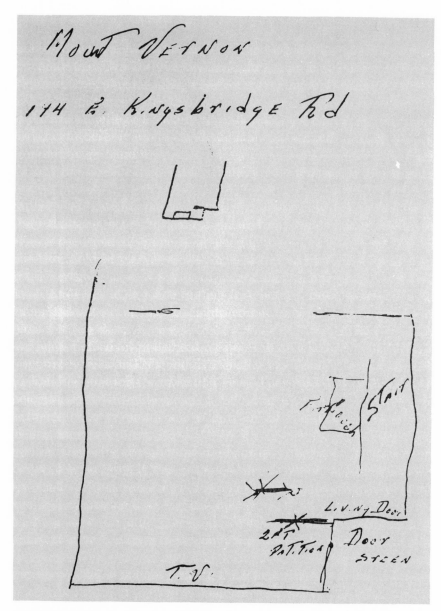

TOP: *Under interrogation by Seedman and other detectives, Winston Mosely sketched the living room where he killed Annie May Johnson. Note the curious handwriting and the stick-figure corpse marked with an X over the genital area.*

OPPOSITE: *How to steal a million dollars: the mastermind behind the Mays Department Store swindle bought business forms printed on the same safety paper used for Mays' checks, then manufactured checks of his own.*

2613

NATIONAL AUTO APPRAISERS
245 EAST 80TH STREET • NEW YORK, N. Y. 10021
APPRAISER'S REPORT

MODEL	SERIAL NO.	ENGINE NO.

OR CONDITION	GOOD	FAIR	POOR
HEADLINING	☐	☐	☐
UPHOLSTERY	☐	☐	☐
FLOOR MATS	☐	☐	☐

OR CONDITION

FRONT RIGHT FENDER	C. REAR RIGHT FENDER
FRONT LEFT FENDER	D. REAR LEFT FENDER

GOOD ☐   FAIR ☐   POOR ☐

MISSION	REAR END	FRONT END	MOTOR
	PAINT	APP. RECONDITIONING COSTS	WHOLESALE VALUE AS IS

DITIONAL REMARKS: GIVE THE GENERAL DESCRIPTION AND CONDITION OF CAR; NOTE, ANY ERASURES OR ALTERATIONS ON THIS REPORT
ES THIS REPORT INVALID.

J. W. **MAYS** INC.   510 FULTON ST. BROOKLYN 1, NEW YORK

1-784
260

HECK NO.	PAY EXACTLY	DOLLARS	CENTS	$	AMOUNT		DATE			
					DOLLARS CENTS SPECIMEN		MONTH DAY YEAR			VENDOR NO.

SPECIMEN

J. W. MAYS INC.

UNDERWRITERS TRUST COMPANY
50 BROADWAY, NEW YORK

SPECIMEN

AUTHORIZED SIGNATURE

⑃0 260 07841⑃

APPRAISER'S SIGNATURE

Bomber Sam Melville and accomplice Jane Alpert converted this East Village apartment into a war center: right, a .30-caliber carbine rifle and two 9 mm "grease guns" (submachine guns); top right, an automatic pistol; scattered around the room, alarm clocks, tape, batteries, boxes of wire, pamphlets and manuals— all bomb-making apparatus. The New York Post *on the table headlines their work.*

The fruits of their labor: (OPPOSITE TOP) *the sixteenth floor of Chase Manhattan Plaza. Melville chose his target carefully—that floor was headquarters for Chase International Operations; directly below was the executive office of David Rockefeller.* (OPPOSITE BOTTOM) *Albert Seedman and New York FBI Director John Malone examine damage at the Whitehall Street Induction Center.*

In eerie silence on an empty Brooklyn street, this packing case stood undisturbed for six hours. Inside was the body of twenty-one-year-old Carmen Roldan.

THE MELVILLE CASE

On the clear moonless midnight of July 26, 1969, a bomb went off on the sagging old United Fruit Company pier that juts off the eastern tip of lower Manhattan into the fast black current of the North River.

Apparently the bomb had been placed against the big steel door to the north bay of the pier's warehouse. Through that door once had passed most of the city's bananas, but those shipments had long since been rerouted to ports as distant as Albany. In fact, United Fruit now leased the pier to a tugboat operator. The bomb was powerful enough to do great damage, except that a shipment of thirty thousand peat-moss planters, piled on the other side of the big steel door, had absorbed the force of the explosion like so much cotton. So had the water beneath the pier. Even so, the blast twisted the steel door into jagged sculpture, splintered timbers all around it and blown-out windows as far away as the guardhouse in front of the pier.

In the morning the Bomb Squad estimated that the job had required twenty-five to thirty sticks of dynamite. "Frankly, I didn't pay too much attention to the report," says Seedman, who had been promoted to Assistant Chief Inspector in June and put in command of Manhattan South. "Nobody was hurt. Nobody was even meant to be hurt, since the bomb had been set well away from the guardhouse. The damage was not extensive. I guess the biggest casualties were those fat gray rats you see waddling around the piers at night or swimming between the pilings.

"But even though this was not a major case, I found myself thinking about it. It was like a puzzle I worked on at odd moments. Why had somebody wanted to bomb this old pier? Further up the river, of course, there were piers worth plundering. I had once seen the warehouse on the French Line pier: at one side ten thousand cases of Mumm's Cordon Rouge champagne were stacked and on the other Michelin tires were piled right up to the rafters. Now, that was a cargo worth blowing a hole in the door for! But United Fruit's pier was a broken-down old wreck with poor security. Its most valuable cargo was the peat moss, and who would bomb a pier for that? During those first weeks I could only imagine one reasonable motive: someone had a grudge against United Fruit or the tugboat company that leased the pier. In any case, the bombing barely made the papers; the big news of that week was that man had walked on the moon.

"Investigating a bombing is difficult," says Seedman. "In a murder case, you may not find the weapon at all, and if you do, it's usually intact. But a bomb usually destroys itself and we're lucky to find any part of it. In the case of United Fruit any possible residue might have dropped into the river. You can usually pinpoint the time of a murder pretty closely, but a time bomb, which normally is set off by the hour hand of a watch or clock, can be left at the bomb site up to twelve hours before the hand closes contact. In that time the pier bomber could have come and gone unnoticed.

"Around eleven that night the guard had seen a boy and girl fooling with a motorcycle across from the pier. But even though the piers are fairly deserted after dark, that did not seem unusual. A West Side Highway exit is just up the street, and vehicles are always limping off with mechanical troubles. Motorcycles are too conspicuous to be used for crime, anyhow. I suspected that whoever placed the bomb had simply walked over from a nearby subway stop. He could have hopped up to the apron of the pier at water's edge, where he couldn't be spotted from the guardhouse, walked fifty feet to the door of the north bay to drop off the package, then left the same way.

"Of course, it was the 'Why?' not the 'How?' that puzzled me. As the weeks went by detectives from the First Squad worked hard looking for leads, but without witnesses, suspects, fragments of the bomb, or letters in which somebody took credit for the act, they got nowhere. Yet this bombing had been carried out for a reason that eventually was bound to become apparent. It was like the snake one of the kids says he saw in the bathroom the day you open up the summer house. You might not see any sign of it for the longest time, but one day, when you've forgotten about it, it will wriggle out from under the bed."

Three and a half weeks after the United Fruit incident another bomb exploded just after eleven o'clock on the evening of August 20. This time it went off on the eighth floor of the elegant new office tower of the Marine Midland Bank at 140 Broadway in the financial district, a five-minute walk from the pier.

Even though all markets have closed, the Wall Street area is not altogether dark at that hour. As the day workers are leaving a horde of clerical workers appears to process the day's checks, transfer security certificates, and generally put accounts in order. On the eighth floor at Marine Midland seventeen women were processing the bank's corporate trust records, when the bomb exploded near one of the elevator shafts. All about them, abruptly, the ceiling tile shuddered and fell, revealing a tangle of wires, metal conduits, and dust and flying paper. Office machines and dozens of typewriters crashed to the floor, a two-ton computer moved three feet, windowglass fell to the street. Beside the elevators a ten-foot hole opened up in the floor, sending tons of debris crashing below, to where fifty more women were at work.

Their faces covered with plaster dust, their dresses shredded by flying glass, the women fled down the fire stairs and out to the marble entrance plaza. There they huddled in a corner across from the huge fiery-red metal cube sculpted by Isamu Noguchi. Looking up, they could see the calm dark façade of the tower marred by the ugly jagged windows of the two floors where they had been working. Remarkably, the worst injuries sustained were one dislocated shoulder and a mild concussion.

"By the time I got there at midnight," says Seedman, "Emergency Service had already set up floodlamps. With all that plaster dust hanging in the light, wreckage three feet deep, the elevator doors blasted apart, and that gaping crater on the eighth floor, I felt I was back in wartime. Except that during the war I understood the reason behind the destruction. Here, in another part of the bank, robbery might have been the motive. All evening long, money and negotiable securities are carted back and forth between Wall Street businesses. Half the trucks on those narrow streets belong to Brink's or Wells Fargo. But these women in the corporate trust department were just keeping the books. They handled no cash, no securities.

"The only other obvious motive was that somebody was mad as hell at the bank. All of us feel that way occasionally, but this was one case when a customer or employee had decided to take action. It wouldn't be unprecedented. Spite was the motive for all twenty-six bombings carried out by George Metesky, the "Mad Bomber" of the late 1950s. He simply felt that his former employer, Consolidated Edison, had done him wrong. But at least Metesky did us one favor: every time he planted a bomb he sent a postcard announcing it. A lieutenant at the time, I spent three weeks in the Motor Vehicle office, thumbing through license applications to see if we could match any of them with the handwriting on one of those postcards. As it turned out, Con Ed finally let us have access to their records and the match to Metesky's handwriting was made there.

"I could see two things for us to do that morning. First, I asked the Bomb Squad to sift through the debris around the crater. Maybe they'd find a clue to what kind of bomb it had been. The second task would also require sifting, except that it would be of people instead of debris. I wanted my detectives to interview every employee on those floors, locate every employee who had been discharged during the last two years under less than happy circumstances, and check out every one of the bank's customers who had been recently turned down for a loan. If this had been a spite-bombing, we might turn up the nut who did it.

"Yet I can't say that I felt optimistic about picking out the culprit through any connection with the bank. In the back of my head, I felt this job had another origin. I also suspected that if we could solve this case, we'd close the United Fruit Company case in the bargain."

Seedman knew that the task he had set for his detectives would take months unless he allotted a major force of detectives to the job. From within his eleven squads he picked twelve men. He favored older men because they had the patience needed to work through so many interviews. But the man who became the master specialist in this case, and in the cases of many of the bombings that followed, was a detective Seedman had transferred from the garment district, Pete Perotta.

"If I needed someone to draw an absolutely straight line down the center of a highway," says Seedman, "I'd pick Pete Perotta. It wouldn't be any straighter than Pete himself. I'd also trust my own books to him, knowing that nothing would ever be astray and the columns would be exactly even. Pete didn't marry until he was forty. Just about the time other men start to go a little flat, Pete got cheerier. He was the man I trusted to do the meticulous work I needed on the Marine Midland case."

Perotta's job was simplified when the bank furnished him with computer printouts listing each employee who had been dismissed, with the notation "voluntary" or "involuntary." Most of the "in-voluntaries" had been let go for too many absences. None provided any leads. In the corporate trust department itself the detectives found the usual webs of dislikes and jealousies among the clerks.

"I know who did it," whispered one woman to Perotta. "For *sure.*" She pointed to one of her co-workers. "She even keeps a gun in her purse. I saw it once when she was at the coffee machine."

The woman readily opened her purse for Perotta. Under the cosmetics was a .32-caliber snubnose pistol. "I leave work at one o'clock in the morning," she told Perotta. "I walk through the dark streets, take the subway, and walk six blocks through the jungle of Brownsville. It's almost two o'clock when I get home. Would *you* do that every night without your gun?"

"No, ma'am," said Perotta. "But you will have to get a license. Right now you're a lawbreaker." But not a bomber, Perotta thought.

Later in the day he talked to a man whose application for a new car loan had been turned down at the branch on the ground floor. As he walked out the loan officer had heard him muttering, "This place ought to be blown up." The would-be borrower turned out to be a frazzled man with too many children to support on his counterman's salary. To Perotta he did not look like a bomber, either.

While the interviews continued, the Bomb Squad was doing its own sifting. After several days all they found was the mangled mainspring from an alarm clock. The clock appeared to have been a Westclox "Baby Ben," the most popular hand-wound model in the country. It had been wired to between twenty and twenty-five sticks of dynamite—about the same payload that had been used at the United Fruit pier.

"For the first time in my twenty-seven years on the force," says Seedman, "I began checking out the availability of dynamite in this city. Upstate, it turned out, a farmer could go to his local building-supply store and buy dynamite simply by signing a log book. In many places a perfect stranger could walk in and buy a box of dynamite without ever showing proper identification. In New Hampshire at the time we discovered it was as easy to buy dynamite as baby food.

"New York City, though, is a different story. For demolition or any other work within the five boroughs, you first need a permit from the Department of Buildings' Dynamite Division. Even with a permit you can only buy from Explo Industries in the Bronx which has been granted a monopoly on dynamite sales for purposes of control. That control is very tight: you can't keep the stuff at a construction site overnight, even under guard. The Explo truck comes and drops it off at six o'clock in the morning, and picks up any leftover sticks that evening. Each stick is controlled by a serial number on the red casing. The whole procedure makes it hard for stray dynamite to get loose in the city.

"But it turns out that back on July seventh something unusual occurred at the Explo yard, a bleak half-acre compound surrounded by a high fence with two concrete blockhouses, one for the dynamite, the other for blasting caps."

The neighborhood is deserted after dark, but Explo had never had any trouble with robbers. The old man who takes the midnight watch, John Katzenberger, used to keep a few stray dogs in the compound, but more for company than to guard the place. Then one night early in July, Katzenberger found one of the dogs poisoned. The next night the other disappeared.

Katzenberger was reading the *New York Post* in the office at one o'clock on the morning of July seventh when he heard noises. As he got up to investigate, three men burst through the door. They were young whites, wearing denim work clothes and with red handkerchiefs over their noses and mouths. They pointed guns at the old man.

"We want dynamite," one said.

They took three boxes from one blockhouse. Manufactured by DuPont in Delaware, each box contained sixty-five sticks. At the other blockhouse they took two cartons of blasting caps, fifty to a box.

"How about detonators?" asked the man with the gun.

"You don't need detonators," snapped Katzenberger. "You can set off the blasting caps only with an electrical current. Anybody knows that."

"Don't be a wiseass," said the man with the gun. But Katzenberger sensed that he would not be harmed even if he did talk back. Two of the men hauled the boxes out the front gate, while the third took the guard out back to keep him from seeing where the others were heading. Then he tied Katzenberger up with a clothesline and left.

"This was a curious robbery," says Seedman. "In the first place, almost nobody knows, unless they take the trouble to find out, that Explo is the only place in town to get dynamite. That was all the robbers were after. They didn't take Katzenberger's money. It was also curious that anyone would take such a risk for only a few boxes of dynamite. Since they had done the research to discover Explo, they must have also learned that outside the city they'd have no trouble purchasing what they needed. Those three fifty-pound boxes plus the blasting caps would sell at retail for less than $200. Who would risk going to jail for a miserable two hundred bucks?

"One other detail stuck in my mind. The watchman said all three men were wearing red bandannas over their faces. That was odd. Usually bandits just wear a pair of sunglasses and a hat. In a bank, where they may be photographed, they'll slip on a skier's wind mask or something left over from Hallowe'en. But red bandannas? That went out with Tom Mix movies."

Nine days after the Marine Midland bombing Pete Perotta laid on Seedman's desk a copy of *RAT*. Several underground newspapers were then thriving in the city, but *RAT* and the *East Village Other* (*EVO*)—named to distinguish it from the "Establishment" *Village Voice*—were the largest. Large or small, these papers served the kids who gravitated to the seamy drug-ridden neighborhood known as the East Village. *RAT* readers could find the latest prices on pot, mescaline, LSD, speed, cocaine, and a full range of "ups" and "downs" quoted as openly as the commodity prices in the *Wall Street Journal*. They could learn how to get on welfare, survive a bad drug trip, and wrest good service out of a hospital emergency room. *RAT* would explain to newcomers how their long hair made them vulnerable to muggers, who could grab it and bring their victim down from behind, while outraged articles printed in more outrageous graphics reviled the United States for its Vietnam policies and domestic evils. The writing was usually crass or obscene; photos and drawings tended to be the same—as befits spokesmen of the "counter-culture."

"What is this piece of crap?" snorted Seedman.

"Take a look at page three, Chief," said Perotta.

There, in a late August issue, Seedman saw the answer which thousands of hours of detective work had failed to produce. Under the heading, "THIS RELEASE IS FOR THE UNDERGROUND MEDIA ONLY— THERE WILL BE NO COMMUNICATION WITH THE PIG MEDIA," was the following letter, which *RAT* claimed to have received in the mail.

> *The explosive device set off at the Marine Midland Grace Trust Company on the night of August 20th was an act of political sabotage. Considerable damage was done to the security files and building structure of the W.R. Grace Company, which extensively controls agricultural and chemical holdings throughout Latin America. . . . This was the third of such acts, beginning with the explosion of a grenade arsenal in New Jersey on July 15 and the blowing up of a United Fruit pier on July 26, commemorating the Cuban Revolution. . . .*

Next to the unsigned letter there was a five-paragraph commentary, written more in the style of *RAT*.

> *. . . U.S. Business spends an enormous portion of its time raping the Third World. . . . If you lived in Latin America, you wouldn't leave out . . . the empire of Peter Grace (which includes, as the banking division, Marine Midland Grace Trust). . . . Grace owns land, shipping facilities, chemical plants, economies, and people.*
>
> *The empire got its start in bird shit. Don't laugh, it's profitable business. Bird shit (guano) is "harvested" off islands in the Pacific and used as fertilizer. But, Grace quickly moved into more dignified pursuits. Grace became The name in Latin American shipping . . . and also owned an airline (Panagra) until recently. It now has extensive interests in sugar . . . liquor . . . chemicals.*

There are reasons why Grace isn't known as a household word. U.S. business is, after all, an elite operation, and people aren't raised to think that business is the sort of thing they should try to understand; it's a given. Grace is just the name on another office building. But for Latin Americans, Grace—W.R. Grace, Marine Midland Grace —is an enemy, an owner. That, apparently, is why the Marine Midland Bank was bombed.

"As I read this," says Seedman, "my first thought was that I should have realized that Castro's revolution was the 'Movement of 26 July.' That might have started me thinking in the right direction a lot earlier. Our best move now was to get the original of that letter. Also the envelope—except I doubted that there ever was one. That commentary beside the letter seemed a giveaway. Whoever had written this knew plenty about W. R. Grace, and, even rarer among these kids, about how business works. This stuff struck me as more than commentary—it had an insider's point of view, as if the writer was telling why *he* did something, not why someone else did. The last sentence explaining 'apparently' why Marine Midland was bombed, rang particularly hollow.

"I suspected this letter and commentary had originated in the offices of *RAT*. If I was right, they'd make sure it was hard to prove. Still, things were looking up. So far the bombers had slipped away each time without a sign. Now they had left us a lead in black-and-white as a pure gift. They were more than confident, they were brazen. In the long run, that's one defect for which they usually pay."

The *RAT* office was on the second floor at 135 East Fourteenth Street, a broken-down building on a block of cheap stores. A large orange-neon sign across the façade of the building had originally said "PHOTOGRAPHS WHILE U WAIT," but certain letters had been tampered with so that now it read, "*HOT** RAT*S WHILE U WAIT." Shortly after two o'clock Pete Perotta climbed the smelly stairway and stood for a moment in the doorway. The place was filthy, with papers scattered around, old food containers in the corners, stacks of old *RAT* everywhere. Staring at him were three bedraggled girls and two longhaired boys. Perotta shook his head. Didn't these kids know they'd feel better if they looked better? But that was not what he was here to say.

"Who's the boss around here?" asked Perotta as the kids continued to stare.

They shrugged. "We don't have a boss," one of the boys answered. "It's one big happy family."

"Families have a boss," said Perotta. "At least they should."

The boy finally pointed to a slender girl with straight dark hair; she was dressed in blue jeans and a man's pin-striped shirt. As Perotta approached, her nearly black eyes did not even blink. Perotta felt uncomfortable addressing himself to a woman who obviously wore no bra.

"May I have your name, please?"

"Jane Alpert," she said, slouching against a battered desk.

"We're investigating that bombing at the bank downtown a couple of weeks ago, and I need to borrow that letter you published on page three of the last issue."

"A letter? . . ." The girl looked blank.

"The letter you got in the mail about the Marine Midland Bank bombing." Perotta took out the clipping.

"Oh, *that,*" said Jane Alpert. "I remember that. I typed it up for the printer myself. But all that stuff gets thrown away as soon as it's used. We'd be up to our asses in paper if we didn't. All newspapers do that."

"Who wrote this?" asked Perotta, pointing to the commentary.

"A fact sheet came along with the letter," she said. "All the information came straight off it. I hardly had to change a word."

"You threw that out too. Right?"

"I'm afraid so."

"Well, listen. You mind if I buy a couple of back issues of your publication? Say for the last four months?"

"Take as many as you want," said Jane Alpert. "They're thirty-five cents each."

Much as he hated giving even a nickel to those kids, Perotta left with $2.80 worth of *RATs.* That evening he showed Seedman an earlier issue, dated August 5. Buried in an underground-news roundup, under the headline "UNITED FRUIT PIER BOMBED," was an article of interest to the detectives:

A pier on the Hudson River owned by the United Fruit Company was blasted by a bomb on midnight of Cuban Independence Day, July 26th. Police said the bomb was either dynamite or a plastic ex-

plosive and that they were investigating the "motives and method."

An anonymous caller verified that the explosion . . . was in "cele-bration of Cuban Independence Day."

This was at least the second act of apparently political sabotage in the New York/New Jersey area in a month. . . .

"The *RAT* story," says Seedman, "was what you might call an exclusive. The city dailies had barely noted the bombing. I never did see anything at all about it in the *Times*. And nowhere did I hear of an anonymous caller's verifying that the pier had been bombed to celebrate Cuban Independence Day. I was also interested to learn that the bomb was 'either dynamite or a plastic explosive' and that we were investigating the 'motives and method.' None of my men had told the press either of those things, so far as I knew.

"Whoever had written this story looked awfully cagey to me. The device of the 'anonymous caller' allowed the writer to spell out the significance of July twenty-sixth without incriminating himself. *RAT* had removed the story one step farther from the truth by attributing it to Liberation News Service (LNS), the underground equivalent of AP or UPI, which packages stories, photos, and drawings that go out twice a month to underground papers everywhere. By quoting police theories about the bomb and using the phrase 'apparently political sabotage'—a phrase echoed in the later Marine Midland commentary—the writer could sock home the point and context of the bombing while keeping himself out of the picture. Somewhere among *RAT*'s many contributors, I felt we would find our bomber.

"As always, it's one thing to suspect people of causing trouble, another to prove it. We could do nothing until we found something specific to link the *RAT* staff more directly to the bombings. So in the weeks after the bank job we kept close watch on the flow of people moving in and out of the *RAT* office. Undercover men kept their ears pinned to the pavements of the East Village streets, listening for the chance remark that would bring us home. By early September, two weeks after the bank job, I still didn't know what I expected first—a break in the case or another bombing. But if I had to make a choice, I was afraid I knew which it would be."

At exactly 2 A.M. on September 19 a powerful bomb went off on the fortieth floor of the Federal Building on Foley Square, not far from the sites of the two earlier bombings. Many noncontroversial government services, ranging from the administration of Social Security to distribution of food stamps, were handled in the tower. But it was not general public knowledge that the fortieth floor was also the domain of the U.S. Army. Seedman rode to the scene on the nearly empty Long Island Expressway, arriving at 3:45 A.M. The wreckage that greeted him hardly looked different from that at Marine Midland exactly one month before. This bomb had exploded in a transformer room close to the men's room, sending pipes gushing, ceiling tile and the vents behind them crashing down, knocking out a bank of elevators and blowing out windows on the eye-jangling grid of the huge building.

"This was an assault on Federal property," says Seedman, "so FBI men were arriving right on the heels of the NYPD and the fire department. Technically, my detectives had no jurisdiction at all, but there was never a thought that we should step away. The FBI had no equivalent in New York to our own Bomb Squad, which had already begun bagging the debris for comparison to the siftings of other bombings.

"The epidemic now spread. On September twenty-fourth, five days later, a bomb was discovered at the Chicago Civic Center, set to go off at 2:30 A.M. It consisted of twenty-four sticks of dynamite wired to a blasting cap, battery, and Westclox alarm clock— just about the same setup that had caused our bombings. In fact, the Bomb Squad had just picked another Baby Ben mainspring out of the debris from the Federal Building. That same day bombs exploded in the Air Force ROTC building at the University of Wisconsin in Madison, a traditional hotbed of radical politics, and at the Federal Building in Milwaukee. I began to wonder if this was ever going to end. Were we doomed to a period of perpetual edginess, wondering when the next bomb would go off? Were we going to have to turn every building where people once walked freely into an armed camp? It was a scary thought.

"Two days after the Federal Building bombing, the *Times* and the wire services received special-delivery letters with identical messages: 'As Richard Nixon was talking "peace" at the United Nations on Thursday, September 18th, and his masters of war were relentlessly dealing out death and destruction throughout the world, a time bomb was placed in the Federal Building as an act of solidarity with our brother and sister revolutionaries all over the world.

The specific targets were the Department of the Army, located on the fortieth floor, and the Selective Service System, located directly below the Army office. . . .'

"This time I didn't expect any report in *RAT* revealing the details of the blast. They probably wished they'd never been so brazen as to publish the pier- and bank-bombing stories. Just the same, on September sixteenth, I'd been able to get a warrant, good for ten days, to search the *RAT* office for any sign of the 'anonymous' Marine Midland letter. On September twenty-fourth, the day of the bombings in Madison and Milwaukee and the near-bombing in Chicago, I ordered a team of six detectives under Pete Perotta to exercise that warrant."

"Hey, *RAT* readers," began the paper's report of the event, "guess who oinked into our office just the other day. . . ." The detectives silently searched file cabinets and desks but found no sign of the bombing letter—no surprise to Seedman, since he doubted that it had ever existed. What they did find was a copy of the United Fruit bombing story, which *RAT* had attributed to Liberation News Service.

To Seedman's eye, this story did not look as if it had been sent out by any wire service. The LNS attribution seemed typed in as an afterthought, off center below the headline, while the copy itself appeared to have been composed and edited directly on the same single page. For example, in the sentence beginning "This was at least the second act of apparently political sabotage in the New York/New Jersey area in a month," the word "apparently" had been inserted in pencil. Other pencil-editing indicated that the writer had composed the story as he went along.

"Just the same, this sheet wasn't any good to us as direct evidence against anybody," says Seedman. "Whoever did the pencil-editing could claim that the copy just appeared on his desk and he had no idea who wrote it. Even if we could match the typing to one of the *RAT* office machines, there was no way to identify the typist. Kids wander in and out all day and from the masthead changes in each issue it appears that the average staffer's stay is less than a month."

Still, Seedman felt, that writer was almost certainly more than a reporter. He was a bomber.

On October 7, as Seedman nursed a late drink in a restaurant with two detectives who had worked late with him investigating a murder, his chauffeur, Freddie, burst in to relay the report of an explosion at the U.S. Army Induction Center on Whitehall Street. Hurrying down to the financial district, Seedman found the by now predictable devastation. It was one thing to bomb a glossy impersonal new office tower. But this handsome old building, erected in 1881 and designed in the classical style with charming details, did not deserve such a fate. Seedman had grown fond of the place from spending several days here in 1968 during antiwar demonstrations held at the Induction Center. The same large sign he remembered was still hanging on the ground floor: "THE SECURITY OF THE WORLD STARTS HERE."

In the morning, the newspapers and the wire services received the briefest announcement so far:

> *Tonight we bombed the Whitehall Induction Center.*
> *This action was in support of the NLF, legalized marijuana, love, Cuba, legalized abortion, and all the American revolutionaries and GIs who are winning the war against the Pentagon.*
> *Nixon, surrender now!*

The Bomb Squad again found a Baby Ben mainspring and fragments of a blasting cap in the debris. The whole business was driving Seedman crazy. "We were dashing around the East Village, checking everywhere, finding nothing," says Seedman. "It was the most exasperating case of my life, and the most ominous. We were always afraid that next time we'd find a bunch of dead people in the wreckage.

"One odd piece of the puzzle did turn up that week, even if it did not immediately fall into place. It came from the Royal Canadian Mounted Police via the FBI. *Le Petit Journal,* an underground newspaper in Montreal, claimed that two political bombers for the Quebec Liberation Movement who were being sought by the Mounties had fled to the United States and were hiding out with some white revolutionaries in the East Village.

"In the middle of the summer, continued *Le Petit Journal,* the two Canadians and an American revolutionary robbed four hundred sticks of dynamite from the Bronx. They split the booty among them, also giving a portion to the Black Panthers. Then the Canadians slipped back into Canada with their share and went back into hiding. The journalist who had written the story refused to give the Mounties any further information.

"The East Village is a Jewish, Slovak, black, and Puerto Rican neighborhood—but not French. You'd think that with dozens of detectives canvassing it block by block, we'd come across a merchant or a janitor who had noted two French-speaking strangers on their block. But the area is just too dense with life to find anybody except by luck. However, this article in *Le Petit Journal* assured us that our focus on the East Village had been correct. It also offered an explanation of one puzzling detail of the Explo robbery: Why had all three men worn red bandannas? Forget Tom Mix—it was a universal symbol to show that they were leftist revolutionaries committing a political act, not a common robbery."

A month later Seedman's investigators were beginning to lose momentum. Though no bombings had occurred since October 7, they hadn't gotten any breaks either. On November 11 Seedman arrived home at about 2 A.M. "I thought I'd listen to the two-o'clock news before rolling over to sleep," he says, "so I turned on the radio. Just as I was drifting off, I heard it: 'Flash! There has just been an explosion in the RCA Building at Rockefeller Center.' I dialed the duty man in my office to see what gives. While the phone was still ringing . . . 'Flash! There has been an explosion in the General Motors Building on Fifth Avenue.' The duty man didn't know what was going on yet. I jumped into my clothes, but before I could knot my tie . . . 'Flash! . . . an explosion at the Chase Manhattan Bank tower in lower Manhattan.' No use waiting the twenty-five minutes it would take my driver to get dressed and come over. I drove in myself."

Seedman arrived at the RCA Building at 3 A.M. to find that the twentieth floor, where the bomb had exploded, was leased to the Standard Oil Company of New Jersey, one of the corporations *RAT* had dubbed a "Hungry Imperialist Corporate Giant."

One radio station had received a call, warning that a bomb would shortly go off in the RCA Building, but the place had not been evacuated. In the Rainbow Room people continued to dance to the music of Lester Lanin's Orchestra; when the explosion finally came, forty-five stories below, the dancers were only faintly jarred. Finding the main elevators dead, they left by freight elevator, except for a few who preferred the twenty-minute walk down the fireproof staircase. In the noble tradition of the sinking Titanic, the orchestra played on until the last guest had gone.

Surveying the massive wreckage on the twentieth floor, Seedman wondered whether, confronted with photos of the various bombing scenes, he could tell one from another. The chaos on the nineteenth floor of the General Motors Building and on the sixteenth floor of Chase Manhattan Plaza, headquarters for international operations of Chase Manhattan Bank, did not change his mind. Directly below this last explosion were the bank's executive office suites, including one belonging to David Rockefeller. Luckily, a switchboard operator, warned that bombs would go off in three office buildings, one of them Chase, called the police, and the thirteen hundred clerks working in the eighty-story building at the foot of Manhattan Island were sent home.

After visiting the three bomb sites, Seedman drove back to the RCA Building and set up headquarters for all the bombings there. At dawn he called Chief of Detectives Fred Lussen to ask for a free hand in dramatically enlarging the group of detectives who comprised his little bombing-investigation team.

"How many?" asked Lussen.

"Twenty-five whom I can hand-pick from anywhere."

"You got 'em," said Lussen.

The men Seedman chose were all in top physical condition—every man on this job would have to be tough enough to hit the streets around the clock, if necessary, checking out leads until this scourge was defeated. While the Bomb Squad crated the debris at the three buildings and the twenty-five members of the special unit were told to report to their new assignment, Seedman went to the home of a friend on Central Park South to shower and shave. When he returned to the RCA building at 8:30, the Associated Press had just turned over a letter it had received from the bombers.

During this week of anti-war protest, we set off explosives in the offices of Chase Manhattan, Standard Oil, and General Motors. . . .

The Vietnam War is only the most obvious evidence of the way this country's power destroys people. The giant corporations of America have now spread themselves all over the world, forcing entire foreign economies into total dependence on American money and goods. Spiro Agnew may be a household word, but it is the rarely seen men, like David Rockefeller of Chase Manhattan, James Roche of General Motors and Michael Haiden of Standard Oil, who run the system behind the scenes.

The empire is breaking down as peoples all over the globe are rising up to challenge its power. From the inside, black people have been fighting a revolution for years.

And finally, from the heart of the empire, white Americans too are striking blows for liberation.

Seedman compared the neatly typed note to the Whitehall bombing announcement and also to the original copy of the *RAT* "news story" on the United Fruit pier-bombing. To his eye, the Whitehall note and the latest communiqué looked as if they were typed on the same machine. If confirmed by the lab, then he would have tangible proof that the city and FBI were looking for the same bombers.

Seedman received a call from John Malone, the dignified director of the FBI's New York office, who, like Seedman, was known as a man who kept his own counsel and listened more than he talked. Next to J. Edgar Hoover, Malone was probably the most respected FBI boss.

Shortly after the Federal Building bombing brought the FBI into the investigation, Malone told Seedman that his people had an informant who might develop leads to the bombers. Malone didn't say who the informant was and Seedman didn't ask. He knew that preserving an informant's cover required absolute secrecy. He also knew that when the time came, Malone would deal him in on any information he received.

"It took a while," Malone was telling him now, "but our informant finally gave up our man."

"Who is it?" asked Seedman, his voice flat.

"His name is Sam Melville. White, thirty-four years old, no visible means of support. He leases an apartment in the East Village, at 67 East 2nd Street. But he spends most of his time with a girl named Jane Alpert, who lives at 235 East 4th Street. She works for *RAT*. Looks like a nice quiet girl, but we think she's part of the plot."

Seedman pulled a copy of *RAT* from his briefcase. On the masthead, beside the title "Hip Princess," was the name Jane Alpert. Because she was one of the insiders at *RAT*, his detectives had already looked for a connection between her and the bombings. But like Malone's men, they had found her to be a quiet, intelligent, level-headed girl. Many others on the staff seemed much likelier to do crazy things and the detectives' attention had shifted accordingly.

"I don't think we can make a case stick on either of them yet," Malone went on. "If we searched their apartments we could probably come up with bombs. But that doesn't prove they carried out these bombings. So far all we've got is the word of the informant. I'd like to watch them for a while until we can nail them good, Al."

"Maybe we can nail them right in the act," said Seedman. "It shouldn't take too long. The bastards have been hitting at better than one job a month. Right now they must think their technique is so perfect that they can speed it up."

Seedman and Malone decided to sit on them together.

Late in the morning Seedman's twenty-five hand-picked detectives and twenty-five of Malone's agents spread out through the East Village in shifts of two-, three- and four-man teams. The detectives were surprised to see that many of the FBI men had allowed their hair to grow out in greasy straggles. They dressed in motorcycle jackets, boots, and genuinely well-worn blue jeans. In fact, several of them drove pin-striped custom-chromed and -lacquered Harley-Davidson and Yamaha bikes. Not many years ago FBI men simply didn't have it in them to melt in like that. As for the detectives, most of them simply specialized in looking like New Yorkers, down-at-the-heels and unremarkable.

Nothing that Seedman could learn about Sam Melville's life marked him as a potential bomber. He had been arrested in 1968 during a sit-in at a residential building owned by Columbia University. The charges were later dropped, though at thirty-three he was older than most of the student demonstrators and not exactly a juvenile offender. He had been arrested in 1961 by an auxiliary policeman for failing to take cover during an air-raid drill. A judge fined him fifty dollars. At that time his name was Sam Grossman, which he soon changed legally to Melville, presumably after his favorite writer. He was divorced from his wife, Ruth, who had custody of their son, Jocko. Though he had never completed his engineering studies, Melville worked on and off as a designer of plumbing hardware.

"If Melville really was our man," says Seedman, "his line of work explained his expertise at messing up those buildings. Twenty-five sticks of dynamite will cause tremendous damage no matter where they explode, but in each of the buildings hit, these bombs had been placed to deliver the most damage throughout the structure. At least one elevator shaft in each building had been thrown out of line. Bombs had been placed in transformer rooms to knock out power, and behind washroom wall panels to flood the area. This was the work of a guy who understood the vital systems of an office building the way a doctor understands a body.

"New York can take most anything in stride, including a bombing a month, but with simultaneous explosions at GM, RCA, and the Chase Bank, the town suddenly got a bad case of jitters. That day, November eleventh, the Bomb Squad was faced with more than 200 bomb threats. Most were clearly from cranks, but the police were running themselves silly just trying to check out the ones that sounded most dangerous.

"To show just how nervous people felt, take the case of this man who worked on 42nd Street. He's walking down the corridor to his office early in the morning, when all of a sudden he stops short. Just inside the door of an empty office he sees a large projectile, about the size fired by a tank. For a moment he freezes. Then, without shouting or scaring anyone else, he picks up this projectile as gently as he can. Trying not to shake it or, God forbid, trip, he slips around the corner and goes down the stairs. He carries the projectile into a men's room on the floor below, sets it down in a corner, then dashes back up to his office and calls 911, the police emergency number.

" 'I've found a live bomb that was planted here during the night,' he whispers to the patrolman who takes the call.

"The floor is evacuated. The Bomb Squad rushes over and two Bomb Squad detectives wearing surgical gloves kneel down in the men's room and examine the projectile with their portable fluoroscope. It is hollow. At about this time the man who owns the projectile turns up at work, and is told to wait with everybody else until the police open the floor again.

" 'Who stole my doorstop?' he yells when he finally gets in. It seems that the 'bomb' is an empty shell from World War Two which he has been using as a doorstop for five years now. The fellow who panicked at the sight of it had been walking by that very same doorway every day of those last five years."

Even as switchboards all over the city lit up with bomb threats, the first joint-surveillance teams faded into the streets of the East Village. Some covered the East 2nd Street block where Melville rented an apartment under the name David McCurdy; others headed for East 4th Street, where he lived with Jane Alpert. They blended in with the drunks staggering by the decaying buildings or nodding in doorways, while others roared by on motorcycles like Hell's Angels. In their pockets they kept pictures of Melville, Alpert, and three others who often came and went at the 4th Street place—a twenty-six-year-old ex-schoolteacher named Pat Swinton; a dark, lean Duke University dropout named David Hughey; and a thirty-seven-year-old sometime machinist named George Demmerle. Like Melville, he had drifted out of marriage and the straight life at a later age than usual.

"Despite our close surveillance," says Seedman, "as long as Melville was on the loose, we were running a risk. Out in the suburbs or at a country hideout a stakeout often can be maintained flawlessly, but on a congested block in New York, it's practically impossible. There was always the chance that in the weeks we waited to catch them planting another bomb, they might slip out of the city, or even drop off a bomb. But the surveillance had two aims which made it worth the risk. One was simply to catch them in the act so a jury would have no reasonable doubt of their crime. The second was to protect the FBI's informant.

"This man had spent years infiltrating the radical underground. If possible, the FBI didn't want to sacrifice his usefulness by revealing him in court. The only way they could hope to avoid that was by building a case 'around' him. If enough evidence—quite apart from the informant's—could be amassed to prove the bombing conspiracy, he would never have to be revealed. He could move on to another part of the underground, always building his credentials, always working for the Bureau. He would be like an eternal worm on a hook. No matter how many fish get caught, this worm stays on the hook to lure the next victim.

"We knew, of course, that sooner or later Melville would pick out our people, no matter how much at home they looked in the East

Village scene. That was why we decided to keep several teams on them all the time. If the suspects felt they had shaken off a tail, they'd be less guarded against a second at the other end of the block."

But while Melville, Alpert, and the others showed no signs of recognizing the tails, they were beginning to act as wary as cats who smell the hunter. They kept the shades drawn and the lights on constantly. At first the stakeout teams took that as a sign that the suspects were home. But then other teams would catch sight of Melville or one of the others disappearing into the subway. They were avoiding the front entrance, skittering across rooftops and dropping into the hallways of other buildings. They were not even sitting back to watch their handiwork on the eleven-o'clock news. They were on the move.

"Our informant says Melville is ready to do another job tonight," John Malone told Seedman in the morning. "This time they plan to place bombs in U.S. Army trucks parked outside a National Guard armory. The trucks will be driven inside late at night, and the bombs will go off a few hours later."

"Which armory?" asked Seedman.

"He didn't say."

"The only three in the city still operating with trucks are at Lexington and 26th Street, Park and 34th, and one out in Jamaica. If I had to guess, I'd say he wouldn't bother to go all the way out to Queens. He'll settle for one of the two closest to his apartment."

"We can cover them all," said Malone. "In fact, we can ask the Army to park plenty of trucks outside each armory. He can have his pick."

Seedman fidgeted all day. According to the hourly reports, Melville was working in the 2nd Street apartment. He kept running in and out, and George Demmerle also showed up there. Jane Alpert was coming and going in her East 4th Street apartment, a ten-block walk from *RAT*. But Seedman was not happy to hear that despite stepped-up surveillance, the teams were not always sure where the suspects were. The one most often lost was Melville.

"I had promised to go to a retirement dinner that night for three detectives from the Eighteenth Squad," Seedman said. "If it had been held in the boondocks, as many of these affairs are, I would have passed on regrets. But since it was at the midtown Park Sheraton, as close to both armories as my own office, I went to that dinner, even though I was as nervous as the first night my wife went into labor. Bill Averill, commander of the detective district where the RCA and GM bombs had hit, went along with me. We got a table near the door and had a phone hooked up so my office could reach me as soon as Melville looked ready to make his move."

At 8:42, just as the waiters were taking away the fruit cocktail cups, the phone rang. Seedman grabbed it.

"It wasn't exactly what you thought it was gonna be, Chief," said the voice from Police Headquarters. "A bomb just exploded on the fourth floor of Criminal Court on Centre Street. That's only four blocks from here, you know? Christ, I heard the explosion myself."

Seedman dashed out with Averill on his heels. For the first time in the years since he had rated a car and chauffeur, Seedman ordered his driver, Freddie, to sit in back while he drove. Keeping the siren at full blast, Seedman made the trip from the hotel at Seventh Avenue and Fifty-fifth Street to 100 Centre Street, about sixty-five blocks, in the record time of exactly five minutes.

Except for a robbery case being tried in Night Court on the eighth floor, the massive gray courthouse, overflowing with people by day, had been nearly deserted at the moment of the blast. The bomb was hidden behind a plumbing access panel in the fifth-floor men's room. As in most of the recent strikes, the blast had sent water gushing through the marble corridors and down the fire stairs to the main lobby. It leveled a terra-cotta wall seventy feet long, tore steel doors from their hinges, showered glass over Centre Street. A young clerk who had been on the toilet in the fourth-floor ladies' room was thrown off the seat with such force that she landed fifteen feet away. Fortunately, the only thing injured was her dignity.

As the Fire Marshal and the Bomb Squad detail began to sift the debris, a disgusted Seedman walked down the courthouse steps, grinding glass particles under his feet. With fifty lawmen watching over him, how had Melville shaken loose? Could he be the wrong man? If any Fed but John Malone had named Melville as the bomber, Seedman would now be inclined to doubt it.

"We may as well drive up and look at those armories," he said to Averill. This time he slumped in the back and let Freddie drive.

If the bomber wasn't Melville, then Seedman was back to that day the report of the United Fruit pier blast had crossed his desk in the dead of summer.

Almost precisely as Seedman and Averill were leaving the Park Sheraton to go downtown, Sam Melville and George Demmerle slipped up to the roof of the East 2nd Street apartment. Scampering across six tenement roofs, they came down through a doorway on East 3rd Street. Demmerle was wearing his usual work pants and denim jacket, but Melville was dressed in an olive-drab wool Air Force uniform with corporal's stripes. A matching duffel bag was slung over his right shoulder.

The two men split in opposite directions. Melville, whistling and jaunty, stopped by the B & H Deli on Fourth Avenue for a sandwich and washed it down with celery tonic. Then he strolled over to Astor Place, a hangout for students from nearby Cooper Union and New York University, and went down the stairs to the IRT subway. It was 9:35. As he rode the No. 4 local train north, Melville continued to purse his lips in a noiseless whistle. Behind his wire-rimmed glasses, his eyes appeared as calm and unclouded as a child's. His long powerful legs straddled the duffel bag.

Three men in a battered blue Chevrolet were watching as Melville came up from the subway exit at 23rd Street and Park Avenue. They followed him cautiously at a distance of fifty yards, driving slowly as if looking for a parking place. Melville walked east on 23rd Street with no sign of concern. Two passengers in the Chevy were FBI agents who had been receiving walkie-talkie reports on Melville's movements from the downtown teams—the most recent report had been transmitted as he stepped onto the platform at 23rd Street. The third passenger was Sandy Tice, a Bronx detective Seedman had called in just that morning for this duty.

Tice looked more like a farmer than a detective. He was tall and gawky, with feckless blue eyes, a spray of freckles, and slightly buck teeth under a thatch of cornsilk hair. At thirty-two, he looked twenty-two. Loping down city sidewalks, he tended to gawk at every sight like a country boy who until now thought Tulsa was about as dazzling as a city could get. The odd thing was that Tice was not putting on an act. Though born and raised in New York City, he had the eye of a country boy, and noticed everything as if seeing it for the first time. On a crowded street he could often pick out a face he had seen months ago on a squad-room bulletin board. He was always turning up suspects other detectives had given up hoping to find.

Tice was also seasoned to violent grabs of suspects. Just a few months earlier he had been shot in the center of the chest by a renegade Mafioso known as Tony the Shrimp (5' 10", 244 pounds), who was trying to blast his way through a roadblock on a quiet street in Queens. Luckily, Tice had thought to wear a bulletproof vest.

Tice suddenly felt uncomfortable in the back seat of the Chevrolet. Tracking Melville via walkie-talkie had been truly impressive, but now Tice wanted to do the job out on the street, on his own two feet.

"I'll be close by if you need me," he said and slipped out the back door as Melville disappeared around the corner onto Lexington Avenue. Tice paused, giving Melville a thirty-step lead, then swung around the corner himself, limping slightly in the right leg. Far from attracting attention, Tice had observed that men being followed would somehow gloss over a fellow with a limp, even while scrutinizing others most carefully. Trailing him along Lexington, Tice noticed that Melville was broad and powerful across the shoulders, perhaps a size forty-four suit. He looked as if he would be fast in a sprint.

At 25th and Lexington, Tice suddenly noticed Demmerle loitering on the corner across the street. Tice immediately crossed over to that side and began to read the menu in the window of an Armenian restaurant. An entree of ground lamb, raisins, and pine nuts in a casserole sounded especially interesting, and he promised himself he'd bring his wife here as soon as this was over.

Tice glanced away from the menu long enough to see that Melville had turned down 26th Street and alongside the 68th Regiment Armory. He wanted to follow him, but right now his only concern was to make sure that Demmerle, still at the corner of 25th Street, did not notice him. They were smart. No wonder Melville had never bothered to look back: one block before he had to turn left for the armory, he had stationed Demmerle as a spotter. A quick shout to Melville on the other side of Lexington Avenue and he would never make that turn into 26th Street. Even if he was arrested as he continued up Lexington, he could be charged only with possession of a bomb—an offense far less serious than bombing.

After three minutes Melville reappeared on Lexington and walked toward Demmerle, whose eyes had been combing the block from the 25th Street corner. Tice, who had retreated a full block to 24th, was glad to see the duffel bag still slung from Melville's right shoulder. The two conferred for a moment, then went back up to 26th and turned left. No matter how great the risk of being spotted, this time Tice knew he had to follow.

As he turned the corner, twenty steps behind them, he noticed how suddenly the block became quiet. On the south side loomed the dark-red-brick armory. Its roof vaulting in a continuous curve, it looked like a hangar or a storage place for dinosaur bones. Three Army trucks were lined up at the curb, two-thirds of the way toward the Park Avenue end of the block.

Tice glanced about for cover, knowing Melville and Demmerle would look back as soon as he turned the corner. He was delighted to see walking toward him a slender blond man dressed in a close-fitting suede suit. His Pekinese was straining at its leash like a lustrous animated mop. Plainly, he was homosexual. Tice winked at him.

"Sir, can you tell me where a fellow might be able to get a little . . . action around here?" he asked hopefully.

"Do you mean . . . ummm . . . oh!"

The man stammered and began to smile, but Tice didn't wait around for his answer. He heard the clatter of running from the far end of the block. Melville stopped digging into his duffel bag and looked up. It was the FBI men Tice had left in the Chevrolet.

"Drop it!" one of them shouted at Melville.

"No! no!" yelled Tice, knowing the stuff could go up if you so much as breathed on it. "DON'T drop it, for Christ's sake!"

He sprinted toward Melville, who was looking first one way and then the other. Judging that Melville would pull no weapon, Tice did not draw his own service revolver. But as Melville and Demmerle froze against the side of the truck, cut off both ways, Tice grabbed the duffel bag. The FBI men, guns drawn, pushed the prisoners against the truck. Tice put his ear to the canvas. Inside, he heard ticking. . . .

"Where's the Bomb Squad?" Tice shouted. He knew they could not be far away. Seedman had ordered a technician team to stand by at each armory all evening, and the Bomb Squad office was just five blocks away. Tice suddenly realized he did not have the slightest idea of what to do next. Where on a quiet city street was the best place to put a ticking duffel bag?

"Relax," said Melville, who was now being searched by four agents and two more city detectives. "They're not set to go off until two o'clock."

Tice and all the others looked at their watches. It was 10:22. Along with a tear-gas pen, he was surprised to see the FBI men remove a .38-caliber revolver from a shoulder holster concealed beneath Melville's Air Force jacket. He was more surprised to turn around and see Albert Seedman standing off to the side, cigar in mouth, staring impassively at Demmerle and Melville.

Melville and Demmerle were driven off to FBI headquarters in the back seat of the agents' blue Chevrolet. Detectives Schmitt and Hornidge removed the four bombs, each of which was constructed from a battery, blasting cap, Westclox alarm clock, and four to six sticks of dynamite. After Detective Schmitt had cut the circuits, he inspected the serial numbers on the bright-red casings.

"This is the Explo dynamite stolen in July," he said, "and those are the Explo blasting caps."

As Tice and the other city detectives turned to go, they were suddenly accosted by the man with the Pekinese. Sizing up Seedman as the man in charge, he pointed out Tice.

"Tell me, sir," he demanded in outrage. "Is this person a police officer?"

Seedman ignored the dog sniffing at his trouser cuffs. "Ask him if he has any identification," Seedman said. The man turned to Tice, who reached into his pocket and produced his gold shield. Tice hoped the man would be amused by the entire incident, but he walked off in a huff.

Shortly after Melville and Demmerle arrived, Jane Alpert and David Hughey were brought into separate interview rooms at the FBI office. They had been arrested in her East 4th Street apartment minutes after the 26th Street incident. The second woman, Pat Swinton, who the FBI felt was part of the conspiracy, had so far eluded arrest. Seedman noticed that while Alpert was calm and hard-nosed, David Hughey's dark eyes were filled with distress and fear.

Seedman walked over to the room where Melville was already

being questioned and stood outside. This was FBI turf, not his own. Traditionally, local law officers never sat in on an FBI interrogation. But this was one time, Seedman decided, he would not observe etiquette. Without knocking, he walked in and took a good look at his bomber.

The surveillance teams had described Melville as an extraordinarily energetic man who walked with the implied force of a locomotive. With four ticking bombs in the duffel bag slung on his shoulder, he had radiated vigor and good cheer. Now his face was slack and his eyes dull. Poorly shaven and dirty-haired, he was collapsed in a chair with no more apparent energy than a beached jellyfish.

The two FBI agents, both in their early thirties, nodded to Seedman to take a chair. They did not seem surprised to see him there.

"I tried never to hurt anyone," Melville was saying in a low voice. "I always called 911 an hour before each bomb blew. But they don't want to hear the time of day from you. The same at the building security offices—they don't want to be bothered. But if they had listened to me at the bank, those seventeen people would have been out of the place."

Seedman remembered that a call had indeed gone to a Marine Midland security station at midnight on August 28, but the station was not at the branch that was bombed. Melville had called the wrong building.

"I called the RCA Building security office *three* times the other night," Melville continued. "They say, 'Sure, fella.' They humor you. But they never want to get off their asses to clear the building."

"How do you know they didn't clear the RCA Building after you called three times?" asked Seedman.

"I was there," said Melville testily, finally showing a little spirit. "I called from a phone booth where I could see the entrance to the building. Nobody came out."

"That's funny," said Seedman. "Yesterday morning I went all around the front of 30 Rockefeller Plaza to find a phone booth that looked out on the front of the building. You know what? There isn't one."

Melville looked at the floor and did not answer.

Out in the hall the two young FBI men asked Seedman if he had actually looked for a phone booth or whether he had just been trying to shake Melville's confidence.

"I looked for a phone booth at dawn," answered Seedman.
"Why?"

"If there was a booth in sight of the entrance, he might very
well have used it. People who cause trouble always like to see the
reaction. Before everybody came to work, I would have had that
booth dusted for prints. The way a person wraps his hand around
the receiver, maybe we could have gotten a palm print as well as
fingers."

"Though George Demmerle was arrested and taken into an
interview room like the others, he just went through the motions,"
says Seedman. "When John Malone and I sat down together shortly
before midnight, he confirmed that Demmerle was the informant.
Melville had already confessed to all the bombings orally, so Malone
hoped he could protect his informant. But in one pretrial hearing
the judge instructed the government to identify its informant and
reveal how long he had been working under cover.

"Demmerle had been a paid Federal informant since 1966. At
the great Woodstock rock festival in September 1969 he showed up
dressed in a purple cape and manned a goodwill booth sponsored
by the 'Crazies,' a drugged-out group too silly to cause any real
trouble. Nobody seemed to like him except Melville, who admired
him for holding down that booth for twenty-four hours straight.
When Melville offered to spell him, Demmerle said no, only a bona-
fide 'Crazy' would do. Apart from his extremism, Melville also may
have liked Demmerle because he was one of the few men at Woodstock older than himself.

"During the next two months, Demmerle made a point to touch
base with Melville in the East Village. He was full of plots that
Melville adored, such as dumping a special chemical down every
manhole in the financial district to eat away every telephone cable
it touched. The others in Melville's 'collective,' especially Jane Alpert,
had always been suspicious of Demmerle. She had tried to persuade
Melville not to let him in on any of the bombings, but Melville
spilled everything about the GM, RCA, and Chase Manhattan jobs
to Demmerle—only too late for him to tip the FBI. He also invited the
informant to help carry out the armory-bombing planned for the
night of November 12.

"Melville did devise one test of his new friend's good faith. On
Wednesday morning he told Demmerle the armory job was set for
that night. Demmerle passed the word to his FBI contact. But early

in the afternoon, Melville casually mentioned that he had just planted a bomb in the State Criminal Court Building, set to explode at 8:30. It wasn't a bad idea. The cops and the Bomb Squad would be running downtown to Centre Street while he and Demmerle headed uptown for the armory job. Demmerle was now in a dilemma. If he warned his contact about the bomb already ticking, the FBI would warn us. We'd clear the court house and begin a search for the bomb. Melville would hear about it on the radio and know that only Demmerle could have tipped us off.

"However, if courthouse business went off as planned in the afternoon, Melville could tell Jane Alpert that she and the others had been wrong about George. Deciding to risk it, Demmerle sweated out the afternoon without transmitting a word about the courthouse bomb. The damage it caused was the price of nabbing Melville in the act—the only sure way to get him convicted."

Early Friday morning, Seedman sent Detectives Schmitt, Hornidge, Tice and James Mohan with their FBI counterparts to search the Alpert and "McCurdy" apartments. At Jane Alpert's place they found stolen passports, mounds of revolutionary pamphlets, a rifle, a box of .38-caliber bullets, and even a map of the Bronx with a circle marking the block where Explo Industries was located. Also a bag of sickeningly dirty underwear.

The "McCurdy" apartment was the warfare center. A small decrepit place, it was crammed full of blasting caps, safety fuses, nine-volt batteries, clocks and clock radios, empty dynamite boxes, a carbine, a 9-mm. automatic, a .45 semi-automatic rifle, soldering iron, wire cutters, voltage testers, a book titled *Military Explosives,* and hundreds of rounds of ammunition. Taped under a sagging cot was a U.S. Army M-26 fragmentation hand grenade— live.

"Melville confessed to the eight Manhattan bombings in the fall of 1969, plus an attempted bombing at the Chicago Civic Center and the bombing of the Milwaukee Federal Building. He refused to name any accomplices, insisting that he had acted alone. He was held without bail, but Jane Alpert and David Hughey each went free on $20,000 bonds, pending trial. A fourth accused conspirator, a seventeen-year-old *RAT* staffer named Jonathan Grell, who was carrying a loaded .38 revolver when arrested at his parents' home in the Bronx, also went free on bail.

"The first weeks she was out we had no trouble keeping track of Jane Alpert. Every day she religiously attended the proceedings of the so-called Panther 21 trial. Using her *RAT* press card, she got a front-row seat among the rest of the reporters. One of my detectives had to go down and testify at that trial. When he got back he told me that during a brief recess, Alpert had put her feet up on the low gate in front of her. She was wearing a short skirt and the guards could not help notice she was wearing no pants underneath. They asked her to put her legs down.

" 'If you don't like what you see,' she had answered, 'don't look.'

"Jane Alpert was hardly an exhibitionist. As far as I was concerned, the act she put on in the courtroom was in the same class with the dirty underwear in the closet: a protest against convention. She had been scholarly and soft-spoken in high school and at Swarthmore College, had taken a job with the Oxford University Press and begun studying for an advanced degree in Greek at Columbia University. But she threw everything over to work ten hours a day without pay for *RAT*. She was rejecting mainline society, in fact and in symbol—such symbols as cleanliness and modesty.

"Melville turned up in court and pleaded guilty to Federal bomb conspiracy and State arson charges. When he found he could be sentenced to three hundred and forty-four years on State charges alone, his resolve to bear all the punishment himself weakened. He asked Alpert and Hughey, who were also implicated in the conspiracy, to cop a plea to lesser charges in return for the DA's promise not to give him what amounted to life imprisonment. His associates agreed to do so, and Hughey was sentenced to four years in a Federal Youth Correctional Facility. Jane Alpert jumped bail before she could be sentenced and has not been seen since. In May 1973 she wrote a public letter from underground to announce she had progressed from 'serious militant leftist to radical feminist.' Her only desire now, she said, was to see women simply 'work for themselves.'

"Melville did his best to escape before his own sentencing, but all his attempts failed. One Saturday, while being taken from his cell in the Tombs to a room in the adjacent Criminal Court Building —the same one he had bombed—he overpowered a guard and dashed down the fire stairs. An alert guard in the lobby stopped him at gunpoint. On another occasion a surprise inspection of Melville's cell turned up a letter explaining what would be the best time to blow out a wall of the prison. Included with the letter was a precise series of diagrams showing the dimensions of the walls, placement of the bars and location of his own cell. On June 19, 1970, he was sentenced to eighteen years in prison on eight counts of State arson. Sentences for various Federal offenses were to run concurrently. With good behavior, Melville might have been free in as litttle as thirteen years.

"George Demmerle was an odd case. Born in Brooklyn, a die-maker by training, he had joined the super-rightist Minutemen, who were as willing to use violence to defend their views as any 'serious militant leftist.' Nobody liked Demmerle—not his ex-wife, blood relatives, Jane Alpert, Hughey, or any of the others on the East Village scene. Nobody except Sam Melville. The Marine Midland Bank had offered a $25,000 reward for information leading to the arrest of its bomber. Even though Demmerle was being paid by the Government, he qualified for the money—and he took it too. He is lost from sight now. I take that to mean that somewhere, right now, he has gone under cover again.

"After the showdown at the 26th Street Armory, *RAT* published a sort of apologia for the bombings which I believe was written by Melville. The article, which was quite sophisticated, detailed the structures of the businesses that Melville had bombed. It pointed out, for example, that a large number of Standard Oil shares are still controlled by the thirteen foundations and seventy-five family trusts maintained by the Rockefeller family. It pointed out that Peter Grace, chairman of Marine Midland's parent company, W. R. Grace, then owned 281,834 shares of Grace stock, that his grandfather had been the first Catholic Mayor of New York City, that Grace owned three thousand A & W Root Beer Drive-Ins, six hundred Baskin-Robbins ice cream stores, Revere Sugar, Right-Away commercial salad toppings, as well as mammoth foreign holdings. The writer pointed out that when a priest named Patrick Peyton campaigned to get more South Americans to say the rosary, Peter Grace supported him, saying, 'If these people didn't have the rosary, they'd have nothing.'

"But what interested me most was the way the writer felt about corporate office buildings.

Each day those buildings suck in human energy and spit it out again in a regular 9-5 rhythm. Then they stand idle and aloof, empty of humanity, while the rest of Manhattan swells to the point of explosion. . . .

"Even before we caught Melville, we knew that our bomber had a feeling for where buildings could be hurt the most, how to knock out lifelines like pipes and elevators. Later, of course, we learned that Melville had worked in plumbing design. But as I read that passage in *RAT* I realized that wasn't the only reason he hit those buildings the way he did. To Melville those buildings were more than brick and mortar and pipes. They were alive. They were dragons for him to slay."

"Sam Melville was a prisoner at Attica when the great riot of September 1971 took place. The blacks were glad to have him. He was one of the few whites they could put on the negotiating committee who was a bona-fide revolutionary. Sam must have felt right in his element. But the negotiations fizzled, and the prison yards were stormed by troopers armed with shotguns. Thirty-one prisoners and the eleven hostages were killed in the attack. When it was all over, they found Melville dead behind a barricade, shot in the chest. Three homemade bombs lay on the ground just beyond his hand."

THE TOWNHOUSE CASE

Butler and Low libraries face each other across a great sweep of lawn at the heart of Columbia University. For years Butler has been used for offices rather than books, so it is mostly administrators who enter beneath its elegant Georgian dome during business hours. But far into the evening students continue to pour into Low through its mighty file of Ionic columns. Overhead, chiseled into its block-long façade, are the names of the seminal Western thinkers: Homer, Herodotus, Sophocles, Plato, Aristotle, Demosthenes, Cicero, Virgil. . . .

It was here that Seedman spent five ugly days in 1968, called away from his post in Brooklyn to bolster the police command team attempting to check the chaos during the student riots of that spring. The phalanxes of waiting cops would have been delighted to eradicate the problem with clubs and tear gas. But the university's own top command preferred to let the uprising play itself out. The administration, from president on down, understood the gut feeling that had fueled the protest was that it had lost touch with students and was scornful of them. What better way to prove them right than by calling in a crushing display of police muscle?

So the police were ordered to stand fast under a steady pelting of obscenities. They even had to stand aside while food was delivered to the student cadres occupying a half-dozen university buildings, among them Butler Library, where the invaders took turns leaning back in President Grayson Kirk's chair, feet on his desk, smoking his quality cigars.

Despite command restraint on the cops, many kids were beaten anyway, and stretcher cases were constantly being moved from the campus to nearby hospitals. It was an angry time. Yet all the bile that spilled out of Columbia during those five days was nothing compared to the genuine horror of this scenario two years later.

Saturday, March 7, 1970. The great lawn is deserted, except for a few students tossing Frisbees and footballs this brisk late-winter afternoon. Inside Butler, a skeleton staff is hard at work, much of it new in the aftermath of the riots. At the other end of the lawn students working on their second-semester term papers make their way into Low Library. The university is again at peace, and the spring of 1968 seems like ancient history.

The first explosions go off almost simultaneously in Butler and Low libraries. The bombs, painstakingly constructed from the condensed innards of many sticks of TNT, are the most powerful ever to be set off in New York City. They are also the first designed specifically as "antipersonnel" bombs, piercing whoever happens to be in their path as they explode with a fusillade of one-and-a-half-inch roofing nails.

The massacre of March 7 was destined to be Seedman's greatest case. Yet because of what happened to the bomb makers the day before, it was the case that never took place.

Seedman was on the phone on Friday, March 6, with his old pal Ed Mooney from the Seafarers' Union when the desk man, Ralph Ronga, slipped a note onto his desk: "12:15 pm from C.B. 2nd alarm, 4 explosions, 18 West 11th St. Cause unknown. 1 Ptl. injured, not serious."

Seedman covered the phone's mouthpiece and asked Ronga, "What am I supposed to do? Run over and help put it out?"

"If you had read about this yourself on the teletype, you'd jump on me for not letting you know first. Right, Chief?"

Through a cloud of cigar smoke, Seedman watched Ronga back out of the office and, still chatting with Mooney, pictured the address: 18 West 11th Street would be just off Fifth Avenue at the north end of Greenwich Village. A year had gone by since he'd been on the block, but he remembered it clearly: a tree-lined quiet row of townhouses and a few small apartment buildings, most still occupied by single families, as they had been in the nineteenth century. It was as classy and serene as any block in the Village. Though theoretically these old houses were firetraps, somehow big fires never seemed to start on this kind of block.

Seedman had just gotten off the phone when Ronga came back. "Sorry to bother you again, Chief, but Captain McDermott from the First District called. He says it's one hell of a fire and maybe you ought to come down."

"Any dead or injured?"

"Not so far."

"Then why would I want to come down?"

Ronga paused. "Captain McDermott just says it's like no gas explosion he ever saw. Like it's—unnatural."

Seedman walked down 11th Street from Fifth Avenue, which was blocked off by fire-fighting apparatus. With its Federalist-style homes in perfect repair, the well-swept stoops, and the buds on the trees just beginning to swell, the block was even lovelier than he had remembered. Nothing much had changed here for a century. Nothing but the scene at number 18.

The flames were not simply licking at the skeleton of what must have been a handsome townhouse. They churned out in rolling white swirls that seemed to eat up the water jets blasting from the firemen's big hoses. Seedman had never seen even a gas fire quite this savage. The place was burning like an ammo dump. McDermott was right: it was unnatural.

"Right after the first explosion, two girls came out the front door," reported McDermott. "They're the only ones we know for sure were in the place. One was tall, slender, and blond, the other short, squarish, and dark. They both came out stark naked and a lady from down the block took them to her house."

"Well, they must know who was in there and what the hell happened."

McDermott looked down. "They probably do, Chief. But as soon as they borrowed some clothes from this lady, they disappeared."

McDermott was braced for his boss's displeasure, but Seedman only stared at him with interest.

"First, something's not right about this fire," he said. "Then, something's definitely not right about these girls disappearing. Give my office a call, Bob. Tell them to send over a couple of detectives from each squad. Ten will do for now."

Seedman turned now to John O'Hagen, the city's Fire Chief, and James Canty, the Chief Fire Marshal.

"What do you think, Chief? Is it a gas explosion?"

"Could be," answered O'Hagen without enthusiasm.

"Looks like an awful big bang, even for gas."

O'Hagen and Canty both nodded.

Though the fire had been blazing for well over an hour, the flames continued to churn without letup. A doctor across the street offered Seedman his waiting room for conducting interviews; everyone on the block had heard or felt the shudder of the first explosion at 12:06. Patrolman Ronald Waite, who had been guarding a nearby school crossing at Sixth Avenue and 10th Street, had raced toward the sound. So had off-duty Housing Authority Patrolman Vincent Calderone, who had just left his doctor's office on Fifth Avenue at 11th Street. Just before they arrived, the two girls had come out the front door. Coats were thrown over them by the first neighbors at the scene, and Susan Wager, wife of actor Michael Wager and ex-wife of Henry Fonda, whisked them off to her home down the block at number 50.

The townhouse was then still intact, though acrid white and yellow smoke hissed out of the windows ominously as if from a newly opened fissure. Patrolman Waite tried to plunge inside to look for others, but was driven back by the thick smoke and coughed until he was sick. Dashing through the house next door, Calderone hoped to enter number 18 through the backyard, figuring the smoke might not be so bad in the rear. But the back door was blocked by a padlocked metal gate and the windows were barred. Calderone was wondering how else to get in, when he was startled to hear voices from inside:

"Where are you, Adam . . . ?"

"In here. . . ."

"Adam . . . Adam. . . ."

Calderone took out his service revolver. Aiming at an angle to prevent ricochet, he fired away at the heavy padlock, but his bullets barely dented it. The smoke, especially from the lower windows, was getting worse and the whole house seemed to be quivering as if possessed. Suddenly fearful, Calderone backed away. In the next instant, the place heaved with a new explosion from somewhere deep inside, knocking Calderone back against the rear fence. Instead of acrid smoke, pure fire now leaped from the windows, singeing his eyelashes. He heard no more voices. Afraid of being trapped, Calderone got out the way he had come.

Meanwhile, the girls were cleaning up in the Wagers' guest bathroom. Susan Wager, a friendly, handsome woman, had rummaged up jeans, sweaters, and shoes for them, and she could hear them whispering excitedly together. But they fell silent when they came out of the bathroom. Mrs. Wager did not expect smiles or thanks—the girls were undoubtedly in some sort of psychological shock—but somehow they did not seem shocked or numb: theirs was more the silence of wary cats.

"We're going to run over to the drug store on Sixth Avenue to buy burn ointment," said the dark girl.

"Oh, I have great stuff in the medicine cabinet," said Mrs. Wager. "I'm forever touching hot pots in the kitchen."

"We've caused you enough trouble already," said the blonde, and before Mrs. Wager could say another word, they were out the front door, dashing toward Sixth Avenue like commuters late for a train. The wail of fire sirens rose from Fifth Avenue. By now number 18 was blazing furiously, but the girls never looked back. Not until they were around the corner did Susan Wager realize that when she had seen them in the nude, they had been covered with a dusting of ash—but neither had showed any sign of burns. Besides, as Seedman pointed out when he heard the story, where could they have been carrying money to buy the ointment?

As is typical of New York, it was easier to gather all these details than to find a neighbor who could tell Seedman who owned number 18. Finally someone identified the owner as James Wilkerson, a former vice-president of the Young & Rubicam advertising agency who had retired several years earlier to oversee the string of Midwestern radio stations he owned. He was married to an Englishwoman named Audrey; she was his second wife and quite a few years younger. The neighbor who identified him thought the Wilkersons had gone to the Caribbean for a few weeks' vacation.

"Do they have children?" asked Seedman.

"Two daughters, I believe, by Jim's first marriage. He doesn't talk about them much."

Seedman rang Wilkerson's midtown office but, getting no answer, sent Detective Joe Gibney to check the place out. Meanwhile, detectives reporting in from other squads copied down plate numbers from all the cars nearby and checked local hospitals to see whether they had treated any unusual injuries that afternoon. Fingerprint men dusted the Wager bathroom but the maid had scrubbed the place thoroughly as soon as the girls had left. She hadn't missed a spot of the walls, knobs, sinks, or doors, the detectives noted ruefully.

At 4:30 Gibney returned to find his boss staring at the townhouse. After nearly four hours of steady hosing, it was finally beginning to burn more stubbornly than savagely.

"Wilkerson's secretary took a long lunch," reported Gibney. "When she got back, she wired him in St. Kitts to come home at once, although he's due back tomorrow anyhow. Apparently his daughter Cathy was minding the house—she fits the description of the tall blonde who lammed out. The secretary doesn't have any idea who the other girl might be."

"Does the daughter work?"

"She didn't say. In fact, she didn't want to say much of anything about this Cathy Wilkerson. I figured she had more on her mind than she was telling, so I checked the kid out. She's got no record with us."

"Better check her out with BOSS [Bureau of Special Services] and the FBI," said Seedman. But he was thoroughly mystified. Why should Cathy Wilkerson be a fugitive from her own house? If only the place would stop burning, the debris might offer some hint of an answer.

Anxious as Seedman and the Fire Department were to search the building for casualties, O'Hagen told him not to count on getting inside for several hours more. Barring an unexpected fast break in the case, Seedman could see that his men would be on this site long after dusk tonight and probably many more nights. They would need an office. The superintendent of the building across the street, where the doctor had temporarily lent his waiting room, offered the basement for as long as it was needed. While detectives continued to bring in witnesses for interviews, five special phones were soon installed on makeshift tables.

Gibney was back again shortly before six o'clock. "Hey, Chief —it took BOSS a little while, but they came up with a hit from

Chicago on this Cathy Wilkerson. She's from the Weatherman faction of SDS, the wildest of the wildest. She's been up front at almost every violent SDS demonstration in the country over the last two years. Right now she's out on $5,000 bail for assaulting a cop during a riot in Chicago last December." Gibney shook his head. "I knew Wilkerson's secretary was holding back on me."

"If she didn't hold back, then you wouldn't have been suspicious—right?"

Gibney nodded.

"Then you ought to go back and thank her, dummy."

Gibney basked in Seedman's sour gaze. He knew he had brought in the first hard lead of the day.

As O'Hagen had predicted, it was dusk before the fire finally subsided at the front of the townhouse, even though it was still being fought in the rear. But the rubble was impenetrable. Three floors of charred wreckage had dropped down in front of the place and for the moment firemen could do no more than pick at the top layer. They had been heaving away for an hour when, amid the debris choking the stairs to the basement entrance, they spotted an arm.

They worked twenty more minutes in silence to uncover the body. It was that of a powerful young man, age perhaps twenty-five. He was lying in a bed of brick and plaster dust, his arching back now frozen in the rigidity of death. His hair, under a heavy powdering of dust, was plainly red. Insulated in that dust packing, the churning fire had not been able to reach him. The body was in no way charred or singed. If anything, the dust gave his face a tanned look. His mouth was wide open, as if frozen into a gasp. Gazing down at him, Seedman suspected he had been killed not by the blast itself, but by the weight of the rubble that had fallen on his chest. Even though he could still suck air into his mouth, his lungs could not expand to receive it—skiers trapped in avalanches under many feet of snow have strangled the same way.

Sam Parola, who had caught the case for the Homicide Squad, knelt and, without moving the body, patted the pockets of the well-cut wool slacks for identification. They were empty. The collar of the white dress shirt was labeled "Saks Fifth Avenue," the tee shirt "Rogers Peet Co., Boston." Before the body had been fully uncovered, Seedman had guessed him to be one of Cathy Wilkerson's

Weatherman friends, but the young man was not wearing the right labels for that—he was too well dressed. Besides, among the hundreds of SDS members and sympathizers Seedman had dealt with at Columbia University, he had never seen one with hair trimmed so short. Probably this young man had simply been walking along 11th Street at the moment of the first, less serious explosion. Rushing in to help, like a Good Samaritan, he had been trapped by the bigger blasts that followed.

It was dark by the time the Medical Examiner okayed removing the body to the morgue. Seedman was anxious now to probe further into the house, but it was simply not possible to penetrate the wreckage packed solidly outside the basement entrance. The going would have been much easier on the main floor, but the Fire Chief forbade it, since much that remained of the upper floors was simply dangling, ready to crash down at the slightest jiggle. Further exploration was postponed until morning while a Con Ed crane set to work knocking down the stubborn remains of the townhouse façade.

By midnight most of the firemen had gone. The gawkers, kept at a distance behind police barricades all day, also had mostly drifted away. But Seedman still found himself staring at the place, its skeleton illuminated now in Emergency Service floodlights, his mind swirling with questions. What had caused this fine century-old townhouse suddenly to quiver, explode, and burn viciously for six hours? It seemed impossible that the whole structure could have contained enough combustibles to fuel that kind of blaze. He did not believe the cause was anything as mundane as a flawed gas line. Was there something extra? How did the fact that Cathy Wilkerson was a member of Weatherman, a group that advocated violence, figure into it? How could blowing up her parents' house serve her cause? And if she hadn't bombed the house, why had she fled? Only those girls could tell why the place had come to such a cataclysmic end, but Seedman did not expect them to turn up very soon. Short of any surprise witnesses who might unexpectedly come forward, the only available answers would be buried in the wreckage of number 18.

The Fire Marshal would conduct his own investigation, of course, but it would stop once the cause of the fire had been pinpointed. Seedman's own Bomb Squad had become skilled at such work in cleaning up after Sam Melville's office bombings. Neither set of experts, though, had ever done what Seedman now proposed.

He had in mind, in effect, a sort of archeological dig to learn the story not just of the fire, but of the people involved in it. He had seen documentaries showing how ancient tombs and even cities had been reconstructed, fragment by fragment. He would do the same with these ruins, all hundred or more truckloads of it. The expense would be exceptional. But Seedman had never felt so sure that a case deserved such effort. Having settled on how to proceed, Seedman finally turned away from the townhouse. It was 3:35 A.M.

In the morning the Sanitation Commissioner lent Seedman a portion of his department's Gansevoort Street pier for the project and assigned special equipment and crew to the Police Department. Several detectives with a knack for carpentry were soon building a set of table frames with wire mesh stretched across them to sift the debris. As it was hosed down the smallest fragments would fall through and could be inspected separately. When the processed rubble was reloaded into sanitation trucks for delivery to the regular dumping grounds, Seedman would know that no townhouse secrets were being dumped too. Exactly a day after the explosion sixteen recruits he had pirated from the Police Academy were at work on the first truckload under the supervision of a single Bomb Squad detective.

Early Saturday morning a tall, stylish, remarkably handsome couple hurried down 11th Street from Fifth Avenue. Their tanned faces drawn tight, they pushed through the police barriers.

"Move back, fella!" shouted a patrolman.

"I'm Jim Wilkerson," he said. "This is my wife, Audrey. It's our house."

He looked at the place with pain. His wife turned away. "*Was* our house," he amended.

Standing on the railing of the Con Ed crane, Seedman had spotted the couple as they rounded the corner and quickly took them down to his basement office. Though Wilkerson talked readily about his daughter, it was easy to see why his secretary had been hesitant. Cathy, his daughter by his first wife, had grown up in the well-to-do suburban Connecticut town of Stamford. At New Canaan Day School and Abbott Academy she had always stood out as an honor student. The change came in 1962, when she had entered Swarthmore College and quickly become caught up in SDS and the politics of the New Left. In those pre-Vietnam years activists had devoted themselves mainly to ending racial injustice; in summer she had traveled around the country, working in minority teaching projects. She had often detoured to the New Hampshire town of Meridan to visit her mother, now married to Harlan D. Logan, speaker of the State House of Representatives.

Cathy's mother was a Quaker pacifist, as staunch an opponent as her daughter of racism and the then-escalating Vietnam war Still, Mrs. Logan was distressed that even after her graduation from Swarthmore in 1966, Cathy continued to be at the most violent end of the SDS spectrum. In 1966 Cathy helped edit the *New Left Notes* at SDS headquarters in Chicago. In 1967 she tried but failed to visit North Vietnam. In 1968 she was arrested for "disorderly conduct" at the Democratic National Convention in Chicago. In 1969, at the SDS national convention in Flint, Michigan, she aligned herself with the splinter faction calling itself Weatherman after a line in Bob Dylan's song "Subterranean Homesick Blues"—"You don't need a weather man to know which way the wind blows." Its aim was pure violence against the system, both planned and impromptu.

In October 1969 Cathy was up front in the gaggle of Weathermen who rampaged through the streets of Chicago with no purpose but pure violence, in what they proudly called "Four Days of Rage." But one of her friends remembered a weary Cathy referring to the event simply as "a death trip." She was arrested on the first day for attacking a policeman with a four-foot club, the charge that Gibney had picked up from BOSS.

Though they disagreed on methods, Cathy and her mother remained close. At Christmas, when Cathy had gone to Meridan for three weeks, she had looked "ghastly." Mrs. Logan had filled her with food and vitamins, and by the time Cathy left on January 15, the day after her twenty-fifth birthday, she had looked healthier and seemed happier. Hugging her good-bye, Mrs. Logan had at last permitted herself to hope that Cathy would not remain a Weatherman much longer.

James Wilkerson, on the other hand, had found it far harder to deal with his daughter. A good Republican, capitalist, patron of good food and wine, art and antiques, general reaper of the fruits of "the system," he simply had no common ground on which to meet Cathy. Though she had no job of her own, she refused the generous allowance he offered.

"Financial problems sometimes make me dysfunctional when I

have to spend my time scrounging around," Cathy admitted to an interviewer from the *Washington Star* in 1968. "But the materialism of society has become repugnant to me. For women especially, liberation from materialism can be a profound thing. When you don't have to consume goods to find your identity, that's important."

Eleven days before her father's townhouse exploded, Cathy had appeared there unexpectedly, as thin, dirty, and sick as she had been when she had arrived at her mother's for Christmas.

"Here it was, the coldest part of winter," said Audrey Wilkerson, "and she did not have a pair of shoes that covered her feet. I gave her money to buy a warm pair of boots first thing. Even then, I had to push her out the door to shop for them."

"We left for St. Kitts the day after she arrived," said James Wilkerson. "I told Cathy to stay as long as she liked. She seemed pleased at that. I don't mind saying I was pleased too. It was nice to phone every few nights from the island and find her home. For the last few years the only places I've ever been able to call her have been SDS headquarters in Chicago, SDS Washington, SDS Pittsburgh. . . ."

"Was anyone else in the house when you called?" asked Seedman.

"She never mentioned it."

"Does any of her girlfriends come to mind who is dark, stocky, not too tall, with curly hair?"

"Well, both times Cathy was arrested in Chicago it was with a girl named Kathy Boudin. She fits that description. Her father is a big civil rights lawyer." Wilkerson shook his head. "They may look like opposites, but these two girls are soulmates."

Seedman had already sent Joe Gibney and Sam Parola to see whether Susan Wager could refine the description of the girl she had brought home with Cathy Wilkerson. In the Wager living room the detectives were served coffee from a silver service. Sitting gracefully on an embroidered French chair, Susan Wager was as beautiful a woman as they had ever seen, and Gibney was finding it hard to press her on necessary details of the dark girl's anatomy.

"Was she . . . did she . . . ?" Gibney motioned with cupped hands to his own chest.

"What my partner is getting at," broke in Parola, "is, did she have a big pair of tits?"

Gibney, who had just taken a gulp of coffee, choked. But Susan Wager threw back her head and laughed.

"You could say that," she said.

"We can't put that in the alarm, ma'am," said Gibney primly.

All weekend rumbling sanitation trucks carried load after load from 11th Street to the Gansevoort Street pier, yet the debris of the townhouse seemed as thick as ever. Working together, the Fire Marshal and detectives were able to trace the paths of what appeared to have been three separate blasts. One had come straight up through the center of the house. The second, further up front, had blown out the façade. The third had blasted a great hole like a cave in the right side of the house and the adjoining ground-floor living room of actor Dustin Hoffman and his wife at number 16. Although the debris had hurtled through the brick wall with such force that it was now imbedded in the opposite wall, much of the Hoffmans' furniture, books, art pieces, and hi-fi equipment was miraculously left in place unharmed.

Con Ed investigators reported that gas had not caused any of the three explosions, yet they had never seen a home blown apart so violently by anything but gas. What else in a normal household could do it? To Seedman's surprise, they were as mystified as the Fire Marshal. Everyone agreed, though, that all three blasts seemed to have originated in the sub-basement, now covered with fifteen feet of densely packed debris. Even with the Con Ed crane digging full time and detectives working by hand, it would take at least two full days before that level could be explored.

"Actually, it's a basement and then a sub-basement," explained Wilkerson. "I had a workbench down there where I liked to restore old American furniture we picked up in the country. I also had a wine cellar, packed with bottles which couldn't be replaced now for triple what I paid for them."

"Maybe your insurance covers it," suggested Seedman.

Wilkerson shook his head sadly. "My insurance isn't going to cover half of what I lost. Just three weeks ago I turned down $220,000 for the place. It's insured for $90,000."

As the weekend closed, Seedman wondered why neither family nor friend had come forward to identify the body of the young man with short red hair. Could they have missed the stories blanketing the newspapers and TV? It was not until late Sunday night that Seedman found out why. Just as he was leaving the on-site office to go home, Inspector Tom McGuire took a phone call from the FBI.

Fingerprints taken at the morgue Friday night had identified the body as that of a twenty-four-year-old Columbia University graduate, Theodore Gold, who had been a campus vice-chairman of SDS. Two months earlier he had been arrested with ten other SDS members for sacking TV station WCAU, a CBS affiliate in Ardmore, Pennsylvania. Calling themselves the "Quaker City 11," they had smashed windows and pulled out phone lines to protest CBS coverage of the Black Panther trial then in progress in Manhattan.

To Seedman, the news was electrifying. Though Cathy Wilkerson was a Weatherman, she was the owner's daughter and had a right to be in the townhouse. Her friend Kathy Boudin had no such privilege. That made two. Now the "Good Samaritan" had turned into a third Weatherman. Three was a crowd. If all had gone peacefully, Seedman might have been willing to concede that the temporarily empty house had been used merely for a social gathering of likeminded young people. But events ruled that out. The Wilkerson house must have been a command center where some kind of specific violent campaign was in the works. Seedman could only hope that as the "dig" slowly proceeded toward the bowels of the house, the nature of that campaign would be uncovered.

Late Sunday night Sam Parola brought Theodore Gold's father to the morgue to identify the body. Ted's uncle accompanied them. Parola figured that Gold, who was a doctor, would keep himself under control better than most civilians did in the morgue, but taking no chances, he pulled out the stainless-steel slab before the two men could prepare for it. It hurt less that way, he'd found—like yanking a Band-Aid, rather than pulling it slowly.

Dr. Gold stared steadily at the corpse, his features almost as rigid as those of the face on the slab. The uncle did not look. The place was silent.

"That is not my son Teddy," Dr. Gold finally said.

Parola did not blame him for wishing it weren't. But the body was not mutilated and there was no reason for Dr. Gold to be uncertain. Parola himself could see the similarity between the living and dead men.

"It *is* your son," he said.

"How would *you* know?" demanded Dr. Gold, turning on him fiercely.

"Ten perfect fingerprints plus a palmprint says it's your son," answered Parola.

"It is *not* my son," repeated Dr. Gold in desperation. "The fingerprints are a mixup. Do you understand? This is not Teddy."

Parola looked at the floor in silence. He waited.

In another instant, Dr. Gold fell on his knees. Putting an arm over the body, he began to weep. The uncle knelt beside him and, embracing each other, the two men sobbed bitterly and loudly.

Kathy Boudin, however, was still alive, and Seedman had hoped that her parents might be as helpful as Cathy Wilkerson's. But at the Boudin home on St. Luke's Place, only a few blocks from 11th Street and nearly as quaint, Kathy's mother referred Seedman's men to her husband for comment. The detectives asked for his office number.

"Look it up yourself," she said, and shut the door.

At his midtown law offices a courteous but correct Leonard Boudin told the detectives he had spoken to his daughter and she was well. He did not know where she was. After promising to ask her to call a special police number if they should talk again, Boudin showed the detectives out. Their request had been almost a formality—neither Kathy's father nor the detectives expected she would ever place a call to that police line.

On Tuesday the Con Ed crane began its fifth day of digging out the rubble of the townhouse. Seedman had ordered one of his detectives to oversee each bite of the bucket, and on this drizzly morning the job fell to Pete Perotta. To Perotta, the dig seemed doomed to uncover nothing but endless heaps of timber, brick, plaster, glass, rags, and mutilated household furnishings. To make matters worse, the excavation had now progressed below ground level, so each bite of the bucket was being dredged up from the murky black water that filled the basement. Everything came up covered with slime. Perotta was not crazy about standing around in hip boots in the drizzle, but the crane operator was liking it even less.

"Suppose there's a fuckin' bomb in this place," he complained at the start of the shift. "One tickle of the bucket and it ends up in my mouth."

"Hey, partner," Perotta answered, "if I'm willing to stand down here in this crap and point out where to make the bite, you can damn well sit in that dry cab and work the stick."

It went on like that, load by dripping load, until just before lunch, when Perotta ordered the crane to dig toward the right front side of the basement. Up came another mass of dripping gunk. But as the crane operator was about to swing it over to the waiting sanitation truck, Perotta held up his hand. As the jaws continued to drip, Perotta's disbelieving eyes began to discern a horrible outline: the remnants of a human being.

Perotta continued to stare, immobile, as the crane operator got out of the cab to take a look.

"Is that . . . ?"

Perotta nodded.

"Holy Mary, Mother of God."

Afraid that the man might plop into the murky water, Perotta moved to support him. But instead of fainting, the man suddenly lit off down 11th Street, his short legs churning madly.

Seedman, his detectives and FBI agents were called up from the basement across the street. All of them stared at what was hanging from the teeth of the bucket. They made out one arm without a hand, a shredded torso, buttocks, one leg without a foot. There was no head.

Working the crane himself, Perotta slowly lowered the remains onto a clean blanket laid out on the sidewalk. Firemen and detectives knelt and gently pulled away the splintered wood and other debris. When the Medical Examiner arrived, they carried the remains in the same blanket to the morgue wagon. As they lifted the bundle into the van, Perotta, who had helped remove the hefty Ted Gold on Friday night, was struck at how what had once been a life now weighed hardly anything at all. As the wagon pulled away, he realized something else—despite their close inspection, he did not have the slightest idea of the body's sex.

A twenty-six-year veteran of the force, Perotta had learned long ago how not to lose his appetite even in the face of the most grisly sights. He went around the corner now for a sandwich and beer in a Sixth Avenue tavern and saw the crane operator slumped at the end of the bar. Though the man had obviously steadied himself with several stiff shots, his face was still heavy with revulsion. In the time it took Perotta to dispose of a brisket of beef sandwich and two Löwenbräus, the man never moved except to call for two more whiskies. Perotta dropped his money on the bar and, walking to the far end, put a calm hand on the crane man's shoulder.

"Come on, old partner. We got work to do."

"Not by me."

"The bad part's over now."

"Till the day I die, I'm not going back there," said the man. But when Perotta took him by the arm, he did not resist.

Nothing but the usual debris came up in the next three hours, and Perotta was congratulating himself that his prediction was apparently correct. The bad part *was* over. The little crane operator actually looked quite chipper when, at the stroke of five o'clock, he pointed to his watch. Quitting time.

"One more bite!" shouted an irritated Perotta, who as a detective had never quit work simply because it was a certain hour.

The bucket splashed down a full seven feet into the black water over a spot just behind the front of the foundation. It came up with the usual clutch of debris, except that between the teeth was a dull gray globe about the size of a basketball. For the second time that day Perotta held up his hand. Moving closer, he noticed what appeared to be nail points bristling just under the surface of the globe. The whole effect reminded Perotta of the oranges his mother used to spike all over with aromatic cloves and hang on the Christmas tree. Then Perotta realized that other mud-encrusted protuberances on the surface were blasting caps.

He felt a quick thrust of pure fear. A nose away, patted into this big ball, was enough dynamite to blow away half the block.

The crane operator was again beside him, peering between the teeth.

"Oh, God. Is that the . . . missing head?"

"Don't worry," said Perotta. "It's only the guts of about forty sticks of dynamite. You picked it up like one big goddam cupcake."

Saucer-eyed and silent, the operator backed up to the sidewalk on tiptoe, as if a normal footfall would be disastrous. As he raced off, Perotta knew that this time it was for good. He shut off the crane's ignition himself and called for the Bomb Squad.

The street now evacuated, detective technicians studied the dynamite ball hanging a few feet over the pavement. To Seedman the thing looked as ominous as a harbor mine. The detectives laid it into a cushioned steel box as gently as a babe and carried it into their special truck, armored with sixteen layers of steel mesh.

"No matter what we put in here," said the driver, "I always felt that if we hit a big bump or picked up a freak radio transmission, this old truck would hold it all in. But with this baby, I'm not so sure."

The truck rumbled down the block like an oversized armadillo and headed for a remote marsh in the Rockaways, where the load could be safely exploded. Seedman could only feel sorry for any gulls that happened to be gliding overhead.

"Okay, forget the crane," ordered Seedman. "Who knows what other stuff is buried down there. It might bend the crane all out of shape. From now on it'll be all handwork."

"Right, boss," said the Bomb Squad men solemnly. "Better us than it."

Wearing chest-high rubber waders, the Bomb Squad men lowered themselves into the section of the sub-basement from which the dynamite ball had been pulled. Since their floodlights did not penetrate one inch of the cold black water, they had to feel around below the surface with greatest care. A jamup of jagged planks and beams which had settled at this level made footing treacherous. But the nails and splinters sticking out of the debris turned out to be the least of the dangers.

In the next two hours detectives pulled out a case neatly packed with fifty-seven bright-red sticks of TNT and five smaller cases containing a total of a hundred and forty-six blasting caps. They fished out sixteen alarm clocks and wristwatches, each fitted with electrical terminals and blasting caps, and found ninety-four feet of waxed, coiled, slow-burning orange fuse.

It had been years since the Bomb Squad's backup armored truck had been in use. Now, at 9:40, it was running a shuttle service between the soggy cache and the marshes. Seedman stopped the shivering detectives as they prepared to go back in.

"We've used up our luck for today," he said. "We'll quit until morning." For the first time in five days the exhumation stopped.

Given the interests of the townhouse visitors, the Chief was not surprised to discover that they had opened a bomb factory. "However," says Seedman, "one aspect of our discovery *was* totally unexpected. The dynamite ball which, miraculously, did not explode when the teeth of the bucket clamped into it, was the most powerful bomb we had ever come across in the city. But apparently its makers were not satisfied with mere explosive force. Therein lay the shocker. They had also studded the bomb with hundreds of one-and-a-half-inch roofing nails.

"This Weatherman bomb was not primarily designed to destroy

property, though it certainly would have done so. It was meant to destroy people, and in a very unpleasant manner. Hurled out by the great force of the explosion, these nails would tear flesh into spaghetti. Since the path of the nails could not be predicted, the bombers could not know whom they were maiming, and we have to assume they did not care. They would surely have been pleased to know their victims almost turned out to be detectives. As it was, the only victims were their own people. The body in the bucket had been so badly mutilated by roofing nails, for example, that only after painstaking examination could the Medical Examiner determine it was female.

"A bomb factory on the scale we had just uncovered probably had required the efforts of more than the two living and two dead persons we had so far accounted for. After all, the explosives we'd found represented only the stock which hadn't blown up. Others beside Wilkerson and Boudin may have escaped, but they would have had to exit during the first few seconds before neighbors rushed up. Given the noon hour, it was also possible that they had just ducked around the corner for lunch. Or they might not have been so lucky, in which case they could still be under the tons of debris burying the foundations of 18 West 11th Street.

"We would have to resume the search, but our work would be complicated by a new consideration. Now that we knew about the dynamite, my own responsibility was greater. Suppose other explosives were down there, ready to go off under the boots of the detectives? The only ones who could tell us what to expect were the fugitives themselves. The next morning I asked the Wilkersons to make a public plea to their daughter to let us know whether I was endangering my men by continuing the search."

Cathy's mother spoke first that day from her home in New Hampshire. "I believe in you so much," Mrs. Logan said in a recorded telephone message. "I know you would not wish to add more sorrow to this tragedy. More lives would be needlessly lost, and only you have the key, Cathy. Please, please telephone or wire or have someone call for you with this information."

Mrs. Logan's voice faltered as she continued. "There is nothing else we need to know except that you are safe, nothing we need to say to you except that we love you and want desperately to help."

That evening James Wilkerson stood before TV cameras on 11th Street to make a similar appeal. "Just let us know how many people, if any, are still left in the ruins of our home," he said. "I am making this appeal to you because I know you don't want to cause any further anguish or loss of life."

Afterward a reporter asked Wilkerson if he had been "communicating well" with Cathy. As he considered the question, the father's handsome features sagged with pain.

"As parents, we'd have to say no, not in recent years. I am not in favor of SDS. It is difficult to discuss with someone who is."

Standing well to the side of the battery of cameras, Joe Gibney watched Wilkerson make his plea. He knew that afterward, as they had done on each of the last three nights, the couple would retire to the small suite they had taken around the corner at the Fifth Avenue Hotel, where they made most of their own meals on a two-burner electric hotplate. During several of his visits to the suite, Gibney had been invited to eat dinner with them, and the Wilkersons had always seemed in reasonably good spirits. Jim Wilkerson had even been ecstatic when Gibney brought over a pair of his favorite shoes, custom-made in England, which Police Academy recruits had retrieved from the debris at Gansevoort Street. But Gibney had never seen Wilkerson look so low as now. He followed the couple to their hotel.

"I know you both like to eat really special food," said Gibney. "But I guess you haven't had the time or the heart to do much about it lately. Anyway, I was wondering whether you had a taste for a nice tender rabbit?"

Wilkerson, plopped in a wing chair deep in a gloom, barely stirred.

"My boys and I keep a hutch in our backyard in Queens and I'd be glad to bring you in a rabbit. And I'll tell you what else I could bring," said Gibney. "Remember I told you about my own little farm upstate near Corning?"

"I remember," said Wilkerson.

"Well, the boys and me go ice fishing up there every winter and we got a freezer full of pickerel. Did you ever taste a pickerel out of ice-cold clean water?"

"Oh, *yeah*," said Wilkerson, rubbing his hands together now. "Sautéed with fresh shallots in butter and wine, a few mushrooms tossed in at the end . . . delicious!"

Gibney drove home that night happy to have cheered Wilkerson up. The man had lost his daughter and his home, and Gibney was glad he could offer him even a small pleasure. He had in mind a particularly plump gray rabbit with one black ear, the very best in the hutch, that he had been saving for his own table.

While bodies and bombs were dramatically being recovered from the townhouse's murky depths, the humdrum sifting of the Gansevoort Street recruits turned up an item that, though far less startling, very nearly produced the biggest break of all: a soaked, blurred, but still legible appointment card reminding Kathy Boudin to visit her dentist at 10:30 on March 9, the Monday after the explosion. Now, first thing Wednesday morning, Seedman sent Gibney to the dentist's fancy East Side office.

"Miss Boudin didn't by chance keep her appointment on Monday?" Gibney said to the receptionist.

"She most certainly did. Right on time."

Gibney was stunned. How had she dared? Either she had terrific guts or her teeth really hurt badly. Or perhaps she wanted to give an aura of normality to those days in case she ever had to deny being at the townhouse.

"Did Miss Boudin make another appointment?" asked Gibney. The receptionist obligingly began to thumb forward in the book when the dentist suddenly appeared and slammed the book shut.

"Can I help you?" he asked tensely.

"I'm trying to locate Kathy Boudin," Gibney answered, flashing his shield.

"What makes you think I know where she is?"

"I don't—but I thought you might have given her another appointment after Monday's."

"That's between me and the patient." Only the intercession of the DA's office could persuade the dentist to reveal that Kathy Boudin was due back for more drilling the very next morning. This time she didn't show up.

They hit another dead end when detectives extracted from the debris a torn white dress shirt laundry-marked "REILLY." Seedman wondered whether it had been left behind by yet another visitor to the townhouse, but local laundries were unable to identify it. Then a detective named Mizzi, pursuing the report that someone inside the townhouse had called out "Adam" just before the final explosion, happened to knock on the door of Jonah and Elinor Raskin at 250 Riverside Drive. A search of known SDS activists had turned up

only one Adam—the brother of Jonah Raskin. Adam Raskin was en-
rolled as a college student in Montreal, but Mizzi had come to
investigate the long shot that on the day of the explosion he had
been in New York instead.

A woman answered the detective's knock.

"Mrs. Raskin?"

"No. They're away."

"Your name, ma'am."

"Barbara."

"Barbara what?"

"Barbara Reilly."

Mizzi remembered the laundry mark on the shirt almost instantly, but tried not to show that he had made the connection.
Then Mizzi heard someone else moving around in the apartment.

"Who else is back there?" asked the detective loudly.

A man came forward. "My name is Robert Reilly," he said.

Mizzi decided to act as if he had come for Reilly in the first
place. "I'd like you to come down to the office to answer a few
questions about the townhouse that exploded last week."

Robert Reilly stared at the detective coolly. "Okay," he said.
"I'll have my attorney meet us there."

Reilly was a schoolteacher. Under interrogation he claimed
never to have been in the townhouse, nor to know Cathy Wilkerson,
but he did admit to knowing Kathy Boudin.

"One more question," said Seedman. "You don't happen to be
missing a nice white dress shirt, do you?"

Reilly stared at Seedman. "Why do you ask?"

"We found one marked 'Reilly.' Just thought it might be yours."

"It's not," answered Reilly quickly. "My God, how many Reillys
do you think there are in this town?"

"Not that many who know Kathy Boudin."

Reilly said nothing, but Seedman saw no point in pressing him.
Even if the shirt did belong to Reilly, that didn't prove he had been
in the townhouse. Adam Raskin could have borrowed it. Judging
by the way Ted Gold had been dressed, the people at the bomb
factory sometimes felt the need to dress "straight," as Sam Melville
had during his bomb deliveries.

"We could have settled the question easily," says Seedman. "All
Adam Raskin had to do was prove he was in class in Montreal on
March sixth. But we couldn't find him. His parents were no help,

and the Montreal police also were unable to determine whether he had been in their city then. Unless Adam Raskin chooses to show up one day and cooperate, we may never learn anything more to suggest his presence than the cry of a name and a shirt he may have borrowed."

The plea of Cathy Wilkerson's parents went unanswered—nobody called or sent word about whether more bombs still lurked in the lowest strata of ruins. Not much more could be done to maximize security, except to pump out the apparently bottomless reservoir of black water from the deepest recesses of the basement. That way, at least, the searchers would be able to see where they were stepping.

The week's digging passed uneventfully until Saturday morning, when Joe Gibney and Sam Parola came upon what appeared to be a small, damp pink and brown rug wrapped around a sewerpipe. Gibney reached to unroll the rug but it came away in his hand. Only then did he realize he was holding flesh. For the first time in his sixteen years as a cop a rush of nausea dropped him in a quivering heap. Even Parola, whose daily life on the force meant going where the gore was, felt utterly revolted.

As Parola was dragging his partner out to the street, Seedman appeared. "What's the matter with *him?*" he asked.

"Joey just needs a little air, Chief."

Parola propped Gibney against a tree and then took Seedman into the ruins. What Gibney had taken for a rug appeared now to be the upper torso of a male—minus limbs or head. After spreading a canvas beneath it, Parola gave the pipe a hard kick. The torso fell off. It was hollow right to the spine. To blow apart a human body like this had taken an incredible force.

"I didn't think anything could be worse than the girl in the bucket," Parola muttered.

Seedman was not entirely surprised at this new finding. Just the day before the Fire Marshal had remarked on the faint smell of spoiled meat around the site. Seedman had kept it to himself, but his own feeling had been that it was the odor of human death.

The next day, as Seedman wondered how the two mutilated bodies would ever be identified, the Gansevoort Street crew came up with their prize finding. Out of the muck from the bottom of the basement they had sifted the skin of the upper joint of an index finger. John Hackett of the Missing Persons Bureau took the print by fitting it around his own index finger, then rolling it out on the ink pad as if it belonged to his own hand.

City and FBI technicians went to work, checking the single print against prints of all known SDS members who had ever been arrested. In just two days the FBI came up with the answer. The print belonged to twenty-seven-year-old Diana Oughton, who had yielded to absolutely no one as a front-line Weatherman. In fact, she had stood out. That brought the number of bombers in the townhouse to five.

Like the others, Diana came from a well-to-do family in the serene country town of Dwight, Illinois, eighty miles outside Chicago. The Oughtons were prominent nationally as well as locally. One great-grandfather established the first hospital for alcoholism in the United States, the other founded the Boy Scouts of America. Diana's father owned thousands of acres of farmland around Dwight and in Likskillet, Alabama, where the property was worked by sharecroppers.

At the exclusive Madeira School in Greenway, Virginia, Diana had been a large, blond, friendly girl with an eager smile. A model student, she had been accepted at each of the elite Eastern women's colleges known as the Seven Sisters. She had picked Bryn Mawr, arriving there in the fall of 1959 with the traditional silver service for afternoon tea.

Diana had majored in German, spending her junior year in Munich. The first sign that she would not return to the good life in Dwight had come at graduation. A strapping Princeton football player had proposed but she turned him down, having chosen instead to work as a Quaker volunteer in the poor Guatemalan mountain town of Chichicastenango. While none of the volunteers lived luxuriously, Oughton's way of life had become increasingly primitive until, at the end of her two-year tour, she was subsisting in a dirt-floor hut as raggedly as the most luckless peasants of Chichicastenango.

Returning to the States in 1966, Diana had wandered into a Master's program in education at the University of Michigan at Ann Arbor, but an experimental free school for young children was soon consuming far more time than her studies. At the school she met Bill Ayers, a spirited, handsome, and radical teacher whose father was chairman of the Chicago Edison Company and a trustee of Northwestern University. Diana and Bill were soon running the free school together. In 1967 she asked her father to have her name removed from the Chicago Social Register.

After the Columbia student riots in the spring of 1968 and the debacle in the Chicago streets at the Democratic Convention in August, Diana and Bill had become leaders of the local SDS chapter. Rough-and-tumble insurgents, they had booted out the gentler idealists who for six years had been the quiet bulwark of campus SDS. At the SDS national convention in June 1969 they had joined the dissident Weatherman faction of several hundred fanatics. Along with Diana and Bill, its members included Ted Gold, Cathy Wilkerson, Kathy Boudin.

"At the Columbia riots," says Seedman, "I had seen that while a large part of the crowd bore no goodwill to President Grayson Kirk or us cops, they were reasonable kids who wanted to vent their feelings, make their point, then get back to the business of studying. Only a minority, whose loudest spokesman was Mark Rudd, insisted on prolonging the confrontation for its own sake. They seemed to need each new spurt of violence like an addict needs heroin, and they were just as desperate to get it. Out of this handful came the Weathermen."

The Weathermen decided to mark the second anniversary of Che Guevara's death with "Four Days of Rage" in Chicago. As a warmup seventy-five women from several collectives traveled to Pittsburgh to "radicalize" South Hills High School. When the local Friends Service Committee refused to let them use the office mimeograph machine, the women held the staff captive while they ran off a leaflet. Two days later the seventy-five women stormed South Hills High, spray-painting "HO LIVES" and "FREE HUEY" everywhere and charging down the halls, screaming "Jailbreak!" But the kids had no idea what was happening. The invaders fled as the police arrived. Cathy Wilkerson was among those arrested; Diana Oughton was among the escapees.

The Weathermen had hoped that as many as fifty thousand sympathizers would pour into Chicago a few weeks later for the "Four Days of Rage." On the eve of the rally Weathermen dynamited a statue erected in memory of eight policemen killed by a bomb in Haymarket Square in the nineteenth century. The next day fewer than four hundred Weathermen gathered in Grant Park for the first ragtag charge through the streets. By the end of the third day most of the participants were under arrest, including Cathy Wilkerson, Kathy Boudin, and Diana Oughton.

According to Thomas Powers' book *Diana: The Making of a Terrorist,* Oughton called her sister Carol in Washington four days later, before the townhouse explosion. She complained that "the pigs [had] been riffling through [her] house," and wanted to send Carol a sealed envelope of her personal papers. (The envelope arrived a few days later, marked "N'ouvrez pas.") The sisters chatted awhile about little things. Then Diana suddenly asked, "Will the family stand by me, no matter what? Will they help me if I need it?"

"Of course," answered Carol, having no idea what her sister was planning. "Anything."

Two weeks after that call, on St. Patrick's Day, three teeth were sifted out at Gansevoort Street and later identified through family dental charts as Diana's. Another of her fingers was also found. It appeared that she had been at Wilkerson's basement workbench, assembling a bomb, when something went wrong. The torso wrapped around the nearby pipe may have belonged to a male working with her.

All during March recruits sifted for a clue to identifying the torso but found none. The most police could do was scrape a few blood samples from the pipe for future comparisons. There was one other possibility. Calling on his most grisly expertise, Seedman was aware that the force of such a terrific blast might literally rip the victim's face cleanly from the bone and hurl it against the nearest surface. Removed with care, this "death mask" might even be restored by a taxidermic process to an approximation of its original features.

The detectives found no such death mask, though they did find bits of flesh imbedded in the far wall of Dustin Hoffman's living room next door. At first the death mask theory had seemed farfetched as well as revolting. But it was proven accurate, at least indirectly, when, twenty-five feet from the nearest body, the searchers found a cleanly severed human heart.

Toward the middle of April rumors from the FBI's huge intelligence network indicated to Seedman that the torso might belong to Terry Franklin Robbins, a twenty-five-year-old radical from Queens. Like the torso, he was large-framed. He was also a violent extremist who had served forty-five days in an Ohio jail for leading the riots at Kent State. He was friends with Wilkerson, Boudin, Oughton, and Gold and had disappeared immediately after his release from jail, two weeks before the explosion. Detectives believed his father and sister when they swore they had not heard a word from him.

Sam Parola took Terry Robbins' father to the morgue where he pulled out the slab quickly, as he had done for Ted Gold's father. But while Dr. Gold had resisted acknowledging Ted's undamaged body, Samuel Robbins merely stared blankly.

"You expect me to say that's my *son?*" he asked in wonder.

"We thought you might notice something which only a parent could identify," answered Parola. He showed Mr. Robbins a shoe found near the torso.

"That might be his size and style of shoe," agreed the father. "But is that proof of anything?"

Parola shook his head and drove Samuel Robbins home.

Like Diana Oughton, Terry Robbins had been a regional organizer for SDS in the Midwest. In 1967 he had taught in the free school she ran with Bill Ayers. In those years he had not been a student himself or worked at any "straight" job. Seedman wondered why such an apparently strong young man had never been drafted.

As it turned out, Terry Robbins had indeed been called up for a preliminary physical exam, but had been rejected when a doctor submitted X-rays showing a badly deformed disc in his patient's lower spine. When those X-rays were compared to the intact spine of the torso, detectives were disconcerted to learn that the disc in the X-ray appeared to be in worse shape than the one in the torso.

"I was so sure we had the right guy," said Parola.

"If I was a kid who didn't want to be in the Army," said Seedman, "I'd find a doctor who'd help me out, maybe by fudging some X-rays."

Though no one could ever prove that the disc in the X-ray had been altered, the Medical Examiner thought it was quite possible.

Members of Terry Robbins' family agreed to submit samples of their hair and blood to compare with those on the body. All

these comparisons pointed to Terry Robbins, but none was con-
clusive. As with so many other questions, Seedman awaited final
word from the survivors of the townhouse explosion.

As Seedman had hoped, the townhouse dig did uncover clues,
not only to their identities, but to how the Weathermen had lived.
Among the most useful artifacts found were a large number of stolen
checkbooks, credit cards, drivers' licenses, and student ID cards. It
was easy to see how the Weathermen could afford not to work.

One waterlogged checkbook, bearing the names of William &
Kathleen Langdon, had been stolen two weeks before the explosion during a party at the University of Pennsylvania. The next
morning at the local Sears, Roebuck a girl had used three Langdon
checks to buy an electric drill, a saw, and a green leather attaché
case. "This is for my husband's birthday," the girl had said. "He'll
be so happy."

That same Saturday morning more Langdon checks were used
to buy shoes, pants, and shirts from four stores in downtown Philadelphia. The forgers had passed all the checks that day, knowing
the stores would not be able to verify the account until Monday,
when it would be too late. Other checks stolen from a student at
Bryn Mawr, Diana's alma mater, were used the week before the
explosion to buy clothes and three LaForge antimagnetic watches at
Macy's in New York. The warranty cards were found at Gansevoort
Street.

An oddly chilling insight into the recklessness of the townhouse
guests came out of an investigation of a stolen credit card found in
Cathy Wilkerson's wallet. The real owner was a New York University student who had reported her purse stolen while she sat in
the university library's reading room.

"I never believed I'd get it back," she told the detective who
came around to her Thompson Street apartment. "Where did you
find it?"

"In that townhouse over on 11th Street."

The girl's face clouded over, but she only thanked the detective
and closed the door. The next morning, however, she called him
back.

"I couldn't sleep last night," she said. "I told a lie about my
purse. It was really stolen from a friend's apartment. I slept over at
his place, and when we woke up in the morning, my bag was gone
from beside the bed."

"Why didn't you say so in the first place?"

"Well, I'm still legally married to someone else, even though we're separated. But if it helps you at all with that townhouse horror, it's worth a little hassle with my husband's lawyer."

Seedman felt the girl's story had filled in a striking detail of the townhouse portrait. Stealing from a room where people are sleeping was the most brazen kind of act, one which few thieves have the courage or stealth to attempt. But these Weathermen apparently had both. One other such thief came to mind. His thievery was also incidental to his real criminal interests. He was Winston Mosely, murderer of Anna Mae Johnson and Kitty Genovese.

"Of all the items recovered at the site," says Seedman, "I was most anxious to trace the fifty-seven sticks of dynamite we pulled out the Tuesday after the explosion. American Cyanamid was able to tell by the crate markings that the shipment had gone to New England Explosives Company in Keene, New Hampshire. That was not surprising, since for years now rural New England has been a prime source for anyone wanting to buy dynamite without answering hard questions. These dealers all seem to have a Yankee philosophy of minding their own business. Sure enough, despite the best efforts of the FBI and my own detectives, no clerk at New England Explosives could positively identify who had bought the townhouse load.

"Dynamite was bought by questionable people all over New England that week. One night, for example, a young man walked into the Kendall Lawson Company in Barre, Vermont, and asked for a hundred pounds of dynamite, blasting caps, and fuses. After flashing identification cards in the name of Rabbi Henry Skirball of the American Hebrew Congregation on Fifth Avenue, he got the merchandise. The clerk never asked why a rabbi from New York would need dynamite and the real Rabbi Skirball didn't, of course. His wallet had been stolen at Columbia University early in March and we found it in the townhouse."

Even if they never learned their lessons, Seedman felt that the townhouse group must have tried to read up on explosives before trying to use them. Where might they go for such information? The obvious first choice was the city's marvelous central library at 42nd Street. Indeed, the records of the Science & Technology reserve shelf did show that on February 4 a book on the chemistry of explosives had been checked out by Kathy Boudin.

Seedman had always insisted that his detectives repeatedly return to the area of a crime and recanvass the ground for witnesses. It paid off in the Townhouse Case nearly a month after the explosion when, two blocks south, on West 9th Street, Joe Gibney discovered a shy young girl named June White. She had usually spent her spare moments in front of 16 West 11th Street in hopes of seeing Dustin Hoffman, but ever since the day of the explosion she had been afraid to go back. Under Gibney's gentle coaxing, she revealed that on the last Saturday morning in February she had noticed a group of six to eight young men and women unloading brown crates from a light-colored car. They carted them quickly into the basement of number 18. The fellow directing the unloading, she remembered, was a musclar young man with short red hair. He kept telling the others to handle the crates carefully. From mug shots June White unhesitatingly picked out Ted Gold.

The Chicago trial of Cathy Wilkerson and Kathy Boudin on charges of assault and riot during the "Four Days of Rage" had been scheduled for March 16, ten days after the explosion. They never showed up, and Wilkerson's bail of $5000 and Boudin's of $10,000 were forfeited. In July they were among thirteen Weathermen indicted by a Federal grand jury on another bombing conspiracy charge; named along with them as conspirators, but not indicted, were Terry Robbins and the late Ted Gold and Diana Oughton. The FBI could locate none of the thirteen.

Late in May 1970 Bernardine Dohrn, one of the missing thirteen, sent the *New York Times* Chicago Bureau a typewritten "Declaration of War" against American society. It said that black revolutionaries would no longer have to fight alone because now Weathermen would be leading "white kids into armed revolution." It said that the Weathermen were now adapting the "classic guerrilla strategy of the Vietcong and the urban guerrilla strategy of the Tupameros" to their own country. It said that, as Che had taught them, "revolutionaries move like fish in the sea," and that the contempt of young people for their society had created such a sea. It promised that the Weathermen would "never live peaceably" under this system. The next paragraph said:

> *This was totally true of those who died in the New York townhouse explosion. The third person who was killed there was Terry Robbins, who led the first rebellion at Kent State less than two years ago.*

"With this admission from the Weathermen themselves," says Seedman, "I closed our investigation of who the torso was. However,

Samuel Robbins refused to take the word of Bernardine Dohrn; the remains have yet to be claimed. If I were the father, I don't know that I'd give up hope, either. Certainly the Weathermen have discarded all traditions, including conventional decency, in the belief that they hinder the 'revolution.' They could have announced Terry Robbins' death simply to stop the law from seeking him out, but I doubt even they would perpetrate such a cruelty on the family.

"On April thirtieth, the recruits at the Gansevoort Street pier sifted out the last piece of human tissue we were to find. Like the rest, it was delivered in a plastic bag to the Medical Examiner. A few days later I sent the recruits back to the Police Academy. It had taken us eight weeks to pick through the debris that had been the townhouse. We had found evidence as small as the hour hand of a pocket watch and large as a case of dynamite. We found more than three dozen stolen credit cards, drivers' licenses, and other personal papers which helped us trace the movements of the townhouse Weathermen before and after March sixth. We learned that besides the three who died and the two who escaped and fled, other Weathermen had been in and out of the place since the Wilkersons had left for St. Kitts.

"But for me the most important moment of the case came on March tenth, when I stepped close to that odd gray globe in the teeth of the bucket and saw it was studded with one-and-a-half-inch roofing nails. Those nails more than justified the massive expense of this investigation. They represented a campaign, not only to destroy property, as Sam Melville had done the previous fall, but to brutally destroy human bodies along with it. That second aim was confirmed by another letter from Bernardine Dohrn in December 1970. She explained that 'two weeks before the townhouse explosion, four members of this group had firebombed Judge Murtagh's house in New York as an action of support for the Panther 21, whose trial was just beginning.' The group had thought this a 'very good action,' but not radical enough. Two weeks later, Dohrn goes on, the group had 'moved from firebombing to *antipersonnel bombs.*' They planned what she calls a 'large scale, almost random bombing offensive.'

"The only big question that remained was what target they had in mind to open this offensive," says Seedman. "Random or not, it was bound to have significance to them, just as the United Fruit Company pier on the Hudson had its own peculiar significance to Sam Melville. From FBI informants we soon learned that the first target had, in fact, been picked with an eye for history. It was the Low Library on the Columbia campus—the last place where SDS could feel it had won the sympathies of a large body of students, the last place it had acquitted itself with its own version of glory. What better spot for this Weatherman remnant to try to recapture the spirit of old.

"They certainly came close. Cathy Wilkerson's parents were due home the morning after the explosion but by then the bomb factory would have been dismantled, the bombs removed, and the house tidied up, just as the Wilkersons had left it. By then, too, my big case would have been uptown, amid the ruins of Low Library.

"So now, kids come and go from the library as they almost always do. The campus feels as peaceful as it did in the years before the Vietnam War. As for the Wilkersons, they have moved to a farm in England. Back on 11th Street, the handsome homes on each side of the townhouse have been rebuilt at the ragged edges. But the lot where number 18 stood is blocked off by a high board fence with a 'For Sale' sign on it. If you peek between the boards, you can see that the land is overgrown with bushes, young trees, vines, and, in season, flowers. It is as green as anywhere I know in New York, and even more peaceful."

A Greenwich Village townhouse glows with almost unnatural flame moments after bombs first explode in its basement.

Assigned the tedious task of sifting the debris, these recruits from the Police Academy—working under the supervision of Det. Sam Parola, right front— discover critical evidence that identified one mutilated corpse as that of twenty- seven-year-old radical leftist Diana Oughton.

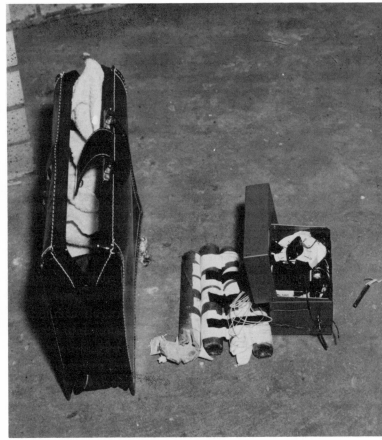

One of two bombs planted by the Jewish Defense League in the Manhattan offices of Amtorg, a Russian freight company. The first exploded; this one, concealed inside the briefcase, was shortcircuited seconds away from blowing up in the faces of several of the police top brass, including Seedman.

Seconds before shooting. This frame from a motion picture taken at the 1971 Italian–American Civil Rights League rally shows Jerome Johnson, posing as a photographer, within a few feet of Joe Colombo. A moment later he replaced his Bolex with an automatic pistol and fired four shots into Colombo's head and neck.

Columbus Circle in turmoil: police and spectators—some wearing red, green and white "Unity Day" caps—crowd around the fallen Joe Colombo.

Though Joe Colombo claimed the Mafia was a myth, this police diagram of the Magliocco Family (formerly the Profaci Family) lists Colombo as a caporegime and the Gallo brothers—Albert, Larry, and Crazy Joe—as soldiers.

THE GIUSEPPE MAGLIOCCO FAMILY

BOSS

GIUSEPPE MAGLIOCCO
"Joe Malyak"
FBI-184224 (2,3,6,8)

Key to Activity Code

1a. Currently in jail for Nar
1b. Awaiting trial for Nar
1c. Previous conviction for Nar
1d. Suspected of being active in Nar
2. Gambling
3. Shylocking
4. Labor racketeering
5. Vending machines and/or juke boxes
6. Extortion, Strong arm and murder
7. Counterfeiting
8. Criminally receiving
9. Alcohol tax violations
* Identified by Joseph Valachi

Successor to:

GIUSEPPE PROFACI
"The Old Man"
FBI-362142a
Deceased

UNDERBOSS

Salvatore Mussachio
"The Shiek"
FBI-191344
(2,3,4,6,8)

CAPOREGIME

Sebastiano Aloi
"Buster"
B-72788 (2,3,4,6)

Leo Carlino
"Big Leo"
B-117290 (3)

John Franzese
"Sonny"
FBI-3400301
(2,3,4,6,7,8)

Simone Andolino
FBI-5064655 (2)

Joseph Colombo
B-415516 (2)

Ambrose Magliocco
(3)

John Oddo
"Johnny Bath Beach"
FBI-349341 (2,3,6)

Salvatore Badalamenti
B-161191 (2,3)

Harry Fontana
(2,3,6,8)

Nicholas Forlano
"Jiggs"
FBI-886909 (1c,2,3,6)

SOLDIERS - BUTTONS

Anthony Abbattemarco
"Shatz"
B-430747 (2,3)

Salvatore D'Ambrosio
"Sally D"
B-253747 (6,8)

Albert Gallo, Jr.
"Kid Blast"
B-34922 (2,6)

Philip Gambino
"Foongy"
B-275897 (6)

Cassandros Bonasera
"Tony the Chief"
FBI-191363 (2,3)

Bartolo Ferrigno
"Barioco Bartulucia"
FBI-1705717 (1d, 6,7)

Joseph Gallo
"Crazy Joe"
FBI-120842A (2,6)

Charles LoCicero
"The Sidge"
Deposed B-168356 (2,3)

Alphonse D'Ambrosio
"Funzied"
B-233838 (6,8)

Cosmo Frasca
"Gus"
FBI-285760 (2,6)

Lawrence Gallo
"Larry"
FBI-392538 (2,6)

Gaetano Marino
"Toddo"
B-45651 (1d, 2,4)

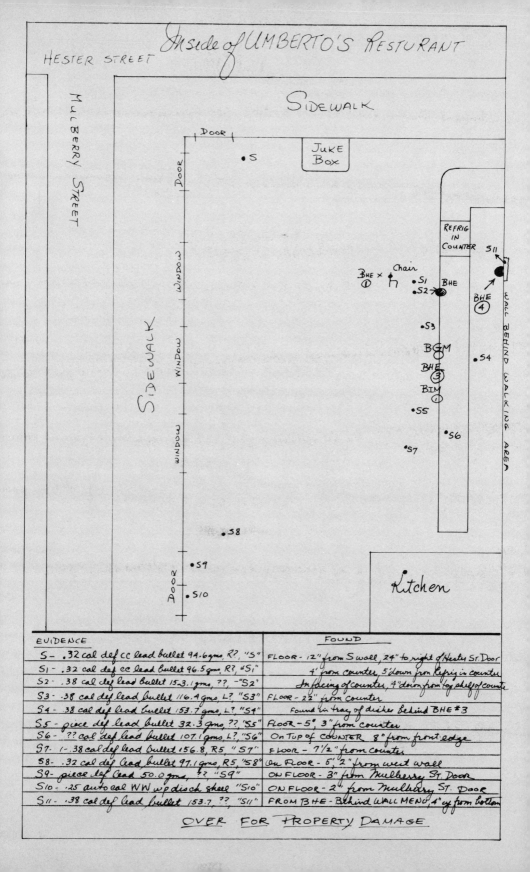

Inside of UMBERTO'S Resturant

HESTER STREET

MULBERRY STREET

SIDEWALK

SIDEWALK

DOOR

JUKE BOX

DOOR

WINDOW

WINDOW

WINDOW

WINDOW

DOOR A

REFRIG IN COUNTER

WALL BEHIND WALKING AREA

Kitchen

• S

BHE × ①

Chair

• S1   BHE

• S2   BHE

• S3

BGM

BHE ③

BIM ①

• S5

• S6

• S7

• S11

BHE ④

• S4

• S8

• S9

• S10

EVIDENCE	FOUND
S - .32 cal def cc lead bullet 94.6 gms, R?, "S"	FLOOR - 12" from S wall, 24" to right of Hester St. Door
S1 - .32 cal def cc lead bullet 96.5 gms, R?, "S1"	4' from counter, 5' down from Refrig in counter
S2 - .38 cal def lead bullet 15.3.1 gms, ??, -"S2"	In facing of counter, 4' down from top shelf of counter
S3 - .38 cal def lead bullet 116.4 gms, L?, "S3"	FLOOR - 22" from counter
S4 - 38 cal def lead bullet 153.7 gms, L?, "S4"	Found in tray of dishes behind BHE #3
S5 - piece def lead bullet 32.3 gms, ??, "S5"	FLOOR - 5', 3" from counter
S6 - ?? cal def lead bullet 107.1 gms, L?, "S6"	On Top of COUNTER 8" from front edge
S7 - 1 - .38 cal def lead bullet 156.8, R5, "S7"	FLOOR - 7½" from counter
S8 - .32 cal def lead bullet 97.1 gms, R5, "S8"	On FLOOR - 5', 2" from west wall
S9 - piece def lead 50.0 gms, ??, "S9"	ON FLOOR - 3" from Mulberry St. Door
S10 - .25 auto cal WW w.p. disch shell "S10"	ON FLOOR - 2" from Mulberry St. Door
S11 - .38 cal def lead bullet 153.7, ??, "S11"	FROM BHE - Behind WALL MENU 4" up from bottom

OVER FOR PROPERTY DAMAGE

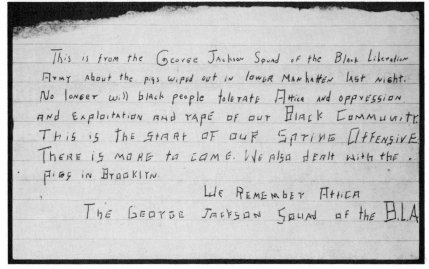

This is from the George Jackson Squad of the Black Liberation Army about the pigs wiped out in lower Manhatten last night. No longer will black people tolerate Attica and oppression and Exploitation and rape of our Black Community. This is the start of our Spring Offensive. There is more to come. We also dealt with the pigs in Brooklyn.

WE REMEMBER Attica

The GEORGE JACKSON Squad of the B.L.A

TOP: *Pursuing a couple of apparent traffic violators in this patrol car, Officers Thomas Curry and Nicholas Binetti suddenly found themselves the victims of a Black Liberation Army ambush. Together they absorbed sixteen bullets from a Thompson submachine gun; somehow, they survived, though neither is expected to fully recover.*

BOTTOM: *"The guns of liberation": after the shooting of Officers Foster and Laurie, this message received by United Press International introduced the Black Liberation Army.*

Scaled-down version of a wall-sized police diagram of Umberto's Clam House, the scene of Joey Gallo's assassination, showing location of bullets and shells found by police, as well as damage done to the restaurant.

As Police Commissioner Patrick V. Murphy (right) looks on, Seedman briefs reporters on suspects in shootings of Police Officers Foster and Laurie.
(Ken Regan/Camera 5)

THE JEWISH CONNECTION

In a burnished and glowing private room of an elegant club on the East Side just off Park Avenue, waiters are draping fresh linen on the long table where a dozen of Al Seedman's friends will soon throw a stag dinner to celebrate his promotion to Chief of Detectives. Though the guest list is short, it includes District Attorneys, judges and other bigwigs, so the manager is personally dusting the silver and checking the crystal for water marks. On this warm April evening in 1971 Seedman will come as close as he ever has to meeting a violent death.

For the moment he is still at work in his office. Across the desk sits Pete Perotta, a balding man whose soft manner and unwary eyes are rare among veteran detectives. Perotta might pass for a pediatrician, but he is talking to Seedman about bombs. Ever since that elegant nineteenth-century townhouse on West 11th Street was blown apart, bombs have been Perotta's specialty. Bombs are what Seedman has called him down to talk about now.

At this same moment, 5:30, chief engineer Frank Hassett is at his own desk in the basement of the thirty-story office building at 355 Lexington Avenue whose tenants include Amtorg, the Soviet trade mission. Hassett, who sits surrounded by dials and valves, is finishing up his daily reports when the phone rings. The voice on the other end is young, high, and straining to be calm.

"Clear the building fast," it says. "You're about to be bombed."

In the next few moments desk men at the Associated Press and United Press International answer their phones and hear a similar voice deliver this message:

"Several time bombs have been placed in the offices of Amtorg. They will go off in less than fifteen minutes." The caller pauses, then adds fervently, "Free all Soviet Jewish prisoners. . . . Let my people go. . . . Never again."

In his office, Frank Hassett sighs and gets up from his desk. The call does not come as a complete surprise. For more than a year, Arab and Russian tenants of the building have been targets of Jewish protest. Just two weeks ago, in fact, several members of the Jewish Defense League slipped into the nineteenth-floor reception room of Amtorg to release a swarm of wriggling mice and frogs; a plague to warn the Russian pharaohs to let the Jewish people go.

Hassett goes up to the reception room, where two city cops have been stationed since the trouble began, and they and Joe Renfro, the elevator starter, clear the floors directly above and below Amtorg of all workers still in the building. At the end of a long day, it seems more trouble than it's worth. Then Renfro opens the heavy steel fire door on the nineteenth floor. On the landing he sees a cheap vinyl attaché case. In the quiet of that concrete-block stairwell he hears it tick.

Seedman was notified of the bomb threat as he talked with Perotta. With as many as a dozen similar threats phoned in every day, his desk men normally would not have bothered him, but whenever the JDL or any other group harassed the Russians, shouts of protest against the "Zionist hoodlums" were sure to be heard from the floor of the United Nations and even from the Kremlin. By now, men on duty at the Bomb Squad would be dashing to 355 Lexington Avenue from their office in the Police Academy, only four minutes away. Emergency Service would be reporting and traffic units standing by, ready to seal off the block if necessary. Duty detectives from the 17th Squad also would be on hand—all for a bomb threat that was almost certain to be false.

But something about this call seemed different to Seedman. The unleashing of the frogs and mice two weeks earlier had been a

lark—good for a laugh, but unlikely to shake the JDL's determination to make trouble for the Russians. If anything, their bravado
would be greater next time. Moreover, the timing of the call itself
disturbed Seedman. Most crank bomb threats come in the morning
when offices are full. If the aim was mischief, why call after five
o'clock, when most people had gone home? Seedman could guess.
An after-hours bomb would cause damage, consternation, and more
howls at the UN, but most likely stop short of doing bodily harm—
an escalation the JDL was probably unprepared for. Besides, the
setup was perfect. Up to 5:30 the bomber could enter the building
without signing in or having his briefcase checked; after planting
the bomb he could leave unnoticed in the after-work rush.

"Nothing will probably come of this goddam thing, Pete,"
grumbled Seedman. "But for the hell of it, let's ride up there."

They stepped into Seedman's waiting black Ford at the same
time as the men of the Bomb Squad were stepping into the elevator
at 355 Lexington. Suddenly the elevator rattled violently as the
briefcase on the fire stairs exploded.

The blast ripped away the heavy steel fire door, splintered the
furniture in the Amtorg reception room, set the carpets ablaze, and
blew out windowpanes all along the nineteenth floor. It was 5:40.
If the bomb had been timed for thirty seconds later, the explosion
would have caught the Bomb Squad on the nineteenth floor. As they
surveyed the damage and checked for more bombs, the Bomb Squad
men were startled to see how many of police top brass were arriving—first Seedman with Perotta, then Chief of Intelligence Arthur
Grubert, then the dignified Douglas MacArthurlike figure of Chief
Inspector Michael Codd.

At 5:50 a 17th Squad detective exploring the twentieth floor
fire stairs yelled shakily for a Bomb Squad man. Everyone rushed
up. There on the landing was another briefcase, ticking coldly. A
young Bomb Squad detective named Gerald Sommerville knelt and
snapped open the case.

With Codd, Grubert, and Seedman looking over his shoulder
in fascination, Sommerville lifted out a gray-enameled steel box.
Inside were a kitchen timer wired to a flashlight bulb, small and
large batteries, and three sticks of dynamite. These components
were carefully fitted and wired as neatly as if the homemade bomb
were a specimen of precision computerware.

As Sommerville reached into the midst of the bomb with his

needlenose pliers, the tiny bulb suddenly lit up cheerily. Seedman remembers that Codd smiled quizzically. He himself understood the significance—but couldn't help thinking that quite a few friends and notables were going to be stood up that night at his promotion dinner.

"That bulb lights up when juice is ready to flow," Sommerville whispered in the sudden silence. "I guess we had half, maybe three quarters of a second until . . . ignition." He looked around him at the Chief of Intelligence, Chief of Detectives, and Chief Inspector. Only then did his face go white.

"Jeez," he whistled. "We wouldn't have had no more bosses."

Later, as his friends sipped brandy at the end of the stag dinner, Seedman bit into a warmed-over filet mignon and thought about how good it was to have teeth.

"By coincidence," says Seedman, "I had originally called Pete Perotta down that evening to talk about finding a better way to set up bomb investigations. I had been aware of the problem ever since the Mad Bomber case in the middle 1950s. With his capture, we hoped our bomb problems were ended. But then in the middle 1960s, as the antiwar movement heated up, bombs went off again in draft offices, recruiting centers and office buildings. From 1965 through 1971, five hundred and five bombs were placed around the city. All but ninety-eight exploded.

"In each case the Bomb Squad reported promptly, and if it was not too late, defused the bomb and hauled it away in their custom-built armored truck to a godforsaken spot at Fort Tilden, where they dismantled the rest of it. Then they turned in a technical report to the squad detectives who caught the case. Therein lay our problem. If some nut planted one bomb in the Bronx, one in Manhattan, and one in Queens, squad detectives from three different precincts would be working on the cases. Unless they got together and compared technical reports, they might never realize that all the bombs were the work of one guy."

The morning after the Amtorg incident, Seedman suggested to the Commissioner and Chief Inspector Codd the need for a new kind of bomb investigation squad to operate citywide, as fire marshals do within the Fire Department.

"Why don't we just expand the duties of the current Bomb

Squad to include looking for bombers?" asked Commissioner Murphy.

Seedman explained that a man could be a marvelous bomb technician without knowing how to sniff out leads that would point to bombers, who were a slippery breed anyhow. Good investigative detectives, on the other hand, were likely to turn butterfingered when it came to deticking a bomb. So two separate units were needed—the existing Bomb Squad and a new unit to coordinate all bombing investigations in the city. But the men were stumped on what to call it. For lack of anything better, Codd dubbed it the "Explosive-Arson Squad."

That week Seedman hand-picked seven seasoned detectives to man the Explosive-Arson Squad. Five, including Pete Perotta, had distinguished themselves in the Townhouse Case. A sixth, Joe O'Dowd, was a fire marshal on loan from the Fire Department. In charge of the new unit Seedman put George Howard, a barrel-chested young sergeant with the close-cropped hair and gruff manner of a drillmaster who had done good work for Seedman as a detective in Manhattan South. By April 25, two days after the Amtorg incident, the Explosive-Arson Squad was fully manned and hard at work.

The Jewish Defense League had been founded in 1968 at a Queens synagogue. Though its members were mostly students, its leaders were a lawyer named Bert Zweibon and an orthodox rabbi named Meir Kahane, both in their mid-thirties. Their goal was to make Jews as tough in defending themselves as any black, Irish, or Italian streetfighters. Members were trained to use chains, karate chops, and guns to fight anti-Semitism. A favorite JDL motto—"every Jew a .22"—reflected the membership base in poorer neighborhoods, especially in Brooklyn, from where wealthier Jews had moved, leaving a remnant to fend off the new minorities moving in. But the JDL's most fervent cry was its only possible response to the finality of Hitler's slaughter of The Six Million: "Never Again."

"In its first three years," says Seedman, "this pack of kids led by Kahane and Zweibon gave us nothing but trouble. They harassed Russians, Arabs, Black Panthers, and even rabbinical assemblies. They threw paint, beat up people, picketed, sloshed blood on Russians, let loose mice and toads—and they bombed Amtorg. I was convinced of that. But they were quick to disown the act. Denying it with a straight face must have taken real discipline, but as long as we had no specific proof, they were free to go about their business. We could only suspect them.

"I needed an informant at the League's action center—a 'Jewish Connection.'"

At this point, the only evidence Seedman had was the unexploded Amtorg bomb itself. The Explosive-Arson Squad had taken it back to their new squad room on 10th Street, hoping it might somehow lead them to the bombers. Since the bomb was expected to explode, the maker had not bothered to dust away his fingerprints. But the Latent Squad could find none, except for those of Detective Sommerville. Since the red DuPont dynamite sticks carried no serial numbers, they were no help either. But the vinyl attaché case seemed more promising. Showing it to the head luggage-buyer at Macy's, detectives discovered that the basic case had been imported from Europe, while the zipper and metal corners could have been put on by any of dozens of manufacturers. Undaunted, the detectives went to the luggage retailers' exhibition at the Coliseum to ask at one booth after another whether anyone recognized the brand of the cheap vinyl attaché case. None did.

Union Carbide knew on what date it had manufactured the 1.3-volt battery in the bomb and even pinpointed the shipment in which it had arrived at the New York distributor. But from there the battery could have gone to any store in the city. However, since its price—eighty-nine cents—had been marked by hand, it had probably been purchased at a small shop.

What interested Seedman most was the white enamel kitchen timer. Stamped with the word "Micronta," it was made in Connecticut exclusively for Radio Shack, a nationwide chain of retail and catalog stores specializing in home electronics. The timer could have been ordered by mail or bought in any of the hundreds of Radio Shack stores around the country with many in metropolitan New York. Each sale over the counter was written up in triplicate —one each for the customer, store, and head office—including the customer's name and address for the catalog mailing list.

These preliminary facts had been chased down by the team of Joe Gibney and Sam Parola who had first become partners in the Narcotics Squad. Gibney was a bald, wizened little man, soft-spoken and deceptively shy-looking; as a boy growing up on the Brooklyn docks, he had learned to handle himself with much bigger men long before he ever became a cop. By contrast, Parola was wiry with dark eyes and lustrous black wavy hair, a flamboyant type who might have been a croupier at Las Vegas.

"If that timer was bought in a local Radio Shack, Chief," Parola reported, "then somewhere there's a sales slip stashed away. The trouble is, one hell of a lot of people bought these timers, especially photographers who use them in darkrooms. First we'd have to riffle through tens of thousands of receipts to pull out the Micronta sales, then go find the buyers one by one. Frankly, sir, me and Joe don't know if it's worth the effort."

"It's worth it," said Seedman. "Maybe lots of people did buy these timers, but how many people buy *two*? I'll give you a tip: you'll know it's the right receipt when the name and address turn out to be fake."

Astonishingly, Gibney and Parola sifted receipts for only two days before apparently hitting paydirt. In a Radio Shack office in Queens they found a sales slip, dated three weeks before the Amtorg bombing, for six Micronta timers. It was made out to a "Father Monoghan" at an Amsterdam Avenue address on the Upper West Side of Manhattan. The address was bound to be wrong and the name was a joke. But the fact that he had used up only two of his timers was not. Did "Father Monoghan" have four more bombs in store?

At the Amsterdam Avenue address Gibney and Parola were startled to find a storefront church. When a middle-aged man in a clerical collar appeared and introduced himself as Father Monoghan, they gaped.

"You happen to have any beefs against the Russians, Father?" asked Parola.

The priest hesitated. "Well," he said, "not against the Russians themselves. But their government is not sympathetic to their belief in God."

Gibney and Parola, both religious men, nodded. It seemed silly to ask the next question, but Gibney went ahead anyway.

"Father, on April second of this year did you buy six kitchen timers from Radio Shack?"

"I did indeed."

"Why did you need six timers, Father?"

Monoghan smiled wistfully. "Well, gentlemen," he said, "a

storefront church has a lot of bills to pay. So on Friday nights we conduct a Bingo game, and the ladies who play like those timers. I use them for Bingo prizes."

Three days later Parola and Gibney were sifting through a large carton of sales slips in a Radio Shack in Borough Park when Gibney pulled out a bill dated April 10. Listing one package of copper wire and two Micronta timers, it was made out to "Feldman" of 6136 Eighth Avenue. The detectives were pleased to discover that no such person had ever lived at that address.

The salesman remembered making the sale to a pair of young men. From an album of JDL activists he tentatively picked out Stuart Cohen, eighteen, and Sheldon Siegel, twenty-five. Both lived in nearby Borough Park.

To Seedman's eye, Cohen had nothing special to recommend him as a bomber. Like most JDL members, he was just a kid with a streak of silliness and some strong feelings about being Jewish. Siegel, on the other hand, was far more interesting. At twenty-five he was older than the others. As an architecture student at Manhattan's City College, he picked up spare cash by working part time in a photography and model-building workshop. When questioned by detectives, his boss described him as an exacting and resourceful technician. Seedman wondered if he was exacting and resourceful enough to make the magnificently crafted Amtorg bomb.

At this point, Seedman felt it would be useless to ask Siegel or Cohen why they had bought two kitchen timers and a hank of wire on April 10. They could dream up a galaxy of reasons why they needed the materials, particularly since Siegel worked in a photography lab. Seedman would have liked to place Cohen and Siegel at 355 Lexington Avenue on the afternoon of the bombing. Since the kitchen timers could be set for a maximum of only ninety minutes, the bomb-carriers had probably entered the building between 4:10 and five, but the elevator starter and two young patrolmen in the lobby could identify no one from the JDL scrapbook. Seedman was scarcely surprised. Like hundreds of others entering the lobby that afternoon, the bomb-carriers wore business suits and carried black vinyl attaché cases.

"I gave the squad two goals," explains Seedman. "I wanted them to run down Cohen and Siegel's friends and activities to see if we could connect them with the Amtorg bombing. But most of all, I wanted to convince the JDL that it was no longer a good time to plant bombs.

"Mayor Lindsay had asked me personally to prevent any more incidents like Amtorg. It was bad enough when the JDL kids threw paint or eggs at Russian diplomats or followed their wives around the supermarket shouting curses at them. But even if it hurt no one, a bomb was a disaster for the city. The Mayor was acutely aware that the United Nations did not have to be in New York. In 1948, when the United States ran the world, it may have seemed natural to establish a world body here. But now a horde of member nations didn't like us and especially didn't like New York. If they voted to move the UN elsewhere, that could be a fatal blow for the city as a great cosmopolitan center. No one was more critical of New York than the Russians. The JDL was out to make sure they liked it even less."

Seedman ordered the Explosive-Arson Squad to put a tail on Cohen and Siegel once every second day—and on an irregular schedule. A pair of detectives could pick one or the other suspect, follow him for a while in the morning, late at night, or on weekends. They could stay with him for one hour or ten, work shifts back to back or ignore the suspects entirely for several days. Seedman wanted to make sure that Cohen and Siegel never felt safe enough from surveillance to take any action against the Russians. He also hoped to learn what kind of young men they were and how resourceful they could be. Maybe Cohen and Siegel just did not have it in them to be bombers.

The two suspects soon made it clear that they had it in them to be or do anything. They quickly detected the tails as Seedman had meant them to. But unlike most suspects in his experience, neither of them got flustered. The first time Cohen and a friend noticed two detectives parked halfway down the block, they walked over to the car and jotted down the license plate number. The first hour he was under surveillance, Siegel snapped away with a 35mm. camera at the detectives who sat expressionless in the car. Just as Seedman had an album of JDL troublemakers, he was sure that they had one of their own, pasted in with all the members of the Explosive-Arson Squad.

One evening in May, Siegel and Cohen were leaving a local delicatessen when they spotted Gibney and Parola across the street in Parola's battered Pontiac. At the same moment, a patrol car came around the corner.

"Officer! Officer!" Siegel yelled out falsetto.

The patrol car backed up to him.

"See those two mean-looking men back there in the beat-up Pontiac?" he asked apprehensively. "Well, I don't know why, Officers, but they're acting like they're out to get me and Stuie here. They've been following us everywhere. We're scared. Do you think maybe you could escort us home?"

Getting out of their car, the two young patrolmen walked over to the Pontiac. "Let's see your operator's license and registration card," one of them asked Parola coldly.

Parola gritted his teeth and flashed his gold shield instead. So did Gibney. Across the street, Siegel and Cohen looked on with straight faces.

On the morning of June 3, six weeks after the surveillance had begun, Seedman got an urgent call from Sergeant Howard at the Explosive-Arson Squad.

"The guy from Radio Shack just called," he said. "Siegel was back. He bought copper wire and electrical tape. This time he gave the name Eddie Stern."

"That message marked the end of our sporadic surveillance of Siegel and Cohen," says Seedman. "Now we had to watch them every moment until we found out what Siegel planned to do with his wire and tape. But the Explosive-Arson Squad consisted of only seven men. They couldn't be expected to stay on these kids twenty-four hours a day, so I decided to augment them with detectives from Safe and Loft, or, as it is now known, Safe, Loft, and Truck Squad. Spending so much of their time tracking hijacked and stolen goods, they were the canniest tailers in the Bureau.

"I knew that from personal experience when I was assigned to the squad as a young detective in 1947. A couple of veterans were then investigating a patrolman suspected of working with a gang of armed robbers. These detectives would pick him up from the instant his own shift was over and stick with him until he reported for his next shift. That went on for months without this rogue cop ever knowing that he was being tailed. Lucky for us he never did, because when we finally caught the gang we learned they had kept a lookout in the rear of the van they used for jobs. He was armed with a machine gun and anyone who looked as if he was tailing them would be shot."

Less than a full day after initiating the continuous observation of Cohen and Siegel, a pair of Safe & Loft detectives followed Siegel's gold Volvo as he and Izzy Danziger, another JDL activist, drove across the Queensboro Bridge into midtown Manhattan. In the wretched crosstown traffic, the two cars crawled westward on 51st Street, six lengths apart. Siegel kept trying to drive into parking garages but they were all full; even the massive Rockefeller Center Garage was crammed. Finally, just west of Sixth Avenue, he found a garage, while the detectives continued on to Seventh Avenue. Racing back around the corner, they were relieved to see Siegel and Danziger leaving the garage empty-handed. That was scarcely surprising. As usual, they had made no effort to hide the fact that they were following the boys. On the way in from Brooklyn, Siegel had doubled back on himself three times, not so much to lose the detectives as to dip wings to them. Held up at a long light, Danziger had scampered back from the Volvo to snap their picture a half-dozen times. But the boys knew the limits of what they could afford to do. Or so the detectives assumed until, on the second deck of the garage, they peered into the gold Volvo.

On the floor between the bucket seats they saw a metal film canister. But instead of the standard screw-on top, it was fitted out with a device that looked like a fuse. Deciding they had reason enough to investigate further, the detectives opened up the car as fast as any thief. The film canister was indeed fitted with a fuse. It was packed with powder and laced with tiny tacks meant to fly out like shrapnel when the bomb exploded. The detectives found a second bomb under the seat, this one a cardboard paper towel tube filled with powder. In the trunk they found a bayonet and Mace, a crowd-dispersing chemical. They also found one dozen empty alarm clock cartons.

The detectives had left Siegel and Danziger in a long line of visa applicants at the Passport Office on Fifth Avenue. When they finally returned to the garage, the Volvo was brought down promptly. But instead of pulling it out to the exit ramp, the attendant parked it at the back of the garage, with the front bumper almost touching a concrete wall.

"What the fuck are you doing?" shouted Siegel. At that instant the Safe & Loft men pushed him and Danziger against the same wall and arrested them for possession of dangerous weapons.

"This was a touchy situation for us," explains Seedman. "Since they had made no attempt to conceal their presence, the last thing these detectives expected the kids to do was risk arrest by traveling with bombs. So they had had no warrant to search the car. But the law does allow officers to search without a warrant if there is reason enough to make an arrest. Seeing that bomb between the bucket seats was certainly reasonable cause to believe Siegel had committed the crime of possessing a dangerous weapon."

Sheldon Siegel did not deny that the bombs, Mace, bayonet, and clock boxes were in the Volvo. But he insisted these items were all out of sight in the trunk.

"Would I really be stupid enough to leave that stuff in plain sight when I knew you were looking to bust my ass?" he asked. That would be for a court to decide. If it believed the boys' version, the search would be ruled illegal and the bombs found by the detectives would be inadmissible evidence.

But before they ever got to court, Seedman wanted Siegel to discover how much grief could come from tangling with the various city, state, and Federal law enforcement agencies which now had an interest in him. The Alcohol, Tobacco & Firearms division of the U.S. Treasury Department had charged Siegel with possession of a bomb, a far more serious crime under Federal than State statute. When his gold Volvo was finally driven out of the parking garage that afternoon, an ATF agent was at the wheel. He took the car straight to a Federal lot in the Bronx, where it was held as evidence.

Whether any of these charges would ultimately stick was not important to Seedman that day. Siegel's and Danziger's tactical mistake had left them vulnerable to legal procedures that could drag out forever or be cut short—depending on the mood of the police and DAs. Seedman had the leverage he had been waiting for. And the man he wanted to use it on was Sheldon Siegel. Now, while the arrest still had him upset, was the moment to persuade Siegel that the various DAs would go easy on him only in return for inside information about the JDL's plans. It would be a delicate negotiation, but if it could be brought off Seedman would at last have his Jewish Connection.

From all reports, Siegel was a highly nervous, quirky man who would require careful handling. For the delicate job of winning him over, Seedman settled on Detectives Gibney and Parola. Gibney was gentle and soft-spoken, a good listener who could put the wildest paranoiac at ease. Parola was just as finely tuned to others' feelings, but Seedman was counting on his lurking Italian temper which, if sprung at the right moment, might provide shock treatment Siegel would respond to.

Siegel was working that summer as a handyman at the Pioneer Country Club, a rambling resort with kosher kitchens in the Catskill Mountains "Borscht Belt." Out on bail but without his car, he was forced to commute whenever he returned to Brooklyn. Just a day after his arrest Gibney and Parola got him on the phone and requested a meeting. Siegel reluctantly agreed, but insisted they stay away from the hotel itself. He would meet them at a tree stump on a dirt road a half-mile away. The detectives did not kid themselves that Siegel was ready to cooperate. But he *was* curious and that was a beginning. At the appointed hour they found him standing alone out by the stump, gangly, droop-shouldered, and laconic.

"We know you believe in what you're doing for the JDL," Gibney began. "To tell the truth, me and Sammy here aren't too crazy about the Russians either. But you got to understand that this crazy stuff with the bombs and crap is only going to *hurt* your people in the end, both here and in Russia. And as long as you're doing this stuff, we got no choice but to hurt *you*. We already have. Even if we decided to lay off this parking garage foolishness, the Feds would keep on pounding you. They'd pound your balls right off. You done enough already to guarantee that."

"Now we'll give it to you straight," Parola broke in. "Do you know who Al Seedman is?"

Siegel shook his head without interest.

"You should," said Parola, his voice rising. "He's the Chief of Detectives of this city and you almost blew his goddam head off."

"What are you talking about?" Siegel's face suddenly prickled with curiosity.

"I'm talking about that night at Amtorg. Your bomb was a split second away from blowing up in the face of Seedman *and* the fuckin' Chief of Intelligence *and* the Chief Inspector too. All the big cheese. Do I have to tell you where you'd be now if that had come off?"

Siegel shrugged.

"Now listen to me," Parola went on. "Chief Seedman is one of your own people. He is also a religious man. But so help me, he will see to it that you get mashed unless you help us and help yourself."

"I'm not buying," said Siegel, "but what's your deal?"

"The only deal is just that we should all help each other," said Gibney. "That's all. Our boss wants to head off any more incidents like Amtorg. Everyone won't always come out as lucky as he did. The next time it could be a bloodbath. You can help prevent that by letting us know when something is going to happen. As for your-self—and we know that's a secondary consideration for you—Chief Seedman will speak to the DA and the Feds and make sure they treat you easy."

As they talked, Siegel had stretched his lanky legs across the back seat of Gibney's car in a relaxed manner. Now he suddenly sprang out of the back seat to the road, slamming the door behind him.

"You guys must think I'm a real asshole!" he shouted angrily. "You give me this sweet talk, but in the end I get fucked. Well, it's not gonna happen because I'm not gonna work for you. I'd rather be dead!"

Gibney and Parola watched Siegel stalk away, then drove morosely back through the mountains to report to the Chief that Siegel was not going to play ball.

"Go back tomorrow," he ordered.

"But, Chief," said Parola, "this kid is just going to tell us to fuck off again."

"I'm telling you the same thing," said Seedman. "Go back."

The detectives placed another call to the Catskills. As they had expected, Siegel told them not to bother coming back. But when Parola threatened to walk right into the Pioneer and grab him in front of all his friends, Siegel agreed to meet them, again at the stump.

"Joe and I had to come back," said Parola. "If you don't do your part in this deal, everyone loses. We also came back because, in all fairness, there's something else you ought to know. You can believe it or not, I don't care. We are developing other leads in the Amtorg case. It may take awhile, but, Shelly we know they're going to lead straight to you. And then there ain't gonna be no mercy on your soul."

The detectives searched Siegel's face for some indication of his thoughts, but he was in such a state of perpetual jumpiness that it was hard to say where one reaction left off and the next began.

"You do whatever the fuck you want with me," Siegel suddenly spit out. "Rake me over the coals. Kill me. I believe what I'm doing for the JDL is right. It's worth dying for. I really don't give one holy shit what you do. Now, let me alone."

Siegel stalked off again. Gibney and Parola drove the hundred miles back to the city in silence. They had tried again. Nobody could say they hadn't worked all the angles. Nobody. Except Seedman.

"Go back," he told them.

"It's a waste, Chief."

Seedman drew a bead on them through the smoke of an unusually nasty cigar. "I'm paying you to go up and breathe that good mountain air and you don't want to go?"

"Hey, Sammy," said Gibney the next morning as they sped along Route 17 toward the mountains. "You know how this kid swore to us he'd rather die than inform on the JDL?"

"Yeah?"

"Well, as long as the Chief made us go back like this, I have an idea. There's no point in going over the same old ground with him. But I have this real nice shovel that I use to dig up the garden every spring. Before we left I put it in the trunk. . . ."

"Don't say any more, Joe," said Parola. "I got the picture."

When the detectives met Siegel that morning, they suggested driving around instead of sitting in the hot sun. In the car they dragged Siegel over and over the same old ground, but he stared silently out the window. Suddenly Parola turned off on a dirt road several miles beyond the Pioneer Country Club.

"Where the hell are we going," Siegel demanded. Ignoring the question, Parola pulled off onto an even rougher road that snaked into a forest of pine. Though it was a bright day, the sun filtered down only faintly. They could hear birds, nothing else.

The detectives motioned Siegel out of the car. As the young man stood watching, Patrola took the shovel from the trunk. It was a heavy-duty job with a big red scoop.

"You gonna plant a tree for Israel or what?" asked Siegel.

Parola smiled. "I'm gonna plant you," he said. He held out the shovel.

Siegel backed away, his eyes wide. "Cut this shit," he said.

"*You* cut the shit," said Gibney. "You better start figuring out real fast where your best interests lie."

Siegel was backed up against the car now. The detectives moved close.

"Goddam it, Shelly," screamed Parola, brandishing the shovel. "You got such a hard head *you* should have been born Italian instead of me. We can treat you the same way we used to treat pushers back in Narcotics. It's up to you. Now, are you fuckin' well going to do right by yourself or aren't you? You gotta decide right this minute."

Gibney threw in the zinger: "I mean, you *said* you'd be willing to die for this."

Siegel looked from Parola to Gibney to the shovel, his face crisscrossed with tics. He took a deep breath. "I did say it and I meant it," he said. "Plenty of Jews are dying because of the fuckin' Russians, while I'm living pretty good. . . ."

Parola raised the shovel.

"Wait, I'm not finished," Siegel said quickly. "I'll also say this. Let me think about if I can give you anything that won't hurt my friends. Because there's no way I'm gonna do that."

"Think how long?"

"Overnight."

"Fair enough, Shelly," said Gibney.

When they returned the next afternoon, they found Siegel sitting on the stump and smiling as they came toward him. From a distance the smile had looked good—but not up close.

"I thought it over last night," he began, his Adam's apple jumping. "I decided that you'd end up fucking me like the rest of those bastards. So I'm not doing a thing for you. Do whatever you want to me."

Siegel began walking up the road, his gangly frame full of tension. Parola drove the car alongside him.

"Just hold your ass on for a minute, Shelly," said Gibney quietly from the passenger's side. "Which bastards are you talking about?"

"All you bastards are the same," muttered Siegel.

"But just *now*, who did you mean fucked you?"

"The city DA . . . the Federal DA—they both did a job on me but good. They broke their promise."

"What promise, Shelly?"

"They promised to give me the goddam car back. It's not even mine. It belongs to my brother, his name is on the registration. But here I am, taking the fuckin' Short Line bus back and forth. I *hate* being without wheels."

"Christ Almighty!" Parola shouted. "Is that what you want? Your car back? Why didn't you say so in the first place?"

Parola wheeled the car around with a screech and took off for the city, leaving the gaunt figure of Siegel standing in the dust.

Hearing this report two hours later, Seedman could see Siegel's point. The Federal and city prosecutors had promised to return Siegel's car, but before handing over the keys they wanted him to cooperate. Seedman called a young Assistant DA assigned to the case by the Federal Prosecutor's office. "Can we give this silly kid back his car now?" he asked.

"Well, we've still got a lot of legal work in which this car figures," answered the DA. "Quite frankly, we're also under pressure from Washington to keep mashing down on these people. We're willing to give the car back, of course, but he's got to earn it. So far, he's given us zero cooperation."

"I understand," said Seedman. "If this was a Cub Scout trying to earn a merit badge, you'd be absolutely right. But Siegel is in a different kind of organization. As much as he wants his car, he'll never knuckle under; he'd rather walk to the Catskills on his hands. Even if we do give him the car there's no guarantee he'll cooperate. But right now it's our best shot at him."

"Strictly as a courtesy to you, Al," said the DA dubiously, "we'll release the car."

"After all the preliminary haggling," says Seedman, "we were now about to make our nuts-and-bolts investment in Sheldon Siegel. It wouldn't take long to learn what the return would be, if any. But if he was going to become an informant, I wanted him to feel as secure as a paranoid kid could. That meant giving him a sense of importance, so I had a special telephone set up for his calls in the Explosive-Arson Squad office. Nobody was to have that number but him. He could call it toll-free from the Borscht Belt or wherever the hell he happened to be.

"We also took another step to protect him by doing away with his name. An informant can't be effective if his name is known to more than a very few people. That's why it doesn't build his sense of well-being to know that thirty lawmen are waiting on his every word. If someone slips up, or deliberately violates his trust, he can be dead in ten minutes. Good informing is almost always the result of a slowly developing one-on-one relationship, and I rarely press a detective to reveal whom his information is coming from. I prefer to let the detective size up the informant while I size up the detective.

"If Siegel was going to produce for us, I wanted him known only to me and those two detectives with whom he seemed to be developing a stormy rapport. From that day on, I decided he would be known only as 'Angelo.'"

That evening Parola called Siegel. "Stop by the office here first thing tomorrow morning," he said. "Joey and I have a present for you."

"What present?"

"Just be here like I say. And be glad there's still a Santa Claus."

Next morning a suspicious Siegel walked into the squad room. "What are you guys trying to pull on me?" he demanded.

"You hollered you were being fucked because they took your car," answered Gibney. "Well, it took a lot of ball-busting, but we convinced the Feds to give it up. So you can turn in your bus tickets. As for the rest, we told you already what you can do to help us, your friends, and yourself."

Gibney handed Siegel a piece of paper. "This is the number of a new phone we had put in overnight. Nobody knows it but you. It sits quiet unless you dial it. We don't want anybody, not even our own squadmates, to know you from the next guy on the street. So we're going to call you Angelo, and that's the handle you're to use when you call us. *If* you ever do. Now let's get cracking and pick up your car."

Two days later the special phone in the far corner of the Explosive-Arson office rang for the first time. Gibney sprang to pick it up.

"This is Shel—ummm, I mean, Angelo."

"Yes, baby."

"Listen, you know that big estate in Glen Cove the Russians bought to play around? Well, I hear some people decided to plant quite a few sticks of dynamite under the fence. It's supposed to go off today, so I hear. Now, don't say I didn't give you guys something back."

Angelo hung up. Almost at once local police and ATF agents notified by Seedman's office were racing up the winding roads leading to the wealthy, woodsy town of Glen Cove, thirty miles from Manhattan on Long Island's North Shore. But a thorough search of the grounds turned up nothing—or so the ATF agents lost no time in reporting to Seedman. He had been pleased to be able to tip the Feds to the impending bombing—information that never would have reached them if Angelo hadn't gotten his Volvo back. Now Seedman knew the Feds were just as pleased to announce they had searched the entire estate without finding so much as a beer can.

Seedman was puzzled. He would not have been surprised if Angelo had come up with nothing. They had taken that gamble when they returned his car. But why would he offer false information?

"What are you trying to do, jerk us off?" Parola yelled angrily into the phone at Angelo.

"After the good stuff I gave you? What do you mean?"

"I mean, you jerked us off. There wasn't any bomb out in Glen Cove."

"Call you back in ninety minutes," Angelo said and hung up.

On schedule, the special number rang again. "It *is* there," he said. "It's a hundred and seventeen feet east of the main gate, under a big patch of poison ivy. I saw it myself, just now. I don't know why you supersnoops couldn't find it yourselves."

Parola sensed that Angelo wanted to say more, but there was only a nervous silence. "You got something else on your mind, Angelo?" he asked.

"Just this. You don't have to worry—that bomb isn't going to go off. It has a lot of muscle but it was made sloppy. If I had made that thing, it would have worked." Angelo hung up.

Poking around warily in the luxuriant poison ivy patch that they had avoided during their first search, Nassau County police and ATF agents found twelve sticks of dynamite attached to a battery and a pocket watch. As Angelo had said, the wiring was sloppy and the circuit had never closed. Though the charge was three times greater than the Amtorg bomb, this one had been planted too far away to damage the huge stone main house of the estate. But if it had detonated, it could have easily blown away anyone who happened to be passing on the road. And whatever the damage, it would have been certain to provoke a major Russian snit, probably the JDL's immediate goal.

"What was important to us," says Seedman, "was that American law enforcement authorities had learned in advance about this bomb and located it before the Russian gardener came across it. It showed we really were working to protect them, and took the edge off their inevitable outrage."

With many JDL members off in Israel or working at camps and hotels, the summer of 1971 was quiet for the Russians in New York. But Angelo himself was in a turmoil. At times he would refuse to see Gibney and Parola, cursing and hanging up when they called. Then, at unpredictable moments, he would call them to arrange a "meet." These calls rarely came during office hours, so both detectives had given Angelo their home phone numbers—something they had never before offered an informant. Often the calls came on weekend evenings, just as the detectives were about to go out. "It's that creep on the phone again," Gibney's wife once said in disgust. "I guess we'll have to cancel the dinner plans again."

Drop by meager drop, Angelo fed the two detectives information about the JDL, its goals, members, and operations. But when questioned on the crucial points—who had done the Amtorg bomb and placed the faulty bomb at Glen Cove?—he was silent. If they pressed him, he only sulked and demanded to be let alone.

Angelo was constantly fearful that other members of the JDL would spot him talking to Gibney and Parola, both of whom looked markedly non-Jewish. To reassure him, meets were always arranged for unlikely places—Italian sections of Brooklyn, or the docks at night. Parked under the West Side Highway or the Brooklyn-Queens Expressway, they would often have to shout to hear each other while the traffic roared by. Eventually they decided the place they all felt safest was the broken-down block of President Street where the Gallo mob was headquartered. Even Angelo agreed it was a place where the roughest JDL types preferred not to tread.

Their conversations slowly came to be almost ritualized. "Shelly," Parola would intone, "I swear on the lives of my children that nobody is ever going to find you out, but you got to give us just a few little things we need to build the case around you."

"You're not ratting on your friends by helping us," said Gibney, joining the chorus. "*They* were the lucky ones when that Amtorg bomb went off. If anyone had gotten hurt, we would've pulled out all the plugs to collar them. And if they'd blown up three bosses and a Bomb Squad detective. . . . Holy smokes! *All* of you wouldn't be worth a nickel together."

Angelo listened. It was obvious the bombings were still on his mind, but as July dragged into August he continued to shy away from giving the detectives any hard facts. Gibney and Parola were not losing patience, but they were losing interest.

One hot Sunday night in August their patience paid off. For a half-hour, the detectives had been sitting under the West Side Highway, chatting with Angelo in his gold Volvo. Nothing seemed different, except that Angelo was in particularly good humor. Then the inexplicable happened.

"You want to go up to your office, maybe?" Angelo suddenly asked.

The detectives looked at each other to be sure they had heard right. Till now Angelo had always recoiled at the slightest suggestion that he come to the office. His only visit had been the day he got his car back, and even then he had acted as if the place were mined. But now, at midnight, the three men found themselves climbing the stairs to the deserted Explosive-Arson office. Gibney spread out an assortment of doughnuts, cupcakes, and coffee they had picked up on the way over.

"If I was to tell you not just crap but the real *good* stuff," asked Angelo for the thousandth time, "how do I know the JDL won't find out?"

Parola gave the ritualized assurances, Gibney echoed the refrain.

Angelo crinkled a cellophane wrapper in his long nervous fingers. He sank deeper into his chair, a slow smile spreading across his face. Parola sighed. They seemed to be losing him again. But this time he looked up.

"I was just thinking about a funny story," Angelo said. "Wanna hear it?" Without waiting, he told how he and Stuie Cohen had once gone to a Russian pianist's concert at Carnegie Hall. For twenty minutes they had sat quietly in their seats. Then, in the middle of the serene slow movement of a Beethoven sonata, they had rolled down the aisles opened bottles of double-strength ammonia. For the first time ever Gibney saw Angelo laugh uproariously. But when they tried to bring conversation back to the Amtorg and Glen Cove cases, he again began to drift.

Parola jumped up. "Do you understand that right now you are looking at ten, maybe twenty years in the can on a Federal rap for bombing?" he shouted. "You want to go through the best part of your life eating out of a tin tray where they slop the food on like garbage? Do you realize that in all that time you'll never get laid?"

Parola's voice had risen to a scream. Gibney placed his hands on his partner's shoulders and gently pushed him down into a chair.

Angelo appeared to be unmoved by Parola's outburst. But the next thing he said was, "If I'm gonna help, you damn well better get me off the hook."

"We got to be honest with you on that, Shel," said Gibney, sensing Angelo's change in attitude. "The DAs carry the weight on that, but they listen real close to what our boss suggests to them and usually go right along. We're pretty sure you'll be granted immunity in return for helping the prosecution. It's almost standard. The only thing is, when we do make the collars on this Amtorg thing, we're gonna have to take you right along with the others. It's the only way to preserve your cover."

Angelo nodded. Haltingly then, with great effort, he began at last to tell them what they had worked so hard to hear. He told them how he had assembled the Amtorg bombs in the apartment of Eileen Garfinkel, Stuart Cohen's twenty-year-old girlfriend. Five other JDL members had watched, anxious to help, but Siegel would not trust them to lay a finger on his work. He told who had delivered the bombs to 355 Lexington Avenue and who had made the phone calls. He speculated on who had been responsible for the dud bomb left at the Russians' estate in Glen Cove, taking pains to point out again that he himself had taken no part in assembling such a "piece of crap."

By the time Angelo and the detectives left the office, it was after 3 A.M. He had insisted on parking the Volvo six blocks away in case any JDL members were in the neighborhood. Now he allowed the detectives to walk him halfway back. Strolling alone through the quiet Greenwich Village streets, the three of them actually felt like friends. It was their twenty-second meeting since the morning Gibney and Parola had first seen Sheldon Siegel waiting nervously by the stump on the dirt road in the Catskills.

"We put our case together as tightly as possible," says Seedman, "before handing it over to Bob Morse, U.S. Attorney for the Eastern District of New York. He was happy to make the indictments. His involvement meant the United States itself was dealing with these crimes against Russians rather than the local police. That was fine with me. But my men on the Explosive-Arson Squad had done an extraordinary job on this case, and I felt they deserved to bask in a moment of public credit. I decided to announce the indictments at a press conference right in the Sixth Precinct station house, where Gibney and Parola had finally broken through to Angelo.

"Naturally, I asked Bob Morse to come. He thought a press conference was a good idea—but he wanted it at *his* office. We finally arranged a compromise: we would have our press conference, then Morse would have his."

Seedman scheduled his for 10:30 on September 8. That morning news-media cars and station wagons packed into the narrow length of 10th Street, leaving even less space than usual for traffic. Slipping through the fifty camera and sound men milling around on the ground floor, Seedman went upstairs to the Explosive-Arson Squad office. Six of the seven JDL members who had been arrested during the night were joking together loudly in the iron-barred cage at the far end of the room. The seventh, Eileen Garfinkel, had been released from the cage and was wandering around the squad room, lounging on desks and wisecracking loudly to the other prisoners. She had been performing nonstop since seven o'clock that morning without attracting the attention of a single detective.

Striding past her, his cigar stub clamped between his teeth, Seedman walked directly to the cage. "Hey," she jeered, "this must be the big cheese." As if he heard nothing, Seedman stood in front of the cage and looked in. The surprised Explosive-Arson men exchanged looks. Seedman usually ignored prisoners. Why was he staring so intently at the six men in that cell?

Seedman was joined outside the cage by the reporter who, a year later, would collaborate with him on his memoirs. Suddenly one of the prisoners, a fat college student, began to giggle.

"Is that your son there, all dressed up," he asked, "or your . . . boyfriend?"

Across the room on Parola's desk Eileen Garfinkel doubled over in mock hysteria. The detectives waited silently for the Chief to put them in their place.

Instead Seedman turned slowly and looked at the boy without expression. All he said was, "Am I making fun of you?" The JDL seven stopped laughing. None of them seemed to know how to answer. A moment later Seedman walked away. He had got what he came for. For the first time, at the very rear of the cell, he had seen for himself the gangly figure and brooding sallow face of Angelo.

The next month was so quiet that Seedman found himself able to accept social invitations. On the night of October 20 he and Henny went to a cocktail party given by his friends Arthur and Esther Lipps. With all the noise inside, he stepped out for a moment on the terrace overlooking Central Park, dark now except for weavings of light from the crosstown roadways. Twenty blocks up a spray of moonlight washed Belvedere Lake. About this hour one month ago, Reuben Ortiz had strolled into the park with the teen-aged girl from South Carolina. At that same hour detectives were also fanning out in Brooklyn to make the Amtorg arrests.

"Phone for you, Al," called Esther Lipps from the terrace door. Only the duty detective in his office knew where to reach him, and he wouldn't interrupt the Seedmans' night out without a very good reason.

On the line was a duty sergeant from the 19th Squad, which covers the poshest area of the East Side. "Hate to say this, Chief," he said, "but somebody just fired four shots into a bedroom window on the eleventh floor of the Russian Mission on 67th Street. Four of their kids were sleeping inside but, thank God, no one was hit. We think the shots were fired from the roof of Hunter College, across the street. Boy, those Russians are mad!"

All summer and early fall the JDL had been quiet, too quiet. These four shots could be the JDL's way of announcing that summer recess was over and they were back to brew up new trouble.

Leaving his wife to wait in the car, Seedman went up to the roof of Hunter College's seventeen-story main building. There John Mahoney, the sergeant from the 19th Squad, pointed out the eleventh-floor window across the street where the shots had gone in.

"Were the lights on?" asked Seedman.

"Yes, Chief," said Mahoney.

That made the act seem more malevolent than the Amtorg bombing. It meant that the sniper crouched on the roof could figure that people were in the room and was willing to risk hitting them. When the rifle was found shortly after midnight at the bottom of an airshaft in the college building, it looked even worse. The weapon was a brand-new .243-caliber Remington fitted out with a telescopic sight.

"This sniper paid quite a few extra dollars to be able to center his target in the hairlines," says Seedman. "Like the Amtorg incident, it was just fantastic luck that nobody had been killed. Or had that always been the plan in both places—to cause damage but not death? All I knew for sure, as I stood on the roof of Hunter College, was that this incident was going to set off a howl and we had better have something to show for our investigation, fast."

The howl came quickly and from several directions. Within seventy-five minutes of the shots Secretary of State William Rogers had called the Soviet Ambassador in Washington to apologize for the incident. Late that night in Moscow, U.S. Ambassador Jacob Beam was summoned to the Foreign Ministry for an extraordinary dressing down. In the morning, at the UN, Yakov A. Malik, the Russian Ambassador to the UN, attacked the United States for failing to curb the "Zionist hooligans" in its midst. Then he turned on Yosef Tekoah, the Israeli Ambassador to the UN, and challenged him to proclaim to the General Assembly that the Jews were a "chosen people" and "closer to God" than all others.

Trembling with anger, Tekoah rose to say that if the Jews had been chosen for anything, it was to suffer. "It was the Soviet Union, not Zionism or the Jewish people, who concluded a treaty with Hitler and Ribbentrop," he said, referring to the Soviet-German non-aggression pact of 1939. One other incident that may have exacerbated the Russians' ire was a JDL threat to kill two Russian diplomats in the United States if a woman named Silva Zalmanson, a Soviet Jew accused of attempting to hijack a Soviet airliner, died in prison. Some suspected that the sniper's shots had been designed to drive that warning home. Even the Saudi Arabian delegate, Jamil M. Baroody, got into the act by attacking Mayor Lindsay as ". . . a sycophant who goes to synagogues and acts like a rabbi to obtain Jewish votes." Under the circumstances, Seedman was desperate for a quick face-saving break.

"We started with the rifle," says Seedman. "Unlike the weapons used in gangland shootings, this rifle had been easily found and could be easily traced. In fact, it was brand new with serial number intact. That was surprising. After the shots had been heard it made sense to get rid of the rifle before trying to get out of Hunter College. But once the decision was made to leave the weapon, why didn't they take advance precautions to keep it from being traced?

"Not that I was complaining. In the morning we were able to

trace the Remington to the firm of Charles A. Greenblatt in Hempstead, Long Island. As it happened, I knew Charlie from the days when his store used to be right around the corner from Police Headquarters. My own hammerless revolver came from his shop."

Detectives drove out to Hempstead with the Explosive-Arson Squad's photo album of active JDL members. When they showed it to the salesman and the gunsmith who had fitted the rifle with its telescopic sight, both men picked out eighteen-year-old Isaac Jaroslowitz. A Brooklyn rabbi's son, Jaroslowitz had been arrested in April during a demonstration at the Iraqi Mission. Detectives rushed to his home but neither his parents nor neighbors were helpful about where he might be. Just the same, Seedman felt he would show up soon. The JDL kids were not the type to dash into hiding. Besides, Jaroslowitz probably would not be able to resist returning to the scene of his crime.

The afternoon after the shooting Seedman ordered Jaroslowitz's photo distributed to the 19th Precinct. Like many JDL kids, he wore a skullcap according to Orthodox Jewish tradition, so he would probably be easy enough to spot. Sure enough, less than two hours after the photos were posted, a 19th Precinct patrolman picked him up at the corner of 67th Street and Lexington Avenue, just down the block from the Russian Mission. He was a bearlike overweight youth with a bushy mustache and a friendly smile. Though initially he made a few stabs at denying any part in the shooting, he did not seem at all upset at having been arrested. If anything, Seedman felt, Jaroslowitz acted as if he had been anointed. Yet the boy clearly was not stupid. How could he behave this way, knowing that he was likely to be jailed for attempted murder? He had to know something that so far the detectives didn't. The whole business made Seedman uneasy.

It was long past dark. Normally Seedman would have waited until morning to see whether the salesman and gunsmith from Greenblatt's could pick out the suspect in a lineup. But he was under abnormal pressure to get results fast. An anxious Mayor Lindsay had called several times for a report on the investigation. The Justice Department had called to relay the Attorney General's concern that all possible measures were being taken to break the case. Seedman decided to have the two men brought in that evening. But even though they had quickly recognized Jaroslowitz in the JDL album, they did not seem eager to come into the city now and pick him out of a lineup. Seedman could understand why. If the JDL was crazy enough to shoot into a room full of children, they might also be ready to go after anyone who identified them. Or worse. Everyone knew the JDL's talent for ingenious harassment.

It was after nine o'clock when the two men finally arrived at the 19th squad office. Jaroslowitz was put into a lineup with nine other young men as strapping as himself. Seedman was dismayed to notice the gun salesman shaking his head every few seconds as if to clear it. He finally did point to Jaroslowitz, but Seedman was not fully satisfied.

"You got problems with your eyesight?"

"Well, I got diabetes," the salesman answered. "It sure hasn't done my eyes any *good.*"

"What would you say right now if I told you your wife was in that lineup?" The salesman squinted. He looked from one man to the next, then went painstakingly back down the line. "I don't think she's up there," he said finally.

Seedman sent him home. He would be hopeless as a witness in court.

Luckily, they still had the gunsmith. A man who did precise up-close work was bound to have good eyes. Kenneth Aull saw very well indeed. With no hesitation, he picked out Jaroslowitz as the man for whom he had fitted a telescopic sight on a new Remington .243 semiautomatic rifle.

"Now we had to decide what to do with Jaroslowitz," says Seedman. "He had been identified as the purchaser of a rifle, but not as a sniper. We had no reason to accuse him of firing the shots and no evidence that he was part of a conspiracy that culminated in the shooting. He had not been discovered carrying a concealed weapon. In fact, he had done nothing to violate local or state law.

"However, under the Federal Gun Control Act of 1969, a purchaser of a gun must fill out a Federal form identifying himself at the time of sale. The purchaser of this Remington had identified himself with a draft card as Henry Faulkner, 830 Arthur Avenue, the Bronx. So once again, as in the Amtorg case, we had to call in the Alcohol, Tobacco and Firearms Division of the Treasury Department to charge Jaroslowitz with purchasing a gun with false identification.

"But the ATF balked at arresting Jaroslowitz, contending that the case against him was hardly overwhelming. They had a point. Under normal circumstances I never would have ordered Jaroslowitz arrested so quickly. But with everyone so anxious to see fast results, the gunsmith's identification would have to suffice. In the morning George Bush could stand up at the UN and mollify the Russians by announcing that an arrest had already been made.

"At midnight I tried to call Bob Morse to see if he would order the ATF to make the Federal charge right away. There was no answer. Then I called George Bush, who had given me his number in case anything important broke after office hours. Not feeling qualified to decide, he called the Attorney General in Washington. By this time—about two o'clock—Bob Morse came home. After listening to the facts of the case, he checked with the Attorney General and then called back to order Jaroslowitz locked up for violation of the Federal Gun Law. By then it was nearly four A.M.

"All that time, Burt Zweibon, lawyer for the JDL, was hollering that his client was being railroaded to placate the Russians. I have heard lawyers yell louder for less reason. But with the President planning to visit Russia later in the year, I was not about to allow a dopey teen-ager from Brooklyn to cast a shadow on that event.

"Before that night was over we had also heard from Meir Kahane, the JDL's founder, leader, theoretician, and chief spokesman. I had met Kahane on several occasions, shortly after the JDL had begun to make news in 1968. The guy looks anything but fanatic. He dresses in quiet well-tailored suits, his hair is short and carefully groomed. It also goes down well with many that he is a patriot, a believer in America, a devoted anti-Communist.

"Still, I had my reservations about Kahane from the first. At the time, of course, the JDL had not yet caused any of the dangerous incidents for which it would soon become infamous. It simply maintained that Jews, traditionally peaceable and book-loving, should now become fighters as well, as the Israelis had done in the Six-Day War. I can't offer any good reason why I did not care for Kahane— nothing that he said or did, just something in his eyes. I know that may sound melodramatic, but a detective learns to trust such reactions, and something in those eyes made me uneasy. I'd call it a lack of reasonableness. I'd seen the look before, in the eyes of other policemen as well as criminals, and no good has ever come from my experience with such people.

"Now, three years later, I found myself asking Kahane whether his JDL was responsible for the sniper attack. He said it was not, he deplored the incident. For legal reasons he obviously had no choice but to deplore it. Still, I wished he could find some way to be less hypocritical. After all, the responsibility for what these silly kids did weighed heavily on him as an adult, whether he was directly involved or not. They looked up to him. Whatever advice he gave they listened to. Yet, as we would learn, bombs were put together right in the Brooklyn headquarters of JDL, on the same floor where Kahane worked.

"The arrest of Jaroslowitz took us off the hot seat in the sniper case. The kid had been identified by the gunsmith, he was a JDL activist, and though he claimed he hadn't bought a rifle, it was plain that he sympathized with what had been done. The case looked even better when, in an address book belonging to Jaroslowitz, we found an entry for Greenblatt's gun shop."

Jaroslowitz was arraigned in Brooklyn Federal Courthouse the day after his arrest for giving false identification when purchasing a rifle and using a forged draft card. U.S. Attorney Morse argued that bail should be set at a whopping $100,000 since JDL members had been known to jump bail set as high as $25,000. As Meir Kahane and a small group of JDL members sat glowering darkly in the empty courtroom, Morse went on to recite one such example after another.

Morse concluded his detailed presentation, and bail was set at $25,000. He turned to leave the courtroom. Blocking the aisle, eyes burning, was Kahane. "Not only don't you help the Jews, you hurt the Jews," Kahane said. "I am ashamed you are a Jew. Your brother wrote about Jews like you."

"The wrong Morse died," added a younger JDL member.

Morse ignored that. He stared at Kahane, his jaw twitching. "I do not lose my temper," he said in a low tight voice. He walked out of the silent courtroom as Kahane continued to glare at his back.

Kahane had been referring to the attorney's brother, Arthur D. Morse, who had been killed only a few months earlier in an auto accident in Yugoslavia. A year earlier he had written a book, *While Six Million Died*, which accused the Roosevelt Administration of doing little to help European Jews, even though it was aware that they faced no future but extermination. When reporters later asked Kahane why he had brought up the matter now, he answered by telling a story. Some young Russian draftees went to their rabbi to ask if they could eat pork while in the army. If they had to eat pork to live, they should do so, the rabbi answered, but they should not suck on the bones. Kahane conceded that it was Robert Morse's duty, as U.S. Attorney, to request high bail for Jaroslowitz. But then he should have shut up instead of hammering away. "He was sucking the bones," said Kahane.

"As suspects go," says Seedman, "Jaroslowitz looked good. Yet even after the arraignment, I didn't have the right feeling about him in my gut. This fat, smiling, relaxed kid, who had appeared to be the only one enjoying himself during the long exhausting night we had him in custody, might have done some silly things, but he had the wrong look and wrong face for a sniper.

"Jaroslowitz's grandmother had come up with one small fact in his favor. She pointed out that Isaac never would have bought a gun on October eleventh. That was the minor Jewish holiday of Sh'mini Atseret, marking the day on which King Solomon dedicated the first temple in Jerusalem. Isaac, son of a rabbi and a genuinely religious kid who attended synagogue services every morning, had been in synagogue all day, she said. Of course, he could have taken time out to buy a gun at Greenblatt's, but I tended to doubt it. The kid was just giving me all the wrong signals. But if he was not the sniper, we had another way to find out who was. Gibney and Parola would have to go to Angelo."

On the evening of Jaroslowitz's arraignment Parola met Angelo at one of their favorite spots, under the West Side Highway.

"I don't know who did it," said Angelo, "except that I don't think it was Izzy Jaroslowitz. I mean everybody thinks it's funny that he got picked up. He doesn't do that sort of thing."

"Sure he does, meatball," said Parola. "The kid's got a sheet."

Angelo looked blank. "A sheet of what?"

"He's got a felony arrest on his yellow sheet in the Police Department, meatball. You must know what he did better than I do."

"Well, I don't know about that but they say he was in synagogue the whole day when he was supposed to be out buying the gun. I believe that."

"So who did it?"

"I don't know, and to tell the truth, I don't even think the JDL was involved."

"Don't give me that, Shel," Parola said. "Let me tell you something. If this is the wrong kid, I want him to get off. And the only way to do that is to find the right kid. You can find out who that is for me, Shelly."

"I told you, I don't know. Maybe give me a few days, and I'll look around to see what I find out."

"That's all I want," said Parola. "I don't expect you to stick your neck out."

The Sunday after Jaroslowitz's arrest Parola and Angelo met again, this time on President Street—the only place he seemed even slightly at ease. In neighborhoods that made him especially nervous he would lie on the rear floor as they drove, his long limbs bent at sharp angles like a broken praying mantis. Here on President Street he was willing to rise to a slump in the bucket seat. Now he told them he refused to cooperate unless he was granted immunity on the charges pending against him, and guaranteed that he would never be revealed as the informant in the Amtorg and Glen Cove cases.

"If you think the U.S. Attorney is going to give you the world on a silver platter," said Parola, "you're a fruitcake."

Parola reported to Seedman that it might be a long time before Angelo gave them anything on the sniper attack. If Angelo was not responding to threats that the U.S. Attorney might throw the book at him, what could get him to talk? Maybe it was time to lean on his special relationship with Parola and Gibney.

"Tell Angelo I'm not promoting you guys unless you break this sniper case," Seedman told Parola. The detective turned red as Seedman let that sink in. "I won't feel sorry for you. But he will. You'll see."

That afternoon at three o'clock, the special phone in the squad office rang.

"Hello, Charlie's Circus," barked Parola.

"Charlie?"

"Yeah, brother, what's doin'?"

"Can we make a meet tonight?"

"Ten o'clock, across from the diner."

That night Parola went through all the old reasons why Angelo should tell him who the sniper was. Then he trotted out this new one. "It's a personal favor to me and Joey," he said quietly. "It's better than even money that we won't get listed for promotion unless we pop this thing."

Angelo didn't say anything, but Parola felt a softening in the tight atmosphere inside the Volvo. The two of them had hard, cold reasons for dealing with each other, but Parola had come to feel as intimate with Angelo as if they had shared a trench in wartime. Paranoid and difficult as Angelo was, Parola liked him not for the usual reasons. The bond that united them was much more substantial, and because of that, Parola could now see that Angelo was genuinely concerned to think he could affect their chances for promotion.

"I don't know what I can do," Angelo finally said. "I mean, I really don't know who did it. Even if I did, how could I fuck my friends? Everybody in the JDL is my friend, whether I know them or not." Depressed, Angelo shook his head. "Maybe I just ought to drive off the end of the pier," he said, motioning to the rickety bulkheads above the black current.

"Hey, wait a minute, meatball, how much did this car set you back?"

"$3600."

"No sense in letting it go to waste. Why not just let me run you over with the fuckin' car. Then I'll give it to my son."

Later in the week, Parola set up a motel-room meeting between Angelo and Assistant U.S. Attorney Pattison, who was handling the Amtorg and Glen Cove cases. Angelo agreed to the meet only after Parola had promised to come along. But Seedman didn't like the idea. Pattison worked out of the Eastern District office that had started off on the wrong foot with Angelo by hedging on returning his car. Then they had promised to send him out to California to start a new life once he testified against the others. He had been given a letter promising him immunity in return for full cooperation. But in spite of all the assurances, Seedman sensed that Angelo would trust only Gibney and Parola with any juicy new plums of information. Right now the Eastern District could only stir Angelo's paranoia.

Nevertheless, as Parola sat glumly by, the meeting took place. Pattison tried to induce Angelo not only to testify on all the JDL matters pending but to do so without immunity. He explained that a jury was always suspicious of a witness who testified against others to save his own skin. If he pleaded guilty in the Amtorg case—thus sparing himself from having to testify about all the damning details of how he made the bombs—and appeared without immunity as prosecution witness against the others, then the court would be far more disposed to pass a lenient sentence. "Get it off your chest like a man," Pattison advised Angelo, who, Parola could not help thinking wryly, was so concave he almost didn't have a chest.

At his next meeting with Gibney and Parola, Angelo was morose. "I'm not going to testify at all," he said. "If I don't testify, those fuckers don't have enough to convict anyone, including me."

Parola looked at him incredulously. "Are you going bananas?" He ticked off how they had him identified as buying the equipment at Radio Shack, how they had followed his every movement. "Jesus, Shel," he lied, "we even got witnesses now that you built the fuckin' bombs."

"I don't care. Whatever they do, they'll do."

"Personally," said Parola, "I think you're stepping on your own prick."

The next day, under the West Side Highway, Parola came at Angelo from a different angle. "It suddenly dawned on me," he said. "I told Joey here, maybe this idiot Shelly went up on that roof *himself* to prove to his friends that he's not a rat."

Angelo's face showed nothing.

"Think about it, jerkoff," Parola went on. "All those four shots zinged right in there. Now, I personally don't believe the rest of those kids have what it takes to get off four good shots like that in a row. You're the only guy who knows anything about rifles, Shel. I mean, the gunsmith said that the kid who bought the rifle was asking stupid questions like he couldn't believe."

Parola leaned forward. "Did you do it, Shel? Tell me now and it'll die right here."

"No," said Angelo.

"Then who, Shel?"

Angelo wriggled. He looked out the window. "I think maybe a guy named Gary did it. That's all I heard."

"Gary Fishman?"

"I don't know. Maybe."

Seedman felt they would have to move as cautiously with this new name as they had moved quickly with Jaroslowitz. They could not afford to release one suspect and arrest another unless the new evidence was absolutely solid. Like Jaroslowitz, Gary Fishman had a "yellow sheet" of previous arrests. In the spring he had been arrested for sitting in with a JDL group at the office of the New York

Board of Rabbis. His signature on file in the Bureau of Criminal Intelligence (BCI) was not at all similar to the "Henry Faulkner" on the gun-purchase application. After his detectives observed Fishman for several days, Seedman was pretty sure he wasn't the sniper.

"Goddam it, Shelly, you embarrassed the hell out of us," said Parola at their next meeting on President Street. "You're gonna jerk us off one time too many, and then you know what happens? I get the fuckin' shovel again. But this time the dig will be for real."

"It was supposed to be a guy named Gary, that's all I know," said Angelo. "Maybe try a guy named Gary Shlian."

That night Parola looked up Gary Shlian in BCI. Seventeen-year-old Shlian lived in Kew Gardens Hills, Queens, far from the Brooklyn neighborhood where the cadre of biggest troublemakers lived. But Shlian had been arrested in the spring, along with Jaroslowitz and Fishman, at that New York Board of Rabbis sit-in. Parola felt his heart beating as he looked at the boy's signature. It almost certainly was from the same hand that had signed the gun application.

"For six weeks Jaroslowitz had been refusing to give us a handwriting sample," says Seedman. "Now, if he wanted to walk away from this charge, he was going to have to provide one—except that it was no longer our place to ask him. ATF had made the complaint and the Eastern District was prosecuting. It was up to them to force the issue. But they were in no hurry, since they were the ones who would look bad if a new culprit popped up—especially one supplied by us.

"On December seventh Jaroslowitz finally gave the U.S. Attorney a handwriting sample. It didn't appear to match the 'Henry Faulkner' on the application. Meanwhile, we had developed a latent palmprint from the lower corner of the application. It was so smudged it was useless for anything except a comparison of the same palm, but when we compared it to the palmprint we took from Gary Shlian's BCI file, they were identical. To top it off, Shlian was a big dark bearlike guy like Jaroslowitz. It was easy to see how the gunsmith had been confused. So now, even though the idea didn't thrill ATF, we were going to have to make an exchange.

"Rather than snap up Shlian right then, I wanted to spend a bit more time making the case against him as airtight as possible. But when we put a tail on him, we learned something we hadn't bargained for. Shlian and Fishman were planning to fly to Israel on Saturday.

"It looked as though we were going to have to arrest them to keep them from leaving. But I was still hoping to postpone the arrest on the gun charge so we could see where Shlian might lead us if we let him run. Luckily, both he and Fishman were due to appear in State Supreme Court on the following Monday for sentencing for their part in the Board of Rabbis' sit-in. I asked the DA to see if they could be arrested for bail-jumping. Even if the airline schedules physically permitted, he felt no judge would believe that someone who left for Israel on Saturday had any intention of returning for a Monday morning court date.

"In order to make the bail-jumping case stick, we would have to make the arrest at the last second," says Seedman. "Otherwise we never would be able to prove they were really planning to use their tickets." On Saturday night at eight o'clock Shlian and Fishman were among the first passengers to board BOAC Flight sixty-two for Tel Aviv via London. But when they got to their seats, they found them already occupied—by George Howard and Joe Gregorowicz of the Explosive-Arson Squad.

"No trip?" said Shlian.

"Not today," answered Howard.

While they waited in the lounge for the boys' baggage, Shlian called Burt Zweibon, the JDL lawyer. When the detectives got back to the 6th Precinct station house, he was waiting for them.

"Are you telling me this arrest is just for bail-jumping on the Board of Rabbis' case?" demanded Zweibon.

"That's it, Burt," said Sergeant Howard.

"Then why are you guys from Explosive-Arson making the arrest?"

"We were ordered to, Burt. What can I say?"

"Did Seedman order this?" asked Zweibon. "Because if he did, you can't tell me there's not more to it than a bail-jumping charge."

"*Is* there more to it, Burt?" asked Howard.

The lawyer did not answer. But on Tuesday morning, February 1, U.S. Attorney Morse announced that the charges against Jaroslowitz would be dropped and almost identical charges made against Gary Shlian.

"With the handwriting and palmprints on the application

matching, Shlian had little choice but to plead guilty," says Seedman. "We were glad of that. It meant that Angelo's cover could still be preserved. I felt he'd help us out again. In fact, he really threw out the name of Gary Shlian only as a favor to Parola and Gibney, asking nothing in return. But some time earlier, in December, the government was ready to start the trial of the Amtorg Seven, and then Angelo had wanted something very badly—to hide his identity as our informant. Since the whole case revolved around him, that wouldn't be easy and I told Gibney and Parola that if he wanted us to try, he'd have to come up with more good information. I wanted to know in advance when the JDL was ready to try something new."

"I told you plenty already," Angelo angrily said to the detectives.

"We've got the DA's guarantee," said Parola, "that you get immunity for whatever you tell us about, even if you are personally involved."

Angelo looked at them hard. "You swear it?"

Gibney and Parola shook their heads. "That's the deal the Chief worked out with the DA."

"Because if I tell you what I'm thinking," said Angelo, "it's gonna knock you through the pavement."

The detectives believed him. They waited.

"Okay," said Angelo, "here goes." As he began to talk Parola took out a pad and pencil and started scrawling furiously, not daring to look up for fear of disturbing the flow. It was the first time he'd ever taken notes during a meeting, but Angelo was going too strong to notice.

The JDL had worked out three new moves against the Russians, Angelo explained. The first was to build a drone airplane, which could be radio-controlled from an automobile. The plane would have a six-foot wingspan and a hollow fuselage packed with six sticks of TNT, cut down to fit inside. The plan was to get the plane airborne at the East River and 67th Street, then drive crosstown to the Mission with the plane flying directly above. Whenever they had to stop at red lights, the radio controller in the car would direct the aircraft to circle around until the light turned green.

As they passed by the Mission the radio-controller would guide the aircraft down to the roof. When it landed, the weight of the plane would fold back the landing gear, closing a circuit with the TNT. In the car the controller would shut off the transmitter guiding the plane and turn on a second transmitter, which would activate the firing circuit.

"The idea is to use TNT instead of dynamite," explained Angelo. "It makes a bigger boom for its weight."

"When is this little outing planned for?" asked Parola, in disbelief. He didn't have to ask who had conceived this attack.

"Frankly, I'm not even sure it can be done properly," said Angelo. "If you ride along 67th Street, you'll notice that the wind currents are real unsettled between the buildings. Drop a Kleenex out of a window and you'll see how the currents swirl it around. I don't know if you could even keep the plane on a steady course. In fact," he said, shaking his head, "the thing might even land right on the roof of the car."

"Just remember," said Parola. "You don't drive that car off a pier, you don't blow it up. It's for my kid."

"What are the other two plans?" asked Gibney matter-of-factly.

The second plan, Angelo explained, involved the parking garage directly under the Mission. JDL observers had noticed that every week at the same time a member of the staff would leave the garage to visit a ladyfriend. Two hours later he'd return. The JDL plan was this: while the Russian was out visiting they would load the underside of his car with dynamite. When he returned, the single Russian guard would open the garage door and minutes later the dynamite would go off, right under the Mission.

The two detectives nodded. Russian cars were a favorite target of the JDL. One of their earliest tactics was to pour water into the Russian gas tanks or stuff them with burning rags. Angelo was a magician with auto engines. He could fix anything. Even for someone with half his talent, attaching a bomb to the underside of a car would be ridiculously simple.

"Okay, what's the third plan?" asked Gibney.

"Well, they tried a couple of times to do something out there at Glen Cove," said Angelo. "But they always messed up. The new plan is going to work. They got some Israeli Army plans for a lightweight portable mortar. They'll set it up in some bushes down the road from the estate and then just lob shells into the place. . . . Boom! Boom! Boom! Boom!"

The detectives were silent for a moment, trying to absorb the enormity of the JDL campaign. All that had gone before seemed like peanuts: this was a guerrilla war. Parola was first to speak.

"Which of these deals might come off first?" he asked.

"I don't know," said Angelo. "It's not in my hands. But I will tell you this. The business with the plane isn't going to happen, if you ask me."

"Why?"

"Well, the plane was all built"—he looked down—"I'm not saying by who. Anyhow, it was taken out to a big park in Queens to test out, complete to a dummy load exactly equal in weight to six sticks of TNT. This little aircraft responded beautifully to the radio commands. Circles, dives, climbs . . . did it all. Everyone wanted to try it for themselves. But the person running it didn't want them to. They kept insisting, they were going wild, so finally, this certain person lets Stuart Cohen take the transmitter for just a few seconds."

"So what happened?"

Angelo glared. "So, that dumb bastard, Stuie, he wrecked it. Bzzzzzzzzzz—poof!"

"Tell me just one other thing, Shel. How come you wanted to land this plane on the roof rather than fly it in the front door?"

"Are you nuts?" asked Angelo incredulously. "You got a cop standing out in front there twenty-four hours a day. Suppose he got wiped out? Then you really *would* make a hole for me with that shovel."

"When Parola explained these three plans to me," says Seedman, "I felt the same way as I had when I got the report from Radio Shack that Angelo had bought more fixings for his bombs. I knew he'd have to be tailed around-the-clock, a job the Explosive-Arson Squad couldn't handle alone. So I had brought in the Safe and Loft Squad to augment them. Now I felt the same way again. Only this time, if these kids had thought out their plans in such detail, they could cause more trouble than *all* my squads could handle. I still doubted they wanted to kill anyone. But they didn't have to go that far to get what they wanted. For months the President had been laying out a delicate rapprochement with the Russians which could be torn apart in seconds because of these dopey but ingenious kids.

"The responsibility for preventing such craziness would have to be spread around, so I called John Malone, director of the FBI's regional office, to suggest we coordinate our efforts. I called George Bush too. The response was fast. The next afternoon, Bush called us together in his apartment on the thirty-fourth floor of the Waldorf-Astoria. He had a full house. There were contingents from the U.S. Secret Service, the FBI, UN Security, the Treasury Department, the New York District Attorney's office, the Justice Department, and U.S. Attorneys from the Eastern and Southern Districts. I brought along John Kinsella, George Howard, Gibney, and Parola.

"Bush stood up as we were served coffee and cake from a silver service like a bunch of old hens. He explained that Attorney General Richard Kleindienst and the President himself were anxious to prevent the JDL from doing anything to cause a major shudder in our relations with the Russians. To spike the JDL guns, he proposed a task force of Federal agents and my own detectives who would act in teams as virtual babysitters for members of the JDL. As long as they were good we would let them alone. But the moment they tried any mischief, we hoped we would be there to stop them. I lent twenty-five hand-picked detectives to the task force. They even got Gibney and Parola. In charge of our contingent I put Paul Reilly, a topnotch sergeant from Safe and Loft.

"It was lucky we overwhelmed the JDL with attention when we did. They were trying. After Stuart Cohen crashed that beautiful plane in the park, another was built in the basement of a Brooklyn home, using the radio guidance gear salvaged from the wreckage. That was the expensive part. Parola priced it at $355. The balsa fuselage came to no more than forty dollars and lots of hard work. But once the second plane had been built, they got no chance to move it out of the basement. The task force was all eyes, all the time.

"Early one morning, at another home in Brooklyn, our stakeout observed two JDL members loading into their car what looked like rifles wrapped in brown paper. They started driving north, up through the city, across the Hudson, up the Palisades Parkway in New Jersey, and back into New York along Route 9W, a curving, treacherous road that hugs the Hudson. By then they were the only two cars on the road. The kids began to take quick little detours and doublebacks.

"Finally, at four A.M., in the middle of Rockland County, the detectives tired of the game and pulled over the JDL car. Inside was

Izzy Danziger, who had been arrested in the parking garage with Angelo, and another member named Gene Kleinhandler. They indeed had a rifle in the car, which the agents suspected them of transporting to the JDL training camp near Woodbourne. Since they had no license for the weapon, Danziger and Kleinhandler were arrested, only to be bailed out the next morning.

"Late one night another group of JDL kids got together in the men's room of a synagogue in Hewlett, Long Island, to make bombs for a new attempt on the Russian estate at Glen Cove. But the project was interrupted by the joint task force and the local police who burst in and arrested them, confiscating their pipes, powder, batteries, and timers.

"In January, Angelo told Parola and Gibney about a new plan. The JDL had managed to buy yet another highly accurate Remington rifle with a telescopic sight. An advance party had then gone down to Washington to case the gloomy old Russian Embassy on 16th Street. Across the street they found a small, expensive hotel with rooms facing the Embassy.

"Once the kids figured out exactly which room had the best sight angle on the Embassy driveway, they planned to rent it, at thirty-four dollars a day, for as long as it took to pick off the Russian Ambassador to the United States. If their purpose was to jolt relations between the two countries, even a shot that missed would have more than done the job. But thanks to Angelo's tip, we never let them shake loose long enough to try.

"The only point of friction between me and the Feds on the JDL task force continued to be Angelo. They wanted him for their own. I've found that the Feds have always placed more reliance on informants than we have, maybe because they have more money to pay them. Most of my detectives keep their best informants happy with an occasional ten-spot, but for crucial information in a big Federal case an informant can walk away with ten grand. If he comes up with more good information in another case, he can end up in a higher tax bracket that year than any of us on the other side.

"Angelo did not react well to the Federal people, never forgetting that if we hadn't interceded, he *still* might not have his Volvo back. But the Feds persisted in messing with him. If they kept at it, he might also back away from Gibney and Parola. That worried me. No matter how closely the joint task force covered the active JDL members, it was always possible they'd get loose for something bad. The only effective warning device we had against that was a cooperative Angelo slumped in a car with Gibney and Parola."

The prospect Seedman dreaded finally materialized on January 26 at the office of eighty-three-year-old impresario Sol Hurok. He had outraged the JDL by continuing to import Russian musicians and dancers to perform in the United States, mostly to packed houses. Hurok had recently moved to sleek new quarters on the twentieth floor of a glass tower on Sixth Avenue. The office had just opened that Wednesday morning when two neatly dressed young men walked in to ask about tickets to an upcoming event.

"If you'll take seats, somebody will help you shortly," said Kelly Brown, the receptionist. Five minutes later he looked up and saw the two young men slipping out the door. Where they had been sitting he was stunned to see a bluish-pink flame dance up the cord of a table lamp. It raced into the center of the lamp, glowing far brighter than any bulb. Before his eyes, genie-like, the lamp melted in the blue-pink flame.

At that moment two other neatly dressed young men walked into the office of Columbia Artists Management, Inc. (CAMI), on nearby West 57th Street. Like Hurok, the organization was an importer of Russian artists. Here too the boys asked about tickets but slipped out before they could be helped, leaving behind an unnatural flame to consume the reception-room furniture. Luckily CAMI was on the ground floor and almost nobody had yet arrived for work. The few people already in the office simply threw open the windows and fled to the street.

But Hurok's sleek glass box was too modern to have windows that could be opened. In a matter of seconds smoke had gathered in thick black billows at the front door and at both fire exits. It snaked through the air ducts to the distant rooms in the Hurok complex. Kelly Brown had shouted a warning to the others, then raced out as his own desk was engulfed by flames. A publicity man named John Gingrich tried to call the Fire Department, but the switchboard had melted and the phone was dead. The two dozen employees on hand were driven back from the exits by the smoke and fire. They filled the air with hacking coughs. Gingrich and the other men used office chairs to smash out the tinted-glass wall panels. A blessing of winter air rushed in.

In the confusion no one realized that three young women from the accounting department had taken refuge in a room at the farthest corner of the Hurok offices. They too tried to knock out the wall panels, but did not have the strength. Petrified, they lay down on the carpet and covered their heads.

One of the women, Virginia Proodian, saw that her friend, twenty-seven-year-old Iris Kones, seemed paralyzed by fear.

"Don't worry, hon, it'll be all right," said Proodian. "Someone will come for us."

Firemen finally arrived and carried out seventeen injured employees, including old Hurok, who was found barely conscious in an armchair. In the far corner office the three women were still lying with their heads buried in the carpet. Two were revived. Iris Kones was not.

"Walking through this wreckage," says Seedman, "I knew that we had seen the end of JDL action, at least for a while. But it was not the result of anything the police had done to them. They had done it to themselves. All their plots to harm the Russians had now climaxed in the death of one Jewish girl. If that didn't take the heart out of this bunch, they didn't have hearts."

The JDL at once denounced the bombings as "insane acts" with which its members were not involved. Meir Kahane sent the same message from Israel, where he was making plans to emigrate. To draw attention from the joint task force, which operated best out of the spotlight, Seedman told the press that he had formed a Major Crime Squad to devote full time to this investigation. But the most critical job for now was beyond their capability. It would fall only to Parola and Gibney. They would again have to make the Jewish Connection.

In the months since the Amtorg indictments the two detectives had hardly seen Angelo at all. That case and the garage charges still hung in limbo during extensive pretrial maneuvers by the Government and defense lawyers. Now they met again on their block on President Street.

"You know what we're here for, Shel," said Parola.

Angelo nodded. "I swear I don't know who did that crazy stuff. Myself, I'm out of it."

"Find out for us, Shel."

"Why should I?"

"Because a pretty little broad died and her family ought to know that someone will answer for it."

"That's your problem, not mine."

"Are you such a total prick that you don't feel anything for that girl?" exploded Parola. "Or if not for her, what about your friends? It'll be better for them if they stand up and take their medicine. After all, it wasn't like first-degree murder, they won't go away for life. They'll be out in a year or two and then they can walk around with their heads up. I'm telling you, Shelly, if we don't catch them, they'll walk around for the rest of their lives in their own head prison."

Angelo's face twitched, but he said nothing. The detectives met with Siegel a dozen more times over the next month with no results. One morning, after a particularly sour meeting, they told Seedman that they were getting nowhere.

"We know that persistence paid off once before with this kid," said Gibney. "But that time we could stick him with the thought that we were getting to him anyway through other evidence. This time Sammy and I don't think he's directly involved, so he doesn't see any reason to talk."

"Let's offer him money," said Seedman.

The detectives looked at their boss reproachfully. "You got to be kidding, Chief," said Parola. "This kid will never, *never* break for money."

"Do what I tell you."

At their next meeting under the West Side Highway, Parola laid $5000 in bills on the front seat between them. "This here comes from Mr. Hurok himself and other folks who are hoping that justice can be done for that poor girl," said Parola quietly. Angelo seemed transfixed by the neat stack of hundred-dollar bills. The detectives knew that he was always in debt; only last fall they had chipped in to help him buy a new door for the Volvo. Now his long fingers brushed over the bills. They waited.

"I'm . . . not talking for money," Angelo said weakly.

Parola riffled the bills like cards. "Look, meatball, this isn't Ronzoni coupons, ya' know." But Angelo had turned away.

The detectives returned the money to Seedman in the morning. "We knew he wouldn't take it," Gibney said.

"I knew that too, you silly bastards," said Seedman. "I just wanted to give him the chance to prove to you, and himself, that he could look at a wad of cash and spit on it. Now everyone knows he can't be bought out for the wrong reason. Maybe now we can come up with the *right* reason."

Seedman had only one wedge that might open up Siegel: immunity was no longer a bargaining tool; Angelo had already won that with the Amtorg information. But the one thing Siegel kept begging the detectives to promise was that no one would find out he was the Jewish Connection. Secrecy could not be guaranteed as simply as immunity, so Gibney and Parola always had promised only to do their best to preserve Angelo's cover. Maybe now, if Siegel supplied them with enough evidence to put the Hurok bombers in jail without his testimony, they could use such a guarantee as a wedge. It all depended on what he had to trade.

"Shelly," said Gibney at their next meeting, "we know you can't be bought for money. We know you fuckin' well can't be intimidated by being thrown in the can. But we do think you care that your friends don't find out who you are. Is that true?"

"You're damn right. And you better not reveal me." Angelo was suddenly on the edge of his seat.

"Take it easy, kid," said Parola. "Now, listen. Give us the names of the kids who did this Hurok thing, and I think we can get a promise that not only will you walk away from everything else— but the DA won't reveal you. Otherwise, Shel, it's going to happen in open court, right out in front of your people."

"Don't squeeze me that way," said Siegel coldly.

"It's them that's gonna squeeze, baby, not me," answered Parola, just as coldly.

Throughout the winter, the three of them huddled, often shivering, in forlorn parts of the city for as much as two hours at a time. In early April windows rolled down now, they were still talking, and Angelo was sulkier than ever. But not always because of bombing matters. The girl Angelo had fallen for, Tova, had been flirting with another JDL member and it was driving Angelo crazy. The detectives hardly blamed him. A beauty with a cascade of blond hair and an upturned nose, Tova reminded Gibney of the Irish girls he went to school with. Often Angelo seemed to want to talk, but something was holding him back. They were willing to bet it was Tova.

But then on May 7, fifteen weeks after the meetings had recommenced, the inexplicable again happened.

"Will you still make good on that promise not to reveal me?" Angelo suddenly asked in the Volvo.

"For the good stuff, we sure will, kid."

"Suppose I tell you who made the bomb they used at Columbia Artists Management."

"That's the good stuff, all right."

"You swear you won't reveal me?"

"We swear, kid."

"It was me."

The detectives were stunned. They had been absolutely certain Siegel would not dare get himself in any deeper. It was not just because he was in a legally precarious position; they felt they had genuinely convinced him of the folly of trying to bomb Russian Jews into freedom. Why else had he given them the name of the sniper who had fired into the room where children slept? Why had he told them about the plot to dynamite the Russian Mission's underground garage? Or to land a drone airplane loaded with TNT on the roof? Or to shoot the Russian Ambassador as his limousine swung into the Embassy driveway in Washington? Angelo did not need to reveal those things to get immunity in the Amtorg case. He had warned them, everyone thought, to prevent the gravest of international incidents.

"How could you do it, Shel?" asked Gibney. "How the fuck could you?"

"They were going to do it anyway," he answered. "I couldn't stop them. I just happened to come across them trying to make this bomb over at a place on New Utrecht Avenue. I'm surprised they didn't blow themselves up. They didn't know what the hell they were doing. Don't forget, this wasn't dynamite like usual; it was an incendiary bomb. They were slopping it together like it was batter for potato *latkes*. The way they were doing it, the thing was going to turn out way too huge. So I told them to get the fuck away and made it for them. Smaller. They kept begging me to pack more in, but I wouldn't. If I'd let them do it, they'd have packed enough heat to send the thing to the moon. Or melt the building down."

"So who were the others?"

"I'm not telling."

"How in hell do you expect us to keep you out of it if we don't know whose heads to knock?"

The detectives soon pried out of Angelo the names of the

delivery teams for the Columbia Artists and Hurok bombings. Though he insisted he had not made the Hurok incendiary bomb, the detectives no longer believed him. But they could understand his reluctance, immunity or not, to identify himself with a case involving murder.

In the middle of June detectives arrested the first of nearly a dozen JDL members on local and Federal charges including conspiracy to bomb, unlawful possession of explosive devices, malicious damage to property used in interstate and foreign commerce, arson, and finally, murder.

Meeting under the West Side Highway for the first time after the arrests the two detectives and Angelo felt strange. Somehow it was not a bad feeling.

"Joey has a farm upstate near Corning, you know," said Parola. "When this is all over, we were thinking, maybe you'd like to come up with us for a couple of weeks during the hunting season. It's real pretty country then. There's deer and pheasant and rabbit and wild turkey and even some bear that comes across the property. So we'll just get up early every morning and hunt and chop firewood and cook up great food on Joey's old cast-iron stove. And we'll clear all this crap out of our heads. . . ."

"That'd be nice," said Angelo.

With all parties too busy, they never got to Corning. The detectives did not even see Angelo again that year. But in the fall they were pleased to hear that he and Tova were planning to be married.

Siegel had always understood that he could not avoid testifying in some manner at the trial. The Government had promised only to protect the nature of his role as much and as long as possible. But as the January 1973 trial date approached, Siegel began to make noises through his lawyers that he would neither testify on any matter pertaining to the bombings nor *ever* take the stand against any member of the JDL. He seemed to be slitting his own throat. Didn't he realize he would lose his immunity and end up going to jail with the others? Even worse for him, the Government would feel no compunction now about blowing his cover by putting him on grandstand display as an informant. Or so it seemed. But neither Gibney and Parola nor Seedman was aware of what Siegel's lawyers were planning. On the basis of pretrial information furnished routinely by the Government to the defense, the lawyers had found a loophole: in the fall of 1971, while Gibney and Parola were locked in almost nightly sessions with Angelo, the FBI had tapped the phone of the JDL's Brooklyn headquarters and Siegel's home phone. This could have been done only by court order, except in cases involving national security where the President could authorize the tap directly, bypassing the courts. However, these taps had been ordered not by the President but by Attorney General John Mitchell. As such they were illegal.

Alan Dershowitz, a young Harvard Law professor who headed Siegel's legal team, now argued before trial judge Arnold Bauman that his client had become an informant only because he was threatened with imprisonment on the Amtorg charges. But Siegel had not realized that he had actually been "discovered" through the illegal FBI wiretaps. Those taps invaded his Constitutional right to privacy, in effect, and therefore constituted an illegal search. To protect himself Siegel felt he had no choice but to give information about his own part in the bombings as well as the roles of others. All this evidence flowed from the secretly carried out invasion of his privacy, a flow tainted at the original source, like a spring that contaminates drinkers far downstream, even as they slake their thirst.

For the Government Assistant U. S. Attorney Henry Putzel argued that Siegel's "stream" of information was not tainted in the least. He had been "discovered" not by the admittedly illegal wiretaps but through good old-fashioned detective work by the Explosive-Arson Squad. They had ingeniously traced the Micronta timer to Siegel, then waited for him to return to the Radio Shack before putting the screws on him.

To counter this argument, Siegel had one more ace to pull out. Ever resourceful, he had "wired" his Volvo to record many of his conversations with Gibney and Parola, beginning in the fall of 1971. One of those tapes, Dershowitz claimed, contained a remark by Parola that could be interpreted to mean that Siegel originally had been found out through FBI wiretaps.

The matter could be easily settled, of course. Judge Bauman would simply listen to the FBI tapes himself. Then came the bombshell. Despite a law requiring that such tapes be "warehoused" for at least ten years, the Government admitted that the FBI tapes had been destroyed. Judge Bauman, a hollow-cheeked and thoughtful man with bushy gray hair, was clearly upset by the Government's admission. But he ruled anyway that Siegel had been "discovered" by timer rather than tape.

Siegel was the Government's first witness. He gave his name, but from then on refused to answer any of Putzel's questions. Bauman formally found him in civil contempt but allowed him to continue under existing bail. But a three-judge panel of the U. S. Court of Appeals looked at Siegel's refusal to answer differently. The defendant had every right to maintain that he had been illegally discovered, they said, just as the Government had every right to dispute him. But how could Siegel prove his claim if the Government, by violating its own statute, failed to provide the crucial wiretaps? The burden of proof was no longer on Siegel. It had shifted to the Government. Yet by illegally destroying the admittedly illegal tapes, the Government had also destroyed their only chance at rebuttal.

Sheldon Siegel, the panel ruled, had suffered a violation of his Constitutional rights. He was within his rights in not answering questions which grew out of that invasion. Judge Bauman's finding of civil contempt against him was "reversed and vacated."

Several other JDL defendants eagerly sought to wash themselves in Siegel's "taint," claiming that if his rights had been violated and he had been coerced into naming them as bombers, then their rights were also violated. The Court of Appeals rejected this argument and ordered the defendants to testify. But when Judge Bauman was finally able to resume the trial, all of them refused to answer any questions, citing the dictates of their religion and maintaining that they could accept only the judgment of a rabbinical court. Obviously simmering, Bauman cited each of the defendants for civil contempt, the sentence for which was far lighter than the one they faced if found guilty of the bombing charges.

After a teen-aged defendant named Richard Huss refused to answer a long series of droning questions put by Assistant U. S. Attorney Joseph Jaffe, his attorney rose testily.

"Excuse me, Your Honor," he said. "The witness has made it clear in my mind he will not answer. I see no purpose in this continuing."

Bauman leaned forward in cold anger. "Let me tell you what the purpose is. Someone has committed a dastardly, vicious, unforgivable, unforgettable crime. Someone is frustrating the administration of justice in a case that in my mind involves murder. People who deliberately do so will learn the power of the law—even if there are those who have literally gotten away with murder."

Huss looked straight ahead, wide-eyed and frozen. In the fifth row of spectators, his mother grasped the arms of the women on either side of her, both of them mothers of other defendants. Farther back, a mere spectator named Sheldon Siegel jiggled his knees, and kept his eyes averted from the Bench.

"Proceed," ordered the Judge.

Q: *Mr. Huss, on the morning of January 26, 1972, did you go in a motor vehicle with Sheldon Davis, with Jeffrey Smilow and Murray Elbogan and with Jerome Zellerkraut, and drive from Brooklyn to Manhattan?*

A: Same declination. [The "declination" was a long statement Huss had read in answer to the first question following his swearing-in.]

THE COURT: I order you to answer.

THE WITNESS: Same declination.

Q: *Had you, prior to the morning of January 26, agreed with Sheldon Davis and Stuart Cohen that you and Jerome Zellerkraut would go to the offices of Sol Hurok?*

A: Same declination.

THE COURT: I order you to answer.

THE WITNESS: Same declination. . . .

Q: *Mr. Huss, did you on the morning of January 26 deliver an attaché case, along with Jerome Zellerkraut, to the offices of Sol Hurok?*

A: Same declination.

THE COURT: I order you to answer.

THE WITNESS: Same declination. . . .

Witness by witness, declination by declination, the Government's case was shattered into ever smaller bits. Without Angelo the prosecution was impotent. After each witness had been cited for civil contempt, all that remained was for Bauman to set their bail. Just as Morse had done, Assistant U.S. Attorney Henry Putzel asked for high bail in every case. The lawyer for defendant Jeffrey Smilow protested Putzel's request that bail be set at $50,000.

"Your Honor," said the lawyer, "on the question of bail, you are fully familiar with the background of this witness. He has been before Your Honor several times. . . . He has been before Judge Weinfeld, I believe, in another proceeding several times. He appeared in court on each and every occasion. He lives at home with his parents. They reside in Kings County. His mother is here in court and has been here each and every occasion. This witness is presently—"

"Do you know who isn't in court today?" asked the judge.

The lawyer shook his head.

"Iris Kones," thundered Bauman.

Gibney and Parola had waited outside the courtroom that day as usual in case they were called to testify. They had never spoken to Siegel. As the place emptied out after the last session they saw him come through the mahogany doors and walked over to him warily. Neither detective stood as high as Siegel's chin.

"Joey and me just thought we'd say . . . now that it's over . . . like the judge said, it's a shame for the girl. . . . But personally, kid, we're glad for *you* it turned out this way. . . . We. . . ."

Aware that Parola's fast tongue had deserted him, Gibney said, "We wish you a lotta luck."

Siegel's mournful wary face ticked uncertainly. It seemed about to rearrange itself into a smile. His wife, Tova, had been staring coolly at the detectives, running her delicate hand across her husband's shoulder blades. Now she ran it down to the small of his back, traced a brush line across his thighs, up his arms and, with the gentlest pressure of a finger, led him away.

The four rode down in silence in the same jammed elevator. Only a few paces apart, they walked through the echoing lobby out to the great portico of the gold-domed courthouse. At the bottom of the thirty granite steps the couple and the pair of detectives turned and walked off briskly in opposite directions. Just as he and Tova were about to turn the corner, Sheldon Siegel turned around. He gave a fleeting wave.

Gibney and Parola turned in time to return the wave. It was their last connection.

THE COLOMBO CASE

You're a smart guy. Play ball with us. Other-wise you can never tell what will happen to you. I have lots of friends. Nobody could ever pin it on me because I would be in California. It would be the perfect excuse.

—JOE GALLO TRYING TO SHAKE DOWN TEDDY MOSS FOR HALF THE PROFITS OF HIS THREE BARS, NEW YORK, MAY 3, 1961

I

"I first heard Joe Colombo's name in 1960, in a cafeteria in Brooklyn just across the Williamsburgh Bridge. I was a brand new captain just assigned to the Brooklyn North detective command after two years in charge of Narcotics investigations in Manhattan East. Over the next nine years, with a brief time out for a tour in Queens, I'd be commanding first a district, then half of Brooklyn, then the other half, then the works. In the process, I'd learn practically every block of that whole fantastic borough, bigger itself than all but a half-dozen cities. But right now, sitting in this cafeteria, I was nothing but a greenhorn.

"It was a plain, inexpensive place with hard edges, but at one table I noticed a bunch of flashy characters—sharkskin suits, mono-grammed cufflinks, the works—just sitting over their coffee cups, not eating any lunch. I asked my driver, Joe McGuinnes, if he didn't think they looked out of place among all the working stiffs.

" 'This is a pickup point for the fast money,' McGuinnes ex-plained. 'What they call a "drop." Guys looking for a crap game come here and are taken by special cars to wherever the game is set up this week—usually in a garage or the basement of an apartment building. This game is always getting busted, but it keeps coming back. It belongs to a soldier for Profaci. His name is Joe Colombo.'

"I never can think of Colombo back then when we were both middle-rungers in our respective organizations without remembering his beautiful set of felt-topped mahogany gambling tables. They were hand-crafted to order; even then you'd pay $500 to have one made up for your rec room. The minute a lookout signaled trouble, the guy in charge of the game just touched a finger to a button underneath. Bingo! In a flash the table folded up on its specially designed legs into a neat package, dice and all. By the time the door came crashing down, the crap-shooters had turned into just a bunch of guys, standing around the basement, whistling a tune."

In 1938 Joe Colombo's father was garroted by a rival in the mob. Joe had to quit high school and went to work in a printing plant to support his mother and sister. During the war he joined the Navy, only to be discharged after three fitful years for "psychoneurosis." He returned to Brooklyn and worked for a while on the waterfront, but around 1950 took his first step toward becoming somebody in the mob: he won appointment to a five-man "hit team" that handled Joseph Profaci's most stubborn problems. At least fifteen killings were flawlessly carried out by the team, which included other young men aching to prove themselves—Larry and Joe Gallo.

Profaci had a reputation for greed in those days, and it only got worse as he grew older. Even though he owned a thriving olive oil and tomato import business, and had a mansion on Long Island and a New Jersey estate with its own airport, he still demanded a twenty-five-dollar "slush fund" contribution every month from each member of his family, high and low. That twenty-five dollars galled the young Gallos. It symbolized Profaci's greed. As good hit men they felt they deserved more of the action, a piece of the rackets for themselves. While they bridled, Colombo was content to run his dice game and let Profaci rake off as much as he wished.

By the time Seedman took command of the 10th Detective District in 1961, Joe Colombo seemed to have reached his own level of maximum competence. Ironically, it was the Gallos' greed that would soon catapult Colombo to unexpected prominence—and would lay the Gallos low.

One morning early in 1960 the Gallo brothers swept five Profaci lieutenants off the streets and held them hostage. They were not released until Profaci promised the Gallos and their men a larger share in his rackets. But it was power, not promises, that counted—a principle which the Gallos, incredibly, seemed to have forgotten. Since Profaci commanded far more muscle than the Gallos and the young hoods siding with them, he simply declared a five-month "peace," and then proceeded to try to exterminate them.

Profaci died of cancer before the war with the Gallos could be resolved. His crime family seemed destined to be passed on to Joseph Magliocco, his underboss and brother-in-law. But the Gallos had caused such a ruckus that three of the other four New York families were hesitant to support Magliocco, a gentleman of the old school. Without their support, the so-called national commission would not support Magliocco either.

Magliocco turned to Joseph Bonanno, the only New York don who supported him. Bonanno's operations had spread farther than any other mobster's—to Arizona, California, Colorado, and Canada —and like any true *conglomerateur,* he felt this was only the beginning. But he suspected that the three family heads resented his expansionist vision. His next move was inevitable. Certain that prison would take care of Genovese, he looked around for someone to kill Gambino and Lucchese. But he did not want to let the contract himself. That would be a job for Magliocco.

Now Joe Colombo's moment was approaching. Magliocco knew that Colombo always had been a faithful soldier of the late Joseph Profaci, never a young upstart like the Gallos. Surely Colombo could be trusted to carry out this most important contract. If he succeeded, Magliocco would take over the mob and be able to return the favor he owed his friend, Joe Bonanno.

But Colombo did not keep the faith. Sensing who had the real power now that Genovese was in prison, he ran to Gambino's side to warn him, not shoot him. Magliocco was called before the national commission. He confessed, repented, begged mercy, went back to his rolling Long Island estate to ride horses sturdy enough to carry his three hundred pounds. A year later, he was dead.

Bonanno now realized he had played his cards all wrong. He had backed Profaci during the Gallo uprising. He had backed Magliocco. Now both were dead. He had called for the extermination of two of the five New York dons, and they were still alive. Survival, not expansion, had become his biggest problem, so Bonanno fled into hiding on the West Coast. He had brought his own house down. But the coup de grâce had been administered by the treachery of Joe Colombo.

Gambino now rewarded Colombo with control of the lucrative Profaci family. As the new kingmaker, Gambino could do that with a wave of the hand. Except that Colombo would not quite be a king. He would always be beholden to Gambino. Who else could have raised him up so swiftly to glory? That knowledge was Gambino's payment. Now he would control his own family and pull strings in a second—the well-oiled apparatus created over thirty years ago by Joe Profaci.

A few years later Sam "The Plumber" DeCavalcante, boss of the New Jersey mob, wondered aloud into his FBI-tapped office phone how a nobody like Colombo could have been elevated to the top of the Profaci family. "He was nothing but a bust-out man"— a small-time gambler—railed DeCavalcante.

"He was always hangin' on Carl's shoulder," answered the voice on the end of the line. But that was exactly it. With Genovese in prison, Gambino knew he was more powerful than any other New York family head. Colombo must have known that too, or he surely would have fulfilled the hit contract.

Now that he was a don, Colombo no longer ran a dice game personally. Starting in 1963, the dice rolled for him. In an effort to appear legitimate, he became a salesman for Cantalupo Realty Company and took equity positions in a florist shop and a funeral parlor, both traditional fronts for men of his position. Back in 1924 Dion O'Banion, Al Capone's predecessor in the Chicago mobs, had been rubbed out while snipping chrysanthemums in his own little flower shop on North State Street. Joseph Bonanno, head of one of the original five families created by Salvatore Maranzano in 1931, was said to have perfected the double-bottomed coffin—the upper section for the official deceased, the lower for a rubout victim—at his own funeral parlor in lower Manhattan.

A few years after his ascension Joe Colombo truly arrived as a

Mafia boss. In the hills of Orange County, New York, he bought a secluded estate complete with tennis court and swimming pool.

Joe Colombo became a don in 1964, the same year Seedman was promoted to Inspector. By 1968 Seedman and Colombo were at the top of their respective professions in Brooklyn—Colombo had been running the Profaci family for five years and Seedman was commander of the borough's detectives. It was inevitable that they would meet.

"One morning in April," recalls Seedman, "a case came up where I thought Joe Colombo could help us out. In fact, I felt he might even *want* to help.

"It concerned an old con named Cologero LoCicero or, as he was known in Borough Park, Charlie the Cidge. As far back as 1925 he had been arrested for murder in the service of Joe Profaci. He had also been a Colombo captain. But now he was sixty-four years old and semi-retired. As was his daily habit, that morning he went over to Calisi's soda fountain at 66th Street and 11th Avenue—a dozen blocks from Dellurnia's candy store—for a strawberry malted milk.

"At nine-fifteen the door opened. As the proprietor and the Cidge looked up, two men with bags over their faces blasted away. The counter, the floor, the walls were shattered—everything but the malted glass and a pack of Lucky Strikes beside it. The Cidge was dead at once.

"Normally, I would have been puzzled by this execution. The average age of mobsters under contract is well below sixty-four, unless they are at the top level. LoCicero was not trying to take over new territory. He was not hired out to do anyone's dirty business. He was just an old man who wanted a malted milk. Why would he be hit in a manner suitable to a rising young muscleman?

"In this case, however, I did have a pretty good idea why. During the summer of 1966 his grandnephew, Richard LoCicero, had worked as a courier for the Wall Street brokerage firm of Paine Webber Jackson and Curtis. About five o'clock one afternoon he was taking a packet of negotiable securities to the bank when a man with a gun forced him into the doorway of a deserted building, tied his hands to the doorknob, and made off with securities valued at $360,862.

"That was the story as Ritchie told it, but it didn't ring true to me. I knew the kid had plenty of bad influences around him. In September 1966, two months after the theft, a detective posing as a fence reported that he had been offered a batch of negotiable securities at cut rate. Two of the six sellers were Charles and Carlo LoCicero, sons of Charlie the Cidge and uncles of Ritchie. Early in 1967 a grand jury indicted them for criminally receiving stolen goods and called Ritchie to testify. He was not very helpful. It was a mystery to him, he insisted, how his uncles had come to be offering the same securities that had been taken from his hands last July. Certainly he would have recognized either of them if they had tied his hands to a doorknob in broad daylight!

"Ritchie kept his mouth shut, but out in Brooklyn somebody must have thought Ritchie told more than he did. I was in the office early one morning a few weeks before the trial when a DOA was reported in a backyard on Bay 16th Street. I went over myself. It was Ritchie, lying face up. I never saw an uglier rubout. He had been stabbed in rows up and down so many times he looked like a strainer. He had also been degutted, like a chicken.

"Yet this was no worse than many other Mafia-style executions. I have seen bodies of men tied up with their legs pushed up under their chins, so that when they try to kick loose they strangle themselves. I have seen men with their own penises shoved down their throats. Forget all the stories about the romance or honor of the Mafia. Forget the tomato plants they tend so lovingly. These people are not satisfied to settle a dispute or betrayal by simple murder. They must also humiliate the victim, even in death. This is how they are in their heart of hearts.'

"Though Cologero LoCicero and his grandnephew Richard were executed a year apart, it was a safe guess that one killing was in return for the other. The men coming to trial in the securities case, Carlo and Charles, were the Cidge's sons. If the Cidge felt Ritchie's loose mouth had caused them trouble, he may have authorized his grandnephew's execution. If others closer by blood to Ritchie felt the Cidge was responsible for the boy's death, then payment had to be returned in kind. In either case we had nothing to go on but theory. Our only witness, the proprietor of Calisi's soda shop, was so petrified he would say nothing at all—he didn't want anyone to think he had spoken out of turn like poor Ritchie.

"I felt nobody would be in a better position to confirm or deny the connection between the killings of the Cidge and Ritchie than

Joe Colombo," Seedman said. "I put the word out through the detectives that I wanted to see him. In the eight short years since I had sat in the dairy cafeteria, watching his dice-game pickups, Colombo had moved a long way up. I expected a big shot like him to balk at coming down to the 66th Precinct station house. But he agreed to appear at one P.M. on Wednesday, April twenty-third.

"Till that day I had never seen a man in Colombo's position enter a station house without lawyers. To them, it's enemy territory. The lawyer shakes your hand and advises you his client will gladly answer questions on any subject except those you are interested in. He sits right beside his client and monitors the conversation—the more the client knows, the less he lets him say. Imagine my surprise, then, when on the dot of one on April twenty-third, Joseph Colombo walked into my office alone. He was wearing a well-cut blue suit, white shirt, muted burgundy tie. He looked like a prosperous banker.

" 'I believe you knew Cologero LoCicero,' I said.

" 'I did know Mr. LoCicero, yes.'

"I told Colombo that quite frankly the murder was a puzzle to us; the man was just blasted off his stool for no apparent reason. 'I know you'd like to see us solve this case as much as we would,' I said. 'I thought you might have heard something about it.'

"Colombo shook his head and looked troubled. 'Chief, I give you my complete cooperation in this. It was a terrible thing. But I do not understand why you're coming to me about it. So help me, I don't have any connection with this.' "

Seedman had played the long shot that Colombo might find it in his own interest to drop some hint of where to look for the Cidge's killer, or at least to affirm the connection between the two LoCicero executions. But Colombo was not going to do either. Instead, as became clear from his darkening face, he was revving up for something else.

"You lean back at that big desk, Chief, and you're thinking, 'This guy is sitting here, feeding me a line. He's nothing but a two-bit greaser trying to look respectable.' Well, you're wrong. I am an American citizen, first class. I don't have a badge that makes me an official good guy like you, but I work just as honest for a living. I am a salesman in real estate. I have a family to support. God willing, the business I do will keep them happy and well fed and put my boys through college."

Colombo leaned forward in his chair. "If I was a Jewish businessman, you'd never dream of calling me down here on a murder I had no connection with. But because my name is Italian, that's different. I'm a goombah mobster, not good people like you.

"But I don't expect you to ever think differently, no matter what I say or do," said Colombo, now shaking his head sadly. He looked as weighed down as Job. "I know that when you're done, I can walk out of here. At least, today I can. But I also know this: as sure as I sit here, I fully expect to be harassed by the law for the rest of my life. Not by you, necessarily—the detectives who work for you are on the whole good guys—but the Federal men are lousy. They are bigots. I expect they will be after me before long. I'd never say this to my family, but I swear to God the FBI is going to frame me somehow. Maybe it will be income-tax evasion, maybe one of those conspiracy deals. Whatever it takes, they will throw me into prison. I expect to die there."

A half-hour after Colombo walked into Seedman's office the interview was over. Seedman had not really expected much help in solving the murders of the two LoCiceros without witnesses, evidence, or informants. Those cases would go unsolved, like most mob executions. But in those thirty minutes he had learned something important two years before it became public—Joe Colombo was planning a whole new strategy for the Mafia.

"By looking me straight in the eye that morning and claiming he was just an honest businessman, I read him to mean that he was not going to carry on in the tradition of first-generation Mafia leaders like Capone, who lived in splendor and flaunted their power, even to the extent of occasionally guaranteeing clean public elections. Nor was he going to follow the example of second-generation dons like Carlo Gambino, who demanded every sign of respect within the organization but in public acted like the humble corner-fruit-market man, always ready to turn the other cheek. Gambino was like the hog snake, which rolls over and plays dead until trouble passes.

"Joe had now shown a third face. He was not going to rule in splendor, he was not going to act humble before the public. Until we could prove differently, he would demand to be treated like a legitimate businessman in real estate brokerage, reject any marketing of organized crime under the brand name 'Mafia,' and dare us to call him a less than honest man. If he was finally nailed on some charge—and he was smart enough to realize the Feds could work more angles than the local cops—why, then, it was a frameup."

Colombo's original new strategy was publicly unveiled early in 1970 when the FBI arrested his son, Joe, Jr., for allegedly melting dimes into silver ingots worth more than the sum of the coins. What the elder Colombo had told Seedman on a personal level that morning in 1968, he now tooled up into a grand strategy. Not only was he personally going to resist this new "harassment" of his family, he was going to hold it up as an example of how the Italian-Americans had become a scapegoat for everyone's crime problems. No longer would they take it lying down, he proclaimed. They had been demeaned long enough. Other minorities had struck back. The Jews had the Anti-Defamation League. The blacks had the NAACP, CORE, SNICK. Now he would form the Italian American Civil Rights League. Now Italian-Americans could stand tall and proud under the red, white, and green banner of the IACRL and the inspirational leadership of Joe Colombo.

His timing was perfect. For almost twenty years news reports had been full of the long intense battle for black civil rights. Now the white middle class was ready to listen to the complaints of other minorities. And Colombo, it seemed to many Americans, had a pretty good case. Everybody had read *The Godfather* and had rooted for the WASP detectives against Italian gangsters on TV's *The Untouchables*. But that was all fiction, figments of a storyteller's imagination. In real life who could recall any recent *hard* news about gang wars or atrocities perpetrated against innocent citizens by the Mafia? Maybe Colombo was right—for too long they had taken fiction for fact.

If that was the reaction of the Average American, hardworking Italians across the country were delighted to hear this well-spoken earnest businessman give 'em hell. In six months forty chapters of the League had sprung up, and dues and donations poured into its national headquarters on Madison Avenue. The flow of donations became an avalanche. Day and night crowds of League members picketed FBI district headquarters on Third Avenue, jeering as well-groomed agents in their suits and ties slipped nervously through the demonstrators' ranks on their way to work. Joe Colombo himself often appeared at the barricades in the evening before rushing off to news and talk shows. There he earnestly preached a gospel that startled men like Seedman, his detectives, and their state and Federal counterparts: the Mafia was a myth created by the media and the FBI. It was time honest citizens called their bluff.

"What made Colombo's pitch so confusing," explains Seedman, "is that he *was* absolutely right. Italians had every right to resent being lumped by the millions into a Mafia whose nationwide membership does not exceed nine thousand men. But however small the organization, Joe Colombo was part of it. We knew him to be the head of a clearly charted family of two hundred exceptionally loyal men dealing in loansharking, gambling, hijacking, and theft. We had arrested him ten times on gambling charges, once for falsifying his real estate broker's license application. The Feds had wrapped him up for income-tax evasion. Of course we were after him, and his latest defense was to ride on the backs of honest people, sucking the decency from their lives like a leech. It was a brilliant ploy.

"What confuses the public further is that the Mafia no longer makes itself visible. It has shape, it has organization, and most important, it has discipline—but it exists mainly in the heads of the members. As we tighten the screws, they have no choice but to make their operations even less visible. Carlo Gambino, for example, commands the largest Mafia family—a thousand members—yet he can't take written reports or even talk to most of his men because we observe each visitor to his home on Ocean Parkway in Brooklyn. Whenever he leaves the house, we follow him. Yet he operates smoothly anyhow. If the Don wants to go somewhere, a chauffeur appears. *Anybody* he wants materializes at once. It's the same discipline and communication codes that help small armies vanquish large ones. It is nothing the public can see when Joe Colombo tells them the Mafia is a myth.

"Colombo went one step further to disguise his own Mafia family: he began to insist that each of his soldiers get a real job— sanitation man, butcher, salesman, guidance counselor, any damn thing as long as it was legitimate. He was asking for a big sacrifice. One of the major benefits of being 'made' as a family member was that nine-to-five jobs were out. You became a man of independent means, a treasured goal for someone whose father had worked like a dog six days a week in the garment or building trades. Now, when every other guy was straphanging on the subway early every morning, you were still in bed. It was the Brooklyn version of *The Great Gatsby*.

"I once analyzed the life of a bookie who had traded under authority of the Profaci family in South Brooklyn. He was a broken-down guy with one shiny old suit and bad teeth who lived in a shabby apartment with a worn-out wife and sloppy kids. Each day from ten to six he hung around a phone booth on Utica Avenue, taking bets. Rain, sleet, heat, or snow he was on that corner at least eight hours a day. But this man would boast proudly, sometimes with icicles hanging from his nose, that he did not have to work for a living.

"Under Colombo in 1970 this man would have to get a night job, maybe as a motorman on the IRT, if he wanted to keep that streetcorner post. Otherwise, wives of working men might see his wife buying steak in the market and ask the logical question: 'How does she pay for it if he doesn't work?' Years ago it would have been accepted that he had 'connections.' But no more. In his new role as debunker of the Mafia and leader of the IACRL, Joe Colombo did not care to explain such mysteries away."

Even Colombo must have been surprised at how easily his cries of discrimination intimidated the forces on the other side in those early days of the League. The producers of the film *The Godfather* promised not to use the word "Mafia," which was like asking the producers of *Patton* not to use the word "Nazi." Astoundingly, certain newspapers, including the *New York Times*, and the networks and even the Justice Department agreed to stop using the words "Mafia" and "Cosa Nostra" ("Our thing"), the term Mafia informer Joseph Valachi told a Senate Committee insiders use among themselves.

"I'd see Colombo on the late news with that overweight son of his beside him," says Seedman. "They'd claim the Mafia was a myth, that we law enforcement officials were pinning all the ills of society on Italian-Americans—this after I might have gotten home late from the office because of problems *his* people were causing us in the city. I could understand why Colombo would want to spin out this line. If people believed him, he could operate easier. What bothered me was something else. Didn't he remember that his own dad had been killed by 'Our thing,' which he claimed did not exist? 'Come on, Joe,' I felt like saying. 'Honor thy father.'"

By June 28, 1970, when the IACRL held its first annual "Unity Day" rally, Colombo was able to look down like Caesar at fifty-five thousand proud Italian-Americans gathered at Columbus Circle on the southwest corner of Central Park. Every place he turned girls wearing hot pants and 'Kiss Me, I'm Italian' buttons waved and smiled adoringly. Politicians of all persuasions turned up to pay him homage. Even Governor Nelson Rockefeller had accepted honorary membership in the League. No one cared to be reminded that day about Colombo's previous arrests, the charts and tape transcripts outlining the structure of his crime family, or about his upcoming trial on charges that he directed a major gambling ring. Today talk was of Joe Colombo going into politics to represent *all* the people. Under the red, white, and green bunting billowing above the speaker's platform, Colombo smiled the smile of a man whose ballooning power and appeal seemed limitless.

If Colombo had been satisfied with the brilliant public relations that culminated in the first "Unity Day" rally, he might have gone out a champion. But he was too enamored at seeing himself on television night after night to give it up. In the whirl of testimonials, interviews, and picketing, Colombo stopped listening in certain important quarters where voices did not have to be raised to be heard.

The first hard sell had made the public aware of their own tendency to lump crime, Mafia, and Italians carelessly in one bag. But once the point was driven home and the media and law enforcement agencies had backed off, the continuing strident tone did not wear well. People originally sympathetic to Colombo's pitch became bored or annoyed by his loud charges of discrimination—and many of them began to have second thoughts about Colombo himself. Maybe the government *had* been right in calling him a Mafioso. On the *Dick Cavett Show* one night, Cavett noted that Colombo earned his living by selling real estate and through his interests in a flower shop and a funeral home. Without a cue sign, the audience snickered.

"Whatever the public might think of Colombo was not our concern," says Seedman. "But late in 1970 we began getting intelligence reports that he was losing support among former backers. This did not bode well for his future. Carlo Gambino, in particular, had at first been as surprised as we were by his protégé's unexpected knack for public relations. As long as politicians were pressuring the police and FBI to step a bit more gingerly, Carlo would restrain his gut feeling that silence was the best policy in his business.

"What bugged Gambino now was that Colombo didn't know enough to take his winnings and go home. He figured correctly that by now the FBI men were getting fed up with crossing Colombo's picket lines every morning and the soldiers back in Brooklyn were bound to suffer for it. Gambino noticed, too, that while Colombo howled long and loud over the arrest of his son, he wasn't wasting his energy defending other Italian sons who were taking their lumps from the FBI.

"In a word, the rest of the mob was jealous of Colombo. The IACRL may have begun as a tool to free his son, but it had turned into something more. Making money on the numbers was nice. Loansharking brought in an even higher return. Hijacking, though more dangerous, was all gravy. But to sit in a sleek Madison Avenue office every morning and open piles of envelopes containing dues and donations from all over the country—this was the greatest racket ever devised. It was even better than the Mafia's old-country practice of selling yards of coarse cotton soaked in chicken blood to pilgrims who thought they were buying genuine shrouds of the martyred saints.

"Not that all the cash went into the pockets of the League's organizers, of course. Colombo and his son Anthony officially paid themselves only $300 per week each. Henchmen of Gambino himself were also on the payroll. After expenses, the IACRL announced, remaining funds would be used to support a summer camp and a children's hospital. But examining their records, a former accountant like me could see ample opportunity for funds to go astray. It happens all the time in far tonier 'nonprofit' organizations. We knew from conversations with Gambino's lieutenants, in particular, that they were sore at Colombo for raking off the top without passing it around.

"One other cloud that came Colombo's way was the return of his old associate, Joseph Gallo. In 1962 Gallo's fight for a better deal in the Profaci rackets was cut short by a conviction for extortion. A dynamic man, he had to languish in prison while Colombo moved to the top. When he was released from prison in 1970, many powerful mobsters did not want to see him cut back in. They were all content to answer to Joe Colombo.

"Gallo understood that he could not waltz back into power, of course, but he made a start. According to informants in Brooklyn, Gallo demanded—as a sign of Colombo's friendship, and as a guarantee Gallo would never be a thorn in his side as he had been to Profaci—$100,000 and a piece of territory to work as his own. Colombo ignored him. It was too bad he had gone to prison; Joey should have used his own muscle more discreetly. Now he could pay the price.

"But Gallo, obviously, would not see it that way. He would be out to get back power in the rackets. How could he do that— start a Joeyburger franchise? His exact method, as always, was bound to be unpredictable. Except on one point. It would be violent."

As the time for the second annual "Unity Day" rally drew near, the good vibrations of the previous year were gone and visible signs of the Mafia's disenchantment were sprouting up all over. Small shopkeepers in Italian sections of the city—butchers, florists, delicatessen owners, dry cleaners— were visited by burly IACRL members who told them to post "Unity Day" notices and to stay closed that day so they and their employees could attend the rally. Many merchants thought it wise to cooperate until a second burly group appeared within minutes and suggested that they strip off the new posters while the glue was still wet and remain open as usual on June 28, 1971.

The shadow of Carlo Gambino fell with particular effect on the docks of the city. Longshoremen who had mysteriously been given the day off with pay to attend the 1970 rally were now being told to keep the cargo moving in 1971. Paul Vario, the League's membership director and a captain in the Gambino family, abruptly resigned a few weeks before the rally, claiming health problems.

"Coming to work on the morning of June twenty-eighth," says Seedman, "I fully expected trouble at Columbus Circle. But we all felt we could anticipate the limits of that trouble. A few spoilsports moving through the crowd would be all it took to ruin the cheerful mood. They could jostle people, start arguments and fights, even hoot down Colombo and other speakers or throw stink bombs. But these were all techniques the Department knew how to handle. The men under the Chief of Patrol are better at controlling crowds than any police force in the world. These men, many in plainclothes for the occasion, would be circulating in the crowd, along with many superior officers. They had guarded everyone from King

Hussein to Elizabeth Taylor. Though Colombo had asked us to minimize the police contingent around the platform, busloads of Tactical Police would still be parked out of sight on the side streets, ready to snuff out any disturbance that threatened to get out of hand.

"My men would also be at the rally, though this wasn't their primary function. Detectives are essentially caseworkers—they need a crime to investigate. Most of the men assigned to Columbus Circle that day were specialists in mob politics, any one of whom could identify hundreds of Mafia figures by the backs of their necks. They were there to tip off the uniform officers whom to watch, who might be carrying an unauthorized weapon, who were known friends and bodyguards of Joe Colombo and who were his enemies.

"The rally was scheduled for noon. I planned to drop in myself at eleven-fifty, but John Kinsella, my top assistant chief, would get there about ten-thirty to watch how the rally was coming along. Meanwhile, my desk was piled with the promotion and transfer recommendations that always accumulate right before the summer. The only way I knew to keep track of the three thousand men in the Bureau was to consider each of these applications myself, though I may have never seen the man for the duration of his assignment or even his entire career.

"At eleven-thirty-five I was considering a detective's request for transfer from the Auto Squad to the Airport Squad at JFK, closer to where I knew he'd just bought a house, when the private line rang.

"'Colombo was shot a few minutes ago,' John Kinsella said. 'A couple of bullets in the back of the head. The guy who did it is dead—a black man. We don't know yet who shot him. They took Colombo to Roosevelt Hospital, but the way he was pouring out blood all over, it didn't look to me like he's going to last out the hour.'

"I was stunned. Not in my wildest dreams did I imagine *this* kind of trouble at the rally. I knew, of course, that many people would dearly love to see Colombo shot—and there were more of them every day. But they have ways they like to do it, ways which make sense for them. They do it in quiet restaurants between dinner hours, on dark streets. Places out of the way. If there was a chance anybody might see them, they wear masks, like the men who hit Charlie the Cidge. They don't even like *one* witness. Had they dared to make a hit now surrounded by police, camera crews, spectators, and Colombo's own guards? It was also not the mob's custom to use black hit men. Plenty of their own young studs were eager for the honor, just as Colombo had been in his youth; Profaci had only to point his finger. Was this black man crazy, or had he acted on his own out of some personal pique? As my chauffeur and I sped uptown to the hospital, I had no answers. No crime in thirty years had left me so totally confused.

"On the third floor at Roosevelt Hospital the chief surgeon, Dr. Halston, showed me the X-rays of Colombo's skull. One bullet had lodged in the upper neck, two in the forehead. Incredibly, there was no sign of fatal subdural bleeding. So Joe Colombo was not going to die. As he was being prepared for surgery, I looked in on him. His color was good and his chest moved up and down regularly. Just the same, it might have been better if he had passed away then. Those shots had made his brains into scrambled eggs.

"I walked down to another operating room. Inside, laid face-down on a steel table, was the body of the black man, still dressed in a polo shirt and light-colored cotton slacks. Two small ragged gunpowder holes showed in the small of his back. According to a notebook and certain other papers removed from his pockets, his name was Jerome A. Johnson.

"I did not know yet whether Johnson had been shot by one of our men or one of Colombo's. I certainly did not know why he had shot Colombo. But whether he acted independently or on orders, I regarded his act and the act against him as more than felonies. They were an insult. They made a mockery of our ability to keep peace at a public assembly. The people of New York would demand action. Beyond that, I felt my own reputation as Chief of Detectives was on the line. However long it took me, I was determined we would solve this case."

II

"Lacking any direct evidence or motives to explain the shooting of Colombo," says Seedman, "I saw two main thrusts for our investigation. First we would reconstruct the events of 'Unity Day' in the greatest possible detail. At the same time we would be exploring the life of Jerome Johnson, going as far back as his first-grade teacher, if necessary, until we understood why he woke up on the morning of June twenty-eighth, determined to shoot Colombo.

"From the moment of Kinsella's call, I could not fathom how Johnson had ever gotten close enough to Colombo to get those shots off. Colombo was fully aware of the danger in any such rally, and he knew from rumblings beforehand that this one was especially dangerous. But he also had an experienced team of bodyguards who had been providing their boss with security for many years. They were sure to put the tightest ring around him ever on 'Unity Day.' So how had an armed black man been allowed to get close enough to shoot their boss?

"The answer was a combination of some sharp work by Johnson and some slack work by the so-called bodyguards. Johnson obviously knew that the trickiest part of his job would be getting into the rally itself, so he took several clever steps. He got himself an IACRL press card—not from headquarters, but from a League chapter in New Brunswick, where they didn't keep close tabs on the cards. Johnson also diverted suspicion by coming dressed in a polo shirt and cotton pants so tight that any spot where he could be hiding a gun—small of back, inside of thigh, under the arm—would have to bulge.

"Where did the gun come from, then? Probably from the most important accessory he thought to bring along with him: a pretty girl. Black, with a modest Afro, she was dressed to show off a great figure that Colombo's bodyguards were sure to ogle. As we put the pieces of Johnson's life together, we'd see that he was a marvelous con man. He'd certainly learned that the best way to enter someplace you're not invited is to turn up with a beautiful woman.

"Johnson also carried a camera, as did the girl. They were both good ones—his was a Bolex worth about $1200 and hers was a 35mm. still professional job outfitted with a 200mm. telephoto lens. A few of the news photographers noted that Bolex since it isn't normally used for this type of work, but the Colombo men had no way of knowing that. Between the press card, the tight clothes, the girl, and the cameras, Johnson had no trouble getting his foot in Colombo's inner circle."

Joe Colombo arrived at Columbus Circle shortly after eleven A.M. in a chauffeured Buick sedan leased to the IACRL. Red, white, and green streamers were strung everywhere and an electric organ

piped out melodies for several thousand early arrivers. It was a
hot day. Colombo wore an open-necked white shirt and dark pants.
He waved to the crowd, chatted briefly with the police, then turned
to his own lieutenants beside the speakers' stand.

From thirty feet away, as Colombo checked over the speaking
schedule and security arrangements, Johnson bobbed and weaved
with the Bolex. Though the bodyguards had let him this close, he
did not pass the boss's muster. Among the dozen or so photographers
surrounding him, Colombo had eyes only for Johnson.

"Watch him," he ordered. Johnson continued to bob and weave.
A moment later, the girl smiled brightly and waved. "Hi, Mr.
Colombo," she piped out. He did not bother to acknowledge her.
Meanwhile, Johnson stopped this fancy footwork and dropped into
a crouch, fifteen feet away; the Bolex was still at his eye. It
was 11:30. Three shots went off, fast ones. An old-time Colombo
henchman named Rocco Moraglia screamed, "Bastards! Bastards!"
Soundlessly Colombo fell, hand to his right cheek, blood pouring
from his mouth and ears. Even as Colombo collapsed, Johnson was
piled on by a horde of bodyguards and police.

Thomas Reed, the first man to tackle Johnson, was not a bodyguard or patrolman. He was a Deputy Chief Inspector of Patrol, one
of its dozen or so highest-ranking members. He grabbed the right
hand of Johnson which still held tight to the gun. The two of them
were instantly buried under a dozen other bodies, but Reed kept
Johnson's wrist locked to the ground. From somewhere very close
behind him, he heard three muffled shots. With all the knees and
elbows digging into him, Reed wondered if he himself had been hit.

Then more cops reached the pileup and began pulling bodies
off, Reed last of all. A patrolman pulled Johnson's hands behind him
and slapped on handcuffs. It was unnecessary. The three shots in
Johnson's back had been fatal.

"It was one thing for Colombo's bodyguards to let Johnson in
close, another to let him actually point a pistol at their boss long
enough to get off three shots," says Seedman. "But Johnson had
several factors working in his favor. Colombo knew that the armed
men hovering around him at a public event would have to be carrying current New York City pistol permits. But because of their arrest
records, most of his veteran bodyguards, men like Rocco Moraglia
and Vincent Vinglio, did not qualify for such permits. Colombo did

not want to be embarrassed that day by any arrests for unauthorized firearms. Or by smartass reporters writing that Colombo was flanked at the rally by rough-looking men known to have long criminal records. He didn't even want *unarmed* old-timers around; that would hardly be in keeping with the spirit of 'Unity Day' and the mythical character of the Mafia.

"Colombo's strategy was to use his unarmed veterans like an early-warning system, stationing them along the outer perimeter of the speakers' area to check out any would-be infiltrator. Colombo surrounded himself with young men without arrest records, men our detectives did not recognize. Many of them were carrying unauthorized weapons, but since they had clean 'sheets' they could afford to chance getting nabbed. The detectives certainly knew the type— young Turks who wanted to make a name for themselves.

"These bodyguards were busy flexing their muscles for the television cameras so their friends and folks back in Brooklyn would turn on the evening news and say, 'Hey, isn't that Louie the Turtle from Bay Eighth Street standing beside Colombo? Jeez—I didn't know he was so close to the boss. . . .' But they could do only one thing or the other—glare at the camera or keep their eyes out for any suspicious person who ventured near Joe Colombo. They chose wrong."

The pretty black girl with the becoming Afro had hovered close to Johnson as he bobbed and weaved with the Bolex. She did not use the 35mm. camera hanging around her neck. None of the witnesses remembers exactly where she was when Johnson magically exchanged the Bolex for the ancient .32-caliber German Menta automatic. Nobody saw her hand him the gun, but as the shots were fired she took off like a deer. A photo taken at that moment shows her body at an angle, slender legs kicking up, as she dashes from the area of the reviewing stand. A powder horn hangs at her waist. She had taken a dozen strides when two young patrolmen blocked her path and ordered her to stop.

She looked at them with round brown eyes. "Are you kidding? Stay there and get my head blown off? No, sir!" She vanished into the crowd.

The escape of that girl was to pain Seedman increasingly as the investigation wore on. "You'd think these two guys would *love* to grab a girl like that," he says. "But like the guys around Colombo, being young, they didn't have the experience to react the right way. A veteran cop would never have let that girl scram. Now all we had was a photo of her kicking up her heels. Other photos showing her full face may exist, but for reasons we'll get to, they were never made available.

"Difficult as it was to believe that Johnson could shoot Colombo at point-blank range, it seems positively unbelievable that Johnson himself could have been shot three times before so many eyes, without any witness to the killing.

"I could see two reasons for that. First, all three shots were fired by someone in direct contact with Johnson's back. To get that close the killer must have burrowed into that pileup like a human drill. It was a professional job—no sooner had those muffled shots got off than a hot revolver popped out of the heap, landing on the pavement a few feet away. It was just as if an ejection button had been pushed.

The gun was a Smith and Wesson .38-caliber nickel-plated revolver. We traced it the next day from the factory in Connecticut to the Arvan Gun Company on Chambers Street in lower Manhattan. In 1952 Arvan shipped it to Finkelstein's Sport Shop in Tampa, Florida, but it never arrived. No record of the gun exists again until 'Unity Day,' 1971. This history is typical of all guns professional hit men use in their work. If ever there was an absolutely professional execution under pressure, this was it.

"The second reason we could find no witnesses to the Johnson murder was the same way all eyes in a football game are on the quarterback when he unloads a long bomb for the winning touchdown. While that pass is spiraling through the air, a beautiful girl could shinny up the grandstand flagpole stark naked and no one in the stadium would notice. It was the same at Columbus Circle. At the moment Johnson's executioner went in for the kill, all eyes were on the star of this show, sinking to the pavement, spurting blood."

Four hours after the shootings, as surgeons extracted two of the bullets from Colombo's head, a caller to the Associated Press, identifying himself as a spokesman for the 'Black Revolutionary Attack Team,' announced: "We have just assassinated Joe Colombo. It is only the beginning. White people will continue to pay for their crimes against black people." Though the police knew little about the group, BRAT had also claimed credit for a bomb that had gone off the previous year in the Rhodesian Consulate.

Soon after that call, Anthony Colombo called a press conference to absolve any and all blacks from the attack on his father. "It was the act of one maniac acting alone," said the young Colombo. "This is what they do now to all civil rights leaders." At a later news conference Anthony Colombo was asked if Carlo Gambino's disenchantment with the League might have been behind the shooting. "The man is the godfather of my six-year-old sister," Colombo shot back. "I don't have to say any more than that." To many reporters it seemed like Colombo was saying enough.

Neither BRAT nor the Colombo statements impressed Seedman one way or the other. A fledgling black revolutionary group stood only to gain free publicity by claiming credit for the shooting. For one ten-cent phone call, they were on the front page of the morning papers. As for Anthony Colombo, he could hardly suggest his father had been the victim of Mafia rivalry when the whole purpose of the rally and the League itself was to deny that the Mafia existed.

Seedman had plenty of unanswered questions. Did Johnson shoot Colombo under contract? If so, who let the contract? Were they whites? Or were they blacks as BRAT had claimed? Was this, as Anthony Colombo maintained, the work of a single individual, or had he worked through intermediaries? If it was a lone assassin, was he insane? He must have been. Even if he had been paid a fortune, a fat lot of good it would do if he ended up the way Johnson had—the way any sane person would have assumed he'd wind up. "Contracted or not," says Seedman, "this had to be the work of a guy whose head was in outer space."

But at this point Seedman could not discount any possibility. So, as he often did with a major crime where no quick solution was in sight, he formed a special squad to work exclusively on that case. The eight-man Colombo Squad was small but select. Since Seedman's biggest question was whether Johnson had acted on behalf of the blacks or the Mafia, he divided the squad between black-militant specialists and those who would lean toward the "mob hit" theory. "I read once that Howard Hughes hired one set of lawyers to defend his interests, another set to attack them," explains Seedman. "That way, he got better work out of everyone. I was applying that M.O. here."

Since Seedman wanted to recreate the life of the dead man in detail, one of the first men he chose was Eddie Lambert, with whom he had worked as long ago as the Fallon–Finnegan murders in 1962. Lambert was particularly well qualified for this assignment. He understood Mafia politics from his days on the Pizza Squad and had better access to Joe Gallo than anyone on the force. He was also a genius at tracking dead men.

"Some years ago, we found a man's body in the Mill Basin in Brooklyn," says Seedman. "He hadn't been in there long, but that didn't matter. If a bulletproof tank fell into that water, it would turn into sponge rubber before they could pull it out. Not much was left of this body—a skeleton and two cement blocks. Nobody would have cared if Eddie had just checked the missing persons file and then sent the remains to the paupers' cemetery. That's what happens to most of the nameless corpses that turn up in the city.

"But Eddie stared down at that pile of bone and ligaments and then borrowed the man's dental plate. He went from one dentist's office to another until, after weeks of flashing his badge and then flashing the teeth, he found a dentist who thought it could be his work. A quick thumb through the records turned up the patient's name—a small-time hoodlum in the Brooklyn rackets. Lambert visited the family. They didn't know where the guy was, but they weren't the sort to turn to the police for help.

"Lambert asked permission to look through the man's car, and in the trunk he noticed a bag of steel washers. He matched one against a dime in his pocket. They were exactly the same size. He called the phone company. Had any coin boxes in this part of Brooklyn been getting a large number of slugs? One pay phone in Bay Ridge had—but the flow had stopped over a month ago.

"Eddie checked with the phone company's business office. Had any long-distance calls been dialed from the phone booth in the drug store? Yes, several, mostly to numbers in the upstate city of Utica. Lambert got in his car and headed upstate. By the time he came back, he had unearthed a corruption-ridden municipal government, including the police, which would later become the subject of a state investigation. He also picked up the trail of the man in the Mill Basin and followed it to his killers."

In charge of the Colombo Squad Seedman put Sergeant John Weber. An expert on black militants, he had a gentle face, mild manner and none of the cold wariness of many veteran detectives.

Sometimes Weber seemed to be drifting on the periphery of a conversation; the meatier the content, the farther he appeared to drift, giving the impression of someone it would be surprisingly easy to put something over on. "In this case we would be asking for cooperation from a much broader spectrum of people than usual," Seedman explains. "We would be interviewing blacks, too much whites, crooks, students, jailbirds, Mafiosi, people with no criminal connections of any kind. Many of these people are not the type to respond to being tough-talked, and Weber could handle these people without turning them off. He could also handle the real bad guys, even though they would think they were handling him. That's what John likes them to think. That's why I picked him to lead the investigation."

The Colombo Squad had little concrete evidence to go on at first. Johnson's press card had not been issued properly; the Bolex had disappeared in the midst of the pileup; the murder gun was a .32-caliber Menta manufactured during the First World War in Germany, a totally untraceable weapon. With the girl missing, that left only the contents of Johnson's slacks—a tattered address book and seven checks imprinted with "B & H Distributing Company" and "Enterprise Modern Service Company," both at 110 West 23rd Street, Manhattan. The prize item was the address book. Sixty-six names were scribbled in it, most of them of women living in New Brunswick, New York, and Boston, though a few were as far away as Los Angeles and Medicine Hat, Alberta. It would take months to systematically track down every name in the book. But even if it did not lead directly to the source of the shooting, it was the best route to finding out what kind of person Johnson had been. "I was particularly interested to see if any drug dealers, black militants, or Mafia figures turned up," Seedman says. "Maybe we'd even unearth a real prize, like the girl who fled from Johnson's side."

By Wednesday, June 30, Lambert and his partner John Ciarski were in New Jersey, checking out the numerous New Brunswick entries in the address book, as well as Johnson's family background. Pairs of detectives were dispatched to Boston and Philadelphia, and in New York other teams worked with the B & H Distributing Company checks and interviewed witnesses at the rally and Johnson's women in Manhattan. The correspondence desk began to check with police departments in places like St. Louis, San Francisco, and

Medicine Hat, where Johnson appeared to have stopped briefly. Backing his own hunch that Johnson's head must have been in outer space, Seedman wanted an especially thorough check of public and private mental hospital files.

At the same time other detectives were working on an even more urgent task: locating all film taken of the scene. Though the shooting had occurred about thirty minutes before the rally was scheduled to start, all the local newspaper and television crews had been on hand, as well as many free-lance and foreign news service crews. Starved for details of what actually happened, detectives were desperately anxious to study every frame of film they could get. But time was critical. The local television stations had only to push a button in their editing rooms to erase their footage forever.

The search for film and photos began to persuade Seedman that neither BRAT nor Anthony Colombo was telling the truth. Detectives would visit the studios of newspapers, television stations, and free-lance photographers only to discover that often members of the IACRL had been there before them. Detectives also learned that soon after the shooting Colombo bodyguards had roamed through the crowds trying to confiscate film of the event. They did not approach obvious professionals, of course; only private individuals who looked as though they might yield to persuasion.

The Colombo men had been particularly interested in a photographer hired by the League itself to make still photos of "Unity Day." As the shots were fired this photographer, here named Cirillo, was up close to the platform. But his teen-age son, who was working with him, had set up on a car roof forty feet to the south. That put him directly in line with the black girl's escape route. Colombo's men were as aware of her importance as the police. They quickly escorted Cirillo and his son to their studio and waited outside the darkroom door while the film was developed.

In the morning Cirillo was brought to the men's room on the third floor of Roosevelt Hospital, down the hall from the room where Colombo lay in the eighteenth hour of a coma that might never end. A moment later Anthony Colombo walked in with Moraglia and Vinglio while two watchdogs stationed themselves at the door. Standing near a toilet stall, ready to duck in if somebody came, Colombo examined the contact sheets. "You got any more sets of negatives or prints?" he asked.

"No," answered Cirillo. "That's it for me and my son."

"We appreciate you helping us out with this," said Colombo, putting the photos in his briefcase. "From now on you'll get exclusive coverage of all affairs at the catering places where we have a say. That's quite a few."

Colombo, Moraglia, and Vinglio walked out of the men's room, leaving a shaky Cirillo free to step out into the morning air.

"It took us a few days to find this guy," says Seedman. "He told us he'd missed our radio and TV appeals to look at any films of the event. He admitted that his son had indeed been on the car roof snapping away. But just as the shots went off, sad to say, the boy ran out of film. Though he remembered seeing a black girl out of the corner of his eye, he had no pictures of her flight. Still, these patrolmen who let the girl escape did see Cirillo's boy snapping away as the girl crossed his path. This kid may not have been the world's most experienced photographer, but he certainly knew whether or not he had film in the camera. I feel he had head-on photos of that girl that still exist, maybe in duplicate. But until somebody gives them up, we'll have to wait.

"The Colombo people insisted that Johnson had acted alone. If they really believed that, why did they go to such lengths to find out exactly who was in those photos? I believe they were looking for enemies from outside the family or maybe even for a traitor in their own midst.

"On the other hand—and this troubled me from the moment of Kinsella's call—if rival powers had decided that Colombo must go, Columbus Circle was a wildly improbable place to put him away. And why pick a black button man? The answer to both those questions seemed to point to only one man—Joe Gallo.

"As a teen-ager, Joe was once given mental tests by court order. The report came back that he was nuts. But I never thought that was why they called him 'Crazy Joe.' He wasn't crazy, he was unpredictable—just like the shooting of Joe Colombo in Columbus Circle.

"As for using a black hit man, that, too, sounded like Gallo. During his nine years in prison, he had enthusiastically taken up the black cause. He ate his meals with the blacks. When white prisoners objected to the way black barbers were cutting their hair, Gallo insisted on having his hair cut only by blacks. In 1967 he sued the Government on grounds that his fellow whites were depriving him of his civil rights because of his public support of black prisoners."

Seedman was well aware that Gallo had not cultivated the blacks at Attica and Greenhaven prisons to further interracial tolerance and brotherhood. He was far more interested in adding muscle to his faltering underworld operations. In the years since the Profaci war death and defections had thinned the President Street ranks. Joe's brother Larry had died of cancer in 1967 and Albert Gallo, Jr., did not have the leadership qualities necessary to take over the family. Meanwhile Colombo was extending his power in all directions, even absorbing the powerful Carmine Persico faction. Now that he was out of prison, Gallo's only hope of regaining a top position in the mob was to augment his tight little President Street group with a raw but carefully controlled dose of black power.

To this end, Gallo kept an eye out for black prisoners whom he might fit into his organization. If they were getting out of jail before him, Gallo would give a "block party" in the man's honor and tell him to head straight for President Street. There he could pick up a cash loan or whatever else he needed to get started again. One black ex-convict told Seedman that he had been given $1000 and offered a job as a truck driver which he turned down only because he didn't have a driver's license. "They'd be delighted to give the guy a job as a truck driver," says Seedman. "Later on, he could pay back the favor by hijacking the truck.

"While Anthony Colombo was beating us over the head for suggesting a gangland link to his father's shooting, unsolicited hints were coming right from within his own ranks that our suspicions about the Gallos weren't so farfetched. One day in Brooklyn the FBI stopped a car in which Rocco Moraglia was riding with several other men. While the men were being searched for illegal firearms, one blurted out, "I hope you guys are doing this to the Gallos too. They're the ones who shot Colombo."

Another pointer in the Gallo direction soon came from a far more bizarre and unexpected quarter: a filmmaker named McMullan, who wanted permission to make a documentary film of the Gallos in their President Street headquarters. Knowing better than to arrive unknown and unannounced, he approached a private investigator named Hall, who had the Gallos' ear. Hall came back with word that he probably could get McMullan into the Gallo headquarters—but not until after "Unity Day," the following week.

"Oh, I'm going to be at the rally to film there too," remarked McMullan.

Hall stared at him. "Don't go," he said. "There's going to be trouble at the rally."

"What kind of trouble?"

"Just don't go," answered Hall icily.

At home that evening McMullan called Ti-Grace Atkinson. A tall, pale, blond woman in her mid-thirties, Atkinson had been raised in Louisiana—her name means "Little Grace" in Cajun. In recent years she had become a leader of the extremist faction of the Women's Liberation Movement. She was so extreme, in fact, that she once announced that she had stopped talking to men altogether, since even small talk would deflect her from work toward a nation of free women.

Early in 1971 Atkinson had approached Joe Colombo about the possibility of a different kind of marriage: that of the Women's Lib Movement and the IACRL. There was a precedent of sorts: Colombo had already joined hands with Rabbi Meir Kahane of the Jewish Defense League, because both men saw themselves as hard-line leaders of kicked-around minorities. In fact, Colombo and Kahane had a golfing date the weekend after the "Unity Day" rally.

For Atkinson to unite with a militant "civil rights" group like the JDL was one thing. JDL women had equality; some had even been indicted as bomb makers. But on the face of it any liaison between the Women's Lib Movement and the IACRL was a mind-bending mismatch. Mafia men had always put up a fist against any change in the old-country tradition of rigid sex roles. A wife had a home, with emphasis on the kitchen. She had a bed to make children on. She had respect. But she was not to delve into her husband's business or be independent in any way. She was not even required to provide sexual recreation for her husband, much less herself—that was the function of the mistress, who could be dealt with in sexually imaginative ways to which a wife of "respect" should not be exposed. If a wife openly didn't like any part of her life, she could expect anything from a laugh to a beating. As for Mafia daughters, it was considered an insult to the family if a girl expressed an interest in leaving the house before she was claimed as a wife herself.

Ti-Grace Atkinson was hardly repelled by the way Mafia men treated "their" women, simply because she saw all women as being oppressed. At least Mafia men oppressed women openly. No, what appealed to Ti-Grace, as a fellow extremist, was the very thing Colombo insisted did not exist. She liked the way the Mafia handled its problems. If women were ever going to make any headway against an entrenched enemy, they just might have to borrow the rubout tactics that the Mafia had refined to both technology and art.

"I never knew Joe Colombo to be at a loss for words," says Seedman. "But if anybody was going to leave him with his eyes rolling and his tongue hanging out, it was this wild broad, Ti-Grace."

A week before the rally McMullan told Atkinson what he had heard from Hall about the rally, thinking she might like to tip off Colombo. She called him back a day later to say that Colombo thanked him for the warning, but he was well aware that trouble was brewing at Columbus Circle. His people had taken steps to handle it. He also knew very well that the source of the trouble was President Street.

Even certain detectives who had grown up in Brooklyn and maintained informal liaison with Colombo over the years suggested to him that it might be unwise to climb up on that reviewing stand. He told them that his own sons had also pleaded with him not to appear at the rally.

"After all the politicians speak, I'm the one the people will want to see," he said. "How could I have respect for myself if I was afraid to show my face? How could my sons? I have to go through with it this time. But I promised them, after this rally—no more."

"Those were the warnings," says Seedman. "We'd heard them, Colombo had heard them. But they told us nothing about how Jerome Johnson had materialized at Columbus Circle. Only by reconstructing his life could we get to the source. Once again, as with the Townhouse Case, we would have to become like archeologists. The time, instead of putting a house back together, it would be like re-assembling the pieces of a Greek statue. Except that the archeologists usually are lucky enough to find all the pieces in one hole."

III

One morning in 1969, two policemen in a patrol car noticed a young black man, wearing skin-tight blue jeans, strolling along a quiet street of elegant homes in Beverly Hills. He did not look as if he belonged on this block. He gave his name as Jerome Johnson, though he had no identification papers at all. Asked what he was doing on this secluded block at four o'clock in the morning, he said he'd been visiting a girl. He showed them a book of poetry the girl had lent him. He didn't remember which street she lived on, having picked her up that evening on Sunset Strip. He smiled man to man at the cops as if they could understand. They took him down to Sunset and told him they'd better not see him back in the hills again.

"I guess that sums up Johnson's life about as well as anything else we picked up," says Seedman. "Popping up on a fancy street in Beverly Hills, where he could always make a contact but never really arrive himself, walking in the middle of the night with no money and a book of poetry."

As the portrait of Johnson began to fill in, Seedman's initial feeling that his head was in "outer space" was borne out. Johnson had gone to public schools in New Brunswick, where his mother still lived. In 1967, after graduating from New Brunswick High, he headed for California and had lived by his wits ever since. At nineteen he had no special plans. Along Sunset Strip he moved smoothly into a druggy, drifty society, living mainly on the flotsam of the wealthy folk in the hills overhead. With his muscular frame and a glib tongue, Johnson found it easy to strike up conversations with the single girls, most of them white, whom he targeted on the street and at the parties he managed to sniff out. Though Johnson never used anything harder than pot himself, he did try selling drugs. He did not do well at it. He also tried check-forgery and burglary, but got caught at both. Seduction was what he excelled at. He drifted from apartment to apartment, living off women. In the two years he was in California, Johnson was never known to hold a job. He was arrested six times for burglary, rape, forgery, and possession of narcotics.

What kept him in California was the film business. It fascinated him, and he desperately wanted to make it as an actor, director, producer—anything to do with movies. But despite all his talent with women, he could not crack the film world; his only connection was Van Kirksey, a black actor and director who often let Johnson stay in his Hollywood apartment.

Johnson returned to New Brunswick early in 1969, bringing back a bag of tricks and con routines polished to slippery perfection. Rather than live with his mother, he hung around the local campus of Rutgers University, striking up conversations at the student union, on sidewalks, and in parking lots with girls who might take him home. His favorite openers were astrology questions. He lived with white and black girls, though again the majority were white. Lambert and his partner Ciarski interviewed more than twenty girls who had taken Johnson in for periods ranging from a day to two months. Seedman waited to hear of any case in which Johnson had been violent with a girl, but the Rutgers women said that was not his style. "He was the best lover I've had, on a technical basis," said a two-hundred-pound blonde, looking down modestly. "He was hung like an elephant."

Johnson was pathetically anxious to play the big-time filmmaker. He had business cards made up for "Johnson Productions, Inc." Sometimes he hired a chauffeured Cadillac limousine and drove slowly around Rutgers, always ready to roll down the window and talk to a girl. He often told a prospect that after a short figure-modeling test she might get a part in the next production of Johnson Productions, Inc. If he saw that the sham would not work, he simply suggested that he would make a very good pimp.

By the spring of 1970 Johnson had become so much of a fixture around the Rutgers campus that he was finding it hard to spin out his line to even the most gullible coeds. He drifted on to Manhattan, trying to cultivate people in the film business, picking up girls in Greenwich Village and Chelsea. He asked many of the girls to work for him as prostitutes. But whatever it took to make women want to do all the work and hand over all the money, Johnson didn't have it. In fact, he hardly ever had a dime.

Johnson soon wandered on to the Harvard campus in Cambridge, where, as usual, the coed pickings were easy. He swung down occasionally to Philadelphia, where his friend Van Kirksey was at work in local prisons, creating drama programs. As 1971 began, Johnson was skittering along month by month, usually broke, sizing up girls on streetcorners, ever watchful for anyone who might get him into the film business.

At his death Johnson was carrying little more than the Beverly Hills Police had found that morning in 1969—a tattered address book and the seven checks imprinted "B & H Distributing Company" and "Enterprise Modern Service Company," both on West 23rd Street. But detectives who turned up there found only a burned-out hulk, which had been the Club Orgy until a fire in April. The bank told them that B & H was the same as Bark Book Company, and the

Metropolitan Review Division of Enterprise Modern Service Company. The B & H account had been closed on June 10, eighteen days before "Unity Day."

Roger Simms and Ted Franks had been authorized to sign checks for B & H and Enterprise Modern Service. Simms had five arrests for "obscenity" and Franks nine. The detectives found Simms at Bleecker Street, the new home of Club Orgy and Adult World. He had never known Jerome Johnson and had no idea how he had gotten the checks, but thought that his ex-partner, Franks, might. Questioned at Actor's Playhouse on Seventh Avenue South, Franks scratched his head. He didn't know Johnson either, but he remembered that several checks had disappeared a few months before the fire.

"I had a model working for me then who also helped out in the office when the massage business got slow," Franks said. "She was a junkie on methadone. She's related to some big shot. Maybe she took those checks. She was living at the time with a black guy somewhere in the Village. I have no idea where she went after I fired her."

After a three-week search, detectives found the girl in a filthy downtown tenement. She was indeed the niece of a local judge. At the 5th Precinct station house, she insisted she had not taken any checks, that she might have once met Jerome Johnson but had no way of knowing for sure. As the interview dragged on, she began to sweat and grow pale. Her eyes glistened. She begged the detectives to let her go. Seeing her misery, they felt almost relieved to know that in the East Village this gaunt girl wearing a long-sleeved blouse on a hot summer night would quickly find a fix.

"We learned plenty when the missing Bolex turned up," says Seedman. "It started off as a puzzle to us. We have motion-picture frames showing Johnson aiming that camera at Colombo thirty seconds before the shots. On the other hand, we have frames of this black broad taking off from the scene with the thirty-five-millimeter still camera over one shoulder, a powder horn at her hip, but no Bolex. Where was it?"

On Thursday afternoon, three days after the shooting, a detective working in Manhattan South received a call from an acquaintance who had been standing fifteen feet from Johnson when the shots went off. His feet rooted to the spot, he had watched the instant pileup on Johnson. While everybody else was scrambling, he noticed the Bolex lying several feet away. "I picked it up," he told the detective, "thinking one of these photogs had dropped it in the scuffle. When they broke it up, I figured the right guy would come over and claim it. I sure wasn't gonna announce it. Then fifteen guys would have piled on top of *my* ass."

Five minutes later they took Colombo and Johnson away, but nobody came to claim the Bolex. The man stood through the whole listless, strangely unhysterical rally with the camera in his hand. It went unclaimed. At three o'clock, over three hours after he'd picked it up, the man locked the Bolex in his trunk and drove home.

"This guy sits in front of the television drinking beer, watching for himself on the evening news," says Seedman. "He doesn't see himself, but he does hear a report that Johnson had come to the rally with a camera, probably a Bolex. 'Holy smokes!' the guy says. He calls over his brother-in-law, who is a camera bug. Down in the basement they unload the camera, but there's no film inside. Johnson had been grinding away with an empty magazine.

"The guy ponders what to do. He doesn't want to get involved, doesn't want to go to the police cold. But he does know a detective. For two nights he mulls it over. On Thursday morning he decides that if he goes to the detective, maybe one day he'll rate a favor in return."

By five o'clock Thursday afternoon the Bolex 8-16 reflex camera was on Seedman's desk. Burned into its brown leather case was the name of the Banner Camera Shop, Cambridge, Massachusetts. The pair of detectives who left for Boston the next morning on the seven-o'clock shuttle were told by the shop's manager that Johnson had walked in on Wednesday, June 23, and asked if he could rent a Bolex 8-16 over the next weekend. When he came back on Saturday morning to pick up the camera, Johnson left a check for $23.80, using a draft card for identification. With the Bolex over his shoulder, he walked out into Harvard Square.

"Here we have a young black male who walks into a camera shop out of the blue, asking not to rent just a camera, but a Bolex," says Seedman. "They don't know him, they've never heard of him, he has no press credentials to suggest he is a legitimate photographer whose equipment has been stolen. Yet they take one of the B and H Distributing Company checks without Johnson's name on it, without as much as a driver's license for identification, without even a cash deposit—that's what they say, no deposit—and Johnson walks out with a $1200 camera. This story had to be a bunch of crap."

Under close questioning, however, the manager of the camera shop stuck to his story. The only additional information he would give was that the check for $23.80 had bounced. Any further insight into what really happened would have to come from somewhere else. That spot, Seedman felt, might be back in Manhattan at the Riverside Drive apartment of a filmmaker named James Hauser. According to one of Johnson's girls, he had worked briefly as an extra in a film Hauser made six months earlier in Greenwich Village. Hauser now admitted that Johnson had visited him and his wife several times in their apartment after the filming. Once or twice, Johnson brought along marijuana, though more as a favor than a straight sale. He would do whatever he could to ingratiate himself with a working filmmaker.

One Sunday evening in May, Hauser had come home after a weekend out of town to find his apartment burglarized. The most valuable item taken was a Bolex movie camera exactly like the one Johnson used on "Unity Day." But the obvious conclusion would be incorrect. It was not the same Bolex. The camera that Hauser had reported stolen to the police was stamped with a different serial number, and experts who examined Johnson's camera were certain that its serial number had not been altered.

Seedman and Lambert puzzled over the riddle of the identical Bolexes, convinced that the camera in Cambridge was somehow connected to the one on Riverside Drive. That connection may well have been explained by a phone call Hauser remembered getting from Johnson a week before the shooting. "I've got a photographic job to do next Monday," he said. "I need a guy to help me out. Can you do it?"

"Whose job?" asked Hauser.

Johnson hedged a moment before claiming he had been hired by the IACRL to record their "Unity Day" rally at Columbus Circle. Hauser was puzzled. Johnson was no professional photographer. How had he suddenly managed to pick up a job on which he could afford to hire an experienced professional as an assistant? Hauser thanked Johnson for thinking of him, but said he had other work that day.

"Looking back over the report of that burglary," says Seedman, "I was struck by the fact that in spite of all the excellent locks Hauser had installed, no force had been used to enter the apartment. Either the burglar was a genius at lock-picking or he had keys. Although Hauser insisted he had never given Jerome Johnson a key to his apartment, I felt he might have lent Johnson one long enough for him to duplicate it. That's easy to do and forget.

"In that week before 'Unity Day,' Johnson called not only Hauser but several other photographers to ask if they would assist him. They were all professionals with access to press credentials, and all but Hauser were women. It would be ideal, from Johnson's point of view, to use both a pro *and* a woman as his best guarantee of getting past the bodyguards. He also must have known that even a good camera at his shoulder was not going to make him look professional. The bodyguards would assume that Johnson was the photographer's assistant rather than the other way around. As long as they gave him shooting room, they could think what they pleased.

"Once the women had turned him down, Hauser was the next obvious choice. But if Johnson *had* stolen Hauser's Bolex, he could hardly dare appear at the rally with it. Hauser would surely grab it in a second to see if it was his own. But suppose before Hauser can blink, Johnson slaps him on the back and says, 'Hey, I love that Bolex of yours so much I got one just like it.' He hands the camera to Hauser, who opens it immediately and sees that the serial number is not his. At least he is satisfied then that Johnson did not break into his apartment, which he certainly must have suspected but could not prove.

"How does Johnson arrange this sleight-of-hand? His best bet is to make a trade, but any legitimate shop in New York is sure to check the police stolen camera list. He could get a better deal in Boston, where it is unlikely that the Bolex will be on any list. So he walks into a camera store in Harvard Square and says, 'Listen, man, I need to do some filming this weekend but this damn Bolex isn't working right. Why don't I rent one from you and leave this one as a deposit?' The fellow behind the counter may decide to deal with Johnson, even though he knows perfectly well the camera is hot. But he'll never agree to an even swap. He'll demand a cash deposit as well, though it doesn't have to be nearly as much as the value of the camera. The black guy's Bolex will take care of that. Now the shopkeeper figures he can't lose, even if the check bounces and the shop's own camera never comes back. So much for how Johnson got the Bolex.

"The first thing I checked out, incidentally, was whether Johnson's old German Menta could fit into the camera's magazine. The ballistics people and I sat at my desk for twenty minutes, all of us trying to wiggle that gun into the magazine. It wouldn't go in quite far enough for the camera to close all the way. Johnson could have handled the camera with the gun inside, but I doubt he'd have risked somebody noticing the crack in the case. The girl probably carried the gun for him jammed in the powder horn, or maybe even in her underwear."

This girl now fascinated the Colombo Squad more than ever. Going along with Johnson without having any inkling of his real plan was one thing. To be his gun moll was another. Yet in the weeks after the rally she remained a phantom. Even a precise description was maddeningly elusive. "With all the people ogling this girl, you'd think she'd be easy to nail down. But one young cop says, 'She was tall, about five foot seven, and she had on a miniskirt and a sweater, very sharp.' His partner says, 'She ran right by me. She was wearing those jeans with lined cuffs turned up. A beautiful girl, kind of petite, I'd say about five foot two.' This from two patrolmen standing not more than ten feet apart. We settled on a composite description of a moderately dark-skinned fine-featured girl with a moderate Afro, wearing blue jeans and a yellow pullover sweater."

Though they had yet to see her, after a few weeks Lambert and Weber soon began to feel they had at least found the girl's name. Scribbled in the address book, it was Marge Reilly. She was a New Brunswick teacher who had left town shortly after the end of the school term—and just after the shootings. At New Jersey state police headquarters the intelligence section reported that Marge Reilly was a black militant. Though they considered her more the brainy type who pulled strings in the background, she had once been spotted in a remote area of the Jersey countryside, driving away from a range where militants practiced small-arms fire. Everyone described her as a fine-featured girl with a moderate Afro.

Nobody Lambert questioned in New Brunswick could remember seeing Marge Reilly with Johnson. But several people thought they remembered a girl of Reilly's description at a party which Johnson had thrown at the home of one of his girlfriends. One guest remembered spotting in the kitchen a carton filled with single-portion boxes of Rice Krispies. But as she reached down to take a box, she saw a glint of metal underneath. Pushing aside the cereal, she was shocked to find a layer of pistols stacked on the bottom of the carton. The detectives had no reason to suspect the owner of the house, who had let Johnson borrow the place while she was away, but they did think the pistols might be connected somehow to Marge Reilly.

Working in Manhattan, John Weber found a New York City Housing Authority patrolman who still accepted Marge Reilly's mail in the building where she had lived before moving to New Brunswick. Casually he mentioned having often seen the girl at a bar on 23rd Street near the Chelsea Hotel, an area where Johnson had also been known to hang out. As the patrolman spoke Weber's eyes drifted upward and he seemed to be tuning out. Actually, he was electrified. Until now, Marge Reilly was just another in the string of Johnson's New Brunswick girls. Now this information moved her into the section of Manhattan where Johnson himself had been living just before the shootings. The 23rd Street bar, in fact, was just a block from the burned-out Club Orgy, from which had come the B & H Distributing checks found in Johnson's pocket.

Weber had never assumed that the Black Revolutionary Attack Team had to be bluffing when it claimed to have shot Colombo. Even if the BRAT boast was fake, he felt that some other black group was probably responsible for the crime. It was unlike the mob to come out shooting on "Unity Day," whereas the blacks might. Now he was hot on the trail of a good candidate for the wanted woman. She fit the physical description, she was deep into militant activities, she had apparently moved close to Johnson in the weeks before Unity Day.

In the deep of summer, the trail of Marge Reilly was picked up in a small town in Georgia where she was teaching in a Head Start program. After two months of being so careful, Weber was more determined than ever not to tip her off. He decided to personally escort the two patrolmen who had seen her best to Georgia. Weber did have some doubts about their eye for detail, since both patrolmen had differed on key points of her description. But now Weber was hoping it would all come rushing back to them as they saw her, and they would firmly point a finger at Marge Reilly.

As Weber and the patrolmen walked out of the Atlanta terminal at 10:20 A.M., they were happy to see a black police sedan and driver awaiting them at the curb. Since it was so difficult to get reimbursed for expenses like rental cars, they knew Seedman had called ahead to his Atlanta counterpart for help. As Weber approached the car, he was surprised to see, behind them in the terminal, the tanned, lanky, unmistakable figure of Mayor John Lindsay. Apparently he had been told that three New York City cops were on the flight, and now he was striding toward them, surrounded by an army of aides. Weber knew John Lindsay was trekking around the country in search of the Democratic nomination for President. He could see the Mayor's campaign smile now.

The two young patrolmen were also watching the tall man loping toward them. "Hey, does that guy look familiar to you?" one of them said, nudging the other.

His partner scratched his head. "Yeah. . . . but I can't quite place him. . . ."

Weber looked over at the patrolmen to let them know he shared their joke. Then he realized they were dead serious. Finally, just as the Mayor reached out to shake hands, the patrolmen lit up in recognition.

"Hello, Mr. Mayor."

Weber cursed to himself. These two were supposedly his best shot at identifying the only girl who might shed light on the otherwise unfathomable actions of Jerome Johnson. He could only feel disgust.

Lindsay's party headed for the black sedan, assuming it was for them.

"I'm sorry, sir," the driver drawled. "But I'm not here to pick y'all up. It's these other gentlemen they sent me to get."

While the Mayor's party hopefully waited for someone else to come, the three cops were driven off toward a tiny town thirty miles from the city. Weber still had no plans to let Marge Reilly learn she was under suspicion. He had worked out a plan in cooperation with the Atlanta police to permit the two patrolmen to get a good look at her. A local cop would drive them out to the small Head Start building, knock on the door and ask whose car was parked out front with New Jersey plates. That would bring out Reilly. He would explain to her in detail when she must transfer registration, how to do it, etc.

Meanwhile, the patrolmen would get their chance. If they could positively identify the girl, she could be extradited back to New York as a material witness. And Seedman might be closer to knowing why Johnson shot Colombo.

On the Head Start porch, Marge Reilly listened, full face to the two patrolmen. Weber leaned on the patrol car's fender, looking bored.

He needn't have bothered with his elaborate plan. If this was the girl who had brushed by the patrolmen on June 28, they were not able to say so now. The patrol car drove them back to the airport and they went home.

"Everything was in favor of them making the identification," says Seedman. "It would have been good for the case, good for John Weber, good for their own careers when they were looking for promotion.

"But they didn't. Those patrolmen may have been blind, but they were certainly honest men."

IV

As in any big case, this one brought in a flood of false leads.

One week after "Unity Day," Seedman sent two detectives to the Union County Jail in New Jersey to hear Gary Paul Klinger, a twenty-four-year-old white man accused of bank robbery, tell this story:

From the fall of 1970 until his arrest the following spring he had worked as a collector in the "shylocking" operations of two Brooklyn mobsters named Vincent Lombardozzi and James Plumeri. More than once Klinger had heard the two men rail at Joe Colombo's duplicity. In October, they told Klinger, $400,000 in bogus twenties had gone astray while being moved to the West Coast under Colombo's protection. Lombardozzi and Plumeri muttered that they ought to hit someone in the Colombo family, maybe one of the sons, to show they knew the loss was no accident.

In December, Klinger was again present one night when the two men were in a stew. A shipment of silk from Italy, with a cache of heroin rolled inside, had disappeared from the docks at Elizabethport. It too had been under the protection of Joe Colombo. When another collector named John Augustine volunteered to hit one of the Colombos for them, Lombardozzi said he would like nothing better, but for the time being it was too risky.

On a Tuesday evening in May 1971 Klinger was sitting with Lombardozzi and Plumeri at the big Busch Terminal waterfront complex when a drug dealer he knew only as Jerry came over. Jerry told them he had tried to convince a pretty blond junkie named Doris Lane to spend the night with him in return for an ounce of cocaine. Right now only black guys were turning her on, she said, and the one in her life at the moment wouldn't dig it. His name was Jerry Johnson.

"He's crazy, but I love him," Doris Lane had said. "In a couple of weeks he's going to shoot Joe Colombo for the Black Liberation Army."

As Johnson explained it to her, Colombo had been allowing the BLA to buy guns from his organization, provided that they were to be used only against other blacks, not members of the white mob. The BLA kept secret target ranges in Secaucus and Kearny, New Jersey, but their sources of illicit arms had been drying up, so they had been happy enough with the arrangement—until one night when they arrived at a garage in Queens to pick up their share of a hijacked shipment of Smith & Wesson revolvers. They found members of the rival Black Panther Party also waiting.

Colombo's men had explained that their leader had offered the Panthers weapons under the same terms. This infuriated the BLA group, many of whom had split from the Panthers after bitter disputes. But the guns were allotted as Colombo ordered—50 percent for himself, 25 percent each for the two black groups. It was then that the BLA had decided to demonstrate its muscle and prevent further erosion of its position by hitting Colombo. But they had preferred to use a man outside their own ranks, a man a little crazier than any of them. Jerry Johnson, a high-school friend of one of the members, was perfect.

"Klinger's story offered an answer to one of the big questions about the Colombo shooting—whether the job had been ordered by black militants or by the mob itself," says Seedman. But I might have gotten more excited if Gary Klinger had not already lied to me once before.

"It occurred back in the summer of 1967, when I was Detective Commander for Brooklyn South. Gary was then seventeen. His parents were divorced and he was living with his father, who was a pharmacist, in an apartment in Sheepshead Bay. About four-thirty on the morning of August seventeenth, Gary claimed, he had been awakened by a gun blast. He dashed from his bedroom into the living room, where his father often fell asleep watching television. His father was lying on the couch with his head blown off. The front door was wide open.

"It isn't every day that a kid kills his father, especially a Jewish kid, but that's what I suspected as I listened to Klinger's story. With detectives from the 61st Squad, I poked around in Gary's room. Pushing away a pile of dirty underwear in his closet, I happened to see a hole in the floor with little splinters of wood still around it. This kid, I told myself, must have come in here to try out the gun before using it on his dad! I told the Emergency Service people that if they looked hard enough, they'd find the gun. Klinger couldn't have had much time to dump it before calling the police. I was just hoping he hadn't run the short distance to the Sheepshead Bay promenade and tossed it over the railing. In that muck we might never find it.

"An hour later the service people turned up the rifle in a storm sewer two blocks from the apartment. When I confronted him with it, Klinger didn't bother to act surprised. He seemed pleased. His father had angered him by refusing to let him raid the pharmacy cash register for money to use on dates. Klinger claimed to be a pre-med student, to have an IQ of God knows how much, but he was actually nothing but a kid with a smirk who had been born bad.

"Murders within a family are common. They are usually set off by jealous rages and drunkenness, but by the time the police arrive, the murderer is usually contrite. Klinger's total smugness shocked me. Even though he was only seventeen, I felt he was a kid who somehow just turned out bad and never would be good. It might be the best thing if he spent the rest of his life removed from society.

"So when Gary Klinger turned up in jail in New Jersey, I was surprised. Apparently, he had convinced the Corrections authorities in New York that he should not be penalized for one mistake for the rest of his life, and he spent only four years in the can. Now he had used his freedom to commit various crimes, most recently a string of bank robberies. Not that this history ruled out the chance he had good information on the Colombo case, of course. But my feeling, which eventually proved out, was that Klinger didn't want us to believe his story. He had gotten the benefit of the doubt once in New York and knew he'd never get it again in New Jersey. So he tried to concoct a whopper that would convince us he should be certified as a nut who deserved to be in a mental hospital. That would be an easier place to make an escape than prison. It didn't work. Considering what an ingenious story he told, I must admit that maybe his IQ *was* pretty high after all.

"A zillion nuts, creeps, and psychos came out of the woodwork in the Colombo case. Even though most were far more pathetic than Gary Klinger, I didn't feel any more charitable toward them. They cost us too many hours of wasted work. Yet we couldn't afford to dismiss any of these stories until we checked them out.

"We got one call from a Long Island woman, for example, who claimed she had observed Johnson's cousin, Richard Garvin, visiting the house next door several times a week in company with whites she believed to be Mafiosi. Despite all the publicity on the case, not many housewives on Long Island—or anywhere else—knew Johnson had a cousin named Richard Garvin. When detectives visited her, the lady showed them dozens of snapshots she had taken of the visitors next door. None were of Richard Garvin.

"Then we had a heavyweight rough-looking fellow who hung out in a garage near Columbus Circle. After swearing us to secrecy, he revealed that mob elements in Brooklyn had paid Jerome Johnson a $5000 'eye-opener' two weeks before 'Unity Day.' Thirty-five thousand more was due him upon fulfillment of the contract. Then the same people had approached this fellow and asked him to station himself on the roof of the garage and pick off Johnson with a high-powered rifle as soon as Colombo went down. They knew he was an ex-sharpshooter for the Marines, and could do the job. This heavyweight certainly knew the mob, he looked the part, but I got the feeling he was a nut and I told him so. He thought it over for a minute.

" 'Yeah, I guess maybe you're right, Chief,' he said."

"One summer my family and I stayed by a lake in the Adirondacks. The place was swarming with fishermen loaded down with expensive equipment, dashing around in motorboats from dawn till dusk. They caught next to nothing. Meanwhile some nine-year-old wandered down to a stream near his house trailer and using a handline, plastic bobber, and a piece of bacon, he caught a thirty-two pound pike, the biggest of the season. No matter how many stories we chased in the Colombo investigation, I tried to keep that kid and his fish in mind. You can never predict where the good stuff is going to come from, or who's going to bring it."

Early in the investigation, a black detective working out of a homicide squad in Harlem got a call from a man who said he had information on the Colombo case. The detective knew the caller's reputation in the street as a triggerman too smart to be caught. When it suited his purposes, he was also a police informant.

"Come over here to the squad room. We can talk in the back room."

"You're outa your fuckin' mind," the informant said. "If I was seen going in there without being dragged I'd get mashed."

"Pick a bar, then."

"Fuck that, man. They all know you."

"What do you want me to do? Meet you in Central Park in the middle of the night?"

It was the middle of the night in the silent park when the detective met the informant on the dark path that circles the reservoir. There the man told the detective how he had been approached two weeks before "Unity Day" by a middle-aged Jewish man named Harvey Turkman, whom he knew from "other business." Turkman had a "big-money" job coming up, but he would not discuss a word of it in New York. They arranged to meet the following night at a motel in Boston; the informant was slipped a hundred-dollar bill for his carfare.

Exactly twenty-four hours later the informant walked into the darkened bar at the motel and was surprised to see a black woman named Esther Spann sitting with Turkman. Esther was married to a good friend of the informant's, a man who was currently in prison at Attica. A second white man whom he did not know was introduced as "Butchie." Turkman came right to the point.

"Next Monday Joe Colombo puts on a rally at Columbus Circle like he did last year," Turkman said. "Except this year we don't want it to ever get off the ground. Take care of Colombo and we'll see to it you cut out of there as soon as it's done. You get $40,000— half before, half after."

"Why hit him at the rally?" asked the informant. "Why not a place where nobody's at?"

"Because," answered Turkman with an edge on his voice, "we feel the effect will be best if we do it the way I just told you."

The informant nodded, putting on a face as if the job appealed to him. Underneath, his gut feeling was that only a crazy man would ever dare try what they were asking.

"How'd you say I'm gonna get out of there?" he asked.

"That's my job," said Esther Spann. "I got a dozen black people lined up to start a commotion. When they do, you shoot. Everybody else is gonna think the shots came from them, not you."

"It's not as hard as it sounds," Turkman added. "You have the element of surprise going for you. Everybody is going to be watching the ruckus the other people are causing." Turkman paused. "We'll give you $10,000 tonight."

It was after midnight. "Let me sleep on it, brother," said the informant. "I want to think how I can do this without getting taken out myself."

"You got until tomorrow afternoon," said Turkman.

The informant was in turmoil. He had the distinct feeling that if he didn't agree to the job, he would soon be crab food at the bottom of Boston Bay. They had made him privy to information too sensitive, too valuable to trust him with unless he went all the way. He was locked in. That, anyhow, was what Turkman would like to think. But he'd rather take his chances with Turkman than try anything as crazy as a public assassination. He was tempted to check out of the motel that very night and flee the city. But that would seal his fate. He decided to gamble that he could slide out of the deal in the morning.

At noon the informant walked into the bar again, a pistol tucked in the small of his back, just in case. To his surprise, Turkman was now drinking with a black man, younger and more muscular than himself—Jerome Johnson, according to the informant.

"You can cool it," Turkman said. "We got someone else here." The informant measured the vibes around him. Were they smiling and relaxed because they knew he was as good as dead? Or was Turkman just genuinely happy to find a guy crazy enough to think he could get away with the job? The informant didn't wait to find out. In five minutes he was on his way back to New York.

"Could we believe this guy?" asks Seedman. "Apart from any details of the story, we had to consider that he was a paid informant, which is not the best recommendation in the world. Detectives are exposed to the rotten side of citizens every day, but I guess the guy they hold in greatest contempt is the informant. Even in the crime world the same feeling goes. The mob can hire a kid with no money to hit a big shot and he'll walk away from the job leaving $10,000 in bills hanging out of the hit's pockets. This kid would steal the hundred dollars in his mother's hope chest, but he wouldn't loot the body. That would turn a respectable business execution into a common robbery-murder, an act deserving no respect. An informant who rats to a detective because he wants to spite an enemy is understandable. But for money? It deserves contempt—from them and from us.

"All the same, we can't ignore helpful information just because of the source. This informant had come up with good facts before. Certainly, the trappings of the story were true. He had a room key and a receipt to prove he had been at the motel the week before 'Unity Day.' He easily could have been at the bar with the people he described. But they could have been discussing other business—maybe even a different hit contract. By changing a few crucial details, he gets extra leverage from the trip.

"This motel was also the right place for wrong people. Local police knew it as a favorite meeting ground for New England crime elements. If a sensitive job had to be set up, this was a good place to do it."

Seedman was willing to accept the mechanical details of the informant's meeting in Boston. But if the real reason was to set up the contract on Colombo, he knew it could be established only through the two white men and the black woman at the bar. What Seedman *really* wanted—even if it came from this unappetizing character—was a connection to the one man his instincts had focused on from the start. Behind that meeting at the bar, he wanted to find the hand of Joe Gallo.

One morning in July, a month after the meeting, a reporter walked into Seedman's cavernous office. Lined up on his desk were eight thick books bound with brown cardboard. The reporter had never noticed them before.

Seeing his curiosity, Seedman smiled amiably. "These are all this year's entries into Pillsbury's Annual Bake-Off," he said. "They asked me to be on the panel of judges. Each night I take a different recipe home and try it out for taste, texture, ease of preparation . . . you know."

A half-hour later the Chief noticed the reporter stealing another glance at the eight volumes. "I told you wrong," he said confidentially. "Actually, these books are the new editions of the Social Register. The publishers want me to check out all these people for bloodlines, social connections, skeletons in the closet. Who could do that job better than the Chief of Detectives?"

Actually, the books *were* a kind of social register—but of a very select society. Seedman had asked the State Department of Corrections and the detective squad attached to the Brooklyn DA's office to compile a list of all the prisoners Gallo was known to have been friendly with, especially blacks, during the highly social nine years he spent in the Tombs, Attica, and Greenhaven. The list, when Seedman received it, included men said to have been "enforcers" for Gallo in prison, men for whom he had given going-away "block parties," men still on the inside. Their profiles filled eight volumes.

If the Colombo contract had really been let at that motel meeting in Boston, Seedman felt sure he could find the name somewhere in those books. It was not the white man introduced as "Butchie," who, with the help of Boston police, had been tentatively identified as an Italian hood. He lived in a black section of town, odd for an Italian in the mob, and in previous months had made many toll calls to New Jersey and Brooklyn, but there was no way of pinning him to the meeting, or even of being sure that he had been there.

At first glance Harvey Turkman appeared to be a typical middle-aged merchant, balding and paunchy, owner of a small yard-goods shop on Orchard Street which did not seem to do much business. He had no police record, but a closer look revealed certain odd facts about Turkman. His wife and daughters lived in Forest Hills, but he lived out of a suitcase in Manhattan hotels, moving to a different one every few days. He drove an expensive Cadillac. On the basis of a sworn statement from the informant, a State Supreme Court judge authorized a wiretap on Turkman's business telephone.

"He seemed to be a cautious guy," says Seedman. "I didn't want to give him a chance to smell us out. Normally we would have tapped his phone from across the street or a few doors down, but just to be safe, I ordered the tap done by men in a telephone company truck from four blocks away. It was a shock, then, several days after the tap went in, to hear Turkman shout into the phone, 'Listen to whatever you want, you bastards, I got nothing to hide!'

"How had Turkman found us out? As it turned out, he hadn't. He thought we were the FBI, which was about to pluck him out of our hands by arresting him for being an intermediary between whites who imported heroin by the kilo and black wholesalers in Bedford-Stuyvesant: in other words, a heavyweight. The investigation was highly confidential, of course, and while the city's Narcotics Special Investigation Unit had worked closely with the FBI, they did not know what the Colombo Squad was doing. They didn't even know they were tapping the same phone. For once, everyone would have benefited from less secrecy."

As for the black woman known as Esther Spann, she looked no more like the architect of a dazzling crime than Harvey Turkman. Overweight and frumpy, her hair done "white" rather than Afro, she might have been a high-school dietician. She had never been arrested either, but her husband, Ralph, had a long record. Nicknamed "Blood," he was currently finishing up a term for armed robbery.

Seedman was pleased to find an entry for Ralph Spann in volume four of the "social register." He had often taken meals with Joey Gallo at Attica Prison in the middle 1960s.

For a while Seedman hoped he had made his connection to Gallo. When Ralph Spann became eligible for parole and was released from Attica late in the summer of 1971, Seedman watched him and his wife carefully, but always on a long leash. "We were sure he'd eventually tip his hand," says Seedman. "But when he finally made a move, it was the wrong one. He tried to hold up a payroll courier in the elevator of a building on Union Square but this courier turned out to be a cool piece of work. He got the drop on Spann and shot him dead. It must have made a loud noise in that elevator. We found no reason to suspect Spann had been killed for any other reason."

The only active remaining active lead was to trace Jerome Johnson to the motel. But trying to plot his movements in those last months was a job that kept several teams of detectives in at least four cities shaking their heads.

One afternoon four weeks before "Unity Day" and several days after a girl in Greenwich Village had dropped rape charges against him, Johnson strolled over to a Radcliffe coed, a plump redhead, curled up reading under a tree in Harvard Yard. He bent close to her, a wooden scimitar dangling from his hip. "I'm a male witch," he whispered. "Can I tell your fortune?"

That evening the girl took him home to the commune in a rambling old house where she and five other students lived. He lounged for several days, smoking pot and talking about making movies. When the redhead lost interest, Johnson switched to another girl in the commune. Early in June he took a bus back to New York, where he had been living on and off with a Slavic girl on Christopher Street in the Village. On June 4 a desk clerk at the Christopher Hotel called police, thinking Johnson was a man he had seen on an FBI "wanted" poster. He wasn't, but the cops had arrested him for possession of hashish instead. The charge did not stick, since the search of Johnson had been based on "false" information and thus was illegal.

Less than a week later, inexplicably, a hospital administrator named Robert McNeil was driving home along a wooded road in Medicine Hat, Alberta, when he came upon Johnson hitchhiking. In the car Johnson had told stories about his production company, about making films in Canada, about the Hollywood and New York scenes. He was so interesting that McNeil had taken him home to have dinner with his family, for whom just seeing a black man was rare. At about ten o'clock McNeil had driven his guest back to the main road. As he was about to get out of the car, Johnson had asked McNeil whether he had some "ups" or "downs" to give him.

"I'm an administrator, not a doctor," McNeil had answered. "I have no access to pills." On that slightly sour note, McNeil had driven off, leaving Johnson with his thumb out. As usual, Johnson had entered his new friend's name in his tattered address book. By the time the police contacted McNeil, he had quit hospital work and was manufacturing hockey pucks.

Johnson had reappeared at the Cambridge commune on June 14, but his welcome had worn out. Two days later he had visited his actor friend Van Kirksey in Philadelphia, borrowed some money, and gone back to Cambridge, where he had no trouble finding another girl to take him home. Using her phone on June 21, he had called the filmmaker Hauser in New York to ask him for help with the camera work at "Unity Day," the job Hauser turned down. The next day, Johnson took the bus back to New York.

"Two interesting things happened on this trip," says Seedman. "Until now Johnson's few possessions had been scattered between a girl's apartment on Christopher Street, another girl's in New Brunswick, even in a spare room at 'The Perfumed Gardens,' a Manhattan massage parlor where the girls had laughed when he volunteered to be their pimp. Now he consolidated what little he had into a trunk and left it in a bare studio he rented on Elizabeth Street which had no light, no heat, no phone. He also closed out an answering-service account he held under the prophetic name 'G and H Exterminating Service.'

"During that same week, an ex-con named Eugene Foreman had visited a used-car lot on Pacific Avenue in Brooklyn to look at a car he was thinking of buying. Standing across the street with three men Foreman later described to us as 'Mafia types,' he was surprised to spot Johnson, an old friend of his from their high-school days in New Brunswick. Johnson scrambled over to him, apparently anxious to keep Foreman from joining his own group."

"Hey, man, let me lay a little bread on you," Johnson had said with a smile. Foreman had lent Johnson twenty dollars so long ago he had almost forgotten and he was surprised to be getting it back now. He had been especially surprised to see his friend peel off the bill from a roll of twenties. Johnson was one of those people who never had any money.

"What 'chu doin' with yourself?" Foreman had asked.

Johnson had given him a knowing smile. "Just hangin'," he had answered. They had exchanged phone numbers and Johnson had walked back to the three white men, who were watching him from across the street.

Foreman's story seemed just as dubious to Seedman as many of the wilder ones he'd heard on this case. Though the man claimed to be a decorated Vietnam veteran, the best that could be said for him lately was that he had been pestering a waitress at a Child's restaurant in Manhattan with phone calls at all hours, demanding that she sleep with him.

"Yet Foreman probably did see Johnson that week," says Seedman. "The phone number he said Johnson gave him is the same that he gave to several other acquaintances—the Madison Avenue office of the Italian-American Civil Rights League. On the other hand, Foreman may have embroidered on having bumped into Johnson. I doubt any group of men of the type he describes would allow themselves to be seen with Johnson on a busy street, particularly if they knew he wasn't 'just hangin'."

Johnson was back in Cambridge on June 23 to make arrangements at Banner Camera to pick up the Bolex on Saturday morning. On Friday, June 25, he had appeared at the door of the home of a girl in Cambridge he met several weeks before. He had a present for her, a scruffy, mustard-colored large-eyed spider monkey in a cage. The girl had laughed and explained that she could not possibly care for a spider monkey. But since she was leaving for the weekend, he could use her apartment while she was gone. That evening Johnson had used her phone to call two professional photographers in Manhattan to ask about the Columbus Circle job. Both were young women and both refused. Johnson had called another girl he had picked up once in Harvard Square and asked her to dinner, but she had other plans. In the morning Johnson had picked up the Bolex and left Harvard Square in a taxi. A pair of detectives from the Colombo Squad were able to locate the driver, who remembered dropping Johnson off on a streetcorner in a Cambridge student ghetto. He could not be traced further that day.

On Sunday evening, June 27, Johnson had called a girl from the Traveler's Aid desk at the Port Authority Bus Terminal. She didn't remember him at first, but he reminded her that they had met at a party in the Village. He had been thinking of her ever since, he said, and now he was in New York with a present for her. She refused to see him. Johnson had then called a black actress who lived in the Village. She told him to come over if he liked, but she was busy rehearsing a scene with another actor. At about seven o'clock Johnson had tiptoed in with the Bolex and the spider monkey. In the bedroom he had made several more calls, one of them to Hauser, who turned down the job for the last time. He asked the actress to dinner but she had other plans.

"I got work to do anyway," Johnson had said. "Got to get myself together for an important job tomorrow."

"Doing what?" asked the actress idly.

"I'm going to shoot Colombo." Seeing the Bolex hanging over his shoulder, she had assumed he meant with the camera.

"The next moment we pick up Johnson's movements," says Seedman, "is five to eleven at Columbus Circle. Sometime in the preceding fifteen hours he picked up the girl with the Afro who had his powder horn at her belt. The other time we absolutely lose track of him is during those forty-eight hours in Boston when the informant claims to have seen him with Turkman at the motel bar. Of course, if we choose to believe the informant, then we *do* know where he was."

"By the end of winter 1972, I felt we had taken the Colombo investigation about as far as it could go. We had run down every available shred of information on 'Unity Day,' on Jerome Johnson's life, on his possible motives for shooting Colombo, on the motives of those who may have hired him. But even after nine months of work by ten of the best detectives I knew in New York and across the country, the three motives that originally crossed my mind as I watched Colombo being prepared for surgery still all seemed plausible. Johnson could have acted on orders from a black militant group, he could have acted alone, he could have been the tool of a rival Mafia leader.

"Though the Black Revolutionary Attack Team first took credit for the shooting, we found no support for that theory as the months went by. Johnson himself had never been much of a militant, preferring to mix with whites and go to bed with white girls. Marge Reilly was his friend, of course, and she was certainly militant. But she was not crazy, as she would have to have been to go with Johnson to the rally. I think those two patrolmen were right not to identify her. Not that we have any lack of crazy and bloodthirsty so-called militants. Killing Colombo would not further their cause any more than killing young patrolmen walking their beat, yet they have killed a number of cops, including black ones. Just the same, nothing but the one BRAT phone call points to these people, and I don't believe it.

"Johnson himself was certainly capable of acting on his own. Soon after the shooting, we found his trunk in the Elizabeth Street loft which the detectives were hoping contained the key to his act. But all they found were a couple of wooden scimitars, a few feathers, a box of incense, a book on astrology, an Indian carving or two, and a few pictures of him in a cowboy getup. It was a pile of stuff that belonged to a dreamer, a guy from outer space. He was the type to act according to his inner voices, like Sirhan Sirhan or Arthur Bremer, the man who shot Wallace. I just don't think he did.

"The final motive seems strongest to me. I believe this was a job masterminded by Joe Gallo. Several facts point his way, and you don't even have to believe them all. We know that Brian Hall conferred with Gallo and then told McMullan, the fellow who wanted to make a film at Gallo headquarters, to stay away from the rally because it would 'never get off the ground.' That is different from saying it would be disrupted, which we all expected anyway. A businessman who patronized a car service run by Gallo people told us he overheard someone remark that Colombo was going to get his—'*from a nigger*.' Even Colombo's man, Vince Vinglio, complained while being searched by the FBI that they ought to be patting Gallo down instead. As for the alleged motel meeting in Boston, the more we tried to knock it apart, the harder it became to discount. Considering how many names there were in the Gallo 'social register,' it had to be more than coincidental that the wife of one of them popped up in the informant's story.

"Apart from these signs pointing in his direction, Gallo had a motive. He may have been the shakedown virtuoso of all time, but his other money-making skills were nil. He had no choice but to return to the rackets in the style that suited him best—fast, unexpected, and brutal. If Joey were looking for a way to vault back into power now, what could be better than something unpredictable, something with flair? A masterstroke that would wipe out the top man and tell the crime world, the people who would understand muscle *and* its meanings, that he alone had the imagination, the audacity and the sheer guts to carry it off.

"To my mind, everything about this plot, from conception to execution, bore the signature of that little guy with steel balls, Joe Gallo. And I felt that, in time, we'd get a sign, from him or the other side, to confirm it."

THE GALLO CASE

At 5:20 A.M. on Friday, April 7, 1972, the detective on duty at the Chief of Detectives' office called his boss to say that Joe Gallo had just "bought his" at Umberto's Clam House, two blocks away in Little Italy.

"Any suspects?" asked Seedman.

"No, Chief."

"Any others hit?"

"Just his bodyguard, a heavy hitter named Pete the Greek. He got shot in the ass."

"Is Gallo where he fell?"

"The sector car took him to Beekman Hospital. They thought he might still be alive."

"Tell the detectives down there not to talk to the press. I'll make a statement when I get there."

"Ever since Gallo walked out of prison in 1971, the word on the street was that his day was coming," says Seedman. "Nobody took it more seriously than Joey himself. While he planned how to vault back to power so that the street would answer to *him*, he had to buy time. He did it with a master stroke that was unpredictable even for Joe Gallo—he simply took himself out of the action."

Deserting President Street, Gallo had moved across the East River into a plush apartment on 12th Street in Greenwich Village, around the corner from the brownstone owned by the actor Jerry Orbach and his wife, Marta. Orbach had portrayed a Gallolike figure in *The Gang that Couldn't Shoot Straight,* the movie adapted from Jimmy Breslin's novel of Brooklyn mob life. Many of the touches in the movie that audiences might have thought fictitious— like the lion the Orbach character kept in his clubhouse basement— were based on fact. Gallo had kept just such a beast in the basement of his President Street headquarters. The Orbachs welcomed Gallo into their social circle. Most of his evenings were now spent at their place or the homes of their friends.

Gallo had no problem in making the transition from President Street, via Greenhaven Prison, to this new life. Unlike many Brooklyn hoods, who were barely literate, if at all, Gallo had always read voluminously. At Greenhaven, as soon as his morning chore of sweeping down the cell block was done, he read the two newspapers he was allowed to receive front to back. He had books sent in several times a week and could fluently discuss Flaubert, Balzac, Kafka, Sartre, Céline. Gallo also had taken up painting at Greenhaven, and, perhaps in return for helping to keep racial peace, rated an extra-bright bulb in his cell to judge his palette better. The homes of several guards and administrators at Greenhaven are hung with Gallo originals.

Joey not only held his own in the highly social Orbach household, he was a unique celebrity in their show-business world. Who else could boast of a house mobster? One night Peter Yates, producer of the smash musical *1776,* was complaining about the trouble he was having in trying to locate his dog, which had been stolen from his apartment the week before along with everything else. He had offered a large reward for its return and was being pestered by dozens of callers who guaranteed to produce the dog if he would pay the reward in advance.

Gallo listened sympathetically. "The next time one of those creeps calls you up," he said finally, "I'll be glad to go meet the guy with you. We can clear it up fast that way. . . ."

The whole idea strikes Seedman as extremely funny. "Can you imagine some two-bit hood thinking he's going to make $500 off this easy mark?" he asks. "The guy meets Yates at the appointed place, maybe in a Laundromat. 'I'm Peter Yates,' his 'mark' says. 'I'm so glad you're going to help get my dog back. Oh, yes, this is my friend Joey Gallo.' Joe smiles the smile he's used to shake down a thousand guys. End of shakedown."

Gallo loved his new life with the Orbachs. It enabled him to lull his enemies into thinking he was no longer a menace. In fact, he even talked about quitting the old life and going into show business himself. "But to those of us who knew him," says Seedman, "that was just talk. For one thing, crime was in his blood. Brooklyn had never developed a more naturally gifted and ferocious gangster than Joe Gallo. In a stable full of talent, he still stood out. Another reason I doubted he'd reform was a simple matter of cash. He didn't appear to have a stash of bills waiting for him when he got out of prison—otherwise why ask Colombo for the hundred grand?—but he always wanted to play the big shot. Whenever the check came for a party of six at the Copa, Joey would grab it and peel off a pair of crisp hundred-dollar bills. But he couldn't go on picking up tabs without a steady source of income.

"But this Friday was special. It was his forty-third birthday and a celebration was a must. Setting out in a new black Cadillac driven by Peter ("Pete the Greek") Diapoulas, his grade-school chum and current bodyguard, Joey had gone to the Copacabana with a party including his bride of three weeks, Sina, her ten-year-old daughter, Lisa, his sister Carmella Fiorello, Pete the Greek, and his girlfriend, Edith Russo. Arriving at midnight, they were joined at a big table by Jerry and Marta Orbach, a crony from the old days named Bobby Darrow, comedian David Steinberg and his date, columnist Earl Wilson and his secretary. Just as Gallo had often done in the past, they drank bottle upon bottle of champagne. At four o'clock in the morning they closed the place up. They had not eaten since an early dinner. Despite his slight wiry frame, Gallo was a voracious, even joyous eater. Shabby as the President Street complex might have looked, he had always commanded the finest commercial kitchen equipment. As the busboys began stacking chairs on the tables and putting away the linen, Gallo piled his birthday companions into the Cadillac and took off for Chinatown and a dawn supper."

At 4:30 the Cadillac prowled the narrow streets of Chinatown, barely able to squeeze past the private sanitation trucks that clear the sidewalks of heaps and crates of garbage at that hour. A few small noodle houses were still open, but none suited Gallo. Then, coming up Mulberry Street, where Chinatown uneasily bumps up against the lower reaches of Little Italy, Gallo noticed a place he had never seen before. It was freshly whitewashed and brightly lighted: Umberto's Clam House.

Pete the Greek nodded coolly to a pair of burly men standing out front in the dark and drizzle. He had seen them both before, but could remember only the name of Matthew ("Mattie the Horse") Iannello, who with his brothers had belonged to the crime family of the late Vito Genovese. He remembered the other paunchy and styleless man only vaguely from West Side bars in which the Iannello brothers had an interest.

"Ask if the boiled shrimps and scungilli are worth eating in this dump," ordered Gallo.

Even before Pete rolled down his window, Iannello had recognized Gallo in the back seat. His car was plastered with stickers for "Americans of Italian Descent," a group Gallo now pushed as a rival to Colombo's IACRL. As a man with roots in the Genovese family, Gallo enemies since the Profaci war, the last thing Iannello wanted was to serve this party. Iannello also realized that Gallo apparently did not know who owned this new place. Otherwise he would be no more anxious to eat here than the management was to have him. But as long as it had gone this far, Iannello could hardly disparage the shrimps and scungilli in his brother's place.

"Everything's good," he answered.

The silent man who had been hanging out in front with Mattie the Horse waited until the Gallo party had seated itself near the side entrance at the rear of the long restaurant, then hurried south on Mulberry Street.

The two men, three women, and little girl made a fast sweep of their first double orders of shrimps, scungilli, and clams. Joey called for repeats of everything and then headed through the place, cheerfully decorated in white tile and butcher-block tables, for the men's room. Even though they were the only customers, the party-goers were feeling in an appropriately festive mood. But when Gallo did not return after five minutes, Carmella leaned toward Pete and said, "I hope nothing happened to Joey. Maybe you should check on him."

"I know my job," he answered with an edge to his voice. Just then Gallo bounded up the stairs, looking refreshed and quite dapper in his pin-striped blue suit.

Behind the clam bar Salvatore LaMonica, the cook, had been no more thrilled than his boss to see the Gallo party enter. He had hoped to clean up early and get out on the dot of six. Now he had to run from the spaghetti-cooker at one end of the bar to the deep-fryer at the other to the clams on ice in between. By six o'clock the place would be a mess.

As most people do under the sudden circumstances, LaMonica at first decided that the noises he heard coming from the vicinity of the side door were firecrackers. But as he started to turn around, a soda glass beside his hand splintered on the bar. Instead of completing his turn, LaMonica threw himself face down on the floor, thus saving his life and making sure he did not see anything he was not meant to see.

Contrary to movieland practice, Gallo and Pete the Greek had not seated themselves with their backs to the wall. This was one time in real life when it might have helped. As the balding man in the sport coat calmly walked in the side door and fired an automatic pistol, it cost them a fatal second simply to turn around. Pete pushed over the table like a barricade. Amid the clatter of plates and gunshots, the screaming women shrank behind it. Pete now finally had his own gun out, a small silver-plated .25-caliber automatic. Screaming curses, Gallo deserted his party, running the length of the bar at top speed toward the front door.

That sprint may have saved the others' lives. Without ever moving from the side doorway, the gunman blasted away at Gallo as if he were a duck in a shooting gallery. Two bullets passed harmlessly through his flying coattails, one hit him in the elbow, one in the buttocks, one in the back. That last shot, the fatal one, ripped the carotid artery, which sends blood to the right side of the brain. Now the blood, three quarts of it, poured into the cavity behind his lungs. Gallo staggered into the street a few feet from his black Cadillac and fell over on his back.

Inside the restaurant the gunman stopped firing the instant Gallo went through the front door. Smiling, he backed out the side door. Sina had thrown her coat over her daughter to block her view; she and Edith Russo now seemed to be in a trance, huddled behind the table, but Gallo's sister was screaming loudly. Pete the Greek finally managed to race to the side door and fire off six shots at a car speeding north on Mulberry Street. Then he vaulted over the clam bar and strode back toward the kitchen.

On the floor Salvatore LaMonica raised his eyes just enough to see Pete the Greek's legs coming toward him and also caught sight of "something shiny" in Pete's right hand. LaMonica decided he better not move or make a sound, even when the Greek's heavy step came down on his outstretched fingers.

Pete found Mattie the Horse cowering in a corner of the kitchen. "If you had anything to do with this, it's gonna be real bad," he said, staring at him with obvious hatred and anger.

"You think I'm crazy, to let this happen in this place?" answered Mattie. "I don't know nothing."

Pete shoved him back against the spaghetti pots and ran back through the restaurant, again stepping on the silent LaMonica's fingers as he vaulted the bar. Out in the street he found Carmella holding her brother's head in her lap and wailing loudly. There was no sign of blood, but Joey's pale-green eyes were unfocused and his breath was dying out in little gasps.

Two patrolmen in a sector car who had heard the wails but not the shots from a block away screeched to a halt outside the restaurant. As one of the patrolmen, Felice Agosta, ran toward the huddle beside the Cadillac, he saw Pete the Greek remove his arm from around Carmella, reach beneath the back of his coat, and throw the silver-plated automatic onto the street behind him.

"Get us to the hospital!" screamed Pete.

Agosta did not know who was giving him orders, but he instantly recognized the dying man as Joey Gallo. He picked up the gun and yelled for his partner to call an ambulance.

"Goddam it, we got no time for an ambulance!" screamed Pete.

Though Agosta did not like being barked at, he looked down and saw that Pete was right. With his partner's help, he and Pete carried Gallo to the back seat of the sector car and raced to Beekman Downtown Hospital, five minutes away. Doctors hooked Gallo to a cardiac-resuscitation unit, but even a mechanical plunger could not keep his heart pumping. Gallo had no blood left to pump.

Not until Gallo had been pronounced dead did Pete the Greek discover that he too had been shot—in the buttocks. "I don't want to give you a hard time," he said when attendants asked his name, "but I can't tell you anything." At 5:45, when the first of dozens of detectives arrived, he did agree to tell them who he was. A few minutes later the women of the Gallo party arrived, the little girl wearing Gallo's gray fedora pulled over her eyes. Her mother and

Edith Russo still seemed numb, but Carmella bellowed loudly: "He was a good man, a kind man. He changed his image, that's why they did this to him. . . ."

In light traffic on the Long Island Expressway at 7 A.M., his first cigar of the day five minutes old, Seedman was pleased to hear on the radio that reporters seeking details of the Gallo assassination were awaiting the arrival of the Chief of Detectives. Too much would be said in any case, he knew. Standing in the drizzling rain outside Umberto's, he satisfied himself that the place was being processed correctly. The corner of Mulberry and Hester was cordoned off. Inside, the Latent Print Unit was dusting for fingerprints, the Photo Unit was making a thorough record, Ballistics men were busy digging nearly two dozen bullets out of the bar, floor, ceiling, walls, and rear table. They had been fired within ten seconds.

"If they stay here all morning, how am I going to do my lunch business?" the manager of Umberto's complained to Seedman.

"You're not helping us get done any quicker by telling us who came in here shooting, are you?" said Seedman.

"I didn't see it."

Seedman glowered. "Then don't complain when we try to find out what happened. Or else this place won't be open for a week."

Seedman called for the Police Engineering Unit to come make charts showing the action at Umberto's which he could use later at the press conference. "A flip chart with neat clear diagrams is a modern management technique to make it look like you know what you're doing," he explains. "That's very important when you don't have a damn thing to go on.

"As usual in Mafia rubouts, we had no murder weapon, but that didn't worry me because even if we did, it wouldn't be traceable. The .38-caliber bullets extracted from Gallo's body and the woodwork at Umberto's were also worthless without a gun to match. We had no witnesses to give us a useful description of the killer, even though a tableful of people were looking right down his barrel. We had no plate number or description of the getaway car, though Pete the Greek stood looking at it long enough to fire six bullets as it drove away.

"It was all typical, except for one point which puzzled me. I wondered why the job had been done at Umberto's. Normally, executioners pick a spot where the victim habitually goes, like the shop where Charlie the Cidge drank his malted milk each morning, or a spot where a double-cross has been set up, like the Sahara Lounge, where Carmine Persico tried to garrote Larry Gallo. Almost invariably they also choose a quiet street at a quiet hour like Bond Street, where Larry Gallo got his revenge by shooting Persico from a pickup truck one Sunday morning. But Joe Gallo had started out at the Copa and then taken his party to Chinatown on the spur of the moment. How did the killers know where to find him?

"However they did it, the fact that Gallo was found and killed just about nailed down the motive behind the shooting of Colombo in my own mind: Gallo had ordered the job to clear the way for his own comeback. In terms of the kind of honor these people worry about so much, it was certainly tit for tat. Gallo had dishonored Colombo by bringing him down in front of a huge audience, including his own sons. By using a black hit man, Gallo had added to the dishonor. Now Joey had been dishonored in turn by getting his in front of his wife, sister, and even a little girl. The fine points of honor cannot be overemphasized in their society. A man like Carlo Gambino will turn his palm under yours while shaking hands to indicate he does so only as a formality. But if he thinks you're truly a hale fellow, he will shake hands by putting his own palm over yours."

"On the evening of April nineteenth, twelve days after the incident at Umberto's, I was addressing a class on municipal government at New York University when my beeper went off. My office wasn't supposed to bother me during that hour except for a real emergency, so I excused myself and went to the phone, wondering who got killed this time.

"Mike Codd, the Chief Inspector, was on the phone. 'The FBI has a guy out in Santa Ana, California, who claims he was part of the Gallo hit, but they don't know enough of the details to check his story out. You'll have to go up to the FBI office and talk to him from their phone.'"

The caller's name was Joseph Luparelli. It meant nothing to Seedman, nor did Santa Ana sound like a likely spot to provide information about the shooting of Joey Gallo on Mulberry Street. Seedman did not have high hopes for the call.

"What is it you've got to say?" he asked when the FBI put Luparelli on the phone.

"I didn't do the Gallo hit, Chief," said a genuine Brooklyn voice. "But I was in my own car outside. I was the 'crash car' driver. I was supposed to block off anybody chasing the real getaway car."

"Who shot Gallo if you didn't?"

"I want to tell you that, Chief. But you got to understand something. These other people want to kill me, that's why I had to come out here. Now, I don't want no breaks for myself, but I had to leave my family back in Bath Beach. If I tell you who did it, you got to promise to guard my wife and kids. I swear I don't want nothing for myself except to stay alive."

"We'll protect them and you if there's reason to," said Seedman. "Now, who shot Gallo?"

"It was Fat Fungy and Sonny Pinto and two brothers named Bennie and Cisco."

"They all shot Gallo?"

"Sonny Pinto done the actual hit."

Seedman was startled. According to certain Brooklyn detectives, who were so secretive about their underworld sources that even Seedman never pressed them, two of the men involved in the Umberto's job were Philip Gambino and Carmine Di Biase. Both men were associates of Joseph ("Joe the Yak") Yacovelli, the acting head of the Colombo crime family since the shooting at Columbus Circle. Their street names were Fat Fungy and Sonny Pinto. In fact, at that very moment detectives were trying to locate them for surveillance.

"Luparelli—do you have a Social Security number," asked Seedman.

"No."

That one fact told Seedman more about Luparelli's background than any series of explicit questions he could ask. To support a wife and children without a Social Security number, which is to say, without ever having held a job in his life, Luparelli had to be a crook. He might know what he was talking about.

"I'll ask the agents with you to put you on a flight back to New York in the morning," said Seedman.

"I'm not gonna go on a plane myself. They're watching me out here. That's why I turned myself in. Somebody will have to come along on the plane."

Seedman could hear the note of stark terror in Luparelli's voice. The man was in fear for his life—the same emotion that had driven

Joseph Valachi, the only other major Mafia informant of recent times, to speak out when he heard that Vito Genovese had arranged for his murder in a Federal prison in Atlanta. Seedman did not want a nervous, maybe hostile wreck of a man to come off that flight straight into an extended interrogation. If Luparelli was really that rare and valuable commodity, a good informant, it would pay to humor him.

"I'm going to send out a Lieutenant Ferguson to bring you back in the morning," said Seedman. "He's a sharpshooter. He'll keep those stewardesses away from you." Ferguson was familiar with the facts of the Gallo case, but his main value to Seedman at the moment was that he was calm and could handle people and would do a good job at soothing Luparelli.

"Tell me one other thing," said Seedman, just to satisfy himself once and for all. "Why did you shoot Gallo?"

"You know why, Chief," snorted Luparelli. "We done it because Crazy Joe put out the contract for that nigger to hit Colombo."

Seedman met the flight from Los Angeles the next evening at seven o'clock, along with Deputy Inspector John O'Connor and Assistant Chief John Kinsella. Ferguson came off the ramp looking fresh in spite of having flown cross-continent twice in a day. But the stocky, heavy-jowled, shabbily dressed man on his arm seemed frazzled and miffed. His eyes darted around the sleek boarding area, noticing all the empty seats.

"I thought you was going to do it different," said Luparelli. "I thought the plane was going to taxi away from the terminal before you took me off."

"What are you, some kind of hijacker?" asked Seedman.

"You don't understand," Luparelli muttered, his eyes sliding around. "They could get me real easy in here."

"They could get us *all*," agreed Seedman morosely. "Two Inspectors and the Chief of Detectives and you. And also poor Lieutenant Ferguson here."

Seedman knew that Luparelli wanted to be taken more seriously. But he felt that the more deference Luparelli received in payment for whatever knowledge he had, the slower he would be in parceling it out. Seedman could hardly blame him. Luparelli was a small-time thug who had probably never been taken seriously by anyone. In fact, Luparelli looked just about as Seedman had pictured him, judging from his police record—arrested once for unlawful entry in 1952 and again for attempted third-degree burglary in 1955. "This guy was a nonentity who was going to grab all the attention he could," said Seedman. "I was determined to minimize it."

On the way back to headquarters Seedman tried to relax Luparelli, assuring him that his family was being carefully guarded. As they talked, first in the car and then for several hours in John Kinsella's office, it became apparent that as dense, paranoid, and self-important as Luparelli might be, he did have first-hand knowledge of how Joey Gallo came to be assassinated at Umberto's Clam House. Here is what he told Seedman:

At four o'clock on that drizzly April mornng Luparelli felt a sudden craving for a bowl of red clam chowder at Umberto's. He never explained exactly why he was in the neighborhood at that hour, except that he often was. Maybe it was because his only real means of support was fencing stolen goods, and he often picked up good tips in the bars and social clubs of Little Italy during those early-morning hours. Luparelli also claimed to be a chauffeur for Joseph Yacovelli, who, unlike most Mafiosi, lived in an apartment on Manhattan's East Side; but he spent a lot of time in Little Italy.

Luparelli had just finished his chowder and walked outside to chat with Mattie the Horse when the big Cadillac swung around from Mulberry Street. He instantly recognized both Gallo and Pete the Greek, a hood much like himself who drifted in the underbelly of the mob, performing the chores of a flunky. Years before, Luparelli remembered, Pete had worked as a bouncer in a midtown bar owned by the Iannello family.

Luparelli and Mattie had exchanged cool nods with Pete. They knew this was not Gallo territory. Yacovelli, in fact, had once invited Gallo's most trusted bodyguard, a tanklike man known as Joe Jelly, to go deep-sea fishing on a private cruiser out of Sheepshead Bay. All that came back of Joe Jelly was his waterproof jacket, wrapped around a large fresh fish and dumped on President Street after dark. It was the real-life precedent for a similar incident in *The Godfather*.

Luparelli remained silent but watchful as the Gallo party, laughing and flushed, left the Cadillac and walked to a table at the rear of Umberto's. Then, whistling softly, he hurried three blocks down Mulberry Street to a drab Chinese restaurant, where he found Philip Gambino, Carmine Di Biase, and two brothers he knew only as Bennie and Cisco drinking beer and eating lo mein. It was a few minutes before five A.M.

"Where is Joe the Yak?" asked Luparelli, who should have known the answer himself if he really was Yacovelli's chauffeur.

"Not here," he was told.

"Well, the *ubazze* is eating over at Umberto's right now."

"*Ubazze*," explained Luparelli to Seedman, is slang for "crazy person."

The four men in the Chinese restaurant had stared expressionlessly at Luparelli, but they had suddenly become tense. According to Luparelli, Di Biase had gone to a phone booth and called Yacovelli at home. The Yak had impatiently asked what they were waiting for.

Five minutes later Di Biase parked his car just beyond the side door of Umberto's on Mulberry Street. One hundred feet behind, Luparelli pulled up with Gambino in his passenger seat. Their job was to keep an eye out for any passing patrol car and to block off anyone pursuing the getaway car. While Bennie and Cisco waited in the first car, Luparelli watched with interest as Di Biase stalked into the side door of Umberto's. He heard almost instant firing. Seconds later Joe Gallo staggered out the front door and fell over on his back. It was just like watching television. Luparelli saw Di Biase race out of the place and jump into his own car. As it screeched away from the curb Pete the Greek stuck his gun out the door and began firing. Luparelli, his own car unnoticed, was afraid that Pete would blow out the tires. But Pete aimed his first shots at the passengers, plugging several holes in the rear window. Not until the last instant did he lower his aim, smacking the right rear tire as the car swerved around the corner.

A half-block south of Police Headquarters Di Biase parked in a legal space. He and the two others jumped into Luparelli's backup car, which headed swiftly up the East River Drive to their boss's 86th Street apartment. There, Luparelli said, Yacovelli congratulated them. It had been eleven years between Joe Jelly and his boss. Yacovelli dialed the home phone number of a commercial tow-truck operator and arranged for Di Biase's car to be towed to a New Jersey junkyard and crushed into a three-foot cube. Then, says Luparelli, he gave the five men the key to a luxury apartment overlooking the Hudson River ten miles north of Manhattan in Nyack, New York. Except for being used for an occasional tryst it had been in waiting for just this moment. Here the men could keep out of sight in case they had been seen by any witness who would be foolhardy enough to identify them. If no trouble came up in the next week or so, they could return in triumph to Mulberry Street.

Luparelli felt exhilarated by the whole train of events. Their plush hideout in Nyack was a far cry from the confines of Little Italy or the dreary block in Bath Beach where he lived with his family. And when the heat was off, maybe he would finally get a break from the mob. For twenty years he had hung on to the fringes of what was now the Colombo family, doing odd jobs, chauffeuring, hoping to become a "made" man. "They got books just like unions, ya know," he told Seedman. "They don't let you in for nothing. They don't care if they *never* let you in. They got to keep it exclusive or it gets loose."

The advantage of being on the books as a bona-fide member of the family, Luparelli explained, was that he could stop hustling so hard. He could quit doing the odd jobs that nobody else would touch, like fencing stolen goods for family members with only a tiny cut for himself, or even dirty work like burying bodies, which he had recently done in a downtown garage basement, he said. Membership would give him the right to do the hijackings rather than the peddling, the rubouts instead of the shoveling. He might even be allotted a loansharking or numbers territory, franchises with a steady income and, because of the family protection, little fear of competition.

All Luparelli felt he needed to be "made" was a break, and act to show his true allegiance, the way Colombo himself had zipped to the top by tipping off Gambino about Bonanno's plan to assassinate him. Now, simply because he had felt like having a bowl of red clam chowder at Umberto's, Luparelli had won his chance. If not for him, Gallo never would have ended up writhing on his back in the middle of Hester Street. Surely the books would be opened long enough to enter the name of Joseph Luparelli.

But after five days in Nyack he sensed something was going wrong. Di Biase, Gambino, Bennie, and Cisco did not seem as friendly as they should, considering what he had done for them. He chalked it up to jealousy. But on Tuesday night, April 11, after eating a dinner they had prepared of pasta and sausage, Luparelli settled back to watch television. Suddenly he felt a jab of pain in his stomach. He ignored it, but after several more spasms, he eyed the other men watching the TV show, which happened to be an episode of *Police Surgeon*. They smiled, drank their beer, rubbed their stomachs with satisfaction. Luparelli was a man with a cast-iron stomach. Had they slipped something into his pasta?

That night he was asleep on his mattress in the living room when the pains came back. He opened his eyes and saw a figure standing over him.

"Who's that?" he rasped.

Di Biase looked down at him. "It's just me, Joe," he said soothingly. "Just wondering if you were all right. You been moaning in your sleep."

Luparelli closed his eyes and began to breathe heavily, pretending to be asleep. But he was in a fright. He was remembering back to a night just before Christmas in 1951. Di Biase had been playing cards with his friend Michael Errichiello in the clubhouse of the Mayfair Boys Civic and Social Club on Mulberry Street, just a block and a half from where Umberto's is now. They had argued and Di Biase had stalked out. At five o'clock on the morning after Christmas he had walked back in the club to find Errichiello asleep with his head on the table. Tiptoing over to his friend, Di Biase, smiling now, had shot him three times in the head. Turning around he had seen a member of the club named Rocco Tisi looking on in horror. Deciding that was the incorrect emotion, Di Biase had shot him also.

Tisi had survived to testify against Di Biase, one of the few occasions when one Mafioso has broken silence. Di Biase had hidden out for eight years, then got "disgusted" and turned himself in. In 1959 he was tried and sentenced to the electric chair, but the conviction was reversed on a technicality. On retrial he was acquitted.

Now Luparelli was wildly fearful. Di Biase had smiled down at him as he must have smiled at the dozing Errichiello. In the morning Luparelli had gone out, supposedly for cigarettes; actually he had jumped into his car and roared out of Nyack. He sped south on the Palisades Parkway to the New Jersey Turnpike, rendezvoused with his wife to exchange cars, and headed on to Newark Airport. He parked in the long-term parking lot and took the next TWA flight to Los Angeles. A distant cousin of his was living in a tract development in the desert near Santa Ana. It was the only place Luparelli had thought he might be safe.

By late afternoon on April 12, Luparelli was staring out his cousin's living-room window at all the identical ranch-style homes, thinking that the dry pink air of Santa Ana seemed worse than what he inhaled in New York. In these streets, children played and women breezed to and from the supermarkets. It seemed safe. But Luparelli was trying to think what the others were thinking. Did they know he had relations in California? They had to. He remembered coming home from his first visit to the Coast and describing to the men on Mulberry Street the mountains, snow-capped even when the temperature was eighty degrees down below, and the freeways, where you could open up and drive like a bat. They'd remember. Suppose Joe the Yak's men drove through the long-term parking lot until they found his car? Then they would know for sure. They could be on their way west right now—or maybe they had already arrived, waiting outside for him now to leave the house.

Suddenly the doorbell jangled. Luparelli slid into a closet in the guest room. It sounded like the voices of children. But was that a ploy? In panic, he escaped through a rear window. He was turning into a regular *ubazze*. But who could blame him? Not only were his hopes of becoming a "made" man dashed, and for no reason, but now New York wasn't even safe for him as a nobody.

That was when the thought of going to the law had first popped into Luparelli's head. Why not? Besides protecting him and his family, they might even start him on a new life in another place. That afternoon, looking to the surprised agents like a man in big trouble, Luparelli had stumbled into the Santa Ana office of the FBI.

"This guy was no Valachi," says Seedman. "But his tale of the Gallo shooting checked out. We put the Nyack apartment under surveillance immediately, and, sure enough, the other men were there. Now we had another problem. Under state law, a man can't be convicted of a crime solely on the testimony of another person involved in the crime. His story must be corroborated by independent evidence or the testimony from another source. If we crashed into the Nyack apartment and collared the Di Biase group, they'd tell us they were conducting a spiritual retreat. As long as they stuck to the story, we couldn't touch them.

"So who else might corroborate Luparelli's account? We started with the little Chinese woman who ran the noodle dump where

Luparelli had contacted Di Biase. If she had overheard them talking about guns, getaways, or actually killing Gallo and then watched them troop out the door at five A.M., she might be the extra bit of corroboration we needed. That is, if she would talk. I sent over a Chinese-speaking detective to feel her out. But just as I feared, she'd learned her lessons from the crowd who hung around her joint. She had seen and heard nothing.

"We could try those who had been in Umberto's during the shooting. They included Mattie the Horse, the cook LaMonica, and the Gallo party of six. Mattie the Horse claimed to have been in the kitchen. LaMonica insisted he had buried his head in the sawdust behind the clam bar for the duration. That left the folks at the Gallo table.

"All five of them lived up to the ancient code. From the time Pete the Greek went to the hospital he refused to tell us anything but his name. Sina Gallo said she had concentrated on shielding her daughter and could offer no help. Neither could Edith Russo. The little girl was confused and vague. Whether it was genuine or by direction, I couldn't tell.

"If anybody was going to break for us, I felt it would be Carmella Fiorello. She had loved her brother and her grief was intense. Apart from that, she knew that the whole incident was highly irregular. Even if the other side wanted a man badly, they would normally take pains not to rub him out while his wife looked on. That offended the sacred separation of family and business. Men might be killed in front of their girlfriends or even along with them, like Joe Colombo's father, but I never heard of it happening in front of wives.

"It was bad enough that Sina and Carmella had to watch the riddling, but a child? To Colombo or Gambino, this would be an incomprehensible breach of etiquette. Little girls were meant for ribbons and frilly dresses on Sunday mornings. Suppose one of those shots had blown the freckles off her face? Since the other side had broken the rules, I hoped maybe Carmella would too.

"She listened closely as detectives who had known her brother tried to persuade her that the indecency done to Joey could best be punished by catching the assassins and throwing them in jail. But they could do that only with her help.

"Carmella was unconvinced. This was an affair for the boys on President Street to settle their own way, she insisted. We explained to her that with Joey gone, the boys on President Street did not have the muscle to do that without shedding a lot of their own people's blood. Besides, she had only one more brother.

"We offered to put her in a private hospital room for the day so she could talk to us in confidence. It would seem a reasonable precaution since she was diabetic and the shock could have been harmful. Carmella pointed out that a day in the hospital cost at least a hundred dollars. Would Blue Cross pay? We assured her it would be arranged. She wavered, but finally elected not to give us one shred of useful information. At the funeral, she screamed out, 'Joey, Joey—the streets are going to run red with blood!'

"It was no more than I expected. After her brother Larry was garroted in the Sahara Lounge by Carmine Persico, we picked up a hood named Anthony Abbatemarco, who had lured Gallo into the trap and then shot a cop in the face as he ran out. The cop identified Abbatemarco, but Larry Gallo wouldn't say a word against his assailant. He just stood mute and stony-faced. It worked both ways, of course. A few months later I visited Carmine Persico in the hospital after Larry Gallo shot him from the back of a pickup truck on Bond Street.

" 'Who did this to you, Carmine?' I asked him as he was being wheeled down a hall.

"Persico's eyes were swollen and caked with blood, but what little I could see of them was hard and bright. He looked straight up at the ceiling and shook his head no.

"Carmella wasn't the only one who showed how well the women can keep silent. Luparelli's wife was distraught over what her husband had done. 'I have the kids, one of them a boy in school,' she said. 'How am I going to explain to him about his father?'

"It was a good question. How *do* you explain to a wide-eyed kid that his father is a hood who helped murder another hood?

" 'That's not what I mean,' she said. 'I mean, how am I going to explain to my boy that his father is a *squealer?*' "

"Luparelli himself was doing nicely in protective custody. Since it seemed advisable to keep him moving, he and his wife got to sleep in half the hotels in town. He ordered what he wanted from room service. When he complained that his leg hurt, we took him to specialists, got him medicine. I asked him how long the leg had been giving him trouble. For years, he said.

" 'Did you ever go to a doctor before?' I asked.

" 'You kidding?' he answered. 'They'd charge me an arm *and* a leg. Better they should charge you.'

"Every once in a while, when he got to feeling we were his service staff, I'd tell him it wasn't worth it. I'd have my car drop him off on a stool at Umberto's and we'd forget the whole thing. That always put his feet back on earth."

Ever since Luparelli's first call, Seedman had kept the Nyack apartment tower under surveillance with the cooperation of the local police and the FBI. It had been unusually easy to tap the phone, once the court gave the order, because an FBI agent already lived in the building. But Di Biase, Gambino, Bennie, and Cisco were not trusting the phone. They did all their talking from booths in drug stores and gas stations near the apartment. Seedman ordered all these pay phones put out of order, except for one, which was tapped.

It would have been easy for the police to "snap up" the four men while they slept. But the D.A., John Keenan, saw no point in taking them into custody yet, since none of the witnesses was ready to corroborate Luparelli's story. Neither, obviously, were the men in Nyack. Seedman could only wait and watch and hope they would give themselves away. But that break never came. Late one afternoon they drove away from the apartment and were soon lost to their tail in the rush-hour crush. They never returned to Nyack.

"Di Biase did the same the last time he was charged with murder," says Seedman. "He was gone eight years before he turned himself in. This time I doubt he'll be so quick. It is highly unusual, actually, for police *ever* to find a fugitive. More often than not they wind up dead. If not, you'd have to mobilize an army just to check all the hiding places on Mulberry Street—forget everywhere else. People don't hide in hiding places, anyway. They hide in the open, and the only way you can get your man is for someone to give him up.

"The Gallo case points up the near impossibility of bringing a mob assassin to trial. In Luparelli we had a unique asset. Yet even with his detailed account of the murder, and the rest of the hit squad pinpointed in Nyack, we *still* lacked the necessary witnesses and evidence to get convictions that would stand up in court. Out of the whole business, the only one we could prosecute was Pete the Greek for possessing an illegal firearm."

At his trial in State Supreme Court in Manhattan, Pete the Greek admitted that he had not filed income-tax returns in ten years. He explained that he had not been able to work because of a war injury suffered in Korea, followed by an auto accident in the States.

"When was this accident?" asked prosecutor Robert Tannenbaum.

"May I have a recess to speak to my lawyer about that?"

"Was your lawyer in the car too?" asked Tannenbaum sarcastically.

"No. But I want to speak to my lawyer about how to answer that question."

Though Pete the Greek was not much more cooperative about answering Tannenbaum's other questions, he did admit that he had worked recently at Pappy's Italian Food Products, Inc., on Route 82 in Fishkill, New York, where he was an officer of the corporation. Tannenbaum asked if he was working at Pappy's now.

"We're in Chapter Eleven," he answered.

"You mean bankruptcy?"

"That's right, Mr. Tannenbaum."

"What is your title?"

"Vice-president."

"Who is president?"

"Frank Compepele."

"How do you spell that last name?"

"C-A-M-P-I . . . C-A-O-M-P . . . C-A-M-P-O-L. . . ."

"He was your partner and you can't spell his name?"

Pete shrugged. "Me and Frank, we don't go formal."

As for the night of April 7, Pete was happy to estimate the value of the Cadillac he had driven at $12,000, though he railed at being called a chauffeur and insisted that he took orders from nobody. With Pappy's "in Chapter Eleven" and no other job in sight, hadn't it been difficult to pay that much for a car? It was on loan from his father, explained Pete, a man in his late seventies. On the night of Joe Gallo's birthday, didn't Pete think it was odd to leave his wife and five children at home in Brooklyn while he celebrated with Edith Russo? She was a "very close friend." He also admitted that, upon his release from the hospital, he went straight to the Gallos' President Street headquarters, where he kept a "change of clothes," and did not go home for several days.

Answering the specific charge of possessing an illegal firearm, Pete the Greek insisted that as shots burst from the side door Gallo had handed him the silver-plated automatic that he then used to defend himself and the others. He had never carried a gun in his life. He also pointed out that he had never been arrested in his life. After two weeks of testimony, Pete the Greek was convicted of illegal possession of the gun and sentenced to one year in prison, suspended thanks to his otherwise spotless record.

Two years after the incident at Umberto's, Luparelli remained in protective custody somewhere in New York, still charged with no crime. Philip Gambino had reappeared soon after leaving the Nyack hideout and was promptly arrested for violation of parole on a hijacking conviction. Di Biase and two men known only as Bennie and Cisco were still at large, if they were still alive. Joseph Yacovelli suddenly turned up on February 28, 1974, explaining that he was fed up with hiding out and running away. His bail was set at $25,000. He posted it and walked out.

Gone with Joe Gallo was the last of the black-shirt white-tie, pure gangster style so popular in movies of the 1940s. He was a man who could carry off the role in life and certainly had in death. He had even kept to the style in dispensing death. One night soon after Albert Anastasia was executed in the elegant barbershop of the Park Sheraton Hotel on October 25, 1957, Gallo smiled his chilliest smile to a barroom friend. "I guess you could say I'm the lead in the barbershop quintet," he said. Few men could have dropped that line without being dismissed as braggarts. Joe Gallo got away with it.

One evening Gallo was eating dinner in a Brooklyn restaurant when at another table he spotted Judge Samuel Leibowitz, who had tried Gallo before. Going over to Leibowitz's table, Gallo said, "It's a great country we live in when a guy like me can walk up to a person such as yourself at dinnertime." Then he said a lot more. As the other patrons gaped, the Judge's party became increasingly uncomfortable. Leibowitz was used to looking down at men like this from the bench; now Gallo was looking down at him and would not stop talking. "I guess he felt that restaurant was his turf," explains Seedman. "He didn't want Judge Leibowitz coming back, and as far as I know he never did. That was 'Crazy Joey'—crazy like a fox."

But when Gallo got too brazen, he could do himself in. Gallo had been prospering right up through the early 1960s by collecting "dues" at taverns for a bartenders' union he had established in South Brooklyn. Each proprietor paid in an average of thirty dollars per week for his bartenders who, unknown to them, already were members. It was a nice income for Joe. It could be expanded a thousand times over without touching a fraction of the bars in the city. But then Gallo picked the one proprietor he should have left alone. His name was Teddy Moss.

It all began one spring morning in 1962 when Teddy Moss was working in his office garret above an umbrella shop on Seventh Avenue at 24th Street. He looked up from the books of the three bars he and his father owned to see some flashily dressed strangers walk in. They offered to sell him $48,000 worth of hijacked whiskey at the bargain price of $20,000.

"I don't want it," said Moss.

"You don't have to pay all cash," said a jowly man named Sidney Slater. "You can have terms."

"I don't want it," repeated Moss.

"You don't have to take the whole load, you can take half. A quarter even."

"I don't want any of it," said Moss. He resumed checking his books and after a moment the men walked out.

The next morning Joe Gallo himself turned up in Moss's office. "Listen," he said, "I sent my friends to see you because I heard you were a bright, ambitious young businessman. My kind of guy. So, why don't you help them out?"

"Why pick on me?" asked Moss. "I didn't send for you. I never even met you."

Gallo leaned forward, his pale-green eyes hard as ice. "You don't send for me. I come to you—when I want, where I want, for what I want. Give my boys a break, Mr. Moss. They deserve it and so do you."

The next morning Slater came back with Mike Albergo, a former bartender at the Rumpus Room, the bar Moss owned in Queens. They both looked at Moss with concern. "This Joey Gallo, don't go against him," they said. "He has friends all over, they can get you. Why don't you just cooperate?" But Moss set his lips and would not listen. Later that afternoon he had just finished getting a haircut when Gallo and a friend walked into the barbershop.

"Wait," said Gallo.

"I don't have time, I have an appointment," Moss said. But he sat down anyway. After twenty-five minutes, when the two men were finished with their own haircuts, Gallo said to Moss, "Did you pay for your friends' haircuts too?"

"No," answered Moss. Gallo smiled. They walked outside toward Seventh Avenue. "I think you can do a better business if I put my own people in your joints, furnish a clientele," he said. "You and I will share the profits fifty-fifty."

"I don't even have profits at two of my places," said Moss.

"Then with the clientele I'll supply you'll do better. Tell you what: Why don't you get your books ready for me to look over tomorrow? Bring in your accountant."

Walking down the crowded avenue in the sunlight, Moss was stunned. He saw now that the liquor deal was only bait, a way to hook him so that he could be roasted, put on the Gallo table, and gobbled up. It was incredible. His father and he had built up their businesses on pure sweat. Could they now lose them to a stranger wearing a black shirt and a white tie?

"What if I don't want your deal?" asked Moss.

"Well, a brick could fall on your head," said Gallo thoughtfully. "You could fall down a flight of stairs. A car might run you over. A lot of things can happen. I have a lot of friends. I could be in California and no one would be able to pin it on me. I'd have the perfect excuse. . . ."

Moss was chilled to realize that Gallo made it sound more like fact than threat. At that moment a Cadillac pulled up to the curb and took Gallo away.

At Moss's home in the Bronx the next morning, the phone rang at two o'clock. "Joey wants to see you downtown at the Luna Restaurant right now," said Albergo. "You better go."

"Okay," said Moss. But when he turned on the light he saw that his wife was shaking, wide-eyed and soundless. After a few minutes, Moss turned out the light and stared into the dark.

In the morning another of Gallo's men called. "Joey had someone waiting for you at your car last night. They were going to break a few bones to get the message across. But nothing will happen if you come down to the J and A Social Club on Park Street at three o'clock—and bring your books."

Moss was greeted by Slater and Gallo's Egyptian friend Ali Waffa when he walked into the J and A. "My friend is the nicest person in the world," said Waffa, a ship's cook who had been best man at Gallo's wedding. "Just play ball with him." But when Gallo walked in a few minutes later and saw Moss without the books, he threw him into a chair.

"If you were me and I was you, wouldn't you say I was stupid to give you all this trouble?" asked Gallo.

Moss could see they were waiting for his response. "Yeah, I guess," he answered.

"Say, 'I'm stupid.'"

"I'm stupid," said Moss in a monotone. Gallo nearly smacked him off the chair. "Say it like you mean it," he said.

"I'm stupid," said Moss. Gallo smacked his face again.

"I'm *really* stupid!" Moss bellowed. When they kicked him out a few minutes later, welts were rising on both sides of his face. He had been told to be at the Luna with his books the next evening, ready to talk details of the partnership then or never.

That evening as he walked into his bar in the garment district Moss was stopped by two rough-looking men. They were new to the cast of characters. But they said they had heard he was having shakedown problems with Joey Gallo. They assured him that while Gallo had a great deal of muscle, others had more, and they were in a position to help him. Moss agreed to meet them that night in a room at the George Washington Hotel on 23rd Street.

Preferring not to go in alone, Moss brought his father along to the meeting. Teddy explained how the load of hijacked liquor had been offered to him as bait, how Gallo had then demanded half the business, how he had alluded to "accidents" that could happen if Moss did not yield. When he had finished the story, the door to the next room swung open. Moss froze, until the two men who stepped out identified themselves as assistant district attorneys. The two rough-looking men who had listened to his story then identified themselves as city detectives.

They had heard about Moss's problem from their informants on the street; now they wanted his cooperation in this rare chance to foil a shakedown in progress. Best of all, they could throw it right back at a top mob goon who considered himself untouchable. With

Moss's help, Joe Gallo would be stewing in prison for years. The DA's office and the police would spare no expense in providing total safety for Moss and his family for as long as he wanted it.

Moss looked at the detectives and assistant DAs. They had the kind of clean-cut Irish faces which were the bedrock of his business. He looked at his father, who nodded back. Moss agreed to do as they asked.

His conversation with the detectives had already been recorded from the next room. Now an electronics specialist appeared and hooked up a recording device to the hotel room's phone. Once it had been installed, Moss dialed Mike Albergo, his former employee and friend, to ask for advice.

"Isn't there any way to stop him?" Moss asked.

"This guy is the top, you have to go with him," counseled Albergo. "Meet with him tomorrow night at the Luna, give him your books, give him what he wants. You'll still do good taking home a third of the business—"

"He only wants half," interrupted Moss.

"That's even better. Just quit fighting these guys and it'll be much better for you in the end."

Moss sighed. "Suppose I get out of the city, take my family to Europe. Maybe this will be over by the time I get back."

"They'll chase you down wherever you go. They'll run you down in their Cadillacs. Give it up, Teddy. You don't have a chance."

That evening at the Luna Restaurant, Gallo tried to get Moss to eat before they got down to business. "They got great steak and peppers here," he said, patting Moss on the back. "You'll love it to death."

"I'm not hungry," said Moss glumly, but at Gallo's insistence he ordered a shrimp cocktail. "Maybe you can outline this proposition to me one more time," said Moss.

"I'm moving in," Gallo said, leaning forward. "That's the proposition."

Moss picked at his shrimp. "Well, I'd like just a little more time to think about it. I mean, this business is my whole life."

Smiling his glinty smile, Gallo turned to Mike Albergo and said something in Italian. At the next table a woman who obviously understood the remark smiled at her male companion, who went on talking about the high cost of getting his house air-conditioned. But even he smiled as Gallo turned to Moss and repeated it in

English: "I told Mike, sure, you could take three months to think about it on me—in the hospital."

Just then a flunky rushed to Gallo's side. "The whole place is crawling with cops!" he whispered. Gallo, Albergo, and Ali Waffa started toward the door, but they were followed by the couple at the next table, who were detectives. In front of the Luna, more detectives arrested them. In the morning, they and several others were booked for attempted extortion and conspiracy to extort.

Gallo wanted a lawyer named David Price to defend him. But Price was a tired man of seventy-three, on a prolonged vacation in Florida. When it was plain that he would not be returning soon, Judge Sarafite appointed another veteran trial lawyer, Irving Mendelson, to defend Gallo along with a lawyer who had represented him before, Robert Weisswasser. But Gallo would not speak to Mendelson, except to accuse him of being part of the "swan song" rigged up for the trial. Infuriated, Mendelson had to be restrained from going after Gallo. He apologized later to the judge, saying, "I don't absorb this sort of thing easily."

In the conferences in Judge Sarafite's chambers, Gallo answered all questions by saying, "Your Honor, I can't answer that without my lawyer." He ignored the judge's reminder that the court was willing to appoint any lawyer in New York City to defend him in the absence of David Price. Gallo's trial began on November 14, 1961, and lasted five days. Throughout that entire time Gallo stood mute. He was convicted on all counts and sentenced to seven to fourteen years in prison.

"It's a rare shakedown that makes it from the street to the courtroom," says Seedman. "What normally prevents it, of course, is the victim's fear of jeopardizing his family's safety by going to the police. It's much better to work out a private peace with the muscle on the street, or so he thinks.

"Since these hoods live off the fears of legitimate businessmen, obviously they have to bloody people up fairly often. But they are just as quick to turn on their own people. Luparelli could hardly be blamed for fearing the worst when he woke up in Nyack to find Di Biase staring down at him. He knew that no matter how unjust his own reversal of fortune seemed, there were plenty of bloody precedents for it. He had only to remember what happened to Joe Gallo's flunkies after the shakedown of Teddy Moss."

Several weeks after the Gallo trial Mike Albergo got a flat tire on a street in Queens. As he knelt with his brother to jack up the car, both were gunned down. A few months later Gallo's close friend Ali Waffa was found floating against the pilings alongside his ship at Hoboken. Sailors trying to stagger aboard drunk at night often fall off the gangway and drown, but Ali Waffa's body was so full of bullets it was a wonder he floated.

Several months after Gallo went to prison Sidney Slater, who had first contacted Teddy Moss and offered him the hijacked liquor, took his girlfriend, a tiny blonde who favored fur collars, to see the Sammy Davis show at the Copacabana. At almost four o'clock a man appeared at their table whom Slater knew as Jiggs Forlano, a member of the Profaci family, which had handled gambling operations in Havana before Castro swept them away.

"Can we step outside for a chat?" asked Forlano. Slater sent the blonde outside instead, at which point they were joined at the table by two other Profaci men, Carmine Persico and Donny Montemarano. They asked Slater a lot of apparently idle questions about Gallo's transfer from the Tombs in Manhattan to Sing-Sing. Meanwhile, all around them busboys were stacking chairs on empty tables. They were the last customers.

"What are you doing in a fancy place like this anyway?" Forlano asked suddenly. Before Slater could ask him the same question, Forlano swung at him. Slater thought the shiny object on Forlano's finger was a ring, but as it brushed just under the right eye, he realized it was a steel hook, the kind newsmen use to cut the string around bales of newspapers.

As Slater held a napkin to his bloody eye, a waiter came over. "Would you gentlemen like a last drink?" he asked. "We're about to close up."

"No, thanks," said Forlano. He and the other two men got up and left wordlessly, leaving Slater holding the napkin to his eye, the linen now soaked red. Later that week Slater decded to become a police informant.

Ten years later Joey Gallo also left the Copacabana as the busboys were stacking chairs on tables. To many of his new friends, it may have seemed that he had given up the rackets and left the boys on President Street behind. After all, he now read French novels and philosophy while they watched *Mod Squad*. Even as a young man he had preferred smoking hashish in Greenwich Village with Ali Waffa to going to the mob's beer parties; and Marta Orbach was supposed to be helping him write a memoir of his seven years in prison.

"But to anyone who believes that Gallo could have stayed away from the rackets, the Teddy Moss affair is instructive," says Seedman. "At that time, in 1962, he was supposed to be pinned down on President Street by the superior numbers of the Profaci army. All the rest of the Gallos certainly were, including his brother Larry. But here was Joey, brazening his way around the streets of Manhattan, attempting to shake down one of the most ambitious tavern-owners in town, in territory which wasn't his even *before* the Profaci war.

" 'Who do you think runs this town, people like you or people like me?' he had asked Moss.

"At the time of his death ten years later, I am convinced, he was determined to answer his own question the old way—not by writing his memoirs but by elbowing himself toward the money and power in the way he knew best. He had made a beginning in prison by selecting a squad of blacks who would augment his own thin forces when he got out. Thanks to the knowledge of Islam he had picked up from Ali Waffa, he was able to make better contact with Black Muslims. To first-generation Italian mobsters, such actions were unbelievable. To them, Italians from villages fifteen miles away were alien as Eskimos!"

But Gallo saw it differently. "You can never tell what will happen to you," he had advised Moss ten years before. "I have *lots* of friends."

"Striking down Colombo on 'Unity Day' through a black man was right in character with what Gallo had told Moss. He was also right in character by going for the top of the same family he had attacked in 1960, when Joe Profaci was don.

"Gallo had earned his nickname by striking when his victims least expected. I guess it was a sort of justice that he met his own end, not from the vicious men who had stalked him in vain, but from an illiterate street thug—a nobody—who felt like having a bowl of clam chowder on the same morning Joey, whose own first craving was for Chinese food, finished up his birthday party with boiled shrimps and scungilli at dawn."

AMBUSH

I. DOCKERY AND FLECK

On the perfect warm morning of May 21, 1971, thumbing the back pages of the *Jerusalem Post* over tea in a café in Tel Aviv, where he was vacationing with his wife, Henny, Seedman noticed a one-paragraph report of the machine-gunning of two patrolmen in New York. Though riddled with bullets, they were still alive. Their attackers, thought to be black militants, had escaped.

If he had been anywhere near the city now, Seedman would be racing back to put the investigation in motion the way he wanted it. Though it was unwritten law in the force that a man's vacation was sacred, Seedman often interrupted his own, just as he always took evening and weekend calls so he could arrive at crime scenes while they were still fresh. As he rose in rank, it got worse, not better. Now, because he was five thousand miles from New York, his office staff probably figured he would not hear about this shooting. Which probably explained why they had not called him about it; they wanted him to enjoy.

Anyway, this was more than a vacation. Only a few months ago he and Henny had been married, after the breakup of their first marriages. She was a fair woman, handsome, even-featured, and erect. Though she smiled more easily, she looked at people with a clear, unwavering gaze that was the counterpart of her husband's. Raised in a tiny French village, where a Jewish family was rare, she had eluded the Nazis and moved on to the United States after the war. Her parents and brother, a fighter pilot, were living now in Israel and she had brought her new husband to meet them for the first time.

Two days later, at the air base where Henny's brother was stationed, Seedman saw another item in the *Jerusalem Post:* two patrolmen were dead after being ambushed by black militants in New York. Seedman assumed that the two patrolmen he had read about earlier had succumbed to their wounds. Probably they had never really been alive after the machine-gunning. The hospitals of the city were full of machines that, for a while, could force even a ruined body to linger.

All day at poolside under the desert sun Seedman thought about those dispatches. Just before dinner he put through a call to New York, where it was noon.

"Who shot that pair of patrolmen?" he asked John Kinsella, the dour Irishman who was standing in as Chief of Detectives.

"*Which* pair?" asked Kinsella over the crackling wire.

"Holy smokes!" said Seedman.

"One pair on Riverside Drive on May nineteenth, one pair outside a housing project up on the Harlem River on the twenty-first," said Kinsella. "A group calling itself the Black Liberation Army claims both jobs. We have very few leads to work with right now."

"Is it like Brooklyn in '68 all over again?"

"Worse," answered Kinsella.

In the morning Seedman and Henny were on an El Al flight back to New York, cutting four days off their two-week vacation. It had been like a rerun of the summer of 1968 to hear from Kinsella about the shootings. With Seedman then commanding Brooklyn South detectives and Kinsella Brooklyn North, they had worried about just such an incident being set off by the Black Panther Party, which had begun to flex its muscle in the borough. As the summer heat moved in, every big city in the country with a local Panther cell was tense. On July 20 eleven cops and Panthers had been killed in a shootout in Cleveland. Nearly every day after that Panthers from the Brooklyn headquarters on Nostrand Avenue skirmished with the New York police.

On August 1 two Panthers were arrested for using a loud-speaker to try to incite a riot. The dingy hearing room on Schermer-horn Street where they were brought for arraignment that night quickly filled up with Panthers and off-duty cops. As the judge entered, the Panthers set off a commotion by refusing to rise or take off their black berets. Choosing not to press the issue, the judge quickly released the two defendants on their own recognizance to await trial. Still rancorous, police and Panthers emptied out of the hearing room into a miserably hot night.

It was still miserable at 2:55, when Seedman was awakened at home by a call from his staff captain, Ken Fitchelman.

"Two patrolmen were hit by shotgun fire less than an hour ago, Chief," said Fitchelman. "At 1054 Eastern Parkway. They were answering a complaint of some real loud family dispute but they never got into the building."

"Dead?"

"They're full of shotgun pellets, but they'll make it."

"Did they see who did it?"

"They didn't see a thing."

Driving the deserted Belt Parkway to Brooklyn a few minutes later, Seedman considered that the Panthers were not necessarily the ones responsible for the shooting. Anyone without an air-conditioner, which meant most of the people on that stretch of Eastern Parkway, would find the sheets too sticky to sleep between, and with nothing good to watch on television, they would have little to do but drink and argue and curse the heat. Family disputes would spring up all over, and in the worst of them guns inevitably would be pulled. Except that people almost always used handguns or knives in family disputes. Shotguns were in a rougher league to which the Black Panthers belonged.

At 2:10 that morning, as the story was reconstructed, a call had come into the Brooklyn Communications Center from a man, apparently black, speaking in a clear voice. "I live at 1054 Eastern Parkway. It sounds like the people next door are fighting. . . . I think it's a man beating the hell out of his wife. . . . I tried but I can't get in."

"What apartment?"

"Apartment Three-E—that's E for Edward."

"What cross street?"

"Wait a minute, I'll find out. . . . Schenectady."

"What's your name?"

"Jones. J-O-N-E-S."

"What's your phone number?"

"I'm calling from an outside phone because my phone is out of order."

Since the sector car that normally would have answered the call was already at the scene of another fight, the dispatcher asked for any other nearby car to volunteer. In the next sector over, Patrolmen Thomas Dockery and Leonard Fleck, cruising Utica Avenue, agreed to take the call. They pulled up to the gray-brick five-story apartment house on the service road beside Eastern Parkway. Once Jewish and Irish, the neighborhood was now mixed, with blacks and Puerto Ricans. Sweating even in their short sleeves, Dockery and Fleck walked side by side toward 1054.

They had gone only a few steps when a tremendous boom exploded out of the dark. Dockery tumbled head over heels. Before he could get out his service .38, a second boom took Fleck down. Full of steel shot, howling in pain, the patrolmen were picked up by other patrol cars and rushed to Kings County Hospital. Interviewed like any other victims by the detectives from the 71st Squad, they said they had never seen their attackers and did not even know where the shots had come from. Detectives rummaging behind a ragged clump of bushes to the right of 1054 Eastern Parkway found two empty shotgun shells. In the rear of the building, at the bottom of a twelve-foot fence, they found a white button imprinted with a black panther.

Ten days after that shooting, at the same hour of two o'clock, a patrol car was cruising past the intersection of Schenectady and Eastern Parkway when three quick shots smashed through the windshield. Seeing nothing to shoot back at in the dark, the patrolmen accelerated and ducked their heads 'and, as glass splintered in on them, sped off. At dawn, detectives found three empty shells on the roof of a building just two doors from the corner. Again the shooters were phantoms.

With attacks on cops now in both Brooklyn North and South, Seedman and Kinsella set up a joint task force to work on the cases. Under a lieutenant named Angelo Galante, the team spent all that winter and fall gathering intelligence on Brooklyn Panthers. Some came from black cops working "deep undercover" within the party— so deep that their own families often had no idea they were even cops. More information came from Panthers who had been nabbed for crimes like robbery, auto theft, and assault and were hoping for leniency. This information, in turn, was used to persuade judges to authorize wiretaps on the phones of known Panthers to pick up yet more information. In line with that strategy, on March 6, 1969, Galante and a black detective named Clarence Crabb drove up to a correctional facility in Bridgeport, Connecticut, to see what they could learn from four Brooklyn-based Panthers, Ron Hill, Nathaniel Burns, Lumumba Shakur, and slender, handsome, and well-spoken twenty-seven-year-old William Hampton, who seemed most cooperative of all.

No sooner had Hampton begun to talk than Galante got the funny feeling that he was listening to a familiar voice. It sounded exactly like the one who had reported the family dispute on Eastern Parkway. If anyone could match that voice it was Galante, since he had listened to the automatic recording of that call at least a hundred times. Galante took Crabb aside.

"I know it sounds crazy, Clarence," he said, "but I swear this is the guy from the tape that night."

Crabb clapped Galante on the back. "I was thinking the same thing," said the black detective.

"So jerk him off a little, Clarence. You'll be better with him than a honky like me."

Crabb smiled and walked back alone to the interrogation room. After chasing out the guard, he turned to Hampton and explained that thanks to new electronic miracles a man's speaking voice could be identified as surely as his fingerprints.

"That's why I have to tell you that we know you put in that call to the Seventy-first Precinct back on the morning of August second," said Crabb.

"I'll tell you this straight, Bill," he continued, putting his arm around Hampton's slender shoulders. "It's bad to rob a bank, because people like their money. But it's like dunking for apples on Hallowe'en compared to setting up cops to be shot. If you did the shooting too, then nothing or nobody can keep your ass off the fire now. But if you *didn't* fire off those shots, you might squeeze out of this okay if you tell me who did. The reason I'm saying this to you, frankly, is that in my personal opinion you didn't do that part. . . ."

Hampton eyed Crabb carefully. "You're right, I didn't shoot them. But I'm going to have to think awhile whether I'm going to tell you who did."

"Take your time," said Crabb, getting up. "Those tapes last forever."

On the morning of March 17, 1969, three days after he was released on two years' probation on the Connecticut charges, Hampton was brought by Galante and Crabb to Seedman's office at Brooklyn South headquarters. Speaking calmly, he told how thirty Panthers had milled angrily outside the courthouse on Schermerhorn Street after the hearing on the night of August 1. They were mad at having been asked to take off their berets and stand for the judge, mad at the heat, mad at the beatings they were sure the cops had given their two brothers who had been arrested for inciting a riot.

"You'll see Panther power tonight!" someone had shouted from the angry knot. But nobody could think of exactly how to express it and the Panthers drifted away. Back at the Nostrand Avenue Panther headquarters Ron Hill finally had said that he would do something even if nobody else would and asked Jordon Ford, the Brooklyn party commander, for permission to "move." Ford nodded but said nothing.

Hampton had chased after Hill to his car. "I haven't got the technical equipment, you know," he said, "but I'll go with you because maybe you'll need cover."

Hampton and Hill had driven alone to Hill's apartment on East 98th Street in Queens where his wife had fixed them coffee and then gone back to sleep. At midnight Hill had transferred a shotgun from the bedroom closet to his car trunk. They had driven to the Eastern Parkway neighborhood where Hill once lived, parking one street over on Union. Through the backyards and over a fence they had traced out an escape route that came out at the gray-brick building at 1054 Eastern Parkway.

"They keep this place crawling with patrol cars," Hill said. "The first one that comes by, we'll take it out. Then back through the yard, over the fence, through another yard, and we're at the car. Nobody on Union Street will know what happened on the Parkway."

They had sat in the heat by the bushes in front of 1054 for fifteen minutes but no patrol car had come by.

"Goddam," said Hill. "Every other night they're crawling around like roaches. Go make a phone call to the precinct, Bill. Tell them some people are drunk and fighting in this building."

Hampton trotted off. He tried a dime in one phone booth after another but none worked. Eventually he found himself in front of an all-night coffee shop on Utica Avenue where he bought doughnuts to bring back to the bushes.

"What took you so long?" Hill demanded.

"If you know this turf so fucking well, then *you* find a phone that works," snapped Hampton. Tired and sticky, he was beginning to feel that the mission was getting to be a drag.

"There's a bar two blocks down on Schenectady," said Hill. "The phone in the back says 'Out of Order,' but it works."

Passing a line of morose drinkers at the bar, Hampton entered the phone booth and dialed 911. Then he walked back to Eastern Parkway, where Hill was sitting like a stone on the steps by the bushes. The unexpected boredom of the mission had gotten to him too. Now that phase was over. They moved behind the bushes. At 2:33 the squad car pulled up along the curb and Dockery and Fleck got out. As they walked, relaxed, up the sidewalk, Hill blasted the first shot. Suddenly fearful as he saw the first cop fall screaming, Hampton bolted toward the backyard before Hill could fire the second shot.

Hampton had scaled the rear fence easily during the practice run but now, grasping frantically, he ripped the pants of his black double-breasted suit and fell backward, jamming his right knee. He grabbed for his black beret and this time scrambled over, with Hill right behind him. As he started the car, they heard shots coming from Eastern Parkway where the wounded officers were trying to attract attention.

They zoomed down Rockaway Avenue to an empty parking lot near the ocean. When their breath no longer came in heaves, they drove to the apartment in Jamaica, Queens, where Hampton lived with his common-law wife, Verna. As she came out to the kitchen table sleepily, the round-the-clock-news radio station WINS was broadcasting a bulletin on the shooting of two patrolmen on Eastern Parkway.

Suddenly wide-eyed, Verna looked from one man to the other.

They smiled at each other but not at her. She asked no questions. As Hampton explained now to Seedman, Panther women, like Mafia women, were trained not to mess in their men's business. In the morning Hill and Hampton had gone to work as usual.

"Where was that?" Seedman asked.

"At Pratt Institute," Hampton answered. "We taught black culture."

"You trained for that?"

"Didn't have to be. It came from, you know, Federal anti-poverty money. We got ninety dollars a week."

The most interesting part of that 1968 conversation seemed even more striking to Seedman now as he flew high over the Atlantic with Henny beside him. He had tried to pinpoint what words had been used by Jordon Ford, the local Panther commander, to authorize the ambush. If the Panther Party maintained a military chain of command, then the brass were more culpable than the soldiers, who just followed orders.

"Did Ford say, 'Go ice those pigs,' or what?" Seedman asked.

"Oh, no, nothing like that," Hampton answered, shaking his head. "He didn't have to. Hill said he wanted permission to 'move.' When a Panther says that it automatically means he's going to hit the Police Department. That's what the entire program is all about."

Hampton leaned forward. "Listen," he said, "the only reason I'm telling you all this is because I don't think that program can help black people any more. If I did, you could fry me and I wouldn't talk. But now I decided that when cops get shot, black people just get crapped on even more. Maybe by telling you this, it'll prevent it from happening next time."

When Jordon Ford was picked up by detectives that night, he sounded unnaturally reasonable for a man commanding a cell of what was then the most militant black organization in America. "When I hear a Panther call just any cop a pig," he told Seedman, "I get upset. Because I never was the type of person to just label anyone automatically. But I go with it because I'm a very organizational person, a Capricorn. If it's the party line, I go with it. If somebody asked me what I felt personally, I'd be glad to explain in detail. But I'd always point out where it diverged from the party line.

As an official Panther, I always stay tight with that line. What I think or what my wife thinks personally just doesn't matter."

While Ford explained how the Panthers had come to hate cops so much, Seedman found himself wondering which side the commander was on. "It started back in Oakland, where the party itself started," explained Ford. "Oakland police were the worst. Their brutality against us was daily. In New York we've had incidents of kids being beaten, but it's nothing like in Oakland. Unfortunately, you have cops here who do act emotionally when they should be acting professionally. Yet you can't say too much about it because they're just human beings. Two hundred cops getting emotional on a hot night is not necessarily an indication of all thirty thousand. . . ."

Hampton was sentenced to seven and a half years in prison for the assault on Dockery and Fleck. Hill, who was by then serving a term in Connecticut, escaped before he could be tried and is still at large. Jordon Ford, who had neither ordered the ambush in so many words nor taken direct part, got off with five years' probation.

In June 1969, three months after the Ambush Case was broken, Seedman was promoted to Assistant Chief Inspector and given command of detectives in glamorous Manhattan South. With this move, he was first in line to eventually succeed the grizzled Dutchman, Fred Lussen, as Chief of Detectives. Hair now graying, shoulders broader, cigar in place as he moved between crime scenes and the squad rooms, Seedman had the look of Lussen's heir. It couldn't be long. Lussen had served nearly thirty-five years on the force, which was about as long as anyone stayed.

In September 1970, an easygoing Irishman named Howard Leary was replaced as the city's Police Commissioner by Patrick Murphy, a very different kind of Irishman. Murphy had been Training Officer of the Police Academy fifteen years earlier when Seedman, one step under him, was Director of Recruit Training. Like Seedman, he had benefited from the high-level contacts he made at the Academy. Unlike Seedman, the new Commissioner had never been a detective and did not want to be; he seemed uninterested in any kind of field work. After a succession of headquarters desk jobs, he had left to become Police Chief in Syracuse, then an administrator for the Law Enforcement Assistance Administration in Washington.

Murphy was coming to his latest job now from Detroit, where he had also been Police Commissioner. He would find a department shaken by allegations of widespread corruption. Its most damaging accusers were two young cops, David Durk and Frank Serpico. Feeling that the police brass had no intention of acting on their charges, they had gone to the *New York Times,* and the story had made front-page news for months. This was the last thing Mayor John Lindsay wanted at the moment. Gearing up for a try at the Democratic Presidential nomination in 1972, he was determined to stifle any hints of corruption in his administration. One of his countermoves was setting up the so-called Knapp Commission to investigate the problem. The other was finding a new Police Commissioner. Stern, religious, scrupulously honest, Patrick Murphy seemed exactly the man to make the specter of corruption go away.

As Seedman lit up his first cigar of the day at 8:15 one morning in late September, the radio in his official car crackled out: "Car Twenty-seven, call your command." At a phone booth on Queens Boulevard, Seedman was told to call the Police Commissioner's office at once. He was surprised to hear, for the first time in nearly eight years, the flat voice of Patrick Murphy.

"Can you spare the time for lunch with me, Al? I'm in from Detroit for a few days to look around."

They lunched at a quiet place called Gasner's, a few blocks from City Hall. Slender, pale, and mild-mannered, Murphy had hardly changed over the years, except that his pale-blue eyes were even more restless than they had been. He wanted to know which of his contemporaries were still on the job, what the food of the force was, above all, where was the corruption. Seedman did not want to hedge, but the fact was that nobody could say for sure. In a department of 30,000 men, corruption obviously existed, as it always had. Obviously too, it crept into certain parts of the department and the city more easily than into others. Yet nobody had ever mounted a massive and sophisticated effort to pinpoint corruption and eradicate it. The biggest problem was that neither corrupt cops nor citizens who were often their too willing victims were about to volunteer help to such a probe unless, possibly, they were caught in the act. But Seedman was sure of one other thing. Most cops were honest, not crooked, and that went double for detectives.

After lunch Murphy surprised Seedman by asking him to come along on the ride uptown to his office. Always shy and uneasy, like a squirrel waiting for a nut but worried that the person handing it over will come too close, Murphy seemed glad to have Seedman lead him from office to office and introduce him to the men he would command.

In the two weeks before he officially took over, Murphy peppered Seedman with calls for advice on who would make good staff men, what points to stress in his acceptance speech. He understood that Seedman was already in line to be the next Chief of Detectives. The move from Brooklyn into Manhattan at the command level was a traditional grooming point for the jump. He asked Seedman when the Chief of Detectives would retire. Knowing that Lussen would retire when the Commissioner wanted him to, Seedman said he did not know. For the beginning of his administration, Murphy talked vaguely about a "staff job" for Seedman.

At first, Seedman thought Murphy might have in mind the First Deputy slot, the top assistant to the Commissioner. But that job went to William Smith, a retired captain who had worked before with Murphy, first in Syracuse and later in Washington. Since the Chief Inspector's slot was now filled by Mike Codd, promotion for a two-star Assistant Chief like Seedman could only be to one of the four three-star jobs in the department: Chief of Personnel, Chief of Inspectional Services, Chief of Patrol, and Chief of Detectives. None was available. So what job could Murphy be thinking about?

One afternoon in late October, Seedman was seeing off the President's party at the Wall Street heliport when an urgent call came through from his office.

"Chief," said the clerical detective when Seedman finally got to a phone, "the word is down from the PC's office for you to report to the Police Academy auditorium tomorrow morning. In *uniform*."

Seedman was mystified. He was going to be promoted, obviously, but to what? He called the Commissioner's office but Murphy had already left.

"You're getting promoted, if that's what you're wondering, sir," said the new staff man on the phone.

"To *what?*"

"Way up, way up," said the smiling voice.

That night Seedman got Murphy on the phone.

"I'm giving you a big new job, Al," he said. "It's called Director of Training. But I don't mean pushing papers at the Police Academy. You'll be empowered to rove over the entire Police Department to evaluate operations wherever you see fit. I want you to hold executive conferences, set up feedback channels to monitor what's going on in the field, organize training programs to increase our efficiency, and stop our men from being killed or injured." Murphy paused. "In short, Al, I'm giving you a mandate to help me bring this vast tradition-bound Department in line with twentieth-century management practices."

A silence fell. "Does that mean," Seedman finally asked, "that I'm not going to be Chief of Detectives?"

"No, no, Al. I know you're the one man for that job. But this is where I need you now."

In the first two months on his new job Seedman found Murphy good to his word. He picked his own staff and explored the Department freely, looking for ways to use men better and cut down their opportunities for graft.

He ordered patrolmen to stop trying to enforce the archaic "blue laws" that prohibit sale of certain items on Sunday. One large area that made Murphy uncomfortable, Seedman sensed, was the Detective Bureau itself. For one thing, Murphy had never been a detective. More to the point, he was determined to put tighter controls on the Department. Yet nobody outside the Bureau knew exactly what detectives did with their days. True, they were an elite force. Since the turn of the century, the second-floor squad room in each precinct house had been the exclusive domain of detectives who went up and down the stairs without so much as a nod to the uniformed desk man on the ground floor. Though they no longer wore broad-brimmed hats or long overcoats, they were still as mysterious to young patrolmen as they had been to Seedman when he reported for his first tour of duty in 1942. Right now, they were hardly less mysterious to the new Police Commissioner.

Seedman himself had been bothered for years by an altogether different problem with a detective's day. He simply had too much paperwork. It prevented him from getting out in the streets, where he belonged. Most of it involved petty cases that did not even require a detective's expertise. They could be handled by patrolmen.

"If a guy comes running into the station house, claiming his wife put a dent in his head," Seedman says, "the desk officer sends him up to the duty detective, who has to spend forty-five minutes typing up a 'U.F. Sixty-one' complaint report even though it's an open-and-shut case that could be handled by a patrolman. Or some guy's in a dither because his car was just stolen. In this city it doesn't pay for the detective to go out looking for it. All he can do is fill out forms and send out alarms, which again patrolmen could do as well. A patrolman would be delighted to get even this small taste of detective work, yet under an old rule, the only crime he is empowered to investigate is the theft of a milk bottle from a stoop! The only reason he was granted even that much authority was because in summer, the milk might have spoiled or been swallowed by the time he was able to summon the duty detective.

"Another problem which bothered me was that detectives were faced with a tremendous variation in work load, depending on where they were working. In the Twenty-eighth Squad in Harlem they could be dashing from one murder to the next on a hot weekend. In the One-eleven, out at the edge of Queens, they could spend the same weekend yawning. Where more crimes were committed, of course, we had more detectives, but the extremes were still too great. Assignments had to be made on a more equitable basis so that every detective caught the same potential work load."

"The answer to all this was the setup called detective specialization. It was already used in several cities, including Chicago and Los Angeles. It meant that almost all crime reports coming in to the switchboard would be channeled to one of four squads: homicide and assault, burglary and larceny, robbery, and narcotics. Under specialization, a detective would no longer have to try to calm down a guy who had the buttons stolen off his coat at twelve-seventeen, then run to a bloody body at twelve-twenty-seven. The button case would go to specialists in the burglary and larceny squad—or even a patrolman—the murder case to homicide-assault.

"The traditional squads would be dissolved to make way for new districts, each of which would include the four specialized squads. Before drawing up the districts, I wanted to make a study of exactly how many hours detectives spend on each type of case. Knowing that, detectives could be allotted to each district so that each one got the same work load. Freed from the cut and dried work that could now be left to patrolmen, they could now do the work they were trained to do best."

Murphy was delighted with the specialization proposal. Besides satisfying Seedman's desire to get more detectives on the

street, it satisfied the Commissioner's own desire for more supervision. Since the new districts combined several of the old squads,
extra sergeants would be on duty to supervise each shift. Under
the old squad system, there were times when no sergeant at all was
available for the night shifts.

During the fall Seedman worked on organizing the specialization plan. Murphy suggested he might visit cities where specialization was working best, including Chicago and Los Angeles. Seedman
made plans to take off after the New Year with John O'Connor, a
curly-white-haired captain whom he had brought from Brooklyn
South to be full time director of the program. One afternoon, about
a week before they were to leave, Seedman was at the scene of a
huge gas explosion in a bar on lower Broadway that had left several
bodies under the debris when Carl Carolla called him from the office.

"The First Dep wants to see you," said Carolla.

Seedman knew Bill Smith from his years at the Police Academy,
where Smith had also been assigned for a stretch. He was going
to college then and always seemed to be off in a corner studying.
That was all Seedman could remember about the man. As Seedman
entered his big office on the third floor at headquarters, Smith welcomed him with a smile. He was a burly man, now with thinning
black and silver hair and shadowy jowls.

"Al," he said, "how'd you like to take over McGovern's job?"

Joe McGovern was the Chief of Inspectional Services, a three-
star job created to handle corruption and other sensitive problems
within the ranks. In theory, whoever had the job could cut deep into
the vast apparatus of the Department to get at any man who was
corrupt. But to do the job right, you had to be more than impeccably
honest. You had to be enthusiastic with a hatchet. McGovern,
plainly, had not been. Otherwise, the need for the Knapp Commission would never have arisen. Now McGovern would have to go.

Smith saw how Seedman was looking at him. "I don't have to
tell you the importance of this job, Al. The PC has come to clean up
this Department. Inspectional Services is the key."

"Whenever I found a bad apple in my command, I always
bagged him real quick," answered Seedman. "I was glad to. But it
only happened once in a while. You're talking about doing it full
time. Somebody's got to. But, Bill, that's not how I dream about
capping off my career."

"It's the best way you can serve the people of the city."

"No. The best way is as Chief of Detectives."

As Seedman was preparing to leave with O'Connor for Los Angeles a few days later, word came over the teletype that Frederick Lussen had retired. Seedman was startled. Lussen was still six months short of thirty-five years on the force. More to the point, the Captains' Endowment Association had yet to negotiate a new contract with the city for senior officers. Normally, an outgoing man waited for that contract so that his pension would be based on the new salary scale. If Lussen left now, Murphy must have given him a strong nudge.

But more startling was the message that followed on the teletype. John Kinsella, who had stepped in as Manhattan borough chief after Seedman left for the training assignment, had been made acting Chief of Detectives. Seedman got on the phone to Murphy. The Commissioner could do what he damn well pleased, of course. But Seedman saw no point in beating around the bush.

"Here I am flying off into the blue tomorrow morning," he said, "and Kinsella is acting Chief of Detectives. What's the story?"

"I want you to make the trip, Al," said Murphy. "But I don't want you to be tied down with other worries. It's a very important mission. Nobody can do this specialization thing but you. When I say this is the most important thing right now, believe me. So relax!"

In the morning, Seedman flew with O'Connor to Los Angeles on the first leg of their tour. Between Smith's proposal and Kinsella's appointment, he was not entirely convinced the way was clear for him. But again, Murphy was as good as his word. On March 18, after the specialization machinery was in place along with several other projects Seedman had been working on as Director of Training, he got a call from Mike Codd, the Chief Inspector, to say that he should again report in the morning to the Police Academy auditorium. In uniform.

The next morning, before his wife and a smiling Mayor, Seedman took command of the city's three thousand detectives. Eight weeks later he had felt settled enough into the cavernous, musty office on the second floor of Headquarters to take the trip to Israel that Henny wanted so much. But now, flying back four days early, Seedman was thinking back to the ambush of Dockery and Fleck in

1968. Since coming to Manhattan he had lost direct touch with Panther activities in Brooklyn. But he was aware that it had become harder to penetrate the party with undercover men.

Maybe the party had begun to dry up and there was no depth to penetrate, but it could be a more ominous phenomenon. Could the action be moving somewhere else? Maybe the real militants had deserted the party to form a compact, angry ball of heat that, like a dying star, would erupt in one last spasm before going out altogether. Seedman remembered William Hampton's answer when asked what words the Panther commander, Jordon Ford, had used to authorize the ambush of Dockery and Fleck on that hot night in 1968.

"He didn't have to use words," Hampton had replied. "It was understood that when you asked for permission to move, that automatically meant hitting the police. *That's what the entire program is all about. . . .*"

II. CURRY AND BINETTI, JONES AND PIAGENTINI

Eleven hours after lifting off in Tel Aviv, the Seedmans were met at JFK by a dozen detectives. Unsmiling and dark-suited, they looked out of place among the excited families, many of them dressed as if they had just come from a backyard barbecue. Rather than listen to all the detectives, Seedman had his chauffeur take Henny home, while he went to the 32nd Precinct to review everything that had been done. There he went over the DD-5s, detailed summaries of each detective's progress on a case, the Medical Examiner's reports, the lab reports, crime-scene photos, intelligence files and dossiers on particular subjects. Normally, Seedman would not have grasped for the paperwork like this. But now he needed to make up for five lost days and five thousand miles.

On the evening of May 19, Patrolmen Nicholas Binetti and Thomas Curry, both thirty-nine years old, were sitting in their idling 26th Precinct patrol car at the corner of 112th Street and Riverside Drive. The spot is one of the nicest in Manhattan. To the west of the Drive, Riverside Park is a fresh green ribbon at this season, blocking out the West Side Highway as the park slopes to the Hudson River. Across the river are the Jersey Palisades. Overlooking this vista, on the east side of the Drive, is a row of still-elegant old apartment houses. Most of the prestigious tenants who moved here in the 1920s when the buildings were new are gone, but one who stayed was Frank Hogan, the slight white-haired man who for thirty-four years had been the universally respected District Attorney of Manhattan. He lived at 412 Riverside Drive, one of the last buildings where maids still unroll canvas awnings over the river-view windows when the afternoon sun backs down over the Palisades and where perfectly groomed old Irish doormen still tip their hats to ladies.

For almost two years Hogan's office had been prosecuting the "Panther 21" for conspiracy to blow up department stores, police stations, government offices, and the Bronx Botanical Gardens. Actually, by the time Judge John Murtaugh convened the trial in March, only fifteen Panthers were on hand, the rest having jumped bail.

The defendants had many sympathizers, by no means all black. They were the darlings of much of the white liberal community. In the months before the trial Hogan had continually received threats against his life. During the trial itself a bomb had gone off on Judge Murtaugh's doorstep. It became necessary to give both men police guards. That is why Patrolmen Binetti and Curry were sitting in front of 412 Riverside Drive on that evening of May 19. Actually, they were only the relief shift while the regular guard went to dinner. They didn't mind. Spring scents wafted up from the park and a faint but rich trace of fire still filtered through the trees from the sun behind the Palisades. The neighborhood was at its quietest and nicest hour.

About 9:35 the patrolmen noticed a light-blue Mustang come down 114th Street, traveling the wrong way. Ignoring the traffic light at the foot of Riverside Drive, the Mustang turned into the main roadway and rolled slowly past Curry and Binetti. Two black men in the front seat grinned at them.

The duty of the guards was to protect Frank Hogan's home, not chase minor traffic violators. But the two black men in the Mustang were too blatant to ignore. The patrol car caught up with them at 108th Street, five blocks south. The Mustang slowed down but did not stop.

After hugging the Mustang's bumper for two more blocks, Binetti pulled his cruiser alongside at 106th Street. With a grass bank buffering the buildings on the left and the park on the right,

Riverside Drive is particularly isolated here—it does not even have a sidewalk.

Curry motioned for the blacks to pull over. The driver, he was irritated to see, was still smiling. Suddenly, the man's head dropped out of sight. In its place, pointed at him by the passenger, appeared the muzzle of a machine gun. The passenger fired continuously into the doors and windows of the patrol car, the blasts tossing Curry and Binetti about like popcorn in a popper. Curry took bullets in his face, right shoulder and upper stomach. Binetti took twelve slugs in the right thigh, knees, both arms and hands, right shoulder, stomach, and back of the neck.

Moments later passing motorists found Binetti crumpled under the steering wheel, Curry lying half in the street on the passenger's side, and the car looking like a sieve. A doctor, out walking his dog in the park, did what he could to stop the bleeding. Patrol cars soon arrived to rush Curry and Binetti to St. Luke's Hospital, ten blocks away, leaving the doctor to return home soaked in blood. In the next hour patrol cars from every one of the city's seventy-four precincts ringed the hospital as officers answered an emergency call for blood.

Astonishingly, Binetti and Curry did not die, but they certainly would never be the same. Though he had been shot only four times, Curry took the worst of it. The bullets disfigured his face, destroying nerves and wrecking portions of his brain. Only Binetti was able to describe what happened. No other witnesses were located.

Two evenings later at 8:30 packets were dropped off in the lobbies of the *New York Times* and WLIB-FM, a black-oriented radio station on 125th Street. Neatly wrapped in copies of the *New York Post* headlining the machine-gunnings, each contained one New York license plate 8373 YR, a set recently reported stolen. Accompanying each packet was a typewritten letter which said in part:

MAY 19, 1971

ALL POWER TO THE PEOPLE
HERE ARE THE LICENSE PLATES SORT AFTER BY THE FASCIST STATE PIG POLICE. WE SEND THEM IN ORDER TO EXHIBIT THE POTENTIAL POWER OF OPPRESSED PEOPLES TO ACQUIRE REV-

OLUTIONARY JUSTICE. . . . THE DOMESTIC ARMED FORCES OF
RACISM AND OPPRESSION WILL BE CONFRONTED WITH THE
GUNS OF THE BLACK LIBERATION ARMY, WHO WILL MET OUT
IN THE TRADITION OF MALCOLM AND ALL TRUE REVOLU-
TIONARIES REAL JUSTICE. WE ARE REVOLUTIONARY JUSTICE.

> ALL POWER TO THE PEOPLE
> JUSTICE

That same evening at 10:30 Patrolmen Waverly Jones and
Joseph Piagentini walked out of the apartment tower at 159-20
Harlem River Drive, part of a public-housing cluster called Colonial
Park Houses, just inside the northern tip of Manhattan. They had
come from the apartment of a woman who had called the 32nd
Precinct for assistance after being knifed in a domestic fight. By
the time Jones and Piagentini arrived, she wanted neither medical
help nor anyone arrested.

Walking toward their patrol car along the curved walk in
front of the building, they passed two young girls who were waiting
for their parents to take them to a restaurant on City Island for
fried shrimp, then a gypsy-cab driver waiting for his wife, then
two men idling against the fender of a light-blue Mustang. It was
fifty-nine degrees with no moon. The two men slipped off the fender
and fell in behind the patrolmen. Padding silently in sneakers, they
caught up quickly until, three feet behind, they reached into their
jackets and pulled guns.

Jones fell flat on his face from the first shots. He no longer
moved. Piagentini crumpled to his knees, but even as the two men
stood over him firing, he tried to rise. "Don't kill me! Please don't
kill me!" he screamed. They fired away until finally Piagentini
stopped pleading and fell on his face. It had taken ten bullets.

The men knelt and took each patrolman's service .38. Kicking
Piagentini over onto his back, they fired two more bullets into his
chest from his own revolver. Holding guns in both hands now, the
men jogged toward the back of the apartment house, where a long
hill led to higher ground overlooking the river.

The first patrol cars arrived moments later. Jones was dead.
Piagentini, despite having taken twelve bullets from three different
guns—two .45s and a .38—was still moaning. As a patrol car raced
toward Harlem Hospital, he died in the back seat, his head in the

lap of a patrolman with whom he had walked out of the 32nd Precinct at four o'clock to begin the evening shift.

While Seedman was airborne from Tel Aviv the following Monday afternoon, a neatly typed special-delivery letter arrived at WLIB.

MAY 21, 1971

ALL POWER TO THE PEOPLE.

    REVOLUTIONARY JUSTICE HAS BEEN METED OUT AGAIN BY RIGHTEOUS BROTHERS OF THE BLACK LIBERATION ARMY WITH THE DEATH OF TWO GESTAPO PIGS GUNNED DOWN AS SO MANY OF OUR BROTHERS HAVE BEEN GUN DOWN IN THE PAST. BUT THIS TIME NO RACIST CLASS JURY WILL ACQUITE THEM. REVOLUTIONARY JUSTICE IS OURS! . . .

ALL POWER TO THE PEOPLE
REVOLUTIONARY JUSTICE

The morning after the arrival of that letter, Seedman and Deputy Chief Sy Silver drove to Unity Methodist Church in the Morrisania section of the Bronx for the funeral of Waverly Jones. Along with five thousand members of his own force, the tiny church on a trashstrewn street was ringed with policemen from many states. The Commissioner, looking pale and uncomfortable, seemed surprised but relieved to see Seedman.

"I thought you were still in Israel," he said as they waited to enter the church.

"Got back last night."

"I guess you'll be briefed after the funeral."

"I'm already briefed," said Seedman. Having read in the morning *Times* that the Commissioner expected the cases to be broken within "days," Seedman wondered if Murphy knew of a lead that he did not. But Murphy volunteered nothing and Seedman did not ask.

That evening, after spending the day with the investigation teams uptown in the 24th and 32nd Precincts, Seedman stopped by his office at headquarters to see what paperwork had accumulated since he left for Israel nearly two weeks earlier. On top of the pile he found a note, dated that afternoon, from the Commissioner:

Dear Al,

I've always known you'd make a great Chief of Detectives and that you'll prove it to me by solving the 32nd Precinct case within the next forty-eight (48) hours so that you can go on being Chief of Detectives. Right on!

Sincerely,
Patrick V. Murphy

"I'd known Pat Murphy for quite a few years at that point," says Seedman. "In all that time I'd never known him to joke about anything and I didn't consider this memo to be his first. Nor did I consider it a threat. To my mind, it was a prayer.

"Murphy had come to the Department to root out corruption, but how could he do that if his men rode the streets in fear of being gunned down at any moment? Survival took precedence over graft. Now he was praying, via this memo, that all this ugly business would go away."

On this Tuesday evening, four days after the murder of Jones and Piagentini, a task force of eighty detectives under Inspector Ed Jenkins still had little to work with but a few witnesses. The teen-age girls who had been waiting for their parents to take them out for fried shrimps had dashed into the lobby as soon as the firing started. They had not seen the killers from closer than thirty feet. The gypsy-cab driver waiting for his wife had been closer, but he had ducked behind his cab when the gunfire started. By the time he looked up the killers were gone.

One potentially key witness had not even seen the shooting. He was Clarence Lee, a seventeen-year-old who had come from Brooklyn to visit friends in the project. He had been walking between two of the buildings when he heard the shots go off, but he had assumed that they were "ladyfingers," a string of firecrackers with interbraided fuses which go off in rapid succession. Then he saw the two men coming around the corner, jogging calmly with guns in hand. Terrified, Clarence Lee lay down behind two trash cans. As the taller of the two men came by, he stopped and looked down. "Be cool, brother," he said. "We don't want you."

Just in case they changed their minds, Clarence had remained behind the trash cans as the men jogged up the hill behind Colonial Park Houses, slipping the guns under their jackets as they went.

They had the service revolvers of Jones and Piagentini as well as their own guns.

In the Riverside Drive case the machine-gunning had taken place in a lonely spot where Curry and Binetti themselves were the only witnesses. Curry was in no shape to remember anything. Binetti thought he might recognize the men in the car, though he was not certain. All Captain Dick Nicastro's Special Squad had in the way of a solid lead were the two license plate packets. But since they had been stolen, plates 8373 YR could not be traced to the Mustang the patrolmen had caught up with at 106th Street. In fact the legal plates had probably been bolted back onto the car within an hour after the shooting. It was hopeless to look for the Mustang among the thousands in the city.

A welter of prints came up from the newspapers used to wrap the plates. Most were "elimination prints," belonging to people who had opened the packets. Some were "P/Vs," or prints of partial value. But working on the center of the front pages, where a reader's fingers normally don't touch, the lab men picked up two full clear prints from one copy and a single print from the other which they could not yet identify.

"I expected the people who did this job to show up again soon," says Seedman, "if only because they could not resist rattling away with that machine gun again. For people who love to shoot guns, that is the ultimate trip. As easy as it is to get handguns in the city, machine guns are scarce. The public can't buy them, so they must be stolen from military armories or direct from the factory."

On June 4, eleven days after the lab had brought up the prints from the *New York Posts*, the FBI informed Seedman that the set of two prints belonged to Richard Moore, who had jumped $100,000 bail in the "Panther 21" case. The single print belonged to Eddie Josephs, a Panther who had jumped $25,000 bail in the same case.

Seedman was startled to hear about the "hit" on Richard Moore. From all reports within the Panther Party, he had jumped to Algeria to be with the Eldridge Cleaver faction of the party. On May 12, exactly a week before the attack on Curry and Binetti, the *New York Times* had published a letter from Moore on the Op-Ed page. Moore had defended his bail jump by claiming he was facing not justice but a "Fascist Farce of a Trial . . . presided over by the Evil Likes of John Murtaugh."

"Moore's prints on that *New York Post* did not prove he'd done the job on Curry and Binetti," says Seedman. "At least, not directly. But even if the BLA hired him only for his writing talents, he was one smart cookie. By sending off that article to the *Times* with an Algerian postmark the week before the ambush, he was throwing us a curve at the right moment. We thought he was still there. Besides, the living was good in Algeria. The 'revolutionary' government in that country not only furnished the Cleaver faction of the Panthers with a hilltop villa, it gave them a living allowance from the public treasury, just like a royal family. Who'd expect Moore to come back home from a deal like that?"

Visiting the Curry-Binetti Case headquarters that Friday when the print identifications came in, Seedman noticed that Nicastro's usually crisp features had gone gray and haggard. He had been working sixteen hours a day on the case for two weeks now. Since coming home from Israel, Seedman himself had worked no less.

"If you're going to have a goddam heart attack," he told Nicastro, "you may as well have it with me on the golf course."

Driving to the course next morning, Seedman was glad they were getting an early start. It was already eighty degrees, far hotter than normal for early June, and by noon it would be a real cooker. Maybe just what they needed was to sweat off two weeks of accumulated tensions. They were walking to the tee after breakfast in the clubhouse when Seedman stopped at the door.

"I'll feel better if you give the office a call before we tee off," he said, even though he had already spoken to the duty detective at 6:45 who said all was quiet. "Just so we'll know nothing came in during the night." During those hours before dawn when the rest of the city slept, the nether world got rolling. Up in Harlem, in fact, detectives normally picked up more information between 2 A.M. and dawn than all other hours combined.

Suddenly Seedman noticed Nicastro in the phone booth start scribbling notes. He waved Seedman over excitedly.

"You're not going to believe this, Chief," he said. "Your man just got word that four guys were picked up this morning trying to take an after-hours club in the Forty-eighth in the Bronx. They came calling with a whole arsenal. Including a machine gun."

"Names?"

"Augustus Qualls, Irving Lee Mason, *and*"—Nicastro's mobile Italian face was triumphant—"Richard Moore and Eddie Josephs."

Back in street clothes, the two officers walked into the 48th squad office just forty-five minutes later. The atmosphere was less than electric. The duty detectives knew ballistics would routinely check the confiscated machine gun to see if it had fired the sixteen rounds into Curry and Binetti. But they did *not* know two of their prisoners had left fingerprints on the *New York Post* wrapped around the license plates. Seedman had ordered that only a few detectives specializing in tracking Black Panthers be furnished with that information. He had wanted Moore and Josephs to luxuriate in the belief they had gotten away clean. Otherwise, they would flee the city, and if they got to Algiers, they would never come back. Now they had muffed the chance and saved Seedman's Panther specialists the trouble of tracking them down.

That morning at 5:15, as the story developed, a cabbie at the end of his ten-hour shift was speeding up a bombed-out-looking stretch of Park Avenue toward the taxi "barn," when he noticed four men stalking up the steps of what appeared to be a dumpy social club at 171st Street. He did not need to slow down to see that they were bristling with firearms. Four blocks away, at the intersection of Third Avenue and Claremont Parkway, the cabbie flagged a patrol cruiser.

"I just saw four guys going into a joint at 171st Street on Park," he said. "They looked like they were gonna stock up a gun store—wholesale." He sped on.

Since the location was just out of their own sector, the patrolmen radioed their sergeant for instructions. Sergeant Wills, an old-timer, knew the Triple O Social Club as a spot with a rugged clientele, especially at 5:15 on a Saturday morning. Wills had seen men shamble out of the place who looked as if they could bite through a pistol barrel as easily as a soggy French fry. Anyone planning to induce those customers to submit to a holdup was right to carry along an arsenal. Now Wills ordered all available units to 171st and Park, including any who could make it from adjoining precincts.

Meanwhile, inside the Triple O, Moore, Josephs, and Qualls had lined up the fourteen male and twelve female patrons against the wall opposite the bar while Mason stood guard on the steps outside.

"Everybody strip off your duds!" hollered Moore. Even though automatic weapons were being pointed at them, several of the women had giggled as they wriggled out of tight-fitting slacks.

"I'm gonna blow some ass away unless you hurry up," said Moore. "Everyone toss the stuff right here in the middle of the floor."

As the clothes had piled up, Qualls riffled through them, throwing valuables on a card table. In one pair of slacks he found a replica of a NYPD patrolman's shield.

"What's this?" Moore said quietly, twirling the owner of the slacks around.

"Hey, brother, I—"

Moore rapped him across the face. The man fell to the floor, nose and mouth streaming blood. "I was saying, brother," he said blearily, "I don't work for the Man. But this little badge comes in handy sometimes."

"Lucky thing you ain't a cop," said Moore. "You'd be iced right now if I thought you was."

Outside, Mason was peering up and down the avenue. Quiet as it was, he was getting nervous. Suddenly, a shot rang out from inside. He rushed up the stairs, wondering what went wrong.

"Cool it," said Moore. "We were only telling them to speed it up. These cats just don't want to strip fast enough."

Mason tarried a moment on his way back out, noticing the backsides of some of the female patrons, stripped to panties except for those who had not worn any undergarments.

"Quit staring at ass and get the fuck out where you supposed to be," said Qualls.

Mason had trotted out the door and taken three steps when he saw patrol cars at each end of the block with cops behind the cars, their guns trained on him. Frozen for a moment, he watched more patrol cars pull up in silence. He had never seen so many at once. How did they know? Didn't they use sirens? Mason scampered back into the Triple O.

"The pigs have got us surrounded!"

Moore, Josephs, and Qualls hardly seemed flustered.

"Everyone get their clothes back on, quick!" ordered Moore. The patrons had knelt to pick out their things from the pile on the floor. As they dressed the four robbers unbuttoned their own shirts so they would also look hastily dressed. The last thing they did was hide their weapons under the tables and behind the jukebox.

"Okay, we're gonna march out with hands up, together," said Moore. "Anyone points the finger at us, we'll see to it you get mashed."

In the littered avenue below, a total of thirty-nine slightly baffled officers from three precincts watched the column of half-dressed blacks march slowly down the stairs to the sidewalk, their hands up.

Cops with shotguns stormed past them up the stairs and into the Triple O. Except for a mess of leftover clothing, a card table piled with valuables, and the guns, it was empty.

"Okay, where are the holdup guys?" shouted the cops. Everyone shrugged.

"Come on, who is it?" asked the cops.

"Maybe they got away out back," one girl volunteered.

"We had the back covered," said the cops. "Besides, it doesn't even have a back way out. Now, if nobody is going to help us out with this goddam problem, then we'll just lock *everyone* up."

"It was him," said one of the group, pointing to a half-dressed man beside him.

"No, sir, it was *him*," that man said, pointing to the next one in line, the one with the bloody face.

"Fuck off, man," he shot back. "You think I hit my own face?"

Sergeant Wills could see this was not a crowd of police boosters, but he could also see that under the glaze of booze and drugs in many of their eyes, they were scared. He ordered the patrolmen to take them aside one by one and ask confidentially who the robbers were. Mason, Qualls, Moore, and Josephs were filtered out.

Now, at 9:15, as the prisoners were being interrogated at the 48th Precinct, Seedman and Nicastro looked over the captured weapons laid out on the squad commander's desk. The cops at the Triple O had found a 20-gauge shotgun and a .357-magnum revolver under one table, a second shotgun under another, a 9-mm. long-barrel gun behind the beer chiller, and behind the jukebox a .45-caliber Colt automatic and the .45-caliber submachine gun.

These last two were the ones that counted. Seedman hoped and even expected that Ballistics would identify the submachine gun as the one that had ripped off thirty-three rounds at Curry and Binetti on Riverside Drive. But he hoped even more devoutly that the Colt .45 had been one of the guns used to take down Jones and Piagentini. That would tie Moore and Josephs into both cases.

Seedman went around to look at the four prisoners, isolated, handcuffed, and closely guarded in separate rooms during the interrogations. Mason and Qualls were busy explaining away their part in the attempted robbery at the Triple O that morning. They kept repeating that killing cops was not their "bag." But Moore and Josephs sat in taut and angry silence, explaining nothing, staring coldly at any detective who addressed them, though the men in the squad room were pleased to see Moore begin to shift in his chair and look away from Seedman's flat gaze.

At first Irving Lee Mason claimed that his arrest had been a mistake. "I was out taking a walk when I came upon these chicks, standing around half-dressed. I moved in a little closer to see what it was about, and all of a sudden they were pointing at me and I was being frisked. . . ." Mason looked up sunnily at the detectives.

"Do yourself a favor. Don't tell us you were taking a walk at 171st and Park Avenue at five A.M. I own a seventy-five-pound German shepherd that would be afraid to do that."

"You got a point," Mason said. Then he explained that at 7:30 that evening he had been eating pizza at a standup counter at 148th Street and Broadway when Josephs, whom he knew as Jamal, had tapped him on the shoulder. They had met a year earlier at the Harlem Black Panther office. When Jamal had told Mason he needed his help that night, Mason had begged off. But Jamal had taken him by the arm and asked him how his wife and child were. Mason got the message.

At 2:30 the next morning, he was picked up in a maroon Buick by a man called Dharuba. Because of the "Panther 21" publicity, Mason knew that Dharuba's original name was Richard Moore. Jamal and a man he did not know were in back. They drove unhurriedly until they came to Park and 171st, where they observed the Triple O and chatted until 4:30. Mason swore that in all that time, the subject of the cop shootings never arose.

Augustus Qualls told the detectives that on Wednesday night he had been walking along Trinity Avenue at 163rd Street in the Bronx when Moore pulled alongside him in the maroon Buick. Though Qualls had not seen him for two years, he had no trouble recognizing Moore: they had gone to school together in Harlem. Moore introduced Eddie Josephs and asked if Qualls knew of a numbers runner or dope peddler they might "rip off." Qualls suggested they try the corner of 115th Street and Lenox Avenue, where an

Argentinian heroin dealer did high-volume business. The man was on station, probably carrying at least $1000 in his shabby clothes. Moore felt the spot was too exposed, however. For the rest of Wednesday night and Thursday as well, they drove around, looking for a suitable place to "rip off," finally settling on the Triple O. But Moore wanted to wait until early Saturday morning, when the take would be higher.

"Moore prepared for this job as craftily as he planted the *Times* article from Algeria," says Seedman. "First, he brought along a professional stickup man—Qualls. He resisted an easy shot at the Argentine dope peddler, undoubtedly because he sensed that dope attracts plainclothesmen, especially on a crowded corner like 115th and Lenox. On the other hand, the Triple O seemed just right. It was a private social club. It was a godforsaken stretch of Park Avenue and by five A.M. everyone planning to drop in already had. Best of all, with all its gambling and cocaine-snorting, neither clientele nor management would be anxious to call the police. You could rob twenty-five people of everything, even their clothing, without risking a single call to 911. These were important considerations for men like Moore and Josephs. Apart from possible involvement with the cop shootings, they were already bail-jumpers. If they got caught this time, they would stay in the can.

"Incidentally, for a man who wrote feelingly about the way police oppressed his people, Richard Moore was no slouch himself. He picked black victims in a black-owned club, he trained more firepower on them than I've ever heard of being used in a robbery, he smacked one of them as hard as if he were a genuine honky. None of this was in the BLA platform, but it was good strategy. The unforeseeable catch was that cabbie flying for the barn.

"Qualls was a heroin addict who began to sweat and twitch early that Saturday morning. We arranged for him to get a methadone fix, but it was hardly the price of making him talk. He and Mason wouldn't shut up. For two men who claimed they'd heard nothing about cops being shot while they sat in that Buick, they seemed remarkably anxious to dissociate themselves from Moore and Josephs. Not that they told the truth—that crept into their stories only where it was convenient—but I didn't care. All that counted was the Ballistics report on those two guns.

"As it turned out, Ballistics had trouble deciding how to test the machine gun. Normally they fire comparison bullets from a hand-gun into a cotton-stuffed box, then microscopically compare the markings on the bullet caused by its journey through the barrel with those on the crime bullets. But a machine gun heats up as it rattles away, causing different stresses in the barrel; moreover, ripping off thirty-three rounds, to duplicate the attack on Riverside Drive, would have torn apart the cotton-stuffed box. They solved the problem by going down to the swimming pool in the Academy basement, hold-ing their ears, and firing thirty-three rounds into the deep end.

"Within an hour their report was in: we had the weapon used on Binetti and Curry. But we had batted only .500. The Colt .45 was not the one fired into the backs of Jones and Piagentini. Had Moore and Josephs used different guns to do that job? Or had it been done by others? On Sunday afternoon, we arranged a lineup to find out.

"We were counting most on Clarence Lee, the seventeen-year-old who had actually been spoken to by one of the killers. Five days after the shooting we had designated Clarence a material witness, but despite our efforts to keep it quiet, the press picked up the news and we were forced to put him in protective custody. If the men he had seen didn't hesitate to kill a black cop, they surely wouldn't draw the line at Clarence. We moved him into a suite in the City Squire Motor Inn on Seventh Avenue above Times Square. As long as he could order steak for breakfast, he loved it. Like every other protective custody deal, this one was a drain on the taxpayer, a drain on detective manpower, a drain on everyone's goddam nerves. It was also useless. At the lineup Clarence Lee could not pick out Qualls, Mason, Moore, or Josephs. Neither could any of the other witnesses. For the time being, we'd have to assume the killers of the patrolmen in Harlem were still at large.

"In the Riverside Drive case, we had to wait until the two patrolmen recovered enough to look over a line up containing Moore and Josephs. As it was, Binetti's knees were shattered so we had to bring him over from the hospital in a wheel chair. He studied the line up for a long time. Finally, he shook his head. Never having gotten a good look at the men in the Mustang, he just couldn't be sure. His partner Curry was still too badly shot up to even try. Luckily, we had that machine gun. Without identifications, we could not place it in either man's hands that night, but it was comforting to know that even if Moore and Josephs were never convicted of that crime they would still have to answer for armed robbery at the Triple O."

In the days that followed, teams of detectives, many with extensive contacts in the black militant community, combed Harlem and the Bronx to find out what Moore and Josephs had been doing in the months since they jumped bail in the "Panther 21" case. The more the detectives searched, the more Seedman's intuition about the Black Panther Party ever since the Fleck and Dockery shotgunnings was confirmed. The Panthers, relatively open to all comers in the late 1960s, were no longer the focus of black militant action. Interminable court battles, publicity, and internal bickering had worn down the party's cutting edge. The blacks who meant business had split off in tight little knots that the undercover men could not penetrate. The specialists who kept detailed dossiers on Black Panther politics had never even heard of the Black Liberation Army until it was too late. Even now, three weeks after the shootings, eighty detectives from the Special Squad plus a swarm of FBI agents could learn next to nothing about the BLA, Moore, or Josephs.

Then on the afternoon of June 13, one week after the Triple O affair, the "hot line" number manned by a bilingual detective at the 32nd Precinct to take citizens' tips on the cases received its forty-seventh call of the day.

"I want to tell you something very important," said a female voice.

"We're listening, ma'am."

"Those four men you arrested in the holdup last week, you can believe them when they say they had nothing to do with those police killings in the housing project. I know. That was a Friday night. I saw them at my girlfriend's house all night."

"What's your girlfriend's name?"

"Pauline Josephs. She lives at 757 Beck Street in the Bronx. I think she's Eddie Josephs' girlfriend. It's just a coincidence they have the same name. . . ." The woman hesitated. "She's a good girl. I know she'd call herself, except that she's too scared." She hung up.

Seedman had just stopped by the 32nd Precinct, as he did at least twice a day, when the call came in. As usual with a "hot line" number, most of the calls had been from kooks, drunks, and lonely people. But this forty-seventh call interested Seedman. He played it back on the recorder which automatically taped all calls. The voice was small and high, with a West Indian lilt. Despite her disavowal, it seemed plain to him that the caller must have been Pauline Josephs herself.

At the ground-floor-front apartment at 757 Beck Street, a slender black woman as tiny as her voice answered the door. Told that her voice had been recorded, she did not try to keep up the charade.

"I only wanted to help them, especially Eddie," she said. "I have a child by him."

Pauline Josephs agreed to go to the 24th Precinct for questioning, where she willingly gave the detectives the following information: She was twenty-three years old and a native of the Virgin Islands. She worked as a doctor's receptionist at Prospect Hospital in the Bronx. Eddie Josephs, who called her his "revolutionary wife," had disappeared without word at the end of January as the "Panther 21" trial was about to begin. In the spring, she went home to the Virgin Islands to deposit their daughter, Brenda, with an aunt. Then she hurried back to her job in New York.

On May 13, the day all the Panthers were acquitted, Eddie Josephs had suddenly appeared at her door. She screamed and yelped in joy.

"I knocked you up, didn't I?" he said, patting her stomach.

"How did you know?" she said. She had never told him she was pregnant. The baby wasn't even showing when he disappeared.

"I have ways of knowing things," he said, but he would not say much about where he had been.

Pauline now calmly rattled off an eye-popping list of top Panthers who had passed through her airy apartment on Beck Street. They included Richard Moore, whose girlfriend, Patricia Greene, came on weekends, Irving Lee Mason and his wife, Ila. Just a week earlier, Mason had been telling detectives how he hadn't seen Moore for months because he was turned off by Panther tactics. According to Pauline they were *all* a close-knit "revolutionary family." Other members included Panthers Andrew Jackson, Michael Dennis Hill, Frank Fields, JoAnne Chesimard, and Robert Vickers. After the "Panther 21" trial, most of them had disappeared.

According to Pauline, any fugitive black militant wanting to flee the country could get help from JoAnne Chesimard or Andrew Jackson who were local contacts for an underground railroad. They would fix up the fugitive with phony identification and put him on a train to Montreal, where the Quebec Liberation Front would supply a fake passport for the flight to Algiers via Paris. For anyone who did not want to flee the country, Chesimard or Jackson offered placement in many out-of-the-way sympathetic communities in the United States.

About ten o'clock on the night of May 19, Pauline recalled, she had been washing dinner dishes when in walked Moore, Frank Fields, and Michael D. Hill, all of whom "related" to her place.

"We need to clean out a car real fast," said Moore. "Give us a hand."

While the others had switched license plates on a blue Mustang, Pauline knelt in front and back to pick up dozens of shell casings, keeping her hands away from the machine gun sticking out from under the seat. Eddie Josephs was sulking inside the house. He was mad at Moore, supposedly his buddy, for not taking him along. Later, they all watched the eleven-o'clock news reports on the shootings.

"You handled the grease [submachine gun] real good," Moore said to Hill, "but not good enough to kill them."

"Maybe we should make a run down to the hospital and finish off those pigs," said Eddie Josephs, brightening up.

"It says pigs from other precincts are pouring in to give blood," Moore said. "The place'll be guarded too tight. Maybe they'll die anyway."

Two nights later, according to Pauline, she and Eddie, Moore, Andrew Jackson, and the Masons were relaxing after a dinner of pepper steaks washed down wtih Boone's Farm Apple Wine when Irving Mason rushed in from the next room where he had been watching television.

"Hey, man," he said, "they had a bulletin on the tube. Two brothers just offed two pigs in Harlem."

As they had done two nights earlier, they gathered around the set for the eleven-o'clock news. While the camera swung over the bloodied sidewalk where Jones and Piagentini had fallen, the men tried to think who might have done it. Whoever the attackers were,

they were acutely aware, they had finished off the job with handguns, while they themselves had failed with the "grease."

"Find the two bloods that iced those pigs," Eddie Josephs told
Mason. "You can get around better than us right now."

"I'll try," he answered. But despite his efforts and much dis-
cussion of the shooting in the house, Pauline Josephs claimed they
never did find out who did it.

"The first afternoon we talked to Pauline," Seedman says, "it
was hard to know exactly how much of the truth she was telling.
Quite a bit, obviously, was intended to establish her credibility so
we would believe her when she insisted that her 'revolutionary
husband' had not been part of the Riverside Drive shootings. She
managed his alibi very delicately. Sensing it would be a bit much
to try to convince us that Eddie would not kill cops, she claimed
only that he had been mad at not being invited along by Moore.
Legally speaking, of course, it didn't matter if he frothed at the
mouth, as long as he didn't do it and didn't know it was going to
happen. By the same token, she was careful to say that he had not
participated in cleaning the Mustang or changing the plates. This
Pauline seemed to have an awfully good sense of what would fry
Eddie in a courtroom. It wasn't intentions, it was participation.

"We needed time with Pauline Josephs. Even if only a fraction
of what she told us that first afternoon was true, she was too valuable to be left in the street. Like Clarence Lee, we had her designated a material witness. To make her captivity as pleasant as possible, we put her up in an expensive suite in the Commodore Hotel
where the room service was quick. We gave her three detectives,
one a woman, for company."

Late that same night Seedman sent a task force of well-armed
detectives under Deputy Inspector Bill Connelie to 757 Beck Street
with a search warrant. Pauline insisted that ever since Moore and
Josephs had been "busted," everyone else had stayed clear of the
premises. The detectives watched the brownstone for several hours,
but by 2 A.M., when no lights had gone on, they entered and
searched the apartment. In a trash can they found four traffic sum-
monses for a blue Mustang. The owner turned out to be Paul
Stuart, a Panther who later admitted having lent his car to Moore
the night Curry and Binetti were shot.

In a vacant apartment on the top floor the detectives found two rooms stocked with medical supplies and a third room in which they found a set of stolen license plates and thirty-six wine bottles fitted out as Molotov cocktails and neatly lined up in rows.

"Pauline had no trouble identifying photos of more than a dozen hard-line Panthers who had passed through her apartment," says Seedman, "but oddly enough, she was in no way militant herself. She was happy enough to hold down her receptionist's job, play hostess to the others, and keep her 'revolutionary husband' satisfied.

"We also heard an intriguing tale from a Bronx hooker named Ima Joe, who came forward at the behest of her current boyfriend. He thought the information was too hot to sit on. Our own reaction was to be more dubious. But as with Pauline Josephs, Ima Joe knew what she was talking about. In time, we'd learn that she knew even more than she talked about."

One night four years ago, Ima Joe explained, on her day off from her job as a live-in maid for a wealthy Queens family, she had dropped in at the Sports Center Bar on Seventh Avenue at 123rd Street where she met a tall, lean black man named Mike Williams. Though he was only seventeen and she was twenty-five, they became lovers. She had a child by him who was now being cared for, along with her three other children, by Ima Joe's mother in Moxley, Georgia.

Ima Joe never found out what Mike Williams did for a living, but it didn't matter. They got along beautifully. The only thorn in the relationship was Mike's half-brother, Reggie Williams.

"I met a lot of mean men in my life—you wouldn't believe some of the things they think they have the right to do to me for a few lousy bucks—but I never met a man who scared me like Reggie," said Ima Joe. "He was always tensed up like he was ready to smack somebody's head off. I knew he would do it too, but Mike thought he was great. Reggie was older and Mike looked up to him. If Mike ever did get in trouble, it was gonna be on account of that Reggie."

Ima Joe had been fast asleep early one Saturday morning when she suddenly awoke to find Mike running around the apartment, slamming drawers and digging in the closet.

"What chu doin', honey?" she had asked blearily.

"Baby, I've got to go—Reggie just shot some cops." And he was out the door with a suitcase. Ima Joe, who had popped a few "downs" before going to bed, sunk back into instant sleep.

"It was hard to evaluate what Ima Joe told us," says Seedman.

"I wouldn't say she was full of crap, but on the other hand, her story was a little too vague. How could she go with this Mike for three years and not have any idea where he hung out, what he did with his days, who his other friends were, where he and Reggie might be hiding now? She didn't even have a photo of him. I was sure she was holding back details. Yet why come to us in the first place if she didn't want to tell the story? I suspected she might be using us to get herself fixed up with methadone at Bellevue Hospital. So after telling her to get in touch with us if she heard from Mike or Reggie again, we put Ima Joe on the back burner.

"Every day of that summer I had as many as thirty detectives combing the city for other leads to the murders of Jones and Piagentini. In the process they solved over two dozen other open cases, including three murders. They seized thirty-seven guns, several pounds of various drugs and the pushers who went with them. All that was great but it was not our main concern. I felt we were working against a fairly specific deadline. If the killers decided that despite our best efforts we were never going to get close to them, they would feel awfully chesty. Their thoughts were bound to turn then to how much fun it would be to kill cops again. Once they decided to 'move,' all our precautions would not help. If a citizen wants to take down two of the twenty thousand uniform cops who ride and walk the city streets, there is no way to stop him."

On Sunday afternoon, August 29, Seedman took Henny to a barbecue in the Long Island backyard of his old friend Milton Baum. Seedman needed to unwind. For the last three months he had been working seven days a week on several important cases. The public had been looking to the detectives he led for solutions that simply had not been forthcoming. The fact that so little was needed to break each case only added to his impatience. Seedman was stretched out in a chaise longue with a steak and a stiff shot of Scotch when Milt Baum called him to the phone. "Long distance," Milt added, handing him the receiver.

That was odd. As always, he had told the office where he could be reached—but long distance?

Seedman found himself talking to a detective chief in San Francisco.

"You're Chief of Detectives in New York, is that right, sir?"

"Right."

"Just want to be sure who I'm giving this information to. We had a little incident here just after midnight."

The San Francisco chief told Seedman that one of his sergeants, George Kowalski, had stopped for a red light when a 1965 black Oldsmobile swung around the corner and stopped broadside to the patrol car. Glancing over, Kowalski had been astonished to see one of the two blacks in the front seat pointing a machine gun at him. Kowalski had ducked. But instead of a blast of gunfire, he had heard nothing but a rapid series of clicks. The gun had misfired. As Kowalski surfaced with revolver in hand, the Olds had sped off.

Kowalski had pursued the Olds, at the same time radioing for help and giving a brief description of the car. Now the passenger in the Olds was firing back at him with a handgun. Kowalski roared across a set of railroad tracks—and his right rear tire blew out. Still, he had continued the chase at hobbling speed.

Seconds later he had heard a terrific crash. Bumping around a corner, he saw that the Olds had bounced off a light-blue Ford with four startled riders inside. Two cops in a patrol car answering Kowalski's call had already headed off the Olds from the opposite direction. Now they jabbed shotguns into the windows of the car, where the two black men sat, too dazed to react. Kowalski stuck his gun into the Olds too. Seeing the machine gun on the floor, he could hardly comprehend that just moments earlier he had been looking down its nasty green barrel, clicking away out of a calm night.

"I believe your people sent out an alarm on the service revolvers taken off the dead officers up there in Harlem," the San Francisco detective chief was saying to Seedman.

"Yeah?"

"Well, we took three guns out of that Olds. The machine gun and two revolvers, a .38 and a .45. This .38 is a Smith and Wesson, serial number CI-177598—"

"That belonged to Waverly Jones."

"That's why I figured you wouldn't mind being bothered on Sunday."

Seedman savored his cigar and the good feelings that were beginning to work inside him.

"Are you there, Chief?"

"I'm here."

"We're not sure of the IDs on the two guys yet. They gave their names as Tony Bottom and Harold Stevens, but the one who says he's Bottom had a driver's license in the name of James Williams. We're checking it all out. By the way, both guys claim they're Panthers."

"Can I send two men out in the morning who know our case inside out?"

"We'd be delighted to have them," said the San Francisco chief.

"One other thing. Can we keep this business about the Jones gun quiet for now?"

"We won't say a word on this end. Anything we can do for you helps us as well now."

"How's that?"

"A couple of these people came into one of our station houses this afternoon. They opened up with automatic weapons and killed a sergeant. The bastards got away."

In the morning Seedman sent William Seffers and William Butler to San Francisco, a black-and-white detective team that had worked from the start on the shootings of Jones and Piagentini. Seffers was so eager to talk to the Panthers that he left without so much as a change of underwear. While the detectives were in the air, San Francisco police called to say that the two men had been identified by an FBI fingerprint check. Tony Bottom was indeed Anthony Leonard Bottom, twenty years old, but Harold Stevens was actually Albert James Washington, Jr., a thirty-year-old New Yorker. In the following days New York and San Francisco police units and the FBI worked together to draw full portraits of the two men who had captured themselves when so many hard-working detectives could not.

Bottom, born in San Jose, California, had been a bright child who caused his divorced mother more trouble than she could handle. Judged to be "beyond parental control," he had been sent to a string of youth farms and by his late teens had been arrested for grand theft, possession of Molotov cocktails, auto theft, burglary —all nonviolent crimes. In recent years he had drifted from coast to coast, with occasional stopovers at Salt Lake City, where his step-father took a new job as a computer programmer. In the fall Bottom had begun working as a social-service aide for the State of California, similar to the job, Seedman noted, that Ron Hill and Bill Hampton had been doing in Brooklyn when they shotgunned officers Fleck and Dockery in 1968. On May 21, the day Jones and

Piagentini died, Bottom was dismissed from his job *in absentia* for excessive unexcused absenteeism. He had not reported to work in California for sixteen straight days.

Albert Washington was ruggedly built with a palpable air of violence about him. He had been in and out of mental hospitals on both coasts, and in 1967 was sentenced to twelve to twenty years for bank robbery in Denver. In the brief time he actually served, he wrote articles for the Panther newspaper, signing one "A. Washington, a Mad Man." His mother was a clerk for the NYPD. When he was a child, his family had lived in the brand-new Colonial Park Houses in Harlem where Jones and Piagentini died.

"Here in New York we had nothing on Bottom," says Seedman. "But two months before, Washington had been one of three men arrested for the June eighteenth holdup of a Beneficial Finance loan office in Harlem, not far from where the killings took place. His partners were Ronald Carter, a Panther, and Robert Jackson, brother of the Andrew Jackson, who frequented 757 Beck Street and worked the underground railroad with JoAnne Chesimard. The bank's office manager had gotten a look at the getaway car and gave us a partial plate number. On June twenty-ninth a Tactical Patrol Force car on routine assignment spotted the car, which belonged to Carter's common-law wife, not far from the Colonial Houses.

"Washington gave his name to the New York police as Lawrence Williams. Lacking any other identification, the processing officers bought it. Although it took Washington five weeks to make his $5000 bail, not until right after he was released did we discover, by a belated fingerprint check, who Williams actually was. As you can imagine, he was gone like a jackrabbit.

"You have to be amazed at the balls of it all. The guy kills cops. After lying back three weeks, he sticks up a loan office in the same neighborhood, probably to make his fare for a trip to California. When he is caught, he blithely lies about who he is. While detectives eat up the streets looking for any hint of our culprits, Washington sits in the Tombs, waiting for his friends to rustle up bail money, probably by more stickups. Then, five weeks later, he checks out and heads for the Coast. Before the end of the month he is pointing the 'grease' at Officer Kowalski. It was exactly what I feared would happen when these guys started feeling unstoppable. Only now it was happening coast to coast.

"As soon as we got mug shots of these two, I knew who I

wanted to look at them first. I sent detectives up to her cruising turf on Westchester Avenue to pick up Ima Joe. At the Thirty-second Precinct investigation headquarters, we had laid out a square of a hundred mug shots. She pointed straight into the pack at Bottom and smiled. 'That's my Mike,' she said.

"Then she saw the shot of Washington. 'And that's that goddam Reggie.' "

Then, without prompting, Ima Joe admitted something else. Even as the detectives talked to her in June, she had been taking food to Mike and Reggie in an abandoned tenement on Simpson Street. She had done it for two weeks. One night, Reggie had grabbed her by the throat.

"You're talking to the cops, aren't you," he snarled.

"They'd love for me to talk," she said as Mike pushed Reggie away. "But if I did, they'd be here in this shithole pointing a gun in your mouth instead of me with this fucking fried chicken."

A technical team hurried to the abandoned tenement, but in the two months since Ima Joe had last been there the city had bull-dozed it down. It was now the neighborhood dump.

"If we'd followed Ima Joe a little closer," says Seedman, "we might have nailed Bottom and Washington at this place back in June. But since she came to us, we never figured she was holding back. After all, why implicate this pair and then shield them? I suppose she was a little like that spiritualist Edith Berrios whose brother, Miguel, had stuffed the girl in the box. Once this woman had taken us halfway to her brother, she found it hard to go the other half. The difference was that we had gone looking for Edith Berrios. Ima Joe had come looking for us.

"One reason I'd been anxious to keep a lid on the news of the recovery of Waverly Jones's service revolver in San Francisco was that mere possession of the gun didn't necessarily mean Bottom and Washington had to be the killers; they could have gotten the gun from others. But that loophole was closed when the FBI reported that the .45 which Washington had fired at Kowalski when his machine gun jammed was the same weapon that had killed Waverly Jones. Maybe someone might have loaned them one gun from the New York ambush. But two?

"At that point we felt confident that all we had to do was get our witnesses out to the Coast to identify these two, and our investigation into the Jones–Piagentini killings would be neatly wrapped up. We had no way of knowing that while only two men had done the shooting, the assassination party consisted of five men, methodically organized into back-up killers and look-outs, and that more than two years would pass before the last of the killers was captured.

"A week later our witnesses appeared for the lineups in San Francisco's Hall of Justice. Bottom was positively identified. Washington was not. I'd counted on Clarence Lee for that, but again he was useless. If they'd made funny faces at him from the lineup, I doubt he would have noticed. Luckily, that same week, we got confirmation of Washington's part in the ambush—from Bottom himself."

It had come out of a conversation with his cellmate which began with the usual jailhouse pleasantries.

"What are you in for, brother?" asked Bottom.

"Receiving stolen property," answered the cellmate, who had been a municipal street cleaner. "What about you?"

"Shootin' at pigs. . . ."

Bottom went on to recount, at meals and exercise breaks, how he, Washington, and "two or three other brothers" had been in the parking lot of a housing project in Harlem when they saw two cops go into one of the buildings. While the others had taken backup positions near where the car was parked, he and Washington had leaned against a Mustang at the curb where they knew the cops would pass on their way back to their patrol car. They had waited twenty minutes. Then the two cops had appeared and Bottom had said, "Okay, let's go." The black cop went down dead from the first shots in the back. The white cop kept trying to get up and begging not to be killed. They took the guns from the bodies and dashed up a hill behind the project. A half-hour later they came back by taxi to watch police swarm over the scene.

"This story was valuable because of its detail," says Seedman. "It matched what our witnesses described, right down to the words Clarence heard Bottom say as he and Washington fell in behind the patrolmen. It was also valuable because this was the first inkling we had that two or three others were involved, meaning that we still had our work cut out for us. You might think, incidentally, that the street cleaner was telling us this in hopes of getting a big reduction in sentence. But since he was only serving a maximum four-month term, he could expect to get very little out of it. He passed on the story, at some risk to himself, because it appalled him.

"The tale that Bottom told was true except for one small detail. We'd eventually learn that Bottom, not Washington, was one of the actual triggermen. It is not strange at all that treachery took place in the San Francisco jail."

Seedman had hoped that Washington, in another part of the prison, also would find a cellmate who was *simpatico,* but he sulked and kept to himself. With the cooperation of the San Francisco police, Seedman sent out a young black detective to pose as a prisoner. He was thrown in the cell with Washington, but before long the guards and nonmilitant prisoners sensed that the new inmate was being awfully friendly to a cop-killer. He found himself getting bumped off his feet in the shower room and slapped around on his way to and from meals. Worst of all, Washington ignored him. After a week the well-bruised detective was returned to New York.

"We tried hard, with FBI help, to find out where Bottom and Washington got that machine gun," says Seedman. "Like any weapon of that type, it could have been manufactured only for the Army. But this model was twenty years old; its serial numbers excised, and its point of theft lost forever. As for the .45 which Washington had fired out the window after the machine gun failed, it had been bought in Salt Lake City by a San Francisco Panther visiting Bottom's sister, a student majoring in physical education at Utah State College. Bottom had once been arrested with Washington in Salt Lake for carrying concealed guns in his car. Bottom's other passenger that day had been a slight little man named Francisco Torres. We knew him in New York as a member of the Young Lords, a militant group centered in the Bronx which was the Puerto Rican version of the Black Panthers. To round off the circle, it had been Gabriel Torres, Francisco's younger brother, who had posted bail for Albert Washington, under the name Williams, in the Beneficial Finance holdup case!"

Shortly after the Torres brothers had been connected to Bottom and Washington, three men walked into the Bank of America branch at Bernal Heights in San Francisco. The two with sawed-off shotguns held the tellers and customers at bay while the third, a handgun in his belt, emptied the cash drawers and vault of $15,123. Picking up a fourth man standing watch outside the door, they raced to a waiting Chevrolet around the corner. The entire thing had taken less than four minutes.

For a job done so quickly and professionally, it seemed surprising that the robbers ignored the surveillance cameras automatically recording the scene. Since it was becoming standard militant procedure to hold up banks to raise bail for jailed "brothers," local detectives wasted no time scanning the footage. Five witnesses confirmed what they saw. One of the robbers was little Francisco Torres.

With the pressure on in San Francisco, Seedman felt that Torres might well slip back to New York. It was still the best place in the country for a man to get lost. Under the supervision of Inspector Ed Jenkins, an exceedingly fine web was drawn across Francisco's home turf in the Bronx. Its center was the apartment of his sister, Maria Bailey, on Crotona Park North. One crisp evening in mid-October a raggedly-dressed detective spotted a tiny, wary figure look both ways and then slip into the building where Maria lived. Within the hour, Seedman gave Jenkins the order to move.

"I didn't want his task force to be so big they could hear it coming like a stampede," explains Seedman. "But I wanted it to be ready for anything. So it included six detectives with shotguns and six men from Emergency Service with tear-gas guns and gas masks. When you're hitting an apartment where the occupants are likely to react violently, it's best to maximize their sense of instant hopelessness, so that any 'macho' ideas of fighting it out just fade away. John Carroll, the lieutenant in charge of the Emergency Service half of the unit, was an expert at this kind of psychological warfare."

At 7:05 Sergeant Carroll thumped five times on the door of apartment 4C, where Torres' sister lived.

"This is the police," he said into a bullhorn. "We are here to arrest Francisco Torres for bank robbery, pursuant to a Federal warrant. We know you're in there, Francisco. We know women and children are in there also. Don't put them in danger. Open the door at once."

Sixty seconds passed. Nothing but silence from inside.

"All right," bellowed Carroll. "BLUE Shotgun Squad . . . GOLD Squad, take your rooftop stations. . . . PARK Unit, cover the windows. . . . TEAR-GAS UNIT, BREAK OUT YOUR CANISTERS, FACE MASKS IN PLACE. . . . ARE YOU READY? . . ."

It was over. The door was opened timidly by a child so small he had to reach up to turn the knob. Standing despondently in the middle of the room was Francisco, surrounded by his common-law wife, Jacqueline Tabb, her three children, and Maria Bailey and her husband, Stanley. In one bedroom they found twenty-four-year-old Gabriel Torres, Francisco's younger brother. In the bedroom closet they found a sawed-off shotgun, and in a dresser drawer, a stash of marijuana and a packet of five fresh hundred-dollar bills.

Though Crotona Park was in the 48th Precinct, Seedman, for the sake of secrecy, had Jenkins whisk off the five adults to the 25th, further south in Manhattan. Francisco was held for bank robbery, the others for harboring a fugitive and possession of the marijuana and shotgun. Linda Torres, Gabriel's legal wife, was also brought down to the squad room for questioning. Seedman's first impression of the Torres brothers was that they were so slight and lacking in the pent-up anger of black militants brought to the station house that he could almost wonder whether they were in that same rough league with Bottom and Washington. Despite their political exhortations that all "oppressed" people must stick together, it was most unusual for militant blacks and Puerto Ricans to be bonded so closely. But as Seedman read a letter found in Francisco's back pocket, he could feel himself just how close these men were. Addressed to John Holmes, one of the several aliases Francisco used, it was signed with a name often used by Albert Washington and said in part:

All Power to the People

> *Where do I start? . . . In the Red Book it says, "Where there is struggle there is sacrifice and death is a common occurrence." Well, as a soldier and Revolutionary it is my duty to fight the enemy of our people. That's what I was doing, fighting. At no time did I beg or ask for mercy even when blood flowed from my mouth and a Fascist kicked me in the ear and another put a .357 in my mouth. . . . Love for my people, a gun, a woman, clothes on my back and comrades who I loved very dearly. Now all I have is Love for my people and faith in their ability to continue to struggle until they are free.*

> *Revolution Until Victory*
> *Your Comrade in Arms*
> *Noah*

At the bottom of the letter was a note in a different hand:

Now look—Blood don't know that I'm sending this but the brother is really hurt and disspirited. . . . I think he's going to try to do some crazy shit.

T.B.

"We had kept a nice tight news clamp on the connection between this operation and the cop killings," says Seedman. "But a story this important can't be kept from the New York press for more than a few hours. About midnight John Keenan, chief of the DA's Homicide Bureau, agreed that we should conduct a lineup first thing in the morning. One of our witnesses positively identified Francisco Torres as one of the men at the Colonial housing project the night Jones and Piagentini were gunned down. With all eyes on the actual shooters, the witness had indeed not even realized that Torres had been involved. What a terrific break! Now we knew for sure, as Bottom had told the street cleaner in his San Francisco cell, he and Washington were only part of the killing party."

"The women picked up at Crotona Park posed a special challenge. After each of these jobs the men who did the shooting headed not to a bar or a whorehouse but straight to their women. It happened that way on the night Dockery and Fleck got it in 1968 and when Curry and Binetti got it in May. It might well have also happened two nights later with the killers of Jones and Piagentini. Talking to Linda Torres and Jackie Tabb didn't change my mind. But getting them to tell it was going to be a problem. We could not hold them as material witnesses, as we had Pauline Josephs, since they weren't telling us what they witnessed, if anything, on the night of the shooting. But that's what I wanted to do—hold them. Or, more precisely, I wanted them to spend a lot of time with some detectives they could learn to trust.

"The only way to do that was to persuade them they were in danger. That was not a fib. Bottom had told the street cleaner that Jones and Piagentini had been killed by a party of five. He, Washington, and the Torres brothers only made four. We had no idea who the fifth man was. But I'd bet Linda and Jackie knew. If Number Five thought they might talk, their lives were indeed in danger. Even Bottom and Washington were leery of being bailed out in San

Francisco, which could only mean that somebody tough was still at large. Shadowy as that person was, I'd figured out one fact about him by elimination. Bottom had been positively identified as one gunman. But no witness thought Washington or the Torres brothers looked at all like the other. While Bottom had had to keep shooting Piagentini as he tried to get up, this other killer dispatched Jones with his first shot. *That* was who the girls had to be afraid of.

"So in return for our not charging them with illegal gun possession and harboring of fugitives, Linda and Jackie agreed to let us guard them around the clock at a comfortable place under the wing of four of the smoothest, most personable detectives I knew: Al Dais from First District Homicide, Leonard Brown from Manhattan North Homicide, Matthew Nichols from Manhattan North Burglary, and Olga Ford from Narcotics who had done such good work with Pauline Josephs. Each of them also had the gift of gab, a talent they would need if they were going to persuade Jackie and Linda to reveal what they knew about the night of May twenty-first. Winning them over would take loads of tact and time. But the payoff, as it turned out, would make it worth waiting for."

After Torres had been identified in the lineup, Seedman called in the four detectives to give them their new jobs. That same evening, October 15, 1971, at 6:58 all the department's teletypes chattered out a thunderbolt of a message which would make the next morning's headlines. By order of the Police Commissioner, Albert Seedman was no longer commanding the Detective Bureau. His duties were to be taken over by Assistant Chief Inspector John Kinsella.

The whole affair had begun over a year before in September 1970, in the lobby of the New York Hilton, where Golda Meir was to be guest of honor at a dinner. After checking the detective contingent assigned to provide security for the Israeli Premier, Seedman stopped to chat with the new manager. He was glad to meet Seedman, who had called a meeting of all the city's hotel security directors—something no Manhattan borough chief had bothered to do before. Not long ago, Seedman had also assigned a detective detail to provide a local hotel with extra security during a jewelers' convention, when the rooms would be full of gems. Seedman had told nobody what he had done, not even the hotel's security director. In keeping with his usual habit, he trusted nobody but his own detectives. The manager thought that was admirable. He didn't trust too many people either. Now he was wondering whether Seedman would be willing to look over the Hilton's own security setup.

"As soon as I get the time," Seedman answered. "This job of running Manhattan detectives, it's the busiest I ever had."

But a month later, Seedman was appointed Director of Training. Freed of an operational command, he now had the time. He and the manager walked around the Hilton for two hours to see how security could be made tighter.

The manager was glad for Seedman's help. He called several times that fall and winter to invite him over to the Hilton for dinner, but Seedman was again caught up in work and could never make it. One day in March the manager called again.

"Come down and have dinner with us Saturday night," he said. "If you say no, I'll never bother you again."

"Can't," said Seedman. "My wife and I are already planning to go out with another couple."

"Bring them along," said the manager. "It's not like we don't have the room."

But when Seedman's party showed up, they found that the manager had been called away. They ate dinner without him, but when Seedman called for a check, the maître d' shook his head.

"You are the personal guest of the manager," he said.

Seedman understood this to be a courtesy extended by the manager, as well as a gesture of apology for not being able to join them. It was all unnecessary, but Seedman was not about to make a scene over it. He tipped the waiter, tipped the wine steward, tipped the maître d', and left with his wife and friends.

A few weeks later Murphy promoted Seedman to Chief of Detectives. The two men were meshing beautifully. Murphy had delivered what he said he would. The detective specialization plan was going off without a hitch, and Murphy understood that no one but Seedman could have accomplished this first major change in decades in the shape of the Detective Bureau without a peep from the Detectives' Endowment Association.

Murphy's other mandate, of course, was to head off the corruption specter. But here Murphy could not call his own shots. The Knapp Commission was already busy looking for dirt on its own. To justify its multi-million-dollar budget, the Commission would surely find it. At full-dress hearings in the fall Knapp hoped to put before the cameras a parade of captive cops who would confess their misdeeds before all the taxpayers.

Murphy, of course, had taken his own steps to root out the corruption that David Durk and Frank Serpico claimed had been ignored before he took over. That job was entrusted to Sidney Cooper, Chief of Inspectional Services, whose own integrity was unquestioned. Still, in a police force of thirty thousand men, it had to be conceded that Knapp might well find people to fry before Cooper got to them.

What worried Murphy more than the capture of a few patrolmen was that Knapp might find corruption in higher places. As long as lieutenants, captains, and deputy inspectors held clean, the public could still believe that corruption was curable. But who would root it out if the top itself was corrupt?

Cooper had been given three-star status to deal with that problem. He could roam all levels of the department with ease because nobody but the Chief Inspector outranked him. Cooper would have much preferred to catch one corrupt lieutenant than a dozen patrolmen or three dozen plainclothes. But as the summer wore on, and his own people began bumping into more and more Knapp investigators, each side with its own hidden tape recorders, cameras and marked bills, Cooper was having a hard time finding corrupt superior officers. Maybe they were not around. Or were they just too clever to be nabbed?

One hot day, Seedman received a sealed memo from the Commissioner, a copy of which had also been sent to Mike Codd, the Chief Inspector. It was titled "Corruption within the Detective Bureau."

Dear Al:

I'm very concerned that the Detective Bureau will be hard hit within the next month or two not only with reference to Knapp revelatons but by indictments, etc.

Of course, the Patrol Bureau won't be immune. Their exposure permits traditional weakness to be exposed that a few commanders have failed to correct. However, a tough new Chief of Patrol (Donald Cawley) strengthens that flank.

A major successful assault on the Detective Bureau, on the other hand, threatens the three of us in a unique way. I never promoted Elmer but I have the two of you. Let me be specific: If a Detective

Bureau captain or higher-ranking superior were to be indicted in the next month—how could we jump on the situation?

One way would be for us to catch a wrongdoer first, either for violations less than criminal but serious—and the higher the rank, the better. Obviously, it would be better if one were caught by his operational command rather than by CIS (Cooper).

I feel it would be wise for the Chief of Detectives and Chief of Inspectional Services to confer and analyze the situation—and if the Chief of Detectives would make an all-out effort to avoid being shown up.

Patrick V. Murphy

"The real message of the memo was clear enough," says Seedman. "Murphy had inside information that Knapp was on to somebody in my Bureau. Sidney and I were supposed to pull the rug out from under Knapp by getting to the guy first. I'd told Smith before that I didn't want to end my career doing professional headhunting, but this I was glad to do. If there was a rotten superior among my own people, I wanted to put him out of his misery myself.

"So Sidney and I started getting together all his files and mine. We went down the list of hundreds of superior officers, man by man, to see who might be suspect. We went back over each word of the allegations made by Durk and Serpico which had eventually spawned the Knapp Commission. For a while it looked as if we might nail one deputy inspector, but the harder we looked at him the cleaner he seemed. At the same time, and unknown to Sidney, I was putting out my own feelers throughout the Bureau.

"But after weeks of this, poring back and forth through the records, we still had nothing on any high-ranking officer. Yet here was Murphy hinting at indictments. What the hell had Knapp found that we couldn't? I wondered if Murphy knew more than he was telling in the memo. It didn't seem likely but there was always the chance that he was testing us. . . ."

But now on this Friday before the Knapp Commission hearings were to start, Seedman felt no sense of foreboding. He and Cooper had done all they could, and he would stake his reputation on the thoroughness of their investigation. This Friday was a good day, the end of a good week. It had brought the capture of the Torres brothers, then an obviously authentic letter connecting them to Washington and Bottom, then the line up placing Francisco at the

Colonial Park Houses parking lot on the night of May 21. If Jackie Tabb and Linda Torres were given the proper tender care, the last member of the killing party might soon be identified and called to justice. A very good week indeed.

Just as Seedman was about to go to lunch, a Knapp investigator named Julius Impellizzeri phoned to ask if he could drop by that afternoon.

"Come now," Seedman answered. The Knapp people had been to his office several times during the summer for help in their own investigation. So Impellizzeri's request seemed in no way unusual except one: What could he want at the end of the last business day before the hearings began?

Seedman was on the phone, talking to the San Francisco detective chief about Torres, when Impellizzeri walked in. He was a tall, sallow man with slicked-back black hair. Seedman could understand that he had not wanted to state his business on the phone. But now, after fifteen minutes of small talk, Impellizzeri was still stretched out chummily on Seedman's leather sofa, rattling on about his exploits as an undercover observer in Harlem and showing no signs of getting to the point.

"Can I help you with something in particular?" Seedman prompted.

Impellizzeri smiled as if a cue button had been pushed. Springing up from the couch, he strode to the desk and threw down a photocopy of two New York Hilton restaurant checks, both dated March 6. One was a bar bill for five dollars, the other was a food bill for seventy-nine dollars. On the back of each, in large block letters, was printed "CHIEF SEEDMAN."

It hit him like a thunderclap. So *this* was it! No wonder he and Cooper couldn't find the culprit lurking within the upper reaches of the Bureau. It was Seedman himself. All those days they had wasted! This was what all the memos and investigations came down to: Had the Knapp Commission spent a million dollars just to accuse him of stealing a dinner at the Hilton!

Impellizzeri was still smiling at Seedman. "What about it, Al? Did you eat dinner at the Hilton on March sixth without paying?"

Of course he had, but those checks signed in block letters by someone else were no proof of it. Besides, his party hadn't even been to the bar and even the seventy-nine-dollar dinner check was inflated to include tips Seedman had himself paid in cash that night.

Seedman did not have to explain any of this to Impellizzeri, of course, but he would not play into his hands.

"Sure I ate that dinner," Seedman said and explained briefly what happened. "Now, you tell me something," he said, picking up the photocopy. "How long have you had this thing?"

"Oh, I just got it," said Impellizzeri diffidently.

Though he did not say so, Seedman knew better. His own intelligence sources had informed him months ago that Knapp investigators were visiting the hotels to see if any cops were demanding favors. But he and Cooper had never considered that this was what they were after. Murphy, after all, was warning of indictable offenses and worse.

Seedman tossed the paper back at Impellizzeri. "I'm going to tell the Commissioner about this right now."

"Wait a minute, Al. Take it easy. It's not such a big deal. Listen, do you know Whit?"

"Who?"

"You know—Whitman Knapp. Our boss."

"I only know half-wits."

"No joke, Al. Listen, you've been real clean with me on this. It's in your favor. Why don't I go back and tell Whit how it went and suggest we don't even go forward with this. No use getting the Commissioner upset if the thing is going to be forgotten. I'll get back to you by five o'clock." He walked out.

Seedman sat at his desk, astonished. The hours he and Cooper had wasted wracking their brains looking for the criminal! It was funny. But could his career really be hanging now on the goodwill of this smarmy fellow from the Knapp staff? He did not care to wait to find out. He walked back through the sagging old passage connecting his office with the Commissioner's to tell Murphy what Knapp was up to.

"Sorry, but he's not in, Chief," said the Commissioner's personal secretary. "He's home babysitting with his youngest kid. He does that sometimes when his wife goes out on errands."

Seedman did not want to break the news to Murphy on the phone. He went down instead to tell Mike Codd, the Chief Inspector, but he was out.

Seedman returned to his own office. Suddenly, it was five o'clock. Impellizzeri called on the button.

"I spoke to Whit," he said. "I'm sorry. He wants to go ahead with it."

"Okay. I'm going to tell the Commissioner right now."

"Whit already did," said Impellizzeri coldly.

"Holy smokes! What'd he say?"

"Well, he was unhappy, to say the least."

"You're goddam right he must have been unhappy. You wouldn't even let me tell him myself."

Seedman hung up. He was infuriated at himself for being hoodwinked. He had let this crafty Impellizzeri drive a wedge between him and Murphy. That was exactly their plan. Knapp knew Murphy would be petrified at any threat of taint, real or imagined. As the memo said, Murphy had personally appointed Seedman. A problem now, real or imagined, would be a reflection on his judgment. Other commissioners Seedman had served might have been only too willing to face down this kind of challenge. But Murphy would hang back in toilsome worry like Hamlet.

As Seedman went back to Mike Codd's office the buzzer rang ominously. "First Dep wants to see me. Be back in a minute, Al." Seedman sat down on the couch to wait. As the evening darkened, Seedman wondered why the Commissioner had not yet called himself.

At 6:30 Codd walked in. His face was ashen.

"They relieved you of your command," he said. "Cooper is going to investigate you. In the meantime, you're assigned to my office."

Codd saw what was on Seedman's face.

"You're goddam right I fought it, Al. But that's the word that came down. What they really wanted to do was *suspend* you. That's right. They wanted to take away your gun and shield."

Seedman sat on the couch stunned. Codd poured him a drink. He could not remember the last time he felt his hand shake. As they drank, the teletypes in all the station houses tapped out the notice of the apparent downfall of the most famous Chief of Detectives in departmental history.

Seedman drove home that night still expecting to hear from Murphy. The Commissioner would surely come forward to defend his own, skewering the Knapp puff ball for what it was. Despite the sympathetic calls that came at every hour, Seedman was depressed.

He was surprised himself at how much. After all, even if Murphy did not come to his defense, Sidney Cooper's investigation would surely exonerate him. But the weekend dragged by and no word came.

On Monday morning, Seedman reported to Mike Codd's office on the ground floor. Avoiding his old friend's eyes, Codd told him to stay in his old office for now. Seedman found Kinsella standing outside. He was another old line detective with a baleful gaze and impassive aura. But now he fudged in the middle of the floor. The way nobody was looking him in the eye, Seedman was beginning to feel he must be disfigured.

"It's okay, John," he said. "Go sit at the goddam desk. I'll sit here in this corner by the window."

"I'm not going to sit at your desk, Al."

"Nobody wants to look at me, nobody wants to sit where I sat. What is this? *Sit down!*"

Seedman knew that Kinsella had wanted to cap off his own career with the Chief of Detectives job. If not for Seedman, he would have. But watching him at that desk, nobody would have guessed it had been his heart's desire. All day detectives filtered in and out stiffly. The office men soon evolved a system of reporting to Kinsella loud enough for Seedman to hear at the far end of the cavernous space. He would shoot back comments on what to do. That is how it went on Monday. Tuesday went the same way.

Seedman understood that none of this, obviously, was happening in a vacuum. Since Friday evening, Sidney Cooper had been directed to work around the clock examining every detail of Seedman's life. Even the FBI had been called in. All this effort was not over the Hilton dinner. Even by the touchiest standard, that was not a heinous crime. What Murphy really feared was that the incident was only an opening jab, that Knapp was now preparing to let go with his knockout punch. That was what Murphy was guarding against in asking for the intensive investigation of Seedman. Until it was over, presumably, that fear was going to keep Murphy from saying so much as a single word to his dangling Chief.

So Seedman was certain that once Cooper's work was done he would be returned to the job he loved. But Bill Seltzer, an old friend from his Brooklyn days, was not so sure.

"Why should this Murphy stick out his neck by standing up for you?" Seltzer asked. "He figures he can only lose. He'll tell you that for the good of the department you should sacrifice yourself and put in your retirement papers. If you say no, he'll still put in a new guy so everyone can see how clean his shop is. He's worried about his career, not yours."

Seltzer had long been involved in New York politics. Now he went ahead and organized a campaign to send telegrams to the Mayor from all over the country. Seltzer had been wasting in the last year with a form of leukemia. It had stripped off eighty pounds, left his hair white and eyes hollowed. But now he seemed filled with a glow of energy. By Monday, more than three thousand telegrams had arrived at Gracie Mansion demanding that Seedman be reinstated. It was all Seedman could do to keep Seltzer from sending out a squadron of sound trucks to roll through the city streets demanding justice.

Whether it was due to the telegrams, or the predictable clean bill of health from Cooper, or the pleas of Deputy Commissioner Robert Daley, or personal intercession by the Mayor, or simply the Commissioner's own considered judgment, at noon on Wednesday, October 20, Seedman was called from the gloomy office he shared with Kinsella to the brightly lighted press room. The place was steamy with reporters. Murphy was smiling.

"I have no reason to believe that Al Seedman is anything other than an honest man," he said, shaking Seedman's hand.

"It's not every man who gets to be Chief of Detectives twice," said Seedman. The press broke into warm applause.

One of Seedman's last acts before Impellizzeri's visit had been to pick the detectives who would guard Gabriel Torres' wife, Linda, and Francisco's common-law wife, Jackie Tabb. But for the time being, they were not telling anything. They had come out of households, after all, where police were held in less than low esteem. The detectives did not press them. A week went by, then two weeks. Each morning, Seedman got a negative report. He began to feel he was hovering over a pair of gestating rabbits.

Late one evening, a detective got to talking about the future with Jackie Tabb. "You're what now twenty-three?" he asked.

"Twenty-four," answered Jackie stonily.

"Well, let me throw something out at you. In the last couple of weeks the DA has been going like wild building up a case against Francisco. They got witnesses here and they also broke some people out on the Coast. I think he's going to be sent away for a long time."

He gave Jackie Tabb a once-over. "So you're twenty-four now," he went on. "That's young. You've got three nice kids, and if you don't mind me saying so, you've sure got your looks. But you haven't got a man any more. He's nailed whether you talk or not. My advice to you is to give the DA a little something. It won't hurt your people any more than they're already hurting, but it'll just get the law out of your hair, give you the chance to find a good man to help you bring up the kids."

Jackie Tabb looked away in silence. But a few nights later, after the children were put to bed, she told him and Olga Ford this story:

On the night of May 21 she and Linda had been lounging in front of the TV in the Torres apartment on Anderson Avenue, when Gabriel, Bottom, and Washington had rushed in, drenched with sweat.

"Make coffee," Gabriel ordered. "We just iced two pigs."

Without a word, the two women went to the kitchen. Five minutes later Francisco Torres burst in with another man they knew only as Herman Jonas. They were also sweating and puffing. As the women passed out coffee, Gabriel flipped on the eleven-o'clock news. The five men watched intently as the camera panned over the bloodstains on the sidewalk and stunned residents tried to think of what to say to the interviewer.

"We got away clean," Gabriel said, clapping his hands exultantly.

"I didn't know one was black," said Bottom. "I felt funny about doing that."

"Well, you're gonna have to live with it, brother," cut in Jonas.

Seeing Bottom look down, Washington slapped him on the thigh. "Don't pout, brother," he said. "Pigs are pigs. So fuck all the motherfuckers. Hey, did you see that white motherfucker? He sure didn't want to die."

"I wonder, did anyone see us?" said Gabriel. "It sure was a long run up that hill."

"You sure were a slow mother," Bottom said, perking up.

"Yeah, you got to get in shape," said Washington. "I'm an old man and I'm in better shape than you."

"You know, I think a brother did see me," said Bottom.

The man called Jonas looked up and saw the women staring at them from the hallway. "It's done now," he said. "We shouldn't talk about it in front of the sisters. Let's 'sham' it." After they had seen all the news there was going to be, the men turned off the TV and got down to the business of cleaning their guns.

They could not have known it, but not many blocks away, in a parlor on Beck Street, another group of men had turned away from this same newscast thoroughly perplexed. They could not imagine who had done this job. But two nights ago, they had watched the news just as excitedly as Washington, Bottom, the Torres brothers, and the one called Herman Jonas. With the help of Pauline Josephs, they had just come in from cleaning the "grease" shell casings out of the blue Mustang. They were Richard Moore and Eddie Josephs and that Thursday night, May 19, 1973, the show was their own. The only difference was that their jubilation was not quite complete. Unlike Jones and Piagentini, Curry and Binetti were still alive.

In the following days Jackie and Linda had filtered out other details of how the men did stickups to support the households, including the Beneficial Finance job on June 18 for which Washington was arrested eleven days later. They told how, one by one, the five men had slipped off for the West Coast, paying for the tickets with the proceeds of the hold-up.

"These girls also answered one question which had bugged me since Bottom and Washington were chased down in California with two guns from the Jones–Piagentini shooting. How did they move them across the country? It would be too risky to carry them aboard a plane. They were dashing back and forth too often to bother stashing them in a car and driving so many miles. Yet we were sure they were moving heavy weapons as well as handguns around the country with ease. Now Jackie and Linda told us the method. A few days before they were ready to take off for the Coast, they simply packed up the short guns in boxes and the long guns in rolled rugs. Then they took them down to Greyhound or Trailways to be shipped aboard a transcontinental bus. By the time they got to the Coast, the guns were already at the terminal. Nobody ever inspects packages in a bus freight system.

"The blank space in this story was the man they called Herman

Jonas. Even to the girls, he was a mystery. But they insisted he was the mastermind of the Jones–Piagentini murders. He was more than that. He was a black militant who didn't mind firing into the back of a 'brother.' He was also smart enough to be the one member of the killing party who still left us totally in the dark."

In California, meanwhile, detectives had been slowly tracing back the life history of the 1965 black Oldsmobile from which Washington tried to shoot Sergeant Kowalski. They finally came up with the proprietor of a used-car lot aflutter with streamers on Mission Street in San Francisco. His records showed the Olds had been sold on August 5 to a young black man named Samuel Lee Penegar, who paid $500 cash. The proprietor could not remember what the customer looked like and none of the photos the detectives showed him refreshed his memory.

Whoever Penegar was, he could not register the car without a driver's license. A check of that file produced a Polaroid photo and a single fingerprint of the applicant. Staring out of the photo was an unremarkable young black face; to the detectives, however, Samuel Lee Penegar was most tantalizing.

"In trying to figure out who this guy was," says Seedman, "I kept thinking of two things. One was that holdup of the Bank of America branch. Gabriel Torres had been identified by the witnesses, but his four partners were still unknown. It was unlikely they were strangers to each other, since the purpose of the robbery was apparently to raise bail money for Bottom and Washington. One of the robbers could have been Gabriel's brother, Francisco. Why couldn't another have been Samuel Lee Penegar?

"The other thing I kept thinking about was this Herman Jonas who Jackie and Linda claimed was the mastermind. If he was nowhere to be found under that name, why couldn't he be the guy who popped into existence as Samuel Lee Penegar?

"It was all a long shot, but at least we had a photo and a thumbprint now from Penegar's license application. We started going through our files again to see who might match that photo and the FBI and San Francisco police did the same. The best we could come up with was a fellow named Herman Bell, a twenty-three-year-old, born in Mississippi, who had been arrested in New York as a juvenile, and in California for bank robbery in 1969. Nothing in Bell's background suggested a career as a member of the BLA.

But that was no drawback. If he'd been a leading light in, say, Panther politics, we'd have picked him out of intelligence files long ago.

"Still, nothing guaranteed that Herman Bell was the Herman Jonas who sat around the TV set with the other four on the night of May twenty-first. So I gave the photo of Penegar to Olga Ford. But not to show to Jackie and Linda. Not yet. I thought we'd get a less varnished reaction from the children. Sure enough, their eyes lit up.

" 'Oh, oh,' they piped up. 'That's our Uncle Jonas.'

"That was a break. But we still had no witnesses to place Bell at the scene. So we made one more check. It was the sort of thing which is so farfetched you can't allow yourself to hope it will work out. You just whistle a tune and do it. We compared the Penegar-Bell fingerprints with two latent prints we had pulled off the blue Mustang the men had been leaning against in the Colonial Houses parking lot. Miracle of miracles, they matched.

"Though not a single witness had yet identified him, we could now place Herman Bell on that fender as Jones and Piagentini walked by even more certainly than if I'd seen him with my own eyes. Eyes make mistakes. Fingerprints don't."

After the happy ending to the Hilton incident on October 20, Seedman plunged back into his cases as if nothing had happened. That first night, he and Henny had gone over to celebrate at the Central Park South apartment of his friend Arthur Lipps. Comedian Jackie Mason was also a guest. He did a double-take as Seedman walked in.

"For twenty years I've been trying to get to the point where it's news when I go out to dinner," he said glumly. "You go to the Hilton one time and it's headlines."

Later, as Seedman stood alone on the terrace, looking out over the park, Esther Lipps called him to the phone. Instead of the duty detective in his office, he heard a well-modulated voice which he recognized at once.

"Hey, Al. Did you see the early edition of tomorrow's *Times?*"

"Not yet, Mr. Mayor."

"They put the story of your reinstatement on the front page, upper left, with a four-column picture of you shaking hands with the PC. It's great, just great! But goddam, Al, I didn't know you could smile like that. Now *that's* dangerous to your image."

Seedman had barely hung up when the phone again rang for him. Forty-five minutes later, after a second call at the Lipps', Seedman was on the roof of Hunter College, checking the sightline along which a JDL sniper had fired four shots into a bedroom of the Russian Mission. At 1:30 the Mayor was back on the phone, this time anxious for Seedman to make a quick arrest and calm down the enraged Russians and the jittery State Department. As Seedman sent out for more cigars at 2:45, it looked as if his life was back to normal.

But if things were normal, they were not quite the same. Seedman understood that Murphy, panicked by the Knapp challenge, had done what he had to do. But suppose Knapp did indeed have an uppercut ready after his Hilton dinner jab? Couldn't Murphy have asked him straight out whether he had anything to hide? Even aspects of Sidney Cooper's intensive investigation, glad as he was to have had it, galled him. He learned, for example, that Smith had asked Cooper to check into a private dinner given by an old friend of Seedman's, a restaurateur, in honor of his promotion to Chief of Detectives. When the host asked for a list of people who ought to be invited, Seedman had included Murphy, Cooper, and Smith himself. Murphy and Smith had sent regrets. Now Smith was angling to find something nefarious in that dinner.

More to the point, Murphy had made Knapp look better than the Commission had been able to make itself look. True, Knapp had dredged up some scum from the lower depths of the Department who admitted being on the take from gamblers, prostitutes and even drug dealers. That effort was not to be slighted. The Department should have dredged up the wrongdoers itself. But given time and a generous budget, Knapp was bound to come up with at least a limited catch from a force of thirty thousand.

What Knapp really wanted, though, was big game. When they could not find graft or other high crimes at the command level, the best they could do was to pick Seedman's name from those of the dozens of cops who had eaten at the Hilton and trumpet it loudly. That was the length and breadth of the corruption they found among senior officers. Yet instead of putting the Knapp charge in perspective, Murphy had slunk back in fear. He had legitimized their failure.

It didn't help, of course, that the very subject of detectives made Murphy uneasy. As Smith had once said, they went out doing things all day, nobody was sure what. Almost as soon as the new

Commissioner was sworn in, Seedman had heard that he planned to gut the Bureau and put detectives under the command of uniform patrol officers. One day he asked Murphy about that to his face. Blue eyes restless, Murphy denied it. The order for Seedman to go ahead with the massive specialization program seemed to put his denial in more than words. Even with that, certain other moves began to plant fear in Seedman about the ultimate health of the Detective Bureau.

Early in 1971, for example, Seedman had asked Murphy what he wanted to do with the Narcotics Division. In some cities, it was part of the Detective Bureau, in others independent.

"Which way do we go?" Seedman asked. "It doesn't matter to me."

"It's going to stay in the Bureau, Al," Murphy said firmly.

The decision gave Seedman no joy. Narcotics was the work he liked least in the Bureau. His two years as a lieutenant in the Division had been enough. Ever since that duty, he had felt the control on the men in the field was too loose. The work was just too sensitive to allow as much leeway as in other lines of detective work. If Narcotics was to stay in the Bureau, Seedman was determined to beef it up with more supervision. He did that by plucking from other squads some first-grade detectives, the elite of the Bureau, to become "team leaders" in Narcotics. He knew each man and trusted him. That trust was more important than any external controls that could be imposed, including fear.

Then, in November, Seedman had returned from a five-day cruise to find that Murphy had pulled Narcotics out of the Detective Bureau. It was now part of Deputy Commissioner William McCarthy's Organized Crime Control Bureau. Seedman genuinely had not cared whether Narcotics stayed under his command. But once Murphy had given his word that it would stay, he had put in his best men as team leaders. Then he cared. Along with the Narcotics Division, they were now gone too.

As the city's detective squads smoothly shifted to specialization on the first day of 1972, Seedman hoped the new system would preserve his Bureau from further predations. But just a week later Smith ordered the whole project surveyed by the newly formed Inspectional Services arm. He would not dare to do that without Murphy's okay. Now the "bank examiners" would find whatever they had been ordered to find. Again, Seedman began to get the feeling they no longer wanted detectives to be the proudest, freest, and best men on the force. They did not want young patrolmen to work toward a gold shield. They wanted the patrolmen themselves to be the new elite. That would not only mean raising up the patrol force. It meant bringing low the detectives.

Seedman did not like to think about that. But if they willed it, he could not stop it. And if he could not stop it, he began to wonder, did he want to preside over it? For the first time in his thirty years on the force, he wondered how much longer he wanted to be a detective.

"We had been introduced to the Black Liberation Army by their releases on the shootings of Curry and Binetti, Jones and Piagentini. Its existence was one of those phenomena which seems logical only once it erupts. In this case, the BLA was a reaction to the 'establishment' Black Panther Party, just as the Weathermen had been a reaction to the 'establishment' Students for a Democratic Society.

"The Panthers made the mistake of being open. At their storefront offices or hawking their newspapers wearing a black beret, they were easy to watch. Naturally, they ended up exhausting themselves in confrontations with police and stultifying court actions. Even worse, they made the mistake of being public relations geniuses. All the fashionable journalists and even socialites wanted a piece of them. Leonard Bernstein threw them a party, for Christ's sake! After that, how could they possibly function as honest revolutionaries?

"Certain people in the Panther Party itself were bound to ask that question. They would answer it by splitting off, just as certain people from SDS did. These were the real baddies. They wanted blood, not publicity. They understood the *caveats*: No storefront offices. No black berets. No written records. No public spokesmen. No open membership. They could not be friendly with outsiders, including blacks. They had to stay highly mobile. Above all, they could not forget their purpose. They wanted to yank down the line between order and disorder in the society. That was best done by shooting at the men in blue uniform who walked that line.

"These people became the BLA. There weren't too many. They did not represent the majority of blacks, and they knew it. They were not even racists in the sense that they didn't mind shooting a black cop like Waverly Jones. As Washington had said in Linda Torres' apartment, 'Pigs are pigs. Fuck all the motherfuckers.'"

By the fall of 1971, Seedman felt that a big bite had been taken out of the BLA. The five men wanted for killing Jones and Piagentini had been indicted. All but the elusive Herman Bell were in jail. Richard Moore and Eddie Josephs, wanted for the machine-gunning of Curry and Binetti, had been nabbed at the Triple O Social Club. The one major source of concern was the Beck Street crowd. Except for Moore and Josephs, they were still on the loose. Even so, fall went by quietly. What was left of the BLA seemed to be out of town. That suited Seedman.

Then at 2:40 on the morning of December 20, came a bad omen. Two patrolmen cruising the Ridgewood section of Queens had just spotted a car reported stolen a few hours earlier. As they pulled up behind it, the car sped off. The woman passenger tossed out a hand grenade that blew up under the patrol car. Though the cops were not badly injured, that was the end of the chase. In the morning they identified JoAnne Chesimard as the grenade-hurler and Andrew Jackson as the driver of the stolen car. Both had been guests of Pauline Josephs on Beck Street.

"I hated to hear these two were back in town," says Seedman. "Jackson, in particular, rivaled Richard Moore for causing pure trouble. He was wanted for a killing in New York in April. He robbed a supermarket in Georgia while on the run in August. He escaped from prison in November. Now, in December, these two cops picked him out from a hundred mug shots as the driver of that stolen car in Ridgewood. And this was only the year's worth of trouble we *knew* about. Besides, 1971 wasn't quite over yet. On New Year's Eve, ten days after the Ridgewood incident, Jackson slipped away from a shootout with FBI agents at a motel in Tampa, Florida. He left a Panther named Frank Fields behind, dead. Fields had also been a guest at Beck Street.

"Chesimard's specialty was providing bogus passports, driver's licenses, credit cards, and other papers for fugitives, but she also had field skills. Surveillance cameras had snapped her robbing a bank in Queens in August. Wounded in yet another robbery, she was reported to have said she was glad she had been hit. Now that she'd experienced the feeling of being shot, her reasoning went, she was no longer afraid to be shot again. This philosophy may have led to serenity for her, but what about us?"

On the cold morning of January 28, five weeks after the Ridgewood incident, two patrolmen in a radio car noticed a 1971 Lincoln go through two red lights on Kent Avenue in the Williamsburgh section of Brooklyn. The car had just been reported stolen. It stopped willingly as soon as the patrol car's red flasher went on. John Bauer and his partner Charles Szoke walked warily up to the Lincoln, one on each side. Bauer asked for the driver's license and registration. The driver, a young black man, appeared to be reaching for it. Then shots boomed out, catching Bauer four times in the arm and groin. Szoke ducked and emptied his own revolver at the fleeing car. It was found abandoned in Brownsville that morning at 3:30. As Bauer underwent surgery, Szoke was unable to identify the two occupants of the Lincoln beyond the fact that they were young and black. Bauer, though he would survive, was not yet in a condition to be questioned.

A wet snow began to fall late the same evening, January 28. Seedman came home tired at 8:30. He planned to go to bed, for a change, before midnight. At eleven o'clock when the phone rang, he was actually in his bathrobe.

"Two cops were walking their beat at Avenue B and East 11th Street, twenty minutes ago," said the detective at his office. "They got shot. They're at Bellevue."

"Tell Charlie to pick me up in half an hour," Seedman said tonelessly and hung up.

He showered and shaved and put on fresh clothes just as if it were morning. From the humidor built into a living-room cabinet he took a half-dozen cigars, then a pair of notepads from the desk. The snow had begun to stick to the roads. Charlie sped him into town in silence. In the Bellevue Hospital lobby, he met the usual crush—the Commissioner, the Chief Inspector, the Deputy Mayor, a welter of underlings. One patrolman, Gregory Foster, was dead. The other, Rocco Laurie, still hung by tubes.

As usual, Seedman felt useless at the hospital. But he always went there first, rather than directly to the investigation, to let the men know that the Chief of Detectives cared more about his men than the crime itself. Now he would head over to the 9th Precinct on East 5th Street, nearest the crime scene.

"I'm going to stop by too," said Murphy, catching his arm. "Ride with me."

Murphy seemed to need the company. He had always seemed most vital when he was talking about concepts, administration, accountability, anticorruption . . . but the blood jolt of violent crime seemed to leave him utterly lost. Slumped in the back seat of his car now, he looked so tiny and slack that Seedman felt the need to bolster the Commissioner.

"If this is another Jones–Piagentini deal, and it sure looks like it," said Seedman, "then we ought to be in good shape. My guys have built up terrific files on just about anyone who could do this. They're all up in the Special Squad office in the Three-two. I'll have them carted down within the hour. This one should break quick."

"I hope so, Al," Murphy said weakly.

They pulled up to the 9th Precinct station house on East 5th Street. It was as decrepit as the rest of the tenements on the block. Murphy stood in the yellow light of the old place. It was always an effort for him to be among the troops. Now they milled about angrily, hardly noticing him. After a few minutes, he left. Seedman asked the desk sergeant to pull the records of Foster and Laurie. He wanted to know, in particular, what weapons the cops carried. As with Jones and Piagentini, they had been brought to the emergency room stripped of weapons.

Upstairs, Seedman found the former 9th squad room and four smaller rooms used by the detectives stripped and abandoned. Just four weeks ago, he had moved the squad out of the 9th as part of specialization. He wanted to keep the old space reserved for cases just like this. Now, in a dank room with the proportions of a coffin, Seedman hung his overcoat on the wire grating of the window at the far end. This would be investigation headquarters.

"Tell Communications to hook us up five phones," he told a detective. "Get three each for the other rooms."

"You think they'll install them *now?*" asked the detective.

"You thinking maybe next spring?"

John Kinsella, Bob McDermott, Dick Nicastro, and Eddie Jenkins, the old stalwarts from the first shootings, were soon seated around a borrowed table on borrowed chairs as the phone lines went in. Up in the 32nd in Harlem, the detectives who had built massive files on the BLA were busy packing them for the trip downtown. Out at the corner of 11th Street and Avenue B teams were already busy searching for weapons, sifting the garbage in the gutters for shells, taking photos under the Emergency Service spotlights. Dozens of other detectives, mainly off-duty men who had heard the news on the radio, were out canvassing the sagging old tenements. Already, they had brought in half a dozen witnesses. When Seedman was satisfied that all the other processes were smoothly under way, he ordered each of those witnesses brought into his own tiny command center. The process of sorting out the story had begun.

Gregory Foster was a black man of twenty-two, Rocco Laurie a white of twenty-three. Both were veterans of Vietnam. While the newspapers picked up noisy stories of racial tensions between soldiers, they were simply two New Yorkers who quietly hit it off. Back in the city as cops, they had asked to be partners. They were assigned to one of the brand-new neighborhood patrol teams in the 9th Precinct. The idea was to get cops out of the isolation of patrol cars and back on the sidewalks. Just as Seedman had done at their age, Foster and Laurie spent their whole shift on their feet.

Only ten by fourteen blocks, the 9th Precinct was among the smallest and most densely peopled in the city. It was also among the most dangerous. Once the neighborhood had been the domain of poor Jews and Slavs. Now they were only aging survivors amid the new generation of poor blacks and Puerto Ricans who had taken over the tenements. As with the older generation, most were hardworking, but the neighborhood was also laced with "bike" gangs, runaways, winos, and addicts who strung ropes between tenement roofs to facilitate their movements. Even on top of the old station house on 5th Street on a summer night, you might find huddles of junkies sometimes nodding on the tar shingles, still warm from the day's sun.

At 10:25, as the wet snow fell, Foster and Laurie had walked into an eatery called the Shrimp Boat, whose exhaust fans hurled a perpetual aroma of grease onto the corner of Avenue B and 11th Street. The patrolmen wanted to know who had left a car double-parked outside. But nobody claimed the car. Foster and Laurie walked out.

Three, possibly four black men fell in silently behind them.
The firing was slightly muted by the snow. Foster and Laurie went
down at once from the first shots to the head and back. They
went down side by side. The black men stood over them, firing
straight down for several seconds. Then they knelt and slipped each
patrolman's revolver out of its holster. Laurie lay crumpled up on
his side. Foster was spreadeagled on his back.

"Shoot 'em in the balls!" shouted one of the blacks.

It was done. They also shot out Foster's eyes. When Laurie
had been hit six times and Foster eight, the men jumped and jigged
over the bodies. But their celebration had to be brief. The shots
would attract a sector car and probably Narcotics plainclothesmen in
barely more than a minute. All but one of the men dashed for the
car double-parked on 11th Street. The last man continued to
dance a joyous high-kicking war dance over the bodies, a long-
barrel gun in one hand and a police revolver in the other. Realizing
that the others had sped off, he sprinted north on Avenue B.

Less than a minute later the first patrol car pulled up. They
found a slight young Puerto Rican kneeling over Laurie. They
grabbed him.

"I no do it—I help, I help," he said. The three of them lugged
Laurie into the back of their car and sped off for Bellevue while a
second car picked up Foster. But the men in that car could tell by
the ooze on the sidewalk that their effort was useless. As they picked
Foster up a bullet fell out of his mouth.

At two o'clock in the morning after the shooting, a gray 1967
Chrysler was spotted idling empty beside the Canarsie Line subway stop at 14th Street and First Avenue. It had been reported
stolen at gunpoint from a garage in Brooklyn two hours before the
shootings. Seedman hustled over three witnesses who had been
warming themselves over a rag fire on 11th Street. As soon as
they identified the Chrysler as the getaway car, it was towed to the
police garage. Mindful of how just two smudged prints on a fender
had been the key to placing a killer at the scene of the last assassination, Seedman wanted to dry the car completely before the
fingerprint technicians began to dust it. Meanwhile, all service was
temporarily held up on the Canarsie subway line while, below the
14th Street platform, detectives knelt between the tracks. They
found more than a dozen spent shells and an empty .38-caliber-

ammunition box. The gunmen had apparently reloaded right there in the subway station as they waited for the escape train to Brooklyn.

By three o'clock that morning, the tiny command office was humming. After preinterviews in the old squad room across the hall, the best witnesses were brought in to be interrogated by Seedman, Kinsella, McDermott, and Jenkins. At the far end of the table the bilingual patrolman sat over a constantly ringing "hot line" phone hooked up to a tape recorder. Opposite Seedman sat Robert Daley, the Deputy Police Commissioner for Press Relations. Though his only prescribed duty was to handle the rugged New York press, Daley had thrown himself with gusto not only into his own job but into the thick of investigations as well. Because of his hair style, he was known around Headquarters as Buster Brown.

Seedman did not dislike the Deputy Commissioner. But at this sensitive point in the investigation, with witnesses already showing remarkable unanimity in picking out photos of suspects, he did not care to have Daley around. No doubt the press would be badgering Daley for tidbits and Seedman did not want anything leaked. It would be much easier for Daley himself if he could say he knew nothing more than the basics. Still, a Deputy Commissioner could not simply be asked to leave. In the midst of the bustle, Seedman picked up the nearest phone. Cupping his hands over the receiver, he dialed the special number.

"Could I please speak to Mistah Robert Daley?"

The patrolman passed the phone to the Deputy Commissioner.

"Yes, this is Commissioner Daley speaking."

"Ah only wanted to talk to you, Mistah Daley, because I heard some of those other jokers can't be trusted. I have a good little tip on one of those killers. But I don't want to give it to nobody but you."

"Yes, yes," said Daley, now cupping his own hands over the receiver.

"Go to 545 East 2nd Street. Apartment Three-C. That's where the girlfriend of one of those bloods lives. Her name is Irma Cantero. I ain't 'zactly be sure how to spell it. Anyway, she be known to turn a few tricks in her time. But she gonna be alone now. Because that blood is *gone*. You bring her a few bucks. She'll tell. But if I was you, I'd go alone."

Daley hung up. He yawned. "Guess I'll head on home," he said nonchalantly. "Got to be fresh to handle the press in the morning."

As Daley walked out, Seedman motioned for a pair of detectives to follow him. He was not about to send a Deputy Commissioner to such a rough block without protection. Instead of heading uptown to his apartment, Daley's car sped south to the bad area around Avenue C. The building at 545 East 2nd Street was a mess. More gingerly now, Daley held the door open with one well-polished shoe and peered at the names on the mailboxes, half of them pried open. Just then two addicts, eyes bulging like guppies, staggered down the stairs. They looked over the clean-cut impeccably-dressed visitor.

"Hey man, got a cigarette?" one said.

"And a quarter for a cup of coffee?" said the other.

The detectives prepared to move in. But Daley was already backpeddling speedily to the curb where the sight of his black sedan and driver gave the addicts pause. Daley jumped in and this time the car headed uptown. The detectives waited until the doorman at his apartment house let him inside before reporting back to Seedman that the Deputy Commissioner for Press Relations was safely home.

At 4:55 word came from Bellevue that the fight to save Rocco Laurie was lost. An hour later, with all witnesses logged and canvasses and technical procedures under way, Seedman rode back to his own office. As he had done many times in the last year, he lay down on the cracked-leather couch and, his overcoat slung over him, slept until 7:30 like a rock.

Seedman had planned to give direct command of the Foster–Laurie investigation to Bob McDermott, the paunchy, slow-moving but quick-witted head of Manhattan Homicide-Assault squads. McDermott had done good work in the massively detailed Townhouse case in 1970. But now, looking at McDermott this morning, Seedman did not see the old luster in his eye.

"Bob, you've got this investigation if you want it. You know that. But if you feel you can't put in twenty-hour days, tell me now."

"For myself, Chief, I wouldn't care about giving out," said McDermott, his voice full of emotion. "But for those two young cops, I care. And to tell the truth, I don't think I can make it all the way. So I better pass."

Though Seedman then gave the job to John O'Connor, Mc-

Dermott continued to work harder than he should have. After McDermott trudged up just one flight to their headquarters in the old station house, Seedman noticed that he was wheezing. Fifteen months later he was dead.

Late on the morning after the shooting, a clerk in a delicatessen across the street from the Shrimp Boat handed a canvas shoulder bag to a detective who came calling. It had apparently been left unnoticed in a corner by a group of blacks who had brought cold cuts and bread about three hours before the attack. It contained two gun stocks and a set of clippings on the killings of Jones–Piagentini.

The next day, UPI received the following letter:

> *This is from the George Jackson Squad of the Black Liberation Army about the pigs wiped out in lower Manhattan last night. No longer will black people tolerate Attica and oppression and exploitation and rape of our black community.*
>
> *This is the start of our spring offensive. There is more to come. We remember Attica.*
>
> *The George Jackson Squad of the* BLA

This time the senders had taken care not to leave any prints, the mistake made by Richard Moore and Eddie Josephs when they wrapped the license plates from the Mustang from which the "grease" had blazed at Curry and Binetti. Seedman could not help but notice that since Moore had been lost as its chief copywriter, the BLA prose lacked pizazz.

As Seedman was leaving the station house at 1:30 the next morning for the ride back home, a young patrolman came up to him.

"I know it's not my place to say this to you," he blurted out. "But my Dad was a cop. He loved this job and I love it. But as rough as it could be for my Dad, he never had to put up with this . . . this. . . ." The young cop shook his head for lack of a word.

"Listen, Chief," he went on, "I'm carrying my police special plus two non-reg weapons and I'm *still* scared shitless to walk on my beat. For my wife and my two kids, I've *got* to be scared. She bites her nails now, my wife, waiting for me to come home. She says to me, 'Jimmy, you know it's going to happen again. If not this month, then maybe six months. But it will happen again.' And the worst of it is that up there"—he pointed in the general direction of Headquarters—"they don't give a good goddam as long as everything looks clean."

Seedman listened until the cop was done. On the way home, he remembered that at Bellevue on Thursday morning, one of Murphy's top men wondered aloud whether Foster and Laurie might have met their end owing to some kind of drug hanky-panky. That possibility always had to be looked into, obviously. But should it be a commander's first consideraton at the hour when one of his young men lay dead and the other dying? Instead of support there was a void of fear. Though this young cop had not been at the hospital, he sensed it, too. More than any fear of the street, it was what he found intolerable.

"By the end of that week," says Seedman, "we knew pretty well whom we were looking for. Witnesses to the shooting had picked out mug shots from the files we brought down from Harlem. Other witnesses to the action, both before and after the actual shootings, did the same. We got fingerprints from the car and from the canvas bag found in the delicatessen. When it was all cross-referenced, we had four suspects in the actual shooting, and five others we had reason to believe were close by. As in the Jones–Piagentini case, the gunmen were apparently covered from behind.

"That weekend I'd confidentially circulated photos of the four prime suspects to precincts where they might be spotted. But on Tuesday, their faces were all over the front page of the *Daily News*. That was a shame. As usual, I'd have preferred suspects *not* to know they were being sought. If these four had still been in town, they'd be gone now.

"Given time, of course, I would have transmitted a nationwide alarm for the suspects through the National Crime Information Center. But I hadn't been quite ready for that. Except for those locked in by fingerprints, the list of suspects was still only tentative. Witnesses, after all, often reverse themselves once they see in the flesh a suspect they had picked out in a mugshot. But now that the *News* had broken the story, we had to go ahead and transmit the alarms.

"Then Bob Daley convinced Murphy we ought to hold a press conference to announce the alarms. I was against it. So was DA Frank Hogan, who felt the publicity would be prejudicial to any eventual fair trial. But Daley persevered with Murphy. So I figured we may as well do it right. I had flip charts drawn up for each of the four suspects and five others wanted for 'questioning.' A final chart diagramed over twenty major crimes for which the nine were wanted, interlocked by colored lines. I let the reporters into my office for the event. Murphy started off with a short statement on the BLA. Then Daley, using a pointer, explained the charts while one of his people flipped them. As far as the press was concerned it was a great show.

"The four wanted for murder were Ronald Carter, Andrew Jackson, Ronald Anderson, and Herman Bell. For 'questioning' we wanted Robert Vickers, Twyman Meyers, Samuel Cooper, Paul Stuart, and JoAnne Chesimard. As I feared, we had been premature. On the day of the killings, two of the four suspects had been working on a tomato farm in Florida. Introducing any new suspects after this list was published could affect our credibility, but we were forced into a position where we had no other choice.

"Getting out those 'wanted' alarms didn't necessarily mean it would be any easier to locate this group," says Seedman. "Every single one of them had already been sought—without success—for previous crimes. I counted more on the valuable data we were accumulating to lead us to our quarry. Every move we made gave us more names and locations which in turn provided further information. As the files and reports kept growing, I yearned to put the data into a computer so that by just pressing a button, we could get a printout telling us where to look next."

From every part of the city detectives supplied information in such quantities that only the most promising could receive immediate attention. One not too promising story came from Lt. Frank Bolz of the 13th Robbery Squad in Brooklyn.

It was a murky tale of strife between factions of "Youth in Action," a federally-funded antipoverty group in Brooklyn. The action included shootings and kidnappings, none reported directly to the police. Bolz had gone to the Union Street apartment of Henry Brown, a suspect in one of the shootings. Welfare had gotten him the place a few months earlier after his release from Greenhaven Prison. Bolz did not find Brown at home, but he did find a fifteen-year-old heroin addict and prostitute who watched glassy-eyed as Bolz looked around. As he was about to go, she suddenly spoke.

"I know why you're here," she said.

"Why?"

"Because of what happened that night?"

"Tell me and I'll tell you if you're right."

The girl told Bolz that she had been watching television with her boyfriend in the apartment one night at the end of January—a Thursday night, she was certain, because of the show they had seen —when "Sha-Sha" had hurried in, about 11:30.

"I just had some static with two cops in Manhattan," he said. "I think they might be dead."

He walked over to the bed and reloaded a police revolver. Then he threw clothes into a suitcase and left.

She did not know Sha-Sha by the name Henry Brown and the Foster–Laurie Squad, for its part, did not know of any reason to put Brown at the scene of the murders. But what caught Seedman's eye was the address. It was a quick walk from a subway stop on the Canarsie Line. If Brown had dropped his token in the slot at 14th Street right after the shooting, he would have arrived home just at the time the girl said he did. But that was only a speculation. If the report had merit, and the killing party found the police before the police found them, Seedman felt that Brown would be with them.

Instead of in San Francisco, it happened this time on a street in a bad part of St. Louis. At 10:55 on Tuesday night, February 15, a pair of patrolmen cruising North Grand Avenue in St. Louis got curious about a gray 1967 Oldsmobile with Michigan temporary plates made of cardboard. They pulled the car over. Inside were four black men. The cops got as far as asking for the driver's license and registration before shots boomed out from all the windows. One cop dropped, hit in both legs and the stomach. The other crawled around to the back of the Olds and began firing as it sped away. The car was pursued by two Narcotics undercover officers who happened to be parked a block away in an unmarked car. They caught up with the Olds a moment after it had screeched into an empty parking lot. Two of the men had already scampered over a high wire fence at the rear of the lot and a third was trying.

"Drop off that fence or we'll shoot you off!" hollered one of the Narcotics men.

He dropped. Five minutes later a second man was picked up a block away, his arm bloody from a bullet in the wrist. In the back of the car, slumped over almost unnoticed, was a third man. Hemmorhaging internally from a bullet through the left nipple, he was dead in minutes. At the base of the fence police found the Smith & Wesson .38-caliber revolver that had belonged to Rocco Laurie.

Just before dawn a U-haul rental truck was found abandoned near a Procter & Gamble plant in a tough part of St. Louis. It had been seen in front of the Olds just before the shooting started. The dead man left behind in the Olds carried a driver's license identifying him as Frank Reese of Detroit. As for the two suspects in custody, they were not giving out real names.

A confused sketch of this story was handed to Seedman as he walked into the office at 8:15 on Wednesday morning. Though the odds were against it by millions to one, experience had taught him that this shootout was exactly the behavior to expect from the fugitives in front of the Shrimp Boat. But with the recovery of Rocco Laurie's gun, he did not have to worry about the odds. Before noon, three case specialists, Lt. Hugh Ferguson and Dets. Roy Ardizonne and Nicholas Cirrillo, were in St. Louis.

That afternoon they helped the local police identify the dead man as Ronald Carter, one of the four suspects on the "wanted" list. The man picked off the parking lot fence was identified as Thomas McCreary of Brooklyn. The one who nearly got away was none other than Henry Brown, known back on Union Street as "Sha-Sha." From prints taken off the Olds dashboard, it appeared that the man who got away, also listed on the original alarm, was Twyman Meyers.

These identifications seemed to clear up less than they opened up. Why was this group in St. Louis? Who was in the U-Haul truck? Had they started from the same place? Where were they going? The men in St. Louis were struggling to get it all straight. But the more they called, the more hamstrung Seedman felt at having to direct the investigation by phone. He wanted to be at the action.

At 6:30 he called Chief Inspector Codd.

"I sent good people out to St. Louis," he told Codd. "That's what an administrator is supposed to do. But they're confused about the work they didn't do. Mike, I don't know how else to clear this up unless I go out myself."

"Go," answered Codd.

Unspoken but sensed in that exchange between two taciturn men was another reason Seedman wanted to go himself. He still felt that the civilian brass was not supporting the men in the field forthrightly when they needed it. It was not just the young cop who had stopped Seedman outside the 9th who had sensed the attitude. They all sensed it. They would also sense that by going off to St. Louis, the Chief of Detectives was putting himself on the case, not just as three-star brass barking orders from the great office, but as a detective, the very best detective in the Bureau, working on his feet.

Seedman took with him Ballistics Detective Al Johnson, whose own suitcase was filled with all the bullets fired at cops since the night Fleck and Dockery were shotgunned in May 1968. Johnson and his St. Louis counterparts would compare them to bullets fired from the guns found in the Olds.

They'd have plenty to compare. Besides Laurie's .38, a Colt .38 had been found under the leg of the dying Carter, along with a 9-mm. Browning automatic and a .357 Colt Python revolver on the front floor. In the trunk were a .44-caliber "Strum Ruger" carbine, a .30-caliber Plainfield, a .30-caliber Universal, a .30–06 Remington, a Belgian "De Guerne" with telescopic sight, and a Colt automatic rifle. Also in the trunk were several hundred rounds of assorted ammunition including three thirty-round "banana" clips for the Remington automatic.

Early the next morning in St. Louis Seedman went to the morgue to look down at Ronald Carter. Having seen him on the slab, he knew he could forget about him. Then he went to the police garage to look at the U-Haul truck. It was loaded with mattresses, garbage cans, mops, toilet paper, soaps, militant pamphlets, and chemicals used to make fire bombs. Wherever they had been going, it was to set up house. The load of guns in the Olds also pointed to that. Even for the BLA, handguns and all these rifles were a bit much just to take out on a spin.

To Seedman, the most valuable item in the truck was a crumpled receipt for furniture from a store in Cleveland. He sent a detective, Lawrence Haviland, from New York, to check out the address on the sales slip. It was a shoddy apartment building. Among the former tenants was Ronald Carter.

The 1967 Olds had been bought for cash by a black woman the salesman identified as JoAnne Chesimard. Andrew Jackson had come along to "kick the tires."

The U-Haul truck had been rented in Cleveland on the day before the shooting. The clerk identified the renter as JoAnne Chesimard, accompanied by Andrew Jackson.

Digging in the trash in back of the Cleveland apartment house, Haviland found an empty Colt revolver box stamped with the same serial number as on the gun under the dying Carter's leg. In all, the purchase of at least a dozen new guns was traced to the group in Cleveland in the month before the shootout. Seedman wondered how many had been unloaded from that U-Haul before it was abandoned.

On his last day in St. Louis Seedman sent for the girl from Union Street and her boyfriend to look at Brown and McCreary in lineups at St. Louis headquarters. Though the other dozen men were bandaged and made up with bruises by a theatrical artist, they had no trouble picking out "Sha-Sha." They also identified McCreary as someone they had seen around "Youth in Action" meetings.

After those lineups, Seedman took his group home. On the plane he sat behind the youthful prostitute, who was under the wing of the ever faithful Olga Ford. At fifteen she had managed to graduate from heroin to black market methadone. Until now, she had never been so near a cop. She had never been out of New York. She was loving every bit of it.

"Do you think . . . I might could do . . . what you do, Mrs. Ford?" she asked.

"Do what, honey?"

"Be a police lady."

"You kick that stuff and get back for a little schooling, and you could do it better than me," said Olga Ford.

In the seat behind, Seedman knew what Olga was talking about. He could use a girl in the Bureau with her background.

Henry Brown was convicted of shooting a patrolman in St. Louis and sentenced to twenty-five years. He was then brought to New York to be tried for the killings of Foster and Laurie. The girl and her boyfriend identified him. But the witnesses on 11th Street did not. The defense also drummed home the fact that Brown had not been on the list of suspects released at Murphy's press conference. As for Rocco Laurie's gun, Brown insisted it had been given to him by Carter, now dead. Deciding that reasonable doubt of his guilt existed, the jury acquitted Henry Brown. He went back to St. Louis to serve his twenty-five years.

A few months after the St. Louis shootout Ronald Anderson was captured by detectives in an apartment on Dean Street in

Brooklyn. In May 1973 JoAnne Chesimard was captured in a shoot-out on the New Jersey Turnpike after the car she was in was stopped for speeding. The trunk of her car was full of blank passports. As Pauline Josephs had said, JoAnne was the one who could help out fugitives. JoAnne also got her wish—she was shot five times and it did not take the hard look off her face. But in the process of getting her wish, she left behind one dead state trooper.

A month later Andrew Jackson was grabbed out of bed where he lay naked with his girlfriend, Denise Oliver, in a Brooklyn apartment. On September 17 a close associate of Henry Brown's named Melvin Kearney was captured after a long shootout at a Bronx apartment. In October, after a tip from New York detectives, FBI agents picked up the phantom of them all, Herman Bell. They surrounded his car at a stoplight in New Orleans while he was out for a Sunday drive. At his arraignment Bell was asked if he had anything to say.

"It's all been said already," he answered.

"What do you mean?" asked the judge.

"I mean, the history of black people says it all."

The last big fish was Twyman Meyers. He had been sloppy with fingerprints but sharp on the getaway. Then, on November 14, 1973, he was followed from an apartment on Tinton Avenue in the Bronx. Though it was warm, he wore a wool cap pulled down over his eyes and a baggy jacket. He saw the detectives moving in on him before they thought he would. "Fuck you, bastards!" he screamed and started shooting. He hit the two officers before being cut down dead on the sidewalk. The 9-mm. gun he used was matched later to the slugs fired at Patrolman Bauer from the stolen Lincoln the night before Foster and Laurie were killed.

The core of the small, virulent BLA had been reduced to nothing.

As spring came Seedman was hard at work on the Gallo case. Since the Mafia was no more Murphy's bag than the BLA, he was comforted to have Seedman answer questions from the press. But in this new season Seedman continued to feel that despite the smooth take-off of Specialization, Murphy, with Smith whispering in his ear, did not wish the Detective Bureau well. Their delight was in a patrol force rigidly regulated and clean as surgical gear.

Seedman could see the time had indeed come for a better patrol force. Once, when crimes in the city were fewer, the emphasis had rightly been on solving them. The public looked forward to reading about how an ace force of detectives moved in to break the big cases. But crime was no longer a spectator sport. It was happening to everyone. The citizens were full of fear. When they were afraid to go out at night for the early edition of the *Daily News,* they forgot about solving crimes. Their first demand had become simply that crime be stopped, or at least slowed down. So now they looked most anxiously for the flatfoot twirling a nightstick on their block, gold buttons on his chest catching the glow of street lamps. Just get him out there.

So the ascent of the flatfoot's star was hardly a remote wish of the Commissioner's office. It issued from the public itself. But why did pulling up Patrol have to mean dragging down the Detective Bureau? What would a sharp young patrolman aspire to if not a traditional gold shield? Yet the feeling had become steadily more palpable that the Bureau was to be pulled down and ground under. The talk floating down from Smith's office was that detective units would soon be put under Patrol commanders. Seedman understood that also meant putting detectives back in uniform. What better way to take out their starch than by lumping them with the lowest common denominator on the beat and having them report to a crusty old desk sergeant?

Seedman did not fail to see, finally, that if any one man represented the classic style of New York City detective, he was it. As long as he was on top, it was still the Bureau of old. He was by far the most easily recognized cop in the city. No single act would break the Bureau's spirit more than seeing him slapped down. In this spring season, he did not care to wait for that.

He had first reported for detective work as a skinny kid assigned to the Scottoriggio case twenty-six years ago. That case had drawn national attention because the fatal beating of a man simply trying to walk to his polling place was a threat to democracy. Now, at the other end of his career, in the BLA cases, Seedman had also been involved with a crime which drew national attention. This time it was because of another threat to democracy: attacks on the cop in blue, the one visible representation of the rule of law in the streets of the city.

In the Scottoriggio case, Seedman's prime role had been to walk the victim's brother home and wait for him to fall asleep. Now, in the BLA cases, he had run perhaps the most complex investigation in any single city's history. Of course, he got plenty of help. All around the country cops had pasted pictures of the killers on their dashboards. Many of those cops, even in the sleepiest places in America, also knew that the cop in command of the fight against the BLA was the tough looking, cigar-chewing fellow in New York.

On April 28, 1972, thirty years after he walked his first patrol in the Bronx, twenty-six years after Ray McGuire took him on as a rookie detective in Safe & Loft, eleven years after he stumbled over the bodies of Fallon and Finnegan, eight years after he held Winston Mosely's fine hands up to the yellow light of the 114th squad room and seen Kitty Genovese's scratches on the tapered fingers, three years after the surreal nights he stood amid the fallen ductwork and smashed Selectrics in the offices bombed by Sam Melville, two years after watching bombs and what used to be bodies shoveled out of the 11th Street townhouse debris, one year after seeing the wires to the Amtorg bomb, so neatly packed by Angelo, snipped with no seconds left on the timer, eleven months after Curry–Binetti, Jones–Piagentini, and the Colombo shootings, three months since the snowy night Foster and Laurie were cut down, and a month since Joey Gallo ate his last clam at Umberto's, Albert Seedman, without warning to anyone, put in his papers.

He was almost the last of the Depression-bred generation to go. With their college degrees in hand, most of those men would not have chosen police work in more prosperous times. But more than a generation of men was gone from the Detective Bureau. The system of picking new men was gone. The gut reaction of superior officers and "rabbis" had given way to written tests and other more objective criteria. The new system would prevent a few of the worst from getting in, and probably a few of the best. Ray McGuire, who was no ace at test-taking, might never have made detective.

Once a man got into the Bureau, he would also be working under a new system. In all his years on the force Seedman never dared assume he had a right to any particular day off. If a case came up, he went to it. To suggest that it was bedtime or his free Sunday morning would have been unheard of. His men felt the same way. None of this was written down on paper. The system lived in them.

But now the particulars were all in writing. Days off, overtime pay, vacations. A cop was expected to work eight hours a day, like a mailman. Not less, not more. Everything else had changed too. The new generation of cops had been brought up in prosperity, not want. They had every right to a new system, a new style, and with the departure of Seedman, the way was clear. The old school was gone.

But to this day, when Albert Seedman walks down the street as a private citizen, young patrolmen who were not even rookies when he left the Department nudge each other and point to him. His detectives, naturally, remember him from particular cases. One reporter who never worked for him remembers seeing him one fall afternoon before he retired, standing on the East River heliport pad with a throng of security men waiting for President Nixon to arrive from JFK. The full range of municipal protective services is on hand for the occasion. Helicopters hover over the river, fire and police boats crisscross the channel, Tactical Police units, uniformly bored, sit in buses under the East River Drive, firemen are massed on the pier. Secret Service men with binoculars scan the endless window grids of the downtown towers.

Suddenly the President's big helicopter dips down toward the pier in a mighty blast of noise and downswirling air that parts the water below in a shivering trough. The cops and firemen, standing in ranks with chests out and chins up, cringe involuntarily. A few heavy fire hats go skittering across the landing area. Even the Secret Service men, who are accustomed to this great wind, hold their hair in place and look down.

But if Seedman does carry on the last of a certain style, he does not abandon it easily. He points his cigar into the wind and, alone on the pier, acts as though there is no great rotor blast at all. And when the President alights and walks to his car, smiling and waggling his fingers in the familiar V sign, there is a brief but unmistakable moment when the smile disappears. Even for someone whose smile is as practiced as the President's, it is still very hard to smile at Albert Seedman when he is not smiling at you.